JOHN MAYNARD KEYNES: CRITICAL ASSESSMENTS

JOHN MAYNARD KEYNES
Critical Assessments

Edited by
John Cunningham Wood

Volume III

CROOM HELM
London & Canberra

Selection and editorial matter
© 1983 Croom Helm
Croom Helm Ltd, Provident House, Burrell Row, Beckenham, Kent BR3 1AT

British Library Cataloguing in Publication Data

John Maynard Keynes. – (The Croom Helm critical
assessments of leading economists)
1. Keynes, John Maynard   2. Keynesian
economics
I. Wood, John Cunningham
330. 15'6   HB99.7
ISBN 0-7099-2729-0

Printed and bound in Great Britain by
Biddles Ltd, Guildford and King's Lynn

Contents

Contents

SECTION THREE: KEYNESIAN ECONOMIC ANALYSIS

Commentary

In 'The Future of Keynesian Economics' D. Wright attempts to overcome the impression that the economics profession is divided into an unabridgable gulf between 'Keynesian' and 'anti-Keynesian' economists. Wright surveys Keynes' essential analysis and concludes that his teaching is a supplemental development of Marshallian theory, rather than a contradiction. He concludes by speculating that as regards the future of Keynesian economics there is room for great development on numerous lines, such as researching the obstacles to supply in addition to those factors that cause deficiency of demand.

The main object of G.W.G. Browne's paper 'The Keynesian Revolution in Economics' is to give a brief account of Keynesian theory and to assess its revolutionary implications for external policy. Browne runs through such Keynesian concepts as savings, investment, liquidity preference, interest, income and consumption and argues that the Keynesian reliance on frictions or rigidities in the economic system was of doubtful validity. After pointing out that the most revolutionary consequences of Keynesian theory can be seen in the field of public finance, Browne asks if Keynesianism can be applied to the South African economy. He argues that many applications of Keynes' theory depended upon the assumption of a mature economy. Since South Africa had not reached maturity, one therefore had to be careful in applying Keynesian ideas. Nevertheless, he feels that the government had to budget for a deficit in times of depression.

In 'Dr Burns on Keynesian Economics' A.H. Hansen attacks sections of the twenty-sixth annual report of the National Bureau of Economic Research, written by A.F. Burns. Hansen attempts to point out the misconceptions contained in Burns' paper and he stresses the flexibilities in Keynes' treatment of such variables as the consumption function, private investment and the practices of businesses.

In 'Keynesian Economics Once More' Burns replies to Hansen's criticisms by noting the essentials and determinancy of Keynes' theory of income and employment, discussing the consumption function in greater detail and distinguishing the Keynesian apparatus from the Keynesian theory. At the conclusion of the paper Burns provides a succinct appendix on Keynes' business cycle theory. In a 'Brief Rejoinder' Hansen welcomes Burns' paper and points out that the consumption function, and its interpretation, is a central issue in their disagreement. Hansen also claims that by using 'intended investment' Burns failed to appreciate that he had made his case less general.

In 'An Exposition of Keynesian Economics' L. Tarshis offers a simple and acceptable account of Keynesian economics. He is not concerned to discuss the fine points but only the broad outline of Keynes' *General Theory*. He develops a model based on the qualifications to Keynes by Robertson, Hicks, Samuelson,

1

Shackle and Lange. Tarshis carefully discusses such concepts as consumption, investment, income, propensity to consume and save, marginal efficiency of capital and interest rates. He concludes that the skeleton of Keynes' theory is simple:

> The national income depends upon investment and the income-consumption function. Investment, or more accurately private business investment, depends upon the marginal efficiency of capital and the rate of interest; the rate of interest depends upon the liquidity function and the amount of money. The determinants of the marginal efficiency of capital and the propensity to consume are very numerous; some of them were listed earlier.

J. Williams' 'An Appraisal of Keynesian Economics' argues that Keynes' greatest virtue was his interest in economic policy. He believes that the paradox of *The General Theory* lies in the fact that its theme is long-run, but its formal analysis is short-run. While Williamson claims that Keynes' law of the propensity to consume was the most important novel feature of *The General Theory*, it has also been the most controversial. He argues that the function does not account for the rise of the car or of new products generally.

In the discussion which follows these papers, L.V. Chandler concentrates on Tarshis' contribution and he agrees that one should divorce Keynesian theory from Keynes' pessimistic views as to the future of private demands for investable funds. C. Warburton argues that the liquidity preference phase of Keynesian theory is not in accordance with the facts and appears to be irreconcilable with them. M.W. Reder, who fails to understand why 'there were ever any anti-Keynesians', claims that Tarshis was overgenerous to neoclassical theory.

J.W. Angell's 'Keynes and Economic Analysis Today' is a review of the books by L.R. Klein, *The Keynesian Revolution* and S.E. Harris (ed.), *The New Economics: Keynes' Influence on Theory and Public Policy*. He notes that although Klein's book is a religious restatement and defence of Keynes' ideas, it is most useful as a teaching device. The Harris work, by contrast, is a collection of essays which also reflect Keynes' influence. Angell believes that in spite of all the re-workings of *The General Theory*, its basic concepts still remain. He adds that a number of questions which Keynes was either confused on or in error have been greatly clarified since 1936, e.g. savings, investment, involuntary unemployment, etc.

Angell predicts that new analytical work on Keynes would develop along four lines: (1) the relaxing of Keynes' restrictive assumptions, e.g. the treatment of investment as a datum; (2) the effects of monopolies and structural maladjustment and different patterns of resource allocation; (3) the manipulation of Keynes' variables to show how they move through time; and (4) the further development of those objectives, criteria and instruments of public and private economic policy.

D. Dillard's 'The Keynesian Revolution and Economic Development' offers a succinct summary and review of three books: L.R. Klein, *The Keynesian Revolution*; S.E. Harris (ed.), *The New Economics: Keynes' Influence on Theory and Public Policy*; and S.E. Harris, *The National Debt and the New Economics*. Dillard considers that the time has arrived for economic historians to take stock of the Keynesian revolution, which he argues has application for students of economic development. Dillard believes that the widespread acceptance of demand-deficiency as a respectable working hypothesis should change the 'tone of investigations in economic history'. He points out that economic historians have frequently argued facts denied by Say's Law and that supply did not create its own demand. He concludes by noting that a major fault with the work of economists such as Klein and Harris is the failure to develop the broader aspects of the Keynesian revolution, such as the underlying social perspective in terms of which Keynes viewed economic conflict.

In 'Lord Keynes' Theory of Wages' R.H. Fields notes that in *The General Theory* Keynes argued that labour works for a money wage rather than a real wage and Fields argues that this has been true for Australia in the past. Fields then discusses Kahn's theory of wages, arguing that both Keynes and Kahn assume a rising marginal cost curve and depend on that particular shape for their validity. He concludes by stating that the worst prediction of Lord Keynes for a system of stable real wages has been avoided in Australia.

In 'Professor Leontief on Lord Keynes' I.O. Scott questions Leontief's argument (which appeared in S.E. Harris' *The New Economics*) that Keynes assumes, as a basic posulate, a downward rigidity of money wages, although Haberler asserts that such a phenomenon actually occurs. He agrees with Leontief that Keynes assumes a downward rigidity in the rate of interest, but questions Leontief's interpretation of liquidity preference. He also argues that (1) full employment can be attained through monetary policy which does not involve a rise in the prices of commodities; (2) an underemployment equilibrium is possible because of the nature of the demand for money; and (3) underfull employment equilibrium in the liquidity trap case is due to a rigidity in the rate of interest, not because of a rigidity in wages.

In his 'Comment' Leontief disputes Scott's argument on Keynes' 'money illusions' and contends that he had not succeeded in overturning the view that Keynesian theory was an ingenious, but not very successful, attempt at treating dynamic problems in static terms. In a 'Further Comment' G. Haberler disputes Scott's argument and points out that competition would drive down money wages and prices so long as there is involuntary unemployment.

In 'Recent Discussion of Keynes' Theory of Wages: A Review' H.W. Arndt notes that of the twenty-five articles in *The New Economics: Keynes' Influence on Theory and Public Policy*, edited by S.E. Harris, *at least* six dealt with (wholly or in part) Keynes' theory of wages. Arndt attempts to gather together these views so as to construct an outline of Keynes' theory of wages. He argues that the task Keynes set himself was to refute the implications of classical theory that general wage deflation was an appropriate remedy for general unemployment. Arndt points out that Keynes, like the classical economists, assumed that employment is inversely related to the level of real wages. However, in Keynes' theory, labour resisted cuts in money wages and, even if they were accepted, this action would not increase employment since prices would fall proportionately, leaving the real wage unchanged.

In 'An Exposition of the Keynesian System' I.O. Scott presents the rudiments of the Keynesian system as applied to a closed economy for 'beginning students' by means of a simple linear model consisting of six variables: $Y =$ aggregate flow of income in a specific period; $C =$ aggregate expenditure by the private sector of consumer goods and services; $I =$ net expenditure by the private sector of consumer and investment goods; $R =$ the structure of interest rates; $M_1 =$ transactions and pecuniary demand for money; and $M_2 =$ speculation. The model has two parameters: $m =$ the quantity of money and $g =$ government expenditure on goods and services. After constructing his model, Scott highlights the following difficulties: (1) inaccuracies imposed by a desire for simplicity; (2) the static method; (3) aggregation and capital accumulation problems are ignored; (4) price flexibility problems are ignored; (5) no account is given between long-term and short-term interest rates; and (6) no acknowledgement that liquidity preference actually pertains to the relationship among all kinds of assets of varying liquidity.

In 'The Re-examining of Keynesian Economics in the Light of Employment Experience' C. Philbrook seeks to conduct an experiment to see how Keynesian economics has survived the employment experience. He points out, however, that in order to agree on the predictions from Keynesians one had to agree on what Keynesian theory involves. Philbrook therefore discusses the subtleties of Keynes' basic model and concludes that critical experiments could not consist of simply observing either employment or money income in the face of the variability of the marginal efficiency of capital schedule in relation to thriftiness.

R. Fels' 'The Re-examining of Keynesian Economics: Comment' is a comment on the article in which Philbrook discussed the controversy between Keynesian and the orthodoxy of Pigou and others. Given that Philbrook's assumptions of each school were identical, Fels finds it not surprising that the predictions from each model are the same. To Fels, one of the most important differences between Keynesians and Pigovians concerns a question of fact, and, in order to choose between the two theories, one needs an experiment to establish the truth.

By way of introduction to his article 'Keynesian Economics in Relation to Underdeveloped Countries' V.B. Singh provides an overview of Keynesian achievements in developing countries. After discussing the impact of Keynes in the developed world, Singh details the leading characteristics of the poor nations to demonstrate how difficult it is to apply Keynes to such nations. He concludes that the nature of developing societies is such as to preclude the growth of Keynesianism.

F.J. de Jong's 'Supply Functions in Keynesian Economics' critically examines and compares some of the supply functions prevalent in the literature of Keynesian economics. He summarises the positions of a range of authors on the subject and presents this discussion in terms of fourteen propositions. He demonstrates the different and, to some extent, contradictory statements of supply.

In 'Keynes and Supply Functions' R.G. Hawtrey agrees with de Jong in that, according to Keynes, employment is determined by a one-sided demand theory. However, Hawtrey argues that de Jong might have found a shorter proof in demonstrating that maximisation of profits by every individual firm does not necessarily make the sum total of all expected profit a maximum. He also points out that Keynes' supply function in terms of effective demand does not differ materially from the 'familiar' supply function in terms of price. In his 'Rejoinder' de Jong stresses that *ex post* concepts are not suitable for explaining how equilibrium is brought about. He contends that if Keynes' theory is to be taken as an equilibrium theory, the kernel of his argument must necessarily be taken *ex ante*, otherwise his theory should fail to determine an equilibrium position.

At the commencement of 'Keynes and Supply Functions' D.H. Robertson notes the following points about Keynes' supply function: (1) it is a curve of aggregate costs, not of marginal or average costs; (2) in 'costs' it includes such profits as emerge when price is equated with marginal factor costs; and (3) it is the 'familiar' supply curve in de Jong's sense that the factor costs included in it are costs as they present themselves to the entrepreneur, not to any other party. In his 'Second Rejoinder' de Jong comments on Robertson's notes as well as offering a brief exposition of Koopman's theory of monetary equilibrium.

In 'On Keynes' Economic System — Part One' E. Lindahl notes that the central lines of *The General Theory* have percolated to the textbook level and he therefore attempts to construct, for pedagogical purposes, a textbook model. Lindahl asserts that the essential features in Keynes' theory are most clearly shown if one investigates the consequences on economics and employment of a change in the given functions. In his representative model Lindahl assumes that Keynes' system was of the long-run type, used in comparative statics for the determination of equilibria.

In 'Part Two' of his article Lindahl attempts to outline the consequences for the Keynesian constructions involved in making a clear distinction between static long-run and short-run functions. He argues that a constant, if somewhat subtle, theme distinguishing Keynes' from the Keynesians is the former's stress on the dynamic elements in his theory. He argues that the most valuable sections of *The General Theory* consist of examinations concerning the 'dynamic factors in our present system'. He notes that Keynes' immense influence on contemporary economic thinking can hardly be understood unless the impulses making economic theory more dynamic which emanated from his work are considered.

In 'Some Critical Observations on the Major Keynesian Building Blocks' M.E. Polakoff presents a brief summary of the more important post-Keynesian contributions which have occurred since 1936. In so doing, Polakoff concentrates primarily upon empirical and theoretical contributions and in the further development and growth of a set of analytical tools which are indispensable for purposes of fiscal and economic policy. He makes a systematic and thorough treatment of the consumption function, the investment multiplier and fiscal policy, the rate of interest and the marginal efficiency of capital.

Polakoff concludes that many of the empirical and theoretical contributions shed a good deal of light on *The General Theory*. In particular, many of the Keynesian building-blocks were found either to be inadequate or lacking the necessary precision which is indispensable for purposes of policy and prediction. Such research has not detracted from Keynes' essential contribution, which rescued economics from Say's Law.

In 'An Evaluation of John Maynard Keynes' J.M. Gillman devotes careful attention to Keynes' three 'independent variables' — the propensity to consume, the marginal efficiency of capital and the interest rate. Gillman also considers Keynes' view of the rate of interest and the relationship between interest and investment. After attempts to test Keynes' concepts against facts and the operation of the economy, Gillman concludes that capitalists are not initially impelled to act in the manner envisaged by Keynes.

W. L. Smith's 'A Graphical Exposition of the Complete Keynesian System' chiefly employs a simple graphical technique to exhibit the mechanisms and workings of the Keynesian model. Smith uses IS and LM curves to clarify a range of issues in the hope that Keynes' leading ideas will be more accessible to students.

In 'What is Surviving? An Appraisal of Keynesian Economics on its Twentieth Anniversary' W. Fellner delineates three forms of Keynesianism: (1) cyclical Keynesianism; (2) stagnationist Keynesianism; and (3) fundamental–theoretical Keynesianism. He argues that cyclical Keynesianism has survived the twenty years and predicts that it will continue to be an influential doctrine in the future. By contrast, stagnationist and fundamental–theoretical Keynesianism have been vigorously attacked and they might not survive. Fellner also argues that the specific analytical tools of the Keynesian system will retain their usefulness in those contexts where it is considered advisable to disregard the equilibrating faculty of changes in the general price level.

In 'The Influence of Keynesian Economics on Contemporary Thought' Dillard outlines the meaning of Keynesian economics to academics and professionals and to the wider community. To academics and professionals the term refers to the tools of analysis, such as the propensity to consume, the marginal efficiency of capital and liquidity preference. To the wider community, Keynesian economics involve quantitative and qualitative judgements about institutional and historical developments. While academics judge the influence of Keynesian economics in terms of the tools of analysis, the wider community judges it in terms of the influence on policy and ideology. Dillard stresses that although academic economists are interested in policy questions, they have a tendency to evaluate Keynesian economics as a conceptual system which *per se* has nothing to do with policy and ideology. Dillard argues that the essential difference between pre-Keynesian and Keynesian economics lies in attitudes towards a solution of the problem of poverty. He contends that this represents a shift from what may be called the economics of scarcity to the economics of potential plenty, and that Keynesian economics reflects the economic developments of the twentieth century. In other words, Keynesian economics reflects nothing less than the recognition on the level of economic analysis of the age of mass production and increased national wealth.

In the 'Discussion' following Dillard's paper, D. Wright seeks to clarify the similarities and differences of the loanable fund and liquidity-preference theories. W. Salant adds another type of Keynesianism to Fellner's three groups, namely 'contingent' or 'conditional' Keynesianism. T. Scitovsky stresses that one of Keynes' main contributions was the notion of underemployment equilibrium, for it harmonised price theory and employment theory.

In 'Malthus and Keynes — A Reconsideration' B.A. Corry argues that the attempt to establish Malthus as a forerunner of Keynes is of doubtful validity on two grounds. First, he believes that the functional relationship making up the theoretical framework of *The General Theory* is absent in Malthus' writings. Second, he objects to the view, so strongly advanced by Keynes, that the virtual obliteration of the Malthusian line of inquiry and domination of Ricardian economics has been a disaster for the advancement of economics. Corry then demonstrates that Malthus was not an analytic forerunner of Keynes, and that victory for Malthus in his dispute with Ricardo over the effects of capital accumulation would probably not have hastened the development of Keynesian economics.

In his note 'Keynes and the Classics: A Dynamical Perspective' R. Clower suggests a straightforward dynamical interpretation of the foundations of Keynesian and classical thought. He observes that while it is possible to draw technical distinctions between modern and pre-Keynesian economics, it is primarily with respect to matters of intellectual orientation that the two are strikingly different. On Clower's interpretation, the essential formal difference between Keynes and the classics is more one of subject-matter than of fundamental underlying postulates.

D.J.J. Botha's 'The Critics of Keynesian Economics' is a review article of H. Haylett's edited book of the same title. Botha argues that since 1936 Keynesian economics has passed through two phases: (1) the more narrow pro- and anti-Keynesian phase followed by (2) the so-called 'post-Keynesian' phase. Botha believes that Haylett's book, which contains twenty-two essays, belongs to the first phase, but is anti- not pro-Keynes. He argues that the editor is wrong in claiming that the early articles were the final reputation of Keynesian economics. Botha concentrates his review on the articles by J. Viner, who defended the classical doctrine of wage flexibility as a means of ensuring full employment and W.H. Hutt, who supports Viner's position.

In 'Keynes' Finance Motive' P. Davidson notes Ohlin's criticism of Keynes' position and how, in a 1937 review and restatement of his ideas, Keynes introduced his finance motive. Keynes argued that if decisions to invest are increasing, the extra finance involved will constitute an additional demand for money. Consequently, the finance motive was an important additional component to the aggregate money demand function, when the decision to change the level of investment occurred. Davidson argues, and shows, that most writers simply ignored the finance motive by popularising in the name of Keynes a macroeconomic system which made it easy to abrogate completely the finance motive. However, by turning to Keynes' 1937 work, Davidson argues that it is clear that the quantity of money demanded for transaction balances is not directly related to output; rather it is associated with planned or expected spending propensities. Consequently the finance motive evolves as one of the dynamic elements in Keynes' static world. Davidson concludes that the implications for the basic model of Keynes' finance motive are threefold. First, one should not expect the income velocity of money to be constant. Second, a shift in any component of the aggregate demand for money formation will induce a concomitant shift in the transaction demand for money function. Third, with the finance motive the system cannot be dichotomised into independent monetary and real markets since the scale of activity is an important determinant of the level of aggregate demand and therefore of the quantity of money demanded.

The purpose of W.H. Hutt's article 'Keynesian Revisions' is to discuss the significance of the symposium of contributions from leading economists which appeared in the edited volume by R. Leckachman, *Keynes' General Theory — Reports of Three Decades*. Each of the contributors (Haberler, Harrod, Lerner, Reddaway, Austin Robinson, Samuelson, Sweezy and Viner) has two articles — a reprint of a paper written for two decades ago and one specially written for the symposium. Hutt is avowedly anti-Keynesian and he looks for criticisms of Keynes in all the essays. He argues that the striking feature of the new essays is the evidence they afford the discerning reader of the gradual abandonment of the critical logical elements in Keynes' argument. Hutt points out that this retreat can be perceived in eight of the nine articles, the exception being Harrod's papers. He argues that none of the contributors has, however, noted the chief reason why the Keynesian system has been abandoned, namely the experience in the real world. Hutt contends that the actual course of contemporary experience, rather than academic criticism, has undermined the doctrine of *The General Theory*.

At the beginning of his article, 'Keynes After Thirty Years' A.H. Hansen gives a neat summary of Keynes' challenge to neoclassical economics, pointing out that Keynes accepted in full the microeconomic foundations of neoclassical economics. He details the progress of the Keynesian revolution over the period 1936 to 1946 and he argues that the United Nations' Monetary and Financial Conference of forty-five nations at Bretton Woods marked a milestone in the acceptance of Keynes' ideas. He discusses the British White Paper on Employment, the Canadian Documents of 1945 and the 1946 Employment Acts as examples of the change in government thinking. Hansen then outlines the influence of the Keynesian revolution on American administrations. He argues that during Eisenhower's presidency the Republicans came to accept fiscal policy as a necessary and effective anti-depression weapon. More importantly, Hansen believes that the inauguration of President Kennedy led to a new group of convinced and highly competent Keynesians filling all the important economic posts in Washington. He concludes that although Keynes had largely revolutionised the way America thought about economic problems, the nation still had a long way to go.

In 'Keynes and the Keynesians: A Suggested Interpretation' A. Leijonhufvud points out that Keynesian economics, in a popularist sense, is far from a homogeneous doctrine. To him, the common denominator of the 'majority' of Keynesians is the class of models generally used. However, he argues that the standard model, stemming from Hicks' 1937 paper, is an adequate vehicle for the interpretation of Keynes' ideas. After noting that Keynes' theory was dynamic, while his model was static, Leijonhufvud argues that in Keynes' analysis: (1) transactors maximise utility and profit in the manner assumed in classical analysis and in making decisions on savings and investment; (2) price-incentives are effective and this includes intertemporal price-incentives; and (3) the existence of a hypothetical vector of non-negative prices and interest rates which would bring full resource-utilisation is not desired.

In 'Keynes and the Monetarists' S. Weintraub argues that Keynes would have approved of the modern monetarist inscription that 'money matters'. Weintraub seeks to examine how and where money enters into Keynes' system, as well as attempting to contrast some of Keynes' ideas on output levels and inflation and their monetary implications with the views of Milton Friedman, the most prominent monetarist. He argues that two core themes are distinguishable in *The General Theory*, one delineating the employment–output determination (the employment or output theory) and the other concerns Keynes' price level theory. The former is given greater prominence in exposition and application in *The General Theory*. Weintraub explores both theories and concludes that in the relation of money to output and employment there was little to distinguish Friedman from Keynes. However, on price level or inflation, two camps are evident — the monetarist and the wage sects. For Keynesians, the wage–productivity mechanism was more decisive, while to Friedman it is the dual of money supply and output. He concludes that the contemporary dispute must ultimately revolve about the respective theories of the price level and the policies advanced to combat inflation.

J.M. Letiche's 'Soviet Views on Keynes: A Review Article Surveying the Literature' presents an extended review of the book *An Analysis of Soviet Views on John Maynard Keynes* by C.B. Turner. Letiche's paper is a most detailed survey of the literature and not simply a review of Turner's book. After an extensive discussion Letiche forms five conclusions. (1) The appraisal of the Soviet economic literature on Keynes from 1917 to 1964 published in Turner's book demonstrates that politico–nationalist forces primarily determined the extent of Soviet acceptance and/or reception of Keynesian economic writings. (2) The ideological factor in traditional Marxian economic theory (especially the labour theory of value) readily lent itself to the political misuse of the Soviet economic profession, and this was particularly true in the harsh interpretation of Keynes. (3) The Soviet advance in modern economic analysis appears first to have substantially spread in the theoretical non-mathematical literature. (4) Since the mid-1950s, when a large body of modern economic principles was introduced into the Soviet Union, there has been a growing recognition that they have nothing inherently 'capitalistic' or 'socialistic' about them. (5) Marxian economists' attention has been riveted to their fundamental law that the evolution of an economic system is a self-generating dialectical process in which contradiction with the system produces continual motion and development.

H.I. Grossman's 'Was Keynes a "Keynesian"? A Review Article' seeks to evaluate critically the arguments proposed by A. Leijonhufvud's *On Keynesian Economics and the Economics of Keynes. A Study in Monetary Theory*. Grossman points out that Leijonhufvud has argued convincingly that popular Keynesianism does not have an adequate choice–theoretic (i.e. microeconomic) basis, and he contends that Keynes would have been unsympathetic with the development of popular 'Keynesian' macroeconomic theory. Grossman adopts a contrary position and he suggests that Keynes' thinking was both substantially in accord with that of his popularisers and similarly deficient. Grossman's paper focuses upon Keynes' treatment of the demand for labour services, a part of Keynes' model neglected in Leijonhufvud's book. Grossman contends that this particular aspect of *The General Theory* is both central and completely unambiguous as well as being inconsistent with Leijonhufvud's hypothesis regarding the basic conceptions of the consumption function which Keynes himself held. Grossman argues that this inconsistency suggests that Keynes' own formulation of the consumption function was simply *ad hoc*.

The first half of G.L.S. Shackle's 'Keynes and Today's Establishment in Economic Theory: A View' surveys the leading features and analytical tools of *The General Theory*. The latter half of the paper is, in essence, a note on A. Leijonhufvud's *On Keynesian Economics and the Economics of Keynes. A Study in Monetary Theory*. In discussing the book Shackle observes that, unlike contemporary professional economists, Keynes was not a narrow specialist but a man of diverse intellectual interests and abilities.

L.B. Yeager's 'The Keynesian Diversion' contains an overview of the leading tenets of the Keynesian and monetarist schools. To Yeager, Keynes' main contribution was to highlight and extend concern for the problem of employment and effective demand. He notes how in re-reading *The General Theory* he was struck by its resemblance to the supposedly vulgar Keynesianism of income–expenditure theory. In order to highlight the diversion Keynes caused in the evolution of economic science Yeager discusses the work of Harry Gunnison Brown, an early twentieth-century economist, who had made great steps towards an integration of monetary theory and disequilibrium theory.

In 'Kuhnian Scientific Revolutions and the Keynesian Revolution' R. Stanfield attempts to demonstrate the applicability of the Kuhnian paradigm to the Keynesian revolution. He reviews the basic Kuhnian model and compares it with the revolution in economics flowing from Keynes' *General Theory*. Stanfield's discussion leads him to the following three conclusions: (1) both absolutist and relativistic approaches to the history of economics contribute to the invisibility of revolutions and, therefore, to the science-as-accumulation illusion; (2) progress in economic science does not involve a teleological movement towards truth but an increase in the number of puzzles provided; and (3) the commitment to a paradigm as an act of faith cannot be overstated, nor can the analogy of scientific revolutions to political revolutions.

In the first section of his paper 'Keynes and Leijonhufvud' R. Jackman discusses Leijonhufvud's criticisms of the income–expenditure theory, especially the position that the IS–LM diagram completely misrepresents Keynes' vision of the economic system. Jackman refutes Leijonhufvud's view and argues that for specific purposes it is useful to represent Keynes' theory within the conventional IS–LM framework. Jackman also challenges Leijonhufvud's interpretation of Keynes as an accurate representation of his vision.

In 'A Contribution to the Criticism of Keynes and Keynesianism' P. Erdös seeks to illustrate, besides some features of the 'new economics' which have affected economic thinking, Keynes' failure to understand deeply enough the mature forces working in a capitalist economy. He also attempts to explain why for decades the Keynesian tools of controlling the economy appeared to be efficient and then argues why these same tools must fail in the future. In Erdös' opinion, Keynes' scientific achievements marked a high point in the history of non-Marxist economic thought. He contends that Keynes, while turning against some neoclassical theories characteristic of the Marshallian–Pigovian school, remained deeply in the captivity of the school. He attempts to demonstrate the shortcomings in Keynes' methodology by examining his formula for the purchasing power of money. Erdös also argues that the Keynesian principle of effective demand usurps the part played in reality by the profit principle. He concludes that the usual Keynesian tools of anticyclic economic policy fall short of a comprehensive socialisation of investment vaguely advocated by Keynes and, thus, capitalism slides into a world of stagnation and inflation.

In the first section of his paper 'Keynes, Inflation and Money Illusion' J.A. Trevithick restates Keynes' theory of inflation, examines the strategy he advocated for controlling inflation and builds a model to represent Keynes' theory. After making extensive use of Keynes' writings in 1940-2, from the Public Record Office, Trevithick contrasts his model with the neo-Keynesians' formalisations of *How to Pay for the War*. He shows that Keynes, unlike many neo-Keynesians, did not invoke the assumption of money illusion as an adjunct to his theory of inflation. Trevithick argues that Keynes proposed a model which relied almost exclusively upon lags in adjustment in avoiding a decline into hyperinflation. Finally, Trevithick contends that, despite its analytical rigour, Keynes' *How to Pay for the War* did little to answer the questions posed by the modern theorist concerning the level of inflation, for the inflations which preoccupied Keynes' attention were normally of the short, sharp variety, which were associated with particular situations of national crisis.

In his article 'Keynes and US Keynesianism' R. Chase argues that the development of the economics of *The General Theory*, particularly in the United States, resulted in a 'variant Keynesianism', which was incapable of achieving a set of predetermined policy objectives. Chase believes that American Keynesianism followed a development path that is fundamentally different from that of Keynes and his perspective. To support this argument, Chase sets forth a general interpretative framework for Keynes' economic vision. He utilises this framework to explain how the macroanalytics of American Keynesianism was at variance with *The General Theory*.

At the outset of 'The Keynesian Light that Failed' S. Weintraub asserts that Keynesianism had 'bumbled the inflation issue' and now stands in disarray. He attacks those Keynesians who have not read *The General Theory*, and many of those who have, for failing to absorb its content. He then argues that the lack of an appreciation for the money wage in inflation and the absence of a serious long-range incomes policy separated Keynes from the Keynesians. Weintraub also lists fifteen points to render Keynesianism more consistent with Keynes' writings. His main points include: (1) any model purporting to capture the flavour of Keynes which omits a money-wage parameter is suspect; (2) attributing Keynes' underemployment equilibrium to 'rigid' money wages is bad theory and worse semantics; (3) diagrams must be drawn correctly, since numerous textbooks abound with diagrams linking labour demand with real wages; (4) acknowledgement is made that wages are the modern causal force of inflation; (5) money supplies are envisaged in a non-monetary fashion; (6) the transcription of Keynes to models with contracts and flexible exogeneous money–wage payments; and (7) the removal of investment from being static. Weintraub concludes by noting that if 'Keynesianism has failed, might we not try Keynes?'

The review article by A.S. Eichner and J.A. Kregel 'An Essay on Post-Keynesian Theory: A New Paradigm in Economics' provides a guide to the diverse post-Keynesian literature, as it notes the basic works and conveys the salient features of the new approach. The paper divides into the following four parts, each dealing with a separate distinguishing characteristic of the post-Keynesian approach: (1) growth dynamics, (2) distributional effects, (3) the Keynesian constraints and (4) the microeconomic base. Although they construct a table which compares and contrasts post-Keynesian with neoclassical theory, Eichner and Kregel discuss the divergences within each group. They conclude that post-Keynesian theory has the potential to become a comprehensive and positive alternative to the prevailing neoclassical paradigm.

In ' "Uncertainty" and the Keynesian Revolution' E. Weintraub examines one innovation that Keynes introduced into economics with his *General Theory*, namely, the relationship of uncertainty to investment. He demonstrates that this theme had existed in Keynes' writings as early as 1908 and was essential to his main thesis of 1936. Weintraub also suggests why this innovation effectively disappeared from view as Keynes' own work was transformed by economists such as Hicks, Hansen and Klein into Keynesianism or Keynesian economics. In this context he argues that a great deal of the Keynes–classical debate shifted the ground from the relationship between interest rates and investment. Weintraub also raises a related question of why Keynesianism was unable to discuss uncertainty problems and he attempts to demonstrate that general equilibrium theory (i.e. the method of analysis which was finally used to adjudicate the Keynes–classical controversy) was insufficiently developed at the time to pose the right questions. Finally, Weintraub indicates the role of a few economists, including Shackle, whose work has been consistent with Keynes' uncertainty motif.

In 'The Keynesian Paradigm and Economic Policy' A.H. Bornemann argues that Keynesian macroeconomic theory and the relatively new theory of public administration were both introduced in the United States around the time of the New Deal. He outlines how Keynesian theory, which emphasised government fiscal policy and deficit spending to counter depressions, maintain full employment and economic growth, became the accepted paradigm in economics and public finance. Consequently, public administration theory developed and held that government agencies, motivated primarily by their own bureaucratic expansionary self-interest, would result in an equilibrium of national self interest.

In 'Economic Methodology in the Face of Uncertainty: The Modelling Methods of Keynes and the Post-Keynesians' J.A. Kregel attempts to show how post-Keynesian theory can be considered a legitimate extension of the basic methodology employed by Keynes in *The General Theory*, and that the nature and use of the concept of equilibrium in post-Keynesian analysis is different from the orthodox position. Kregel argues that the methodology Keynes chose in incorporating the analysis of an uncertain world was in terms of alternative specification about the effects of uncertainty and disappointment. He points out that this procedure can be characterised in terms of three models of equilibrium — static, stationary and shifting. Each model depicted different assumptions about the effect of uncertainty and disappointment. The paper also argues that Keynes' own view of his general theoretical approach was that it could be used to analyse a range of problems in addition to that which he found most pressing.

M.R. Fisher's 'Professor Hicks and the Keynesians' is a review article of *The*

Crisis in Keynesian Economics by J. Hicks. Hicks' book is a revision of three lectures given in Helsinki in 1973, the first two covering the multiplier, the marginal efficiency of capital and liquidity preference, the final one being devoted to wages and inflation. Fisher's review is exceedingly comprehensive and he carefully weighs and assesses Hicks' modifications to the Keynesian framework.

In their article 'Keynes' Employment Function Re-examined' B. Henneberry and J.G. Witte note that a great deal of the discussion concerning Keynes' aggregate supply and demand functions in the 1960s and early 1970s concerned an endless manipulation of identities, with little of substance emerging. To them, the issue at stake was whether or not the real wage is determined by the level of employment, or vice versa. In an attempt to repeat the identity conjugation they use Keynes' own text as a framework. They claim that while Wells, Weintraub and Leijonhufvud argue that the real wage is a function of employment, which is determined by the autonomous element in total spending, nothing of substance is altered if, with appropriate adjustments, employment were made a function of the real wage rate.

In 'Keynesian Economics: The Search for First Principles' A. Coddington considers three varieties of Keynesianism — fundamental, hydraulic and reconstituted. He then locates each one in relation to a reductionist programme. He concludes that (1) the fundamental approach rejected choice and equilibrium market theory; (2) the hydraulic approach short-circuited reductionist market theory and eschewed formal choice theory; and (3) the reconstituted-reductionist approach attempted to make room for Keynesian ideas within the reductionist programme by refocusing the market theory on disequilibrium states while retaining the standard choice–theoretical foundation. He contends that the three approaches are largely complementary in their contribution to an understanding of Keynesian economics.

In 'Institutionalism, Keynes, and the Real World' W.C. Peterson views Keynesianism and institutional economics as two trains which started on parallel tracks towards a common destination of understanding the workings of a complex, capitalistic system. He considers that Keynesianism developed much more rapidly than institutionalism, but was shunted onto another track and synthesised with neoclassical analysis. He argues that Keynes was institutionalist in the sense that his important behavioural relationships (consumption and investment spending and the demand for liquidity) are embedded in the institutions of our age. Peterson discusses a number of seminal ideas common to both Keynes and institutionalism in his attempt to attain a better appreciation of the workings of the real world economy.

In 'From Pre-Keynes to Post-Keynes' A.P. Lerner argues that pre-Keynesian economics unduly concentrated on microeconomics, while Keynesians devoted too much attention to macroeconomics. To Lerner, post-Keynesians had integrated macroeconomics with microeconomics to cope with the combination of depression with inflation. He maintains that the 'fundamental' Keynesian revolution was essentially a *policy* revolution, based on a theory which showed that, if money wages were rigid, then increasing the real purchasing power of the stock of money by decreasing the price level was impossible. Lerner also suggests that the previous policy problems of 'Keynesianism' stem from a lack of microeconomic analysis, both in the application of 'demand management' and in the attempt to apply incomes policy. He contends that an incomes policy to control wages, based on a recognition of microeconomic forces and principles, should produce better results in controlling inflation.

In 'How Dead is Keynes?' J. Tobin seeks to answer the question as to whether events have refuted Keynes. In an attempt to arrive at a conclusion, Tobin recalls four central propositions of *The General Theory*. (1) In modern industrial societies, prices and wages respond slowly to excess demand or supply, especially slowly to excess supply. (2) Economies are vulnerable to lengthy bouts of involuntary unemployment. (3) Capital-formation depends on long-run appraisals of profit expectations and risks, and on business attitudes towards risk. (4) Even if money wages and prices were responsive to market excess demands and supplies, their flexibility would not necessarily stabilise monetary economies subject to demand and supply shocks. Tobin submits that none of these four central propositions is inconsistent with the contemporary economic scene. After examining why there is great resistance among economists and men of affairs to a Keynesian diagnosis of the present economic situation, Tobin argues that Keynes is most relevant to a situation of increasing prices and increasing unemployment. He concludes that the only way out of the dilemma is to establish an incomes policy.

The main object of H. Minsky's paper 'The Financial Instability Hypothesis: An Interpretation of Keynes' is to state succinctly the financial instability hypothesis and to indicate briefly why it is better suited to contemporary economics than the dominant neoclassical synthesis. Minsky points out that Viner's review of *The General Theory* was the only one to draw a rebuttal from Keynes. Minsky summarises the leading features of this rebuttal and relates how Keynes insisted that the main proposition of *The General Theory* centred around the disequilibrating forces that operated in financial markets. Moreover, these forces directly affected the valuation of capital assets relative to the prices of current output, and this price ratio, along with financial market conditions, determines investment activity. Minsky then details the 'financial instability hypothesis' and argues that it is a theory which endeavours to explain the phenomena of the trade cycle.

V. Chick, in 'The Nature of the Keynesian Revolution: A Reassessment', argues that Keynes' revolution lay in his choice of analytical method, and she demonstrates that Keynes applied a rudimentary process analysis to an economy characterised by a definite sequence of decisions and events through time. She contends that, as a result of this change of method, it is no longer appropriate to treat 'equilibrium' as synonymous with the absence of excess demand or supply in every market. Chick also demonstrates that R. Clower's analysis is neoclassical in structure and hence is unable to illuminate the nature of the Keynesian revolution. Contradicting Clower, Chick argues (1) that the general equilibrium equations are quantity-constrained; hence quantity-constraint cannot be an innovation of Keynes; (2) that the dual-decision hypothesis is inconsistent with Keynes' method and is a misspecification of the behaviour of households; and (3) that Keynes' analysis is inconsistent with general equilibrium analysis but not with the theory of household behaviour and the consumption function is firmly rooted in standard value theory.

In 'Keynes and the Multiplier' D. Patinkin establishes the evolution of Keynes' notion of the multiplier. Patinkin argues that the first hint of the multiplier in Keynes' writings dates back to May 1929, when he wrote a pamphlet with Hubert Henderson on *Can Lloyd George Do It? An Examination of the Liberal Party*. Four years later in *Means to Prosperity* Keynes estimated the United States' multiplier. Patinkin also considers the relationship of Kahn's 1931 article on the multiplier and Keynes' discussion of the concept. He argues that Kahn's article did not recognise the theory of effective demand, and it was Keynes who incorporated this concept into lectures to his students in 1933 and 1934.

In 'Keynesian Economics, Equilibrium, and Time' A. Asimakopulos notes that H. Johnson had conveniently identified two theories in Keynes' *General Theory*: (1) the equilibrium model elaborated by Hicks with his IS–LM diagram and (2) the 'other' theory which attempted to introduce historical time into the analysis. However, Asimakopulos argues that Johnson's writing concentrated on the equilibrium model and omitted important aspects of Keynes' theory, which underestimated the revolutionary nature of that theory. He demonstrates that Keynes considered the role of time and uncertain expectations to be the crucial message of *The General Theory*.

At the outset of her article 'Keynes and Equilibrium Economics' N. Shapiro claims that one of the critical aftermaths of the Keynesian revolution has been a re-examination of the characteristic methodology of modern economics, the equilibrium method. In this context, Shapiro takes up the question of the conceptual underpinning of the equilibrium methodology, which she argues was intrinsically associated with the neoclassical conception of economic life. More significantly, however, Shapiro argues that Keynes broke with the equilibrium methodology and she contends that this involved a break with the neoclassical conception of economic life, especially its treatment of capital and capitalist production.

In 'Patinkin, Keynes, and Aggregate Supply and Demand Analysis' D.L. Roberts praises Patinkin's discussion of Keynes' thinking on monetary problems but attacks his evaluation of Keynes' aggregate supply and demand analysis. Roberts' paper seeks to correct Patinkin's view that Keynes was confused on the matter, and he attempts to show that many of the ambiguities which Patinkin attributed to *The General Theory* emanated from his inadequate interpretation of Keynes' aggregate supply and demand functions. He concludes that if one adopts alternative definitions of aggregate supply and demand, then most of Patinkin's criticisms are unjustified.

In his response to Roberts, Patinkin devotes considerable attention to the meaning of Keynes' aggregate supply function. He argues that there have been numerous interpretations of Keynes' aggregate supply functions and he doubts if Keynes himself knew what it was. In discussing what was involved in this function Patinkin contends that if there is disagreement on the nature of the supply curve in Keynes' *General Theory*, then there must, of necessity, be disagreement about the nature of equilibrium and the adjustment process.

In 'Has Keynes Failed?' Joan Robinson recalls how at a dinner in Washington with his converts, Keynes expressed scepticism about the possibility of achieving full employment and how next morning he told Austin Robinson, 'I was the only non-Keynesian there'. Joan Robinson argues that Keynes foresaw that if a long-run of near-full employment was achieved, inflation through increasing money wage rates presented an awkward political problem for which there was no solution. Robinson argues that Keynes overestimated the power of reason and that his vision of a rational economic policy was muffled and distorted when it became a new orthodoxy. Although he failed in the sense that he thought he was living in a sensible community, Robinson believes that the academic teaching profession failed Keynes, for they did not radically consider the whole corpus of orthodox doctrine, dividing economics into micro and macro courses. She also notes that there is still a great deal to be worked out in *The General Theory*, e.g. the long-period analysis of distribution, technical development, theory of capital, normal profits and the theory of international trade. Robinson concludes that while the task of Keynes' successors has been to amend, elaborate and develop his ideas, their efforts have been frustrated by the 'determined obscurantism of the mainstream of the profession'.

In 'Keynes and the Steady State Economy' S. Peitchinis argues that the Keynesian model is an appropriate model for a steady-state economy. He says that Keynes offered no guidance on how to maintain full employment in the absence of a growth in output and on when output can be increased substantially with the same numerical labour force. Peitchinis contends that Keynes assumed that growth in the aggregate volume of output was always possible, it being a matter only of appropriate stimulative measures. He concludes that the prolonged periods of limited growth and the failure of a variety of expansionary measures have raised questions about the effectiveness of Keynesian postulates.

In 'Keynes as New Dawn' E. Nell refutes Lerner's position that Keynes' true contribution was to revolutionise policy. Nell argues that this is not how Keynes himself saw his mission, for he advanced *theoretical* as well as practical arguments. To Nell, Keynes' contribution was to open up a new perspective in economic theory and he developed the theory of effective demand as an alternative to the neoclassical theory of employment based on marginal productivity.

In 'From Post-Keynes to Pre-Keynes' J.A. Kregel suggests that a broadly accepted interpretation of Keynes, such as that set out by Lerner, fails to comprehend the crucial 'micro' problems which concerned Keynes and his followers, because the interpretation ignores the basic methodological innovations underlying the suggestions for full-employment policy. He argues that Lerner ignored the wider political and social aspects of Keynes' analysis. Contrary to Lerner, Kregel contends that Keynes did not ignore market phenomena or assume wage or price rigidity and, hence, rigidity could not be primarily responsible for either wage inflation or unemployment. He points out that Lerner's remedies for a situation or stagnation cannot be derived from Keynes' view of the determination of wages and employment, and that they would be inadequate to produce wage stability. Finally, Kregel notes the extreme difference between the method of analysis employed by Keynes and that of 'Keynesian' theory.

J. Halevi's 'Comment on Professor Lerner's Paper: A Marxist View' notes that the important point of Lerner's argument (in which he fully agrees) lies in having stressed the fact that a cut in monetary spending generates unemployment rather than a decline in the rate of inflation. However, Halevi argues that wage flexibility is not a necessary prerequisite for achieving full employment, and that equilibrium should not be thought of in 'abstract' but in relation to the structure of the economy. He also notes that Keynes, while aware of the problem of the structure of investment in relation to the level of effective demand, adopted a somewhat ambiguous position. On the one hand he acknowledged that there was no clear evidence from experience to indicate that the investment policy which is socially advantageous coincides with that which is most profitable. On the other hand, he maintained that there is no reason to assume that the economic system seriously misemploys the factors of production which are in use.

A. Lerner's 'On Keynes, Policy and Theory — A Grumble' is a reply to criticism by Nell, Kregel and Halevi, who argued that his earlier 1977 article had completely misunderstood and misinterpreted Keynes' basic economic theory. However, Lerner asserts that all three agreed with his main thesis that Keynes' most important practical contribution lay in showing how unreasonable was the policy of waiting for the natural working of the laws of supply and demand to cure general unemployment. Lerner attempts to refute the claims of his three critics that he had assumed or attributed to Keynes the hypothesis that wages are absolutely rigid downwards. Lerner then sets out his basic grumble, which concerns the alleged contrast between theory and policy. He fails to understand how anyone can doubt that Keynes strongly advocated a policy of adjusting money to wages, rather than the 'flexible wages policy' of the government trying to make wages adjust to the money supply. He agrees with Keynes that the resistance of workers to wage cuts makes the flexible wage policy unviable.

In his short note 'Post-Keynesian Economics, Abba Lerner, and his Critics' D. Collander argues that, contrary to the claims of his critics, Lerner's proposal for a market-based incomes policy is in no sense a departure from Keynes' approach to economic problems. Collander stresses that Lerner's interpretation of Keynes is not severely at odds with that of his critics. He notes that it merely emphasises different points which focus on Keynes' realytic and not on his analytic contribution.

The purpose of A. Coddington's 'Hicks' Contribution to Keynesian Economics' is to examine Hicks' contribution to macroeconomic theory in those respects in which it constitutes a response to, or a development of, Keynes' work. Coddington is concerned with what Hicks obtained from Keynes' writings and what he did with it, rather than with what was really in Keynes. Coddington chose Hicks for his study because of the role he played in making *The General Theory* accessible to the economics profession at large. Coddington examines four aspects of Hicks' work: (1) the writings in which Hicks provides a reconciliation of the Keynesian treatment of motives for holiday money with textbook treatment; (2) Hicks' choice–theoretic formulation of the concept of liquidity; (3) his decisive dismissal of the possibility of reaching stagnationist conclusions with the aid of Keynes' marginal efficiency of capital concept; and (4) Hicks' characterisation of Keynes' work as a method of approaching the problem of economic dynamics. Coddington concludes that on the one hand Hicks was a most severe critic of Keynes' own analysis and, on the other, he was one of the most vigorous and persistent of those who tried to refine and strengthen Keynes' basic ideas. In sum, Hicks restated Keynes' ideas with an increased degree of analytical purity.

In his 'Reply' Hicks points out that he did not easily recognise himself as a 'whole-hearted Keynesian'. He also outlines how it was not until he wrote a paper on 'Methods of Dynamic Analysis' in 1956 that he realised that the most fundamental contribution of *The General Theory* was Keynes' decision to use the business accounting framework as an instrument of analysis.

At the commencement of his article 'Marx, Keynes and the Possibility of Crisis' P. Kenway points out that his research is the product of two 'apparently unconnected lines of enquiry'. The first is of the nature of the puzzle, for Kenway is extremely interested in resolving the question of why Keynes' simple manipulation of aggregate variables yields results which appear quite extraordinary compared with those of orthodox economics. The second question is one of exposition. Ricardo was a strong supporter of the argument which showed that the capitalist economy would not suffer a general glut of commodities. Marx challenged the position and, in so doing, outlined his ideas on the 'possibility of crisis' which highlights the elements within a capitalist economy for which a breakdown could develop. To Kenway, Marx's 'possibility of crisis' theory provides an answer to 'the Keynesian puzzle' and shows why the level of aggregate demand is important. He stresses that it is quite separate from Keynes' theory of effective demand, since Keynes did not require such a theory to justify his effective demand concept. Yet Kenway concludes that Marx and Keynes occupy substantially the same ground on the question of the nature of the problem, though their treatment is entirely different.

S.C. Tsiang's paper 'Keynes' "Finance" Demand for Liquidity' argues that Keynes' 1937 concessions on the finance demand for liquidity made in response to Ohlin's criticism of *The General Theory* provides the key for the reconciliation of the liquidity preference theory to the loanable funds theory and the stock approach with the flow approach. Moreover, on a range of practical issues, D.H. Robertson, who expounded traditional monetary theory, is shown to be right, and Keynes wrong. Tsiang's paper also seeks to demonstrate that Milton Friedman, the modern arch-critic of Keynes, is under Keynes' influence in relying exclusively upon the stock, or portfolio, approach to the neglect of the influences of flow decisions on the money demand. Tsiang argues that Friedman's attempt to combine the work of Keynes and Fisher is unsuccessful. Finally, he claims that Keynes' concession on the demand for finance made his position on savings untenable and in his counterattack on Ohlin he had manoeuvred himself into D.H. Robertson's position without even realising it.

In 'Post Keynesian Economics: A Promise that Bounced?' L. Tarshis considers that post-Keynesian economists have attempted to extend, clarify and bring up to date Keynes' *General Theory* and, in addition, they have sought to develop the microfoundations of macro theory. These attempts have found guidance in two important features of Keynes' writing: (1) his view that economic processes occur in historical rather than logical time; and (2) practically all decisions at firm, household and government levels must be made in the face of serious uncertainty. Tarshis points out that the post-Keynesians have also been concerned with problems stemming from Keynes' work which he did not tackle, e.g. the theory of the distribution of national income and the theory of economic growth and accompanying fluctuations. Tarshis concludes, however, that, with a few notable exceptions (e.g. Minsky's contribution to an understanding through which growth may lead to financial crisis) the ambitious claims of the post-Keynesians 'seem empty of substance'.

In 'On Keynesian Economics and the Economics of the Post-Keynesians' J.L. Yellen compares the new post-Keynesian economics of Davidson, Eichner, Harcourt, Kregel, Minsky, Weintraub and others with the standard Keynesian macroeconomic model which these authors have criticised. In particular, Yellen examines post-Keynesian views on pricing, output, income distribution, inflation, money and finance. She points out that, to post-Keynesians, the competitive firms for which price equals marginal cost are the exception rather than the rule. They note the existence of 'megacorps' and 'administered prices', and conclude that realism demands a scrapping of the perfect-competition paradigm. Yellen also notes that the post-Keynesian model requires as a condition of short-run equilibrium that desired expenditure be equal to output and that a notably absent feature from the model is a labour supply function. He concludes that no post-Keynesian has shown how money should be incorporated into their model of distribution and growth. However, Yellen contends that if they were to incorporate money, then the model would be indistinguishable from standard Keynesian theory.

In 'Post-Keynesian Economic Theory: An Overview and Evaluation' J.R. Crotty offers a succinct discussion of the two main wings of neo-Keynesianism. First, he discusses the neo-Keynesians, a label which refers to the largely Cambridge-based or Cambridge-inspired set of growth-theorists such as Robinson, Kaldor and Pasinetti, who have built on the works of Keynes, Kalecki and Harrod. The second group, the post-Keynesians, includes Davidson, Minsky, Shackle, S. Weintraub and the ubiquitous Robinson. Crotty argues that the neo-Keynesians attack the realism of logical consistency of the neoclassical theory of growth, while post-Keynesian theory focuses on the distributive role of factor prices in adjusting savings to investment. They stress the central features of real world capitalism which makes them suspicious of any macro theory characterised by a stable equilibrium perspective. While the post-Keynesians revived the argument presented by Keynes that the investment function is unstable, the neo-Keynesians have placed the process of capital accumulation, *per se*, at the centre of economic dynamics, with savings decisions seen as adaptive and largely institutionalised.

In his article 'The Microfoundations of Keynes' Aggregate Supply and Expected Demand Analysis' C. Casorosa advances three arguments: (1) that Keynes' supply and expected demand analysis is the extension to the system as a whole of the theory of the competitive firm; (2) at the point of intersection of the aggregate supply and demand functions the entrepreneurs' expectation of profit is maximised, and therefore the criticism of, for example, Patinkin, that the Keynesian theory of effective demand is incompatible with the profit maximisation of marginal analysis is groundless; and (3) there is no microeconomic foundation for the idea that in an atomistic market the expected demand function is the entrepreneurs' expectation of the expenditure function. In sum, Casorosa concludes that the Keynesian short-run theory of the firm is a reformulation, in terms of aggregate supply and expected demand functions for the firm, of the Marshallian theory of the competitive firm, and that the theory of effective demand extends such analysis to the system as a whole. Finally, he argues that the aggregate expected demand function for the economy as a whole is not the producer's guess of the expenditure function and that, even when the entrepreneur's expectations are right, the two functions are distinct.

74

The Future of Keynesian Economics*

D. Wright

Economic theory, like the Supreme Court of the United States, often reflects the state of public opinion, while public opinion is well known to be related to fluctuations of economic activity. At the present time increasing prosperity seems to be bringing with it a growing reaction against Keynesian teaching.[1] Criticism of policies and theories, sometimes rightly and sometimes wrongly attributed to Keynes, reaches from newspaper columnists of various degrees of economic training through the academic work of von Mering and Hahn to the fundamental theoretical dissent of Professor Frank Knight.[2] Under the circumstances, it seems likely that the present trend will go considerably further before it is reversed.

That a theory so obviously depression-born as Keynes's should lose some of its appeal in prosperity is not surprising. When we are struggling with labor shortages and inflation, references to unemployment and deflation seem out of date. Nor can the Keynesian theory — any more than any other — claim a complete immunity from error. The present paper will attempt to develop some of its shortcomings. Nevertheless, a fundamental question presents itself: Shall we allow ourselves during prosperity to forget the problem of effective demand which forms the core of Keynes's teaching? That is the real problem.

There is a tendency occasionally present today, especially in the popular press, to divide economists into two classes, "Keynesian" and "anti-Keynesian", or "orthodox", and to imply that an unbridgable gulf lies between them. Such a mode of thought seems both inaccurate and unfortunate. It is inaccurate, because it would be difficult to find an American economist today, of whatever shade of political opinion, who does not make use of some elements of the Keynesian schema. It is unfortunate, because it leads to loose generalization and, by giving a spurious appearance of disagreement, undermines the prestige of economics in the vitally important fields in which there is substantial unanimity.

*Source: *American Economic Review*, Vol. 35 (3), June 1945, pp. 284-307.

The present essay is to be viewed as an attempt to overcome this impression of fundamental cleavage and to reconcile some of the apparently wide divergences of thought. No one can deny that there are great differences today regarding proposed economic policy. But that such divergences reflect a basic theoretical cleavage seems to the writer much more doubtful. If economists would only state the sort of world at which they are aiming, and the conditions which they are assuming regarding the present one, they would find themselves, it is submitted, in very considerable analytical and theoretical agreement — whatever differences in emotional attitude, social aim, and factual assumption might still survive. Have we not reached a point in which Keynesian theory can be viewed in accurate proportion? Let us try in this paper to relate the system to the views which preceded it, evaluate its policies, and reach some conclusions regarding its future.

I

It is probable that the Athenians did not execute Socrates so much for the things he had said as for the things they thought he had said. The analysis presented in the *General Theory* is widely disliked because of certain supposed doctrines which in fact form no part, or, in some cases, no essential part, of the basic analytical structure. In particular, in business circles in this country, it seems often thought that there is something occultly "radical" or anticapitalist about the Keynesian schema. This is scarcely justified. In criticizing the *General Theory* it is important to distinguish between (1) a body of authoritative scientific analysis and (2) the personal opinions, as of 1935, of one Mr. Keynes, a somewhat discouraged liberal, regarding fact and policy. The difference is almost always clearly labeled. Most of the points particularly criticized today come in Chapter 24, "Some Notes on the Social Philosophy Toward Which the General Theory *Might* Lead" (italics added), and this chapter clearly belongs to the second category I have named. It is not an integral part of the scientific analysis which precedes it, and, moreover, if the writer interprets it correctly, is rather tentative in nature. Let us then, excluding this chapter for the time being, run over some of the main conclusions which are often erroneously thought to be an inevitable concomitant of the Keynesian method.

1. The Keynesian analysis does not in itself "prove" that we "have" to have socialism, or socialized investment, or that capitalism is "bound" to destroy itself.[3]

2. The Keynesian analysis does not necessarily prove that there will "certainly" be long-range unemployment after the war (or at any other time).[4]

3. It does not necessarily depend save in a purely formal sense either on rigid prices, rigid wages, or "hoarding" to show possibilities of unemployment

equilibrium.[5]

4. It does not say that a rising national debt is always necessary or that there is no burden to the national debt.[6]

5. It does not say that spending is always a good thing or that "saving" is always bad.[7]

6. Keynes does not believe that every dollar spent by the government necessarily "multiplies" itself several times.[8]

7. Keynes's analysis in the *General Theory* is not an argument for indiscriminate money wage increases to "redistribute" wealth, or "increase purchasing power." On the contrary, he very explicitly favors there a policy of stable money wages.[9]

8. Keynes's analysis does not deny that wage and/or price reduction can at some times and under some circumstances cure unemployment; nor need the argument necessarily be a matter of liquidity preference.[10]

9. Keynes does not favor protectionism or tariffs *per se.*[11]

10. He does not "disregard" in the *General Theory* the possible adverse effects of taxes on profits and of high, progressive income taxes generally.[12]

11. The *General Theory* is filled with references to the importance of business expectations and business "confidence." There is no ground for saying that these factors are omitted. In fact, a conservative candidate could conduct a political campaign largely on quotations from the *General Theory.*[13]

When this list is read over, and when it is remembered that most of the really startling Keynesian theoretical propositions, as for example on the "equality" of saving and investment, have been shown to be largely matters of definition, the question naturally arises why is Keynes's teaching so disliked in some quarters today? To answer this we must first give as simplified an account as possible of what that teaching is. With so much misunderstanding evident regarding conclusions, it seems plain that there must also be a widespread misunderstanding of the analysis itself.

II

Following the lead of Lord Keynes, the Keynesian schema is usually treated, by opponents and adherents alike, against a background of so-called "classical" thought. The resulting impression is apt to be first, that there was prior to the *General Theory* some single homogeneous body of doctrine regarding the relationship of employment, interest and money, and, second, that Keynesian teaching represents a marked divergence from that body. Neither of these ideas is wholly accurate and their joint effect seriously warps our perspective on the problem. Both prior to Keynes and today the widest divergences may be found regarding basic factual assumptions connected with the employment puzzle.

Nevertheless, the writer submits that it is possible to piece together a composite picture not inaccurately representing the views of a majority of English and American economists prior to the *General Theory*, and he feels that it is in the light of such a picture that the nature of the Keynesian contribution can best be judged. The tradition, submitted to have been probably the prevailing one in this country, will be found (typically) more hinted at than stated by Marshall, and usually developed in American elementary texts in eclectic combination with some of the views of Böhm-Bawerk, Fisher and Wicksell.[14]

Everybody agrees that in full-employment equilibrium the labor and other resources of society may be thought of as being distributed between two groups: makers of investment goods and makers of consumers' goods. Everyone further agrees that under such circumstances the proportion which one group bears to the other is roughly determined by the consumption habits of the economy — in Keynes's system measured by the "propensity to consume."

To the English classical writers the rate of interest was, of course, set by the supply and demand for loanable funds but on analysis this will be found to have been usually only the most superficial aspect of their theory. Fundamentally these monetary transactions were symbols expressing: (1) the supply of the commodity real saving — a flow of resources currently set free for investment uses by the failure of society to consume its entire output; (2) the demand for this commodity fixed by current investment opportunities – in the last analysis the current net marginal value product to be derived from the use of newly produced investment goods.[15] The money rate on loanable funds merely expresses the "real" rate — the excess, figured in some ideal numeraire, of real purchasing power returned to the lender, by the borrower, over that which the lender had originally parted with in making the loan.[16] Monetary changes might distort this "real" relationship but, when equilibrium was once more reattained, the real rate would be reëstablished.

So far we are on fairly firm ground but just at this point one encounters a basic cleavage of economic thought which underlies nearly all approaches to the problem and which crops up again and again. To one group of writers – for example, Professor Frank Knight — there is no limit, or virtually no limit, to the uses to which additional increments of capital (the current flow of net new investment) can be put.[17] It follows that, barring "frictions," it is practically impossible to have too large a proportion of the resources of society devoted to making investment goods, and no need to vary this proportion, certainly not to decrease it. Unemployment is to be cured by removing "frictions" of various sorts — as by wage reduction, or lowering interest. To another group current potential uses for additional capital may vary greatly over time, necessitating changes in consumption habits and/or state investment.

While one cannot be too dogmatic in this matter it is submitted that prior to Keynes probably the larger number of American and English economists believed that the *current* demand for loanable funds (essentially for the most part demand for the real resources they represented), varied over time with changes in invention, expansion, growth, etc. While John Stuart Mill's view of developed industrial countries as habitually on the "verge" of the stationary state might have been considered extreme, most economists in this country — with varying degrees of optimism regarding the investment outlook at particular periods — nevertheless felt that outlets varied over time, and that a naturally stationary state was at least a theoretical possibility.[18] But if investment outlets varied, how could full employment be maintained?

While the problem was seldom explicitly faced, the answer, it is submitted, would probably have been along the following lines. Current saving behaved like "any other" commodity. When new inventions, etc., temporarily raised the marginal productivity of capital and made it desirable, for the time being, to divert a larger proportion of resources from consumption to investment, the demand for loanable funds (under the assumed conditions thought to be little more than the symbol of the demand for free resources, released by current saving), was raised, and as a result the rate (both real and money) of interest went up. With an increased "price" paid for current saving the amount of current saving "naturally" would increase.[19] Men would be shifted from making consumption goods to making investment goods and all would be well.

If this process should be reversed, when the new opportunities were substantially exploited, and if no new ones had appeared, a greater proportion of consumption would be desirable. This too would automatically be provided for. As investment opportunity declined the rate of interest would decline. Consumption would rise as investment fell and surplus laborers in the investment industries would be moved back into making consumers' goods.

Full employment, then, barring "frictions" of adjustment, and the business cycle, would always be maintained by means of a supposed functional relationship between profits, interest, and current savings. If the economy reached a stationary state consumption would rise and the rate would: (1) fall to zero, with no net savings-investment, as maintained by Schumpeter, Irving Fisher and some of the English writers; (2) following some Austrian and Swedish writers, consumption would rise so high, due to time preference, that a certain minimum rate would be maintained since below it there would be capital consumption; (3) other writers, as J. B. Clark, spoke of a "minimum" without giving any explicit analysis as to what that minimum was or why it would arise. But in any event there would no longer be any net savings-investment and there would be full employment.[20]

Keynesian teaching diverges from the foregoing in three important ways. First of all, as with many other modern writers, emphasis is placed not so much on the technical conditions of production as on the "marginal efficiency of capital" — the *subjective expectation* of future profits to be derived from a newly produced capital asset. This is merely an elaboration of what earlier analysis, if properly interpreted, had meant to say, but it gives a place for the "confidence" and speculative factors which are so important in any real situation. Next, and more important, the Keynesian analysis denies any strong functional relationship, such as has been explained, between the rate of interest and the propensity to consume. To Keynes neither observed aggregate consumption nor the propensity to consume necessarily rises when the interest rate falls. Thirdly, the Keynesians set up a "purely" monetary theory of interest by means of which it is shown that the rate will not fall to zero even when there is unemployment and a "surplus" of free resources.

In addition to these three points the *General Theory* gives such special emphasis to one explanation of the decline in the "marginal efficiency of capital" that many people mistake this explanation for *the* general theory itself. I refer, of course, to the idea that, as production increases, consumption rises but not as much. This concept is the customary point of departure for the most usual account of Keynesian underemployment equilibrium. Because consumption does not keep pace with output, it is said that profit expectations on new investment — the "marginal efficiency of capital" — will eventually be forced to fall, but since the rate of interest does not necessarily fall with it, a point is reached at which the inducement to invest becomes zero. Were consumption to rise all might yet be well but, since the propensity to consume in the short run is relatively invariant, consumption is not likely to rise. A deflationary gap appears, secondary deflation begins, and the economy is forced down to a point at which either the refusal of people to curtail their standard of living further or the intrusion of new dynamic factors brings the contraction to a close. New dynamic factors, or capital consumption, may then induce some recovery, but there remains a body of men unemployed and, unless something happens to raise sufficiently either the inducement to invest or the propensity to consume, *average* unemployment, despite cyclical variations, is indefinitely prolonged. On one side there is usually, but *not* necessarily, a block of "idle" money; on the other, there is always a block of idle men.

The sequence of events just given is by no means the only possible way in which Keynesian unemployment equilibrium could arise but it is the most usual manner of explanation and will serve as a good point of departure for our appraisal.

III

Our task in this paper is to see whether the foregoing analysis should properly be called "radical" and whether it represents a marked divergence from, or contradiction of, the main current of previously existing economic thought. But first of all, whether radical or not, a large part of it, even on first examination, is obviously true. Of the three main points mentioned above, the first, the concept of the "marginal efficiency of capital," and Keynes's brilliant bull and bear analysis have roused little opposition and are generally accepted. The second, the failure of the propensity to consume in the short (five- or ten-year) period to move inversely with the rate of interest, to any important extent, is so well established empirically as to be incontrovertible. On the other hand, the behavior of the longer-run propensity to consume is more problematical and, as Dr. Samuelson points out, it appears at times to rise spontaneously, so as to overtake output.[21] The views, however, most often challenged in the Keynesian theory are the special theory of the fall of profits, the "purely" monetary interest theory, and the attitude toward price and wage reduction.

Keynes's "normal psychological law" that in the short period, as income rises, consumption rises, but not as much, is probably on balance nearly as well established empirically, as a statement of general tendency, as the broader statement that consumption does not vary inversely with the rate of interest. Yet somehow it has roused much more antagonism. The writer suggests, however, that conservatively inclined writers would accept the doctrine much more readily if they realized that is not put forward as an *exclusive* business cycle theory, or theory of the collapse of marginal efficiency of capital. Keynes is perfectly well aware that there are any number of other forces which might affect business expectations. Though he does not consider the effects of new invention in the *General Theory* (and this, as we shall see shortly, is a very important point), Keynes certainly does not deny that they must be reckoned with in any actual situation.[22]

One does not, in order to follow the Keynesian analysis, have to feel that the failure of consumption to rise, as output rises, is always the sole cause of the collapse, or even in many instances the most important cause. A decline in the rate of invention, or of population growth, or a simple shock to "confidence" might all, at times, be equally important. What one does have to believe is that current investment opportunities *vary*, or rather that they are not "boundless" and in a "given" situation and over longer or shorter periods can be exhausted. Failure of consumption to rise is merely one of many forces which, in a particular case, may potentially cause trouble.[23]

In considering the "purely" monetary theory of interest, this would appear to be the most radical departure from accepted doctrine in the Keynesian system and it has certainly given rise to the greatest amount of misinterpretation. The truth of the matter is that in full-employment equilibrium the Keynesian interest rate theory is supplementary, rather than contradictory, to that of Marshall. Since this point is so widely misunderstood, particularly by many writers influenced by Keynes, it is worth some elaboration.[24]

Keynes, as is well known, says that the rate of interest is "solely" determined by the interaction of "liquidity preference" and the quantity of money. But let us suppose that we have full-employment equilibrium and that some massive new invention is made which greatly increases profit expectations on the use of additional capital. Business men as a result bid against one another for current real savings — *i.e.*, for free resources to be used in producing additional investment goods and exploiting the new opportunity. Pre-Keynesian writers would argue that, unless current real saving increased, the money rate of interest would have to rise, sooner or later, or else there would be an inflation.

But Keynes's theory would reach exactly the same conclusion. *At the same time* in which business men are bidding against one another for free resources they are also bidding against one another for increased transactions and precautionary cash balances.[25] That is to say, "by definition," liquidity preference has increased — therefore the interest rate — barring an increase in $M\ V$ — must rise.

Some Keynesians, however, might object that if liquidity preference, due to the "speculative" motive, declined at the same time in which the demand for transactions balances rose, there might be no change in aggregate liquidity preference and hence, barring an increase in M, no change in the interest rate. This argument, however, could be true only for a short interval. At best the process would operate only as an increase in the velocity of money. Now, as everyone knows, increases in M or in V can hold down the money rate below the "real rate" — but, *in* full employment, only at the expense of a price rise. If a limit to monetary inflation is reached, the "real" relationships once more reassert themselves.[26] All this may be put in terms of liquidity preference without in any way altering the essentials of the problem. One can say that, until the "money" rate equals or surpasses the "real" rate, liquidity preference for transactions balances to use in exploiting investment opportunities will be "insatiable."[27]

It is in the case of unemployment that Keynes's interest theory makes its greatest contribution. For if the rate of interest be explained primarily in terms of demand and supply for free resources, or "capital disposal," how can one explain the existence of a rate at a time when "free resources" (starving men) are walking the streets unclaimed? The Austrian minimum rate knows no such problem. With the Austrians, barring frictional and cyclical problems, there is always full employment and free resources are always kept scarce by "time preference" — *i.e.*, too high a rate of current consumption to allow a full realization of productive possibilities. Only by some such analysis as Keynes's can one explain why the rate does not go to zero in times of unemployment.[28] The Keynesian theory of the *minimum* rate of interest is therefore a real, a substantially new, and a valid addition to the body of economic science. For the rest the "purely monetary" Keynesian theory is largely a matter of definition, calling attention to certain important short-run speculative factors but not seriously varying the ultimate essentials of the problem.

Keynes's criticisms of Marshall for attempting to derive a theory of interest from the marginal efficiency of capital are not very fair and should apply only to the minimum rate under more or less stationary conditions.[29] It is true, as Keynes says, that, barring change, expansion, etc., and the effects of liquidity preference, investment, under Marshall's line of reasoning, would be carried to the point at which both the marginal efficiency of capital and the rate of interest would be zero. Therefore the marginal efficiency of capital cannot explain a minimum rate in the absence of dynamic factors. But what seems overlooked is that, with dynamic factors and *constant* change, a constant flow of invention, etc., can create new investment opportunities as fast as the old ones are exploited and thus, if invention keeps ahead of accumulation, a permanent scarcity premium on free resources or capital disposal (the "real" rate of interest) could be maintained *though the economy uses no money whatever.*[30]

Once we understand the basic factual assumptions of the Keynesian interest theory in this way, even the much criticized observations regarding interest in Chapter 24 can be given an interpretation which, in the writer's opinion at least, serves to reconcile them with much pre-Keynesian thought. In Chapter 24 Keynes is assuming that "contemporary conditions" are virtually those of a stationary state. Population is not growing very much, foreign investment is not growing, important new inventions are not being introduced, tastes are not changing significantly. Yet the propensity to consume remains low. If we think of England in 1935, these assumptions are not without support. If there were full employment, a flow of new capital instruments would be possible which might soon reduce the pure rate of interest to zero. But interest does not fall because, and only because, of liquidity preference. Nothing but the excessive holding of money and other liquidity substitutes prevents a zero rate. Further (though this point is not much developed), there is an implication that even with a zero rate, profit expectations might not be high enough to call forth sufficient investment.[31] Under these assumptions the advocacy of the euthanasia of the *rentier*, of the socialization of investment, etc., all follow quite logically. But *only because of the facts assumed.* The policies suggested in no way follow from the Keynesian theoretical analysis *per se* and if one believes, with the present writer, that these particular assumptions of fact need not be generally true, then quite different results could follow. Keynes did not say that "interest rewards no genuine sacrifice" or that "there are no intrinsic reasons for the scarcity of capital." He said, "Interest *today* rewards no genuine sacrifice" and the word *today* applies to all the discussion which follows.[32] But now in 1945 when "today" has faded into "yesterday," we are entirely free to revise our estimates of "tomorrow" — and with them our suggestions for economic policy.

A survey of the Keynesian analysis would not be complete without mention of price and wage reduction. Here, too, there is much less real conflict in *analysis* between Keynes and most other economists than is usually thought. Keynes admits regarding both price and wage cuts that the release from active circulation of transaction balances may help satisfy liquidity preference, due to the speculative motive and bring down the rate of interest, with, *ceteris paribus*, favorable results.[33] Regarding wages he also admits that wage reduction may help by producing an "optimistic tone in the minds of entrepreneurs which may break through a vicious circle of unduly pessimistic estimates."[34] Nor does the Keynesian view conflict with Professor Slichter's "selective" wage cut theory.[35]

Furthermore, Keynes's analysis does not necessarily deny, though it leaves largely unmentioned, those ingenious sequence constructions by which (provided only that one accept the hypotheses) it can be shown that the general wage level will fall faster than prices and income, or prices faster than income, or whatever sequence the particular writer chooses in order to show that investment may increase as the result of a temporary rise in profits. True, Keynes does not consider that these policies, practically speaking, are very promising, but he does not deny their possible utility under appropriate circumstances, and conservatives should admit that, at least on a purely analytical plane, Keynes's case in which prices fall indefinitely *pari passu* with wages is just as hypothetically possible as their own.

What Keynes is fundamentally attacking is the attitude which blames all, or nearly all, unemployment on the insistence by labor upon "too high" a real or money wage level. If only labor would take a low enough wage, it is said, there would always be full employment. As a consequence it is easy to decide that virtually all unemployment is "voluntary" since, however innocent in intent laborers may be, if they were not "voluntarily" insisting upon too high a wage men would find jobs.

Such a point of view is always a plausible one. First because of mistaken analogies from partial-equilibrium demand-curve analysis, but second, and more important, because it is undeniable that, if men would work for nothing (zero wages) or pay to be employed (negative wages), they *could* all find jobs. Such contentions are true; but what practical relevance do they have? Since of course what people want is not work but work plus pay, since in fact it is only in rare instances that men work for zero or negative wages, the zero or negative wage argument seems irrelevant. Once it is ruled out, circumstances are clearly conceivable in which the most drastic wage reduction (short of zero) would not increase employment. Under such circumstances it is submitted that it is permissible to speak of "involuntary unemployment" and to say that it exists.

The contrary view may be largely traced back, it is submitted, to the basic cleavage of assumptions regarding investment outlets already spoken of. Should one accept or approximate Professor Knight's implication that investment opportunities are always "boundless," or nearly so, one may indeed maintain that relatively small wage cuts would serve to break log jams of entrepreneurial activity and put people back to work.[36] Thus, without being either inhuman or cruel, one might well say that most unemployment was "voluntary." But if one follows Marshall, Taussig, Schumpeter and many others in believing in the possibility of a stationary state, then during periods of slack investment demand it might well be the case that drastic wage reduction would not increase employment. Once a considerable variability of investment outlet, relative to the propensity to consume, is assumed, the desirability of wage cuts as compared with other policies turns (barring debates of social philosophy) upon the fundamental investment outlet situation. Such I believe to be the position taken in the *General Theory*.

Coming to the matter of price reduction, we must not overlook the suggestion offered, for example, by Haberler that "sooner or later" price cuts will present the hoarder with such bargains that he will find an "irresistible temptation" to dishoard.[37] In the writer's opinion this idea is probably correct, analytically. If one has a million dollars in cash and can buy the Empire State Building for a dime, it is quite likely that one would "take a chance" and do so. But to use this idea as a justification for sole reliance upon wage or price reduction as a cure for depression implies a faith in the strength of the institutional structure of the present system which few people can share. During a violent depression the statement that "sooner or later," some day, at some indeterminate point, things will stop getting worse is more likely to produce revolution than reassurance. Furthermore, even on a purely theoretical plane, dishoarding may stop a contraction, it is true; but there is absolutely no guarantee, if estimates of the future are pessimistic, that dishoarding, induced by price reduction, will make the system expand sufficiently to reattain full employment. One must distinguish between the price cut which impels a man to buy an *existing* real asset and the price policy which will induce him to embark upon the creation of a new one.

Finally, there is a sort of mystical association in many people's minds between Keynesian unemployment equilibrium and "hoarding," and this association lies at the bottom of much of the current cry for the taxation of idle hoards. However, it is perfectly conceivable Keynesian unemployment equilibrium could both arise and continue without the slightest change in MV ever having occurred. Suppose some shock to the system which greatly increases the risks of net new investment. As a result people decide not to save but to spend all their incomes. As a result prices in the consumers' goods industries go up, but since no one will expand his scale of operation on any terms, investment goods industries remain depressed and men are unemployed. There is no hoarding, and no change in velocity, but merely a rise in the price of consumers' goods.[38] Some of the more enthusiastic adherents of the idea of taxing idle hoards have forgotten that merely increasing monetary demand does *not* mean increasing employment if risks are simultaneously increased. But this mistake is not fairly attributable to the essential body of the Keynesian analysis.

IV

From the foregoing survey of the essential framework of Keynes's analysis we may conclude that his teaching is not so much a contradiction of Marshallian theory, or its modifications at the hands, say, of Taussig, but a supplemental development. Keynes does definitely break with the idea that (short period) aggregate consumption will rise as the interest rate falls and vice versa, but, save for this, his theory of interest and Marshall's do not contradict each other – rather they deal with different worlds. Keynes's monetary theory (in a non-tautological sense) applies to conditions of less than full employment. Marshall's theory remains correct (as far as Keynes's theory is concerned) in a world in which there is full employment and a brisk demand for capital.[39] Again in the matter of wage and price policy the differences between Keynes and modern economists who disagree with him are often not differences of analysis, but differences of opinion. The dispute concerns which policy, in a given institutional environment, is most *likely* to yield good results. In other words, both sides should grant the theoretical *possibility* of each other's hypotheses under appropriate circumstances. The important problem is which set of assumptions most nearly fits the actual situation at a given time.

Yet despite the extremely large area of agreement which we have discovered, there are many economists to whom Keynesian economics remains distasteful and who tend to regard it as being, in large part, a depression vagary. In the remainder of this paper the writer wishes to develop two reasons, one justified and one mistaken, which lead many people to dislike Keynes's teaching. He wishes further to offer some suggestions regarding the effect of these two attitudes upon the future of Keynesian economics and economic thought in general.

We have already seen that there are economists who believe that current investment outlets are virtually always and *per se* boundless. If this idea were true, Keynes's teaching would largely be nonsense. The writer has given reasons elsewhere for disagreeing with this doctrine; nevertheless, the matter of investment outlets is absolutely basic and does call attention to one of the most vulnerable points of the Keynesian school.[40] If one were to summarize the weaknesses toward which the Keynesian point of view inclines, as compared with the weaknesses of pre-Keynesian theorists, it is submitted that the divergent tendencies could be compressed within a very simple formula. The "classical" writers tended to pay too little attention to obstacles to effective demand; the Keynesians tend to slur over obstacles to supply. But, as Marshall pointed out in his famous scissors analogy, *both* supply and demand must be considered in any real situation. Here there is certainly much ground for criticism, and the Aristotelian golden mean appears now, as ever, indeed difficult to achieve.

To develop what the writer believes to be the chief weakness of the Keynesian approach we must make use of a not very satisfactory distinction between "institution" or "ideological" barriers to investment, on the one hand, and "objective" ones on the other. Many writers using large elements of the Keynesian analysis tend to consider that "shortages" of investment outlet trace ultimately to "objective" factors — as population growth — largely beyond the reach of policy. Other writers place primary emphasis upon "institutional" factors such as taxation, foreign trade policy, unwise wage policy, etc. It is obvious that practically everything is in the last analysis institutional or ideological – and not least of all the propensity to consume and the birth rate. But when we apply the distinction indicated in a common sense manner, what are the repercussions upon Keynesian theory?

The writer believes both in the theoretical possibility of a stationary state and in the variability over time of actual investment outlets. Nevertheless, it is submitted that usually, and certainly at the present time, the ultimate source of "shortages" of investment outlet is more likely to be ideological or institutional than objective. But does such a point of view destroy the usefulness of the Keynesian system? To the writer it does not. The real distinction should be not between "objective" barriers and "institutional" barriers but between barriers which can be *quickly removed* and barriers which can not. The fundamental problem with which Keynes is concerned is that of effective demand. The basic contention of his theory is that the propensity to consume and the inducement to invest must stand in proper relation to each other if there is to be full employment. The essential weakness of the exchange economy which he stresses is the problem of secondary deflation. The theory is, in itself, as good an argument for trying to increase the inducement to invest, as the propensity to consume. But whatever we do we must act *in time*.[41]

It may very well be true under "given" circumstances that the "shortage" of investment outlet originally precipitating the crisis is due to institutional disorganization (*e.g.*, currency difficulties, etc.) which might eventually be removed, or to international rivalries of a similar character. But while we are waiting for these longer-run policies to take effect, the economic structure may be wrecked by deflation. We must attack both problems at once. A truly rounded policy seeks *both* to maintain effective demand and to bring about a basic adjustment.[42]

It is a weakness of some followers of Keynes — notably Mrs. Robinson — that they tend to see but half of the problem. Such an attitude may be grounded in implicit hostility to capitalist mores, or spring from other sources, but whatever the reason, the result — if applied to a capitalist economy — must be interpreted either as faulty economics or mistaken policy. Such an attitude, for example, easily converts some American applications of Keynesian doctrine into a species of economic isolationism. For even if investment outlets in the United States are insufficient relative to the propensity to consume, due, say, to declining population growth, that still does not explain why we cannot find foreign investment. Again, the monopoly problem, though easily fitted into the Keynesian scheme, is largely left aside in the *General Theory*. The absorption of increased demand by pressure groups of labor and capital, and the consequent failure of employment and output to increase proportionately to a given monetary stimulus, are often slurred over.

Keynes himself could well say that he could not be expected to cover the whole field of economics in one book. However, in the hands of some of those using his analysis, the slurring over of monopoly problems, the ignoring of his warnings as to the adverse effects of excessively heavy progressive income taxation upon the marginal efficiency of capital, the disregard of his cautions regarding money wage changes in *either* direction, have all had serious effects. Few economists, "Keynesian" or otherwise, in this country at least, go so far as to say that we do not need to worry about investment incentives. Nevertheless the idea has been put forward, at times, and derives a certain amount of support from Mrs. Robinson's *Essay on Marxian Economics*. She writes, "With the notion of the supply price of capital, the moral justification of profit as a necessary cost of production disappears, and the whole structure of the orthodox apology falls to the ground."[43]

The genesis of this doctrine is to be found in some unguarded statements by Keynes himself in his "concluding notes." As earlier pointed out, the weakness of that chapter is that it disposes toward incautious generalization from the particular English institutional framework, as of the period between world wars. It is very true that the modern large scale corporation may maintain its business for a long time, and even expand considerably with internal funds, without having any very large, and in some cases without having any, profit expectations. It may also be true (though I think the point overstated) that many entrepreneurs get so much fun out of their work that they would be willing to work virtually for nothing. But these two statements do not add up to the conclusion that profits is not needed in a dynamic economy or that we do not need to worry about investment incentives.

We must be careful to distinguish between investment and *net* new investment; between "rents," wages of management, and monopoly gains, on the one hand, and risk-profits on the other. Whether the entrepreneur enjoys his life so much or not, unless he is working with internal funds *quasi* automatically flowing in to him, he has to borrow or to sell stock, and in order to do so he must offer the would-be purchaser of equity capital some expectation of profit. It is indeed paradoxical that anyone should maintain that investment incentives are not needed, at a time when the scarcity of venture or equity capital has been one of the most vexatious problems of corporate finance in the United States. We need not discuss here the moral pros and cons of capitalism. The only question is: "*Given* the capitalist institutional set-up, are not high profits required in risky net new investment?"[44]

Problems like these may more plausibly be brushed aside in England where net new investment has been proportionately less important than in the United States. The truth seems to be that Keynes's entrepreneur, who needs very little profit incentive to keep him at work, is not the Schumpeterian entrepreneur — the innovator, the moving spirit in a rapidly growing new corporation, in a dynamic capitalism — but a Schumpeterian "manager" — head of some semi-monopolistic trustified, "rationalized," well-entrenched English firm with ample internal funds — one of the uncrowned but probably titled rulers of what has been called the "conservative corporative state."[45] But in America where net new investment is still important, where the arteriosclerosis of capitalism is less advanced, one deals still, in many cases, with a very different problem.

Unless we socialize investment it is still necessary to consider profit expectations and the inducement to invest. The Keynesian schema, if such points be overlooked, does contain an implicit possible stalemate. If demand is raised by drastic redistribution, supply may be so discouraged that no new real investment will be forthcoming, and no increase in real consumption.[46]

The fact of the matter is that economists influenced by Keynes have been little, if any, more immune to humanity's incurable weakness for false generalization than any others. Some pre-Keynesian writers were guilty of erecting special cases into universal laws. Keynes showed the falsity of their generalization by working out special cases of his own. But he had scarcely done so before some of his disciples showed a tendency to ascribe to Keynes's special cases an equally false generality.

As an example, Mrs. Robinson in reviewing Professor S. E. Harris's *Economics of Social Security* rebukes him for holding contradictory ideas at the same time. "He accepts," she writes, "in the main Mr. Keynes's system of ideas, but also accepts the view that high wages cause unemployment, and that an increase in thriftiness has a direct effect (apart from its reaction on the demand for money) in lowering the rate of interest."[47]

The first of these criticisms illustrates very well the pitfalls of the simplified, aggregate, static technique. There is nothing in Keynes's analysis to prevent one from feeling that too high a rate of wages in some *particular* industry or too rapid a rate of *increase* in money wages generally *may* at some times and under some circumstances cause unemployment.[48] That is what Professor Harris was implying and Mrs. Robinson is quite unwarranted in waving such considerations aside. In the same way an increase in thriftiness could conceivably have, at times, a direct influence on the rate of interest apart — excepting always, of course, "by definition" — from the demand for money. The Keynesian "purely" monetary interest theory, as we have seen, is sometimes and in some senses (but by no means always) a mere logical quibble or tautology.

To summarize, there are many way in which dogmatic simplification and the slurring of obstacles to supply might prejudice a conservatively minded economist against the Keynesian analysis — especially in the light of certain offshoots which have grown from it. But none of these points touch the basic Keynesian schema. They do indicate an important error of emphasis and, if capitalism is to survive some of the outgrowths of Keynesian doctrine, this lack of proportion must be corrected. But the essential Keynesian framework remains unaffected. It is entirely neutral and may be accepted as scientific truth by economists of the most diverse political bias.

V

Yet again we are left with the question: Why is the essential Keynesian schema still attacked today? To answer I believe we must probe some of the less justifiable grounds for criticisms. If writers — such as Professor Knight — who approach the problem on various basically different factual assumptions and hence differ from Keynes in essential scientific analysis are left aside, the explanation of much opposition to Keynesian ideas lies, it seems to me, not so much in the specific weaknesses just reviewed as in the uncomfortable nature of the theory itself, especially in the light of traditional American legal and political theory. One can follow the main outlines of Keynes's doctrine and still believe in capitalism, but one canot follow Keynes's doctrine and believe that capitalism will always and "automatically" cure itself of disturbance and unemployment. There lies the rub.

For if one assumes, as most economists do, that the intensity of demand for new capital instruments varies greatly over time; if one concedes, as statistical figures make unavoidable, that the short-run propensity to consume does not rise as interest and profit expectation fall; if one feels that even drastic reduction in the rate of interest (supposing it to be obtained) does not in the short period necessarily give rise to adequate investment demand; if one admits, with most economists, that wage and/or price reduction cannot *always* be relied upon to remedy the difficulty, then a case is necessarily made out, from time to time, for government intervention of some sort.[49] Mere uncritical reference to "insatiable" wants or unused productive possibilities is no longer possible.[50]

True, it may be argued that much of the variation in investment outlets is institutional in character and that our fundamental task is the removal of these institutional frictions. Again Dr. Samuelson's distinction between the long- and short-run behavior of consumption furnishes a line of possible reconciliation between Keynes and Professor Knight. Knight's view regarding "boundless" uses for capital would be correct if tastes, or if consumption, changed adequately, and perhaps in the long run they might. But whether the trouble be due to institutional barriers or to a temporary failure of consumption to rise, or of wants to change, there remains an interval in which demand must be maintained or deflation will ensue. *Something* has got to be done.

Certainly, as has been indicated earlier, there are other policies besides increasing the money supply which are theoretically adequate under proper circumstances. It is a matter for the specific analysis of particular situations.

But to return specifically to attacks upon the Keynesian schema, it may not surprise economists, particularly European economists, to learn that we cannot always trust the competitive mechanism to straighten things out. In more popular conservative circles, however, especially in the United States, I believe that Keynes's ideas derive much of their unpopularity because they form the most widely known arguments for intervention even though such intervention may be quite capitalist in nature.

The trouble with the Keynesian solutions, both for the cycle and for stagnation, is that they imply effort, thought, policy and discretion. No one policy can have eternal validity in a changing world. As the business situation alters, it is necessary to swing from encouraging expansion to discouraging it — and back to encouraging it again — and to use a whole battery of weapons at appropriate times. True, all this may be done toward preserving adequate general security in a competitive, democratic capitalism; but that will never satisfy individuals who yearn for the automatic self-regulating system which the *laissez-faire* economists thought they had found. "Government of laws and not of men," is an idea deeply rooted in the American mentality, and cherished by nearly all of us, but only in the most ultimate sense is such an ideal possible in a developing economy. Where policies must be changed from time to time, someone must do the changing.

It is because the Keynesian analysis brings out this fact so clearly that it is so disliked by the ultra-conservative. Whenever prosperity appears, even momentarily, there are always people to exclaim that "happy days are here again." We are in a "new era." There will be no more depressions. Such an attitude is both childish and dangerous. By encouraging excessive optimism it induces inordinate despair. The true friend of capitalism does not try to claim for the system a performance which it is obviously impossible for it to give. He is on sound ground in pointing out that cyclical fluctuations are an inevitable concomitant of *rapid* technical change; that we cannot avoid one without destroying the other; that nevertheless the proper use of compensatory financial techniques, capitalistically orientated, can reconcile to a considerable extent, within the capitalist framework, the conflicting aims of security and progress; that such a more-secure society would be likely to leave much less room for individual tyranny and oppression than the completely planned state; that the advantages of comprehensive planning and the number of difficulties which it would avoid are absurdly overexaggerated at the present time — all these things the believer in capitalism can say. But he cannot follow the main lines of Keynes's argument and say that the system, left to itself, will always, and "automatically," bring forth sufficient effective demand, for — if we accept Keynes's teaching — that is obviously not true. And if the case for capitalism is made to turn upon a supposed "automatic" power of general adjustment, and if people really try to follow such a policy, a breakdown, it is submitted, is inevitable and the capitalist system will become progressively discredited. We must face the fact that if the case for capitalism is always kept tied up with the case for complete non-intervention, the case for capitalism, in a world demanding security, will be lost.

Thus, in speculating on the future of Keynesian economics, there is room for tremendous development on many lines without destroying the fundamental fabric. There is a need for continued sequence analysis. There is need for less facile manipulation of large aggregates and more particular research. We need less tautology and more investigation. We need a more explicit recognition of our hidden biases and (if we wish to keep the present system) a greater understanding and regard for the essential institutional requirements of capitalism. Obstacles to supply must be given consideration as well as failure of demand. Along these lines the future of Keynesian economics should be one of steady development and synthesis with what has gone before.

But a great danger to Keynesian economics, and economics generally in the United States, is that unwillingness to recognize the nonautomatic nature of capitalism may lead us in prosperity to discard or ignore the greater part of the Keynesian system. Shall we be like army officers always preparing to win the last war? During a boom, will our graduate students be trained primarily to prevent inflation — and hence be unprepared in slump? Will they in slump be trained primarily to prevent slumps and so let the next boom become an inflation? When will the public and many economists discover that in the realm of policy there is no single eternally valid measure and all is relative? In the future of Keynesian economics there is much room for improvement. But if we turn away from the fundamental system and neglect the warnings which it gives regarding effective demand, it will be a major scientific disaster — a disaster furthermore which, I submit, will appreciably reduce the chances for a survival of capitalism.

Notes

The author is associate professor of economics at the University of Virginia.

1.   By "Keynesian teaching" and Keynes's theory I shall mean in this article the body of analysis presented in the *General Theory of Employment, Interest and Money.* In other words, I am not attempting to discuss the private personal views of Lord Keynes at the present or any other time but only to evaluate the body of analysis presented in a specific book.

2.   As an example of criticism of "Keynesian" ideas on a more popular level see J.H. Crider, "It's Your Money, Brother," *Saturday Evening Post,* February 26, 1944. For academic criticism, see L. Albert Hahn, "Deficit Spending and Private Enterprise," *Post-War Readjustment Bulletin* No. 8 (Chamber of Commerce of the United States, Washington, 1943); Otto von Mering, "Some Problems of Methodology in Modern Economic Theory," *Am. Econ. Rev.,* Vol. XXXIV, No. 1 (Mar., 1944); Harold G. Moulton, *The New Philosophy of Public Debt* (Washington, 1943); Harold G. Moulton, George W. Edwards, James D. Magee and Cleona Lewis, *Capital Expansion, Employment, and Economic Stability* (Washington, 1940); on a still more technical level, see Frank H. Knight, "The Business Cycle, Interest, and Money: A Methodological Approach," *Rev. Econ. Stat.*, Vol. 23 (May, 1941). These particular articles are mentioned only by way of instance. Numerous others could be given and other writers mentioned but the writer does not feel any useful purpose would be served thereby.

3.   See Parts III and IV this paper.

4.   *Ibid.*

5.   *Ibid.*

6.   See my "Moulton's *New Philosophy of Public Debt*," *Am. Econ. Rev.*, Vol. XXXIII, No. 4 (Dec., 1943), p. 573.

7.   See, for example, J.M. Keynes, *The General Theory of Employment, Interest and Money* (New York, Harcourt Brace, 1936), p. 377.

8.   *Ibid.*, pp. 122-23.

9.   *Ibid.*, pp. 270-71.

10.   See Part IV this paper; also Keynes, *op. cit.*, p. 264.

11.   Keynes, *op. cit.*, p. 338 *et seq.*

12.   As one example among many, see *ibid.*, p. 372.

13.   For example, see *ibid.*, p. 162.

14.   Alfred Marshall, *Principles of Economics*, 8th ed. (London 1936), p. 534. "A strong

balance of evidence seems to rest with the opinion that a rise in the rate of interest, or demand price for saving, tends to increase the volume of saving."

15.   It must always be remembered — *vide* Schumpeter and Böhm-Bawerk — that mere physical productivity cannot explain the existence of any *permanent* value surplus from which interest would be paid. See J.A. Schumpeter, *The Theory of Economic Development* (Cambridge, Harvard Univ. Press, 1934).

16.   The term "real" rate of interest is subject to a variety of interpretations. It may be used *ex post* simply as meaning the actual "real" return from a given loan allowing for changes in the value of the money unit; or, more usually, it may be given a Wicksellian connotation as (a) the rate at which the demand for loan capital just equals the supply of (real) saving, or (b) the rate which would prevail in a barter economy where loans are made *in natura*. Compare Gottfried von Haberler, *Prosperity and Depression* (Geneva, League of Nations, 2nd ed., 1939), p. 32 *et seq*. The Swedes have elaborated these concepts still further with reference to particular credit and price policies which individual writers have thought desirable. Further complication arises from the fact that actual loan contracts are made for a given length of time and that in the interval the "going" rate may change considerably.

17.   *Cf.* F.H. Knight, "Interest," *Encyclopaedia of the Social Sciences*, Vol. VIII (1932), p. 134. D. McC. Wright "Professor Knight on Limits to the Use of Capital," *Quart. Jour. Econ.*, Vol. LVIII (May, 1944).

18.   J.S. Mill, *Principles* (Ashley ed.), p. 731. Much the same idea is embodied in D.H. Robertson's reference to "inevitable discontinuities of investment outlet."

19.   Marshall, *op. cit.*, p. 534. since the first draft of this paper was prepared Dr. Allan Sweezy has presented a similar analysis. See Sweezy, "Secular Stagnation" in S.E. Harris, ed., *Postwar Economic Problems* (New York, McGraw-Hill, 1943).

20.   This classification excludes writers who like Frank Knight apparently deny the possibility of stationary equilibrium.

21.   Paul A. Samuelson, "Full Employment after the War" in Harris, ed., *Postwar Economic Problems*.

22.   Keynes, *op. cit.*, p. 245.

23.   But see the distinction between "objective" and "institutional" shortages developed below, Part IV.

24.   For a point of view on the problem of Keynesian interest theory rather similar to the writer's, see D.H. Robertson, "Mr. Keynes and Finance," *Econ. Jour.*, Vol. 48, No. 190 and 191. Also *Essays in Monetary Theory* (London, 1940).

25.   Haberler, *op. cit.*, chap. 8.

26.   In this discussion I use the term "real" rate in the first Wicksellian sense mentioned *supra*, note 16.

27.   Lord Keynes, it is true, has written, "I hold that we can be quite sure that a rise in the rate of interest (assuming no favorable changes in the demand schedule for investment) will decrease the actual aggregate of savings. This last statement embodies an essential element in my doctrine and offers a useful shibboleth for distinguishing those who fundamentally agree with the underlying thesis from those who differ." ("Mr. Keynes' Consumption Function Reply," *Quart. Jour. Econ.*, Vol. LII [Aug., 1938], p. 708.) But this statement in essentials reduces to the proposition that, if the money rate were raised above the "real" rate, there would be a deflation and unemployment.

Furthermore, many pre-Keynesian writers would probably see little point in it for they might ask why the rate would go up unless there *were* a favorable change in the demand schedule for investment. Most economists, however, can easily conceive of short-term speculative fluctuations in the demand for money by which the money rate might temporarily rise even though there had been no fundamental change in the investment demand schedule. Practically everyone would concede that under such circumstances deflation would be likely to follow, accompanied by a probable reduction in actual saving. By stressing these possible speculative increases the Keynesian liquidity preference analysis does make a worth-while contribution, but the extent to which it represents any really new discovery, in this respect, can be considerably exaggerated.

28.   Keynes's exposition in the *General Theory* occasionally gives the impression of implying that he believes reduction of the rate of interest to zero would suffice to set free adequate investment without increasing the propensity to consume. But such an interpretation seems counter to the whole general tenor of his point of view and Marshallian inheritance.

29.   Keynes, *op. cit.,* p. 184.

30. Compare Silvio Gesell, *The Natural Economic Order* (San Antonio, Free Economy Publishing Co., 1934), p. 260. "Let us assume that a costly machine is discovered with which everyone can double his present production. This would cause an unprecedented demand for loan-money to purchase the new machine. . . . Even if interest upon loan-money had disappeared this enormous new demand would cause its reappearance . . . interest might even reach an unprecedented height."

Gesell's famous "economic parable" so highly praised by Keynes (see Keynes, *op. cit.*, p. 356), tacitly assumes that there are no competing *borrowers.* Even if a man *cet. par.* were willing to give away a store of real wealth without demanding any real premium (interest) in return, in order to save deterioration and storage charges, the appearance on the scene of a crowd of borrowers clamoring against one another and offering higher and higher percentages of the prospective real gain would soon bring about the existence of a real rate of interest — an excess of "value" in the commodities returned over that lent.

Even though one set of opportunities were exhausted, *constant* changes, the appearance of new machines as the old were installed, could forever maintain a real rate of interest. The difficulties of figuring this value excess *in natura* are obvious but do not go to the essence of the problem.

31. Keynes, *op. cit.*, p. 372. There is some apparent inconsistency between Lord Keynes's admission, on the page referred to, that the "motive towards risk-taking" might be "unduly diminished" by high progressive income taxes, etc., and his later implication, p. 376, that the entrepreneurs are so fond of their work that they do not need the profit incentive. This paradox can be solved, however, I believe, by realizing that Keynes is tacitly assuming an institutional framework in which there is little net new investment. See the discussion below, Part IV.

32. *Ibid.*, p. 376.

33. *Ibid.*, p. 263.

34. *Ibid.*, p. 264.

35. For Slichter carefully faces the problem of effective demand. See S.H. Slichter, "Labor After the War," Harris, ed., *Postwar Economic Problems.*

36. In fairness to Professor Knight it should be remarked that his doctrine that there is no limit to the use of capital need not necessarily be taken to mean that there is no limit to *current* investment.

37. Haberler, *op. cit.*, p. 403.

38. In terms of the quantity equation P will rise, T will fall and MV remain unchanged.

39. This point is well illustrated in Mr. E.V. Morgan's article, "The Future of Interest Rates," *Econ. Jour.*, Vol. LIV (Dec., 1944), p. 340. After a long discussion on Keynesian lines one finds the following: "If on the other hand a high level of employment is maintained, then the importance of the rate of interest as a selector between investment projects will be greater, and if it is necessary to restrict investment in order to prevent inflation it would be better to allow interest rates to rise rather than reimpose controls." (p. 350).

40. D. McC. Wright, "Professor Knight on Limits to the Use of Capital," *supra* note 17.

41. Which does not mean to say that we necessarily should act *at once.*

42. I wish to make it clear that this point of view in no way represents a change from the ideas I have been trying to express since I first began to write on economic problems. The charge is sometimes made that certain American authors, including the writer, who use large elements of the Keynesian analysis, favor spending "without adjustment." Such a charge is completely unwarranted as may be seen from the following quotations from my *Creation of Purchasing Power*, Chapter LX: "Purely monetary problems are not to be compared in magnitude with the problem of possible inflationary demands from organized groups." "The constant demands on the part of labor for higher money wages are an obstacle which practically every writer on purchasing power stabilization has mentioned. . . . Hansen . . . Meade . . . Kaldor . . . Ezekiel." "The problem of the labor unions is, however, only one aspect of the general monopoly problem. If we spend money to increase purchasing power, special groups . . . may raise their prices and absorb the additional funds without any real increase in consumption"; or again in Chapter III: "If too enthusiastic a program of progressive taxation were imposed, the inducement to invest might be seriously reduced and the stimulus to consumption"; or in Chapter VIII, "It should be clear though that no program of purchasing power injection which expects to avoid inflation can entirely escape the necessity of taxation at some point of time." Or Chapter IX, "We in the United States are also too prone to minimize the international aspects of the problem. . . ."

43. Joan Robinson, *An Essay on Marxian Economics* (London, Macmillan, 1942), p. 74.

44. Since the original manuscript of this article was prepared, Mr. G.F. Shove has made the

same point. See Shove, "Mrs. Robinson on Marxian Economics," *Econ. Jour.*, Vol. LIV (Apr., 1944), p. 47.

Mr. A.P. Lerner argues that high progressive income taxes do not hurt the inducement to invest if gains and losses can be made to cancel one another out. The investor is then working "on commission" for the government. But compare this doctrine with Sir William Beveridge's recent statement (*Econ. Jour.*, Vol. LIV [Dec., 1944], p. 161): "The government . . . are fighting unemployment. They ought to be planning for productive employment. But one cannot do that unless there is something one desires *passionately* (italics added) to see accomplished. . . . Experience in peace time has shown that the desire of men who are already above want to increase their profits by investment is not a strong enough motive or sufficiently persistent . . . to produce a demand for labor which is strong enough and steady enough." But after all do men desire *passionately* to work "on commission" for the government at one or two per cent? Furthermore Lerner's doctrine entirely overlooks all the considerations regarding the family motive adduced by Schumpeter.

45.   Compare Keynes, *op. cit.*, p. 373: "Experience suggests that in existing conditions savings by institution and through sinking funds is more than adequate."

46.   Lord Keynes cannot be charged with *overlooking* this possibility in the *General Theory*, but the writer does suggest that he tended to underemphasize it.

47.   Joan Robinson, "The Economics of Social Security," a review, *Econ. Jour.*, Vol. LII (1942), p. 242. S.E. Harris, *The Economics of Social Security* (New York, McGraw-Hill, 1941).

48.   Regarding the possibility of too rapid an increase in the general money wage level, it may be true that in the "long run" all values tend roughly to arrange themselves about the wage-unit *if* there is no further disturbance. But a money wage increase might put a special premium on labor saving devices and aggravate short run, technological, frictional, unemployment. Further, if the *trend* upward is too rapid, adjustment may always lag behind. Compare Professor Frank Graham's discussion of some of these points, "Keynes v. Hayek on Commodity Reserve Currency," *Econ. Jour.*, Vol. LIV (Dec., 1944), p. 422.

49.   Certain conservative writers might deny this conclusion and say that the thing to do is to prevent the boom by high interest rates instead of "filling in" in a slump. Were one to assume that the economy was initially in perfect adjustment, with full employment, this doctrine might be correct. But our society is already permanently distorted with a relatively overbuilt capital goods industry. Full employment only comes (if then) in a boom. The result is that a policy of preventing a boom would leave us in prolonged slump and unemployment. Furthermore, due to the acceleration principle, any expansion to full employment that is at all rapid would be likely to produce further distortion. See my *Creation of Purchasing Power* (Cambridge, Harvard Univ. Press, 1942), p. 29 *et seq.*

50.   Of recent critics Dr. L. Albert Hahn seems to be among the few willing, apparently, to challenge the Keynesian treatment of this fundamental point. In his brochure, *Deficit Spending and Private Enterprise*, Post-war Readjustment Bulletin No. 8 (Chamber of Commerce of the United States, Washington, 1943), he writes (p. 26): "How is it that no production gets started for articles which would be consumed by the former unemployed? For we cannot seriously maintain that the unemployed, if converted into laborers, would save to such an extent that the product of their labor would not meet demand." As to this it may be said, first, that if reliance is made upon the demand of the newly employed *alone*, then if they save *anything* it will prevent receipts from covering costs. Next, part of the money costs of selling a given output of goods, under the private enterprise system (which Dr. Hahn is defending), are *profits* accruing to entrepreneurs. If *they* do not spend their receipts, costs and receipts will not be equal. Dr. Hahn's argument, in this respect, would only be correct under communism or some non-profit state in which there was no net saving.

75

The Keynesian Revolution in Economics*[1]

G.W.G. Browne

Biographers of the late Lord Keynes will be struck by the element of paradox in his character and career. He was a product of Cambridge and a pupil of Marshall, yet orthodox economic theory never had a more dangerous opponent. A man of affairs and a prominent figure in the City of London, he did much to undermine the economic philosophy which the City for generations had accepted without question. Though he identified himself with no political party, he left his mark on political programmes throughout the western world. He was the least dogmatic of men, but he founded the creed of full employment which, if we are not careful, may become one of the principal intellectual bigotries of our age. Paradox, however, is characteristic of revolutionaries, and Keynes was a true revolutionary. Posterity may yet decide that he did more to change the face of our society than — paradoxically — any cloaked and bearded plotter against the established order.

The main object of this paper is to give a brief account of Keynesian theory and to assess its revolutionary implications for economic theory and policy. It would be a pity if the fame of Keynes' last major work, "The General Theory of Employment, Interest and Money", were to cause his earlier publications to fall into neglect. The "Treatise on Money" is in many respects a more satisfying book, and while much of its monetary theory is now obsolete, its analysis of many aspects of banking and currency is still invaluable. Nevertheless, the "General Theory" is the father of the Keynesian revolution and our principal subject this evening.

One of the best summaries of the "General Theory" is contained in Chapter III of the book itself. Those who find mathematics an aid to clarity may prefer the versions of Professor Hicks[2] or Professor Lange[3]; the outline which follows is based largely on the latter.

The aim of the book is to find out what determines the value of three fundamental economic quantities, viz., the total income of the community, the total amount of investment, and the rate of interest. As in the case of most

*Source: *South African Journal of Economics*, Vol. 14, December 1946, pp. 237-52.

economic problems, these quantities are mutually dependent. Where we have three unknown quantities, we need three and only three equations in order to determine their values. Keynes supplied these three equations in the form of a theory of interest, a theory of investment and a theory of consumption. One of these was a completely new contribution to economics, another was a recent product of the Cambridge school, while the third was an old friend in a new suit of clothes. Before we go on to examine these three theories, however, we must first dispose of another Keynesian contribution which at first looks like a fourth equation, but which is really only a matter of definition. This is, of course, the famous definition that savings equals investment.

The identity of savings and investment gave rise to a great deal of fruitless discussion at the time, perhaps because in his "Treatise on Money" Keynes had defined them in such a way that they could differ. But the matter is really quite simple. In any given period, the total income received by a closed community must either be spent on consumption goods or else saved in some form. But the income received must be earned either in the making of consumption goods or in the making of investment goods. Income earned in making consumption goods must be equal to the total amount spent on consumption goods. The balance of income received, i.e., total savings, must therefore be equal to the income earned in making investment goods, i.e., total investment.

Keynes had, however, previously shown that the individual act of saving was not necessarily linked *directly* to any individual act of investment; the saver might, for example, hoard cash in a stocking or buy Union Loan Certificates, neither of which lends directly to equivalent new investment. Nevertheless, by definition, saving must be equal to investment in the aggregate. How are these two facts squared? The best explanation was given by the Swedish economists, who, building on the work of the great Wicksell, had anticipated many of Keynes' ideas. They distinguished between *planned* savings and investment, and the aggregate of savings and investment actually realised in any period. The latter must necessarily be equal, but planned saving need not be equal to planned investment. If planned savings exceed planned investment, income will be less than expected and people will therefore save less than they intended; if planned investment exceeds planned savings, total incomes will rise and actual savings will be higher, while merchants' stocks will be reduced below the level expected, thus reducing investment.

The identity of savings and investment immediately raises difficulties with regard to the theory of interest. Broadly speaking the classical theory was that the rate of interest is determined by the supply and demand for loans. If, however, savings and investment are identically equal irrespective of the rate of interest, how can we say that the rate of interest is the price which brings savings and investment into equilibrium?

Keynes' solution was a strikingly original theory of interest, which, if perhaps not quite so revolutionary as at first thought, forms an essential contribution to economics. He perceived first of all that interest cannot be the reward of abstinence, or waiting, or saving, as the older economists maintained, since one could save money in the form of cash and yet earn no interest on it. Interest is in fact the reward for holding assets in any form *other than* cash. Keynes therefore turned the whole problem upside down and enquired why people should hold cash when they could lend their money at interest.

The essential quality of cash (with which we include bank deposits on current account) is the liquidity it confers on its owner; Keynes in fact calls the desire to hold cash "liquidity-preference". People desire to hold cash for three main reasons, firstly, to keep a small balance for current transactions, like the few pounds we carry around in our pockets; secondly, to hold a small liquid reserve against unforeseen contingencies, and thirdly, for speculative reasons. Suppose, for instance, an investor expects the price of securities to fall in a month or two: if the fall is expected to be appreciable, it will pay him to hold cash in the meanwhile, since the loss of interest on his cash holdings will be more than balanced by his gain in being able to buy bonds at a lower price. Keynes lays special emphasis on this last motive for holding cash, the speculative motive. If it were the only motive, we could say that the rate of interest depends solely on the quantity of money, i.e., cash and bank deposits. If the quantity of money is taken as given, the rate of interest will be such that the people are willing to hold exactly this quantity of money. The quantity of money which people wish to hold for transactions purposes, however, depends on the total income of the community, so we may say that the quantity of money is related both to the rate of interest and the total income of the community — the higher the rate of interest, the smaller the quantity of money which people will wish to hold; and the higher the total income, the larger is liquidity-preference.

This theory, while undoubtedly original, stems from the classical Cambridge theory of money developed by Marshall and Pigou. Long ago students of economics were taught that money had three main functions — as a unit of account, a medium of exchange, and a store of value. Economists varied in the stress they laid on these different functions. In particular, Professor von Mises[4] attempted to reduce the functions of money to one, viz., as a medium of exchange. His views had great influence on the Austrian and later the London school of economists. The Cambridge school, however, developed what became known as the "cash-balance approach" to monetary theory. Whereas the so-called "cash-transactions approach" used the familiar form of the quantity theory, $MV = PT$, the Cambridge school put the quantity theory into a form which laid stress on the average cash balance held by the individual. Keynes himself had contributed to Cambridge theory in his earlier books, and now he built essentially on this foundation.

There is still some controversy as to whether the Keynesian theory represents a complete break with the classical theory of interest, or whether it is merely a refinement and a restatement in another form. In one respect, however, it is a definite advance — it brings the quantity of money right into the middle of the picture. It is no longer possible to regard money as something which can be disregarded in analysing the structure of the economic system, or only introduced in the last chapter to determine the general level of prices. It used to be the hallmark of the trained economist to tear aside the money veil which confused the inexpert observer and to concentrate on the real factors; Keynes has shown that, as a consequence of liquidity-preference or the tendency to hold cash balances, money is as real a factor as any other, and that, through its effect on the rate of interest, it influences the whole structure of the economy.

The second of the three equations on which the Keynesian system is based sets out the relation between investment, interest and consumption. Investment will take place as long as the investor expects to make a profit, i.e., as long as the expected return on his investment exceeds the rate of interest. The expected return on the last unit of investment is termed by Keynes the marginal efficiency of capital, and it is equivalent to what Professor Irving Fisher many years ago called the rate of return over cost. Keynes' theory is in fact identical with Fisher's. With a given schedule of the marginal efficiency of capital, the higher the rate of interest, the smaller will total investment be, and *vice versa*. The marginal efficiency of capital will itself depend largely upon the rate of consumption, since investors will be influenced in their decisions by the prospects of sale for consumption goods.

It will be noticed that the marginal efficiency of capital is what the investor *expects* to realise, not what he actually does realise. The concept of expectations is thus introduced into the Keynesian system. Strictly speaking, it is already present in the Keynesian theory of interest, since the concept of liquidity-preference must really be expressed in terms of expectations. Nevertheless, Keynes' treatment of expectations cannot be regarded as complete; it was left to Professor Hicks[5] to develop this idea more thoroughly. Keynes' theory is, indeed, a mixture of the static and dynamic; at one moment he seems to be speaking of a static system without movement over time, but of course whenever expectations are brought in, time is an essential element. Time has proved quite as much of a bugbear in economics as in philosophy or, at least until Einstein, in physical science, and I do not think the last word has yet been said on the subject.

The third equation defines the relation between consumption and income, while interest may also be a relevant variable. Here Keynes built on the work of R.F. Kahn, a member of the Cambridge school who, in a famous article,[6] developed the theory of the multiplier, to which we shall presently return.

The relation between income and consumption is enunciated by Keynes as follows:—

"The fundamental psychological law, upon which we are entitled to depend with great confidence both *a priori* from our knowledge of human nature and from the detailed facts of experience, is that men are disposed, as a rule and on the average, to increase their consumption as their income increases, but not by as much as the increase in their income." (General Theory, p. 96.)

In Keynes' own terminology, the marginal propensity to consume is positive but less than unity.

It is possible that the rate of interest will also affect consumption through its effects on saving. Formerly it was generally believed that a high rate of interest would encourage saving and discourage consumption. But this is not so certain as appears at first sight. Many people, for example, aim to save a definite sum of money for their old age; if the rate of interest falls, they will have to set aside a larger sum of money annually and decrease their consumption, while if the rate of interest rises, they will be able to reduce their annual saving and increase their current consumption. This tendency therefore works in the opposite direction to the one mentioned above, and the relation between consumption and the rate of interest is therefore uncertain.

Long before Keynes' time it had been widely held that, in time of depression, public works tended to stimulate private industry and that their effect was "like throwing a stone into a pond which makes ripples spread all over it."[7] But a study of the exact nature of these ripples and of their magnitude had to await the development of the multiplier theory by Kahn and Keynes.

The relation between the marginal propensity to consume and the multiplier arises in the following manner. Suppose that, in a time of unemployment, an increase in income accrues to a section of the population. It does not matter for the moment what the cause of this increase is; it may be the result of a public works programme, or reduced taxation, or increased social security allowances, or it may even be brought about by printing bank-notes and placing them in the hands of consumers. The receivers of the additional income may save part of it, or use some of it to repay bank debts, or spend part of it on imported goods, but in accordance with Keynes' law they will spend at least a part of their new income on the consumption of locally produced goods. This means in turn increased incomes for the consumption goods industries, and probably an increase in employment in those industries. The workers who receive increased incomes will again tend to save part of their new earnings or use them to pay off bank debts, but again they will spend a part on increased consumption. Thus a further rise takes place in the demand for consumption goods, and so the process continues — though with ever-diminishing force, since at each round the portion of the additional income which is not spent on the consumption of locally-produced goods leaks out of the process. The main leakages are due to savings, repayment of debt and expenditure on imports. The multiplier is defined as the relation between the aggregate increase in total income and the initial increase in investment.[8] Clearly the value of the multiplier is directly related to the marginal propensity to consume; if the value of the latter is denoted by K, the value of the multiplier is in fact equal to $\frac{1}{1-K}$. The higher is the marginal propensity to consume, the larger is the multiplier.

These three equations, representing respectively the Keynesian theories of interest, of investment and of consumption, are the foundation of the Keynesian system; from them, if we assume that the total amount of money is given, we can determine total investment (which is equal to total saving), total consumption, and hence, by addition, total income. These quantities are homogeneous and may be measured in any convenient *numéraire*; Keynes uses "wage-units". A further object of the "General Theory" was, however, the determination of the level of employment, which is governed by the "effective demand", i.e., the amount which the community is expected to spend on consumption and new investment. Keynes recognises that the level of employment is not a homogeneous concept, but, as Professor Hutt has shown, his attempt to overcome the difficulty of measurement fails to take account of changes in the degree of monopoly.[9] Nevertheless, I feel that Professor Hutt's objection is not conclusive; Keynes' formulation is still valuable in showing that, with a given degree of monopoly in the labour market, an increase in employment depends on an increase in effective demand.

This sort of theory had never been worked out in quite the same way before. Economists like Marshall had developed an economic theory which dealt mainly with the individual producer or consumer, while others like Walras and Pareto extended this type of economic theory from the individual to the community as a whole. But that latter is a dangerous method, since what is true for each part separately is not always true for the whole — we have already noticed, for example, the divergence of individual saving and investment despite the identity of aggregate saving and investment. Keynes, on the other hand, *starts* from aggregate concepts; the revolutionary nature of Keynesian theory derives largely from this "macro-economic" approach, in contrast to the classical micro-economic theory. Keynes has been criticised on the ground that his theory is over-simplified, and that the movements of the broad aggregates with which he deals conceal a multitude of divergent movements in their components. To my mind this criticism misses the point. The simplification which Keynes carried out was an essential step in the advancement of economics. The most significant advances in knowledge often depend on giving something a name and bringing it into the discussion; by making it possible or respectable for economists to talk about total employment, total investment, and the like, Keynes has opened a most fruitful line of progress for economics. I do not imply, of course, that it is not now desirable to analyse the broad Keynesian concepts and to trace economic movements in greater detail; it is most desirable, but the Keynesian simplification was an essential first step.

The general theory which we have built up so far does not depend on any frictions or rigidities in the economic system; the only essential is that the economy must use money, i.e., a medium of exchange which can be used as a store of value. Nevertheless, Keynes did rely upon the existence of certain rigidities for some of the practical applications of his general theory. The first of these is the downward rigidity of money wage rates, i.e., the assumption that wage-earners will resist a reduction in their money wages, whereas they would not resist a fall in their real wage brought about by a slight rise in the cost of living. This assumption is given great prominence in the "General Theory", although actually its validity is rather doubtful. The history of industrial relations shows that strikes are very common in periods of rising prices, while, even where trade unions are strong (as in Britain between the World Wars), reductions in money wage rates are not infrequent.[10]

More important is the rigidity in the rate of interest. Clearly the rate of interest cannot fall below zero, for, if it did, everybody would prefer to hold cash rather than buy securities. For technical reasons, it is probably impossible for the rate of interest to fall below a small positive figure. In slump conditions, where the marginal efficiency of capital falls to a very low level, this rigidity may check investment and hence impede recovery.

The third and perhaps most important rigidity is implied in the theory of "secular stagnation" or the "mature economy" — i.e., the theory that in the western world investment opportunities have become so limited that, given the present propensity to consume, the attainment of full employment is impossible. The theory is implicit in certain parts of Keynes' work, but has been most notably developed by American economists, particularly Professor Alvin Hansen. There are two principal reasons for a decline in investment opportunities — the slowing down of population growth, and the exhaustion of new lands where expansion can take place — such as existed in the Western United States throughout most of the 19th century. The only remaining major opportunities for private investment arise from technical progress and industrialisation of undeveloped countries; Professor Hansen is doubtful whether these will be sufficient to ensure full employment in America. The secular stagnation thesis is still a matter of keen controversy. Its critics aver that the theory betrays a lack of imagination with respect to the growth of wants, the development of technology, and consequently the creation of new investment outlets. But Hansen has a strong reply in his estimate that population growth and territorial expansion accounted for some fifty per cent. of total investment in the nineteenth century.[11] If the bogey of economic maturity becomes a reality, we shall indeed be faced with the paradox of poverty in the midst of (potential) plenty; those countries which are potentially the richest will be in the gravest peril of chronic unemployment and stagnation.

The consequences for policy of Keynes' general theory and of the rigidities to which he attaches special importance are truly revolutionary. Take for example the question of wage policy. This problem illustrates very strikingly the superiority of the Keynesian macro-economic approach over the classical micro-economic method. In the case of any single firm or industry, a reduction in money wage rates is likely to lead to an expansion of employment, since the marginal production costs will be reduced while it is unlikely that the reduction in the average incomes of the employees of that firm or industry will have much effect on the demand for its products. But as soon as we extend the argument to *all* industries together, i.e., as soon as we say that a reduction in *all* wage rates must lead to an expansion in *total* employment, we fall into the fallacy of composition. For when all wage rates are reduced, the effect of the reduction on the total demand for all goods *must* be taken into account. I do not imply that the classical economists completely overlooked this aspect of the problem, but I doubt whether it received the attention it deserves. In Keynes' analysis, however, simply because total income and total consumption are integral parts of the system, it is impossible for this aspect to be overlooked.

Some economists take the line that the Keynesian preference for expansionary monetary action to increase employment, rather than reductions in money wage rates, is the result of "an unwillingness to face the necessity for all-embracing price adjustments"; that in fact the object of such monetary action is to reduce real wages — presumably by raising prices — and that "the frank and open adjustment of money wage-rates so as to increase the flow of real wages" would be a far better method of increasing employment.[12] In my view this line of thought is based on a misunderstanding of Keynes and of the important part which total income must play in determining the general level of employment. To some extent this misunderstanding may arise from the undue emphasis which Keynes placed on the rigidity of money wage rates. This rigidity, however, is *not* an essential part of the argument. In fact, Keynes himself has shown that there may be *no* method of adjusting money wage rates so as to alter real wage rates and increase employment; the argument has been repeated many times by his followers, and even Professor Pigou has acknowledged that a reduction in money wage rates cannot as a rule increase employment directly, but only when accompanied by a reduction in the rate of interest.[13]

Suppose that all factors of production except labour are fully employed, and that there is perfect competition in the hiring of the factors of production. Then if money wage rates fall, there will be a tendency to substitute labour for the other factors of production, and the prices of these other factors will also fall. If there is perfect competition in the sale of the products, their prices will fall too. If all prices fall proportionally, clearly no progress will have been made; employment and real wages will be unchanged. If, however, money wage rates fall in greater proportion than other prices, effective demand at once comes into the picture. Even on the most favourable assumption that entrepreneurs respond to the wage cut by an immediate increase in outlay on investment or consumption, part of the increased income put into circulation will not be spent by its recipients (assuming that the marginal propensity to consume is less than unity); the expectations of entrepreneurs will be disappointed and employment will again contract.

Eventually, however, the fall in prices will lead to a fall in the amount of money which people desire to hold for transactions purposes. People will be more willing to lend, and — unless it is prevented by the rigidity mentioned above — the rate of interest will tend to fall. This again may lead to an increase in investment — provided sufficient investment opportunities exist — and consequently to an increase in total employment.[14] The latter is therefore the last stage of a very devious process — a stage which may never be reached, since the process may strike a snag and come to a stop long before it is completed. Certainly the relation between money wage rates and total employment is anything but direct.

A corollary of this is the revolutionary conclusion that there is no direct and automatic tendency toward the establishment of full employment. If, as a result of disequilibrium between planned saving, investment and consumption, employment is less than full, there is no rapid automatic correction. The downward pressure which unemployment exerts on money wages is *not* necessarily a correcting factor; it may indeed be better if the pressure is successfully resisted. Only by stimulating effective demand can this type of unemployment be counteracted.

Keynes may have contributed to the misunderstanding by his statement that, "in general, an increase in employment can only occur to the accompaniment of a decline in the rate of real wages".[15] The meaning here is not, however, that a decline in real wages *causes* employment to increase; the latter may rather be said to arise from the increase in effective demand. Keynes bases his statement simply on the familiar law of diminishing returns; as total employment rises, the marginal product of labour falls, so that total production increases less than employment. This is the grain of truth in the use by Keynes' opponents of the word "inflationary" to describe programmes of monetary expansion designed to combat unemployment. But, until full employment is approached, every increase in monetary circulation must as a rule be accompanied by *some* increase in the quantity of goods produced, and while some rise in prices may take place, no runaway inflation is conceivable.

In fact, empirical studies have shown that increases in employment may not be accompanied by increases in prices sufficient to cause real wages to fall, and vice versa.[16] Apparently the operation of diminishing returns may be suspended because of variations in the degree of monopoly, though it is not quite clear why the degree of monopoly should change in this way. The point here is that a rise in total employment is *not* dependent on a fall in real wages.

It would be wrong to conclude that wage policy is unimportant. It will always have important distributive effects. Particularly as full employment is approached, it may become more difficult for employers to resist the demands of trade unions for wage increases, and, if these demands are pressed too far, a genuine inflationary situation may develop. A full employment policy will therefore require a great sense of responsibility among trade union leaders and possibly some modification of the principle of collective bargaining.

Perhaps the most revolutionary consequences of Keynesian theory are seen in the field of public finance. Here again the advantage of approaching the question as a whole, rather than extending theory from the individual to the community, is evident. The individual, for instance, must try to conduct his affairs so as to show a profit; he should avoid incurring unproductive debt and try to balance his budget. But what is good policy for the individual is by no means always the right policy for the State. Clearly it is inappropriate for the State to aim at maximising the excess of its receipts over its expenditure. Again, the analogy between the private debt of an individual and the internal public debt of the State is false; the public debt is owed by the State to its own citizens; there is no transfer outside the nation and no net burden on future generations — though this does not mean that the existence of debt has no effects whatever. The conclusion is that the State's decision to raise revenue by loan or taxation should not be based on whether the expenditure is of a current or capital nature, but on the effects on production and distribution which it is desired to create. Secondly, public debt should not be repaid for its own sake, but only as part of general economic policy.

All this is not actually dependent on Keynes' theory, though it is in line with the general Keynesian approach. When, however, we come to the purposes for which fiscal policy should be applied, we find ourselves deeply involved in Keynes' ideas. For, if the aim of fiscal policy is not to be the blind one of balancing the budget at all costs, it may be used as a potent weapon to promote a high level of employment. The latter depends on maintaining aggregate outlay. If outlay falls off, the State can help to maintain it by increasing its own expenditure. It will not help, however, if the rise in State expenditure is accompanied by an equivalent fall in private outlay. There is a danger of this if the State meets its increased expenditure by means of additional taxation. The danger is usually believed to be much smaller if the additional revenue is raised by loans — presumably on the assumption that money invested in government securities is not as a rule diverted from consumption or active investment, though this assumption seems to merit further examination. The danger is perhaps least of all if the money is obtained by means of bank credit or by simply printing additional paper money.

There is another very important application to fiscal policy. One of the chief arguments against progressive taxation in the past was the danger of discouraging investment by the wealthier classes and so "killing the goose that laid the golden eggs". In a mature economy, however, where investment opportunities are limited, mass unemployment can best be avoided by maintaining the marginal propensity to consume, and as the marginal propensity to consume will generally be higher for the poor than for the rich, there is a strong case for the redistribution of incomes through progressive taxation. One of the last defences of inequalities of wealth may have to be given up.

There is practically no end to the practical applications of Keynesian theory. Keynes' strong practical bent is a distinguishing feature of his work; like Ricardo he has blended a knowledge of affairs with a knowledge of theory, with the happiest results. Unfortunately, the general result of his teaching — like that of other recent developments in economics — is to make life more difficult for the economist. There can no longer be any easy rule-of-thumb judgment on wage policy, on fiscal and monetary policy, on international trade policy or even on monopolies. But the economist should look upon this, not with resentment, but as a challenge to perfect his technique and to improve the statistical data required as a basis for policy.

How far can Keynes' teachings be applied to our own country? It must be remembered that many applications of Keynes' theory depend upon the assumption of a mature economy with limited investment outlets. Keynes was writing principally for the economic conditions of his time in the highly industrialised countries of the west, just as the classical economists, who emphasised the law of diminishing returns in agriculture and the pressure of population, were writing for the economic conditions of *their* time. These latter conditions are still present over large areas of the globe; in India and China, for example, the Malthusian pressure of population is still the most important factor in economic life.

It may be assumed that South Africa has not as yet reached the stage of a mature economy suffering from secular stagnation, and care is therefore required in applying the Keynesian analysis to our own conditions. Some of the reservations necessary in the application of a full employment policy have recently been ably analysed by Dr. van der Horst.[17] Still, there is no reason why we should not adopt Keynesian ideas in our tax and fiscal policy and in our public works programme. We shall not go far wrong if we budget for a deficit in time of depression and if we concentrate our public works programme as far as possible in times of unemployment.

The efficacy of public works in combating unemployment depends on the value of the multiplier. No accurate calculation of the value of the multiplier for South Africa has yet been made, but we can make some estimate of the forces determining its value. Firstly, the marginal propensity to consume is probably rather high; the poverty of the great mass of the population, and the lack of thrift among the well-to-do classes, make it probable that a comparatively large proportion of any addition to the community's income is consumed. This will tend to increase the multiplier. On the other hand, a large part of any additional income will probably be spent on imported goods, and this expenditure may not have any direct effect on employment in South Africa.[18] During the pre-war years nearly 30% of any increase in national income was actually spent on imports, and during the period immediately after the 1929-32 depression the percentage was higher. Nevertheless, it seems likely that at least 50% of any additional income in time of depression will be spent on locally-produced goods. This would yield a multiplier of at least 2 — in other words, an expenditure of £1 million on public works would, in time of unemployment, lead to an increase of £2 million or more in the income of the community, provided private investment remained unaffected.

The importance of this may be judged from the fact that the South African national income at current prices fell from £271 million in 1928/9 to £217 million at the bottom of the depression in 1931/2.[19] If allowance is made for price changes the fall is not so great, but is still about 12%. No accurate unemployment figures are available, but there are indications that European unemployment alone ran into tens of thousands during the depression. Yet public investment acctually fell from £12.1 million in 1928/9 to £6.8 million in 1932/3.[20] The policy followed — which was similar to that pursued by most other countries — was based on the false analogy of the individual, who in bad times tends in common prudence to reduce his expenditure. If public investment had instead been increased, even if only to the 1928/9 level, the national income would (on the conservative assumption of a multiplier equal to 2) have been approximately 5% higher in 1932 than the level actually reached, and the soul-destroying effects of unemployment on thousands of South Africans might have been avoided.

It is perhaps necessary to make it quite clear that it is only possible to speak of the multiplier effect on employment with reference to a net increase in total expenditure during a period when resources are not fully employed. There has, for instance, been much loose talk recently about the multiplier effect on the gold mining industry. I do not question for a moment the vital economic importance of gold mining to South Africa, nor do I deny that the revival of the mining industry after 1932 had a very pronounced multiplier effect on the Union's economy. But it is incorrect to speak of the multiplier effect of gold mining during, for instance, the last few years, when resources have not been idle.

In view of the importance of gold to the Union, it is interesting to recall that it forms the subject of one of the most ironical passages in the "General Theory". In Keynes' words, "Just as wars have been the only form of large-scale loan expenditure which statesmen have thought justifiable, so gold-mining is the only pretext for digging holes in the ground which has recommended itself to bankers as sound finance".[21] I think this is a little unjust to gold. The demand for some commodity as a store of value may be irrational, but the fact remains that the demand exists, and it is just as well that there is some convenient means of satisfying it; if there were not, economic conditions might be even less stable. Keynes expressly recognises that the effects of gold production have in fact been economically beneficial to the world.

The reference to war as a good promoter of full employment is a sad reflection. But we may console ourselves with the thought that real peace may be just as good as war in this respect. There are likely to be two great economic problems in the world for the remainder of this century — the problem of a shortage of investment opportunities in the highly developed countries, particularly the United States, and the problem of industrialisation in the relatively undeveloped countries, particularly India and China. International lending will help to solve both these problems. But clearly it will require a high measure of political stability. The atmosphere of uncertainty and fear which characterised the nineteen-thirties, and which unfortunately seems to be arising again, is certainly the enemy of full employment — at least until preparations for war are being actively pressed forward.

Keynes' place in the history of economic thought will be decided by coming generations, but I shall, perhaps rashly, venture a few observations. It is characteristic of Keynes that while most schools of thought agree on his greatness, they do so for very different reasons. Socialists regard him as an economist who exposed the bankruptcy of the capitalist system, while at least some liberals look upon him as one who has shown how some of the worst evils of capitalism may be avoided without risking the regimentation of collectivism. Here is a great disputed question; can we have both full employment and a free society? Or is Keynes a false prophet who will lead us down the road to serfdom? There is no time this evening for a full analysis of this fascinating subject; briefly, my own view is that full (or, at any rate, "high and stable") employment is compatible with a free society, but that the harmonisation of the two will be a most difficult and delicate task for political and economic science. To ignore the necessity for avoiding mass unemployment will certainly be disastrous to free institutions, and it is most unfair to brand Keynes as "recklessly collectivist" simply because the measures which he recommends may, if unwisely handled, impinge on the freedom of our society. Some of Keynes' followers may not, however, be free from suspicion in this respect; in the very last article he wrote, Keynes was moved to protest against the volume of "modernist stuff, gone wrong and turned sour and silly, (which) is circulating in our system, also incongruously mixed, it seems, with age-old poisons."[22]

I have already tried to show how far Keynes' economic theory, and particularly the implications of his theory for policy, are in a high degree revolutionary. The revolution has been remarkably successful. The influence of the "General Theory" has been so far-reaching that it is difficult to realise that it was published only a little more than ten years ago. Its significance for economic theory is evident from almost any current number of the leading economic journals, which are full of articles developing and refining Keynes' ideas. Its significance for economic policy may be seen from the British, Canadian and Australian White Papers on Employment Policy and from the Wagner-Murray Act in America, all of which, whatever their imperfections, are based fundamentally on Keynesian concepts. The story is told that, when he was appointed a director of the Bank of England, Keynes was accused of turning orthodox in his old age. "Not so," he replied, "orthodoxy has caught up with me." That is even more true to-day. Ten or twelve years ago, the term "orthodox economist" would scarcely have been applied to Keynes or his followers; to-day, his opponents are the heretics.

John Stuart Mill defined a wise statesman in the following terms:—

> "History shows that great economic and social forces flow like a tide over communities only half conscious of that which is befalling them. Wise statesmen foresee what time is thus bringing, and try to shape institutions and mould men's thoughts and purposes in accordance with the change that is silently coming on. The unwise are those who bring nothing constructive to the process, and who greatly impede the future of mankind by leaving great questions to be fought out between ignorant change on the one hand, and ignorant opposition to change on the other."[23]

Keynes without doubt conforms to this criterion of a wise statesman, but it must be admitted that, on a strict interpretation of this definition, wisdom comes perilously close to opportunism. The adaptability of Keynes' opinions is well known, and while due allowance must be made for the flexibility and vigour of his active mind, it is not always easy to banish the suspicion that he was writing with an eye to current political and economic trends.

An indication of Keynes' strength and weakness may be gleaned from his own brilliant comparison of Jevons and Marshall. Dealing with Jevons' "Theory of Political Economy", he wrote:

> "It lives merely in the tenuous world of bright ideas when we compare it with the great working machine evolved by the patient, persistent toil and scientific genius of Marshall. Jevons saw the kettle boil and cried out with the delighted voice of a child; Marshall too had seen the kettle boil and sat down silently to build an engine."[24]

There can be no doubt that Keynes was a Jevons rather than a Marshall. The "General Theory" will be read by scholars for generations as an interesting landmark in the development of economic thought, but it will not be used, as Marshall's book was used, as a University textbook for nearly half a century.

Though only ten years old, the "General Theory" is already somewhat out of date — though a recent re-reading of it has led me to think that it is not quite so outmoded as is sometimes thought; many of the ideas which have recently been advanced as refinements, criticisms or developments of the Keynesian doctrine are actually to be found in the original. Nevertheless, its difficult style, its somewhat haphazard arrangement, its irrelevant carpings at the classical economists, and a certain incompleteness about its analysis reduce the permanence of its value.

It is only fair to add that Keynes provided his own defence against this charge. In the same essay from which the above comparison of Jevons and Marshall was taken, he wrote:—

"It was Jevons' willingness to spill his ideas, to flick them at the world, that won him his great personal position and his unrivalled power of stimulating other minds. . . . Economists must leave to Adam Smith alone the glory of the Quarto, must pluck the day, fling pamphlets into the wind . . . and achieve immortality by accident, if at all."

In all probability, Keynes' choice was deliberate. He rejected — possibly he was not suited for — the long, quiet, scholarly research which characterises the work of a Marshall; his numerous outside activities can in any case have left him hardly sufficient time for really profound academic research. He chose rather to fling himself into the controversies of the day, and much of his work bears the stamp of the polemical pamphlet rather than of the scientific treatise.

Perhaps one reason for this lies in the fact that he never exaggerated the importance of economics. In one of his essays he said:

"Do not let us overestimate the importance of the economic problem, or sacrifice to its supposed necessities other matters of greater and more permanent significance. It should be a matter for specialists — like dentistry. If economists could manage to get themselves thought of as humble, competent people, on a level with dentists, that would be splendid."[25]

It is certainly rare for a scientist to see the value of his science in proper perspective. Keynes went further — he actually looked forward to the disappearance of economics! For economics is the science of scarcity, and technical progress may remove material scarcity altogether. The possibility of adapting atomic power to industry makes this prospect less fanciful than when Keynes first suggested it, sixteen years ago. The world is still a wretchedly poor place, but the hope of eliminating want is one which may now be reasonably cherished. Keynes points out that, if that hope is realised, we shall have to revise many things. Many of the old vices, such as avarice, ambition and usury, which during the rise of capitalism acquired a measure of respectability, will again become major sins. We shall have to emulate the lilies of the field, who toil not, neither do they spin. Economists will be out of a job. But this happy state of affairs is not likely to be realised in our lifetimes, and during this period the economic theory which we owe to Maynard Keynes should prove very useful indeed.

Notes

1.   Based on a paper read before the Pretoria Branch of the Economic Society of South Africa, 13th September, 1946.
2.   "Mr. Keynes and the Classics", Econometrica, April, 1937.

3. "The Rate of Interest and the Optimum Propensity to Consume", Economica, February, 1938.

4. Theory of Money and Credit.

5. Value and Capital.

6. "The Relation of Home Investment to Unemployment", Economic Journal, June, 1931.

7. Proceedings of the First Annual Conference on the Prevention of Destitution, London, 1911, p. 543.

8. This is the "investment multiplier". Other definitions are appropriate when the initial stimulus is provided by factors other than increased investment — see Oscar Lange, "The Theory of the Multiplier", Econometrica, July-October, 1943.

9. Theory of Idle Resources, pp. 31-33.

10. *c.f.* A.C. Pigou, Employment and Equilibrium, pp. 82-84.

11. "Economic Progress and Declining Population Growth", American Economic Review, March, 1939.

12. W.H. Hutt: "Full Employment and the Future of Industry", S.A. Journal of Economics, September, 1945.

13. Economic Journal, March, 1938.

14. It is an over-simplification to speak about "the rate of interest" and the relationship between the complex of short-term and long-term rates is by no means simple. Further, there is room for doubt whether interest rates have much effect on investment at all — *c.f.* J.E. Meade and P.W.S. Andrews, Oxford Economic Papers, No. 1.

15. "General Theory", p. 17.

16. *c.f.* the discussion between Dunlop, Tarshis, Keynes and Richardson, Economic Journal, 1938-39.

17. "Some Reflections on Full Employment", S.A. Journal of Economics, March, 1946.

18. It *may*, of course, stimulate the demand for South African exports and so increase employment in the Union.

19. "An Analysis of the Growth of the National Income of the Union", by Prof. S.H. Frankel assisted by H. Herzfeld, S.A. Journal of Economics, June, 1944.

20. *Ibidem.*

21. General Theory, p. 130.

22. "The Balance of Payments of the United States", Economic Journal, June, 1946.

23. Quoted by J.G. Winant, Survey Graphic, June, 1946.

24. Essays in Biography.

25. Essays in Persuasion, p. 373.

76

Dr Burns on Keynesian Economics*

A.H. Hansen

The Twenty-Sixth Annual Report of the National Bureau of Economic Research, written by the Bureau's new Director of Research, Dr. Arthur F. Burns, carries the intriguing title, *Economic Research and the Keynesian Thinking of Our Times*.[1] In Dr. Burns' own language, the theme of his first report "is to relate the work of the National Bureau to the Keynesian thinking of our times." The "opinion," he says, "is widespread that Keynes has explained what determines the volume of employment," and "this opinion reflects a pleasant but dangerous illusion."[2]

Unhappily the history of economic theory and empirical research suggests that ours is a field of study in which we shall never be able to reach perfectly *definitive* conclusions. As economists, we have to be content with something less than that. There is very much in pages 11-27 which suggests that Dr. Burns believes that once the massive studies of the Bureau are completed this situation will be remedied. Perhaps; but one is entitled to be skeptical. The mere accumulation of "precise and tested knowledge" of a limited set of facts, important as this is, will not provide us with a definitive understanding of economic developments which is no longer subject to doubt by competent economists.

On page 13, for example, Dr. Burns refers to three widely differing hypotheses with respect to the thirties. Now the plain fact is that an enormous amount of research on this period has already been done by economists and research agencies all over the world, private and governmental (including invaluable researches of the National Bureau). These have yielded a vast knowledge of the thirties. Yet interpretations and judgments differ. Dr. Burns, however, roundly alleges that "no one has as yet presented an interpretation of the thirties that weighs carefully and dispassionately the many conflicting pieces of evidence" (p. 13). And the inference plainly is that as soon as this is done there will no longer be room for divergent views, or differences of competent opinions. The evidence to date is against this overly simplified view. Economics is not that kind of subject. We need only call to witness any of

*Source: *Review of Economic Statistics*, Vol. 29, November 1947, pp. 247-52.

the vast researches of the last decade, including the recent important work of Burns and Mitchell on *Measuring Business Cycles*. We shall never reach a point when competent judgment will not widely differ, nor shall we ever be able to achieve a truly "scientific guide to governmental policy" (p. 11). Economics can nevertheless be useful even though it cannot reach that level of perfection.

Competent and honest opinions will differ in the future as in the past. The value of Keynes' work, as of any other contribution to economic knowledge, has to be judged on a less pretentious plane than that of some of the more exact natural sciences. The only realistic question is whether or not Keynes has given a fruitful direction to the study of income determination and employment.

It is not altogether clear from the pamphlet what role Dr. Burns assigns to theory. He says (p. 20) that the studies of the Bureau "abound in subtle theoretical analysis," but on page 21 he scorns "speculative excursions from the dreamland of equilibrium." Yet, apart from the somewhat colorful language used, this phrase suggests to me precisely the central concern of theoretical economics, namely analysis of the equilibrium between conflicting forces and tendencies.

Dr. Burns begins with the statement that Keynes and his followers, by and large, "still seek to arrive at economic truth in the manner of Ricardo and his followers" (p. 4). This evidently means by the method of theoretical analysis, i.e., by searching for fruitful general hypotheses whose deductive implications are carefully assessed. Fortunately, this charge is indeed true as far as it goes. It is, however, only fair to add, as Professor Schumpeter has recently pointed out, that Keynes' theoretical work has given a tremendous stimulus to empirical research.[3] No inconsiderable amount of current econometric and statistical studies stems from the Keynesian analysis; and the methodology, and validity, of this empirical research, quite properly, is continuously subjected to vigorous critical analysis. Nevertheless, it is quite true that economists, whether Keynesian or non-Keynesian, do indeed "seek to arrive at economic truth in the manner of Ricardo"; they have, however, at their disposal statistical tools and a wealth of empirical data unavailable to Ricardo and his followers.

In this first section of the pamphlet there is, I feel, a methodological misconception with respect to theoretical analysis; this applies to Ricardian theory no less than to Keynesian theory. The validity and usefulness of the Ricardian analysis does not depend, as Dr. Burns suggests, upon whether per capita income rose or fell in the 19th century (see pamphlet p. 4). Nor would the Keynesian analysis be proven false if during the next fifty years we should experience sustained full employment (p. 8). Indeed Keynesians are perhaps the most optimistic (possibly quite wrongly) with respect to such a possibility. Theoretical analysis is one matter; speculation about the future course of events is quite another. The "correctness and the scientific character" of the

Keynesian (and Ricardian) theoretical apparatus has nothing to do with speculations about fifty years hence. Indeed, Dr. Burns himself at one point in effect recognizes this (p. 8, 8th line from bottom). But then why did he write the section dealing with the "fate of the Ricardian system" (p. 5)? Individuals may use wrong data in their analyses; they may misuse theory. If so, that would be a proper subject for criticism. But this would have nothing to do with Keynes' theory of income determination. And even if Keynes himself could be shown (as may well be the case) to apply his theory at times wrongly, that would not invalidate the theory itself.

If the Keynesian tools of analysis stand up as well as the Ricardian (which, while greatly improved are still the *foundation* of all modern price and value theory), they will have a useful future. And, of course, the theory is far from being final, any more than Ricardo's system was final. A distinguished English economist recently said at Harvard that every economist in Britain is now a Keynesian (including Pigou) in the sense that all use the Keynesian terminology and the Keynesian theoretical apparatus. That, of course, does not mean that they are all followers of those economic policies which Keynes espoused during the Great Depression.

The central part of Dr. Burns' critical analysis of Keynes' theory is continued in pages 5-11. The theory, he says, can be simply put without misrepresenting its essence. But he begins straight away with a marked departure from Keynes' terminology. He uses the words "planned"[4] and "intended investment." Keynes, however, uses the words "rate of new investment," "volume of investment," and "current investment" (Chapters 3, 18). This means the actual investment made in the period in question. Consider now Burns' illustrative figures. With an initial income of $16 billion, with new investment of $2 billion, and with a marginal propensity to consume of ½, income would rise to $20 billion. Now in his interpretation of Keynes, on page 9, Dr. Burns first assumes that "intended investment" (whatever that may mean) is $2 billion as indicated in the figures cited above. Later, he assumes, (p. 9, lines 13, 14) that the "intended investment" changes. Accordingly, in the period in question it turns out that the actual investment was not $2 billion and therefore, of course, income would not rise to $20 billion as first suggested. "Our data (what data?) therefore do not determine a unique size of national income" (p. 9). This "now you see it, now you don't" business is a very strange affair. The illustration is far from putting forth the Keynesian theory "without misrepresenting its essence" (pamphlet, p. 5).

If by "intended investment" is meant investment plans which are not carried out, such "intended investment" has obviously no relevance for income determination. Investment actually made in fixed capital was presumably "intended", while part of the net investment in inventories may at times be "unintended." In any event, the actual investment in any given period is the relevant factor. This does not mean, however, that I regard investment as an unexplained and unexplainable datum given by some *deus ex machina*. On the contrary, significant analysis can be made of the factors affecting its behavior over time.

If Dr. Burns merely wishes to stress the volatile character of investment outlays, he will find numerous passages in Keynes which discuss this matter with unsurpassed clarity. Keynes is well aware that the "volume of investment is subject to highly complex influences" (*General Theory*, p. 314). Expectations of the future, subject to sudden and violent shifts (Chapters 12, 15, 22) play an important role. But whatever these influences, it is the investment actually made in a given period which is relevant. Dr. Burns' statement in this section (pp. 5-11 of the pamphlet) does not, I believe, accurately take account of Keynes' writings.

As time unfolds from day to day, the rate of investment at any moment is a given amount; and whatever that given amount is, the flow of income is affected by the magnitude of the actual rate of investment. The rate of investment may indeed be constantly fluctuating, rising or falling, or it may run along for a time at a fairly stable level. Any change in the rate of investment is likely to induce, after some time lag, changes in the rate of consumption, the magnitude of such changes depending in large part upon the behavior pattern of the community with respect to the effect on consumption expenditures of changes in income. And various factors, both long-run and short-run, may modify from time to time this relationship. Thus, as the flow of investment unfolds, income rises or falls by a magnified amount according to the actually prevailing marginal propensity to consume.

Consider Dr. Burns' statements (pp. 9-10) concerning the indeterminacy of Keynes' income system. If he believes that the consumption schedule and levels of actual investment must be moved capriciously by the dynamic process of adjustment of the equilibrium level, I am forced to disagree both on the basis of theoretical and statistical studies. If he is saying simply that there are dynamic effects of the approach to equilibrium, he is saying nothing that is not already admirably stated in Keynes. In this connection the reader may find it interesting to turn to Professor Taussig's[5] temperate remarks concerning the "penumbra" area of price determination. These highly interesting comments, elaborating dynamic aspects of the problem, were, however, not believed by Taussig himself to be damaging to the Marshallian theory of supply and demand. Similarly, researches all over the world, including no doubt studies by the National Bureau, are hourly engaged in elaborating and improving the Keynesian income theory.

There is, I feel, a misconception with respect to Keynes' view that the consumption function is fairly stable. Keynes never held that it is rigidly stable or cannot be changed. Moreover, the *shape* of this function need not be linear in order to be stable. The marginal propensity to consume may vary with each stage of the cycle, as indeed Keynes believed it did (see *General Theory*, p. 120). Seasonal movements (of a nonfortuitous and therefore fairly dependable character) might conceivably, as Dr. Burns suggests, be found to exist.

Moreover, the *secular* upward shift of the consumption function referred to in Burns' pamphlet (p. 19) has long been recognized (see, for example, my own *Fiscal Policy and Business Cycles*, p. 233, and Paul Samuelson's chapter in *Post-War Economic Problems*).[6]

About these matters there are I think, misconceptions of the Keynesian theory notably on pages 8, 11, and 19, in Burns' pamphlet. Note, for example, such statements as that the consumption function is "fixed" (p. 8); that it has a "certain shape" (p. 8); that the consumption function is "practically invariant" (p. 11); that the savings of business enterprise are correlated "simply and uniquely" with income payments (p. 11); that "monopolistic practices of business firms can safely be neglected" (p. 11); that "private investment will not be influenced appreciably by the character of fiscal policy pursued by government" (p. 11).[7]

Let the reader compare the highly rigid picture which he gets from the discussion of the Keynesian determinants of income as stated in Burns' pamphlet, with the flexible treatment found, for example, on pages 119-25, 147-64, 194-208, 245-71 of the *General Theory*. Expectations, waves of pessimism, and optimism, psychological factors play an important role in Keynes' analysis. Note, for example, the following from page 249 of the *General Theory*: "Thus the position of equilibrium will be influenced by these repercussions; and there are other repercussions also. Moreover, there is not one of the above factors which is not liable to change without much warning, and sometimes substantially. Hence the extreme complexity of the actual course of events." There is a shocking difference between the real Keynesian theory as found in the pages cited above and the statement which Burns gives of the theory. This any reader can verify for himself. Evidence of any close reading of the *General Theory* is not apparent at any point in Burns' pamphlet.[8]

It may be added that the means of changing the consumption function as discussed in the literature are far more complex than indicated in the pamphlet.[9]

The discussion (pamphlet, pp. 20-21) of Keynes' chapter on the Trade Cycle is, I feel, particularly unhappy, and contains, moreover, some misconceptions of Keynes' view. An author may rightly be criticized on what he sets out to do, but not on something he makes no pretense of doing. Keynes' chapter does not pretend to set out definitive statistical conclusions. Note that in the introductory section of his chapter (*General Theory*, p. 313) is the statement: "To develop this thesis would occupy a book rather than a chapter, and would require a close examination of facts. But the following short notes will be sufficient to indicate the line of investigation which our preceding theory suggests."

This statement represents a moderate and cautious attitude. Yet Dr. Burns refers to Keynes' "disregard of elementary precaution." Keynes' theory, says Burns, "should account for *the* sharp and sudden transition" (pamphlet, p. 20, italics mine). But Keynes only refers to the "fact that the substitution of a downward for an upward tendency *often* takes place suddenly" (*General Theory*, p. 314; italics mine). That is quite different and is not disproved by what Dr. Burns says. Again, according to Dr. Burns' version, Keynes says that the duration of the contraction is "about three to five years" (pamphlet, p. 20). But Keynes in fact does not say this, and in terms of the criticism contained in the pamphlet the difference is highly important. Keynes says that there are reasons "why the duration of the downward movement should have an order of magnitude which is not fortuitous, which does not fluctuate between, say, one year this time and ten years next time, but which shows some regularity of habit between, let us say, three and five years" (*General Theory*, p. 317). Dr. Burns has not shown this statement to be wrong. If someone, for example, could show that the facts are that the duration ranges from 18 months to 24 months, Keynes might well have replied: "Fine, that fits quite well into my theory." The version of Keynes which Burns criticizes is a straw man; it cannot be found in Keynes.

This section contains another misconception. Dr. Burns cites three facts (top of p. 21) that are alleged to collide with Keynes' cycle theory. Not one of them collides with Keynes' cycle theory, and certainly not with the general Keynesian theory of income determination. Take Dr. Burns' third fact, that the stock of durable goods (capital goods) increases, as a rule, during contractions as well as during expansions. This means that net investment in fixed capital is usually positive even in depressions. Everyone knows that. Keynes (and most other cycle theorists including Wicksell, Spiethoff, Cassel, Robertson, etc.) does hold that the *rate* of investment fluctuates in the cycle. Kuznets' data show that this is true. Thus the sentence beginning in line 8, page 21, reveals a serious misconception of Keynes' theory. Burns asks the question how Keynes' theory can be reconciled with the "fact that the stock of durable goods in a growing society is virtually free from any trace of business cycles, increasing as a rule during contractions of business activity as well as during depressions." I had to read, I confess, this sentence several times to be convinced that it was actually there in black and white. Keynes' theory on this point is not novel. It relates, of course, to fluctuations in the rate of investment, and such fluctuations may be quite violent while still permitting some increase in the total accumulated stock of capital goods in typical depression periods. In the deep depression of the thirties, however, there was actual disinvestment for the economy as a whole.

The latter half of Burns' statement quoted above is quite all right, though he is certainly wrong, I repeat, when he asserts that it conflicts with Keynes' theory. But the first half is definitely in error. In view of the violent fluctuations in net investment, shown by Kuznets' data (and that of many others), it is simply not possible that the stock of durable goods can be "virtually free from any trace of business cycles."

Dr. Burns' pamphlet raises important issues concerning the value and validity of theoretical analysis,[10] and particularly the character and usefulness of a theoretical apparatus of the Keynesian type. The issue should not be subserved to the question of being "pro-Keynesian" or "anti-Keynesian." I am not interested in classifying economists in Schools. Labels are misleading and had better be avoided. The defense of "received doctrine," whether Keynesian or otherwise, is no concern of the scientific pursuit of knowledge; and I am not writing this note in that spirit. What is important is to make progress by utilizing to the full all available tools which promise to be useful. Most economists, I believe, are convinced that the "consumption function," for example, is a tool from the Keynesian kit which is useful. And it is, I believe, a safe forecast that it will be extensively and fruitfully used by economists and econometricians in the decades that lie ahead. Dr. Burns' pamphlet would, I feel, have been very different had it been written from the standpoint of sympathetically exploring to the utmost extent the possible contributions to economic research which the Keynesian approach has to offer.

Notes

1.   Twenty-Sixth Annual Report of the National Bureau of Economic Research, Inc., New York, 1946.

2.   In this connection, attention may be called to the statement (p. 11) dealing with Keynes' great influence during the past decade, stimulated by the depression and the war experience. "This experience has convinced many that democratic governments can, if they only have the will, readily subdue business depressions." Dr. Burns refers in this connection to the various White Papers (British, Canadian, Australian) announcing the assumption by these governments of responsibility for the maintenance of a high and stable level of employment. I am not certain what impression other readers may have gotten from this section, but to me the inference appears to be that Burns believes that these governments, misled by Keynes, have embarked upon a mistaken policy. A clarification of his position on this issue, in view of what is said in various sections of the pamphlet, would be helpful.

3.   See this REVIEW, XXVIII (1946), p. 196. Also in *The New Economics*, the volume on Keynes edited by S.E. Harris, Professor Tinbergen shows that Keynes has given a great stimulus to econometric research.

4.   The Swedish economists have used the concept of "planned investment" but that would be another story. Also Harrod in his *Trade Cycle* uses "intended investment" in a special sense.

5.   *Quarterly Journal of Economics*, April 1921, p. 394-41. Taussig modestly begins his criticism of the theory of demand (which resembles somewhat current criticism of the consumption function) with the statement that his suggestions do not alter "the essentials of received economic theory." He concludes by saying: "No one supposes that economics is an accurate science." The "mathematical equations and deductions . . . stand for tendencies: they are compact statements of the underlying trend." Thus he ends by defending the theory of demand. The words just quoted could quite properly be applied to the consumption function. It may be added that in this article, Taussig anticipates some of the things so admirably said by Keynes in his famous chapter 12 in the *General Theory*.

6.   S.E. Harris, editor (New York, 1943). In this connection note the following from the *General Theory* (p. 95): ". . . the propensity to consume may be considered a fairly stable function, provided that we have eliminated changes in the wage-unit in terms of money". See my discussion of this in connection with the secular upward drift of the consumption function in this REVIEW, XXVIII (1946), p. 184.

7.   On the last point, for example, compare with the following from Keynes: "This means, unfortunately . . . that economic prosperity is excessively dependent on a political and social atmosphere which is congenial to the average business man" (*General Theory*, p. 162). And again: "With the confused psychology which often prevails, the Government programme may, through its effect on 'confidence', increase liquidity-preference or diminish the marginal efficiency of capital, which again may retard other investment unless measures are taken to offset it" (p. 120).

8.   The last paragraph on page 7 relating to recent developments in income theory discloses a mistaken view with respect to the nature of these contributions. From the *General Theory* on, it has always been recognized that expenditures financed by progressive taxation (effecting a redistribution of income) may raise income and employment. The authors of new contributions (see Trygve Haavelmo, "Multiplier Effects of a Balanced Budget," *Econometrica*, October 1945 and the literature there cited; also Haberler, Goodwin, Hagen, and Haavelmo in *Econometrica*, April 1946) take this for granted, and go on to discuss the question whether tax-financed expenditures may be expansionist even though there is no re-distributional effect upon the propensity to save.

9.   It is only fair to add that I myself, apart from the violent distortions caused by a great war and the reconversion period, regard the schedule of consumption in relation to disposable income (corrected for the secular upward drift) as one of the most stable regularities in all economic behavior. But I do not hold that it is "fixed" or that it is "practically invariant," or that it could not be changed by a change in the tax structure, by social security measures, by minimum wage legislation, by changes in the ratio of wages to profits, by sustained and continuing full employment, by institutional changes affecting savings such as payroll deduction plans, by life insurance reaching an asymptotic level, etc.

The demand functions, for individual commodities or groups of commodities typically reveal a lower order to regularity than does the consumption function. Yet these relationships disclose ordinarily sufficient regularities to make the demand schedule concept a useful and valid tool for economic analysis.

10.   See T. Koopmans' review article on Burns and Mitchell's *Measuring Business Cycles*, in this REVIEW, XXIX (August 1947).

77

Keynesian Economics Once Again. (Followed by A.H. Hansen's Rejoinder)*

A.F. Burns

Professor Hansen's paper in this number of the REVIEW deals with important issues of economic theory. It expresses the judgment of a leading Keynesian thinker, who has had full opportunity to weigh and refine his reasons for repudiating my interpretation of Keynes.[1] Every mature economist knows how barren controversy can be and, in fact usually is. But Keynes' theory is now at the center of much of our economic thinking, and Hansen is its outstanding exponent. Under the circumstances, it may serve the interests of economic science to examine Hansen's strictures with some care. I am grateful to the Editors of the REVIEW for according me the opportunity.

In the following pages I shall consider the major issues raised by Hansen. Section I is devoted to the essentials of Keynes' theory of income and employment, Section II to its determinacy, Section III to the consumption function, and Section IV to the Keynesian apparatus as distinguished from the Keynesian theory. An appendix on Keynes' business cycle theory brings the paper to a close.

I. Keynes' Theory of Income and Employment

In the essay on *Economic Research and the Keynesian Thinking of Our Times*,[2] I boldly attempted to set forth the essence of Keynes' *General Theory* in a few paragraphs. To enable the reader to follow closely the questions raised by Hansen, I reproduce the main part of the original sketch before taking up the criticisms:

> Keynes' theory of underemployment equilibrium ... attempts to show that a free enterprise economy, unless stimulated by governmental policies, may sink into a condition of permanent mass unemployment. The crux of this theory is that the volume of investment and the 'propensity to consume'

*Source: *Review of Economic Statistics*, Vol. 29, November 1947, pp. 252-68.

determine between them a unique level of income and employment. The theory can be put simply without misrepresenting its essence. Assume that business firms in the aggregate decide to add during a given period 2 billion dollars' worth of goods to their stockpiles, using this convenient term to include new plant and equipment as well as inventories. This then is the planned investment. Assume, next, that business firms do not plan to retain any part of their income;[3] so that if they pay out, say, 18 billion to the public, they expect to recover 16 billion through the sale of consumer goods, the difference being paid out on account of the expected addition to their stockpiles. Assume, finally, that the 'consumption function' has a certain definite shape; that if income payments are, say, 18 billion, the public will spend 17 billion on consumer goods and save 1, and that one-half of every additional billion of income will be devoted to consumption and one-half to savings. Under these conditions, the national income per 'period' should settle at a level of 20 billion.

The reason is as follows. If income payments were 18 billion, the public would spend 17 on consumer goods. But the firms that made these payments expected to sell 16 billions' worth to the public and to add 2 billions' worth to their stockpiles; the actual expenditure of 17 billion on consumer goods would therefore exceed sellers' expectations by 1 billion, and stimulate expansion in the consumer goods trades. On the other hand, if income payments were 22 billion, the public would spend 19 on consumer goods; this would fall short of sellers' expectations by 1 billion, and set off a contraction in the output of consumer goods. In general, if income payments fell below 20 billion, the sales expectations of business firms would be exceeded; while if income payments rose above 20 billion, the expectations of business firms would be disappointed. In either case, forces would be released that would push the system in the direction of the 20 billion mark. Hence, in the given circumstances, 20 billion is the equilibrium income, and it may be concluded that the basic data — that is, the volume of investment and the consumption function — determine a national income of unique size. If we assume, now, a unique correlation between income and employment, it follows that the basic data determine also a unique volume of employment — which may turn out to be well below 'full' employment.[4]

This theoretical sketch can be readily translated into the language of diagrams, and it may perhaps prove helpful to some readers if I do that. In Figure 1 line *CC'* represents the consumption function, or the propensity to consume at levels of income specified along the horizontal axis. *DD'* represents the aggregate demand — that is, consumer outlay plus intended investment — at the specified levels of income.[5] *YY'* represents the aggregate supply function — that is, the sum that is just sufficient to induce business firms to pay out to the factors of production each sum along the horizontal axis. At *B* income payments are 20 and *DD'* equals *YY'*. At lower levels of income *DD'* exceeds

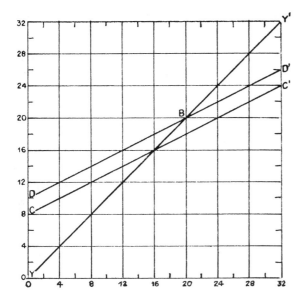

Figure 1

YY'; at higher levels DD' is less than YY'. Hence, as said above "if income payments fell below 20 billion, the sales expectations of business firms would be exceeded; while if income payments rose above 20 billion, the expectations of business firms would be disappointed. In either case, forces would be released that would push the system in the direction of the 20 billion mark." Figure 2 illustrates the same relations in another way. Here II' represents the volume of intended investment, and SS' the propensity to save at specified incomes. At L income payments are 20 and the intended investment equals the propensity to save. At other levels of income, the two are unequal. Since, in the given circumstances, any discrepancy between II' and SS' merely expresses in a roundabout way the excess of DD' over YY', and deviation of income from L will set forces in motion that will tend to restore this level of income. Hence L, or the point of intersection of II' and SS', defines the equilibrium income. And since employment and income are assumed to be uniquely correlated, it defines also a unique volume of employment.

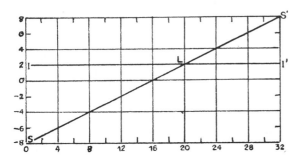

Figure 2

Turning now to Hansen's paper, I am forced to point out that Hansen has not made a single explicit criticism of the substance of my summary of Keynes' theory. Hansen begins by saying that I depart seriously from Keynes' terminology. He then makes miscellaneous remarks, some of them critical of certain portions of my essay, but says nothing in explicit criticism of pages 5-7 where I summarize Keynes' theory of income determination. If my terminology were all that troubled Hansen, there would be no cause for concern. For when I speak of 'planned' or 'intended' investment, I imply merely that 'actual' investment *may* be something different; I do not imply that it *will* be different. If the reader will substitute 'actual' for 'intended' whenever I refer to 'intended investment,'[6] he will discover that the only consequence is that business firms can no longer experience surprises with regard to their inventories. My sketch of Keynes' theory is perfectly general on this point — that is, I deliberately do not specify whether surprises are absorbed in price changes or in inventory movements. Hence anyone who wishes to rule out unintended changes in inventories, regardless of the fact that Keynes himself did not,[7] is entirely free to do so. This restriction will make the Keynesian theory less general; it will have no other effect.[8]

Can it be, then, that Hansen's trouble is not merely my terminology: that despite his failure to specify error, Hansen feels that my summary sketch misses something vital in Keynes' theory of income? There can be no serious doubt on this matter. Hansen says more than once that I have failed to present Keynes' theory accurately, and actually makes an effort — I wish it had been more systematic — to put down his own understanding of the theory. The drift of Hansen's thinking on Keynes' theory of income is indicated by statements such as these: "With an initial income of $16 billion, with new investment of $2 billion, and with a marginal propensity to consume of ½, income would rise to $20 billion." "Investment actually made in fixed capital was presumably 'intended,' while part of the net investment in inventories may at times be 'unintended.' In any event, the actual investment in any given period is the relevant factor" for income determination. "As time unfolds from day to day, the rate of investment at any moment is a given amount; and whatever that given amount is, the flow of income is affected by the magnitude of the actual rate of investment... Thus, as the flow of investment unfolds, income rises or falls by a magnified amount according to *the actually prevailing marginal propensity to consume*" (my italics).

Now the remarkable thing about this representation of Keynes is that Hansen does not feel impelled to say anything about an economic process whereby one level of income supplants another, that he eschews all analysis of expectations or motivation, that he omits any reference to incentives that may induce business firms to maintain employment at one level or to shift from that level to some other; in short, that he sees no need for inquiring whether the balance of forces is such as to produce an equilibrium. He says blandly that if investment rises by 2 billion, and the marginal propensity to consume is ½, income will rise by 4 billion. Given equality between saving and investment, this statement is, of course, arithmetically incontrovertible. But so also is the proposition that if income rises by 4 and the marginal propensity to consume is ½, then investment must have risen by 2. If the first statement expresses Keynes' theory of income determination, as Hansen seems to suggest, then by parity of reasoning the second expresses a theory of investment. And indeed, if it were as simple as all this, we would have at hand a veritable machine for grinding out theories on significant economic problems. Thus if we craved a theory of the propensity to consume, we could find it in the suppressed syllogism that if investment rises by 2 and income by 4, the marginal propensity to consume must be ½.

There is something — one might say a good deal — in Keynes to support such tautological propositions, but it is a little strange to find a devoted follower of Keynes giving them prominence. Obviously, Hansen is echoing *one* of Keynes' theories of the multiplier — specifically, "the logical theory of the multiplier, which holds good continuously, without time-lag, at all moments of time."[9] Need I say that Hansen is not honoring Keynes by identifying this unfortunate appendage of the *General Theory* with Keynes' theory of income? While Keynes at times lapses into tautologies, there can be no doubt that he sought to explain the level of income and employment in terms of underlying human motives and expectations. In seeking to establish "what determines the volume of employment at any time,"[10] Keynes recognized that a solution requires proof. He therefore attempted to show that the factors isolated by his theory were sufficient to establish a "unique equilibrium value" of income and employment; that is, a value "at which there is no inducement to employers as a whole either to expand or to contract employment."[11] When the task was done, Keynes felt justified in remarking that the *General Theory* offered, "properly speaking, a Theory of Employment because it explains *why*, in any given circumstances, employment is what it is."[12]

In condensed and non-technical prose, Keynes' proof is simply the sketch that I gave in my essay on *Keynesian Thinking*. In this proof two propositions are crucial, and both relate to the consumption function. The first is that consumption is a fairly stable function of income in experience; hence, what is actually a fuzzy band may be treated, for analytic purposes, as narrowing to a line. This proposition fixes the consumption function as such, and sets the stage — so to speak — on which investment can play. The second proposition is that as income expands, consumption also increases but by less than the increment of income. This proposition limits the shape of the consumption function. It is necessary if an equilibrium solution is to emerge, just as the first proposition is needed if the equilibrium is to have some relevance to the actual world.

Let Keynes now speak for himself:

> The amount of labor . . . which the entrepreneurs decide to employ depends on . . . the amount which the community is *expected* to spend on

consumption, and . . . the amount which it is *expected* to devote to new investment. . . . When our income increases our consumption increases also, but not by so much. *The key to our practical problem* [i.e., what determines the level of income and employment] is to be found in this psychological law.[13]

But why is this the key to the problem? Let Keynes continue:

What the theory shows is that if the psychological law is *not* fulfilled, then we have a condition of complete instability. If, when incomes increase, expenditure increases by more than the whole of the increase in income, there is no point of equilibrium. Or, in the limiting case, where expenditure increases by exactly 100 per cent of any increase in income, then we have neutral equilibrium, with no particular preference for one position over another. Neither of these conditions seems to be characteristic of the actual state of affairs. . . .[14]

Keynes' meaning is conveyed simply by Figure 1. Given the 'psychological law,' *DD'* must be (as drawn) above *YY'* to the left of *B* and below *YY'* to the right of *B*. It follows that profits of entrepreneurs as a class will be maximized at the point of intersection of *DD'* and *YY'*; that is, when income is the abscissa of *B*. Given the propensity to consume and the intended investment, any erratic displacement of *B* is self-restorative; that is, *B* defines a position of maximum profit, or of stable equilibrium. But if the marginal propensity to consume exceeded unity, the slope of *DD'* would exceed that of *YY'*; hence *DD'* would cut *YY'* to the left of *B* from below. Any displacement of *B*, whether erratic or systematic, would now be cumulative; in other words, profit-seeking entrepreneurs would drive the system to full employment or to extinction, depending on whether the displacement was to the right of *B* or to the left.

It should now be clear that Hansen's purely arithmetic reasoning[15] fails to convey Keynes' fundamental meaning. It is possible, however, to bring the one into harmony with the other. First, the "actually prevailing marginal propensity to consume," if it is to be taken as a historical datum at all, must be treated as a property of a stable consumption function; for, otherwise, it cannot have causal significance. Second, the marginal propensity to consume must be less than unity. Hansen reasons that if the initial income were 16, new investment 2, and the marginal propensity to consume ½, income would rise to 20. If the Keynesian theory of income were reducible to a formula of this type, we would have to say that if the marginal propensity to consume were $3/_2$, other circumstances of the case remaining unchanged, income would fall to 12.[15a] This statement, arithmetically, is on a par with the preceding one. But whereas the first statement makes economic sense in Keynes' basic scheme, the second does not; for, as we have just shown, new investment in the second case will set off a cumulative movement that in real terms has no stopping point short of full employment, and in monetary terms no stopping point whatever.[16]

I have only one additional comment at this juncture. Hansen advises the reader to "compare the highly rigid picture which he gets from the discussion of the Keynesian determinants of income as stated in Burns' pamphlet, with the flexible treatment found" in different portions of the *General Theory*. If by this warning Hansen means merely that my summary fails to convey much that is contained in Keynes' book, I of course agree. My summary was designed to convey the "theoretical skeleton that underlies the Keynesian system,"[17] not as an abstract of the *General Theory*.[18]

There are, to be sure, numerous and enlightening asides and qualifications throughout the *General Theory*. But Keynes was much inclined to operate with the bare bones of his system, and the Keynesians have done so preponderantly. My summary represents rather faithfully, I think, the analytic foundation on which the Keynesian school has built its theories, prognoses, and programs.

II. The Determinacy of Keynes' Theory

My essay on *Keynesian Thinking* carried a warning against what I consider to be the oversimplified doctrines of Keynes, especially as they are being used by his more zealous followers. I asserted that the widespread opinion "that Keynes has explained what determines the volume of employment at any given time . . . reflects a pleasant but dangerous illusion."[19] After pointing out the essentials of the Keynesian theory and its structural similarity to the Ricardian model, I made the following comment:

> Let us go back to the theoretical skeleton of the Keynesian system and examine it more carefully. Suppose that the volume of intended investment is 2 billion dollars, income payments 20 billion, and consumers' outlay at this level of income 18 billion. On the basis of these data, the economic system is alleged to be in equilibrium. But the equilibrium is aggregative, and this is a mere arithmetic fiction. Business firms do not have a common pocketbook. True, they receive in the aggregate precisely the sum they had expected, but that need not mean that even a single firm receives precisely what it had expected. Since windfall profits and losses are virtually bound to be dispersed through the system, each firm will adjust to its own sales experience, and within a firm the adjustment will vary from one product to another. Under the circumstances the intended investment cannot — quite apart from 'autonomous' changes — very well remain at 2 billion, and the propensity to consume is also likely to change. Our data therefore do not determine a unique size of national income; what they rather determine is a movement away from a unique figure. Of course, we cannot tell the

direction or magnitude of the movement, but that is because the basic data on which the Keynesian analysis rests are not sufficiently detailed for the purpose.

I have imagined that Keynes' aggregative equilibrium is realized from the start. But suppose that this does not happen; suppose that, in the initial period, the intended investment is 2 billion income payments 16 billion, and that savings at this level of income are zero. Will income now gravitate toward the 20 billion mark, as the theory claims it should? There is little reason to expect this will happen. In the first place, windfall profits will be unevenly distributed, and the adjustment of individual firms to their widely varying sales experiences will induce a change in the aggregate of their intended investment. In the second place, unemployed resources will exercise some pressure on the prices of the factors of production, and here and there tend to stimulate investment. In the third place, if an expansion in the output of consumer goods does get under way, it will induce additions to inventories for purely technical reasons; further, the change in the business outlook is apt to stimulate the formation of new firms, and to induce existing firms to embark on investment undertakings of a type that have no close relation to recent sales experience. In the fourth place, as income expands, its distribution is practically certain to be modified; this will affect the propensity to consume, as will also the emergence of capital gains, the willingness of consumers to increase purchases on credit, and the difficulty faced by consumers in adjusting many of their expenditures to increasing incomes in the short run. These reactions, and I have listed only the more obvious ones, are essential parts of the adjustment mechanism of a free enterprise economy. Under their impact the data with which we started — namely, the amount of intended investment and the consumption function — are bound to change, perhaps slightly, perhaps enormously. It is wrong, therefore, to conclude that these data imply or determine, even in the sense of a rough approximation, a unique level at which the income and employment of a nation will tend to settle. In strict logic, the data determine, if anything, some complex cumulative movement, not a movement toward some fixed position.

If this analysis is sound, the imposing schemes for governmental action that are being bottomed on Keynes' equilibrium theory must be viewed with scepticism. It does not follow, of course, that these schemes could not be convincingly defended on other grounds. But it does follow that the Keynesians lack a clear analytic foundation for judging how a given fiscal policy will affect the size of the national income or the volume of employment.[20]

This criticism can be summed up in a sentence: viz., the consumption function and the volume of intended investment, which are impounded in *ceteris paribus* by the Keynesian theory, *cannot* (except by accident) remain constant, since the very process of adjusting to the data (the consumption function and the volume of intended investment) will, quite apart from independent influences that may operate on these data, induce changes in them. Nevertheless I have thought it well, for reasons that will become apparent, to reproduce the original criticism in full.

Hansen observes that if my criticism simply means "that there are dynamic effects of the approach to equilibrium", that much had already been "admirably stated" by Keynes. I do not think it worth while to dwell on this comment.[21] The important thing is Hansen's attempt to dismiss the criticism on the ground that it is not basic. Hansen does not argue the case directly, but proceeds by analogy. He invites attention to Taussig's "temperate remarks concerning the 'penumbra' area of price determination," and informs the reader that Taussig's "highly interesting comments, elaborating dynamic aspects of the problem, were, however, not believed by Taussig himself to be damaging to the Marshallian theory of supply and demand." The reader is left to infer that my criticism, which elaborates dynamic aspects of the income problem, is likewise not damaging to Keynes' theory of income. And has not the reader been gracefully prepared for this inference by Hansen's earlier remark that the substance of my criticism had been "admirably stated" — and presumably properly handled — by Keynes himself?

I can explain Hansen's dialectical feat only on the ground that he has not fully understood my argument.[22] I shall therefore try again, and this time guard against deceptive analogies. Let us consider the output of a firm operating under conditions of pure competition. With minor modifications, Figure 2 will serve as an illustration of the case. Assume that the horizontal line *II'* represents the demand curve facing the firm, and that the rising line *SS'* (the vertical scale being adjusted to eliminate negative values) represents the marginal cost of different possible quantities of its output (indicated on the horizontal axis). According to the standard theory, these data suffice to determine the output of the firm "in the short run." The solution is indicated by the abscissa of the point of intersection of *II'* and *SS'*, which in our diagram is 20. The proof is simple. If output were smaller, an extra unit of output would add more to revenue than it would to costs; while if output were greater, a reduction of output by one unit would cut costs more than revenue. Since profit is at a maximum when output is 20, any deviation from that figure will stimulate a movement towards it. In this sense output is uniquely determined.

Within its own framework, this theory of the firm is strictly valid. There is nothing in the situation surrounding the indicated equilibrium output that could of itself induce changes in the demand curve facing the firm (the market price) or in its schedule of marginal costs. Hence the theory cannot be challenged on the ground that if output happened to be at the indicated equilibrium value, it could not be maintained. Nor can the theory be challenged on the ground that if output happened to be out of equilibrium, the process of adjusting to the data — that is, to the demand and supply schedules of the firm — would of itself modify these data. Any criticism along these lines would overlook the condition of pure competition — which reduces the firm to an atom. To be sure, as output varies, there will be changes in the resources employed and in income payments. But since the firm can have only a negligible influence on the demand for resources or on the industry's output, it cannot perceptibly influence any price; in other words, the demand curve facing the firm and its schedule of marginal costs can remain virtually intact as its output undergoes variation.

Let us now return to Keynes' theory of income. In essence, it is an extension of demand and supply analysis to output as a whole. The vital factors in this analysis are the consumption function and the intended investment. These are the data to which business firms, in the aggregate, are supposed to adjust. These are also the data that the theory impounds. But processes of reasoning that are valid for the output of a single firm or small industry cannot be carried over mechanically to output as a whole. Indirect effects can be ignored or slighted in the case of an economic atom, but not for the economy taken as a whole. Infinitesimal adjustments, which might still save the situation formally, are of no practical relevance. By failing to analyze the far-flung repercussions of adjustment processes, Keynes' theory of aggregate income moves on a superficial level, and misrepresents the forces at work. This is the upshot of the criticism of the determinacy of this theory, quoted at the beginning of this section. To dispose of the criticism it would be necessary to show that the induced changes in the consumption function and intended investment are inappreciable, or that they are self-correcting even if large. I suggest that the reader, whether or not he thinks the criticism justified, now turn back and see whether Hansen has come to grips with the issue.[23]

While I concluded in my essay that Keynes has failed to justify his claim of explaining what determines the volume of employment at any given time, I did not claim that my criticism was decisive. Let the reader note carefully the following sentences, which express the essence of what I tried to convey in the essay:

> The problem of unemployment facing our generation calls for realistic, thorough, and unceasing investigation. The great and obvious virtue of the remedies proposed by the Keynesians is that they seek to relieve mass unemployment; their weakness is that they lean heavily on a speculative analysis of uncertain value. This weakness attaches also to my critical remarks on the theory of underemployment equilibrium. Granted that the simple determinism of Keynesian doctrine is an illusion, it does not follow that secular stagnation is another, or that the consumption function may not be sufficiently stable in experience to enable public officials to forecast reliably some consequences of their policies. These questions raise factual issues of the highest importance. . . . [24]

III. The Keynesian Consumption Function

I have already suggested how important the consumption function is in Keynes' scheme. This was emphasized in *Keynesian Thinking*, where I argued that the consumption function occupies much the same place in Keynesian economics as the agricultural production function in Ricardian economics. Since the Ricardian parallel is not immediately relevant, I shall confine quotation to the passages on Keynesianism:

> The most important proposition in Keynesian economics is that the consumption function has a *certain shape*, that is, consumer outlay increases with national income but by less than the increment of income. . . . The Keynesians treat the consumption function as *fixed*, and deduce the effects on the size of the national income of an increase or decrease in private investment, or of an increase or decrease in governmental loan expenditure. . . . To be sure, the . . . Keynesians . . . recognize that the consumption function is not absolutely rigid, and they frequently insert qualifications to their main conclusions. But I have formed the definite impression that the Keynesians — except when they discuss changes in personal taxation — attach even less importance to their qualifications than did the Ricardians. . . .[25]

I have put in italics the words singled out by Hansen as evidence of my "misconceptions" with respect to the consumption function. That these words do not suffice to convey my meaning is evident from the context in which they appear. I charged the Keynesians with minimizing the importance of shifts in the consumption function; I did not claim that Keynes or his followers believe that the consumption function is "fixed." Once more, I do not say merely that Keynesian economics postulates a "certain shape" of the consumption function. The rest of the sentence, which identifies the meaning of "certain shape" reads: "that is, consumer outlay increases with national income but by less than the increment of income." Since this is nothing other than Keynes' 'psychological law,' which in Keynes' own words[26] is the "key" to the problem of income determination and "absolutely fundamental" to his theory, is it not strange that Hansen sees a misconception in my statement?

The best interpretation I have been able to put on Hansen's strictures is that he is concerned less with what I actually say about the Keynesian treatment of the consumption function[27] than with the general drift of my remarks. I suspect that Hansen is troubled because my essay conveys the impression that the Keynesians are excessively mechanical in their thinking, that they gloss over the turbulent life that goes on within aggregates, that they give little heed to adjustment processes in our society, that they subject *ceteris paribus* to excessive strain, that they slight in particular the instability of the consumption function; and that while Keynes is guilty on all these counts, the Keynesians —

among whom Hansen is outstanding — are guiltier still. If that is what is troubling Hansen, I do not think the fault is mine.

Keynes says quite definitely: ". . . we are left with the conclusion that short-period changes in consumption largely depend on changes in the rate at which income (measured in wage-units) is being earned and not on changes in the propensity to consume out of a given income."[28] Keynes did not stop with this generalization. He proceeded to build a system from which "changes in the propensity to consume" were excluded. To be sure, the "changes" are brought in, now and then, by way of qualification. They are also brought in, now and then, in comments on policy. But they do not enter the grand theorems. The 'blade' of investment carves out economic fortune; the 'blade' of the propensity to consume remains stationary while the carving is done. Or to change the metaphor, investment is the actor in the drama of employment, and the consumption function is the stage on which this actor — a rather temperamental one — performs his antics. Why is national income a function of investment? Why is Keynes equipped with an investment multiplier, which accomplishes wonders, but does not even mention a consumption multiplier? Why should an extra Ford car fructify income if acquired for business use, but not if acquired for pleasure? To these questions there is only one logical answer: in Keynes' scheme investment is a free variable, while consumption is rigidly and passively tied to income.[29]

But what of Hansen's views on the consumption function? Taking his extensive writing of recent years as a whole,[30] I feel that he is more prone to identify the formal Keynesian model with the operations of the actual world than was Keynes himself. To Keynes a stable consumption function is an analytic convenience, as I mentioned earlier. True, he sometimes loses sight of the restriction. But when he is explicitly engaged in empirical generalization, his characteristic phrase is a "fairly stable" function. To Hansen a stable consumption function seems to be a tight description of reality, at least in the short run. His characteristic phrase is "highly stable." The following is a typical specimen of his thinking on the subject:

> There is no evidence that the cyclical consumption-income pattern *has shifted, or is likely to shift in the near future*, so as to increase consumption and reduce savings. . . . The fact is that, at moderately high income levels, persistent institutional factors determine within *rather rigid limits* the ratio of consumption to income. . . . The superficial view that the persistence of vast unsatisfied consumer wants is an answer to the problem of limited investment outlets — outlets inadequate to fill the gap fixed by the consumption-savings pattern — overlooks the *stubborn fact* that this pattern is, according to all the available evidence, a *highly stable* one. It is not likely to be radically changed from one decade to another except by important modifications in fundamental institutional arrangements. . . . But whatever the net trend . . . there can be little doubt that *no important shift* in

the consumption-income pattern can be expected within a short period. We have to recognize that we are dealing here with a function that is *highly stable and is not easily changed*.[31]

In his present paper Hansen protests that he does not hold that the consumption function is "fixed." The above quotation would definitely support him in that statement. Hansen also protests that he does not hold that the consumption function is "practically invariant." Whether the quotation supports also *that* statement, I must leave to the readers' own sense of adjectival subtlety. Hansen protests that he has himself called attention to the upward secular shift in the consumption function, and indeed he has. He even grants that seasonal movements in the function "might conceivably . . . be found to exist."[32] All this is to the good. I prefer, however, to stick to the issue, which is not that the Keynesians regard the consumption function as fixed, but that they attach slight importance to its wanderings.[33]

I know of only three ways of testing the position of an author. The first is to determine whether his writing as a whole has a definite pattern. The second is to examine with special care what he says when he attempts to sum up his own thinking.[34] The third is to observe how he handles major economic problems. The last test is the most important of all. I judge that if shifts in the consumption function over the course of a business cycle seemed at all significant to Hansen, he would not assert unequivocally that "it is just because of the *high stability* of the consumption function that fluctuations in the rate of investment *produce* the business cycle."[35] Nor would he say, without further ado, that the "essence" of the depression of 1929-32, "as indeed of *all* depressions, can quite simply and plainly be stated"; this essence being the decline in private capital outlays, which "*caused* unemployment in all the heavy goods industries, and in turn *induced* a decline in consumption expenditures."[36] Again, I judge that if Hansen took the upward secular drift in the consumption function seriously, he would not have ignored it in his Presidential Address (American Economic Association, 1938), which dealt with the forces that shaped national income in the "nineteenth century" and how these forces have lost strength in "our times." In this important paper — still the fountainhead of stagnationist thinking — Hansen freezes the consumption function almost at the start,[37] then (quite logically) maintains silence on its part in economic evolution.

There is much more that might be said of the manner in which the consumption function is handled by the Keynesian school, but I think I have gone far enough to indicate that the "rigid picture" of Keynesianism in my essay — while displeasing to Hansen — is painted from life. I wish merely to add a few methodological remarks on the consumption function *per se*, which is a schedule or curve relating aggregate consumption to aggregate income. If the curve is to mean more than a line on a piece of paper, time must somehow enter. It does so in three ways, as in a demand curve of the Marshallian type.

First, the curve relates to a definite period — day, year, or something else. Second, both consumption and income are rates per unit of time, which of course need not be the same as the given period. Third, the curve shows the response of consumption to income after a certain period of adjustment, which may be 'short' or 'long.' These simple observations have several significant implications: (a) The curve shows a relationship between hypothetical — not existential — magnitudes. (b) For any given period there is not one curve relating consumption to income, but a family of curves, each corresponding to a different period of adjustment. (c) Since there is no fast line[38] between consumer and investment expenditure, another family of curves — one for each reasonable pair of definitions of income and consumption — corresponds to every member of the first family. (d) Finally, since tastes, technology, and resources keep changing in the world we know, the ensemble of curves may be expected to shift from one period to the next.

This, I think, expresses the essentials of the theoretical framework that faces the economist who seeks to determine the empirical properties of the Keynesian consumption function. Quite obviously, vigorous shortcuts must be taken, if anything useful is to be accomplished on the problem. I take it as a reassuring sign of our times that the *General Theory* was promptly followed by efforts to measure the consumption function; that there was no gap of a quarter century, such as separated Moore from Marshall. But I feel that it is regrettable that some of the work has been done in haste, and that much of it has been used uncritically. Man is a slave not only to his theories, but to the very words in which theories are expressed. I venture the guess that if Keynes' theory had been worded in terms of a 'propensity to save' instead of a 'propensity to consume' (which would not of itself change the theory one iota), some of his doctrines would have fewer adherents today. My reason is simply that the evidence which *seems* to support a "stable" consumption function would less readily support a "stable" savings function.

IV. Keynesian Apparatus vs. Keynesian Theory

A considerable part of Hansen's paper is devoted to methodological questions. Here I see no great issues raised. When all is said and done, there is no methodological problem in economics other than straight thinking and the competent use of evidence. The important question always is whether this or that theory is sound, not what role this or that investigator assigns to economic theory. I have, perhaps, more faith in the possibility of a science of economics than Hansen.[39] I surely think that economists should work unceasingly toward that end, and that they fail to do so when they grow impatient with their intractable material. I look forward to the day when economists will not rest content until they have at least specified the observable conditions that would contradict their theories, when the conformity of a theory to facts is respected no less than its logical consistency, and when carefully formulated theories are tested promptly and thoroughly in a score of research centers. But my views on economic methodology, such as they may be, are quite apart from the issues of Keynesian economics raised in my essay and so roundly challenged by Hansen.[40]

I do not see that Hansen's methodological comments have anything to do with the validity of Keynes' basic theory of underemployment equilibrium. Nevertheless, it may be worth while to clarify the distinction between "theory" and "theoretical apparatus" which seems to underlie Hansen's methodological remarks. This distinction is blurred in Hansen's account, with the result that my views, if not also his own, are not represented accurately.

I have no quarrel with the Kyenesian theoretical apparatus as such, any more than with the Ricardian or Marshallian. The Keynesian theoretical apparatus is merely an analytical filing case for handling problems of aggregate income and employment, and is logically akin to Marshall's filing case for handling problems of price. Marshall's files are labeled 'demand' and 'supply,' and there are subdivisions in each on the 'length of the run.'[41] Keynes' files are labeled 'propensity to consume,' 'marginal efficiency of capital,' 'liquidity preference,' and 'supply of money.' The usefulness of Marshall's files in facilitating orderly analysis of price problems is, I think, universally recognized. Keynes' filing case is a more brilliant construction; it is also more novel, and is still fighting its way.[42] On its effectiveness in handling some problems, especially those of short-run change in income and employment, I happen to have serious doubts.[43] But I should readily grant its promise for analyzing certain broad problems of economic organization and evolution, and I think that much more experimenting needs to be done before its range of usefulness can be justly appraised.[44]

But the Keynesian *theoretical apparatus* is one thing, the Keynesian *general theory of income and employment* is another, and the Keynesian *theory of income and employment in the current institutional setting* is still another. My essay was concerned with the second and third, not the first. I questioned the determinacy of Keynes' general theory on the ground that it proceeds on a *tacit* assumption that is open to grave doubt — namely, independence of the consumption function and intended investment from the adjustment processes of a free enterprise system. If the criticism is valid, it bears also on the doctrine of secular stagnation, which I consider the characteristic expression of the Keynesian theory of income and employment in "our times." But two *explicit* assumptions of the stagnationist doctrine have a more vital bearing on its validity. The first is that "consumer outlay is linked fairly rigidly to national income and is unlikely to expand unless income expands," the second that "investment opportunities are limited in a 'mature' economy such as our own."[45] Since these assumptions raise factual issues of the highest importance, it surely is desirable to put them to a thorough test.[46] "A scientific theory cannot require the facts to conform to its own assumptions," and to urge this homely truth — I have now put it in Keynes' words[47] — is not to raise, as Hansen seems to believe, "important issues concerning the value and validity of theoretical analysis."[48]

An economic theorist is justified on many occasions in oversimplifying facts to clarify in his own mind what he believes to be significant relationships.[49] He is likewise justified in bringing the results of his speculative inquiries before his colleagues, whether to seek their critical appraisal before going further or to stimulate them by his work. As long as the economist moves within these boundaries, he may be excused even for not making a strenuous effort to discover how seriously he has distorted the facts by his simplifying assumptions. But when he attempts to give practical advice, he loses his license to suppose anything he likes and to consider merely the logical implications of untested assumptions. It then becomes his duty to examine with scrupulous care the degree in which his assumptions are factually valid. If he finds reason to question the close correspondence between the assumptions and actual conditions, he should either not undertake to give any practical advice, or should frankly and fully disclose the penumbra that surrounds his analysis and the conclusions drawn from it. Better still, he should rework his assumptions in the light of the facts and see whether he is justified on this new basis in telling men in positions of power how they should act. Economics is a very serious subject when the economist assumes the role of counselor to nations.

I cannot agree with Professor Hansen that "the only realistic question is whether or not Keynes has given a fruitful direction to the study of income determination and employment." To this question a hearty affirmative is the only answer, but it is not the only realistic question. In view of the part that Keynes and his school have played in the theoretical and practical worlds, it is not unrealistic to inquire whether their theories bear out the claim that they explain what determines the volume of employment at any given time.[50] I do not think this claim could be readily accepted, even if my doubts concerning Keynes' general theory of underemployment equilibrium — or its special variant, the theory of secular stagnation — turned out to be baseless. Somehow the business cycle, and the various technical and institutional lags on which it so largely rests, would have to be brought into the theoretical system. But as Professor Hansen himself suggests, Keynes' theory of business cycles is a mere sketch, quite incidental to the theory of underemployment equilibrium. In my essay I had something to say about the loose relation between Keynes' thinking on business cycles and the facts of experience, and Professor Hansen has challenged my interpretation. While our differences on Keynes' business cycle theory must not be overlooked, they have practically no bearing on the Keynesian doctrines that have stirred the world, and I therefore relegate this theme to an Appendix.

Notes

1.   In the November 1946 issue of this REVIEW Professor Hansen comments on the great difficulty that economists have experienced in grasping Keynes' *General Theory*. In this connection he makes the following pronouncement: "A recent example disclosing a number of elementary misconceptions is the pamphlet by Arthur F. Burns, on *Economic Research and the Keynesian Thinking of Our Times* (National Bureau of Economic Research, 1946). However, the pamphlet does strikingly reveal (perhaps inadvertently) how economic theory — whether Ricardian or Keynesian — serves the highly useful purpose of pointing up what factual data are relevant to a useful investigation" (p. 187). Since this statement was not accompanied by any evidence, I was of course interested and eager to know what my misconceptions may be. In the course of the ensuing correspondence, Hansen eventually set forth his views in some detail. I replied as fully. Hansen's paper in this REVIEW presents the critical remarks that he developed in correspondence, with such elaborations and modifications as he has deemed necessary to present his case properly before the scientific public.

2.   Hereafter referred to as *Keynesian Thinking*.

3.   This assumption is not essential to the Keynesian system; I make it here in order to simplify the exposition. The figures used throughout are merely illustrative. Further, the exposition is restricted to the proximate determinants of employment in Keynes' system; this simplification does not affect the argument that follows. (This note appeared in the original essay.)

4.   *Keynesian Thinking*, pp. 5-6. In later paragraphs, I distinguished between this general theory of income and employment, and its characteristic special variant — the theory of secular stagnation.

5.   Of course, DD' and CC' need not be linear, see note 3.

6.   At one point I speak of 'planned investment' in an equivalent sense.

7.   See *General Theory*, for example, pp. 123-24, 288.

8.   To illustrate in terms of the preceding example: Assume that income payments are 24 billion. This would imply that business firms expect to recover 22 billion through the sale of consumer goods and to add 2 billion dollars' worth to their stockpiles. The consumption function being what it is, they can recover only 20 billion from the public. Under the present restrictive hypothesis they cannot absorb the difference by leaving an extra 2 billion dollars' worth on the shelf; hence (barring destruction of unwanted goods), they must slash prices. The outcome for the given period is as follows: consumption 20, investment 2, income 22, income payments 24, consumer saving 4, business dissaving 2, aggregate saving 2. In the next period, investment being a datum, business firms will presumably curtail the output of consumer goods. And so they would also under the less restrictive hypothesis; that is, if inventories in the given period piled up, or if the failure of expectations to be realized led partly to price cuts and partly to a piling up of inventories.

9.   *General Theory*, p. 122.

10.   *Ibid.*, p. 313.

11.   *Ibid.*, pp. 26, 27.

12.   J.M. Keynes, "The General Theory of Employment," *Quarterly Journal of Economics*, February 1937, p. 221. The italics are Keynes'.

13.   *General Theory*, pp. 29-30. My italics.

14.   See Keynes' letter to Elizabeth Gilboy, *Quarterly Journal of Economics*, August 1939, p. 634. The italics are Keynes'. Cf. *General Theory*, pp. 117, 118, 251-52.

15.   I am referring to Hansen's explicit argument. He may well have taken some things for granted.

15a.   To explain: since new investment is 2, a reduction of income by 4 and of consumption by 6 is necessary to satisfy the assumption that the marginal propensity to consume is 3/2. In a more technical jargon, if the marginal propensity to consume is 3/2, the marginal propensity to save is — 1/2, and the investment multiplier — 2; hence, if investment goes up by 2, income must come down by 4.

16.   Keynes was an extraordinarily effective teacher, but a poor pedagogue. A good one would have defined the stability conditions of his system with some care. It is not necessary to assume (though there is a gain in realism in doing so) that the marginal propensity to consume is greater than zero and less than unity (*General Theory*, p. 96); it is sufficient to assume that it is less than unity. If the marginal propensity exceeded unity, the system would be completely unstable, as Keynes states. If the marginal propensity equals unity, three cases are possible: neutral equilibrium as defined in the quotation in the text (i.e., when $II' = SS'$ for all values of income in

Fig. 2), progressive inflation (when II' exceeds SS' by a constant), progressive deflation (when SS' exceeds II' by a constant). Keynes doubtless was aware of these possibilities. Thus he writes: If the public seeks "to consume the whole of any increment of income, there will be no point of stability and prices will rise without limit" (*ibid.*, p. 117). This statement does not contradict the quotation in the text; the two treat of different cases in the event of a marginal propensity of unity. But both statements also illustrate Keynes' carelessness about proper qualifying clauses (cf. *ibid.*, p. 261). This, indeed, is the main reason why the *General Theory* is difficult and so frequently misunderstood.

17. *Keynesian Thinking*, p. 6.

18. The proper comparison is with the summaries of fundamentals sketched by Keynes himself, not with the parts of the *General Theory* selected by Hansen (though I hope that these parts as well as the rest of the treatise will receive the reader's attention). I refer to pp. 25-30 of the *General Theory*, and to pp. 219-21 of Keynes' paper in the February 1937 number of the *Quarterly Journal of Economics*. See also pp. 247-49 of the *General Theory* (contained in one of Hansen's recommendations), though this summary is less successful in exposing the skeleton of the system than the summaries just cited. Cf. the following: A.P. Lerner, "Mr. Keynes' General Theory of Employment," *International Labor Review*, October 1936, especially pp. 446-47; P.A. Samuelson, "The Stability of Equilibrium: Comparative Statics and Dynamics," *Econometrica*, April 1941, pp. 113-20, and "Lord Keynes and the General Theory," *ibid.*, July 1946, especially pp. 192 and 199; O. Lange, "On the Theory of the Multiplier," *ibid.*, July-October 1943, pp. 227-28; L. Klein, "Theories of Effective Demand and Employment," *Journal of Political Economy*, April 1947, pp. 109-17, and the review in the same, pp. 168-70; L. Tarshis, *The Elements of Economics* (Houghton Mifflin, 1947), Part IV, especially pp. 346, 360-65. (As far as I know, the sympathy of these authors for Keynes is not suspect.)

19. *Keynesian Thinking*, p. 5.

20. *Ibid.*, pp. 8-10.

21. However, I wish to note, first, that Hansen gives no reference to Keynes' statement; second, the faint suggestion on p. 249 of the *General Theory* (if this is the statement Hansen has in mind) hardly covers the case; third, it would be impossible to show, on the basis of citations from Keynes, that he submitted his work to the criticism I make; fourth, while Hansen's phrasing of my criticism (in view of the surrounding text) suggests that, in a general way, he has grasped my meaning at this point, it is not the phrasing I would use. (I should not speak of "dynamic effects of the approach to equilibrium," since the very point of the argument is that there are no good theoretical reasons for believing there will be such an approach.)

22. Of that there is some evidence, apart from what I say in the text and in the preceding note. (1) When I assert that "our data . . . do not determine a unique size of national income," Hansen inquires "what data?" The answer is the consumption function and the intended investment assumed in my example. (2) In commenting on my illustrative figures Hansen fails to notice that, when I suppose that "in the initial period, the intended investment is 2 billion, income payments 16 billion," etc., I explicitly proceed from a position of disequilibrium. (3) Hansen asserts that he is "forced to disagree both on the basis of theoretical and statistical studies" if, in questioning the determinacy of the Keynesian theory of income, I believe "that the consumption schedule and levels of actual investment must be moved *capriciously* by the dynamic process of adjustment" (my italics). I am puzzled how Hansen could have imagined I meant any such thing, since I at no time referred to capricious movements but did suggest that the "data" determine a cumulative movement.

A parenthetic item remains: what theoretical and statistical studies does Hansen have in mind? I do not know of any statistical studies that indicate absence of capricious shifts in the consumption function. It seems to me that it is exceptionally difficult to determine short-run shifts (other than seasonal) of the consumption function empirically, and that this seriously limits the effective use of the Keynesian analytical apparatus for many problems of short-run economic change.

23. The Taussig analogy, as used by Hansen, skirts essentials: (1) Taussig assumed that the *underlying* conditions of demand and supply in a given industry were independent of adjustment processes. Can a similar assumption be reasonably made for the economy as a whole? (2) Taussig did not assume independence in the short run; on the contrary, he emphasized changes in the "data" induced by adjustment processes. If this much be granted for the Keynesian theory, can it be claimed that it explains what determines income and employment at any given time? (3) Taussig considered the indeterminacy of the Marshallian price theory in the short run (days or weeks or months) a matter of real importance. Can it be argued that the indeterminacy of the

Keynesian income theory in *its* short run (surely a longer span) is of slight consequence? (See F.W. Taussig, "Is Market Price Determinate?", *Quarterly Journal of Economics*, May 1921, especially pp. 401, 402, 405, 411. Compare the passages quoted by Hansen with Taussig's conclusion in full.)

24. *Keynesian Thinking*, p. 12.

25. *Ibid.*, p. 8 (italics added).

26. *General Theory*, p. 29, and "The General Theory of Employment," *loc. cit.*, p. 220.

27. Thus Hansen alleges other misconceptions of Keynes' views (or is it the views of Keynesians?) "about these matters," and quotes four statements from p. 11 of my essay as evidence. By "these matters" Hansen is apparently referring to the consumption function, since that is the subject he is discussing. But three of the quoted statements do not even relate to the consumption function. (For example, the statement that "monopolistic practices of business firms can safely be neglected.") Hansen also claims there is a misconception — or is it misconceptions? — on p. 19, but fails to specify what it or they are.

The four statements on p. 11 which Hansen construes as misconceptions "about these matters" are lifted (a bit inaccurately) from my analysis of the types of assumption needed to reach a conclusion — of which much has been made lately by Keynesian writers — concerning different fiscal paths to 'full employment'; namely, that the loan-expenditure method "avoids . . . the excessively large expenditures" of the tax-financing method "and the excessive deficits" of the tax-reduction method (*Keynesian Thinking* pp. 10-11). This conclusion is advanced, among others, by Hansen in "Three Methods of Expansion through Fiscal Policy," *American Economic Review*, June 1945. Since Hansen did not indicate how he reached this "highly suggestive conclusion" (*Keynesian Thinking*, p. 10), I tried in my essay to pin down the theoretical steps that would lead rigorously to his assertions, and that apparently underlie them. My analysis may be right or it may be wrong; instead of dealing with it, Hansen amasses phrases without regard to the context, and declares they are misconceptions "about these matters" — by which he seems to mean the consumption function, though what he actually means is uncertain.

However, Hansen makes one comment (later and quite incidentally) that possibly relates to this fiscal analysis. The comment begins as follows: "The last paragraph on page 7 relating to recent developments in income theory discloses a mistaken view with respect to the nature of these contributions." (In the paragraph cited, which runs over a page in length, just two sentences bear on recent developments in income theory: "Of late this theory [of the Keynesians on employment policy] has been refined and elaborated, so that 'deficit financing' need no longer be the key instrument for coping with unemployment, and I shall refer to one of these refinements at a later point [this comes on pp. 10-11 of the essay]. But the *practical significance* of the modifications of the theory is problematical, and in any event the theory as I have sketched it still *dominates* the thinking of the Keynesians when they look beyond the transition from war to peace" [italics added].) Hansen then refers to Haavelmo's paper on "Multiplier Effects of a Balanced Budget" (*Econometrica*, October 1945), which takes for granted "that expenditures financed by progressive taxation (effecting a redistribution of income) may raise income," and goes on to discuss (as do the papers it stimulated) "the question whether tax-financed expenditures may be expansionist even though there is no redistributive effect upon the propensity to save." Hansen stops abruptly at this point. The best I can make of this incomplete argument is that Hansen sees an inconsistency between my method of handling the effects of taxation on the propensity to consume on p. 11 of the essay and Haavelmo's method. But there is no inconsistency, since my schedule of the propensity to consume is tied to income before taxes (as is Hansen's in "Three Methods of Expansion through Fiscal Policy," *loc. cit.*), while Haavelmo's is tied to disposable income.

28. *General Theory*, p. 110. Cf. *ibid.*, pp. 95-97, 248. I do not believe that in expressing the consumption function in wage-units, Keynes meant more than that consumption "is obviously much more a function of (in some sense) *real* income than of money-income" (*ibid.*, p. 91, Keynes' italics). I do not know of any evidence that will support Hansen's tentative suggestion that Keynes meant to allow by this device for secular shifts in the consumption function. See Hansen's "Keynes and the General Theory," this REVIEW, XXVIII (1946), p. 184.

29. Samuelson has put the matter accurately: "The crucial assumption upon which it [the doctrine of the investment multiplier] stands or falls is that consumption expenditures and savings are rigidly related to the level of national income. The passive character of consumption cannot be sufficiently stressed." See his "Theory of Pump-Priming Reexamined," *American Economic Review*, September 1940, p. 498.

30.   I have not, however, as yet examined with any care Hansen's recent book on *Economic Policy and Full Employment.*

31.   *Fiscal Policy and Business Cycles*, pp. 247-49 (my italics). See also *ibid.*, pp. 62-63, 237, 238, 250.

32.   Hansen's caution here is admirable, even if a little excessive. Of all the positive propositions that have been laid down in the literature on the consumption function, its seasonality is almost certainly the one that can be most firmly buttressed by statistical evidence on the American economy.

33.   Except, perhaps, "when they discuss changes in personal taxation" (*Keynesian Thinking*, p. 8).

34.   See the above quotation, identified in note 31, which comes from the concluding section of Hansen's fullest discussion of the consumption function, Ch. XI of *Fiscal Policy and Business Cycles*. I may add that much of that chapter seems to me to be in conflict with the conclusions quoted above.

35.   *Ibid.*, p. 249 (my italics).

36.   See Hansen's essay on "Stability and Expansion," in *Financing American Prosperity* (edited by P.T. Homan and F. Machlup), p. 210 (my italics). On the stability of the consumption function, see also *ibid.*, pp. 219, 225.

37.   This is accomplished in a single sentence (which purports to sum up both the thinking of economists and the economic past): "Thus we may postulate a consensus on the thesis that in the absence of a positive program designed to stimulate consumption, full employment of the productive resources is essentially a function of the vigor or investment activity." This, of course, is the kernel of Keynes' short-run theory, and Hansen makes it serve a theory of long-run economic development. See p. 372 of the Blakiston volume on *Readings in Business Cycle Theory*, where Hansen's paper on "Economic Progress and Declining Population Growth" is reprinted from the *American Economic Review*, March 1939.

Can it be that Hansen was not aware of the upward secular drift of the consumption function at the time he wrote this paper? His first mention of it, as far as I know, comes in Ch. XI of *Fiscal Policy and Business Cycles* (1941), p. 233. Ch. XVII of that book reprints the Presidential Address, with various modifications. The sentence quoted at the beginning of this note does not appear in Ch. XVII. Was Hansen led to make the omission by what he says on p. 233? If so, he must have felt that, as far as the consumption function was concerned, no further change was necessary; for he did not add one word on the role of the upward drift in the consumption function in economic development. (The new paragraph inserted on pp. 357-58 is of some interest in this connection.)

38.   Keynes says that "any reasonable definition of the line between consumer-purchasers and investor-purchasers will serve us equally well, provided that it is consistently applied" (*General Theory*, p. 61). This is entirely proper for a formal system. But Keynes' "fairly stable" consumption function is not a property of his formal system; it is an empirical generalization as is Hansen's "highly stable" function. Can the empirical properties of the aggregate consumption function be determined reliably unless the parts that make up the whole — especially the parts that shade into the volatile category of investment — are analyzed?

39.   That does not mean I believe that massive statistical studies will provide us with "a definitive understanding of economic developments which is no longer subject to doubt by competent economists." See, for example, p. 19 of *Keynesian Thinking* ("The data necessary to develop adequately the secular aspects of consumption and saving will not be easy to find or to interpret when found, but the importance of the question may justify our taking the risk") or p. 27 ("True, the most painstaking studies of experience will not always lead to conclusive answers; but they should at least narrow the margins of uncertainty, and thus furnish a better basis than now exists for dealing with grave issues of business-cycle theory and policy").

40.   See above, note 1.

41.   The sublabels on time are indistinct for demand, but I think they are there; in any case, they can be put there (as they can and should be throughout the Keynesian file).

42.   No one questions Keynes' enormous influence, but there are better sources than gossip for ascertaining its extent. The files of the *Economic Journal* and other English periodicals do not support Hansen's report (based on what he heard from an unnamed English economist) that "every economist in Britain is now a Keynesian . . . in the sense that all use the Keynesian terminology and the Keynesian theoretical apparatus."

43.   I have in mind here the apparatus as a whole. Chapters 19 and 22 of the *General Theory*

deserve very careful study from the viewpoint of the effectiveness of the Keynesian theoretical apparatus, as do also some later contributions — among them the treatment of business cycles in Tarshis' recent *Elements of Economics*.

44. I have the impression that the Keynesian file itself is being recast: that the files on 'liquidity preference' and 'supply of money' are fairly inactive, and that the file on 'marginal efficiency of capital' now usually carries the label 'investment'.

45. *Keynesian Thinking*, p. 7.

46. See *ibid.*, pp. 11-19.

47. *General Theory*, p. 276.

48. When I assert that "Keynes and his followers . . . by and large . . . still seek to arrive at economic truth in the manner of Ricardo and his followers" (*Keynesian Thinking*, p. 4), I mean that the Keynesians manifest a strong tendency to take logical consistency with *explicit* assumptions as their criterion of economic truth and that this is insufficient, first, because the *explicit* assumptions may collide with facts of experience, second, because the *tacit* assumptions (they are always present) may do likewise. Hansen is not concerning himself with my views when he first interprets the above quotation to mean "searching for fruitful general hypotheses whose deductive implications are carefully assessed," then adds "fortunately, this charge is indeed true as far as it goes."

Noting my statement on p. 8 of the essay that "there is, of course, nothing unscientific about Ricardianism [i.e., the deductive method] as such," Hansen inquires why I wrote "the section dealing with 'the fate of the Ricardian system'." The answer is contained in the beginning words of the next sentence on that page: "But *ceteris paribus* is a slippery tool. . . ." Hansen has apparently been misled by the phrase "the fate of the Ricardian system," which occurs at one point in the section on "The Lesson of Ricardianism." The context makes it plain (I think) that in that section I was concerned exclusively with Ricardo's *dynamic* theory (in Mill's sense), not with his *static* theory.

49. See *Keynesian Thinking*, pp. 10-11.

50. Hansen asks whether I meant to imply that various governments "misled by Keynes, have embarked upon a mistaken policy" in announcing their assumption of responsibility for the maintenance of a high and stable level of employment (the quoted words are from Hansen's paper). I meant to convey merely that in view of the existing state of knowledge governments are assuming a responsibility they may be unable to discharge adequately, and that broken promises may have serious social repercussions; hence "the need for authentic knowledge of the causes of unemployment in modern commercial nations is now greater than ever" (*Keynesian Thinking*, p. 12).

Appendix on Keynes' Theory of Business Cycles

After considering Keynes' theory of underemployment equilibrium and the issues of fact raised by the Keynesian doctrine, I went on to stress "the need for tested knowledge of business cycles."[1] I tried to develop the simple but fundamental proposition that unless "precise and tested knowledge of what the business cycles of actual life have been like . . . is attained, any explanation is bound to bear an uncertain relation to the experiences we seek to understand or to guard against." Keynes' theory was brought in only incidentally, to illustrate "the consequences that may flow from a disregard of this elementary precaution." In a single paragraph I informed the reader of my purpose (just quoted), informed him also — on the chance that he did not already know it — that Keynes' theory is a "sketch" put "at the end of his long treatise on underemployment equilibrium," summarized the essentials of the sketch, and commented on its failure to square with experience. I then noted that "Keynes' adventure in business cycle theory is by no means exceptional. My reason for singling it out is merely that the *General Theory* has become for many, contrary to Keynes' own wishes, a source-book of established knowledge."[2]

It will help to clarify the substantive issues if I reproduce my account of Keynes' point of departure:

> Keynes starts by saying that a theory of business cycles should account for a certain regularity in the duration and sequence of cyclical phases — that the duration of contractions, for example, is *about three to five years.* Second, the theory *should account for the sharp and sudden transition* from expansion to contraction, in contrast to the gradual and hesitant shift from contraction to expansion.[3]

I have placed in italics the phrases singled out by Hansen for criticism. They seem brittle to Hansen and inspire this conclusion: "The version of Keynes which Burns criticizes is a straw man; it cannot be found in Keynes."

But is not Hansen's verdict too sweeping? In reviewing the *General Theory*, Hansen had this to say about Keynes' view on the duration of cyclical contractions:

> The carrying costs of surplus stocks is the second important factor, *in Keynes' view*, which determines the *duration of depression*. The carrying charges tend to force the absorption of surplus stocks within a certain period, *usually within three to five years.* While the process of stock absorption is going on there is . . . deflation and unemployment.[4]

Hansen not only found in Keynes a contraction of about three to five years, but also that his theory was designed to explain *the* sharp and sudden transition from expansion to contraction. Hansen put Keynes' view as follows:

> A complete explanation of the cycle must, moreover, involve an analysis of the crisis — *the sudden and violent turning point* from boom to depression.[5]

In a later paper, Hansen found once again the sudden transition, not in any straw man, but in Keynes. Hansen even nodded in approval:

> The reason why *the spurt comes to a sudden halt* is well stated by Keynes in his chapter on the Trade Cycle when he says that the essential character of the Trade Cycle is mainly the result of the way in which the marginal efficiency of capital fluctuates.[6]

I do not know Hansen's reasons for shifting his position, but I am reasonably confident that he was right the first time. When Hansen was trying to summarize Keynes' business cycle theory, he adopted the same interpretation that I did. The passages he now cites from Keynes are isolated remarks, which do justice mainly to Keynes' mischievous style; they do not convey his meaning faithfully. Take the following sentence by Keynes:

> There is, however, another characteristic of what we call the Trade Cycle which our explanation must cover if it is to be adequate; namely, the phenomenon of the crisis — the *fact that the substitution of a downward for an upward tendency often takes place suddenly* and violently, whereas there is, as a rule, no such sharp turning-point when an upward is substituted for a downward tendency.[7]

Hansen lifts one clause (the words in italics) from this sentence. To be sure, this clause suggests that downturns are merely *often* abrupt; but the sentence as a whole, I think, suggests the interpretation that downturns are *as a rule* abrupt. This is the interpretation Hansen put on Keynes originally, and it is also the interpretation against which the critical remarks in my essay were directed.[8] And can there really be much doubt on this matter, in view of Keynes' theory that the (typically) sudden break in prosperity is caused (typically) by a "sudden collapse in the marginal efficiency of capital"?[9]

And what shall we say of Hansen's contention that when Keynes spoke of the duration of contractions as being "between, let us say, three and five years," he did not mean "about three to five years"? Hansen bases his argument on a part of this sentence from page 317 of the *General Theory*:

> There are reasons, given firstly by the length of life of durable assets in relation to the normal rate of growth in a given epoch, and secondly by the carrying-costs of surplus stocks, *why the duration of the downward movement should have an order of magnitude which is not fortuitous, which does not fluctuate between, say, one year this time and ten years next time, but which shows some regularity of habit between, let us say, three and five years.*

Now it is possible, to be sure, to interpret Hansen's quotation (I have italicized it) as meaning merely that the longest contraction is less than twice the duration of the shortest.[10] But does this interpretation seem plausible? Did Keynes mean nothing by the "length of life of durable assets" or by the "carrying-costs of surplus stocks"? Hansen overlooks the fact that the sentence from which he quotes is part of a discussion of the factors that render "the slump so intractable." The discussion starts on page 316. Keynes first expresses the view that a "considerable interval of time" must elapse before a recovery can get under way. The passage quoted by Hansen comes a little later, and should be read against the background of Keynes' obvious concern with the *absolute* duration of contractions. This, I think, narrows the uncertainty. If doubt remains concerning the meaning of the phrase "between, let us say, three and five years," it is whittled away by a similar phrase on page

318, which definitely refers to the absolute period required for the absorption of stocks during a slump.[11] And there is additional evidence of Keynes' meaning. He makes a recovery wait not only on the absorption of stocks, but also on the "shortage of capital through use, decay and obsolescence" causing "a sufficiently obvious scarcity to increase the marginal efficiency" (p. 318). In view of the great durability of 'fixed' capital and the sharply reduced demands upon it during depression, can it be seriously argued that Keynes meant that this process could work itself out in a period much shorter than "say, three to five years"?

So much for the issue of the "straw man," which Hansen raised in connection with my account of the starting point of Keynes' theory. The theory itself I summarized as follows in the essay:

> His [Keynes'] theory is that a collapse of investment brings prosperity to a close; that this in turn is caused by a collapse of confidence regarding the profitability of durable assets; and that the contraction which follows is bound to last, say, three to five years, since recovery is possible only after stocks have been worked off, and more important still, after the 'fixed' capital of business firms has been reduced sufficiently to restore its profitability.[12]

Hansen passes over this summary, but attempts to refute what I say of the collision between Keynes' theory and the facts of experience. I cited three such facts. Hansen asserts that "not one of them collides with Keynes' cycle theory," but he stops to examine only one — namely, that "the stock of durable goods in a growing country is virtually free from any trace of business cycles, increasing as a rule during contractions of business activity as well as during expansions."[13] Hansen's argument, as best I can make out, is that this fact does not collide with Keynes' theory, since everyone — including Keynes — knows that net investment in fixed capital is usually positive even in depressions.[14]

If this is Hansen's argument, it is needlessly indirect. The question at issue is simply whether I am right or wrong in reporting Keynes' theory to be that "recovery is possible only . . . after the 'fixed' capital of business firms has been reduced sufficiently to restore its profitability." If I am right, Keynes' theory requires that net investment be, typically, negative in depressions. I maintained that this did not happen. Since Hansen agrees, the way to redeem Keynes is to demonstrate that I misrepresented his theory of recovery. Hansen has not tried to do this, and I do not believe that he would find the task especially easy.[15]

Notes

1. *Keynesian Thinking*, pp. 19-27.
2. *Ibid.*, pp. 20-21. In reading Hansen's critique, the reader may find it useful to take cognizance of this background.

3.   *Keynesian Thinking*, p. 20 (italics added).

4.   See, for convenience, A.H. Hansen, *Full Recovery or Stagnation?*, p. 33 (my italics).

5.   *Ibid.*, p. 32 (my italics).

6.   *Ibid.*, p. 51 (my italics).

7.   *General Theory*, p. 314. (Italics mine. In Keynes' text, crisis is italicized.)

8.   My statement that in Keynes' view "the theory should acount for the sharp and sudden transition from expansion to contraction" can of course be read (as can the citations from Hansen just given) as implying that Keynes meant that downturns are *invariably* abrupt. Had I wished to convey this meaning, I need not have cited more than a single exception. Instead, I referred to Keynes' "rule," and cited several exceptions (four out of a possible seven during the period covered) to show that there was no such systematic difference between the upper and lower turning points as Keynes had supposed (*Keynesian Thinking*, p. 20).

9.   *General Theory*, p. 315. Cf. *Keynesian Thinking*, pp. 20-21.

10.   On this interpretation (which seems to be Hansen's now) Keynes happens to be as wrong on the facts as in my interpretation (and Hansen's of earlier date). One can escape the discomfort once for all: if the passage quoted by Hansen is taken literally, I doubt if any facts could ever contradict it. There is, unhappily, a great abundance of ambiguous remarks throughout Keynes' chapter on business cycles. Under the circumstances, it is essential to work patiently, back and forth, over the text as a whole.

11.   See also *General Theory*, pp. 331-32, where stocks are further discussed.

12.   *Keynesian Thinking*, pp. 20-21.

13.   *Ibid.*, p. 21. Hansen disputes a portion of the statement just quoted. He states that the latter half is "quite all right," but "the first half is definitely in error." Here the difficulty rests on a purely verbal misunderstanding. The latter half of the statement, modifying as it does the first half, merely serves to explain the first half. If, therefore, the latter half is "quite all right," there is no real difficulty.

Although I meant to convey no more than what I have just stated (nothing else was required by the question under examination), it may be well to note that statistics (expressed in a physical unit, for individual industries) suggest that the stock of industrial facilities not only increases, as a rule during contractions as well as expansions of business cycles, but that the rate of increase itself is not systematically higher during a business-cycle expansion than during adjacent contractions. How can this happen in view of the large fluctuations in the output of investment goods and of their close relation to business cycles? The reasons, put briefly, are as follows: (1) If the output of investment goods ascended linearly from the trough of a business cycle to a peak, then descended linearly to the date of the next business-cycle trough; if, further, the output at successive troughs were identical, and likewise at successive peaks; if, finally, retirements were zero; then (barring qualitative distinctions) the stock of industrial facilities in place would increase at a consistently higher rate from midexpansion to midcontraction of business cycles than from midcontraction to midexpansion. (2) None of these assumptions is fulfilled in fact; and a little experimenting will indicate to what extent plausible departures from the model will introduce a haphazard element in the cyclical interval during which the rate of increase in the stock of industrial facilities is especially high or low. The most important randomizing factor in practice (I think) is the unevenness of the successive troughs and of successive peaks in output; for this means, roughly speaking, that the *level* of output of investment goods is in some business cycles greater during expansions and in others during contractions. (3) The preceding statements are based on the tacit assumption that the output (in the sense of value added, in constant prices) of investment goods and the installation of completed facilities are coincident. Of course, there is apt to be here a substantial and highly variable lag, which serves powerfully to distort and diversify the timing of the accelerations and retardations in the stock of industrial facilities.

The whole subject of the cyclical behavior of the stock of industrial capital requires extensive statistical and theoretical analysis. What I have said merely scratches the surface. But I have thought it advisable to indicate that Hansen's remarks concerning what is possible and what is not possible are very hasty.

14.   An earlier statement of Hansen's may be of interest: "The depression is a period of cessation of growth. There need be no actual relapse in capital formation — the existing stock being fully maintained" (*Full Recovery or Stagnation?*, p. 51). See also *General Theory*, p. 329.

15.   On this question, see *ibid.*, especially pp. 105, 253, 317-18, and the Keynesian primer by Joan Robinson, *Introduction to the Theory of Employment*, p. 116. Cf. Tarshis, *op. cit.*, pp. 384, 444, 448.

Brief Rejoinder by Alvin H. Hansen

Dr. Burns' paper is long and this issue of the REVIEW is already over-expanded; space permits very limited comment from me at this time. I warmly welcome his paper which represents, I feel, a remarkable advance over the pamphlet and reflects, moreover, a somewhat more sympathetic attitude toward current economic thinking and analysis. From this paper one gets the impression (much more than in the pamphlet) that the consumption function is not a mere ghost, without corporeal embodiment; though even in the pamphlet Dr. Burns was prepared to entertain the presumption that it has sufficient substance and reality to deserve exhaustive statistical research. The consumption function is indeed the crux of the matter, and so long as it remains a major area for research, as it doubtless will for many years to come, we can be sure that the Keynesian theory of income determination will continue to play an important role in economic analysis. I believe the reader will agree that the issues, while by no means resolved, have been in some measure clarified; and I am content to leave it there for the present. Others will doubtless wish to participate in future symposia on some of the problems raised. They are many and complex.

I am still of the opinion that the pamphlet (see pp. 9-10) strongly suggests that the consumption schedule and levels of investment are moved *capriciously* by the dynamic process of adjustment. Burns now explicitly disclaims this, and I welcome his statement. But this is, in fact, the pivotal issue at stake. If the movement is not *capricious*, then regularities can be found in the relationships of the relevant variables; and if this is so, we *do* have a basis for a theory of income determination.

Dr. Burns fails to see that by using "intended investment", he makes *his* case less general. It is Keynes' formulation (not Burns') which is the more general, since actual investment will at times include unintended inventory accumulation, while intended investment can, in the nature of the case, not do so. Whether or not the term "intended investment" (to which I have no objection as such) is helpful depends of course upon the context in which it is employed. The use made of it in the pamphlet leads, I feel, to confusion.

Dr. Burns suggests that the thesis advanced in my Presidential Address becomes untenable once an upward secular drift in the consumption function is granted. This is not correct. My Address was devoted to the problem of investment opportunities. The gap between (a) investment and (b) the volume of saving which the community wishes to make at full employment, might be due either to a secular decline in investment outlets, or to the absence of a secular rise in the consumption function. Had I made both these assumptions I should have had *two* grounds for secular stagnation — first, from the investment side, and second, from the propensity to save side. My thesis related only to investment. The secular upward drift in the consumption function, in fact, appears, on the basis of available data, to have been such that the *per cent* saved over time has remained about constant. The question then remains, what about adequate *investment offsets* to saving? This was the question to which I addressed myself.

In the next issue of this REVIEW, I shall publish a "Note on Savings and Investment" (not directed at Dr. Burns and written before I had had an opportunity to read his paper) in which I hope to clear up, in a measure at least, some controversial issues with respect to alleged inconsistencies in Keynes' double use of the term "saving" and the related question whether his multiplier analysis is, in situations subject to time-lag, purely tautological.

78

An Exposition of Keynesian Economics*

L. Tarshis

In this paper I shall attempt to give a simple and acceptable account of Keynesian economics. I have no particular qualifications for this task; there are many others who know more than I about *The General Theory* and the writings that derive from it. But since my responsibility is, as I understand it, to discuss not the fine points but only the broad outline, this lack of special knowledge may not be a serious handicap. My hope is to present a picture of Keynesian economics that will be found generally accurate by most of you, and helpful, as a review or refresher, by a few.

I cannot expect this account to appeal to economists as accurate in its detail. The very development of Keynesian doctrine would make any such expectation unreasonable. The doctrine had, for most of us, its beginnings in *The General Theory*; it was molded and qualified in the writings of Robertson, Hicks, Lange, Samuelson, Shaw, and many others; and it has been modified still further in our minds by the events of the last decade. It would be strange, consequently, and indeed disappointing, if *The General Theory* said the same things to us today that it did on its publication. And it would be strange too if this account of contemporary Keynesian doctrine conformed in all details to yours. But perhaps the essential points of the outline will not be challenged.

I. Dependence on Neoclassical Doctrine

Before introducing the novel aspects of Keynesian economics, I should like to emphasize its considerable dependence upon classical and neoclassical tradition. That this dependence should exist will not surprise those who know of Keynes's background. He was surrounded by and he lectured on the Cambridge version of neoclassical economics for many years. A strong reliance on these doctrines is consequently to be expected. That he himself did

*Source: *American Economic Review,* Vol. 38, May 1948, pp. 261-72.

not in *The General Theory* point out this dependence — but, instead, sought to emphasize his break from the earlier doctrines — must be regarded as a tactic of persuasion rather than as an objective statement of the relation between his own work and conventional doctrine. His *Treatise on Money* marks his greatest departure from neoclassical economics and by the time he wrote *The General Theory* he had found a way to reconcile his monetary theory and the neoclassical tradition. Indeed, a good case can be made for the assertion that the doctrine of *The General Theory* was mothered by the *Treatise* and fathered by neoclassical economics. If so, we should have to admit that the child suffered from an extreme Oedipus complex.

The Aggregate Supply Function and Classical Economics. There are two points in particular at which classical doctrine enters. Let us consider them briefly. Keynes introduces the first of them under the title "the aggregate supply function." His concept is obviously closely related to the familiar supply function of neoclassical economics. This function expresses the relation between the output of a firm or industry and the price offered; normally, the higher the price, the greater is the output. His concept though it differs in minor ways is basically similar. In place of the output of a single commodity, he deals with the total production of the economy; instead of measuring total production in physical units, he measures it in terms of total employment; and finally, rather than expressing the independent variable as an offer price, he uses for his variable, businessmen's expectations of sales receipts. His aggregate supply function is, then, a generalization of the substance of the classical function. While the latter gives a determinate answer to the question as to how much a firm with given costs will produce when the demand for its product is known, the aggregate supply function implies that there is a determinate answer to the broader question of how much will all firms produce, or how many men will they hire, given their costs, when the size and composition of the aggregate demand are known?

The General Theory, I believe, marked a great advance over the *Treatise*; and this advance depended to an important degree upon a shift in emphasis. In the *Treatise*, Keynes was interested directly in the general price level; and in *The General Theory*, in the national income. The shift in his emphasis occurred, according to my lecture notes, in 1932, or possibly earlier, and it was at this time that he introduced the aggregate supply concept. The significance of this common date should be noted.

Income, the Value of Output, and Classical Economics. The second aspect of classical doctrine that Keynes adopted consists in his use of a part, though certainly not the whole, of the classical law of markets. He does not, of course, go as far as Say; he rejects Say's law that supply creates its own demand. But he goes part of the way; if supply does not create its own demand, at least it creates the income from which a part of the demand stems. This statement, that production is the source of all income, or more precisely, that the national income or social dividend equals the value of current output, has been accepted generally by classical economists. Moreover, the equality of the value of output and the national income has long been recognized by national income statisticians. For instance, in its first publication, *Income in the United States – 1909-1919*, the National Bureau of Economic Research stated: "The fundamental concept of the National Income which underlies the Estimate by Sources of Production is the same as that underlying the Estimate by Incomes Received. In both estimates the National Income is taken to consist of the commodities and services produced by the people of the country or obtained from abroad for their use."[1] Or again: "Hence it seems that an estimate of the incomes received by all individuals, plus the undistributed incomes of business enterprises, should produce the same figures as the Estimate by Sources of Production, were the data complete and correct on all heads."[2]

At this point some must be asking which of the many available income concepts is concerned in this equality. The answer that I prefer (the gross national product) cannot, I regret, be developed in the time available. Keynes did not, of course, when he was writing *The General Theory* have the valuable July supplement to the *Survey of Current Business* and it is not easy to match his income concepts to the newer ones. But in any case a clear understanding of Keynesian doctrine can be got without examining these technicalities.

The main points of Keynesian doctrine are developed upon these classical foundations — the aggregate supply function and the equality between national income and the value of output. Indeed, starting from the neoclassical position, we can go much of the way towards a formulation of income theory in Keynesian terms before we have to introduce anything that explicitly contradicts other parts of the classical doctrine. Let us see what kind of structure we can build upon these foundations.

II. Income and Aggregate Spending

In accordance with what Keynes accepted of the law of markets, we conclude that when the value of the economy's output in a year is, say, 225 billion dollars, the national income is 225 billions. Our first step, then, is that the national income varies directly with, and indeed equals, the value of output.

What then determines the value of output? Output is valued in the only possible way — by what buyers pay for it. If the value of current output is 225 billion dollars, it indicates that buyers paid 225 billions for it. The national income for a year equals the annual spending of all buyers on current output.

In accordance with the aggregate supply function, output and employment are seen to vary directly with total purchasing, or, looking at it from the buyers' viewpoint, with total spending. Therefore we may conclude that output and employment vary directly with the national income and this, as we have already seen, equals aggregate spending on current output.

Our problem is to discover the factors that determine the size of the national income and the level of employment. The first stage on the way to a helpful answer is reached when we see that the sought-for determinant is aggregate spending. But this does not go far enough, and further analysis is needed. Before taking this next step, however, it is desirable once again to emphasize that there is nothing especially Keynesian about our answer — certainly not in this formulation. While a classical economist would perhaps not find it helpful, he would, I believe, be forced to recognize that it was consistent with at least a part of classical theory.

III. Further Analysis of Aggregate Spending — Consumption and Investment

The objection to ending the analysis here is this: aggregate spending covers such a multitude of activities and it is guided by such a variety of motives that it seems impossible to say anything meaningful about the factors that cause it to vary. After all, a business decision to order a new rolling mill rests upon considerations as different as possible from a government decision to hire school teachers or a consumer decision to buy more clothing. Since the spending stream is made up of such diverse elements, we can expect to find an explanation for changes in its volume only by looking into it more carefully.

The obvious next step is to divide the spending stream into its relatively homogeneous components, which means to classify spending by type of buyer. While buyers could be divided in various ways — for example, as they purchase durable or nondurable goods — Keynes finds it useful to separate them into four groups: consumers, business concerns, government bodies, and foreigners. The sums spent by consumers, he calls consumption; the amounts spent by the other types of buyers are, in order, private investment (normally this category includes housing), public investment, and foreign investment. Consequently, total spending on current output equals consumption plus investment, private, public, and foreign. And total spending on current output also equals the national income. Hence, the national income is equal to consumption plus investment.

It is doubtful whether anything novel, or at any rate at variance with the classical tradition, has been introduced up to this point. If a classical economist can accept the equality between the national income and the value of output, he should have no difficulty, once that output has been classified into goods for consumers, business, government, and foreigners, in accepting the above formulation. Though the formulation at which we have arrived sounds somewhat Keynesian, the sense can still be derived directly from classical teachings.

IV. Reformulation: Income, Investment, and the Propensity to Consume

But this formulation is also open, as we shall see, to a serious objection, and a different way of putting it is called for. We substitute for the statement, income equals consumption plus investment, the statement, income depends upon the propensity to consume and investment. In this form we say no more than before, and the transformation is straightforward once we have introduced the propensity to consume. Why then, we may ask, should we bother to introduce this confusing concept, and simply restate a truism?

The answer, I believe, would run as follows: because in the revised form it discloses factors that are operationally significant; secondly, because it gains in simplicity and elegance.

The objection to the formulation "income equals consumption plus investment" is easily seen. Income depends partly upon consumption, but obviously consumption depends amongst other things upon income. Hence income depends in part upon income. Evidently one avenue in the maze through which we are trying to thread our way leads promptly back to the beginning, which is awkward. Moreover, this false trail diverts attention from other paths that do lead to a solution. What we have, to use an analogy with elementary algebra, is an equation with an unknown that is represented at least by implication, on both sides. It is not a fatal difficulty — the circularity is benign rather than malignant — but it is inconvenient. By re-expressing it, we can avoid this inconvenience, and at the same time provide helpful guidance to the investigator — guidance that will keep him from wandering up blind alleys and along roads that lead only to the starting point.

The Propensity to Consume. It was noted above that consumption depends, amongst other things, upon the national income; these other things, or rather their joint influence, Keynes brings together under the title "The Propensity to Consume." This is the name, then, for the function that relates consumption and income. It is not of course the *ratio* of the two, unless the function can be expressed in this simple form — and there is no statistical evidence that it can. It is simply, to repeat, the relation between consumption and income — the income-consumption function or the income demand for consumers goods. It follows, of course, from the definition of the propensity to consume that consumption is determined by it and the national income, and by these two factors alone.

Now let us return to the formulation to which we objected earlier: income equals investment plus consumption. We can bring out into the open and thus rid our formulation of the element of circularity present in it, if we substitute for consumption its two determinants. Doing so we have: income depends upon investment, the propensity to consume, and income. Now that we have isolated the unknown on both sides of the expression, we can simplify to: the national income depends upon the propensity to consume and investment.

This is the formulation at which Keynes arrives in *The General Theory*. I think it is worth emphasizing that while a classical economist may not find it useful, he would agree that it is based upon an equality accepted in conventional, pre-Keynesian theory. The dependence of the national income upon investment and the propensity to consume is derived directly from the fact that the value of current output equals the income earned in producing it. Once that fact is accepted, the final statement follows.

But to say that this statement about the determinants of the national income can be derived from pre-Keynesian doctrine is not to imply that Keynes said nothing new, or that the classical economist must accept the Keynesian position. What it does suggest is that the points of substantial difference are to be found elsewhere. They will be found, I shall try to show, in the analysis of investment, or rather in the relation between consumption and investment. It is here that the Keynesians and those who do not accept his analysis are farthest apart.

V. Analysis of the Propensity to Consume

Before explaining these differences it is desirable to examine the Keynesian doctrine more carefully. Since income is seen to depend upon the propensity to consume and investment, we shall have to investigate each of these determinants in turn.

What Keynes has to say about the propensity to consume is straightforward. This function, since it covers the effects of all the factors that influence consumption except for income, will be affected in many ways. To indicate some of them, it will be affected by a change in the price level, in the distribution of income, in attitudes towards thrift, in holdings of liquid assets, in the state of the stock market, in the tax structure, in the interest rate, in the dividend policy of corporations, and by changes in many other variables. In fact the list is as long as the list of forces that determine consumers' spending. To say that the national income depends, in part, upon the propensity to consume does not provide a complete answer to our question, but it does suggest directions for further analysis.

VI. Analysis of Investment

The analysis of investment is rather more complicated. Investment can be broken down, as we have seen, into three components: private, public, and foreign. The economist in his professional capacity can say very little about the forces that determine the second of these — public investment — except possibly to point out that his voice is normally not heeded when such investment decisions are made. Keynes had very little to contribute to conventional doctrine on the determinants of foreign investment. Exchange rates, comparative prices, costs of transport, and so on, are the critical factors. His major contribution — and most important break with earlier doctrine — is in his analysis of the determination of private investment.

Private investment consists of the spending of business concerns, except for expenditures that just maintain working capital inventories, and in addition of the spending on private housing. Private business investment — the spending of business firms — is directed towards the acquisition of plant and equipment (including repairs) and to the building up of inventories of raw materials, goods in process, and finished goods. Of course, when inventories are allowed to run down, this part of private investment is negative.

Since private business investment is undertaken by firms generally seeking to maximize their profits, it follows that the amount of their expenditures will depend in some way upon profit considerations. A firm will embark upon an investment project when it expects that course of action to be profitable; otherwise, it will not undertake the project. It will, to put this concretely, order an extension to its plant, or arrange to have its equipment repaired, order new equipment, or build up its stocks of raw materials when it expects to earn more by doing any of these things than it would earn by doing nothing.

Hence the test an investment project must pass if it is to be carried out is this: the money invested in the project must be expected to yield a rate of profit before paying interest that exceeds the interest rate applicable to the firm. If money can be borrowed by a certain firm at 3 per cent, and if that firm believes it can acquire investment goods that will, over their life, return 4 per cent annually on their original cost, after allowing for depreciation but before subtracting the interest charge, it is worth while for the firm to make the investment expenditure. It will, by doing so, add to its annual profits during the life of the asset a sum equal to 1 per cent of the original outlay. Thus, at any date it is worth while for firms to initiate, carry on, or complete every investment project whose anticipated yield measured against the cost of acquiring the good exceeds the particular interest rate facing them.

The Marginal Efficiency of Capital. Keynes names the anticipated yield over the cost of any particular project "the marginal efficiency of capital of that type"; while the schedule of yields anticipated on all possible projects he calls "the marginal efficiency of capital." We have already seen that a project will be undertaken if its marginal efficiency exceeds the rate of interest; hence the dollar value of projects to be carried on depends upon the marginal efficiency of capital, in the schedule sense, and the interest rate.

As Keynes has pointed out, his marginal efficiency of capital concept is identical to Irving Fisher's "rate of return over cost," and it is similar to Marshall's "marginal utility of capital." Because of its familiarity, there should be no serious difficulty in grasping it.

The factors that determine the marginal efficiency of capital are as numerous as those that determine the propensity to consume, though they are, perhaps, more uncertain in their operation and more sensitive to sharp shifts of judgment. For instance, if it is proposed to put up a new plant, it is necessary in estimating its lifetime per cent return over cost to guess about the market for its product for perhaps forty years into the future, and to do the same for the cost of operating the plant. It is obvious that any long-term market or cost forecast of this kind will be uncertain and subject to drastic revision. Some of the factors that could be expected to condition these forecasts are: the existing market for the product, the likelihood that new competitive products will be developed, the productive capacity of the industry, the cost of the capital goods, the general state of business confidence, and so on. In brief, we should want to include in the list all but one of the factors that determine how much expansion it is profitable to undertake, that one being the interest rate, which is considered separately.

VII. Analysis of the Interest Rate

The marginal efficiency of capital is but one of the determinants of private investment; the interest rate is also important. Hence, if we are to round out this analysis we must analyze the forces that set the interest rate. In Keynes's account, its determination rests upon monetary factors — as it should, so he thinks, since it is the price paid for holding wealth in the form of money or, in other words, for borrowing.

When the interest rate is set at any level — that is, when the prices of bonds and other debt instruments are established — it shows that the market does not wish on balance to alter the form in which it is holding its wealth. Those with wealth are content to maintain the existing distribution of their wealth as between money, bonds, and other assets. This must be so for, if they were disposed to change that distribution, they would, in attempting to do so, bid up or reduce the price of bonds. Hence, when the interest rate is set, it means that the economy does not wish to hold either more or less of its wealth in the form of money. It is satisfied, in the circumstances, to hold the amount of money it has. And of course the amount of money it has is precisely the amount that has been created by the monetary system, since after all every bit of money in existence must have a resting place somewhere. Thus we may conclude that the interest rate is determined by two data: the strength of the economy's desire to hold its wealth in money form and the amount of money in existence.

A more detailed examination of the considerations that determine how much of their wealth the members of the economy wish to hold in the form of money will show more clearly how the interest rate enters into the picture.

The Liquidity-Preference Function. The motives for holding *money* are threefold: first, to provide convenience in transactions; second, to provide protection and the means to exploit opportunity in an uncertain world; and, third, to avoid a capital loss feared because of an expected decline in securities' prices. In other words, money is a desirable form in which to hold some wealth, because bonds cannot be spent and they may sometimes be expected to fall in price. Bonds are neither a medium of exchange nor a satisfactory store of value, and money is both. But money, unlike bonds, does not yield anything except the convenience and speculative utilities already noted. Hence against these advantages of liquidity, the holder of money must set the disadvantage that it does not multiply, that his wealth held in that form does not grow. Consequently, we should expect the economy to choose to hold less of its wealth in liquid form when interest rates are raised, and vice versa. This conclusion is, I believe, obvious insofar as it concerns the convenience — and precautionary — motives for liquidity. In considering the amount of money held for speculative considerations, we must remember that that depends upon expectations as to the future course of bond prices. When the views of a part of the market shift to the bearish side, and bond prices are expected by that part to fall, there will be a tendency to move out of bonds and into money, and a shift in the opposite direction will occur when a part of the market comes to expect bond prices to rise. We can suppose that market opinion will become more bearish when interest rates fall to an abnormally low level; that is to say, when bond prices rise to a figure that seems abnormally high; while we may expect the market to become increasingly bullish as interest rates rise towards a level that appears abnormally high. This means that at very low interest rates the speculative motive for holding money will strongly reinforce the convenience motive and the economy will accordingly want to hold a great deal of its wealth in liquid form; at very high rates, the amount of liquidity desired on this account will be much lower.

The relation between the amount of liquidity desired and the rate of interest, Keynes calls "liquidity preference" or the "liquidity function." And since, as we have already seen, the interest rate is determined at the point that equates the amount of money people wish to hold with the amount in existence, it follows that the interest rate depends upon the liquidity function and the amount of money.

VIII. Relation Between Consumption and Investment — Contrast with Classical Doctrine

This analysis of the determinants of the interest rate, perhaps re-expressed in terms of loanable funds, could be expected to appeal to specialists in money and banking. But economists who prefer to explain the interest rate in *real* terms would obviously be less happy with it. There are, of course, many reasons for this, but one of them is particularly worth noting. In the Keynesian account, an increased *desire to save* which, of course, is not at all the same thing as a reduced *desire for liquidity*, would not be expected to lead to a lower rate of interest, or if it does so, only by bringing about a fall in business activity and the national income. If the interest rate does not fall or falls only because of a decline in the national income, investment will not increase by enough to offset the decline in consumption. Indeed we may go further. If consumption expenditures should decline, businessmen would normally consider the inducements to purchase investment goods weaker. Hence, there is no reason to expect the interest rate to act as an equilibrating force that serves to maintain a full prosperity national income, when for instance thriftiness increases.

When the demand for consumers goods falls, we may then expect a reduced demand for investment goods; and as the multiplier process suggests, when the initiating force is a decline in investment, we can expect a decline in the demand for consumers goods. Instead, then, of a model in which a change in the demand for, say, consumers goods is likely to be offset by a change in the opposite direction in the demand for investment goods, Keynes proposes a more realistic model, one in which a change in the demand for the goods of one type is likely except when we start with full employment, to cause a change in the same direction in the demand for the other. Consumption and investment, in the normal case, move together. The economy does not normally, if it cuts down the output of one, find a motive for increasing the output of the other.

IX. Summary

Before considering some of the implications of this analysis let me briefly summarize.

The skeleton of the theory is simple: The national income depends upon investment and the income-consumption function. Investment, or more accurately private business investment, depends upon the marginal efficiency of capital and the rate of interest; the rate of interest depends upon the liquidity function and the amount of money. The determinants of the marginal efficiency of capital and the propensity to consume are very numerous; some of them were listed earlier.

X. Some Implications

The skeleton alone gives us some suggestions for policy; for instance, that when there is unemployment, efforts should be made to increase investment (private, public, and foreign) and the propensity to consume. It also implies that an economy can be in equilibrium at less than full employment, that circumstances can rule in which there is no natural tendency towards peak prosperity. I am sorry that I have no time to consider the other alleged equilibrating factor — changes in wage rates. Keynes's conclusions on this are, I suppose, well known.

The application of this analysis to an actual situation requires judgments as to the quantitative response of the determinants to various changes. How greatly, for instance, can we expect investment to be affected when the interest rate is lowered? How would a change in the wage rate affect investment and the propensity to consume? Is investment greatly influenced by the rate of growth of population? Would a 50 per cent increase in the stock of capital goods bring about a large reduction in the marginal efficiency of capital or a small one? These are important questions and the answers put flesh on the skeleton of Keynesian economics. But Keynesian economics does not consist in the answers to these questions. An economist who accepted the Keynesian outline could claim, though most Keynesians would disagree, that private investment could be greatly increased by a minor reduction in the interest rate, and he would then urge a mild expansionist banking policy during depression instead of a policy of, say, public works. Or one might support a wage cut if he believed that it would favor investment and the propensity to consume. Keynesians do not all have to prescribe the same medicine.

It is commonly believed that Keynesian economics should be identified with the "mature economy thesis," or with a predilection in favor of government controls. This is nonsense. Not all who accept these insidious, as they are now regarded, views are Keynesians. And likewise it is not necessary for all those who are optimistic about our long-term prospects, who wish to encourage private investment, and who abhor government intervention, to oppose the central themes of Keynes's doctrine, though obviously many of them will do so.

Keynes's account of the determinants of the national income in terms of investment and the propensity to consume seems to me to represent his important contribution. His views about the quantitative aspects of the implied relations should be judged separately. Perhaps they were right for England in 1936; perhaps they were applicable to this country in the thirties. Perhaps they are applicable today and will continue to be. But in any case these matters should be kept quite separate from his account of the determination of the national income in a capitalist economy. Whatever our views on, say, the interest elasticity of the demand for investment goods, on the significance of business confidence in determining the marginal efficiency of capital, or on the prospects for important technological improvements in the next decade or two, I think we can regard the Keynesian statement that the national income depends upon the propensity to consume, the marginal efficiency of capital, the liquidity function, and the amount of money as true and useful. That is the final test.

Notes

1. *Loc. cit.*, p. 42.
2. *Ibid.*, p. 43.

79

An Appraisal of Keynesian Economics. (Followed by Discussion)*

J.H. Williams

I

The topic assigned to me is, I am afraid, much too ambitious. I cannot do more than select some questions that seem to me important for an appraisal of Keynesian economics. I shall in part be going over ground I have already tried to explore at some of our earlier meetings and elsewhere, but I do hope to make some further progress.

Keynes's greatest virtue, I have always felt, was his interest in economic policy. Economic theorizing seems to me pointless unless it is aimed at what to do. All the great theorists, I think, have had policy as their central interest, even if their policy was merely laissez faire. If, nevertheless, I have been skeptical of theory, in its traditional form, it is because of its pretension to universality. Economic theory is an exercise in logic, involving abstraction from what the theorist regards as nonessential. Added to the simplifications of selection and emphasis is that involved in the one-thing-at-a-time method of analysis. Our dilemma is, and has always been, that, as Keynes said, without theory we are "lost in the woods." Without hypotheses for testing, we have no basis for economic inquiry. But one can reject with Bagehot what he long ago called the "All-Case" method of the German historical school, while questioning, as he did, the range of validity of what he called the "Single-Case" method of English political economy.[1] This is the kind of question that has chiefly interested me with regard to Keynesian, as well as classical, economics.

As the reference to Bagehot indicates, Keynes was not the first great English critic of classical economics. As a graduate student, nothing interested me more than the writings of the heretics. I found no more penetrating discussion of the relativity of economic concepts than Bagehot's *The Postulates of English Political Economy*; and I returned repeatedly to ponder over Cliffe Leslie's savage outcry against "generalizations . . . which have passed with a

*Source: *American Economic Review*, Vol. 38, May 1948, pp. 273-98.

certain school of English economists for economic laws . . . generalizations which were once useful and meritorious as first attempts to discover causes and sequence among economic phenomena, but which have long since ceased to afford either light or fruit, and become part of the solemn humbug of 'economic orthodoxy.'"[2] The weakness of such men, from the standpoint of the impression they made on later generations of economists or their own, was that they set up no rival system.[3] By the nature of their objections they could not, and had no interest in trying. The strength of Keynes, again from the standpoint of the impression he has made, stems from the fact that he did set up a rival system, for which, like his classical predecessors, he claimed universal validity. To reduce classical economics to the status of a "special" case under his "general" theory, as he so dramatically did in his single-page first chapter, was to stake out his claim on what he undoubtedly regarded as the highest conceivable level; it probably has no parallel in economic literature. But the questions remain: how valid is his system as a picture of reality, what is the range of its application, how useful is it as a guide to economic policy?

In one of the most interesting essays in *The New Economics*, Arthur Smithies, whom I have always considered a good Keynesian, says that Keynes's theory must be regarded as the beginning rather than the end, and calls upon us to construct a really "general" theory, in which Keynes's theory would be a "special" case.[4] This is welcome evidence — and one could cite much besides in the recent work of men who have been ardent Keynesians — of a willingness to appraise Keynesian economics more critically than was apparent in the first wave of enthusiasm that greeted the appearance of *The General Theory* in the thirties. Perhaps it will help us to get away from the tendency to classify everyone as Keynesian or anti-Keynesian. That never seemed to me a helpful starting point for considering objectively either what Keynes's contribution has been or what its limitations are. I doubt, however, whether "dynamizing" Keynes's static equilibrium analysis, which is what Smithies, Klein, and other mathematical economists seem to have in view, will remove the limitations. To my mind, they are inherent in the nature of equilibrium analysis, especially when applied to income as a whole.[5]

II

Keynes leaves no room for doubt that, in his view, his principle of effective demand revolutionized traditional economic theory. In the preface to *The General Theory* he speaks of "treading along unfamiliar paths," and of his long "struggle of escape." It is clear, too, that he regarded his contribution as monetary. The evolution of his thinking covered the greater part of the interwar period, and the stages in it were marked by the *Tract on Monetary Reform* (1923), the *Treatise on Money* (1930), and *The General Theory* (1936). It is clear all the way through that he was intensely concerned with the problems of his day, and particularly with those of England. In this sense all his books are dated. The first deals with the monetary disturbances of the early twenties, with a large emphasis on international monetary policy; it is dedicated to the "Governors and Court of the Bank of England, who now and for the future have a much more difficult and anxious task than in former days."[6] The second is a monumental work — analytical, statistical, historical — whose central theme is a monetary theory of the business cycle (mainly on closed economy lines) and a policy of control of the cycle by the central bank. There is no evidence as yet of preoccupation with unemployment as a chronic tendency, booms are emphasized quite as much as depressions (nothing interested him more than our stock market boom), underconsumption and oversaving theories are given only passing reference.

In a famous passage of *The General Theory*, every sentence of which has a special relevance for his own theory, Keynes refers to "the completeness of the Ricardian victory" as "due to a complex of suitabilities in the doctrine to the environment into which it was projected."[7] It was, I have always felt, a similar complex of suitabilities that accounted not only for the great impression made by Keynes's theory but also for its origin. It was not a coincidence, or a misinterpretation of Keynes, that the first great development of the theory by his disciples was the stagnation thesis, that the war was regarded as a superlative demonstration of what could be accomplished to sustain employment by a really adequate volume of effective demand, and that the weight of expectation of Keynesian economists was that we would relapse after the war into mass unemployment unless vigorous antideflation measures were pursued. There is no better short statement of the stagnation thesis than that given by Keynes: "The richer the community, the wider will tend to be the gap between its actual and its potential production; and therefore the more obvious and outrageous the defects of the economic system . . . Not only is the marginal propensity to consume weaker in a wealthy community, but, owing to its accumulation of capital being already larger, the opportunities for further investment are less attractive."[8] In an article in the *New Republic* which I have often quoted, Keynes concluded: "It appears to be politically impossible for a capitalistic democracy to organize expenditure on the scale necessary to make the great experiment which would prove my case . . . except in war conditions."[9]

I find it increasingly suggested that we should distinguish between Keynes's "personal opinions" and his "theory." I agree there is often a real point in the distinction between what Keynes says and what his theory says. The book contains many obiter dicta which do not fit into the skeleton of his theory, and indeed provide in some cases valid grounds for objection to it. But it has been my belief that the stagnation thesis constitutes the essential content of the theory, and that as we move away from the circumstances that thesis envisaged, the difficulties for the determinancy of the theory are increased and its force as a formula for economic policy is decreased. I have, however, been skeptical of the stagnation thesis, and some of my reservations about Keynes's theory date back to that phase of the discussion.

III

Keynes's main interest was in monetary theory and policy. The development of his thinking was directed towards "pushing monetary theory back toward becoming a theory of output as a whole."[10] His progress can be traced in the transition from $MV = PT$ to $I + C = Y$. There is the question in each case of distinguishing between the truism and the theory. In the traditional quantity theory (which Keynes endorsed without reservation in the *Tract*),[11] V and T were assumed constant, or independently determined, though in the later writings on the subject this is qualified by such statements as "normally," "except in transition periods," "apart from the business cycle." On these assumptions M affected only P (though some thought the connection often ran the other way), which was a complete demonstration that money was merely a *numéraire* and could be ignored in real analysis.

The main concern of business cycle theory, whether monetary or non-monetary, has been with fluctuations of income, output, and employment. In this sense, we had half a century and more of "macro-economics" before *The General Theory* appeared. But there have been formal difficulties with both sides of the quantity equation. In Keynes's *Treatise*, so far as the "fundamental equations" were concerned, the effects of monetary changes were registered exclusively in P. As he later said, the equations "were an instantaneous picture taken on the assumption of a given output."[12] Moreover, as his critics pointed out, they were identities, his excess of investment over saving (via the quantity of money and the interest rate), his windfall profit rise, and his price rise being the same thing, with no causal relationship disclosed, so far as the equations were concerned.[13] There has been difficulty also in the business cycle literature with MV. V has often been treated as a constant (whatever the writer may have said about it in chapters outside his formal theory), or as reinforcing the effects of changes in money quantity. But there is also discussion of demand for money as a factor to be offset by control of the supply, and of the concept of the natural rate of interest as the equator of saving and investment. All these versions, I think, appear in the *Treatise*, though the last undoubtedly interested Keynes most and constitutes a main theme of the book. But the chief emphasis is on business deposits. Regarding income deposits, so crucial for his later theory, his statement in the *Treatise* is: "I incline to the opinion that the short-period fluctuations of V^1 (velocity of income deposits) are inconsiderable," which appears to mean that consumers' demand for money is not a determinant of prices or output (consumers spend what — or in proportion to what — they get), and contains no hint of the later marginal-propensity-to-consume analysis.[14]

In *The General Theory*, $MV = PT$ is replaced by $I + C = Y$, but one can readily see the old equation underneath. Y is PT. Investment and consumption are the components of income through which monetary changes register their effects. Though not in the equation, the quantity of money (together with "liquidity preference") determines the interest rate, which (in relation to the expected profit rate — "the marginal efficiency of capital") determines the volume of investment. The demand for money is broken down into the three strands that had been implicit in the analysis since Marshall. Velocity becomes the multiplier, command-over-consumption-units becomes the propensity to consume, and the distinction between the decision to save and the decision to invest becomes liquidity preference. The identity equation $I + C = Y$ becomes the causal equation $I + C(Y) = Y$. It is the development of the analysis of demand for money which constitutes, I think, the chief innovation of *The General Theory*, and upon it, and the use Keynes makes of it, mainly turns the answer to the question whether he has succeeded in "pushing back the theory of money to becoming a theory of output as a whole." But a question hardly secondary is what has become in the new theory of P. In the *Treatise*, as I have said, T was constant; in the new theory it is P that has become constant, or neutral.

Having shown the development of Keynes's income equation out of the quantity equation, I must add a brief statement of the theory in his own terms. As he sums it up on page 29, "the essence of *The General Theory*" is that "the volume of employment in equilibrium depends on (i) the aggregate supply function, (ii) the propensity to consume, and (iii) the volume of investment." The supply function is the supply price of total output, measured in unit labor costs, assumed (up to full employment) to be constant or neutral. With the cost-price level thus stabilized, changes in effective demand are registered in output and employment. Of the two components of effective demand, the schedule of the relation of consumption to income is a stable function (which may, however, have a characteristic cyclical pattern) determined by the "psychological law" of the "marginal propensity to consume," which is that as income rises a part of the increment is saved. It follows that for every point on the schedule a multiplier can be computed. With consumption and the multiplier thus given, changes in investment (the "autonomous" factor), together with their multiplied effect, determine changes in the level of output and employment, which may settle at any point (up to full employment as the limiting case) determined by the quantity of effective demand. Thus, the lower the marginal propensity to consume, at a full-employment level of income, the greater will need to be the volume of investment if that level of income and employment is to be maintained. As a society grows richer, its marginal propensity to consume grows "weaker . . . but, owing to its accumulation of capital being already larger, the opportunities for further investment are less attractive." Therefore, the state must intervene, through monetary and fiscal policy, to compensate for the widening "gap between actual and potential production" and maintain a full employment level of effective demand.

IV

I have stated the theory baldly because that, I think, is the only way to get at its logic. After that has been done, the rigor of the assumptions may be relaxed, but this is a process of relaxing also the conclusions, and leads back to the questions I asked earlier about the validity of the theory as a picture of reality and a basis for policy.

The paradox of the book (and one of its chief weaknesses) is that while its central thesis is long run, its formal analysis is short run, not in the business cycle sense (to which Keynes devoted only a chapter of "Notes"), but, as Hicks pointed out, in the sense of Marshall's short-run equilibrium. It is in this sense a special rather than a general theory, and a theory more static than the classical theory it was intended to supplant. Moreover, as has been shown by various writers,[15] some of the more novel features of Keynes's interest and wage theory rest on special assumptions, and are less damaging to classical theory (on the appropriate "level of abstraction") than he supposed. In this sense, too, he falls short of presenting an acceptable general theory.

But much of the formal wage and interest theory seems to me secondary. Keynes's main concern was monetary, and it was the quantity equation, and particularly his long meditation over the Marshallian K (plus the impact upon him of the Great Depression), that led him to formulate his income equation and his income theory. Having done so, he worked out the interest theory that seemed to him appropriate, took over such parts of traditional wage theory as seemed to fit and rejected those that seemed not to fit. His great contribution was in focusing attention upon income and in challenging on monetary grounds the assumption, implicit in classical economics, of a full employment level of income automatically sustained. But the important question to ask, I think, is not how much his theory differs in its formal logic from classical economics but how much it differs from business cycle theory, the relation of which to classical equilibrium theory had been becoming increasingly tenuous for at least half a century; and whether in attempting to push the analysis of economic fluctuations back into an abstract framework of equilibrium theory he has done economics a service or a disservice.

As I said earlier, the study of economic fluctuations had of course been concerned all along with "macro-economics." But the main emphasis had been placed on fluctuations in investment. To this Keynes adds little that is conceptually new, unless it is the emphasis on expectations, which comes oddly in a book that is otherwise not only static, with constant technique, but very short run. The emphasis on declining investment opportunities, though part of his central thesis, is certainly not new; it had made its appearance in each preceding major depression. As a practical problem it seems remote today, as it has in each previous period of renewed expansion.[16] Yet as a statement of a long-run tendency (wars apart) it has seemed to me not only plausible but desirable that new investment should become a decreasing part of total income in an advancing society, with qualitative technological change taking over more of the role of progress on the side of supply, and the benefits going increasingly to consumption on the side of demand. But Keynes himself did not discuss technology, and in any case the real seat of his pessimism and the core of his theory lie in his views about consumption. It is here, too, that his theory differs fundamentally from business cycle theory.

V

Keynes's law of the propensity to consume is the important novel feature of his theory. It has been also the most controversial. It was the main question raised by my paper on "Deficit Spending" at our meeting in 1940,[17] by Kuznets' review of Hansen's *Fiscal Policy and Business Cycles* in 1942,[18] and (along with his attack on equilibrium economics generally) by Burns's recent papers on Keynesian economics.[19]

As a first statement, apart from the business cycle or other special circumstances, Keynes's "law" that as income rises consumption rises by less than unity is a plausible hypothesis; but it does not mean, necessarily, that consumption is the "passive" factor or that the consumption function is stable. These two assumptions — (1) that consumption is dependent on income and (2) that there is a "regular" or "stable" or "normal" relation between them, such that the consumption function can be derived as a given datum of the system and used as a basis of policy and prediction — constitute the essence of Keynesian economics. They bear a striking resemblance to the basic assumption of the quantity theory, that demand for money could be treated as a given factor, with the difference that, whereas that assumption was used to support the classical conclusion of full-employment equilibrium (apart from the business cycle), the new law of demand for money becomes the basis of the new equilibrium theory in which full employment is merely the limiting case. The whole structure rests upon the validity of the new law of the demand for money.

Historically, there seems to me to be ample grounds for doubting both the assumptions I have stated. They do not, for example, account for the effect of the rise of the automobile, a consumption good — or of new products generally — upon the growth of national income, where we have had a dynamic response of consumption and investment, each to the other. The application of an investment "multiplier" to consumption as a passive, given factor in order to account for such changes seems wholly unrealistic. Nor would, I think, any "dynamizing" of Keynes's technique by mathematical methods get us much further. Keynes's proposition that autonomous changes in investment determine changes in income, and hence in consumption (according to the "law"), is probably no better than its opposite, that spontaneous changes in consumption determine changes in income, and in investment. The *inter-*

dependence of consumption and investment, each responding to the other —
and both responding (spontaneously rather than systematically) to changing
ideas, methods, resources — seems to me to be the essence of economic
progress. But it does not lend itself readily to equilibrium analysis, which is
probably the reason why it has been the concern of the historians and the more
imaginative kind of statisticians rther than of the pure theorists. As between
Keynesian and classical economics, however, the latter provides, in many
respects, a more realistic point of departure for a study of progress.

The rise of consumer durable goods had been the outstanding economic
phenomenon of our times. From the standpoint both of long-run growth and of
business cycle behavior it raises serious questions for Keynesian analysis.
Between the two wars expenditures on such goods were fully as large as those
on capital goods, and their fluctuations fully as great; nor can we make any
clear generalization as to which played the greater role in initiating cyclical
changes. As "outlets for saving" they played as large a role, and the same kind
of role, as new investment; nor is there any more reason for applying a
"multiplier" to the one kind of expenditure than to the other. They make the
Keynesian statements about "oversaving," or "institutional factors which
retard the growth of consumption," or consumption as the "passive" factor,
seem much less realistic than they might otherwise.

Historically, however, the growth of consumer durable goods accounts only
in part for the rise in real consumption. Kuznets' paper on "Capital
Formation, 1879-1938," at the University of Pennsylvania Bicentennial
Conference constitutes an important landmark in the modification of
Keynesian theory.[20] He demonstrated that, while national income rose greatly
during that period, standards of living rose correspondingly, and the great bulk
of the increase in income went into consumption. Saving, as measured by real
investment, remained a constant fraction of income, with an apparent
moderate tendency in the twenties (on which he does not insist) for
consumption to increase relative to income.[21] In England before the war,
according to Colin Clark's data, saving had been a diminishing fraction of a
growing national income for at least a generation.[22] Since Kuznets' paper, the
"secular upward drift" of the consumption function, to which no reference is
made in Keynes,[23] has become a standard part of the statement of the
consumption function. Its practical effect has been to bring the plane of
discussion (the possible "gap between actual and potential production") back
pretty much to where it had been before Keynes wrote, by disposing of the
more serious version of his law and the one which I think he himself believed —
that consumption, as a society grew richer, became a diminishing fraction of
income — and limiting the stagnation thesis to a discussion of declining
opportunities for investment.

But while the "secular upward drift" is now regularly included in
consumption function formulae, its implications for the analysis have not been
sufficiently examined. One thing it means, I think, is the point mentioned

earlier, the dynamic interaction of consumption and investment. No application of the growth of investment and a multiplier to the consumption existing at the beginning of Kuznets' period, on the assumption of passivity (in the way that was so commonly being done in the thirties) could ever account for the income-consumption relation at the end; and if instead we take a historical regression of the previous relation and project it forward, we are merely begging the question.

Another part of the explanation, without doubt, has been the cost reducing function of investment, with which, because it is too short run, Keynes's analysis does not deal. As I tried to show in an earlier paper, investment is significant, not primarily because of the money income and the employment provided by the capital-goods industries themselves, but because of the fact that by producing consumer goods in more efficient, and therefore cheaper, ways it releases consumer income for expenditure on other goods and services, and by increasing productivity per worker makes possible upward adjustments of income and increased voluntary leisure. This has been the heart of the productive process under the free-enterprise system. It points to the importance of price-wage-profits relationships which in the Keynesian system become submerged, and to the inadequacies in these directions of the Keynesian monetary and fiscal policies as the means of sustaining full employment in an advancing society.[24]

VI

Since the war Keynesian economics has undergone a number of significant shifts. Faced with a condition of inflation as alarming, and seemingly as intractable, as the deflation Keynes faced when he wrote his book, the stagnation thesis has receded into the background of the theory. This is mainly what is meant by distinguishing between Keynes's opinions and his theory. But, as I said earlier, the difficulties for the determinacy of the theory have been increased by the new conditions, and its applicability to policy has become less clear cut. One of the new questions is the relative importance of monetary and fiscal policies — control over the broad aggregates of the income equation — as against more specific (including direct control) policies. Is Beveridge's program for full employment,[25] and that of the six Oxford economists,[26] a logical following out of Keynesian theory (as they assume) or a contradiction of it? Keynes did not favor a planned or regimented economy (except in war), and regarded his theory as a defense against it. Another important set of questions relates to the cost-price effects of monetary expansion, which seemed secondary in deep depression when there were large unemployed resources. Another relates to the longer-run relations of costs, prices, profits, productivity which Keynes's analysis ignores, but which seem to me more important for stability and progress than the short-run monetary factors which his theory selects for emphasis.

Most interesting has been the postwar development of the consumption function. Keynes's book, despite his distrust of mathematics, has undoubtedly given a great impetus to the study of econometrics, and the consumption function in particular has given the mathematicians, whether Keynesian or non-Keynesian, an ideal concept for building models of national income and making forecasts. Thus far, the forecasts have been almost uniformly bad. Though I am quite incompetent to judge, my suspicion has been that the explanation is twofold: first, the stagnation bias carried over from prewar Keynesian economics; second, the fact that in the depressed thirties the income-consumption relation (as well as investment) was abnormally low, reflecting consumers' insecurity and pessimistic expectations. In any event, it does seem significant that the chief error made in the forecasts has not been in the estimates of postwar investment but in the consumption function, the one element theoretically derivable from within the Keynesian system.

After the appearance of the "secular upward drift," the emphasis was on the assumed short-run stability of the consumption function. But postwar experience has cast doubt also on this. It seems now to be agreed among econometricians that the "simple relation" between income and consumption, as Keynes stated it, is unstable. In searching for a more complex relation which may have some promise of greater stability, hypotheses have been introduced which contradict Keynes's own theory. For example, liquidity is now commonly accepted as a factor affecting consumption, whereas in Keynes's theory liquidity affected only investment. Such a change strikes at Keynes's whole structure of demand for money, with its elaborately worked out separation into the three distinct strands I discussed earlier. Instead of the simple relation between current income and current consumption on which Keynes built his theory, we are today working with various hypotheses, including saving out of past income, liquid assets, capital gains, the last highest income reached in a boom, expectations of future income, and other possible factors affecting the income-consumption relation. That expectation should be brought in to explain consumption, whereas with Keynes it affected only investment, is surely a major departure. But it seems unnecessary, and even misleading, to pick out any particular points of difference. The broad fact seems to me to be that we have nothing left of this basic concept of the Keynesian theory other than that consumption is an important component of income and deserves all the study we can give it. The same is of course true of investment, the other component of income. That this is not now being studied with equal intensity by the econometricians is doubtless due to the fact that the changes in it are not derivable from within the system and do not lend themselves as readily to mathematical manipulation.[27]

Scarcely less significant among the postwar developments is the growing recognition of Keynes's underemphasis on the price aspect of monetary changes. As I said earlier, in deep depression this could be ignored, but the practical problem that confronts us, except in that unique condition, is that a volume of effective demand that is adequate for full employment appears to have cost-price effects which not only expand money income at the expense of real income but create a highly unstable economic situation. In other words, Keynes's stable equilibrium (even if we could concede it on other grounds) would seem not to include full employment as the limiting case, but something substantially short of that. This seems to me our most serious practical dilemma. It has both short- and long-run aspects. It presents a question whether we have to make a choice between allowing for a certain amount of slack (and fluctuation) in our use of resources, in a free-market system, or, if we insist on continuous full employment, recognizing the need for more specific controls. But this leads on to the question, not only of our scheme of values (political and social as well as economic), but also of the vitality of the system, whether in a more planned and controlled system we would not weaken the dynamic forces which promote growth and which might, with further study, be directed toward the achievement, not of stable equilibrium in any exact sense, but of a less unstable economy than we have had hitherto. Much, I think, could be accomplished through the further study of price-wage-profit practices and policies. As I said in an earlier paper, though these relations have long been a main concern of (classical) economic theory they have been overlaid in recent years by preoccupation with monetary and fiscal analysis, and the tendency has been to regard price-cost behavior as a kind of *force majeure* to be "offset" rather than corrected. It is surprising how little we know, and can agree upon, with regard to these relationships, and what course to steer in order to avoid merely (a) letting them take their course, (b) compensating for them by monetary and fiscal manipulation, or (c) subjecting them to direct control.[28]

Chapter 21, on "The Theory of Prices," is for me one of the high spots of *The General Theory*. One of Keynes's characteristics was that while he was as sharp as anyone could wish in seeing possible qualifications and objections to his theory, he never permitted them to interfere with his conclusions. Chapter 21 (in which occurs the passage on mathematical economics) is an excellent discussion of the reasons why before full employment is reached, monetary expansion affects prices and costs as well as output and employment. It is interesting that the chapter runs in terms of the quantity theory of money, which suggests again that his own theory is a recast version of the quantity theory.

If there is perfectly elastic supply so long as there is unemployment, and perfectly inelastic supply so soon as full employment is reached, and if effective demand changes in the same proportion as the quantity of money, the quantity theory of money can be enunciated as follows: "So long as there is unemployment, *employment* will change in the same proportion as the quantity of money; and when there is full employment, *prices* will change in the same proportion as the quantity of money."[29]

Inserting Keynes's new concept of demand for money, this is not a bad statement of his own theory. But he goes on to introduce five qualifications: effective demand will not change in exact proportion to the quantity of money; resources are not (a) homogeneous, and (b) interchangeable, so that their supply elasticities vary; the money wage-unit will tend to rise before full employment; the remuneration of the factors entering into marginal cost will not all change in the same proportion. I cannot reproduce the discussion here. It contains references to bottlenecks, collective bargaining, boom and depression psychology, and other factors. One would need nothing more than this chapter to explain not only the kind of dilemma that confronts us today, but the inflationary conditions of 1936-37 on a comparatively low level of employment.[30] But so far as I can see, Keynes does nothing to resolve the dilemma, and this chapter has no place in either the logic of his theory or his policy prescription. It is on a par with similar qualifications of his fundamental equations in the *Treatise*, which he said did not "affect in any way the rigor or validity of our conclusions."[31] In distinguishing between what Keynes says andd what his theory says, it is this kind of difference that seems to me significant. I can offer no explanation of it except that it is what equilibrium analysis seems to do to us. The key, I think, lies in what Keynes says about the rise of money wage rates before full employment (he might equally have said it of any of the other qualifications): "They have . . . a good deal of historical importance. But they do not readily lend themselves to theoretical generalizations."[32]

VII

I am afraid I am outrunning the space assigned to me, but some other topics must be briefly mentioned. Keynes's claim to having put monetary analysis into real terms depends largely on his assumption of constant prices; price and wage changes would affect the consumption function, liquidity preference, and investment. He overstated his point (with which I have long sympathized) that the interest rate does not determine saving. He was wrong in saying that investment does not affect the interest rate but is only affected by it, though we had a striking demonstration during the war of how far an easy money policy can go in freezing the rate at a low level. His point that there is a minimum rate below which liquidity preference will not permit the rate to be driven is valid but needs elaboration. So far as the time risk is concerned, our experience with a frozen pattern of rates demonstrated that rates on long-term governments would fall progressively toward the shortest. But so far as the income risk is concerned, an easy money policy widens the gaps in the interest-rate structure and suggests the need of other methods of attack. An all-out easy money policy, such as some Keynesians have favored, designed to saturate liquidity preference, carries both short-run inflationary dangers (as we are now recognizing) and longer-run dangers of undermining the whole fabric of the private capitalistic economy.[33]

Keynes's emphasis on wages as income and on the downward rigidity of money wage rates and his insistence that unemployment could not be cured by a policy directed primarily at cutting wage rates are among his most important contributions from a practical standpoint, whatever their theoretical merits on some abstract level. But as related to monetary business cycle analysis they have always seemed to me less novel than he supposed. Monetary policy had not run primarily in terms of wage cuts in terms of compensating for wage and price rigidities. His conclusion, moreover, is subject to two large reservations: the effect of cost reduction on investment and its effect (which he recognized) on foreign trade. Moreover, from a purely economic standpoint, there is no reason why cost-reduction policies should not be combined with monetary policies of expansion, as Sweden and Australia did with notable success in the Great Depression.

One of the points most commonly agreed upon, even by Keynesians, is that the aggregates of the income equation must be broken down. A point that has especially interested me is the need of breaking down the saving function to differentiate between business and consumers' saving. I have never understood how Samuelson's findings could be offered in verification either of Keynes's propensity to consume or of Hansen's chapter to which they are appended. His analysis yielded the striking conclusion that consumers in the aggregate spent virtually all their increases in money income and that any additional saving accompanying rising income almost wholly took the form of business saving.[34] The implications of such a conclusion for economic policy are of course very great.

Finally, there is the now familiar point that the Keynesian saving-investment concept (like so much else in the analysis) has tended to submerge the study of the *process* of economic change. We have again, as in the *Treatise*, "instantaneous pictures." How saving and investment must always be equal in real terms, and yet how sometimes the equality denotes equilibrium and sometimes it does not, has caused endless confusion. We can make some headway by differentiating between a "normal" income-saving relation and a process of adjustment to the normal relation. But Keynes does not discuss process, and "normal" saving begs the questions I raised earlier. For a study of change the Swedish *ex ante, ex post*, or Robertson's time-period analysis seems much more realistic.[35]

VIII

As I look back over my paper, my appraisal of Keynesian economics seems to be mostly critical. The most difficult thing to appraise is one's own bias. No doubt my appraisal has in it some element of unfavorable reaction, both to Keynes's own showmanship and his tendency to oversimplify and overstate his case, and to the sheer mass and exuberance of the claims made by his followers in his behalf. I admit all this has been working on me for a long time. Economic instability is equaled only by the instability of economists; what we need most, and often seem to have little of, is perspective. While I have no fondness for prediction, I do not believe that the wave of enthusiasm for the "new economics" will, in the longer perspective, seem to us extravagant. And perhaps it will be only then that we shall be able to appraise objectively Keynes's contribution.

Beyond question it was very great. No one in our time has shaken up economists as much or been as influential in bringing economic analysis to bear on public policy. What he has given us, in particular, is a much stronger sense than we had before of the need for consumption analysis. It was the combination of the man and the times that did it. But I do have to insist again that it was policy, in Keynes's case, that led to theory, and that the weakness (as well as the strength of the impression made) lies in the overgeneralization. What we shall probably find ourselves doing is bringing back the things he temporarily submerged, the study of the processes of short- and long-run change, the emphasis on productivity, and on price-cost-profit relationships. If the conditions to which his theory was mainly directed should reappear, we shall probably find ourselves swept far beyond the kinds of remedies he favored, and forced into things he thought his theory and policies would avoid. But if we can maintain reasonable stability and, by the study of forces and relationships he largely ignored, continue to promote growth, his policies should play an effective role in a more rounded economic policy. I have sympathized all along with the idea of a cyclically unbalanced budget and with tax policies designed to promote stability and growth. But these, for Keynesians, at least before the war, were relatively mild objectives. Moreover, these are not exclusively Keynesian policies, but have been quite as popular with economists in Sweden, for example (where Keynesian economics has never really taken hold), as anywhere else.

What I find increasingly said, as the stagnation thesis recedes into the background, and the postwar questions about the consumption function, the price effects, and the like cast further doubts upon the theory as Keynes stated it, is that (and here the analogy with the quantity equation is striking) he has arranged the elements affecting the income equation in a useful form. This, I think, is true, with all the qualifications I have made. Undoubtedly, his formulation has greatly intensified the study of national income and its composition, though it is interesting that, as I indicated earlier, men like Kuznets and Colin Clark, who have pioneered such studies, dissented from his theory.

What it comes down to is that Keynes's analysis would appeal to me more if he had not claimed too much for it. As with his predecessors, it is the pretension to universality, and the equilibrium technique, that offend me, with the further point that in his case the defect seems to me worse. There is a legitimate and important role in economics for partial equilibrium analysis but the analogy with it of the Keynesian type of total equilibrium analysis seems to me most imperfect, because in the nature of the case the "other things equal" condition is invalid. Consumption, investment, total income interact, and they comprise all the "other things." Until, at least, the econometricians make more headway in deriving them (and their parts) from "within the system," this will be the nature of my skepticism.

Discussion

Lester V. Chandler: Not having had a chance to see Professor Williams' paper I shall comment only on the paper by Professor Tarshis.

I was much heartened by the general tone and content of Professor Tarshis' remarks, the more so because of their contrast with the arguments that we have so frequently heard from Keynesians, especially during the early days of Keynesianism. On far too many occasions, Keynesians have denied the validity and usefulness of almost all neoclassical theory, have claimed for Keynes an excessive degree of originality for the ideas advanced in his *General Theory*, have been too reluctant to accept corrections or supplements to his theories, and have been prone to believe that Keynes's ideas, without further analysis or empirical research, offer an adequate basis for public economic policy. Professor Tarshis has done none of these things. He has emphasized the extent to which Keynes leaned upon and borrowed from neoclassical theory — not always to the benefit of his own theories; he has noted, at least by implication, the advances in the theory of national income that occurred before the appearance of *The General Theory*; he has indicated a willingness to divorce Keynes's basic theoretical formulations from some of Keynes's own speculations concerning the future of Western economic systems; and he has emphasized that the basic Keynesian theory, though simple and valid, is but a theoretical skeleton which must be filled out with much more analysis and empirical study before it can offer a full explanation of the behavior of national income and employment and before it can serve as an adequate guide to public policy. It seems to me that Professor Tarshis' evolutionary and open-minded approach offers hope for a future integration of neoclassical and Keynesian ideas, to their mutual advantage. It also forecasts an increased usefulness of economic theory as a guide to public policy.

This does not mean, of course, that Keynes's contributions were or are unimportant. Though Keynes should not have claimed originality for many of the individual elements of his theoretical structure, the broad framework itself is a major contribution to economics. The same is probably true of Adam

Smith, and of Chamberlin and Robinson who made such important contributions to the other major theme of this convention — the theory of monopolistic and imperfect competition. The implications of Keynesian theory for public economic policy are enormous. Even if we divorce Keynesian theory from Keynes's pessimistic views as to the future of private demands for investable funds — and I agree with Professor Tarshis that the two should be separated — we cannot accept Keynesian theory and still confidently assume that private investment will always be just sufficient to offset savings out of full employment incomes. His discussion of the motives behind saving and behind investment, though incomplete, should have made this clear.

The present period of inflation in no way refutes the basic Keynesian theories as presented today by Professor Tarshis. In the first place, the present situation can itself be explained in Keynesian terms. Keynes did not feel it necessary to reject his own theories in the face of war and early postwar inflation. The present inflation can be used to cast doubts on Keynes's basic theories only by improperly identifying them with an extreme and incautious form of stagnationism. In the second place, we are by no means assured that the present high level of private investment will continue indefinitely. Even the most ardent stagnationists have not claimed that full employment will never be attained; instead, they have indicated merely that on the average unemployment will be higher in the future. We must remember that at the end of the war housing had been in the doldrums for more than fifteen years, that private investment in commercial construction and producers durable goods had been far from satisfactory since 1929, that consumer durables had been unavailable for about three years, and that inventories were at a low level. With these conditions, plus monetary and fiscal policies that assure very low interest rates, the current inflation is certainly understandable, but we cannot be sure that private investment will continue to be even adequate into the indefinite future. Keynesian theory shows its usefulness in dealing with both types of situations — a high rate of investment relative to the propensity to save as well as a low rate of investment relative to the propensity to save.

This brings us to another of the points made by Profesor Tarshis: that the basic Keynesian theory — with its emphasis on the aggregate supply function, the consumption function, the complex of factors which he calls the marginal efficiency of capital, the liquidity function, and the amount of money — is only a skeleton or framework of analysis. It calls our attention to strategic relationships, but it does not supply all the factual, or even all the theoretical, material necessary to make the theory into a complete description of the behavior of income and employment. We know far too little about the key functions in the Keynesian theory — the actual determinants of aggregate supply function, the consumption function, the determinants of enterprisers' expectations as to the prospective yield of new investment, and the behavior of the supply schedule of investible funds in the market. Keynesian theory emphasizes the crucial importance of these functions, but it does not at the present time offer an adequate explanation of their actual behavior, much less provide us with a ready-made formula for securing optimum relationships among them.

For example, what are the effects of the various kinds of monopoly and monopolistic practices on the rate and stability of private investment as well as on the propensity to consume? What are the broad effects of the various industrial price policies? What influences are exerted by the various provisions of tax laws on the consumption function, on enterprisers' estimates of the marginal efficiency of capital, and on the liquidity function? When we face questions like these we realize that the framework of the Keynesian theory has not yet been filled in completely, and that in many respects Keynesian and neoclassical economics are not mutually contradictory; instead, they supplement and give meaning to each other. Professor Tarshis has told us that "Keynesians do not all have to prescribe the same medicine." I agree. But I also suspect that we should not prescribe just one medicine. Rather, we should put ourselves in a position to offer many specific remedies to correct the many specific ills that contribute to the instability of national income and employment. We cannot do this until we have accepted Professor Tarshis' invitation to fill in the Keynesian analytical framework with much material from other schools of economic thought and with further studies and research.

Clark Warburton: Professor Tarshis and Professor Williams have made many interesting observations on Keynesian theory with which I am in agreement. The comments which I shall make relate to Professor Tarshis' closing statement; namely, that the final test of Keynesian theory is the truthfulness and usefulness of the statement: the national income depends upon the propensity to consume, the marginal efficiency of capital, the liquidity function, and the amount of money.

This statement lists four variables upon which national income depends. Earlier in his paper Professor Tarshis summarized the Keynesian theory in the statement that "the national income depends upon the propensity to consume and investment." If these two statements are placed in juxtaposition, they appear to mean that investment depends on the three variables — marginal efficiency of capital, liquidity preference, and amount of money — but that the propensity to consume may be treated as relatively independent of each of these variables. Is this correct? Do changes in the quantity of money or in the preference for liquidity influence consumption expenditures only as a result of changes in national income resulting from a change in investment? Or is it equally true that changes in the quantity of money and in the desire to hold it affect consumption expenditures directly, with resulting effects on the prospect for profit and therefore on investment? And if the latter is equally true, may it not be more important than the former because consumption is a much larger fraction than investment of national income?

One of the variables assumed to influence investment — the marginal efficiency of capital — is an effective stimulant in the form of a differential between the rate of interest and the prospective rate of profit in a business undertaking. Changes in this differential undoubtedly influence the amount of investment, but the Keynesian analysis gives little consideration to the forces at work underneath changes in this differential. On this point pre-Keynesian theory is more explicit, assuming that the differential depends upon the intensity of demand for consumers goods (i.e., income and the propensity to consume); on changes in prices of output relative to prices entering into costs, especially wages; and on changes in the rate of interest other than those induced by change in the prospective rate of profit. Furthermore, according to pre-Keynesian theory, the latter two conditions — changes in prices of output relative to wages and deviations in the rate of interest from the "natural" rate — are in practice sequential results of changes in the quantity of money other than those in accord with trends in productive capacity and habits of use of money. Keynesian economics, so far as I am aware, does not contradict the validity of these propositions. They are simply ignored in *The General Theory* and in the subsequent theoretical developments based thereon. We are not, I think, doing violence to the Keynesian way of thinking, but amplifying it, to reintroduce them. But when we do, the marginal efficiency of capital appears to be a redundant variable, for we may substitute other variables already in the equation. This leaves us with the formulation: national income depends on the propensity to consume, liquidity preference, and the amount of money.

The propensity to consume, or consumption function, is commonly measured by Keynesian economists as a relation between aggregate consumption expenditures and aggregate disposable personal income. When we examine this relationship over a period of years, we find that the propensity to consume is a little higher in times of depression than in times of full employment, excluding war periods; that is, the propensity to consume moves inversely, though mildly, with departures in national income from the upward secular trend associated with a growing population and advancing techniques of production. It is the cause of such departures — particularly in the cases of prolonged lapses from full employment – upon which *The General Theory* is focused. To me it does not seem helpful, when stating the factors causing a slump in national income, to include a factor operating to mitigate, just a little, that slump. We can, then, omit this factor when we apply the Keynesian theory to the practical problem of changes in national income associated with periods of unemployment. We are left with the formulation: national income depends on liquidity preference and the amount of money.

This formulation is not a modification of Keynes's theory. Except for formal details, it is his own formulation in Chapter 15 of *The General Theory*. Let us rewrite the liquidity function, as stated by Keynes, to conform with his assumptions regarding (a) the direction of casual relationships in time, (b) the constancy of income-velocity, except for long periods, with respect to a portion of the monetary stock, and (c) the zero income-velocity of a variable portion of the quantity of money held for speculative purposes. We obtain $Y = vM$, meaning that national income is a function of liquidity preference and the quantity of money — with liquidity preference in the form of its effect on income velocity (i.e., as the reciprocal of holdings of cash balances relative to income).

This formulation of the functional relation between national income and selected variables is a form of the old equation of exchange applied to sales of the final output of the economy, and states the basic thesis of the dominant strain in pre-Keynesian business fluctuation theory; namely, that the value of output is a function of the quantity of money and of its velocity in transactions related to output.

The agreement between pre-Keynesian and Keynesian theory on this formulation is important, not because it means that Keynesian theory of the cause of departure from full employment is essentially the same as pre-Keynesian theory, which is not the case, but because it enables us to locate the difference between the two theories in such a way that they can be tested for their consistency with factual data. This difference resides in the assumptions regarding the interrelations of v and M. In Keynesian theory, changes in circuit velocity of money are positively correlated with changes in the rate of interest, and changes in the rate of interest are negatively correlated with changes in the quantity of money. This means that changes in circuit velocity are negatively correlated with changes in the quantity of money, that is, v and M are compensatory, with additional supplies of money becoming "idle" money. This contrasts with pre-Keynesian theory, according to which monetary expansion in excess of a normal rate of growth is accompanied, with some lag, by higher monetary velocity, and monetary contraction by hesitancy in the use of money; that is, changes in v were regarded by pre-Keynesian economists as a force accentuating rather than compensating the effects of changes in M.

At the Federal Deposit Insurance Corporation we have been engaged for several years in analyzing the conditions precedent to business depression, with emphasis on severe cases like the thirties. The burdens of the Corporation and its solvency both depend upon the frequency and severity of future depressions. We are therefore vitally interested in the theory of lapses from full employment and in proposals designed to maintain full employment, and have assembled and examined with considerable care the factual data regarding the timing and interrelations of changes in the quantity and circuit velocity of money. Our study has covered the period since 1918. The facts, we find, are in conformity with pre-Keynesian theory. The liquidity preference phase of Keynesian theory is not in accord with the facts, and appears to be irreconcilable with them.

Melvin W. Reder: After reading Professor Tarshis' interesting and useful exposition of Keynesian economics, it is difficult to understand why there were ever any anti-Keynesians. But by the same token, it is hard to understand why *The General Theory* was such a controversial and important book. The main reason for this difficulty is, I think, that Tarshis has given a rather overgenerous description of neoclassical theory.

Actually, prior to *The General Theory*, there was no coherent theory of the level of (national) income and employment in existence. Certainly, the writings of Marshall, Pigou, Robertson *et al.* abounded in references to the national dividend or income, but they hardly ever regarded it as an unknown to be determined by the equilibrium conditions of the system. They regarded it as a parameter (entering into various supply and demand functions) which had the following properties: it increased with (1) technical progress, (2) population, and (3) the stock of capital; it also served as an indicator of welfare. That it was not treated as a variable to be determined explicitly by the equilibrium conditions of the system was not an oversight; implicitly it was already determined. It could be found (roughly) by multiplying the equilibrium quantities of the various outputs by their equilibrium prices and summing the resulting products. The level of national income could thus be derived from the equilibrium conditions of the system; but it was not, itself, an unknown.

To develop a theory of the level of income and employment (in static terms) it is necessary to suppose that the system might be in equilibrium with various levels of employment of resources; particularly of labor. Neoclassical economists failed to make this supposition and consequently they were prevented from developing a static theory of employment. For the neoclassical economist, if laborers were unemployed but wished to work at the going wage rate, it meant that the wage rate was above the equilibrium level and that the unemployment could be eliminated by a reduction in the (money) wage rate. Thus, given the usual assumptions of neoclassical theory, the level of employment in equilibrium had to be the "full employment" level.

Now it is, of course, true that in their writings on the business cycle Pigou, Robertson, and others spoke (at least by implication) of changes in the level of national income and employment, and Pigou even argued that if a fall in wage rates leads to expectations of further declines, employment would decrease rather than increase. But these "dynamic" arguments were not integrated with the main body of static theory.

Keynes, in developing a theory of employment, had at least several choices. He could have accepted the neoclassical position that involuntary unemployment was incompatible with stable equilibrium, but argued that either the system did not tend to a position of stable equilibrium or that, even if it did, the position kept shifting through time and that it was the process toward the position (and not the position itself) that was interesting. To have proceeded in this fashion would not have involved contradicting the conclusions (or modifying the assumptions) of neoclassical theory; but it would have involved (1) denying that the conclusions of static theory in this area were important and (2) asserting that a dynamic theory was required. However, as Professor Tarshis' remarks would suggest, Keynes was too much of a Cambridge economist to accept this alternative.

Instead, he chose to pour his wine into Marshallian bottles. He confined himself to static theory, but determined to modify its assumptions in such a way that underemployment equilibria were possible. To accomplish this result, he made a tour de force that has generally been considered quite unsatisfactory. He assumed that the elasticity of supply of labor was infinite (over a sizable range) with respect to the current money wage rate; i.e., that a sizable part of the work force would refuse to work for a money wage less than that currently prevailing. Consequently, if the demand schedule for labor (with respect to the money wage rate) should happen to intersect the supply curve somewhere to the left of the upper limit of the flat range (of the supply curve) part of the labor force would become involuntarily unemployed, but with no tendency for the money wage rate to fall. This is theoretically possible, but not very likely, and it is certainly not the basis for a "general theory of employment."

In the models that have been constructed by Hicks, Lange, Lerner, and others, this aspect of the Keynesian system is virtually neglected and the wage rate is taken as a datum. In Professor Tarshis' exposition this is also done in effect. By implication this defines another Keynesian model — the one with which we are most familiar and with which Keynes himself worked through most of *The General Theory*. Professor Tarshis gives an excellent brief description of this model; it is necessary to note only that it implicitly assumes the money wage rate to be constant. (Keynes's own use of wage units reflects this same assumption.) The short-run equilibrium with which Keynesian analysis is concerned is thus a short run during which the money wage rate is constant; it is also a "Marshallian" short run during which the stock of capital is constant. Whether these two different definitions of the "short run" would always be compatible, is an interesting question, but one which cannot be discussed here.

Keynes's loyalty to the neoclassical tradition is exhibited in other ways. For him, as for his predecessors, the rate of interest was the instrument by which investible funds were rationed. The rate of investment was determined by the equilibrium condition that the marginal efficiency of investment equals the rate of interest. The main difference between his theory andd those that preceded it, is (in this respect) that in his system an increased desire to hold cash balances may, *ceteris paribus*, lead to an increase in the rate of interest and a resulting reduction in investment, while this could not happen in the others. Put in a somewhat more technical way, in the neoclassical system, k (in the Cambridge quantity equation) is not dependent on the rate of interest, while in the Keynesian system it is. But such differences are minor, as compared with the differences between either of these systems and those used by many econometricians in applied work. In these systems the rate of interest is virtually (sometimes completely and explicitly) abandoned as a determinant of investment. The attitude that leads to the adoption of such models has been well expressed by Hicks (*Value and Capital*, page 225): "Interest is too weak for it to have much influence on the near future; risk too strong to enable interest to have much influence on the far future." Hicks himself, for other reasons, did not wish to discard the interest rate entirely as a determinant of investment.

In these econometric models, it is implicitly assumed that the demand schedule for investible funds has, for a considerable range of yields, virtually a zero elasticity. Investment is restrained by considerations of risk, of market limitations, etc., but not by limitations of investible funds. To my way of thinking, it is quite improper to eliminate availability of funds as a determinant of the rate of investment. However, the model that seems to me correct is neither Keynesian nor neoclassical.

Such a model would be based squarely upon the fact of capital rationing. Each firm would have its own sources of capital, the supply of which would not be closely related to the rate of interest it must pay. The rate of interest would be only one, and perhaps not a very important, term in the loan contract; other terms, involving the security of the borrower, etc., might well be more important. In such a model, it would be possible to have low open-market rates coupled with a shortage of available funds for borrowers whose securities did not qualify for the open market.

This type of theory would have given Lord Keynes all the latitude he needed to develop a "general theory of employment." But to have accepted such a theory would have involved a sharp departure from the neoclassical assumption that the rate of interest allocates investible funds. That Keynes chose a path much closer to that of his predecessors is further evidence of the intellectual paternity of *The General Theory* to which Professor Tarshis has referred.

Now for a brief comment on Professor Williams' paper. If I am not misinterpreting him, his remarks are directed not only at "Keynesian economics," but at all formal systems that attempt to explain the behavior of one set of economic variables in terms of the behavior of another set of variables. Professor Williams' skepticism undermines neoclassical theory as well as Keynesian. To him, both theories are oversimplifications; in fact all explicit theories are. And, if I interpret him aright, adding more variables would not improve matters, for no theory involving a finite number of variables could possibly be adequate; reality simply cannot be interpreted in these terms.

In this contention Professor Williams is, I think, correct. His correctness is evidenced by the fact that when econometric models are constructed, no matter how many explicit variables are inserted, it is always necessary to insert one or more terms to take account of errors and shocks; i.e., to take account of all the unspecified independent variables that affect the system. To the econometricians, Professor Williams, and the many economists who agree with him, would say, in effect, that the usefulness of their models as explanatory devices will depend upon the adequacy with which they can specify the probability distribution and estimate the parameters of the system; and, I think, they would be inclined to express skepticism as to the ability with which these tasks can be performed. With this skepticism I should be, at present, inclined to agree, although the researches of the Cowles Commission may force me to change my mind.

But although Professor Williams' skepticism concerning formal methods may be very well taken, it does not help us decide the question of how to proceed in economic investigations. If the formal methods common to both neoclassical and Keynesian theory are inadequate to serve as guides to policy, and if the improvements in model construction introduced by econometricians are not a substantial improvement, then what methods are we to use? It is this question that Professor Williams, and those who believe as he does, must answer if they are to be constructive, as well as wise.

Notes

1. Walter Bagehot, "The Postulates of English Political Economy," in *The Works of Walter Bagehot* (Hartford, Conn., 1889), Vol. V, pp. 249, 253.

2. Thomas Edward Cliffe Leslie, "The Movements of Agricultural Wages in Europe," *Essays in Political Economy* (Dublin, 1888), p. 379.

3. How they affected my own thinking about international trade theory I tried to show in my old paper, "The Theory of International Trade Reconsidered," *Economic Journal*, June, 1929. Reprinted as Chapter 12 in my book, *Postwar Monetary Plans and Other Essays* (3rd ed., New York, 1947).

4. "Effective Demand and Employment," in *The New Economics: Keynes' Influence on Theory and Public Policy* (New York, 1947), Ch. XXXIX.

5. The limitations of mathematical economic theory were never better expressed than by Keynes himself: "It is a great fault of symbolic pseudo-mathematical methods of formalising a system of economic analysis . . . that they expressly assume strict independence between the factors involved and lose all their cogency and authority if this hypothesis is disallowed; whereas, in ordinary discourse, where we are not blindly manipulating but know all the time what we are doing and what the words mean, we can keep 'at the back of our heads' the necessary reserves and qualifications and the adjustments which we shall have to make later on, in a way in which we cannot keep complicated partial differentials 'at the back' of several pages of algebra which assume that they all vanish. Too large a proportion of recent 'mathematical' economics are mere concoctions, as imprecise as the initial assumptions they rest on, which allow the author to lose sight of the complexities and interdependencies of the real world in a maze of pretentious and unhelpful symbols." *The General Theory of Employment, Interest and Money* (London, 1936), pp. 297-298.

6. Preface, p. vi.

7. Pp. 32-33.

8. P. 31.

9. July 29, 1940.

10. *The General Theory*, Preface, p. vi.

11. P. 81: "This theory is fundamental. Its correspondence with fact is not open to question." But in the accompanying footnote he quotes with approval a statement by Pigou which seems to me to raise rather than settle the essential question: "The Quantity Theory is often defended and opposed as though it were a definite set of propositions that must be either true or false. But in fact the formulae employed in the exposition of that theory are merely devices for enabling us to bring

together in an orderly way the principal causes by which the value of money is determined."

12. *The General Theory*, Preface, p. vii.

13. I agree with Lawrence Klein's statement (*The Keynesian Revolution* [New York, 1947], p. 17), though it comes oddly from a mathematician, that there is more to the *Treatise* than the equations. In my own review (*Quarterly Journal of Economics*, August, 1931), I referred only briefly to them, though pointing out their truistic nature, and dealt chiefly with the responsiveness of investment and the price level to the interest rate (which seemed to me the core of the book), his monetary analysis, and my reasons for doubting the effectiveness of his central bank policy.

14. *Treatise*, Ch. 15, p. 246. It is not possible to find a consistent monetary analysis in the *Treatise*. Sometimes he speaks of business deposits A as interacting with income deposits, as though it were merely the quantity of the former (in response to the central-bank-determined interest rate) that mattered; at other times the main emphasis is on business deposits B (a part of the financial circulation); at other times, and particularly in the statistical and historical chapters, it is on transfers between "cash deposits" and "savings deposits," a part of the analysis that always seemed to me particularly oversimplified and unrealistic; see my review above. In the "bear position" there is some anticipation of liquidity preference, but, as Keynes pointed out, they are by no means the same thing (*The General Theory*, p. 173). For an interesting and suggestive interpretation of the extent to which the *Treatise* foreshadowed *The General Theory* (as Keynes thought it did), see John Lintner, "The Theory of Money and Prices," *The New Economics*, pp. 515-526.

15. E.G., Schumpeter, Hicks, Lange, Leontief, Tobin, Modigliani.

16. The reader is doubtless familiar with the literature of the controversy over declining opportunities for investment. In addition to the references elsewhere in the paper, I should mention (among others) Terborgh, *The Bogey of Economic Maturity* (Chicago, 1945), and Wright, "The Future of Keynesian Economics," *American Economic Review*, June, 1945, and " 'The Great Guessing Game': Terborgh versus Hansen," *Review of Economic Statistics*, February, 1946.

17. *American Economic Review*, February, 1941; see my *Postwar Monetary Plans, op. cit.*, Ch. 9.

18. *Review of Economic Statistics*, February, 1942, pp. 31-36.

19. Arthur F. Burns, *Economic Research and the Keynesian Thinking of Our Times* (New York, 1946), and also his paper on "Keynesian Economics Once Again," *Review of Economic Statistics*, November, 1947, pp. 252-267.

20. *Studies in Economics and Industrial Relations* (Philadelphia, 1941), pp. 53-78.

21. Had residential housing been counted as consumption rather than investment, the upward tendency of consumption would have been more marked.

22. His figures on net investment as a percentage of national income show a decline from 12.2 per cent in 1907 to 8.1 per cent in 1924, 7.2 per cent in 1929, and 6.9 per cent in 1935. His conclusion was: "I believe the facts have destroyed the view up till now generally prevalent, that the rate of economic growth was primarily dependent upon the rate at which capital could be accumulated. The very rapid expansion at the present time [before the war] is taking place at a time of heavily diminishing capital accumulation. What is more remarkable, practically none of the capital which is being saved is being put into productive industry proper." *National Income and Outlay* (New York, 1938), p. 270.

23. Hansen's *Fiscal Policy and Business Cycles* (New York, 1941), Ch. 11, p. 233, contains, so far as I know, his first reference to it. It is accompanied by a footnote referring to Kuznets' forthcoming data (the paper mentioned above); they were both present at the Pennsylvania Conference.

24. "Free Enterprise and Full Employment," in *Financing American Prosperity* (New York: Twentieth Century Fund, 1945), pp. 360-373; see also William Fellner, "The Technological Argument of the Stagnation Thesis," *Quarterly Journal of Economics*, August, 1941; and E.D. Domar, "The Prospect for Economic Growth," *American Economic Review*, March, 1947. This is a point I have emphasized in virtually all my papers on Keynesian economics since my review of the *Treatise, op. cit.*, pp. 554-555.

25. Lord Beveridge, *Full Employment in a Free Society* (London, 1944).

26. *The Economics of Full Employment* (Oxford: Oxford Institute of Statistics, 1944).

27. Lawrence Klein has recognized that for a true equilibrium system both investment and consumption should be determinable from within the system, see "A Post-Mortem on Transition

Predictions of National Product," *Journal of Political Economy*, August, 1946, pp. 302-303. He lists the relations we must know before we can make good forecasts: "A principal failure of the customary models is that they are not sufficiently detailed. There are too many variables which are classified as autonomous when they are actually induced . . . The surplus of autonomous variables results from a failure to discover all the appropriate relationships constituting the system. In addition to the consumption function, we should have the investment function, the inventory function, the housing function, the price-formation equations, etc." In *Econometrica*, April, 1947, he made his own forecast for the fiscal year 1947, and said that if he were wrong the reason would probably be his failure to take account of the further rise of prices. (Why should not prices be predictable from within the system?) The actual price level was not significantly different from the one he chose to use; his estimate of investment was too high (though not seriously); but his forecast of national product was too low because he underestimated the consumption function.

28. See my statement on "The Employment Act of 1946" before the Joint Congressional Committee on the President's Economic Report, July 2, 1947, reprinted in my book, *Postwar Monetary Plans, op. cit.*, Appendix I, p. 240.

29. Pp. 295-296.

30. One of the peculiarities of an inflationary volume of effective demand is, apparently, that the slope of the consumption function is no longer necessarily less than unity. For a discussion of this and other aspects of the behavior of the consumption function under war and postwar conditions, see a forthcoming paper, "Use of the Consumption Function in Economic Forecasting," by Robert V. Rosa.

31. See my review, *op. cit.*, pp. 556-558.

32. *The General Theory*, p. 302.

33. In my last talk with Keynes, a few months before his death, it was clear that he had got far away from his "euthanasia of the rentier." He complained that the easy money policy was being pushed too far, both in England and here, and emphasized interest as an element of income, and its basic importance in the structure and functioning of private capitalism. He was amused by my remark that it was time to write another book because the all-out easy money policy was being preached in his name, and replied that he did think he ought to keep one jump ahead.

How greatly Keynesian fiscal policy (and war finance) have complicated the problem of varying the interest rate as an instrument of cyclical control (because of the public debt), we are only now beginning to recognize fully.

For a discussion of these and other aspects of the interest-rate problem, see my paper, "Implications of Fiscal Policy for Monetary Policy and the Banking System," *American Economic Review*, March Sup., 1942, reprinted as Ch. 10 in my book, *Postwar Monetary Plans, op. cit.*; see also H.C. Wallich, "The Changing Significance of the Interest Rate," *American Economic Review*, December, 1946.

34. See Alvin H. Hansen, *Fiscal Policy and Business Cycles, op. cit.*, Ch. 11, Appendix, pp. 250-260, by Paul A. Samuelson.

Samuelson's analysis is based on Kuznets' data (1919-35). For consumers he finds a marginal propensity to consume of 0.97, and for business enterprises a marginal propensity to save of 0.49. "This [business saving] accounts for most of the leakages incident upon net investment: as far as these data go, the leakages incident upon household savings are much smaller and possibly negative" (p. 257). In his conclusion (p. 260) he again emphasizes "the very sensitive relation of consumption to aggregate income payments."

35. See, among recent discussions of this point, David M. Wright, *The Economics of Disturbance* (New York, 1947), Ch. II.

80

Keynes and Economic Analysis Today*

J. W. Angell

Lord Keynes died just ten years after the publication of his great book, at the very peak of his professional and public career. Both his death, and the simultaneous conclusion of "the first Keynesian decade," make the preparation of the two volumes, here reviewed,[1] timely and a fitting tribute.

No one man in the history of economics had so great an effect upon the minds and daily lives of so many people in so short a time as did Keynes. Although students have disagreed to a remarkable extent about which one of several possibilities is "the" crucial feature of the Keynesian Revolution, and although Keynes operated in only certain fields of economics, the reality of the revolution itself is beyond discussion. Both the science and the art of economics, at least within capitalist societies, have been permanently changed — and one can only say enormously advanced — by his work. With respect to the major analytical concepts which Keynes developed or reformulated, it is almost as pointless to talk today of "pro-Keynesians" and "anti-Keynesians" as to say that particular individuals are for or against the multiplication table. The shapes and values to be assigned to particular relations, such as that of consumption to income; the particular analytical conclusions drawn, such as that concerning underemployment "equilibrium"; and above all the resulting policy proposals, such as those concerning government deficit spending — these are another matter, and have precipitated tremendous amounts of discussion. But the very discussions themselves have been largely couched in Keynes' own terms, have been centered around his particular conceptions and formulations of the problems in issue, and in their whole character have differed in remarkable degree from those of the preceding periods.

Dr. Klein's book is in the main a restatement and defense of Keynes' ideas, done with almost religious enthusiasm but nonetheless on a high level of scholarship. I have already tried parts of it in a graduate class, and found it extremely useful. It covers, if not always systematically, the whole range of Keynes' ideas on monetary and general economic analysis from his earliest

*Source: *Review of Economic Studies*, Vol. 30, November 1948, pp. 259-64.

writings, and touches on much of the relevant work of others. Perhaps the most illuminating sections are the chapter on Keynes as a classical economist, especially the sections on the *Treatise*; the summary of the argument of the *General Theory*; and the technical Appendix. The first of these undertakes, and with great success, to build a continuous bridge of ideas from the older forms of monetary theory to the equations of the *Treatise*, to explain each stage in terms of what had gone before, and to lead into the foundations of the *General Theory*. The *Treatise* equations are described as pretentious, and Hansen's criticism is of course admitted, but, it is argued (I think correctly) that they are not the essential contribution of the *Treatise*, and that their defects do not impair the determinacy of prices in the system — which was here Keynes' main goal (pp. 17, 24, and the Appendix). The Appendix is especially interesting for its examination of Pigou's attempt to rehabilitate the classical doctrine, at least for the problems of long-run equilibrium. The other chapters consist in the main of a relatively brief but excellent re-presentation of the essential analytical argument of the *General Theory*, largely as systematized and expanded by Keynes' followers (little is said of the confusions and contradictions of the *General Theory* itself!), and a series of reviews of certain of the main controversies. Despite Dr. Klein's almost excessive zeal in defending Keynes at some points (cf. p. 154), and despite a certain lack of integration and order (surely Chapter V is misplaced?), the book is an important addition to the literature because, though hardly exhaustive, it brings much of the analytical content of the Keynesian discussions together in a compact form convenient for university students. The collection of diagrams is particularly helpful. A number of specific points in Dr. Klein's argument will be referred to below.

The volume of essays which Professor Harris has edited, and in part written, is on a different level. In terms of total space, nearly a sixth is Professor Harris' own skillful introductions and summaries; another third is reprints of papers and speeches which have been published elsewhere (but which, inconveniently, are not identified in the text proper as being reprints), and is made up largely of a number of the classical articles in the post-*General Theory* development and systematization of Keynes' ideas — but with some striking omissions, notably (as Harris points out) Lange's essay on the optimum propensity to consume; and roughly half is new contributions, written expressly for this volume, which re-appraise, criticize, or further extend Keynes' propositions and suggestions. There is also an exhaustive bibliography of Keynes' own writings.

The volume as a whole is a magnificent job, and reflects great credit on the constructive imagination and drive of its assembler, editor, and co-author. It has an essential unity and force which are rare in such collections; it has rendered a great service to all students by bringing so much that is valuable together within one set of covers; and a number of the essays contain very substantial new contributions. Moreover, a smaller yet important matter, most of the papers are admirably written in point of style and clarity.

To comment in brief compass on the detail of so complex and varied a body of material, or even on individual essays, is not easy and perhaps would be of little value. Of the essays dealing with the broader aspects of Keynes' work, those by Professor Schumpeter, Samuelson, Haberler, and Leontief, and by Dr. Paul Sweezy, seemed to me especially admirable. Professor Schumpeter's is surely among the most skillful, subtle, and beautifully written estimates of a man in the literature of economics, or indeed of any discipline. If he perhaps over-stresses the insularity of Keynes' orientation (p. 85), which was so much abated later, his balanced appreciation of the analytical content of the *General Theory* (pp. 91-97) is masterly, and a useful counterweight to the sometimes uncritical enthusiasm of certain of the other papers. Professor Samuelson's essay is intellectually far more sympathetic to Keynes, but he too is refreshingly outspoken about Keynes' confusions of concept and other defects in clarity of thought (e.g., pp. 148-49, 155-57; and compare Klein, in the other volume here under review, pp. 19, 20).

Professor Haberler, on the other hand, if not explicitly anti-Keynesian, is at most an admiring critic. His thoughtful paper rejects many of the claims to novelty made by or for Keynes (he should perhaps have taken account, also, of Keynes' very substantial though largely indirect debt to Robertson). It also attacks — to my mind convincingly — the tenability of that concept of under-employment equilibrium, even with *flexible* wages and prices, which was one conspicuous hall-mark of the early Keynesian enthusiasts (pp. 166-72). The proposition was long troublesome, though it is not central to the main Keynesian argument. Professor Leontief, in his brilliant examination of Keynes' postulates, likewise criticizes the concept of "involuntary" unem-ployment so far as based only on the theory of money wages (pp. 235-39), but unlike Haberler does not go on to attack also its alternative liquidity-preference support (also see Tobin's subtle and penetrating analysis, pp. 576-87; Klein's excellent discussion, *op. cit.*, pp. 80-90; and the recent debate, rather differently oriented, between Professors Hansen and A.F. Burns[2]). Finally Dr. Sweezy, in his short but stimulating chapter, views Keynes against the socio-economic framework as a whole and concludes, as a Marxian must, that even the most ingenious Keynesian devices and stratagems will not cure the basic social disease.

Nearly all of the newly written essays on special aspects of the Keynesian system undertake not only to review, but also to push on into new territory, and all are written at a high level. For sheer lack of space, I shall comment on only a few. Professor Nurkse's study of domestic and international equilibrium is a remarkably lucid statement and extension of the results of applying the income approach, and of the practical devices by which the two sorts of equilibria may be maintained. Much of the development of these ideas, of course, was carried out chiefly by Keynes' followers (including Nurkse himself), but the new orientation as such traces largely to Keynes. I am left, however, with two queries. First, what happens to adjust matters when the income effect is exhausted but international payments are still out of equilibrium? Proximately, of course, foreign "investment" changes (p. 268, n. 5); but what keeps these latter changes, as a rule, within bounds? There is perhaps still something left of the classical problem. Second, I am far from being as confident as Professor Nurkse appears to be in the actual speed and accuracy of operation, and hence in the over-all efficacy, of some of the theoretically adequate control devices. Can the complex questions of administration and psychology be solved so easily?

Professor Goodwin's essay on the multiplier is an outstanding contribution to a problem which seems to have dropped rather into the background recently, except for a short paper by Professor Smithies.[3] It is especially notable because it recognizes so explicitly both the phenomenon of lags, and the fact that these lags may be long (p. 491). If long, it is clear that they may tremendously influence the short- and middle-run quantitative results, and hence the practical desirability, of particular policy measures. Goodwin's development of formulae for the lags is ingenious and persuasive. He also presents one of the very few analyses by a Keynesian in which the multiplier process is tied in with the concept of and the data on the income or circular velocity of money (compare Klein, p. 213), a coordination which I attempted to sketch some years ago (*Investment and Business Cycles*, p. 197 *et passim*; and for an earlier statement of the identity, under certain conditions, of what Goodwin calls [p. 484] the "forward" and the "backward" multipliers see my study, p. 137). It is also interesting to see him conclude (p. 491) that the Robertsonian definitions of saving and investment are more useful than the Keynesian; this view is gaining increasing acceptance.

Professor Smithies' paper on effective demand and employment sets out the main Keynesian and classical assumptions, and then explores the effects of relaxing the Keynesian restrictions: notably with respect to constant equipment and techniques (also see the recent discussions on this problem started by Domar); the transition-period problems of adjustment in reaching new equilibria (despite all his qualifications and implications, Keynes never faced squarely the task of explaining in any detail *how* changes come about); and the effects of *relative* changes in wages and prices. Smithies' comments are often highly suggestive, yet they are tantalizingly brief; one wishes that he had pushed them farther.

Finally, Mr. Tobin's analysis (referred to above) of the relation between money wage rates and employment alters Keynes' conclusion on internal grounds, by showing that unless the "money illusion" is confined to the sellers' side of the labor market, labor *can* increase employment by reducing its money wage demands. This line of argument is different in important respects from Haberler's and Leontief's, but also helps dispose of the more extreme forms of the involuntary unemployment proposition. He might also have made the obvious point that since labor's spending commonly lags behind wage receipts, a material decline in money wage rates could under certain conditions induce employers to increase employment almost at once, and thus expand the total wage bill again *before* any substantial decline in aggregate demand can appear. The proposition can perhaps be regarded as implicit in his argument, but the matter of timing the wage cuts may be crucial. If a self-stimulating decline in aggregate spending is allowed to get a real start, money wage cuts may be powerless to arrest further contraction short of a cyclical bottom.

Taken together, Professor Harris' and Dr. Klein's volumes present an admirable series of reviews, appraisals, and extensions of Keynes' main analyses and proposals. They also suggest certain further comments on the over-all results of the post-1936 discussions, however, on the gaps in the present neo-Keynesian structure, and on some of the problems whose solution should constitute the next major step forward.

Since the publication of the *General Theory*, the whole argument has been reworked again and again by students whose skill and interest in logical consistency far exceeded Keynes's, and who have also added innumerable contributions of their own to the edifice. Sagging walls have been straightened, the floors have been trued up, piles of builder's debris have been neatly removed, and even parts of the foundations have been rechiselled. A streamlined structure has emerged which in many minor respects bears little external resemblance to the original. This is itself a notable achievement. But the structure remains completely Keynes', both in basic concept and in all its main elements.

A number of questions, on which Keynes was either confusing or even in error, and which gave rise to debates that in retrospect are often wearisome, have been disposed of or at least greatly clarified since 1936. Among them are the definitions of saving and investment, and the schedule as versus the observable meanings of the terms; "involuntary" unemployment and underemployment "equilibrium," referred to above; the multiplier and its general relation to income flows (the process as versus the instantaneous sense); the relation (far from satisfactorily described even yet, however) of interest rates not only to liquidity preference and money supply, but also to investment demand and to the supply of investible funds; and above all, the special and peculiarly restrictive character of Keynes' explicit and implicit assumptions. As these assumptions were relaxed and replaced by others which are less limiting and more realistic, much of the apparently irreconcilable opposition between Keynes and the "classical" propositions has been seen to blur, if not to disappear. The two systems of ideas are in large part essentially complementary, not mutually contradictory. Moreover, as his own assumptions are relaxed, the extent to which Keynes' original system was inherently static becomes clearer, and the need for its extension into dynamic problems more imperative.

Many of the very problems and terms around which these controversies were centered represent, in the main, ideas which were either new in economics, or which at least owed to Keynes an illuminating reformulation and a promotion to the center of the stage, and their clarification has itself constituted great forward progress.

But it is obvious that enormous amounts of work remain to be done. Keynes' achievements were the beginning, not the end. He found what he thought to be a reasonably adequate explanation and solution for the great analytical and policy problem of present-day capitalist economies, and his followers have greatly refined his results, but these results have in turn opened up vast stretches of territory for further exploration.

The new analytical work, as it seems to me, is likely to develop along three or four major lines in the next few years. First, the rigidly restrictive assumptions which Keynes used enabled him to sidestep a number of problems, in addition to those referred to in the preceding pages, that are likewise extremely important in the real world. Solutions which are at least preliminary must be found for a number of these problems before the Keynesian theoretical system as a whole can be moved forward much further. The most conspicuous of the problems, I think, arises from Keynes' treatment of investment as virtually a given datum. The Keynesian system requires preliminary (and as a first step perhaps still essentially static) accounts of the effects of income on investment; of the effect of today's investment on tomorrow's (through changes in the stock of capital); of the effects of even quite short-run changes in techniques, equipment, and other elements which may influence the actual and the expected productivity coefficients; of the relations between the endogenous factors as a whole and the exogenous factors; and of all the other major elements affecting the efficiency-of-capital schedule. Other leading problems which have also been largely untouched by Keynes or his followers include the effects or rigidities, monopolies, and structural maladjustments in general; of different patterns of resource allocation; of relative price changes; of variations in the relation of employment to income; and of the familiar fact, reiterated in these essays by Haberler and Hart, that liquidity preference relates to the total of all assets in a more or less graduated scale, not merely to money. Keynesian economics is not the sum of all economics, but it should be reasonably comprehensive with respect to the questions which can properly be regarded as falling within its orbit.

Second, a great deal more information is urgently needed on what may be called "specific" relations in the Keynesian and neo-Keynesian system. I include here, of course, the three basic schedule functions, of consumption, efficiency of capital, and liquidity preference. I also include such things as the various multipliers; the relation of money wages to real wages, and of both to prices and national income; changes in the shapes and positions of the saving and investment schedules, both in the aggregate and for various parts of the economy; the relation of interest rates to productivity; the elasticity of a number of other variables with respect to interest rates; the relation of changes in money supply to various "real" factors; the relation of foreign exchange rate depreciation to trade and income; and a variety of other items. Both extensive further *a priori* analysis and extensive statistical testing are required. No one of these relations, of course, is actually independent of all or most of the others, but they are sufficiently distinguishable quasi-entities to make treatment in isolation a permissible and fruitful first step. It is especially urgent that the studies which are now in progress on the marginal propensity to consume should be brought to a more definitive result. If this propensity proves highly variable and effectively unpredictable in the short run, the implications both for theoretical analysis and for policy purposes will be large and serious.[4]

Third, it is trite yet necessary to reiterate that our actual knowledge of economic dynamics — of how the real world really works — is still at a very early stage. This is in part, of course, simply one aspect of the problems listed in the preceding paragraph. We do not know from observation what the lags and leads are among most of the important sets of presumably related variables in the Keynesian system, we do not know how most of them shift through time, and therefore we do not know whether they are sufficiently stable (either in absolute terms, or in terms of a pattern of change) to be usable for analytical and predictive purposes. Hence we also really do not know very much, in the sense of possessing empirically tested knowledge, about the specific channels and processes through which economic change comes about. Consider particularly the processes involved in the business cycle. Although *a priori* hypotheses of explanation have been familiar for decades, and although vast quantities of statistical material have been assembled, we are still very far from having a *comprehensive* explanation which has been even roughly tested. Indeed, we have not worked out a satisfactory integration of "exogenous" and "endogenous" or self-generating elements even at the level of preliminary hypothesis. And the true origins and effects on business-cycle processes of changes in expectations, which seem to me likely to prove crucial, are still far from being completely explained on even a trial basis (but see Professor Hart's well-known work; and I may be permitted to refer again to the hypothesis sketched in my *Investment and Business Cycles*). Keynes hardly touched on most of these problems; despite his many side observations on dynamics, his formal analysis was largely either very short-run or timeless. Yet he forged an armory of powerful new tools which both theorists and statisticians have been quick to seize. The further application of Keynesian concepts to business-cycle analysis seems likely to be among the most fruitful lines of work in the coming period.

Fourth and last is the further development of those objectives, criteria, and instruments of public *and private* economic policy, whether "interventionist" or *laissez faire*, which are the capstone achievement of socially useful economic analysis. I have hitherto said nothing about these problems, although they are ably discussed in the books here under review, chiefly because their solution depends on the solution of the antecedent analytical problems. The policy proposals worked out to deal with that major disease of the advanced capitalist societies of today which Keynes diagnosed — the dominant general tendency of private investment to lag behind what would be the full-employment level of savings — are extraordinarily rich and varied. It even looks now as though nearly all the *major* possible types had been at least tentatively explored, as long as we stay in what is predominantly a private-capitalistic framework (in a completely socialized economy, the problem would not arise). The intellectual content of the proposals, however, is far ahead of the practical devices available for their implementation. We need a far more flexible and quick-acting administrative apparatus; and, what is more directly the concern of the economist, we need far more adequate and accurate forecasting instruments, that will help us to determine *when* to do *what* and to do it soon enough. The recent essays in model-building, and the admirably objective examinations by some of their authors (notably Dr. Hagen) of the reasons for their failures, are a great advance, yet are obviously only a first step. For the economist with a taste for the "real" world, this must be one of the most alluring of all the new fields — even though, in Keynes' last article, the shadow of the rejected invisible hand once more came creeping over the edge of the page!

The advances made in the last ten years, built so largely on Keynes, have thus been tremendous. Yet one other very grave weakness and potential danger, which many others have also pointed out, still confronts us. A student from the natural sciences who reads the studies here under review will be forcibly and unfavorably struck by one characteristic which runs through nearly all of them. Like Keynes' own work, most of them make little *direct* use of data derived from observation to support the detail of their analyses, and they really state rather few of their conclusions (hypotheses) in forms now susceptible of direct testing and refutation. A number of the authors, perhaps all, are entirely aware of the problems of testing (for example, Lintner in the Harris volume, pp. 531, 536-37, and Klein, p. 19), but they have not attempted to meet it on any very broad front in these essays. Instead, as is still true of most of the work on the central body of economic theory, in the main they have used initial assumptions which have become generally accepted, but which are actually derived largely from (untested) "common" sense and intuition; they have tried to build internally coherent logical structures on these assumptions, and to draw more general inferences; and then they have asserted, on one set of grounds or another, that observed human and social behavior is, in the mass, at least not inconsistent with these inferences. Statistical and other historical observational material is used to some extent, but much of it, like the inferences themselves, is not in forms directly suitable for testing purposes. This procedure as a whole is not "unscientific," of course, and part of the difficulty arises from the limitations of the observational data which are as yet available for exploitation, but the procedure itself obviously constitutes a relatively early stage in the evolution of scientific methods and results.

In these latter respects, of course, it is the recent work of the econometricians which is most "advanced" and most promising. But the econometricians themselves need a wide array of adequately formulated and refutable hypotheses as their raw material. To provide such hypotheses, they and the "pure" theorist-logicians must work together even more intimately, in a ceaseless process of testing, reformulation and new testing. Only in this way can we discover the true character of the operations of our present economic system, and only by these processes can we determine whether its modes of behavior are sufficiently uniform to permit socially adequate control devices to work successfully. If that decision is adverse, and if in consequence we abandon the battle to deal effectively with the prevention of mass unemployment, with wide swings in real economic activity and in monetary values, and with individual economic insecurity, then socio-political pressures are virtually certain to force radical structural changes in the present system itself. Keynes began a new phase of this battle, but he did not win it.

Notes

1. Seymour E. Harris, editor, *The New Economics* (New York, 1947); Lawrence R. Klein, *The Keynesian Revolution* (New York, 1947).
2. This REVIEW, XXIX (1947), pp. 247-68.
3. *American Economic Review*, May 1947.
4. Also see John H. Williams, "An Appraisal of Keynesian Economics," *American Economic Review, Proceedings*, May 1948, pp. 282-85.

81

The Keynesian Revolution and Economic Development*

D. Dillard

The time has arrived for economic historians to take stock of the "Keynesian Revolution" or the "New Economics," as the latest major innovation in economic theory is commonly called. Following the lead of monopolistic competition about ten years ago, the Keynesian analysis is now making its way into sophomore textbooks on the principles of economics. While it will supplement rather than replace the neoclassical economics of Alfred Marshall, which has dominated textbook writing since 1890, it is competing with the latter for priority of importance and stands an excellent chance of winning. By most tests the Keynesian Revolution is a more fundamental innovation than the theory of monopolistic competition. The latter has been handled by adding new chapters in the sections on price and value theory, but the new economics requires a new section on the theory of what determines the level of output and employment in the system as a whole. Certainly this should have a salutory effect in making economic analysis more useful in relation to what have become the major problems of contemporary economic policy.

Three recent books on Keynesian economics suggest an opportunity to explore the meaning and significance of the Keynesian Revolution, with special reference to economic history.[1] Several years ago The Economic History Association held a symposium on "Historical Aspects of Imperfect Competition," which revealed the fruitfulness of utilizing in historical research the ideas and concepts derived from the theory of monopolistic competition. If a minor innovation like monopolistic competition is fruitful for economic history, a major innovation like the Keynesian Revolution may prove even more fertile in extending and enriching investigations of long-term economic development. The three books under review are illustrative of the growing literature that constitutes the carrying through of the revolution.

In a competent little volume, Lawrence R. Klein has attempted to reveal the genesis and nature of Keynes's fundamental contribution. Among the

*Source: *Journal of Economic History*, Vol. 8, November 1948, pp. 171-7.

anticipators of Keynes's theory he discusses Malthus, Marx, Hobson, Foster and Catchings, C.H. Douglas of the social-credit school, and N. Johannsen, who published in 1908 what Klein calls a "complete anticipation" of Keynes's theory of savings and investment. In tracing the development of Keynes's own thought, Klein concludes that the revolution occurred during the great depression of the early 1930's, approximately with the publication of his famous pamphlet, *The Means to Prosperity*, in which use is made of the theory of the multiplier in a refined form and in which a proposal is made to the World Economic Conference that it assist in restoring prosperity by a simultaneous increase in loan expenditures throughout the world.

What is the Keynesian Revolution that was born of the last great world economic crisis? Klein seems to mean by it the formulation and widespread acceptance of a theory of the relation between savings and investment. It involves a change from the classical view that savings and investment are brought to equality via changes in the rate of interest to the new view that savings and investment are brought to equality via changes in the level of national income. New investment in capital assets is a more or less autonomous and unstable variable that does not necessarily rise when income rises or fall when income falls. Saving is viewed as a function of national income rather than of the rate of interest, such that when income increases, savings will increase in a regular fashion. Yet savings cannot exceed investment, because as soon as savings *tend* to exceed investment, income tends to fall; equilibrium is reached only when realized savings are equal to actual investment. High levels of employment are dependent on offsets to savings in the form of investment, by which is meant output in excess of that which goes into current consumption. In this new mechanism of national-income determination through the savings-investment nexus, Klein discovers the essence of the Keynesian Revolution (pp. 9, 14, 37, 42, 86, 110).

In the volume edited by Seymour Harris, the term "New Economics" is equivalent to the "Keynesian Revolution" in Klein's book. The Harris volume is divided into ten parts: (1) seven introductory chapters by the editor; (2) three views of "Keynes, the Economist"; (3) five views of the *General Theory*; (4) four chapters on special aspects of Keynes's work, including public policy and econometrics; (5) ten chapters on international economic relations; (6) seven chapters on business cycles and fiscal policy; (7) one chapter on money and prices; (8) three chapters on effective demand and wages; (9) six reprints of earlier reviews and discussions of the *General Theory*; (10) bibliography of Keynes's writings. Of the forty-six chapters, thirty are newly published and sixteen are reprints of articles, reviews, and speeches. The contributors are all specialists on Keynesian economics, although some are not "Keynesians," either in policy or in basic economic theory. The predominating social philosophy may be described as "saving American capitalism through fiscal policy."[2] Most of the discussions are on an advanced level and should prove of great assistance to graduate-student groups whose members already understand the essentials of Keynes's theory. The volume is indispensable to all specialists in Keynesian economics.

Unfortunately, *The New Economics* does not contain a full-length, systematic discussion of the basic framework of Keynes's economics. It would have much greater value to the beginner if the editor had used the introduction to present a simple exposition of Keynes's economics, the more specialized aspects of which are reviewed and discussed in the rest of the volume. There are, however, a number of excellent, if brief, expositions of Keynesian economics. The best statement of Keynes's fundamental ideas is presented in a reprint of Keynes's own article that appeared originally in the February 1937 issue of the *Quarterly Journal of Economics*. Another outstanding summary reprinted in this volume is A.P. Lerner's review from the 1936 volume of the *International Labour Review*. This statement was read and approved by Keynes before its original publication and hence enjoys a semiofficial status. *The New Economics* makes readily available for the first time the several speeches that Lord Keynes delivered before the House of Lords, and elsewhere, in connection with the British loan, the International Monetary Fund, and the International Bank for Reconstruction and Development.

In some respects the volume is disappointing. Although the contributors are able economists, they were apparently too busy to investigate the many unexplored phases of Keynes's work. For the most part, the contributions that are not reprints are rehashes of things the authors have written elsewhere. Certainly it is convenient to have these brought together into a single volume, but one also has the right to expect more than this from such a brilliant assemblage of economists. There is nothing of significance on the methodological and philosophical aspects of Keynes. Except for Alan Sweezy's ten-page chapter on "Declining Investment Opportunity," there are only occasional references to the secular aspects of Keynes's work.

The bibliography in *The New Economics* is the first attempt that has been made to present a complete list of Keynes's writings and as such is a very useful contribution. Yet I have never seen a bibliography that contains more errors, many of which could have been avoided by thoughtful reading.

Differences between the old and the new economics are perhaps nowhere better illustrated than in attitudes toward the role of the public debt. Adherents of the old economics and its general support of laissez faire believe in annually balanced budgets and abhor a large national debt, whereas the Keynesians take almost the opposite position. The attitude of Keynesians toward fiscal policy generally and toward the national debt in particular is shown in Seymour Harris' *The National Debt and the New Economics*. The Keynesians, who reject the presuppositions of laissez faire, believe that full employment without inflation can be achieved by compensating for fluctuations in private spending by counterfluctuations in government spending. In times of deficiency of private demand, the government should spend more than it takes away from the public in the form of taxes; and in times of inflation, it should take away from the public in the form of taxes more than the government spends. As Harris says, the essence of the problem is: "Repay debt when demand is excessive; incur debt when demand is seriously deficient" (p. 19). He concludes that in the United States in the future, beyond the postwar spree, the level of private spending probably will be inadequate to provide full employment, and therefore the national debt will and should increase above its present level. Under wise management there is no reason to fear the consequences of a steadily rising debt. Good management means, among other things, keeping down the rate of interest, a wide distribution of ownership of the debt, a progressive tax system, and, above all, economic policies designed to encourage high levels of productivity, employment, and national income.

The rate of interest is of prime importance in assessing the burden of the national debt. One of the virtues of the new economics is that it is theoretically consistent with the idea that there is no need for interest rates to rise just because the size of the debt increases. The rapid rise in the size of the debt has been accompanied by a fall in the interest rate. Harris estimates the net rate of interest on the debt of World War II at only 1.5 per cent, after allowing for tax collections on the interest income derived from ownership of the debt.

Mr. Harris' optimism regarding the future of the debt is predicated not only on rising productivity and rising levels of potential national output, but also on a faith in the wisdom and adequacy of fiscal policy to maintain a high actual level of national income. This is difficult to accept in the light of past economic experience with deep depressions and the inability of fiscal policy in the thirties to lift the economy to anything approaching full employment. Even if fiscal policy could do all that its champions believe, if it is permitted to work, present political trends in the United States raise serious doubts that it will be given a chance to work. While the transfer payments from tax payers to bondholders is insignificant in relation to income at full employment, the transfer might become very embarrassing if the national income were to fall as precipitously as it has in the great depressions of the past. I am not questioning the correctness of the policy that Mr. Harris advocates, but I do entertain doubts concerning the justification for his optimism.

In addition to the light which he sheds upon the present and the future of the national debt, Mr. Harris makes some interesting observations concerning debt policy in the past. For example, he considers rapid repayment of the national debt in the decades following the Civil War to be one of the main reasons for the shortage of money between 1873 and 1896 and the falling general price-level which tended to add to the real burden of the debt. Despite the fall in prices, however, he concludes that the burden of the Civil War debt was considerably less in terms of goods and of man-hours of work in 1893 than it was at the end of the Civil War, because of rising productivity and a rapidly growing population (p. 131).

The National Debt and the New Economics is a valuable contribution to one of the most important, yet one of the most commonly misunderstood, issues of public life. It gives a fundamentally sound and detailed analysis of this complex problem, and is projected at a level that should bring it within the reach of a wide audience. There are helpful summaries throughout, and every effort is made to point up the argument. The writing has obviously been done in considerable haste.[3] Although a better book may be written on the public debt, so far none has appeared.

What significance has the Keynesian Revolution for students of economic development? While it should find considerable application in the field of economic history, the narrow way in which the substance of the "revolution" is conceived by economists like Klein and Harris may preclude an appreciation of its importance by those outside the field of economics. Therefore, it should be worth while to point out some of the most useful applications to economic development.

I have interpreted the Klein-Harris concept of the Keynesian Revolution as the invention and widespread acceptance of a better technique for explaining the deficiency of demand. The notion of deficiency of demand is not new, but its wide acceptance by economists is new, and in the field of policy this has undermined the theoretical support that economists have traditionally given to laissez faire. Although economic historians as a group have always been closer than economists to the facts of experience and have probably never been much impressed by the myth of laissez faire as the practice of governments or by the belief in its benevolence if it should actually be achieved, their thinking has undoubtedly been conditioned to some degree by the prevailing state of theoretical opinion. The backwash of the Keynesian Revolution will undoubtedly splash over into the field of economic history. Widespread acceptance of demand deficiency as a respectable working hypothesis should change the tone of investigations in economic history. It will have a beneficial influence if it does no more than relieve the economic historian of the fear of criticism by his sophisticated brethren in economic theory for his failure to see that "supply creates its own demand," even if the facts of experience have seemed to deny this sacred tenet of classical and neoclassical economics. There should result a psychological release in the form of greater eagerness to pursue hypotheses that seem reasonable in the light of the Keynesian analysis, but that seemed unreasonable in the light of the classical theory.

Deficiency of demand, however it be explained, has been especially important in economic development since the beginning of the age of mass production around 1870. The Keynesian hypothesis is consistent with the promise of an age of plenty. It emphasizes the need for consuming more rather than the need for saving more. Common to all theories of demand deficiency is the suggestion that supply tends to outrun demand, that savings tend to outrun investment, that finding markets is more important than finding new means of production, and that mass production requires mass purchasing power. Keynes's theory, which assigns to new investment the special role of distributing demand, is useful in explaining the economic consequences of the close of the frontier, of a declining population growth, the "new" imperialism, the greater severity of depressions since 1873, wartime inflation, the pattern of primary and secondary postwar depressions, the significance of employment of a "favorable" balance of trade, the positive role of the public debt, and, perhaps most important of all, the incidence of inequality of income distribution as the chief source of demand deficiency. Acceptance of the theory of effective demand by academic economists has given this important aspect of economic analysis a respectability it never enjoyed when confined to the underworlds of Karl Marx, Silvio Gesell, and C.H. Douglas.

The Keynesian theory suggests that inequality of wealth and income promoted accumulation of capital during early capitalism but retards accumulation in the later phases of capitalist development. In the relatively poor world of the sixteenth-century price revolution, savings constituted a relatively small part of total social income, and the outlets for investment were virtually unlimited. There was no lack of offsets to savings. In the modern age of mass production, on the other hand, the potential savings that require outlets, if they are to be realized, are tremendous and the inducement to invest is weakened by virtue of the vast accumulation of past centuries. In such a society, the inequality that tends to promote saving also tends to promote unemployment, and when there is unemployment the incentive to invest is further weakened. Hence, the degree of inequality that is consistent with a maximum rate of capital accumulation decreases with every increase in social wealth.

Keynes's analysis focuses on the process of investment as the prime mover of capitalism. With the classical economists, accumulation was important as the source of more means of production to serve as the basis for greater *future* consumption; whereas with Keynes, accumulation is important as the source of demand to serve as the basis of greater *present* consumption. Marx's theory of the role of capital accumulation as the inner dynamic of capitalism is much more complete than that of Keynes, but Marx's explanation of the deficiency of demand in terms of the failure to realize surplus value after it has been produced is a more cumbersome tool than Keynes's principle of effective demand. In Sombart's analysis, the accumulation of capital nourishes the capitalist spirit in its boundless striving toward an infinitely removed goal, but accumulation is unimportant as a distributor of demand. Although theories of capitalism like those of Marx and Sombart are much more impressive than anything Keynes provides, it must be said of Keynes's principle of effective demand that nowhere is there to be found so simple, yet so cogent, an instrument for explaining what appears to have been the general over-all pattern of behavior of the capitalist economy. Nowhere in economics does so little go so far toward explaining so much.

A major fault in the work of Klein and Harris is the failure to develop the broader aspects of the Keynesian Revolution. I refer especially to the underlying social perspective in terms of which Keynes viewed economic conflict. As he envisaged the process, the great problem of the age is to free modern industrialism from the fetters of financial capitalism. His antipathy for the rentier and his belief in the desirability of its elimination carries over into his attitude toward property institutions, since the elimination of the rentier involves also the elimination of income from mere ownership. In this setting Keynes is a less important personality in a much more important revolution than that discussed in the work of Klein and Harris. The savings-investment model becomes a detail in the broader perspective of what C.E. Ayres calls the dichotomy between the accumulation of capital funds and the heritage of improvement, which is another name for the Veblenian dichotomy between the pecuniary and the industrial phases of modern capitalism, that is, between making money and making goods.[4]

In protesting against the narrow view of the Keynesian Revolution, I am, of course, protesting against the narrow view of economics that is characteristic of the volumes under review. The Keynesian Revolution is more than the invention of an abstract, logical set of relations. It is more than an event that occurred in the spring of 1933. The Keynesian Revolution is a further step in the critical phase of a process of changing social and economic relations among individuals and groups. The mathematical, nonhistorical, noncultural concept of economics which is explicit in Klein and implicit in Harris is what renders the work of most economists barren for economic history. For the student of development, the circumstances that nurture the revolution are more important than the strategy of its triumph. The interpretation of the Keynesian Revolution in the narrower sense — in the sense of Klein and Harris — tends to overstate the importance of Keynes to economics (in the narrower sense) and to understate his significance for those outside the field of economics. Yet within the broader reference of the Keynesian Revolution, within which Keynes's theory is more a symptom than a cause, there is a vitality and a promise that merits further exploration by students of economic development.

Notes

1. Lawrence R. Klein, *The Keynesian Revolution* (New York: The Macmillan Company, 1947), pp. xii, 218. $3.50. Seymour E. Harris, ed., *The New Economics: Keynes' Influence on Theory and Public Policy* (New York: Alfred A. Knopf, 1947), pp. xxii, 686, ix. $4.50. Seymour E. Harris, *The National Debt and the New Economics* (New York: McGraw-Hill Book Company, 1947), pp. xix, 286. $5.00.
2. A recent volume under the editorship of Mr. Harris is entitled *Saving American Capitalism.*
3. According to my calculation, Seymour Harris has written and edited no less than fourteen substantial books since 1941.
4. C.E. Ayres, "The Impact of the Great Depression on Economic Thinking," *The American Economic Review, Papers and Proceedings*, XXXVI (May 1946), 112-25.

82

Lord Keynes' Theory of Wages*

R.H. Fields

It is the normal case, according to Lord Keynes,[1] that 'labour stipulates (within limits) for a money wage rather than a real wage.' 'To resist a reduction of money wages but not to resist a reduction of real wages' is not only, according to Lord Keynes, the policy of labour in fact: it is also, in his opinion, the logical course for labour to pursue.

A well-known Trade Union leader,[2] on the other hand, recently said that he would gladly recommend a basic wage of £3 a week to his members, if a corresponding increase in the real purchasing power of money went with it.

One expression of opinion cannot be interpreted as a new approach to wage demands, but it is interesting to investigate the implications of a union policy of securing a certain real wage.

In his *General Theory*, Lord Keynes argued that labour works for a money wage rather than a real wage, as shown by the fact that it does not withdraw its labour when prices rise, although this reduces real wages (p. 9). This has been true for Australia in the past. But what would union leaders have said in 1913 if it had been explained that, although money wages were going to be reduced, prices would fall faster so that real wages could be expected to rise? Keynes went further by saying (p. 13) that 'there may exist no expedient by which labour as a whole can reduce its real wage to a given figure by making revised money bargains with the entrepreneurs.' He wrote this treatise at a time when the only movement in wages being discussed was a reduction, whereas we think now only in terms of increases. But it follows that he meant labour may not be able to raise real wages to any given figure either.

Using the instance of falling money wages he argued that lower money wages and higher real wages are each, for different reasons, likely to accompany a fall in employment, 'labour being readier to accept wage-cuts when employment is falling off, yet real wages inevitably rising in the same circumstances on account of the increasing marginal return to a given capital equipment when output is diminshed' (p. 10). He took the converse to be true also and stated (p. 14) 'resistance to every reduction in real wages raises an

*Source: *Economic Record*, December 1948, pp. 284-9.

insuperable bar to an increase in aggregate employment.' He pointed out that workers in the past had been willing to accept the lower real wage necessary to allow employment to increase. The Australian system of varying wages in accordance with movements in the price index appears to guarantee a fixed level of real wages and this, coupled with a possible new attitude of union leaders, may make it difficult to raise employment if Keynes's arguments hold.

Before proceeding to investigate the possibilities it is interesting to note an article by the economist, L. Albert Hahn, in the *American Economic Review*, March 1945.[3] Hahn argued on much the same lines as Keynes, but thought that in these days, when everybody understands how to use price indexes, falling real wages would be detected and opposed by labour. He therefore propounds the theory that it is possible, even while there are idle resources, for all of an increase in spending to go into raising prices instead of partly to raising prices and partly to increasing employment. He thinks this would happen because employers would refuse to increase employment without the incentive of higher prices relative to wages to cover increasing marginal cost. Keynes, of course, assumed that the fall in real wages would be accepted by labour since they had shown themselves 'more reasonable economists than the classical school' (p. 14). It follows that he thought the inflationary stage would only develop after full employment had been reached.

These arguments of Keynes and Hahn assume a rising marginal cost curve and, in fact, depend on that particular shape for their validity. If it can be shown that that shape is not applicable over a range of output, then the conclusions of Keynes quoted above are also subject to qualification. It is worth spending a little time, therefore, on discussing the likely shape. Keynes assumed it slopes upwards in the short period. He spoke of 'the familiar proposition that industry is normally working subject to decreasing returns in the short period during which equipment, etc., is assumed to be constant' (p. 17). This is perhaps the traditional concept of the shape of marginal cost curves, but it seems to ignore the extent of unused resources available. Experience in some specific industries as well as some general data on marginal cost has been collected below and nearly all fail to show the traditional shape.

In an investigation into costs in a furniture factory by Joel Dean published in the *Journal of the American Statistical Association*, March 1937, it was found that marginal cost appeared to be constant over the range of output included in the study.

The second report of the Econometrica Committee on Source Materials for Quantitative Production Studies, *Cost Categories and the Total Cost-Function*, July 1936, gives some data on costs of production per tonne-km. of air transport. While output nearly doubled, average cost fell by 5 per cent. Marginal cost was stationary except in cases where an additional tonne-km. made another plane necessary.

In engineering, figures published by Pearson, *Journal of the Royal Statistical Society*, 1921, p. 409, show that both repetitive and miscellaneous engineering work is subject to increasing returns at all levels of output within the author's experience. In both types of work marginal cost fell as output rose, the fall being greater for repetitive work as might have been expected.

Production costs in a large English motor manufacturing concern for different levels of output showed a gradually rising marginal cost. Doubling the output increased marginal cost by nearly 40 per cent. This was an odd case, however, as average cost fell and marginal cost rose over the whole range of available information due to the large commencing disparity between the absolute levels of average and marginal cost.

Figures of real labour cost of production of manufacturing industry in the U.S.A. taken as a whole were given by Colin Clark in *Economic News*, April 1941. The figures suggest that increasing average returns prevailed over the period from 1909 except for the period 1936-37, when production was rapidly expanding, and again in 1939-40. In these cases the average real labour cost began to rise and, of course, the marginal cost curve was rising more steeply. But apart from such periods marginal cost seems to have been stationary or falling as output rose. For manufacture as a whole, rising marginal costs in the short term are only likely when employment is high and production is expanding rapidly.

In *Economic Fluctuations* Kalecki discusses the likely movement in marginal cost. He dissects cost into materials, wages, and overheads, the most important from the point of view of marginal cost being wages. He considers that the bulk of industry operates at practically constant returns up to the point of 'practical capacity,' when marginal costs begin to rise steeply. He distinguishes primary industries and mining, which operate under diminishing returns, and railways, etc., which operate under rapidly increasing returns up to the point of capacity. Balancing these out he concludes that industry as a whole operates under conditions of approximately constant returns in the short period. This agrees with the other opinions collected. They all indicate that marginal cost is steady or falling in the short period except when plant is operating near capacity and, perhaps, production rapidly expanding.

We would expect these conclusions to apply to Australia. Normally there is no reason to expect marginal cost to rise in the short period, at least up to the relative level of production before the war. Shift work was not in operation to any extent, overtime was not particularly prevalent, and there were sufficient unemployed (about 10 per cent. of working population) to provide some labour (though of uncertain efficiency) for increased production.

A survey of the efficiency of unemployed tradesmen in the building trades and of unemployed engineering fitters was made by the Queensland Bureau of Industry in September 1938 and published in *Economic News*, April 1939. This showed that the reserve of labour, which was as skilled as the less efficient employed tradesmen, ranged from less than 1 per cent. to under 2 per cent. of the total tradesmen employed. This represented about a quarter of the unemployed tradesmen in the occupations covered. Efficiency of the remaining unemployed fell rapidly, down to about half that of the normal employed tradesman, the average efficiency being about 80 per cent. The trades surveyed may not have been typical but they indicate that, after allowing for the reserve needed for changing jobs, the number of skilled men employed could not have been very greatly increased without calling on the less efficient workers. This supports the contention that marginal costs will rise as practical capacity is reached. But at this stage it is a debatable point whether it is worth trying to push the last few per cent. into employment rather than to pay them unemployment benefits.

The Australian system of variation of wages in accordance with cost of living was not unknown to Lord Keynes since he mentioned the system in Chapter 19. Theoretically, he said, the system of fixing real wages by legislation as in Australia would result in violent oscillation between no employment at all and the level compatible with the real wage, depending on the level of investment. Prices would race from zero to infinity depending again on the level of investment being below or above the critical level which at best could provide an unstable equilibrium. In fact, he said, the escape was found 'partly of course in the inevitable inefficacy of the legislation to achieve its object, and partly in Australia not being a closed system' (p. 270).

One point to be noticed is that the Australian system of wage variation does not ensure a fixed real wage, since only the 'needs' portion of the wage is varied by the price index. It has been estimated that only half the aggregate wage and salary bill would move with the price index.[4] The remainder is made up of margins for skill, wages not subject to awards such as earnings of farm workers, fixed salaries, and so on. A 10 per cent. rise in the price index would raise the basic wage by 10 per cent. and leave the real basic wage unchanged, but average real wages and salaries would fall by about 5 per cent. Perhaps it is as well this is so, otherwise inflation would always be just around the corner, since the spiral of wages and prices would be more imminent.

Another factor not taken into account by Keynes was control of prices and profits. Normally price control is a purely nominal restriction since there is no great disparity between demand and supply, and no economic or political ends to be served other than protection of consumers from the more flagrant abuses. But it has been used for much more positive purposes than that during the war and has become a potent economic weapon in its own right. Theoretically, by strict price and profit control, it is possible to redistribute real income in favour of the worker and fix any level of real wages desired. This, of course, may merely lower the employers' incentive to work but, in fact, control is more likely to be ineffectively enforced. Present company dividends of 20 per cent. or more indicate how difficult control is.

Whether it is because our wage system is not as rigid as usually imagined or because marginal cost does not usually rise in the short term, the system has avoided the worst predictions of Lord Keynes for a system of stable real wages. It has also given employees a share of increased productivity. In fact the arbitration system has increased real wages over the twenty years before the war at just about the rate of increase of productivity. This is perhaps no more than could have been expected under a system of direct bargaining but it has been obtained with much less dislocation and loss of pay.

It is generally recognized that under full employment workers will be in a very favourable position for wage demands to give a certain general level of real wages, as well as sectional increases. To permit a high level of employment without excessive price rise union leaders may need to restrict their demands to the extent found necessary. Unreasonable sectional demands should be avoided, as should real wage increases not justified as labour's share of increasing productivity per man hour. Attempts to secure further real wage increases through increased money wages will lead to price increases which favour monopolistic institutions at the expense of fixed incomes and export industry. Taxation could be relied on to some extent to rectify any redistribution of income in favour of entrepreneurs. Full employment is an explosive state in some ways and it is hoped that workers will continue to prove themselves as good instinctive economists as Lord Keynes judged them to be.

Notes

1.   *General Theory of Employment, Interest and Money.* p. 9.
2.   Mr. R. Leggat, Organizer for the Amalgamated Engineering Union, in a recent address to the Queensland Branch of the Economic Society of Australia and New Zealand.
3.   Incidentally, Hahn claims to have anticipated many of Keynes's ideas in writings in 1920 and later, but had recanted by 1930 on the grounds of this very objection, that labour would not be fooled by high wages but higher prices. He concludes: 'If Lord Keynes has discovered the mechanism of lowering real wages through monetary manipulations, he has at the same time destroyed the working of the mechanism by drawing attention to it.'
4.   H.P. Brown's evidence to the Arbitration Court in the 40-hour-week case.

83

Professor Leontief on Lord Keynes.
(Followed by Comments)*

I.O. Scott

I

In Chapter XIX of *The New Economics*,[1] Professor Leontief examines what he considers to be the fundamental postulates of Keynes' *General Theory*. As a modern classicist, he is concerned with evaluating the Keynesian assumptions and their effect upon classical doctrine. He imputes to Keynes two postulates which, he alleges, Keynes substitutes for the single underlying assumption of the traditional theory. The Keynesian postulates concern the supply of labor and the demand for money, respectively.[2] Professor Leontief asserts that the Keynesian theory is not more but less "general" than the classical theory, because the two postulates in question replace — in his view — the single classical assumption regarding economic choice, which, of course, if true would be contrary to the principle of parsimony.

According to Professor Leontief, Keynes assumes, (1) that money wages are rigid downward, and (2) that the rate of interest is insensitive to an increase in the quantity of money and is also, therefore, rigid downward. I wish to question the assertion that Keynes assumes, as a basic postulate, a downward rigidity in money wages; though, on the other hand, I wish to assert that the phenomenon actually occurs. I shall agree that Keynes does assume, as a basic postulate, a downward rigidity in the rate of interest; but, I also propose to question Professor Leontief's interpretation of liquidity preference and to restore the Keynesian theory of the demand for money to its proper station in economic theory. *In fine*, I must add that even if the *General Theory* should be shown to rest upon a greater number of assumptions than the classical system, the principle of parsimony is a monitory rather than a prohibitory commandment.[3]

Although Professor Leontief deals first with the supply of labor and then with the demand for money, his argument would proceed more logically in the opposite direction. That is to say, he would be more methodical were he first to

*Source: *Quarterly Journal of Economics*, Vol. 63, November 1949, pp. 554-71.

imply the fallaciousness of the theory of liquidity preference, then to insert the postulate of rigid wages in order to enable the Keynesian model to be at underemployment equilibrium, and finally to occupy himself with a destructive analysis of the latter assumption as it appears in his special context. However, I shall follow the order employed by Professor Leontief.

II

To let Professor Leontief introduce his case, I may quote: "Traditional analysis considers the aggregate quantity of labor supplied, in the case where this supply is a competitive one, to be a function of the *real* wage rate; Keynes on the contrary assumes that up to a certain point — defined by him as the point of full employment — one particular level of *money* wages exists at which the supply of labor is perfectly elastic and below which no labor can be hired at all. The deliberate exclusion of the cost of living as a determinant of labor supply makes the latter independent of the level of *real* wages."[4]

The first Keynesian postulate then, according to Professor Leontief, is that wages are rigid downward.[5] But Keynes at no point in his writings explicitly states such an assumption.[6] Professor Leontief does not say that Keynes makes an explicit statetment to that effect; he imputes the postulate to Keynes in what he considers to be a logical clarification of Keynes' thesis. I believe the supposed logical necessity for the postulate, which seems obvious to Professor Leontief, to be invalid; and I shall attempt to show that it is a result, in Professor Leontief's mind, of his misinterpretation of the other matter of liquidity preference; that, in short, if this misinterpretation is corrected, any logical necessity for a postulate of wage rigidity disappears.

Parenthetically, I wish to account for the space which the subject of wage rigidity occupies in *The General Theory*. Keynes devoted many pages to the subject, but he probably did so because he wrote with one eye cocked in the direction of the counsels of state. In other words, Keynes felt it would be politically inexpedient to ask the labor unions to accept lower money wages. In the first place, he realized that it would be foolhardy to expect a single labor union to accept lower money wages; for it would thereby suffer a loss in real wages to the benefit of the rest of the economy. In the second place, Keynes was, if anything, not a socialist; and he undoubtedly abhorred the thought of a wage deflation at the behest of an authoritarian government. It was as a result of his personal predilections, therefore, and of political realities in the Great Britain of 1935, that Keynes concentrated his attention on alternative avenues to full employment.

However, Keynes not only rejected the classical prescription for full employment on practical grounds, but for theoretical reasons as well. He knew that if labor unions voluntarily accepted lower money wages, full employment would not necessarily follow.[7] Keynes reasoned as follows: Given a condition of less than full employment, if unemployed workers offer themselves at a wage less than the going rate, wages and marginal costs would necessarily fall. But since incomes would fall, *pari passu*, with the decline in the marginal cost of labor, there would be a commensurate decrease in demand, and entrepreneurs would have no reason to increase total employment over the given under-employment level.[8]

Keynes was aware, of course, of the fact that a reduction in money wages might have the indirect effect of increasing employment via the rate of interest. To follow the argument employed by Keynesians and modern classicists alike,[9] as incomes fall, less money is needed for transactions, hoards increase, the rate of interest falls, and investment and employment rise. However, I have already noted the impracticability of such a policy. Furthermore, it takes no great imagination to visualize the damage probably sustained by the schedule of the marginal efficiency of capital were such a program to be embarked upon. And furthermore, to clinch the Keynesian argument from a theoretical standpoint, the road to full employment may be blocked by the nature of the demand for money.

I must postpone until later a consideration of the Leontief version of the demand for money. It is sufficient to say at this point that the postulate of wage rigidity is a gratuitous one. Keynes was motivated by considerations other than theoretical in calling our attention to wage rigidities. Moreover, as has been suggested, I shall show that this postulate is not only not explicit but, in addition, that it is not implicit in the Keynesian system.

Surprisingly enough, after attributing the assumption of rigid wages to Keynes, Professor Leontief proceeds to deny its empirical validity.[10] But ironically, excepting, of course, the case of the totalitarian state, the existence of wage rigidity may be asserted.

If money wages are rigid downward — and a cursory survey of labor management relations will show that they are — the worker's behavior may not be completely consistent with the assumption regarding economic choice which underlies classical economic theory. In this respect, I believe Keynes' insight into the worker's psychology was superior to the hedonistic calculus which is fundamental in the traditional doctrine. Even though we treat all workers as *economic men* or more correctly, as human beings endowed with as much irrationality as the rest of us, I cannot accept a supply of labor theory cast in the classical mold as empirically sound. In the first place, a bargaining worker always hopes that his cut of the "economic pie" will be larger if he obtains a higher money wage.[11] In the second place, even though the worker be forewarned that his realization of higher money wages will leave him no better off, he (and certainly I should share his irrationality in a comparable situation) would be irrational enough to choose the higher absolute level of wages and prices. This would be the case, I believe, if for no other reason than that the worker would *feel* better off with the inflated pay check. These facts of worker psychology, which will not be denied by many, are overlooked by Professor

Leontief.

In the following paragraphs he describes and criticizes a Keynesian utility function. "In contrast to the classical, this Keynesian utility function would include, among the ultimate constituents of an individual's preference varieties, not only the physical quantities of (future and present) commodities and services but also the money prices of at least some of them. In particular the *money* wage rate would be considered as entering directly the worker's utility function: confronted with a choice between two or more situations in both of which his real income and his real effort are the same, but in one of which both the money wage rates (and, consequently, also the prices of consumers' goods) are higher than in the other, he would show a definite preference for the former. A classical *homo economicus* would find neither of the two alternatives to be more attractive than the other.

"From such a monetary utility function, a monetary supply curve of labor can be easily derived. In contrast to its classical counterpart, it will show the labor supply as dependent not only on the relative but also on the absolute prices and wage rates . . .

"Although neat and internally consistent, such 'psychological' interpretations of the monetary element of the Keynesian theory of wages are hardly appropriate. They contradict the common sense of economic behavior. The reference to the fact that no worker has ever been seen bargaining for real wages — even if true — is obviously beside the point, since while bargaining in terms of dollars the worker, as any one else, can still be guided in his behavior by the real purchasing power of his income. Moreover, the 'psychological' interpretation of the monetary element in consumers' behavior deprives Keynes' unemployment concept of its principal attribute. Why should any given rate of employment or unemployment be called 'involuntary' if it is determined through conscious preference for higher money wages as against larger real income?"[12]

The underlying implication in these paragraphs to the effect that laborers calculate according to strict economic choice is simply not warranted by the facts of economic experience. It is precisely this kind of inflexible thinking on the part of classical economic theorists that renders economic theory so vulnerable to attack by specialists in other social sciences. If the economic theorist aspires to a position of influence in public policy he must sufficiently complicate his theory so as to give proper recognition to the irrational elements of society's economic behavior. This is not the place to dwell at greater length on the shortcomings of classical economic theory with respect to modern psychology. It is enough to underscore the superior insight evinced by Keynes and revealed so clearly in a comparison of the Keynesian theory of the supply of labor with that of the classicists.

It must be admitted that management and labor alike are hardly unconcerned about real wages, though they deal in terms of monetary units. This is not to say, on the other hand, that the worker has not usually found his real income rising, at least temporarily, with an increase in money wages. Consequently, he is primarily concerned with money, rather than real, wages. As for the perhaps unnecessarily obscure Keynesian definition of unemployment, the Keynesian worker obviously associates a higher real income with a higher money income, whether his expectations are fulfilled or not. It is elementary that the breadwinner is more conscious of the monetary value of his take-home pay than of its real value, subject, as the latter is, to the erratic movements of the prices of thousands of commodities.[13]

Professor Leontief is doubtless correct in criticizing Keynes' use of the word, "involuntary," when he asks: "Why should any given rate of employment or unemployment be called 'involuntary,' if it is determined through conscious preference for higher money wages as against larger real income?"[14] However, I should parry with the question: "Has Professor Leontief, or anyone else, ever seen a worker confronted by such a choice?" But on with the Leontief case.

In order to make *The General Theory* more palatable, Professor Leontief posits a minimum wage law in deference to the Keynesian wage rigidity.[15] With the minimum wage law, Professor Leontief is on familiar ground. All that is necessary now, says our modern classicist, is to inflate all prices except wages. However, Professor Leontief must dispose of one more obstacle, liquidity preference, which, if unexorcized, would render nugatory the classicist's prescription of inflation. The discussion must turn, therefore, to the second basic postulate, which pertains to the demand for money, and which I must investigate to some extent before completing my evaluation of Professor Leontief's treatment of the Keynesian supply of labor.

III

Professor Leontief is, I believe, correct in assigning liquidity preference an important role in the Keynesian system. I feel, however, that certain aspects of the Leontief interpretation merit further reflection. In Professor Leontief's eyes, liquidity preference is nothing more than the velocity of the circulation of money in new, if less fashionable, dress. Before stating my most serious objections to the Leontief interpretation of Keynes, I wish to examine his confusion of the velocity of the circulation of money with the demand for money.[16] In Keynes, all money is divided between that used to satisfy the transactions motive on one hand and the speculative and precautionary motives on the other hand, M_1 and M_2 respectively. We have:

$$M = M_1 + M_2$$
$$M_1 = T(Y)$$
$$M_2 = L(r)$$

The demand for money for transactions is then a function of income; whereas, the demand for money as an asset is a function of the rate of interest.[17] The V of the quantity equation, to the contrary, does not provide us with such useful tools of analysis, for it is the velocity of circulation of all money in the system. It is in this confusion of V with M_2 that we shall find the key to the error in the Leontief interpretation.

According to Professor Leontief, " The theory of liquidity preference provides the Keynesian system with a deflationary mechanism which defeats, through the process of automatic hoarding, every tendency toward inflationary reduction of involuntary unemployment."[18] In this statement Professor Leontief betrays his classical bias and preoccupation with inflation as a prescription for full employment.

It will serve my purpose to consider the Leontief interpretation in two parts, depending on the position of the rate of interest relatively to the liquidity preference schedule. Let us first assume the rate of interest to be above the level where it becomes insensitive to the quantity of M_2, i.e., above the point where the interest elasticity of the liquidity preference schedule approaches infinity. In this range, it is certainly correct, to quote Professor Leontief again, that " The theory of liquidity preference provides the Keynesian system with a deflationary mechanism which defeats . . . every tendency toward *inflationary* reduction of involuntary unemployment."[19] True, in Keynes we do *not* reach full employment through inflation.[20] However, this is not to say that Keynes denies that the prescription of increasing the quantity of money achieves full employment. It is only with regard to the mechanism by which an increase in the quantity of money affects the price level that Keynes parts company with the classicists. And here the divergence between the two systems is clear!

Let us grant for purposes of the argument the wage rigidity of the Leontief interpretation. The classicist recommends an increase in the quantity of money. Then, according to the classicists, people will find in their possession a quantity of cash greater than their accustomed holdings. In trying to rid themselves of the excess, they will force up the price level, Professor Leontief's supply and demand curves for labor are raised, and involuntary unemployment is wiped out.[21]

It is at this point that my earlier reference to the Keynesian treatment of money becomes significant. Starting again with the assumption of unemployment and rigid wages, the Keynesian agrees to an increase in the quantity of money. But, contrary to the classical belief, this expanded money supply will *not* result in inflation. Let us suppose the central bank expands the quantity of money in circulation by purchasing securities on the open market. Former security holders find their cash holdings increased above their accustomed level. Do they then make haste to the consumers' market to exchange their excess holdings of cash for goods? Of course not![22] They try to get rid of their excess money assets by bidding against each other and the central bank for securities, thereby driving the prices of securities up and the interest rate down to a level where they are content to hold the increment to the money supply. Investment increases, and equilibrium at full employment is obtained without inflation.

The point is that in the classical system the holders of the increment to the money supply treat this increment as income. The fallacy in this presumption is clearly revealed in the Keynesian analysis. This increment of money is treated as an asset, not in the general accounting sense, but as an asset in the Keynesian sense of money held to satisfy the speculative or precautionary motives. The V of the quantity theory equation, then, does not provide us with a microscope of sufficient power to detect the fundamental workings of the economy. The superiority of the Keynesian instrument should be obvious.

I shall turn briefly to the situation wherein the rate of interest is rigid downward, i.e., the case in which the interest elasticity of the liquidity preference schedule approaches infinity, and an increase in the quantity of money has no effect on the rate of interest. This case is sometimes referred to as the *liquidity trap* or *two per cent case*. It is evidently this *trap* which Professor Leontief has in mind when he refers to the ". . . *deflationary mechanism which defeats, through the process of automatic hoarding*, every tendency toward inflationary reduction of involuntary unemployment."[23]

If I understand him correctly, Professor Leontief denies the very existence of the *liquidity trap*. Evidently, in his opinion, people hold money to buy commodities. If the prices of commodities rise or fall, people hold more or less money, respectively, in order to keep the purchasing power of their holdings constant. If this be the case, liquidity preference cannot vitiate the inflationary process, since individuals would be willing to increase their holdings of cash only as the price level rises. In other words, if the quantity of money is increased, people will try to rid themselves of the increment of cash. In so doing, they will force prices up to a level at which they are willing to hold the increment of money. That is, prices will rise to a point where the purchasing power of their cash holdings is the same as it was before the quantity of money was increased.

Here again the unsurmountable obstacles which modern classicists necessarily encounter when they attempt to reduce Keynes to classical stature become apparent. The Leontief delineation of the Keynesian system is inaccurate, as he refuses to pay close attention to the respective roles which $M_1 = T(Y)$ and $M_2 = L(r)$ play in the Keynesian system. He insists on defining liquidity preference in terms of the k of the Cambridge cash balance version of the quantity theory.[24] In Keynes, of course, the increment of money is not treated as income. The investor finds the prices of securities, land, housing, *et. al.*, too high. Consequently, he adds to his holdings of cash anticipating an eventual upswing in the rate of interest, thereby nullifying the effect of an increase in the quantity of money on the rate of interest.[25] Hence, this is one[26] of the Keynesian *cases* in which fiscal policy must be substituted for monetary policy if equilibrium at full employment is to be attained.

IV

It has been my purpose to question the Leontief interpretation of *The General Theory* on the following grounds. First, Keynes realized that rigid money wages must be taken into account by the practicing economist. However, he did not postulate wage rigidity, for it is not essential to his theoretical structure. Secondly, full employment may be attained through monetary policy which does not entail a rise in the prices of commodities. Thirdly, among other reasons, we may have an unemployment equilibrium because of the nature of the demand for money. Finally, I wish to reiterate that we were in equilibrium at less than full employment in the *liquidity trap case* due to a rigidity in the rate of interest, not because of a rigidity in wages.[27] Obviously, the wage rigidity plays such an important role in the Leontief version of Keynes only because of the former's conception of liquidity preference and his denial of the *liquidity trap*.

Comment by W. Leontief

Mr. Scott's comments on the Keynesian theory of wages bring to my mind the story about the woman who when accused of having returned a borrowed crock in damaged condition defended herself by claiming that first of all she had not borrowed the crock; secondly, the crock was already broken when she borrowed it; and thirdly, that it has been returned in perfect condition. After admitting, as Keynes did himself in his answer to my earlier reference to that particular point, that the "money illusion" plays a prominent part in *The General Theory of Employment*, and conceding that without it the very concept of involuntary unemployment becomes meaningless, Scott denies that it constitutes an indispensable element of the Keynesian argument. His reference to Lawrence Klein's success in "*relieving*[28] the Keynesian model of any theoretical dependence upon the definition of involuntary unemployment" hardly makes my critic's position any more consistent.

Considering the singularly elusive character of many of his theoretical formulations and the impressionistic nature of some of Keynes' writing, I feel that simple quotations from *The General Theory* will be of little use in settling the present controversy. Let it be noted however that James Tobin, whose article on "Money Wage Rates and Employment" is recommended by Scott as a definitive treatment of the problem, flatly states that "clearly one of Keynes' basic assumptions . . . is that 'money illusion' occurs in the labor supply functions."[29]

Turning now to his discussion of liquidity preference, I still do not see that Scott succeeds in shaking my fundamental contention that Keynesian theory represents an ingenious but not very successful attempt at treating essentially dynamic problems in static terms. He does not contradict my observation that the relationship between the quantity of money and the rate of interest is due entirely to the operation of the speculative motive. On the contrary, his insistence on what I cannot but consider to be nothing more than a typical pedagogical simplification — the conceptual division of all available money into two *additively* combined parts — M_1 and M_2 — only serves to emphasize that particular point. Unfortunately, he does not say "yes" or "no" to my contention that under stationary conditions, (i.e., a situation in which none of the relevant economic variables such as the rate of interest, prices, etc., are changing or are expected to change over time) nobody would hold any money for speculative purposes; that is, that in such a situation M_2 would be *identically* zero. But this is the crux of the whole matter. If the foregoing observation is correct, then in a truly stationary situation, the cornerstone of the Keynesian theory of interest — the direct relationship between the quantity of money and the rate of interest — falls to the ground. (M_1 is assumed not to be a function of p.)

Mr. Scott's plausible description of the sequence of events which would follow an expansion of the money supply by the central bank might be right or wrong; insofar as it refers to an obviously dynamic process, it does not and cannot contribute to the clarification of the theoretical issues involved in this particular controversy. Had he tried to analyze this loosely depicted process in terms of an explicitly formulated dynamic model, he would have found that (a) either the original or the final position of his system must prove *not* to be a truly stationary equilibrium position, or (b) the existence of speculative money holdings, M_2 under purely stationary conditions would have to be assumed.

In the two per cent or the "liquidity trap" case, Mr. Scott explicitly refers to anticipation of an eventual upswing in the rate of interest as the reason why the investors are ready to absorb and immobilize any additional supply of money. This clearly is a dynamic phenomenon. Under conditions of truly stationary equilibrium, characterized by constancy over time of the magnitudes of all relevant variables including the two per cent rate of interest, there would be no reason to expect its "eventual upswing" and to hold on to additional cash for speculative purposes. To justify the existence of a liquidity trap as a long run stationary phenomenon, one would have to give up any reference to expected changes and fall back, as in the case of the labor supply, on some kind of a money illusion, i.e., a demand for money assumed to be independent of its purchasing power. This is essentially the position explicitly taken by Don Patinkin in the article quoted by Scott.[30]

Further Comment by G. Haberler

In note 5, pp. 162-3, Mr. Scott tries to refute my contention that the existence of underemployment *equilibrium* depends on the assumption of rigid wages and that underemployment equilibrium is impossible, if there is competition among wage earners. My reason was that competition would drive down *money* wages and prices so long as there is involuntary unemployment — a situation incompatible with an equilibrium position. It should be noted that real wages need not go down. In fact within the simplified frame of the Keynesian system where prices are supposed to fall parallel with wages, real wages would not fall at all. Mr. Scott holds that if the liquidity trap prevents a fall in the rate of interest or if the elasticity of demand for capital with respect to the rate of interest is zero, "the unemployed would not, theoretically at least, continue to offer themselves at lower money wage-rates" and "the economist would no longer be justified in advising the labor unions to accept lower money wages." (By the way, who are the economists who advise unions to accept lower money wages? It is surely not those economists to whose advice unions are at all likely to listen.)

Taken literally, Mr. Scott's argument moves in a curious kind of circle: Economists would not be justified in recommending wage reductions and the unemployed would not be willing to work at lower wages, because there "would be nothing further to be gained from a reduction in money wages," meaning obviously that employment would not increase. In other words, my theory is wrong, because economists and the unemployed have convinced themselves that it is wrong and prevent it from being tested by keeping wages rigid!

It is hardly necessary to say that this kind of argument does not prove anything. It does not even come to grips with the issues involved. But let me point out the obvious fact that if the unemployed "do not offer themselves at lower money wage-rates," they are either not involuntarily unemployed or there is no competition in the labor market.

That Keynes' theory of underemployment equilibrium depends on the assumption of rigid wages should by now be clear to everybody. I feel embarrassed by saying the same things over and over again, but since again and again there appear articles which overlook or ignore the most obvious considerations, I feel constrained to repeat a few things which I have said already in the first edition of my *Prosperity and Depression*[31] and repeated in later editions and elsewhere.[32]

The proposition that there can be any amount of unemployment with rigid wages is entirely compatible with classical and neoclassical economics. On the other hand, if there is competition in the labor market and elsewhere[33] and if, hence, wages and prices fall continuously or at least spasmodically so long as there is involuntary unemployment, the real value of the quantity of money increases without limit and, assuming that the liquidity preference curve is perfectly elastic or the marginal efficiency entirely inelastic, it is clear that something in the Keynesian system has to give way, for instance, the propensity to consume. What Don Patinkin[34] somewhat pompously enunciates as "the Pigou effect," viz. the proposition that the consumption function will shift upward, if the real value of liquid assets (or assets in general) reaches a certain level, is just common sense which must have been in the minds of many writers. At any rate, when I stated it in the first edition of my *Prosperity and Depression*, I thought that I expressed an obvious fact. Furthermore, it is only one possibility. For example, exactly the same argument that holds for the propensity to consume applies also to the marginal efficiency of capital.

It is true, of course, that all this is not the whole story and that it does not settle all problems of policy. Dynamic repercussions upon the marginal efficiency of capital, changes in the income distribution due to the increased real value of money debts and similar frictions are vastly more important than the mechanics of the static Keynesian system. Surely Keynes would have been the first to acknowledge that. It is high time that Keynesians recognize the inability of the Keynesian system to cope with the problem of wage and price flexibility so that the discussion can be moved out of the dead-end track on which it has been shunted by those writers who take as the last word the static Keynesian system which its author, if he had lived longer and had not been preoccupied with other matters, would have abandoned long ago as an untenable intermediate station.

Notes

I wish to acknowledge the assistance gained from innumerable conversations with Professor Richard S. Howey, University of Kansas, and to thank Doctor James Tobin, Harvard University, who read the manuscript and made many helpful suggestions. Responsibility for the views expressed in the paper is, of course, my own.

　　1.　A collection of Keynesian literature, edited by Seymour E. Harris (New York: Alfred A. Knopf, 1947).

　　2.　"The nature of the supply of labor and that of the demand for money are the two principle points of divergence between the basic postulates of the *General Theory* and the teachings of the classical doctrine." *Op. cit.*, p. 233.

　　3.　Though it is not the purpose of this note to discuss the relative "generality" of the two systems, the following observations appear to be pertinent. Manifestly, there is no definition of "generality" generally accepted by economists. Professor Leontief measures "generality" in terms of fundamental postulates, Keynes in terms of employment equilibria.

Professor Leontief does perform a great service in distinguishing between postulates and deducible conclusions when he reprimands those of Keynes' disciples who maintain that the classicists assume unemployment to be nonexistent.

　　4.　*Op. cit.*, p. 233. The downward rigidity in money wages is, it is true, indispensable to Keynes' definition of involuntary unemployment. I am not concerned in this paper, however, with the role that wage rigidity plays in this context. Rather, I am interested in examining the contention of neoclassicists to the effect that the Keynesian system requires such a rigidity in order to be at underemployment equilibrium. Dr. Lawrence R. Klein, in his admirable tract on the nature of *The Keynesian Revolution* (New York: Macmillan, 1947), has clearly relieved the Keynesian model of any theoretical dependence upon the definition of involuntary unemployment which appears in *The General Theory*. Cf. *The Keynesian Revolution*, pp. 80-90.

　　5.　Cf. also *The New Economics*, Chapter XIV, "The General Theory," by G. Haberler. Professor Haberler apparently agrees with Professor Leontief. Quoting from p. 167 in the Haberler chapter: "Keynes assumes that (money) wages are rigid downward. If this assumption, which is certainly not entirely unrealistic, is rigidly adhered to, most of his conclusions follow: Under-employment equilibrium is radically changed. Obviously, under-employment equilibrium with flexible wages is impossible — wages and prices must then fall continuously, which can hardly occur without further consequences and cannot well be described as an equilibrium position."

Manifestly, Professor Haberler is tying the Keynesian argument to the postulate of rigid wages. He continues in a similar vein on p. 169: ". . . it is pointed out (in Chapter 19 of the *General Theory*) that a reduction in money wages will usually influence employment, but in an indirect fashion, through its repercussions upon the propensity to consume, efficiency of capital, or the rate of interest. The last mentioned route, via the interest rate, is the one most thoroughly explored by Keynes and the Keynesians. As wages and prices are allowed to fall, money is released from the transactions sphere, interest rates fall, and full employment is eventually restored by a stimulation of investment. This amounts to giving up the idea of under-employment equilibrium under a regime of flexible prices and wages except in two limiting cases: Full employment may be prevented from being reached via this route, (a) if the liquidity trap prevents a fall in the rate of interest . . . or (b) if investment is quite insensitive to a fall in the interest rate. Keynes himself regarded both these situations not as actually existing but as future possibilities. But what if we do regard them as actually existing — which as a short-run proposition, allowing for dynamic disturbances through unfavorable expectations, etc., would be by no means absurd? We would still not have established a stable under-employment equilibrium, for wages and prices would still continue to fall."

There seems to be some difficulty here with the meaning of equilibrium. I should presume that by an equilibrium at less than full employment, Keynes simply meant the condition where there are no forces inherent in the economic system which tend to raise the level of employment to that of full employment. This is precisely the condition which exists when the liquidity trap halts the decline of the rate of interest, or when the schedule of the marginal efficiency of capital has an interest elasticity of zero. That is to say, in either of these cases, there would be nothing further to gain from a reduction in money wages. It would follow, perforce, that the unemployed would not, theoretically at least, continue to offer themselves at lower money wage rates. If the unemployed blindly did so, the fact that prices and wages would continue to fall, approaching zero as a limit, is irrelevant. For there is nothing in Keynes' definition of underemployment equilibrium that precludes such a downward spiral of prices. The point is that in these two situations, the economist would no longer be justified in advising the labor unions to accept lower money wages. It follows that in these limiting cases cited by Professor Haberler we have conditions of underemployment equilibria *without* the assumption of rigid wages. It is the rigidity in the rate of interest or the perfectly inelastic schedule of the marginal inefficiency of capital which brings about the condition of equilibrium.

6. Cf. *op. cit.* Chapter XI, "The General Theory," by Abba P. Lerner, reprinted from the *International Labour Review*, October 1936.

7. On this account Keynes considered the workers in their intuitive apprehension, to be superior as economists to the theorists who embrace the classical doctrine. Cf. *The General Theory*, p. 14.

8. Similar reasoning, of course, applies to the correlative but equally fallacious argument sometimes made by labor leaders: an appeal for higher wages on the ground that an increase in wages would increase effective demand and employment.

To deal sensibly with the relationship between a change in the wage rate and the level of employment, a general equilibrium model is required. The dichotomy of price and distribution theory according to the traditional approach, with the oversimplification implicit in economic analysis which artificially separates the producers' and consumers' market, necessarily yields a meaningless solution.

9. Cf. note 5 above; also *Lapses from Full Employment*, (London: Macmillan, 1945) for the Pigovian version.

10. Professor Haberler evidently would not agree with Professor Leontief on this point. Cf. note 5, above.

11. Moreover, a higher money wage received by a single labor union will mean higher real wages for that segment of labor. To this extent, the money illusion is not a manifestation of irrationality, but rather of rationality on the part of the worker.

12. *The New Economics*, pp. 235-6. In this passage, Professor Leontief reiterates a stand on *The General Theory* taken earlier in his article, "The Fundamental Assumption of Mr. Keynes' Monetary Theory of Unemployment," this *Journal*, November 1936, pp. 192-197. At that time, Professor Leontief imputed only one basic postulate to the Keynesian system: that pertaining to the supply of labor. It was Professor Leontief's contention that the fundamental difference between Keynes and the classicists lay in the former's refusal to accept the latter's *homogeneity*

postulate as applicable to the supply of labor.

If we let z represent the supply of labor, y the wage rate, and $x_1, x_2, \ldots x_n$ the prices of wage goods, the classical supply function may then be expressed as

$$z = f(y, x_1, x_2, \ldots x_n)$$
$$f(ty, tx_1, tx_2, \ldots tx_n) = t^b f(y, x_1, x_2, \ldots x_n)$$

where $b = 0$.

That is, the classical supply function is homogeneous of the zero degree.

The reference made by Professor Leontief to the *homogeneity postulate* is simply an econometrician's way of saying that the money illusion of *The General Theory* amounted to a serious departure from the fundamental assumption regarding economic choice of classical economic theory. In a later rejoinder, "The General Theory of Employment," this *Journal*, February 1937, pp. 209-223, Keynes agreed that this difference between the two systems does exist. (For an evaluation of the relative importance of this difference, see *The Keynesian Revolution*, p. 83.)

Assuming that the validity of the money illusion, or rigidity in money wages, is accepted, this same money illusion, Professor Leontief argues, must logically be applied to all supply and demand functions in the Keynesian system. The same view is expressed by Dr. James Tobin in his article on "Money Wage Rates and Employment," *The New Economics*, pp. 572-587 — a definitive treatment of the nasty problem of tracing the effect of changes in money wage rates on the level of employment. To quote Dr. Tobin: "Without the retention of the 'homogeneity postulate' for all supply and demand functions except the labor supply function, the Keynesian money wage doctrine cannot be maintained . . . When the existence of variable factors other than labor is admitted, Keynesian theory requires that these factors be fully employed and that their prices be perfectly flexible. This is where the 'homogeneity postulate' — the assumption of 'rational' behavior — enters with respect to the supply functions of these factors. If the sellers of these factors were, like the sellers of labor, influenced by the 'money illusion', their prices would be rigid like wages and there could be unemployment of these factors. A change in the money wage rate could then alter the employment of labor by causing a substitution between labor and other factors."

"Keynes, since he assumes away the existence of other factors, presents no reason for this distinction between labor and other factors. Lerner, however, asserts that it is 'plausible and in conformity with the assumption of rationality of entrepreneurs and capital owners, who would rather get something for the use of their property than let it be idle, while labor has non-rational money-wage demands.' " (*op. cit.*, p. 582). Dr. Tobin, however, takes issue with Professor Lerner and argues that it is just as reasonable to expect the sellers of these other factors to have nonrational money price demands as wage earners.

Similarly, with the consumption function, Dr. Tobin argues: "The Keynesian consumption function, which is crucial to the Keynesian solution to the money wage problem, is framed in real terms . . . This is the application of the 'homogeneity postulate' to the consumption function. If 'money illusion' occurred in consumption and saving decisions, real consumption expenditure would depend on the level of money income as well as on the level of real income . . . a change in the money wage rate, changing the level of money incomes and prices, would alter the real demand for consumption goods and therefore, affect the volume of both output and employment. Here again, therefore, retention of the 'homogeneity postulate' is an essential assumption for Keynesian money wage doctrine.

"But if wage-earners are victims of a 'money illusion' when they act as sellers of labor, why should they be expected to become 'rational' when they come into the market as consumers?" (*op. cit.* p. 583.)

Although it is my purpose in this paper to show that the Keynesian system is not dependent, fundamentally, upon the wage rigidity, it is interesting and useful to deal with the problem posed by the countless rigidities which, of course, exist in the real world. As for the Tobin application of the money illusion to supply functions other than labor, it seems obvious that the homogeneity postulate correctly describes the supply of the fixed plant and equipment. Once the entrepreneur is saddled with fixed costs he will operate as long as he can defray variable costs. Rigidities in the prices of variable factors other than labor are irrelevant, since if labor is to be substituted, it will be substituted for plant and equipment, not for raw materials or goods in process.

But suppose we admit, what I do not believe to be true, that the suppliers of capital equipment are beset by the money illusion, and if you please, in the short run! Even in this situation, can anyone soberly maintain that, say, ten millions of unemployed laborers could be brought into employment by accepting lower money wages? Anyone making such a plea would have to show that the elasticity of the demand for labor is sufficiently greater than unity to make up for the decrease in expenditures on capital equipment in order to maintain the level of effective demand. To my knowledge, the discovery of this fact remains for the economist of the future. Surely, the burden of proof lies on the shoulders of him who makes the plea.

In any event, in a world of imperfect markets and rigidities in price policies, the entrepreneur is more sensitive to changes in effective demand than to changes in marginal costs. Even if wages fall, the entrepreneur is not likely to increase employment in the short run unless effective demand increases.

Of course, in a sense, all unemployment is voluntary. That is, full employment could always be achieved by reducing money wages sufficiently to cause a reversion to a handicraft society. But such a solution to the problem of mass unemployment implies the untenable assumption of a change in tastes involving a transference of demand from the highly fabricated goods of the roundabout process of production to goods which can be produced by a handicraft society. Needless to say, the solution of the problem of unemployment by means of a "Molly McGuire" movement on a mass scale would be intolerable.

As for the Tobin consumption function, it seems to me that more is being made out of the money illusion than should be. All that the money illusion means when applied to the suppliers of labor is that they associate a higher real wage with a higher money wage. In reality, this does not amount to irrational behavior, but rather rational behavior; because an individual worker or labor union that obtains an increase in money wages will find its real wages have risen above what they would have been had the increase in money wages not been achieved, at least momentarily.

It is of interest to note, as Dr. Tobin has done, that, abstracting from expectations, consumers' real wealth might be increased, possibly leading to increased consumption expenditures, by a general deflation of wages and prices. (Cf. *op. cit.* p. 584. Also, James Tobin, "The Fallacies of Lord Keynes' General Theory: Comment," this *Journal*, November 1948, pp. 763-770, esp. p. 769.) This is the 'Pigou effect,' investigated by Professor Don Patinkin in his recent article, "Price Flexibility and Full Employment." (*American Economic Review*, September 1948, pp. 543-564.) In other words, abstracting from expectations, a reduction in prices may have a stimulatory effect via the propensity to consume as a consequence of an appreciation in the value of assets held in the form of cash."

13. It is true that labor unions are presently paying closer attention to changes in price indices than formerly. Whether or not this fact will eliminate the downward stickiness in wages remains to be seen.

14. Cf. footnote 12, pp. 163-5.

15. This he does while at the same time scorning Keynes' reluctance to clothe his wage rigidity in institutional raiment (*op. cit.* p. 239). A case in point is Keynes' lengthy digression on labor union strategy noted above.

16. Cf. *The New Economics*, Chapter XLI, "Keynes and Traditional Theory," by R.F. Harrod, p. 603.

17. For a statistical investigation of the shape of the "L" function see James Tobin, "Liquidity Preference and Monetary Policy," *Review of Economic Statistics*, May 1947, pp. 130-1.

18. *The New Economics*, p. 238.

19. Cf. preceding footnote. Italics mine.

20. By *inflation*, I mean a rise in the money prices of commodities. Hence, an increase in the quantity of money would not entail inflation unless accompanied by an increased demand for commodities, or unless there is full employment and the interest rate falls, thereby causing an increase in the rate of investment. Abstracting from frictions, such increased investment could take place without causing inflation if there were unemployed resources in the economy.

21. *Op. cit.*, p. 236.

22. Cf. *op. cit.*, Chapter XIV, p. 170. Professor Haberler apparently shares, to some extent at least, Professor Leontief's view on this subject. Quoting Professor Haberler: . . . "we must assume, it seems to me, that consumption is not only a function of income but also of wealth (and *liquid* wealth in particular)." (Italics mine.)

Strictly, consumption (that is, the absolute magnitude of expenditures on consumer goods) is some function of income. We have:

$$C = F(Y)$$

The shape of the consumption function is in turn determined by a host of other variables, which we would normally take as parameters, such as wealth, the tax structure, the social security system, expectations regarding the future availability of consumer goods, the stock of consumer durables on hand, price expectations, government policy (e.g. "E" Bond campaigns), advertising, the status of thrift as a social virtue, the extent of national self-sufficiency, the ratio of dividends to corporation profits, the relation between urban and rural population, the extent of education, expectations as to the future level of incomes, and perhaps (cf Harold Lubbell, "Effects of Redistribution of Income on Consumers' Expenditures," *American Economic Review*, March 1947, pp. 157-170) the distribution of income. All of these factors combine to determine the public's attitude toward saving or consumption at various levels of national income. Professor Haberler evidently wishes to include in this list of variables which determine the shape of the consumption function, not only wealth, but also some variable reflecting the proportion of wealth held in liquid form. He apparently feels that the post-war inflationary trend in prices was due in part to holdings of wealth in the form of cash and in the quasi-liquid form of government bonds. (Cf. "Causes and Cures of Inflation," by Gottfried Haberler, *Review of Economics and Statistics*, February 1948, pp. 10-14). It seems more plausible to me that the post-war upward shift in the consumption function be explained by the dearth of consumer durables sustained by the war, plus expectations of further price rises. In other words, it does not seem necessary to concede that people have suddenly decided to convert their assets into consumer goods in order to explain the upward movement of the consumption function following in the wake of war.

Of course, if monetary policy is successful in stimulating new investment, incomes and consumption will rise. And if the economy is at or approaching full employment, prices will rise. But this price inflation is due, directly, to the increment to income flow and only indirectly to the increase in the quantity of money. In this event, and particularly if open market operations are accompanied by additional income stemming from deficit financing on the part of the government, the marginal propensity to consume may approach unity due to price expectations, with a runaway inflation in the offing. It would surely be agreed, however, that such a state of affairs would be abnormal, e.g. of the catastrophic German monetary experiment following World War I, and need not detain us further at this juncture.

23.   Cf. note 18, p. 165. Italics mine. It should be pointed out that Keynes envisaged this rigidity in the rate of interest as only a remote, but probable eventuality. Despite this fact, Professor Leontief apparently devotes his entire attention to this case.

24.   Where all $M = kY$ and k is defined as the constant proportion of their incomes which individuals hold measured in real terms.

25.   It is true that in a purely static model the demand for money would be proportional to prices. But abstraction from uncertainty is unthinkable. Hence, Professor Leontief suggests (*op. cit.*, pp. 238-40) that Keynes should have written *The General Theory* in dynamic rather than comparative static form. Certainly, it would be exceedingly helpful to have at hand a dynamized, general equilibrium model encompassing all important economic relationships. However, the dearth of dynamic economics, combined with data showing the relatively large number of students in the field of economics, clearly indicate something more than the dereliction of economists as the source of the difficulty.

26.   Cf. footnote 5, pp. 162-3 for the Haberler version of other *Keynesian cases*.

27.   In *The Keynesian Revolution*, p. 89, Dr. Klein concludes: "In order to show that full employment is not automatic in a perfect world subject to the Keynesian conditions, it is necessary to assume nothing whatsoever about rigidities in the system, but only to make plausible assumptions about the interest-elasticity of certain basic relationships." In the *case* of the perfectly inelastic marginal efficiency of capital, no rigidity is involved. In the *liquidity trap case*, on the other hand, there is a downward rigidity in the rate of interest.

28.   The italics are mine.

29.   *The New Economics*, p. 580.

30.   Passing from the defense of the Keynesian position to a counterattack, Patinkin presents in a later article, "The Indeterminacy of Absolute Prices in Classical Economic Theory," (*Econometrica*, XVII, No. 1, January 1949) what he considers to be a proof of internal inconsistency of the classical position. I am dealing with his arguments in a note in the January 1950 issue of *Econometrica*.

31.   Chapter X, §9 (in later editions, Chapter XI, §9).

32.   *Op. cit.*, Chapter I, §5, and Chapter XIII, §6, and the essay quoted by Mr. Scott.

33.   There is no space here to explain in detail that it is not necessary that there should be *perfect* competition. Some flexibility of wages which is quite compatible with considerable

deviations from perfect competition would be sufficient for the argument.

34. "Price Flexibility and Full Employment," *American Economic Review*, September 1949, *passim*.

84

Recent Discussion of Keynes' Theory of Wages: A Review*

H.W. Arndt

In a symposium on "Keynes' Influence on Theory and Public Policy"[1] which was published in the United States in 1947 both to mark the occasion of the tenth anniversary of the *General Theory* and as a Memorial to Lord Keynes, one aspect of Keynesian theory receives, apparently by accident rather than design, an unexpectedly large amount of attention. Of the twenty-five or so new essays of substance contained in the volume, at least six deal wholly or in part with Keynes's theory of wages.[2] These six essays do not in themselves form a well-arranged symposium. But if one takes the trouble to piece the arguments together, one finds in them a useful starting point for a summing-up of the prolonged discussion which this part of the *General Theory* provoked.

The task which Keynes set himself in his treatment of wage theory in the *General Theory* was to refute the implication of classical theory that general wage deflation was an appropriate remedy for general unemployment. His special problem was to perform this task while retaining one of the basic assumptions of classical theory, the assumption that employment is inversely related to the level of real wages (from which it follows that unemployment is involuntary only if labour is willing to accept work at a lower real wage). His solution was expressed in two propositions. First, wage deflation is difficult because labour resists cuts in money wages even though it would be prepared to accept an equivalent reduction in real wages through rising prices (and would, therefore, qualify as "involuntarily unemployed" in the classical sense). Secondly, even if labour were willing to accept reductions in money wages, this would not increase employment since prices would fall proportionately, leaving real wages (and therefore output and employment) unchanged.

Both propositions and particularly the more far-reaching second one, were qualified by Keynes himself in the *General Theory* and have been subject to criticism ever since. Much of the discussion in these essays summarizes and

*Source *Economic Record*, Vol. 25, December 1949, pp. 77-83.

elaborates these qualifications and criticisms.

Keynes' own qualifications of the second proposition related to four main points. (a) The argument applies only in a closed economy. In an open economy, a reduction in money wages will improve the balance of trade and thus increase employment, although these effects may be nullified by similar wage reductions (or tariffs) abroad or by changes in exchange rates. (b) A general fall in money wages and prices, by releasing cash balances from the transaction sphere, may reduce the rate of interest and thus stimulate investment. But this effect, on which Keynes — one cannot help feeling, with his tongue in his cheek — placed chief emphasis, is likely to be nullified either by the "liquidity trap" (at low interest rates) or by the tendency for investment to be interest-elastic. At best, "monetary management by the Trade Unions" would be a singularly clumsy solution. (c) A reduction in money wage rates may have a favourable effect on business confidence. But if the general thesis is correct, any additional investment stimulated by the favourable impression made by cost reductions is bound to lead to losses, even if the wage cut is expected to be once-for-all and permanent. If, as is more likely because of resistance of labour, it is merely one stage in the process of a "sagging wage level" the effect will certainly be unfavourable. (d) Lastly, Keynes considered possible effects on the propensity to consume, through redistribution of income from wage-earners to other prime factors or from entrepreneurs to rentiers. The second of these Keynes thought doubtful and unimportant, while the effects of the first would be unfavourable.

At least four of the six contributors to the "symposium" on Keynes' wage theory seem prepared to follow Keynes up to this point. The chief exception is Professor Haberler who in his generally critical essay makes a root-and-branch attack on Keynes' position.[3] Professor Haberler is primarily concerned to demonstrate that Keynes' theory of under-employment equilibrium depends on his postulate of (downward) rigidity of money wages. He has little difficulty in showing that a completely unstable Wicksellian system could hardly be said to be in under-employment *equilibrium*; though, as Professor Hansen points out, that is hardly relevant to Keynes's main problem. Professor Haberler also advances two arguments against the thesis that employment is independent of the level of money wages. The first, to the effect that a continuous rise in the value of money would increase the real value of cash balances held in the form of gold and may thus raise the consumption function, is not taken very seriously by himself. The second would seem to be a mere reassertion of the classical position against Keynes. No Keynesian denies that "a reduction in the cost of certain consumption or investment goods may well stimulate demand for them"; but when Professor Haberler adds ". . . and for the consumption and investment as a whole" he surely begs the central question. The argument which he advances in support of this proposition is little more convincing. "Assume that the elasticity of demand for some of these things, and therefore incidentally for labour, is unity. Then the wage bill remains unchanged and there are no adverse effects through a fall of consumption demand of the workers. Then employment will clearly rise" (p. 172). This assumes that the additional output (investment) will generate equivalent additional income before cost reduction has any effect on consumption; it is merely one hopeful version of the argument that cost reduction will increase business confidence, the marginal efficiency of capital and investment. Professor Haberler's further point that the additional output must be interpreted as due to a rise in the marginal efficiency of capital or the consumption function, according as to whether the newly produced goods are consumption or investment goods, is even more difficult to accept. Professor Haberler's oblique claim, later in the essay (p. 175), to have shown that Keynes was unable to reconcile "a competitive system (flexible money wages) with the existence of unemployment" can hardly be substantiated.

Even those, however, who broadly accept Keynes' argument so far, and Dr. Tobin and Dr. Smithies in particular, insist that it is acceptable only on the special assumptions on which the whole model of the *General Theory* was worked out, especially the short-period assumption of constant techniques and equipment, the assumption that consumption is entirely a function of *real* income, the assumption of perfect competition, the neglect of variable factors other than labour, of changes in relative prices and wages, and of the role of Government and finally, the predominantly static character of the model. Their further elaboration of the argument proceeds primarily by an analysis of the consequences of relaxing these assumptions.

Dr. Tobin is led by his analysis to add two further qualifications to Keynes' thesis. First, Keynes' neglect of prime factors other than labour led him to ignore the possibility of substitution of labour for other factors in the event of a reduction in money wages. Substitution will take place, and thus increase employment, unless the other prime factors are totally immune to the "money illusion" which, according to Keynes, is a characteristic of labour. Dr. Tobin's subtly developed argument is unexceptionable. One may yet doubt whether the technical obstacles to substitution in the short period in most modern industries do not deprive this qualification of any very serious significance.

Secondly, Keynes' definition of the consumption function in real terms led him to ignore the possible effects of falling money incomes (with stable real incomes) on the propensity to consume. Dr. Tobin argues that these effects may be expected to be favourable to employment (a) because, if wage-earners in their capacity as consumers are subject to the same money illusion as afflicts them in their capacity as sellers of labour, a decline in their money incomes should make them *feel* worse off and thus tend to raise their propensity to consume; (b) because, if consumers' price expectations are inelastic, a rise in the value of money will lead them to anticipate purchases; while, if they are not, the increase in the real value of past savings will tend to depress wage-earners' propensity to save. Here again, the net effect is probably (though not so obviously[4]) in the direction which Dr. Tobin indicates; but it is hard to believe that this effect would be of practical importance.

As against these two favourable effects of wage deflation, Dr. Tobin points out that, since the assumption of pure competition (or at least a constant degree of monopoly) is abandoned, price rigidity may lead to a redistribution of income in favour of (monopoly) profits which would have an unfavourable effect on the consumption function and employment.

Dr. Smithies, incidentally to his main argument, adds two further points. First, if the role of Government is taken into account, a general fall in money incomes will automatically reduce the yield of progressive income tax and, since some parts of Government expenditure are fixed in money terms, is likely to bring about a budget deficit with favourable effects on effective demand. Dr. Smithies, however, would probably agree that this effect is likely to be more significant in the reverse case of wage inflation (which is in the context in which he raises the point) than in the case of wage deflation with which we are here concerned. Secondly, changes in relative wages between different industries which Keynes's aggregate analysis ignored may have important effects on the propensity to consume though, in the nature of the case, their direction cannot be determined in advance.[5]

It is doubtful whether analysis of this often analysed question can fruitfully be carried further than it has been in these essays. What then are we to conclude? On the one hand, there is no question that the bold thesis of Keynes' formal system that real income and employment are independent of the level of money wages is untenable even in a closed economy. There is a large number of ways in which changes in money wages can, and are likely to, bring with them consequential changes in real wages, real income and employment. What cannot be said to have been shown by Keynes' critics is that these effects will necessarily yield a negative correlation between money wages and employment, or, if they do, that they will be sufficiently certain and significant to justify a policy of wage reduction in a depression. As a theoretical foundation for the "presumption against wage-cutting" Keynes' simplification would seem to emerge remarkably unscathed from the ordeal.

What of the other part of Keynes' wage theory, the proposition that "labour stipulates (within limits) for a money-wage rather than a real wage"?[6] This is a question of fact, not of economic analysis; a matter for empirical verification rather than for theoretical reasoning. The contributors to the symposium seem, on the whole, agreed that Keynes' hunch was sound.[7] As Dr. Tobin puts it, "his denial of the 'homogeneity postulate' for the labour supply function constitutes a belated theoretical recognition of the facts of economic life" (p. 581). Here, too, however, the symposium clarifies a number of issues. It also stimulates one or two doubts about the soundness of the traditional formulation of the thesis.

The most interesting contribution is Dr. Tobin's demonstration that the acceptance of Keynes' postulate about the behaviour of labour does not, as has commonly been held, require the assumption that labour behaves irrationally, that labour is "naively deceived by the 'money illusion.' Judged by labour's consciousness of the cost of living in the United States in 1946, this explanation, if it ever was important, is not now significant" (p. 581). Dr. Tobin mentions at least three major rational (or at least institutional) reasons which would explain a tendency of labour to resist money wage cuts where it would not resist an equal reduction of real wages through rising prices.[8] First, in a system of sectional wage bargaining, a cut in money wages for one section means a *relative* reduction in real wages. Secondly, "the cost of living is a remote phenomenon, apparently beyond the control of organized labour, certainly beyond the control of any single bargaining unit" (p. 581). It is obviously easier to organize strike action against a definite decision by a definite employer to cut wages than for a demand for higher money wages to catch up with a creeping, at best roughly measurable, rise in the cost of living. Thirdly, workers fear that wages will not rise again when prices rise in future. In other words, it is on the whole easier in the face of public opinion to resist a cut than to obtain a rise in money wages.[9]

Here is a convincing rational explanation of Keynes' postulate about the apparently irrational behaviour of labour. Yet it does not altogether allay one's uneasy feeling that Keynes overstated the extent to which labour pays attention to money as contrasted with real wages. Undoubtedly labour does, probably for the reasons just given, resist money wage cuts more strenuously than equivalent reductions in real wages with stable money wages. But is this more than a perhaps slight matter of degree? To Keynes the validity of his postulate was a matter of great theoretical importance. For on it depended his demonstration of the possibility of "involuntary unemployment." Having accepted the classical doctrine that employment is a function of real wages, he had to show that labour, despite its resistance to money wage cuts, was prepared to accept lower real wages. That doctrine, however, as Keynes later conceded,[10] depended on the assumption of short-period diminishing returns and, therefore, on the two further assumptions of absence of excess capacity and perfect competition. As soon as one abandons these unrealistic assumptions, the dependence of "involuntary unemployment" on the willingness of labour to accept a lower real wage falls to the ground. Since an increase in employment is possible without a fall in real wages, labour cannot be denied the right to demand jobs for the unemployed without cuts in current levels of real wages. "Involuntary unemployment" can legitimately be defined, without any reference to changes in the level of money or real wages, as any unemployment which could be absorbed by increasing the aggregate level of effective demand.

A similar point might be made about Keynes' formulation of the labour supply function. Here, too, he retained a "classical" concept without inquiring very seriously whether it was reasonably realistic. Take Dr. Tobin's paraphrase of Keynes' thesis: "Labour does attach importance to the money wage *per se* and more labour will be supplied at the same real wages the higher the money wage" (p. 580). It is one thing to insist that labour resists money wage cuts; it is quite another thing to postulate a smooth supply curve of labour with a certain elasticity in terms of money wages. To reinterpret labour's resistance to money wage cuts in terms of a labour supply schedule which is "perfectly elastic with respect to money wages below the current level," as is commonly done in theoretical models of Keynes' theory, obscures the fact that, after all, wage-earners cannot afford to withdraw their labour from the market as a whole indefinitely. They may resist wage cuts by withdrawing their labour (striking) for a time; but if their resistance is broken they willy-nilly work at the reduced wage. Similarly, it is surely a little unrealistic to represent a situation of mass unemployment in a depression as one in which the supply of labour would increase with increasing money wages. The outstanding fact is that the unemployed are "in the market" regardless, within limits, of the level of money wages. No doubt, the aggregate supply of labour always has a certain elasticity (though, if war experience is anything to go by, this elasticity is rather more likely to be with respect to real than to money wages). But if a bold generalization is wanted, the assumption that the labour supply schedule (representing what happens to the supply of labour when money wages change, rather than the fact that it may be difficult to change them) is highly *inelastic* would seem to fit better into the general framework of Keynesian theory than the conventional assumption of an elastic labour supply schedule. But here theorizing had better stop and make way for further empirical study of how labour really behaves.

Notes

1. *The New Economics: Keynes' Influence on Theory and Public Policy*. Edited by Seymour E. Harris (New York: Alfred A. Knopf), 1947. All page references in this Note are to this volume.
2. Wage theory is the subject of Dr. J. Tobin's essay on "Money Wage Rates and Employment" and, from a rather different angle, of Dr. A. Smithies's essay on "Effective Demand and Employment." It also forms the main theme of one of Professor S.E. Harris's introductory essays ("Keynes' Attack on *Laissez Faire* and Classical Economics and Wage Theory") and of Professor Leontief's essay on "Postulates: Keynes' General Theory and the Classicists." Finally, it is one of the parts of Keynes's theory which is criticized by Professor Haberler and defended more briefly by Professor Hansen.
3. Professor Leontief does not deal with this aspect of Keynes's theory directly, but his general unsympathetic position suggests that he would side with Professor Haberler rather than with the Keynesians.
4. To mention but one point, the fact that nowadays a large proportion of (institutionalized) saving is fixed in money terms may well outweigh the factors mentioned by Dr. Tobin.
5. In a further argument, Dr. Smithies seems to get close to Professor Haberler's position. He argues that statistical evidence suggests that in 1937 money wage increases increased labour's share in the American national income and that this contributed to the subsequent depression, (partly) because prices adjust themselves only with a lag and because during that lag "lower profit rates may become reflected in investment plans and a lower rate of investment in future" (p. 568). This effect, which could only be expected to follow a quick and drastic change in wage rates, is less unlikely in the case of wage inflation than in the case of wage deflation; but in either case, the probability that the new favourable (unfavourable) expectations will be disappointed as prices

catch up surely sets narrow limits to the chances of a decisive effect on the rate of investment.

6. *General Theory*, p. 9.

7. Except Professor Leontief. He attributes Keynes's thesis to the fallacy of short-term interpretation of a time lag which "leads easily to treatment of the lagging variable as if it were a constant. A dynamic relationship between money wages and the cost of living, considered from the point of view of supply of labour, implies the existence of a definite lag between the former and the latter. Hence the short-period assumption that the wage rates are constant" (p. 239). If this means that labour will concede reductions in money wages *following* a fall in the cost of living, it may be right but is irrelevant to the problem with which Keynes was mainly concerned. Keynes's question was whether labour would be willing to accept wage cuts in the hope that these would be *followed* by an equivalent reduction in the cost of living — a very different proposition.

8. Dr. Tobin's list is here rearranged, with some change of emphasis.

9. Dr. Tobin mentions two further, less plausible, explanations. (a) Wage-earners have obligations fixed in money terms (i.e., to some extent they share the attitude of debtors to deflation). (b) If their price expectations are inelastic, workers will resist money wage cuts because the expected future price rise would diminish the real value of current savings out of reduced money incomes. One wonders whether workers are even unconsciously influenced by such subtle calculations.

10. "Relative Movements of Real Wages and Output," *E.J.*, March, 1939.

85

An Exposition of the
Keynesian System*

I.O. Scott

I

The rudiments of the Keynesian system as applied to a closed economy may be presented to beginning students by means of a simple, linear model consisting of six variables, two parameters, and six equations. The variables are Y, C, I, R, M_1 and M_2. Y is the aggregate flow in income during a specific period. C represents aggregate expenditures by the private sector of the community on consumer goods and services. I represents net expenditures by the private sector of the community on investment goods.[1] R, the rate of interest, symbolises the structure of interest rates rather than "the" rate of interest.[2] M_1 stands for that portion of the money supply held for the purpose of satisfying the transactions and precautionary motives. M_2 represents money held as an asset — that is, to satisfy the speculative motive.

The parameters of the model are m and g, representing the quantity of money and government expenditures on goods and services, respectively. These parameters are, consequently, exogenous to the private economy. Changes in the parameters indicate intervention by the government through monetary and fiscal policy.

The system of equations which connect and determine the six variables is:

(a) $Y = C + I + g$
(b) $m = M_1 + M_2$
(c) $C = F(Y)$
(d) $I = E(R)$
(e) $M_1 = T(Y)$
(f) $R = L(M_2)$.

Equation (a) states that aggregate income is composed of consumption and investment expenditures on the part of the private economy plus total government expenditures on goods and services.[3] Equation (b) gives us the

*Source: *Review of Economic Studies*, Vol. 19 (1), 1951, pp. 12-18.

Keynesian classification of money balances.

The consumption function, equation (c), is a schedule of consumption expenditures at various levels of income, where $0 < dC/dY < 1$. The shape of the consumption function depends upon a host of other variables assumed to be constants in the model. These constants include: the community's attitude toward thrift; expectations regarding prices, the supply of consumer goods, and the level and certainty of income; the tax structure; the social security system; the distribution of income and wealth, and the form in which wealth is held; population size and distribution; the extent of foreign trade; corporate dividend policy; education; and advertising.

Equation (d) is the investment demand function, or the schedule of the marginal efficiency of capital. This function shows the relation between R and I. That is, given the schedule of the marginal efficiency of capital, the rate of interest determines the rate of investment. Other variables, for our purposes assumed to remain constant, which determine the shape of this function include: entrepreneurial anticipations with respect to market demand, the algebraic rate of change in the level of income,[4] the community's stock of capital, the rate of innovation, the marginal physical productivity of capital goods, and the tax structure.

The two remaining functions explain the disposition of money balances. The transactions function, equation (e), says that the portion of the money supply devoted to transactions is determined by the level of income. An increase in spending, or income flow, is a manifestation of an increase in activity and, hence, involves an expansion in the community's requirements of money for transactions. The linearity of this function and its zero intercept mean that the velocity of active balances is assumed to be invariant with respect to income. An increase in the slope of the function implies an increase in this velocity of circulation. In addition, the shape of the transactions function is affected by the community's credit structure and system of payments.

The liquidity function, equation (f), shows that the rate of interest is determined by the schedule of liquidity preference and the quantity of money held as an asset. At a low rate of interest, the liquidity function becomes perfectly elastic,[5] portraying the tendency for the rate of interest to be rigid downward at low levels. The shape of this function reflects the community's preferences with respect to the risk and inconvenience which accompany illiquidity as compared with the cost of maintaining liquidity. Any change in the community's expectations as to the prices of assets other than cash will also affect the shape of the function.

It is assumed throughout that the prices of commodities and services are constant, perfect competition reigns in all markets, the stock of capital is quite large relatively to its annual increment, and that the rate of technological change is zero. Then, given values for g and m, the six equations determine the level of income and employment.

II

Substituting $F(Y)$ for C in (a), we may write:

$$Y = F(Y) + I + g;$$

or, since g is a parameter,

$$Y = H(I).[6]$$

Employing this new relation between Y and I, we have a system of equations:

(1) $M_1 = T(Y)$
(2) $Y = H(I)$
(3) $I = E(R)$
(4) $R = L(M_2)$
(5) $M_2 = m - M_1$

which is more suitable for a diagrammatic solution of the model.[7] These equations appear in geometric form in Fig. 1. R, I, and Y are measured out

Figure 1

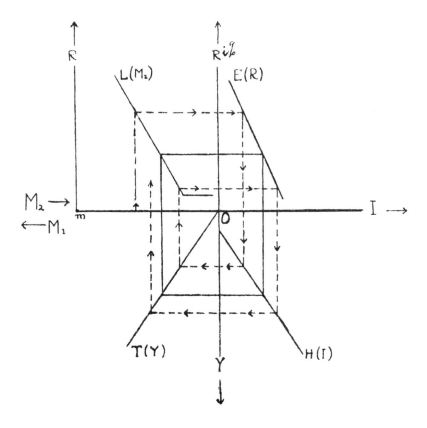

from the origin, 0, in the northern, eastern and southern directions, respectively. Both M_1 and M_2 are measured on the western axis, M_1 being measured in a westerly, M_2 in an easterly, direction. The total quantity of money is given by the segment $m0$. The reader will recognise the schedules drawn in the south-western, north-western and north-eastern quadrants as those which represent equations (1), (4) and (3) respectively. The new function, $H(I)$,[8] appears in the south-eastern quadrant.

In order to find a geometric solution to the model, one may choose at random a point on the $m0$ axis and proceed in a clockwise direction around the diagram until all of the values of the variables are consistent with one another. In Fig. 1 the broken line represents the path to the solution. This line approaches as a limit the heavily lined box, the corners of which determine the equilibrium values of the unknowns.

Let us define:

$$\Delta M_1(t) = M_1(t) - \overline{M}_1,$$

where $\overline{M}_1$ is the equilibrium value of M_1. Similarly, we may set:

$$\Delta Y(t) = Y(t) - \overline{Y}$$
$$\Delta I(t) = I(t) - \overline{I}$$
$$\Delta R(t) = R(t) - \overline{R}$$
$$\Delta M_2(t) = M_2(t) - \overline{M}_2$$

Since we are dealing with linear functional relations throughout, we have from the equations of the model, respectively:

$$\Delta M_1(t) \quad = \quad \frac{dM_1}{dY} \cdot \Delta Y(t-1)$$

$$\Delta Y(t-1) = \frac{dY}{dI} \cdot \Delta I(t-2)$$

$$\Delta I(t-2) = \frac{dI}{dR} \cdot \Delta R(t-3)$$

$$\Delta R(t-3) = \frac{dR}{dM_2} \cdot \Delta M_2(t-4)$$

$$\Delta M_2(t-4) = \frac{dM_2}{dM_1} \cdot \Delta M_1(t-5)$$

By substitution, we finally obtain the algebraic equivalent of the cobweb:

$$\Delta M_1(t) = \frac{dM_1}{dY} \cdot \frac{dY}{dI} \cdot \frac{dI}{dR} \cdot \frac{dR}{dM_2} \cdot \frac{dM_2}{dM_1} \, \Delta M_1(t - 5);$$

or, since $\dfrac{dM_2}{dM_1} = -1$, letting $\eta = \dfrac{dM_1}{dY} \cdot \dfrac{dY}{dI} \cdot \dfrac{dI}{dR} \cdot \dfrac{dR}{dM_2}$, and

compressing one revolution of the cobweb into a single time period:

$$\Delta M_1(t) = -\eta \cdot \Delta M_1(t - 1).$$

The usual assumptions made regarding the shapes of the Keynesian propensities imply $\eta > 0$; therefore the path to the solution is oscillatory.

The first order condition for equilibrium is, of course:

$$\Delta M_1(t) = \Delta M_1(t - 1) = 0.$$

The requirement for stability is evidently:

$$|\Delta M_1(t)| < |\Delta M_1(t - 1)|,$$

or,

$$\left| \frac{\Delta M_1(t)}{\Delta M_1(t - 1)} \right| < 1.$$

But

$$\left| \frac{\Delta M_1(t)}{\Delta M_1(t - 1)} \right| = |\eta|;$$

therefore, $|\eta|$ must be less than unity in order to have a convergent solution.[9]

In the event the cobweb diverges, the equilibrium is unstable. In order to obtain a geometric solution in this case, one would have to move in a counter-clockwise direction, or, alternatively, interchange dependent for independent variables in the original set of equations. Of course, the structure of the economic system determines the causal relationships between the variables and the direction in which the cobweb *must* move. Since the direction of causation indicated above seems more plausible than a causal movement in the opposite direction, we must conclude that such a solution is unstable.[10]

The student may work out the geometric solutions corresponding to various fiscal and monetary policies to his own satisfaction.[11] He is warned, however, that any change in the quantity of money involves an extension or contraction in the $m0$ axis. Since the L function is oriented toward the origin m, rather than 0, it must move accordingly.

III

In order to analyse the operation of the model more completely, equations (1),

(2), . . ., (5) may be expressed in slightly different form, as follows[12]:

(1') $M_1 = \alpha\gamma$
(2') $H\ (I) - Y = -\beta$
(3') $\bar{E}\ (R) - I = -\gamma$
(4') $L\ (M_2) - R = -\delta$
(5') $M_1 + M_2 = m$

An increase in α, β, γ, δ and m will thus denote a decrease in the income velocity of transactions balances, an increase in g or upward shift of the consumption function, an upward shift in the marginal efficiency of capital schedule, an increased liquidity preference, and an increase in the money supply, respectively.

It will evidently be instructive to determine the relationship between each of the variables on the one hand and each of the parameters on the other. Differentiating each variable with respect to each parameter and solving the resulting systems of simultaneous equations, we find:

$$\frac{dM_1}{d\alpha} = \frac{1}{\Delta}, \frac{dY}{d\alpha} = -\frac{H'E'L'}{\Delta}, \frac{dI}{d\alpha} = -\frac{E'L'}{\Delta}, \frac{dR}{d\alpha} = -\frac{L'}{\Delta}, \frac{dM_2}{d\alpha} = -\frac{1}{\Delta};$$

$$\frac{dM_1}{d\beta} = \frac{M_1}{Y^2\Delta}, \frac{dY}{d\beta} = 1 - \frac{H'L'E'M_1}{Y^2\Delta}, \frac{dI}{d\beta} =$$

$$-\frac{L'E'M_1}{Y^2\Delta}, \frac{dR}{d\beta} = -\frac{L'M_1}{Y^2\Delta}, \frac{dM_2}{d\beta} = -\frac{M_1}{Y^2\Delta};$$

$$\frac{dM_1}{d\gamma} = \frac{M_1H'}{Y^2\Delta}, \frac{dY}{d\gamma} = H'\left[1 - \frac{H'E'M_1L'}{Y^2\Delta}\right], \frac{dI}{d\gamma}$$

$$= 1 - \frac{H'E'M_1L'}{Y^2\Delta}, \frac{dR}{d\gamma} = -\frac{L'M_1H'}{Y^2\Delta},$$

$$\frac{dM_2}{d\gamma} = -\frac{M_1H'}{Y^2\Delta};$$

$$\frac{dM_1}{d\delta} = \frac{M_1H'E'}{Y^2\Delta}, \frac{dY}{d\delta} = H'E'\left[1 - \frac{H'L'E'M'}{Y^2\Delta}\right], \frac{dI}{d\delta} = E'\left[1 - \frac{L'M_1H'E'}{Y^2\Delta}\right],$$

$$\frac{dR}{d\delta} = 1 - \frac{L'M_1H'E'}{Y^2\Delta}, \frac{dR}{d\delta} = -\frac{M_1H'E'}{Y^2\Delta};$$

$$\frac{dM_1}{dm} = \frac{M_1 H'E'L'}{Y^2 \Delta} , \frac{dY}{dm} = H'E'L'\left[1 - \frac{H'L'E'M_1}{Y^2 \Delta}\right],$$

$$\frac{dI}{dm} = E'L'\left[1 - \frac{H'L'E'M_1}{Y^2 \Delta}\right],$$

$$\frac{dR}{dm} = L'\left[1 - \frac{H'L'E'M_1}{Y^2 \Delta}\right], \frac{dM_2}{dm} = 1 - \frac{H'L'E'M_1}{Y^2 \Delta};$$

where $\Delta = \dfrac{1}{Y} + \dfrac{M_1 H'E'L'}{Y^2}$.

Making the usual assumptions regarding the Keynesian propensities — that is, $\alpha > 0, H' > 0, E' < 0, L' < 0$ — and assuming $M_1 > 0$, we find the signs of the derivatives determined unambiguously as follows:

	α	β	γ	δ	m
M_1	+	+	+	−	+
Y	−	+	+	−	+
I	−	−	+	−	+
R	+	+	+	+	−
M_2	−	−	−	+	+

With reference to income, this tells us that a decrease in the income velocity of transactions balances and an increase in liquidity preference will have dampening effect; whereas an increase in g or upward shift in the consumption function, an upward shift in the marginal efficiency of capital schedule, and an increase in the money supply will have an expansitory effect. In a similar manner, we can tell at a glance the impact of a change in each parameter upon each of the other variables in the model.

In the first *Keynesian case*, where the interest-elasticity of the liquidity preference schedule is assumed to approach infinity $(L - 0)$, the signs of the derivatives become:

	α	β	γ	δ	m
M_1	+	+	+	−	0
Y	0	+	+	−	0
I	0	0	+	−	0
R	0	0	0	+	0
M_2	−	−	−	+	+

In the second *Keynesian case*, the schedule of the marginal efficiency of capital is assumed to be perfectly inelastic with respect to the rate of interest $(E' = 0)$. In this *case*, the grid becomes:

	α	β	γ	δ	m
M_1	+	+	+	0	0
Y	0	+	+	0	0
I	0	0	+	0	0
R	+	+	+	+	−
M_2	−	−	−	0	+

It is of particular interest to note the ineffectiveness of monetary policy in these two *cases*.

IV

For the sake of completeness, certain of the well-known deficiencies of such a rudimentary income model will be enumerated. In the first place, the model shares with other forms of elementary economic analysis the inaccuracies imposed by a desire for simplicity. The whole range of difficulties involved in the use of a static model for the purpose of explaining essentially dynamic processes is present. The method of employing unexplained shifts in functions — the method of static analysis — leaves much to be desired.

All of the problems of aggregation and capital accumulation are ignored.

Because of the absence of prices, not only the allocation problem, but also the problem of price flexibility — structural and cyclical — fail consideration. The absence of markets compels us to neglect the role of imperfection in determining the level of employment.

Since only the "structure" of interest rates is represented in the model, no account is given of the relationship between long and short term rates. Nor is it acknowledged that liquidity preference actually pertains not only to the relationship between cash and non-cash assets, but to the relationship among all kinds of assets of varying liquidity.

Despite these and other deficiencies, the model may be useful as a basis for further refinement and criticism of the Keynesian system.

Notes

1. "Investment" in the sense of an addition to real capital should be distinguished from "investment" in popular usage which includes the purchase of securities and existing real assets.

2. It would perhaps be more realistic to treat R as an index of the availability of capital rather than as a structure of posted interest rates.

3. Since taxes have not been introduced explicitly, government expenditures are financed by borrowing or by printing paper money. Hence a change in g may effect a change in m.

4. It follows that the acceleration principle appears only implicitly in the model.

5. Inasmuch as a piece-wise linear function has been postulated, this characteristic of the liquidity schedule results in a discontinuity.

6. Any change in g or shift in the consumption function will cause a shift in $H(I)$.

7. After preparing the first draft of this paper, the author benefited greatly from reading an unpublished manuscript in which Professor Goodwin presents a slightly different version of the Keynesian system in diagrammatic form.

8. That $dY/dI > 0$ follows from the hypothetical shape of the consumption function and the identity, $Y = C + I + g$. This slope is, of course, the instantaneous multiplier. It may be desirable to introduce induced investment (equal to some constant times income) into the H function. In this case, the instantaneous multiplier equals:

$$\frac{1}{1 - \text{marginal propensity to spend}}$$

9. The reader may object that η is identically equal to a minus one. However, note that:

$$M_1 = m - M_2;$$

but, in addition:

$$M_1 = T\left\{H\left[E\left\{L\ (M_2)\right\}\right]\right\}$$
$$= \phi(M_2).$$

There are three possibilities. If $\phi(M_2) = m - M_2$, there is an infinitude of solutions. If the equations are the loci of parallel lines, there is no solution. Except in these trivial cases, $\dfrac{dM_1}{dM_2}$ when evaluated

from $M_1 = m - M_2$, will not be identically equal to $\dfrac{dM_1}{dM_2}$ when evaluated from $M_1 = \phi(M_2)$.

10. In the non-linear case, locally linear behaviour will give *stability* in *small* also when $/\eta/ < 1$.

11. The so-called *Keynesian cases* — a perfectly elastic L function, and a perfectly inelastic E function — may be depicted by appropriate assumptions regarding the data of the model.

12. For a description of methods employed in this section, see P.A. Samuelson, *Foundations of Economic Analysis*, pp. 276 *et seq.*

86

The Re-examination of Keynesian Economics in the Light of Employment Experience*

C. Philbrook

If the plenitude of observations since 1940 were equaled by the ease of discovering their total meaning, we should perhaps be able by a few twists of the time series to lay to rest the controversy between Keynesism and old-fashioned orthodoxy. But choice between theories requires the "critical experiment," and one of the most difficult of tasks is the designing of such — especially those of the sort available in the laboratory of history. So it is not strange that students of society — most of us — fall into one or two categories of imperfect scientists. One group, much concerned that the bases of experiment design be sound, rightly devote great effort to exploring the internal logic of theoretical systems but, wrongly from an ideal standpoint, often stop short of discovering new experiments or even of repeating old ones. The other group, in proper eagerness to look at the world in order to know the world, often "settle cheap" with regard to making sure the "experiment" is a significant one, and so allocate effort unduly in favor of observation or statistical manipulation.

Both groups are proper objects of concern, but at present the latter will serve as my whipping boys. I shall not dwell on oversimple conclusions from employment experience, although, however absent they may be from the formal positions of members of such groups as this, they have, one suspects, been rather influential on the climate of thought. (I have in mind, for example, the conclusion that our high employment since the early forties proves Keynes wrong, or that the same thing in its relation to government spending proves Keynes right.) However, with deliberate naivete, I have for the most part followed the "simple" lead and taken literally "employment experience" as the thing from which light is presumably to be shed upon Keynesian economics, and for two reasons. First, this approach has enabled me to run through an exercise which may serve to discourage oversimple "tests" while restating a central part of an orientation making for sound union between

*Source: *Southern Economic Journal*, Vol. 19, July 1952, pp. 21-7.

reasoning and observation. Second, it has furnished me an excuse for bringing up issues which most desparately need to be fought through to consensus.

We cannot, of course, assure ourselves that any theory tells the ultimate truth; and scientific study becomes a matter of trying to discover which of the many theories we can devise is the least bad one — to a large degree a matter of finding which best fits the observations. A critical experiment, then, will consist of an event from which two or more theories respectively predict observable consequences which are different in observable ways.

To agree on predictions from Keynesism, we must agree on what Keynesian theory is; and we shall be lucky if we do not get stalled here. We can presumably agree that, at its most general level, the theory is that income and employment constitute a variable which must adjust until it brings into being a set of values of the fundamental functions — liquidity preference, consumption, and marginal efficiency of capital — which will be mutually consistent and consistent with the quantity of money.

As to substance, it is *not* the stagnation hypothesis, although our "hunches" about economic progress will influence the amount of worry engendered by Keynesian theory. As a theory of underemployment, the essence of Keynes is that, should full employment exist and full-employment savings *ex ante* come to be an amount which, if invested, would drive the marginal efficiency of capital below the current rate of interest, employment would not automatically be maintained, or restored from the decline which would occur. The stagnation hypothesis does dramatize the crucial nature of the position of the curve of marginal efficiency of capital, which, tossed about as it is in the laps of the gods of economic progress, may perchance stand at a level resulting in full employment but by no means need do so and, if it fails, carries in its failure no seed of a cure for the defect.

I therefore assume (1) that, with a constant population, for some time economic progress has been such that the marginal efficiency curve for capital has stood just high enough to absorb full-employment savings at a constant rate of interest and (2) that suddenly this progress declines so that the marginal efficiency of capital curve stands lower and (3) that we are able to observe the facts. The question is, will the consequences predicted by Keynesian theory and those predicted by orthodox theory differ in such a way that each set can be compared with the actual consequences and one or the other be found inferior?

In contrast to the "natural" Keynesian forecast, the prediction presumed "natural" to orthodox theory is that employment would be restored to the old level. (We are, of course, leaping over the painful adjustment, to the new equilibrium expected by each.) But we must tread carefully lest we stumble over assumptions. If we are to find a historical development from which the two theories lead to different predictions, we must make sure it is under identical assumptions that the clashing predictions arise.

In the first place, consider the assumptions concerning the quantity of money.

The assumption "natural" to orthodox theory is that the quantity of money has some lower limit to its contraction. It is probably useful to regard the idea as logically derived from contemplation of a "natural" economy. By this loaded term I mean primarily a monetary garden of Eden in which the snake of acquisitiveness has not yet led us to taste the poisonous fruit of banking. Here incipient unemployment would not drastically curtail the money commodity, and indeed would rather increase it. A constant quantity will represent adequately the old orthodox implied assumption.

The assumption "natural" to Keynes too often slips out of the foreground where it belongs: the quantity of money remains constant in a very special sense — that is, when measured in wage units. Thus, in our hypothetical case if we saw unemployment which we thought reflected "Keynesian" equilibrium and also observed that wage rates fell during the period, it must be true also that the number of dollars fell proportionately; or, if we observed that the number of dollars rose, it must be true also that wage rates rose proportionately.

To look for clashing predictions under identical conditions we must on grounds of monetary assumptions, then, consider two questions. First, with a constant number of dollars would Keynesian theory deny restoration of full employment? Second, with a constant quantity of money in wage units would orthodox theory deny underemployment equilibrium?

Next, as to wage rates, the assumption natural to orthodoxy is some flexibility, and apparently natural to Keynesism is rigidity. However, we need not on this account proliferate our questions. A constant number of dollars along with wage rigidity yields, of course, a constant quantity of money in wage units; and if orthodoxy did not deny underemployment equilibrium where the constancy of money in wage units was achieved in this manner, it would not do so where this was achieved by reducing the number of dollars in proportion as wage rates fell.

Thus, still two questions are necessary. First, would Keynes deny that full employment would be restored if the number of dollars remained constant and wage rates were flexible? Second, would the orthodox deny underemployment equilibrium if the number of dollars were constant and wage rates rigid?

What does Keynesism say of a constant number of dollars and flexible wage rates? Keynes's own discussion, as well as the clear logic of the case, makes evident that, as wage rates declined and the quantity of money in wage units, therefore, increased, the rate of interest would decline to whatever extent was necessary to absorb savings. (The theory under consideration refers, of course, to the "general case" of sloping liquidity preference, and not to the essentially unrelated case where the rate of interest has reached an ultimate "lenders' minimum.") Thus, what liquidity preference will affect is, not employment, but the degree to which wage rates and the price level must fall. One might add a force which common sense calls for, which has been increasingly hard for Keynesians to neglect, and which has been admitted by various Keynesians such as Lange and Lerner: namely, that the increasing value of cash balances must raise the consumption function. Thus, since both theories predict the same thing with regard to employment — namely, its restoration, — then even in a neat world where we found money constant and wage rates flexible mere observation of the employment index would not furnish a critical experiment, a basis for choice between the theories.

There remains the second question, whether orthodox theory would deny underemployment equilibrium if wage rates remained rigid and the number of dollars were constant. Here we seem at least to be approaching an area where critical experiments may be found. For in this context it seems at first, or second, blush fair to hold orthodox theory to an implication that unemployment would not continue, even in a world which was "Keynesian" in the sense that *prices* did not fall. The force to restore employment would be of the following nature. Existing cash balances would, of course, have no greater real value than before the unemployment began. But real and money income would be lower, making real balances a larger proportion of real income than before. This should have effects of two sorts. As to consumption, real expenditure should increase (in relation to the new, lower level). As to investment, part of the cash balances could then be described in old-fashioned terms as uninvested savings — a part made larger by the fall of real and money income; and these would be thrown on the loan market, driving down the rate of interest.

Yet the way is not clear to a critical experiment. In the first place, the leaders of orthodoxy would grant, although Keynes did not rest upon the idea, that the curve of marginal "convenience and security" of cash balances would be less than perfectly inelastic, so that, when the offering of loanable funds drove down the rate of interest, somewhat greater cash balances would be planned for. If so, total expenditure, and hence employment, would not be fully restored. Thus, taking orthodoxy in this "Pigovian" form, we fail again to get a critical experiment. For the issue cannot be assured of hinging upon anything but matters of *degree* of unemployment; and how shall we know what degree of unemployment arising in the conditions under discussion would force acceptance of an orthodox interpretation in preference to a Keynesian, or vice versa? And this point is reinforced by thoughts on expectations, presented below.

It might be supposed, however, that we could succeed, at least if we took as orthodoxy the "extreme" hypothesis that the quantity of real balances demanded is absolutely unaffected by the rate of interest. For, according to this notion, old cash-balance habits should re-assert themselves, and it might appear that employment should be fully restored. But if the demand for capital is quite elastic, as orthodoxy would suppose, then, even though money income were restored, more of it would go to capital and the demand for labor would be lower. Thus, again we are left with differences of only degree, and the questions raised above on such differences apply, as does the point yet to be made on expectations. It seems indeed questionable, then, that we shall derive a critical experiment in terms of employment experience as such.

But perhaps we have merely cleared away the distractions to deriving a test purely in terms of money income, which would serve for at least the more questionable form of orthodoxy. For, if money income stays down, will not any economist-pilgrim seeking an orthodox heaven of theory feel, hot upon his neck, the breath of the Prince of Stagnation? Must he be dragged down to the Keynesian abyss, or will the grace of Pigou, Robertson, and Knight suffice for his salvation? The kindly light should lead, I believe, along at least two paths.

The first path may be approached by asking *at what time* money income would be expected to return to its old level and, more specifically, what is the role of expectations in determining the time. That role is affected by the complex of "exogenous" factors by reference to which expectations are in notable part formulated. Was the constancy of the quantity of money predictable — that is, guaranteed by any element in the institutional framework? How much was the government toying with the idea of nationalized industry, increasing business taxes, encouraging labor monopoly, and doing other things which raise questions about the future of business earnings? And indeed, one ought to add, how much influence was enjoyed by new theories which lent themselves to prediction of permanent depression? Unfavorable elements of these sorts may create stagnation for a period which is of unassignable limit and unamenable to measurement. Before deciding that even the "extremely orthodox" force for income restoration was absent, one would have to satisfy himself that such elements were no stronger than before the decline.

The second path is rough and, I think, not thoroughly marked in spite of the notable pilgrims who have set foot upon it. If saving is done "through the banks," savers are letting their deposits grow. If the banks "pass on the savings to industry," they must do so by expanding the total of outstanding loans — that is, by increasing the quantity of money. Thus a constant quantity of money "as determined by the banks" would not in the first place have sustained money income. Moreover, if the banks had been expanding to match these savings and our case of fallen marginal efficiency of capital developed (or if thrift increased), is there any mechanism (at least in our case of rigid wage rates) through which surplus reserves would assuredly be made sufficient, or through which such surplus reserves as existed would "make their weight felt" to such a degree as to induce bankers to put them to work even at the necessary, lower rate of interest? Before capitulating to the "liquidity-trap" explanation, our orthodox theorist ought to satisfy himself whether there is a banking trap which, to be sure, would constitute a liquidity trap but which would have different bases and call for entirely different analytical treatment from the Keynesian.

The conclusion, then, would seem to be that critical experiment cannot consist of simply observing either employment or money income in the face of that widely feared phenomenon, misbehavior of the marginal efficiency of capital in relation to thriftiness. Obviously this does not close off the avenues of enquiry. Although the two theories permitted the same directional effects, each often presented a different route by which the economy was said to arrive at the end point. When the rate of interest fell with dollars constant, Keynesism said this change was due to an increased quantity of money in real terms in conjunction with a sloping liquidity preference curve, while orthodoxy said the rate fell because savers threw their funds on the market. Keynes thought the brunt of maintaining employment would then fall on the investment effect of the change in the rate of interest, while orthodoxy said that also the increased real value of cash balances would raise the consumption function. Each difference of route is likely to offer pairs of different hypotheses. Each pair of hypotheses may be inspected to see whether the implications of one fit the observations while those of the other do not. The examples cited suggest many statistical studies in which economists are trying to do just that; and all who would be worthy of the tradition of Smith and Marshall, great observers both, must cheer for the effort.

But painful care is required in formulating the question. What much of the endless theoretical controversy is basically about is, what would constitute critical experiments. And the prospects are not always bright either for successfully conceiving these or for carrying them out. Certainly to furnish sound hope of success, careful inspection of the internal logic of the parts of the two theories is necessary. Indeed, I suspect that so far the greater part of such progress as we have achieved toward consensus has come through students' forcing each other to reappraise the significance of "things that everybody knows."

Especially because we cannot be sure when, if ever, we shall by statistics settle all the questions we might wish to, it seems well to expand the theme that it is *critical* experiments which must be sought — that is, questions the answers to which will do some good: let us use theory fully to avoid dwelling on unnecessary issues. We might ask whether the very question of which is the correct theory is necessary. For surely the overwhelming obligation of economists today is to reach the utmost consensus on policy which their individual visions of truth permit. These two theories point to the same policies, provided only that we mean what we say about wishing to maintain a system of free enterprise, while agreeing that downward pressure on wage rates is to be avoided as far as possible.

The essential policies may be indicated under the following heads:

(1) Aggregate demand: control at some level no more inflationary than that needed for a constant price level nor less so than that required by constant wage rates.

(2) Expectations: unmistakable announcement of the aggregate demand rule.

(3) Implementations: (a) the fixing of total government expenditures without reference to unemployment as such, although not without reference to relief of distress as such; (b) for secular increase of money, revenue deficits; (c) for cyclical offsets, open-market operations, with revenue variations aiding

in any case and available for greater use if necessary.

(4) Wage rates: encouragement of practices such that wage rates rise wherever at the current wage the number of workers demanded exceeds the number available, and fall in the opposite case.

A sufficient reason for making public expenditure variation a device only of last resort is that no one — Professor Hansen no more than others — seriously means to *reduce* expenditures when aggregate demand needs reduction. A one-way control is no control; and, by adopting this device with the now-popular perspective, we should be lucky indeed to escape a fair formula for inadvertent development of collectivism: namely, against inflation, raise taxes — against depression, raise expenditures.

As to wage policy, there are those who will wish to regard the essence of Keynesism as consisting of the statement that wage rates *are* rigid and nothing can be done about that. These persons will emphasize that they are realistic, that they are studying "things as they are." This suggests a parable of the staff of mechanics called to inspect a stalled automobile. Imbued with the spirit of realism and so knowing that only ivory-tower mechanics studied ideal or "normal" machines, they, of course, went out and got the facts about this particular machine and took them as given. These facts included that one passenger, because his comfort really was best served by doing so, kept his foot under the accelerator pedal, which therefore could not be depressed. The mechanics' prognostication was that the car could only be pushed about. True, one mechanic timidly suggested that the logic of this machine called for having no feet under the accelerator; but his colleagues, noting the large size and irritable disposition of the owner of the foot, assured him that such a notion was not to be mentioned, since the other occupants could never sufficiently influence the crucial passenger, and customers were already too few to risk making an enemy. The armchair mechanic ventured that perhaps the other occupants could decide for themselves how much they could influence the large passenger, and indeed, if the alternatives were put clearly before him rather than obscured, even the large passenger might yield; but of course this foolish idealism led no one astray from hard-headed practicality.

The reason for the policy of encouraging flexible wage rates is simply that a free-enterprise system cannot long function without it, according to Keynesian or any other reasoning. The much-misinterpreted wage-price spiral has brought that fact nearer home to even many Keynesians. (The evolution of Professor Lerner's thinking should be highly instructive.) A nominally free-enterprise society repudiating the market criterion here must, lacking as it will other definite criteria, eventually find itself in the position to which we seem now to have attained, where no policies adequate to continuance of free enterprise are politically feasible.

If the arguments brought together here are sound, consensus on policy is logically possible. We should like to know as much truth as we can; therefore, let us work toward more, and especially better, empirical studies. At the same time let us not hide in such studies from the even more pressing obligation of trying to see the picture whole. Let us rather gird ourselves grimly and spring to battle in those figurative armchairs where, contrary to public impression, the most strenuous and agonizing of struggles occur. And let us bring the prizes of our struggles together, in conclaves such as this, there to see them torn from us and mangled, to the hurt of our superficial pride, but yet remolded to help make a better weapon against the army of errors which attack us in our search for the means to the good society.

Note

A paper presented at the Twenty-first Annual Conference of the Southern Economic Association on November 16, 1951. For stimulating discussion bearing on the content of this paper, I am indebted to my colleagues, Mr. George M. Woodward, Major Robert L. Bunting, and Professors Thomas M. Stanback and Dudley J. Cowden. Mr. Woodward has increased my debt by his judicious criticism of form.

87

The Re-examining of Keynesian Economics: Comment. (Followed by Philbrook's Reply)*

R. Fels

In a recent thoughtful article, Clarence Philbrook discussed "the controversy between Keynesism and old-fashioned orthodoxy."[1] By "old-fashioned orthodoxy" he apparently did not mean pre-Keynesian or classical economics but rather the reconstruction of pre-Keynesian theory that has been attempted by Pigou and others. Since that reconstruction is too recent to be called old-fashioned and too little accepted to be called orthodoxy, we shall here refrain from using Philbrook's phrase.

According to Philbrook, the choice between Keynesian and Pigouvian theories "requires the 'critical experiment' . . . ," which he defined as "an event from which two or more theories respectively predict observable consequences which are different in observable ways."[2] But "we must make sure that it is under identical assumptions that the clashing predictions arise."[3] In seeking a possible critical experiment, therefore, Philbrook took care to make the assumptions identical, with the result that the two theories yielded remarkably similar predictions.

This should not have been surprising. It is difficult to see how two theories which are logically sound could yield different predictions unless one or more of their assumptions differed. In economics the difference between two competing theories typically is the ease with which they can handle different assumptions — not the same assumptions — and a critical experiment would be one which determines which assumption or set of assumptions yields better predictions. For example, let us take two theories: Keynesism and the quantity theory of money. The essence of the old-fashioned quantity theory of money was something more than the quantity equation; it was the assumption that the quantity of money is constant or at any rate stable. Now we could put the assumption of a constant velocity of money into the Keynesian framework. It would be a little clumsy to do; it would mean that the liquidity preference schedule would be absolutely inelastic; and it would further mean that there

*Source: *Southern Economic Journal*, Vol. 19, January 1953, pp. 377-82.

would be a different schedule for each level of income, with the whole family of schedules related in a certain way. But we do not want to do that if we want to get at the root of the difference between Keynesian theory and the quantity theory. Much of the point of Keynesism is an implicit denial that the assumption of a constant or even stable velocity of money is a useful assumption to work with. Hence, Keynes designed a framework which could permit a different assumption, namely a liquidity preference schedule which has some elasticity with respect to the rate of interest, so that in his system an increase in the quantity of money might lower velocity, though he would not have discussed the problem in these terms. So if we wanted to devise a critical experiment to decide between these two theories, we would want to start with different assumptions about the behavior of the velocity of money, even though we might want as many of the other assumptions as possible to be the same.[4]

But a critical experiment would not be likely to destroy either theory completely. Thus many who, like the present writer, doubt if the velocity of money is stable nevertheless find the quantity equation a useful tool with which to work. The choice between theories in economics often is a matter of convenience rather than correctness. Thus in a recent controversy, Milton Friedman pointed out that he could state his analysis in terms of either Keynesism or the quantity theory.[5] He would have preferred the latter, but since he was arguing against Keynesians he used the Keynesian apparatus instead.

Let us now apply the above conclusions to the dispute which Philbrook discussed. One of the most important differences between Keynesians and Pigouvians concerns a question of fact. Pigou assumed that if prices fall, thus increasing the real value of privately held wealth, the consumption function rises. In this way he and others have tried to revive the classical contention that a free enterprise economy with flexible prices has an automatic tendency toward full employment. Hansen, the well-known Keynesian, doubts if this effect, if it exists at all, is strong enough to matter.[6] If we want to choose between these two theories (if that is the right word), we need an experiment in which prices fall, other things remain equal, and we can observe the consumption function. Pigou would predict that the consumption function would rise significantly. Hansen would predict that it would rise negligibly or not at all. The experiment, if it could be performed and repeated often enough, would settle an issue that has been widely discussed in theoretical literature during the last decade. But it would only determine what assumption should be used by theory, not what theoretical apparatus is "correct."

Towards the end of his article, Philbrook said, "We might ask whether the very question of which is the correct theory is necessary. For surely the overwhelming obligation of economists today is to reach the utmost consensus on policy which their individual visions of truth permit."[7] The present writer feels that the overwhelming obligation of economists is to seek truth, particularly, truth that is relevant to important policy problems. If finding truth contributes to a consensus among economists, that may be well and good, but if the two objectives conflict, surely the search for truth must come first. In fact, too much consensus can be bad. Economics is not like medicine. Physicians may hope to reach a consensus on the diagnosis and cure of a certain disease, but they usually have a single well-defined goal — the health of the patient.[8] In economics the goals are numerous and conflicting. There are bound to be genuine differences of opinion on economic policies. Such differences arise from different value judgments and therefore cannot be resolved by science. If the people are to be properly informed, it is desirable that their different value judgments be reflected among economists. It would be as bad for all economists to have the value judgments of Robert A. Taft as for them all to have the value judgments of John L. Lewis. In either case, consensus on policy problems could be hoped for, but in either case it would be dearly bought.[9]

Method, Implications, and Consensus: Reply to Professor Fels

I had supposed that Keynes, when he inveighed against a tradition holding that a free-enterprise economy with flexible prices has an automatic tendency toward full employment, was speaking of something which actually had existed; and apparently Professor Fels agrees with me after all, for he refers to efforts to revive that "classical contention." In a world in which "modern" and "revolution" are prestige words in intellectual circles, it appeared to me that my term "old-fashioned orthodoxy" might, in the eyes of critics, clothe the contention in opprobrium sufficient to render the term unobjectionable.

Two points concerning method are brought up by my critic. First, citing my faithfulness to the precept that "we must make sure it is under identical assumptions that the clashing predictions arise," he says by implication that on account of this faithfulness the fact that "the two theories yielded remarkably similar predictions" is without significance: "It is difficult to see how two theories which are logically sound could yield different predictions unless one or more of their assumptions differed." My own difficulty is in seeing how there could *be two* theories unless one or more of their assumptions differed. And, since I was discussing two theories, perhaps most readers will have discerned this clue to reading sense rather than nonsense into my words and hence will have seen I was merely stating and respecting the proposition that ordinary principles of experiment must be observed.

The second question of method concerns what a critical experiment might prove, and appears largely in the two paragraphs beginning with the statement that the results "would not be likely to destroy either theory completely." Two thoughts, possibly three, appear in a manner which leaves it hard for me to be sure what is the total message intended. None of them contradicts anything I said — or, as far as I can see, adds anything essential — and I mention them only because the tone of the passage suggests contradiction. The order is selected for my convenience. First, the experiment would determine only which theory — or assumption — should, because it is the more nearly correct, be used. Second, it *may* be that the discussion of the Pigou effect was meant to bring out that a test of two opposing assumptions need not prove critical as between two theories respectively employing them. Third, if I appraise properly the role of the words "convenience rather than correctness" and "theoretical apparatus," Professor Fels' main point here is that the showing of which theory or assumption is better need not determine "what theoretical apparatus is 'correct'": that is, it might remain possible to express oneself in terms which made use of the "apparatus," or language, of the theory believed to be inferior — as in rejecting the quantity theory but yet using the equation of exchange. This matter was of course not at issue in my paper.

Although not for Professor Fels' reasons, it is nevertheless true that the "remarkably similar predictions" from the two theories "should not have been surprising," for the analysis fundamental to my exercise has been available for quite a long time. Still, it is by no means without interest that, under like conditions as to monetary and wage-rate policy, results so similar to those of old-fashioned thinking follow from a theory which was said to constitute a "revolution" and which fostered a general conviction that "free enterprise cannot supply full employment," that downward-rigidity of wage rates is desirable, and that expansion of government expenditure is the natural first resort against unemployment. The lines of thought upon which rests recognition of this similarity establish that the direction of effect of policies flowing from the old-fashioned logic are not denied by Keynesian theory. It follows that if, with respect to other ends, we consider free enterprise to offer the least bad society, we need not for technical reasons use, in order to have satisfactory employment, the now popular devices which will beyond reasonable doubt destroy that system. All economists, Keynesian or not, who believe in free enterprise logically ought to join in advocating employment policies which give the fullest opportunity to devices which least threaten free enterprise, holding back for last resort those which are inimical to it. All economists of both schools, regardless of preference in systems, ought to join in making clear that clashes in end-value judgments, not simply disagreement on technical limitations, account largely for differences in their choices of policy. My paper was largely a plea that members of the profession do their best to make known just how unoriginal, how unsurprising, these conclusions are.

Although the Pigou effect was used merely as the subject of an exercise in the interpretation of critical experiments, I judge that Professor Fels' justifiable intent was, in part, to raise a substantive issue, the role of the Pigou effect in the whole controversy. Little can be said here. It should be recalled, however, that unless the Pigou effect is absolutely nil, Keynesian under-employment equilibrium under the stipulated conditions falls to the ground. Policy argument could go forward over the values at stake in drastically changing price levels; but that there is, with a constant quantity of money, some set of prices which would result in full employment could not be denied. And the policy argument referred to would be irrelevant unless the "orthodox" decided we literally could not trust men with any power whatever to control the quantity of money, even under the most explicit laws. So long as this not unnatural despair is staved off, no one wishes the recipe for employment maintenance to consist of adjusting of wage rates to wild vagaries of aggregate demand. In reasonable policy discussion, the importance of acceptance of any Pigou effect at all is twofold: first, the reciprocal of agreement that a full-employment set of prices exists for any given quantity of money is the concession that for any given set of prices there is a quantity of money which will maintain them; second, to establish firmly that, with any but a mad monetary policy, wage-rate declines relieve rather than worsen unemployment, is to remove an intellectual support from the ideal of wage rigidity which, being a repudiation of market criteria, bids fair to destroy our allocational mechanism and, by inviting upward-pressingness, to render nugatory any aggregate-demand policy whatever.

The far-reaching implications of a finding that the Pigou effect is nil ought to be pondered. If marginal adjustments are not made with respect to the value of cash balances vis-a-vis expenditure, I see no reason to take for granted any of the numerous manifestations of "marginalism" which are integral, not only to the thinking of the "orthodox," but also to that of Keynes, both with respect to the relative pricing process which he assumed and with regard to his theory of employment. The common idea — reflected in Professor Fels' comments — that the conception called the Pigou effect is something new never ceases to astonish me. It is the equilibrating force in the "ancient" real balances theory of the value of money; and, in spite of the textbook verbiage on different "approaches," no theory has been offered which, without resting upon this effect, seriously faces the question of why the observed range within which the familiar oscillations of the price level took place in any period was itself not one thousand times higher or only one-thousandth as high.

My final comments, on truth-seeking and consensus-seeking, must be inadequate. I have hoped to say elsewhere more about policy selection by economists, and apparently such efforts are not uncalled for. If men revere truth above all and seek, in words of Professor Fels, "particularly truth that is relevant to important policy problems," I take it they will be seeking "the utmost consensus on policy which their individual visions of truth permit," of which I spoke, and we shall both be satisfied. I am puzzled, however, by the notion that too much consensus can be bad, although I have often heard it. Uncritical acceptance is bad. But if the truth-seeking of individuals leads them to consensus, they can no more reject the outcome than in the opposite case they could force it. That science cannot say the last word on value judgments is true but irrelevant; if we seriously enter upon policy discussion, we must use such means as are appropriate, even though doing so should class us with that all-but-forgotten man of the academic world, the philosopher. True, "if the people are to be properly informed, it is desirable that their different value judgments be reflected among economists" — but not through special pleading. Each economist must be aware of conflicting values; and the very essence of the study of social economy is a search for mechanisms which will "correctly" adjudicate conflicts in the light of consensus upon higher values.

Notes

1. "The Re-Examining of Keynesian Economics in the Light of Employment Experience," *The Southern Economic Journal*, Vol. XIX, No. 1 (July 1952), p. 21.

2. *Ibid.*, pp. 21-22.

3. *Ibid.*, p. 22.

4. The present writer, who is profoundly ignorant of the physical sciences, suspected that Philbrook had borrowed the term "critical experiment" from them and therefore consulted a physicist. The latter said that in physics the two theories to be tested by the critical experiment would include a number of hypotheses. Some hypotheses might be identical for the two theories, but at least one would have to be different if the two theories are to yield different predictions. If hypotheses are for physicists what assumptions are for economists, the parallel between our discussion in the text above and what this physicist told us is striking.

5. "Comments on Monetary Policy," *The Review of Economics and Statistics*, Vol. XXXIII, No. 3 (August 1951), p. 189.

6. Alvin H. Hansen, "The Pigouvian Effect," *The Journal of Political Economy*, Vol. LIX, No. 6 (December 1951), pp. 535-6. See also Lloyd A. Metzler, "Wealth, Saving, and the Rate of Interest," *ibid.*, Vol. LIX, No. 2 (April 1951), pp. 93-116.

7. *Loc. cit.*, p. 26.

8. An exception occurs when in childbirth the physician can save either the mother or the baby but not both. Here the medical profession encounters the kind of problem typical in economics. They are under no compulsion to reach a consensus about whether the mother or the child should be saved but rightly let those concerned make the decision.

9. In the specific context of Philbrook's article, he is to some extent free of this criticism since he has specified or implied certain goals: full employment, survival of free enterprise, avoidance of downward pressure on wages. We might very well want consensus among economists whenever such a list of goals is handed to us, provided the list is complete and the goals do not conflict. But in fact, the goals are always numerous and conflicting, and choices among policies involve choosing how much of one goal to give up for the sake of achieving more of another.

88

Keynesian Economics in Relation to Underdeveloped Countries*

V.B. Singh

I

Professor Hansen is correct in saying that "the influence of Keynes permeates all official international gatherings grappling with economic problems."[1] It is so because, as Professor Knight says, "the practical significance of economic theory is in the field of social action."[2] Therefore, no wonder that the various specialized agencies set up by the United Nations are busy in applying the teachings of Lord Keynes to the varied problems of contemporary economic life. Hence, the choice of the subject for a discussion before a gathering like this is only in the fitness of things.

The title, probably, is likely to indicate that Keynesian economics had a fair trial in the developed countries; therefore, it should be applied to under-developed countries. This apart, even from the point of view of finding out the directions of its applicability in under-developed countries, it is necessary to know the achievements (or otherwise) of Keynesianism in the industrialized countries. The *General Theory* is the child of the Great Crisis which posed the problem of unemployment in sharp contrast to the conditions prevailing under socialism. Since the General Theory promised an alternative to socialism, it has found a prompt response from an audience which was all too ready to receive such a message. Thus, observes Lord Keynes: "the authoritarian state systems of today seem to solve the problem of unemployment at the expense of efficiency and freedom. It is certain that the world will not much longer tolerate the unemployment which, apart from brief intervals of excitement, is associated — and, in my opinion, inevitably associated — with present-day capitalistic individualism. But it may be possible by a right analysis of the problem to cure the disease whilst preserving efficiency and freedom."[3]

Like the older theories, this is also a theory of equilibrium. But its novelty is that it postulates that equilibrium is possible at any level of employment which depends on effective demand. Another novelty of this theory is that it treats the

*Source: *Science and Society*, Vol. 18 (3), 1954, pp. 222-34.

rate of interest as a pre-eminently monetary phenomenon, determined by the liquidity preference.[4] Hence the rate of interest can be manipulated by the monetary policy of the Government and the Central Bank. In turn these novelties have led to practical policies like the financing of investment by the expansion of the bank-credit, the cheap-money policy and deficit public spending. Lord Keynes himself said that: "the theory can be summed up by saying that, given the psychology of the public, the level of output and employment as a whole depends on the amount of investment. I put it in this way, not because this is the only factor on which aggregate output depends, but because it is usual in a complex system to regard as the causa causans that factor which is most prone to sudden and wide fluctuations."[5]

In the Concluding Notes Lord Keynes wrote that this theory was "moderately conservative in its implications."[6] He accepted "the socialization of investment" as a powerful weapon to fight unemployment and economic stagnation as "it seems unlikely that the influence of banking policy on the rate of interest will be sufficient by itself to determine an optimum rate of investment."[7] But promptly he contrasted such a measure with "socialization of production." "This need not," he wrote, "exclude all manner of compromises and of devices by which public authorities will co-operate with private initiative." "Beyond this no obvious case is made out for a system of state socialism which would embrace most of the economic life of the community. It is not the instrument of production which it is important for the State to assume."[8] To this he adds: "I see no reason to suppose that the existing system seriously *mis*employs the factors of production which are in use . . . It is in determining the volume, not the direction, of actual employment that the existing system has broken down."[9]

Expressing his views on capitalist exploitation Lord Keynes says: "for my part, I believe that there is social and psychological justification for significant inequalities of incomes and wealth, but not for such large disparities as exist today. There are valuable human activities which require the motive of money-making and the environment of private wealth-ownership for their full fruition. Moreover, dangerous human proclivities can be canalised into comparatively harmless channels by the existence of opportunities for money-making and private wealth, which, if they cannot be satisfied in this way, may find their outlet in cruelty, the reckless pursuit of personal power and authority, and other forms of self-aggrandisement."[10]

Therefore, the following characterisation of Keynesianism by Professor Harris seems to be very correct: "Keynes would indeed try to preserve capitalism by ridding it of its parasitic elements: Excess savings, high rates of interest, the hereditary principle and its debilitating effect on capitalism; the preference of the future over the present. . . ."[11] This can be better summed up in Mr. Dobb's words: ". . . he [Keynes] thought he could separate the parasitic elements of capitalism from capitalism itself in order to save the life-blood of the system from exhaustion."[12]

This poses the most important question before us: can there be full employment (even in the Keynesian sense)[13] under capitalism?

Space does not permit any detailed discussion of the problem which is implicit in the above question. A reference, however, may be made in passing to the following arguments advanced by Mr. Dobb in a discussion on this problem.[14]

1. Keynesianism does not take into consideration the basic contradiction of capitalism (*viz.*, conflict between enhanced productive power and profitability), and focuses attention upon measures which are within the orbits of financial and exchange relationships. On the theoretical level perhaps this may not look so serious, but its devastating consequences are seen in the practical sphere.

2. Under conditions of capitalism a level of full employment (or anything near it) is an exceedingly unstable position: "unstable in the sense that a small pressure in either direction is likely to give rise to a rapid cumulative movement, uphill (into inflationary conditions and subsequent collapse) or downhill (into falling production and falling demand)." Therefore, stabilization policies framed in terms of "aggregates (*e.g.* certain investment totals) will be too general and unselective to smother the *de*stabilising tendencies at (or even near) their source." They will fail to control the situation. Pointing out the inadequacy of measures at the financial level, Mr. Dobb says that they "imply (because of their indirectness and remoteness) dealing in terms of aggregates, as well as the converse."[15]

3. The above may be illustrated by an example given by Mr. Kaldor. It so happens that there is a large amount of excess capacity in industries producing capital goods and relatively little in consumer goods industries (or vice versa). Unless the increase in demand is distributed in a manner which will create an appropriate proportion in capital goods and consumer goods, expansion is likely to lead to full capacity output in one department of the industry, while substantial unemployment will remain in the other department. Even if we assume that full employment has been achieved in both the departments, any shift of expenditure between investment and consumption may upset the position and start a tendency to decline in one of the two departments, which will later have its serious repercussions on the other. "Full employment, therefore, not only means a certain level of real income; it also implies a real income of a certain composition . . . [it] presupposes a division of real income between real consumption and real investment in a certain proportion."[16]

4. Connected with this difficulty is the question of the giant monopolies which control industries. These monopolies have in responding to increased demand uniformly adopted the policy of price-raising and thus enhancing or preserving their profit-margins. This has meant that expansion of output has been artificially checked. Motivated by the desire to maintain their profits at the maximal level the monopolies are not likely to listen to the advice of investing in a particular direction. Thus, under capitalism where private

enterprise predominates, the investment by the State will be too weak to influence the main sector. So long as the crisis-breeding tendencies in capitalist economy — due to the conflict between enhanced productive power and profitability — remain, crisis can only, at best, be postponed. It cannot be eliminated. This conclusion is supported by Mr. Kaldor in the following words: "As investment activity continues at a high level, excess capacity of equipment is bound to make its appearance. Once redundant capacity appears, it will be almost impossible to maintain activity undiminished, unless state investment activity is extended so wide as to replace private investment."[17]

5. According to Lord Beveridge and American economic opinion, even under full employment millions would remain unemployed. Moreover, the evidence that is available goes to show that the level of employment which was maintained during the war can no longer be kept intact. In fact, the crisis is being postponed by the production drive in war industries. This supports the view of Lord Beveridge: "the only sovereign remedy yet discovered by democracies for unemployment is total war."[18] This is fatal, especially in the atomic age, to all such values that society ought to preserve. This underlines the argument of Professor Pigou that "the analytical apparatus developed in it [the *General Theory*] is explicitly designed to deal with problems of fluctuation over short periods. . . . Thus, questions about the ultimate equilibrium, if there is one, to which the whole creation moves, cannot be treated *directly* by Keynes's apparatus . . ."[19] (Emphasis not in the original). Elsewhere Professor Pigou adds: "In a moving world, therefore, Keynes's short period equilibrium positions are not the positions which are at all likely ever actually to establish themselves."[20]

Lastly, it needs to be added that the Keynesian concept of the state has not been fully appreciated in relation to the economic policy that it may enunciate. He assumes a state which is not only above the class interests of the conflicting groups — the laborers and the capitalists — but is in the general interest of society as a whole. This assumption is wholly unreal. The class affiliation of the modern state is so vital that it can only work in the interest of the capitalist class.[21]

In conclusion, I should like to quote Mr. Dobb again: "once economic theory is allowed to employ the deus ex-machina of an impartial state, a classless state, actuated by social purposes and ironing out the conflicts of actual economic society, all manner of attractive miracles can be demonstrated, even without the aid of algebra. One might dismiss such attempts as harmless pastimes, were it not that ideas play a role in history, and can not only disseminate the opium of false hopes, but in the cold war of today more dangerous illusions about the grim realities of present-day capitalism."[22]

II

Now, we may turn to an application of Keynesianism to under-developed countries, whose problems are more complex than those of the industrialized countries, where Keynesianism, as we have seen, has not achieved any notable success. Here it may be said in a cursory way that the completion of the Industrial Revolution in certain countries divided the world into two parts: the industrialized (or developed) and the unindustrialized (or under-developed) countries. Among the complex problems of the under-developed countries are: predominance of agricultural and pastoral occupations; export of raw materials and import of mill-made goods; absence of heavy industries and predominance of foreign capital in the others; deterioration and destruction of artisan economy; top-heavy tax structure; lack of integration and existence of "plural" societies; direct or indirect political dependence.[23] These features are also shared by colonial countries — which go with Imperialism.

The wave of nationalism in the under-developed countries has created the desire of having a national economy — which presupposes political independence. On the economic plane it means a vigorous scheme of industrialization round the hub of heavy industries. Be it noted that any scheme of industrialization in any under-developed country cannot succeed unless the present agriculture, which is dominated by small peasant economy, is transformed into an agricultural industry. Therefore, agricultural and industrial development must be dovetailed.

Putting it more simply, it may be said that such a development implies the modernization of agriculture; industrialization; improvement of the technique and organization of artisan economy; cooperative endeavor in every sphere of production (all of this implies emancipation from foreign capital); development of national banking, shipping and insurance; stabilization of prices; guaranteed minimum wages and extension of educational and medical services.[24]

III

Let us now examine the solution provided by Keynesian economics to the problems of under-developed countries. We have already seen that Keynesianism fails to ensure full employment even during prosperity in the industrialized countries. That does not increase our faith in it for the under-developed countries. Moreover, the most important difference between the industrialized or developed countries and the unindustrialized or under-developed countries is that in the latter small peasant economy predominates; production is largely for home consumption rather than for the external market; and so market economy remains relatively under-developed; capital equipment is low and the technological level is almost primitive; consequently the composition of capital is such that fixed capital plays a very unimportant role. In these circumstances the effects of the multiplier are quite different than those envisaged by Keynes. Dr. V.K.R.V. Rao has discussed this problem in one of his recent contributions and it would be fruitful to emphasize the following points:[25]

First, in countries like India the secondary, tertiary, and other increases in income, output and employment do not operate despite the high rate of marginal propensity to consume.

Second, because of the rigidities offered by the economic organization, the primary producers cannot, even if they want to, increase their output in proportion to their income. We may say, therefore, that the income multiplier is higher in money terms than in real terms.

Third, since the marginal propensity to consume is high, the major portion of the increased income would be spent on consumption goods, which will diminish the marketable surplus of the food grains. This will have a serious repercussion on non-agricultural prices. Thus, the forces operating in the under-developed economies neither lead to high income nor to higher employment.

Fourth, the process of economic development can take place on two different levels, and it is important not to confuse these two types of economic development. Firstly, we can speak of developmental processes within a given economic structure. Here the level of economic activity may move from a lower to a higher level without the economy as a whole moving. Secondly, the economy as a whole may move from a lower to a higher stage of economic organization. This would mean structural changes: the replacement of one type of economic organization by a higher one. The Keynesian principles are applicable in the first case and not in the second. Therefore, the desire of the under-developed countries to attain the status of an independent national economy presupposes structural changes, and this aim cannot be fulfilled by Keynesianism.

Lastly, in conclusion, I may say that the environment suitable for the growth of Keynesianism is not to be found in the under-developed countries. Here we have not involuntary but disguised unemployment;[26] not food industry but subsistence farming; not adequate industrial capital but foreign and usurious capital which drain the life-blood of our economy. Hence I should like to say what Lord Keynes himself said about the classical theory: "I shall argue that the postulates of the classical theory are applicable to a special case only and not to the general case, the situation which it assumes being a limiting point of the possible positions of equilibrium. Moreover the characteristics of the special case, assumed by the classical theory, happen not to be those of the economic society in which we actually live, with the result that its teaching is misleading and disastrous if we attempt to apply it to the facts of experience."[27]

Is not this truer of the Keynesian theory than it might have been of the classical?

IV

The above conclusion is also supported by the practical measures that should be taken and the inadequacy of such measures suggested by some Commissions. Be it noted that Articles 55 and 56 of the United Nations Charter make it obligatory for this mighty organization and its members to work for full employment and other allied goals, and the members have pledged themselves to take joint and separate action for the aforesaid purpose. This pledge is based on the conviction that "full employment can and must be maintained within each of the different economic systems under which countries have chosen to live. . . ."[28]

The Report on *National and International Measures for Full Employment* (which did not include any member from the under-developed countries) unanimously assumes that every type of unemployment cannot be eliminated and suggests the desirability of defining the "meaning of full employment in the country concerned in operational terms. . . ."[29] The remaining recommendations do not go beyond fiscal and monetary measures[30] and fail to visualize a program for the development of under-developed countries without the "stabilization of the flow of international investment" "over substantial periods,"[31] which clears the way for the lending countries to penetrate into the borrowing countries. And so the Report suggests that "Governments of lending countries should take direct responsibility for a considerable volume of future international investment."[32]

Another Report by a committee of experts (including representatives of under-developed countries as well) on *Measures for the Economic Development of Under-developed Countries*[33] devotes a chapter to the "Preconditions of Economic Development" and observes that: "Progress occurs only when people believe that man can, by conscious effort, master nature"[34] and concludes that feudal or aristocratic societies do not provide the necessary atmosphere for economic development.[35] Therefore, some of the major recommendations of this Committee are land reforms, abolition of privileges based on race, color, caste or creed and the introduction of progressive taxation,[36] a scheme of industrialization. The Report further recommends that leaders at various levels of society must be prepared to "inspire the masses with an enthusiasm for progress."[37] Such ideals can only be realized through democratic planning.

Similarly, the International Labor Office Report on *Action against Unemployment* specifically recommends that to remove unemployment the countries "have to alter their economic structure, to revolutionize their techniques of production and, above all, to achieve a sufficiently rapid increase in capital accumulation to counteract the depressing effects of a rapidly growing population."[38] "The second method of relieving chronic underemployment is industrialization."[39] Even for absorbing the surplus agricultural labor — which is mistakenly taken to be a symptom of over-population

— remedial measures are to be taken "simultaneously in two main directions: land settlement and industrial development."[40] The Report further recommends that "the speed of industrial development in the under-developed countries will be governed mainly by the supply of entrepreneurship, capital and industrial skill. A basic aim of their policy will be, therefore, to expand the supply of all these three factors of production. A lag in the supply of any one factor would retard the whole process."[41]

The conclusion that follows from the analysis of the Reports of the three Committees mentioned above is that in the capitalist countries a certain type of full employment may be achieved by applying the Keynesian principles, but this is true only for the short period. Even this limited objective cannot be achieved in the under-developed countries without a fundamental change in the economic organization. Furthermore, the problem before the under-developed countries is not merely one of full employment but of an all-round economic development.

V

Now, the question is, how to industrialize the under-developed countries? Here, the application of the Keynesian principles (centering round the spiral of saving and investment) means that in order to raise the level of saving more *net* investment is necessary. But in these countries the per capita real income is low, therefore, only small savings are effected: which in turn, become a limiting factor on higher investment. To meet this situation remedies such as inflation, deficit financing and foreign investments are being suggested. Inflation is the mistress which devours its own lovers. How deficit financing will be a magical solution for the industrialization of the under-developed countries remains to be proved by its advocates. The political aspect of foreign investments is that the borrowing countries have to subordinate — openly or tacitly — their political and social judgments to the lending countries. Moreover, the post-war trend of foreign investment in India shows that such investments are not for developmental purposes but for war needs. For example, Professor Nurkse says: "over 90 per cent of the direct investment in under-developed countries went into petroleum production."[42] Thus in case we assume that the problem of industrialization is *essentially* financial, the under-developed countries would have to face certain rather humiliating economic, political and social consequences.

The alternative theory postulates that industrialization is *essentially* a matter of economic organization and if the people make this choice industrialization can be effected without foreign capital and making heavy sacrifices with regard to consumption.[43] The central theme of this theory is that capital accumulation can be effected by mobilizing the forces latent in disguised unemployment and surplus agricultural labor. Starting with large-scale constructional work we can be in a position to increase our marketable surplus — which according to Mr. Dobb is the single fundamental limiting factor upon the pace of development[44] — and thus reorganize our foreign trade so as to import heavy industry and power-generating plants and these should be given top priority. Thus, the ball of economic development is set rolling and the pace of industrialization is much higher, and also free from violent fluctuations, unlike the former case. We see some countries marching ahead on this path. The essence of this theory is gaining support even in American academic circles and Professor Nurkse's latest book[45] is a testimony to this fact. It is this approach, and not Keynesianism, that promises a solution of the basic problems of the under-developed countries.

Notes

This paper was read before the 36th Annual Conference of the Indian Economic Association, Jaipur, December 1953.

1. A.H. Hansen, *The New Economics* (New York, 1947), p. 143.
2. F.H. Knight, "Realism and Relevance in the Theory of Demand," *Journal of Political Economy*, Vol. LII, No. 4, p. 311 (1944).
3. *The General Theory* (New York, 1936), p. 381.
4. As Lord Keynes says: ". . . the rate of interest is the reward for parting with liquidity for a specified period." *Ibid.*, p. 167.
5. *The New Economics*, ed. Seymour Harris (New York, 1947), p. 191.
6. *General Theory*, p. 377.
7. *Ibid.*, p. 378.
8. *Ibid.*, p. 378.
9. *Ibid.*, p. 379.
10. *Ibid.*, p. 374.
11. *The New Economics*, p. 544.
12. *Modern Quarterly*, 1950, Vol. V, No. 2, p. 129.
13. Cf. A.C. Pigou, *Lapses from Full Employment* (London, 1945).
14. "Full Employment and Capitalism," *Modern Quarterly*, 1950, Vol. V, No. 2, p. 125-135.
15. *Ibid.*, p. 132.
16. N. Kaldor, *Economic Journal*, Dec. 1938. p. 644.
17. *Ibid.*, p. 653.
18. *Full Employment in a Free Society* (London, 1944), p. 112.
19. *Keynes' General Theory: A Retrospect* (London, 1950), p. 3 f.
20. *Ibid.*, p. 62.
21. This point has been fully dealt with by Professor Laski in his *Trade Unions in the New Society* (New York, 1949).
22. *Modern Quarterly*, p. 135.
23. *Proceedings of Asian Relations* (New Delhi, 1948), p. 121 f. See also D.R. Gadgil, "Preconditions for Economic Development," *Indian Economic Review* (Feb., 1952), Vol. I, No. 1, p. 14-20.
24. *Proceedings of Asian Relations*, p. 122 f.
25. "Investment, Income and the Multiplier in an Under-Developed Economy," *Indian Economic Review*, (Feb. 1952), Vol. I, No. 1, p. 55-67.
26. See Joan Robinson, *Essays in the Theory of Employment* (London, 1937), p. 84. United Nations, *Measures for the Economic Development of Underdeveloped Countries* (New York, 1951), p. 7; Bhabtosh Dutta, *The Economics of Industrialization*, ch. iii.
27. *General Theory*, p. 3.
28. United Nations, *National and International Measures for Full Employment* (New

York, 1949), p. 6.
   29.   *Ibid.*, p. 11.
   30.   *Ibid.*, p. 76-81.
   31.   *Ibid.*, p. 54-56.
   32.   *Ibid.*, p. 56.
   33.   *Op. cit.*, ch. III.
   34.   *Ibid.*, p. 13.
   35.   *Ibid.*, p. 13 f.
   36.   *Ibid.*, p. 93.
   37.   *Ibid.*, p. 16.
   38.   *Report on Action against Unemployment* (Geneva, 1950), p. 128.
   39.   *Ibid.*, p. 149.
   40.   *Ibid.*, p. 212.
   41.   *Ibid.*, p. 212 f.
   42.   Ragnar Nurkse, *Problems of Capital Formation in Under-developed Countries* (London, 1953), p. 82-3.
   43.   See Maurice Dobb, *Some Aspects of Economic Development* (London, 1951).
   44.   *Ibid.*, p. 45.
   45.   *Op. cit.*

89

Supply Functions in
Keynesian Economics*

F.J. de Jong

One of the most puzzling elements in Keynesian economics is the nature of the supply function and its place in the macro-economic system. Small wonder that several attempts have been made in current literature to comment on this question. These comments, however, are to some extent contradictory: the result has been that different concepts of supply are presented in Keynesian economics as it now stands.

This paper is intended to present a critical examination and comparison of some of these supply functions in Keynesian economics.[1] Of course, this purpose obliges us to devote considerable space merely to summarising the positions of some authors on the subject, in order to make our own argument more readily comprehensible.

The fourteen points which I have to make are presented in the form of so many italicised "Propositions." These Propositions together form a summary of this article: therefore, no separate "Summary" is appended.

1. A Simplified Keynesian Model

The core of Keynesian Economics is the Principle of Effective Demand. This Principle may be summarised in the widely known graph of Fig. 1, which runs in real units, so that by definition it holds good that

$$Y = p \cdot Y_r \qquad (1.1)$$

where $Y =$ money national income, $p =$ the general price level and $Y_r =$ real national income.[2]

The simplified Keynesian model of Fig. 1 represents two independent and mutually consistent equations:

$D_r = D_r(Y_r)$ macro-economic real demand equation $\qquad (1.2)$

$D_r = Y_r \qquad$ 45°-line $\qquad (1.3)$

*Source: *Economic Journal*, Vol. 64, March 1954, pp. 3-24.

Since there are also two variables, viz., D_r and Y_r, the model is determinate. Point E represents the Point of Effective Demand: it determines real national income $_E Y_r$, which in its turn determines employment N_E *via* the production function $Y_r(N_E, \bar{K}_r)$, where $\bar{K}_r$ represents the stock of real capital in the economy.

Since Keynesian economics is essentially short-run economics, $\bar{K}_r$ is a given magnitude.

For $Y_r = {}_E Y_r$ it holds good that

$$S_r = I_r \, (= BE) \qquad\qquad (1.4)$$

where S_r = real savings and I_r = real investments; this equation represents a necessary and sufficient equilibrium condition.

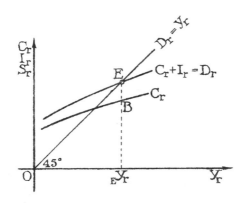

FIG. 1 The Principle of Effective Demand.

Symbols:

C_r = real consumption expenditures;

I_r = real investment expenditures;

D_r = total real expenditures,

$\quad D_r = C_r + I_r$;

S_r = real savings;

Y_r = real national income;

$_E Y_r$ = real national income determined by Effective Demand.

It strikes one that in Fig. 1 no supply curve is plotted,[3] whilst the model is none the less "complete" in the strict meaning of "determinate."

Real national income — and therefore employment — seems to be determined by a one-sided demand theory: thus by something *à la* von Böhm-Bawerk. Apparently we are to think of Keynes as a kind of "macro-economic Austrian economist."

2. The Patinkin Supply Curve

Precisely the latter point was made some years ago by Don Patinkin.[4] I feel obliged to summarise his argument as briefly as possible and only in so far as I need it for the purpose of my own exposition; afterwards this summarised part of his contribution will be examined critically.

Patinkin's criticism of "traditional Keynesian economics" is that two problems have remained unsolved. In the first place the supply side of the system has been neglected, and in the second place the concept of involuntary unemployment has not been defined in Fig. 1 — neither quantitatively with respect to the amount of unemployment, nor qualitatively with respect to the problem why this unemployment should be called "involuntary."

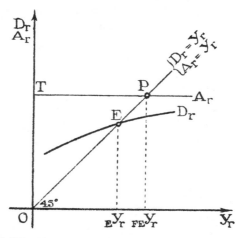

FIG. 2 The Patinkin Supply Curve $A_r(Y_r)$. This curve is drawn here exactly horizontal.

Patinkin solves these two problems together at a blow by means of introducing a supply function — *i.e.*, A_r in Fig. 2 — which he characterises as "the aggregate desired-supply curve"; for the sake of brevity, I suggest calling it "the Patinkin Supply Curve." The function depicted by this curve is obtained by adding up all entrepreneurial micro-economic Walrasian supply functions; it is something like a horizontal — or perhaps somewhat increasing — line.[5] The Patinkin Supply Curve intersects the 45°-line at point P in Fig. 2. Analytically, the model of Fig. 2 runs as follows:[6]

$D_r = D_r (Y_r, p)$ demand behaviour equation (2.1)
$A_r = A_r (Y_r)$ supply behaviour equation (2.2)
$D_r = A_r$ equilibrium condition (2.3)
$Y_r = A_r$ 45°-line. (2.4)

There are four mutually independent equations and also four variables (D_r, A_r, Y_r, p); but, as Fig. 2 shows, the equations need not be mutually consistent; if they are not — as in the case of Fig. 2 — the equilibrium condition will not be fulfilled: the model is indeterminate. In the latter case, point E will be relevant: point P will not be reached.

The economic significance of this inconsistency of the model is in the first place that entrepreneurs are not on their behaviour equations; this means by definition that they do not act "freely," in the economic sense; their desired-supply A_r is larger than their actual time rate of turnover D_r. The result of this fact will be a downward pressure on the price level p. According to the classical outlook as this is interpreted by Pigou,[7] the fall of p will cause the D_r-curve in Fig. 2 to shift in an upward direction until points E and P coincide, that is, until the model is no longer indeterminate. According to Keynes, on the other hand, price elasticity of demand will probably turn out to be too small for any fall of p — provided the price level be reasonably flexible, which is, however, generally not the case — ever to push up point E as far as point P. If effective demand is not enlarged by other expedients, such as, *e.g.*, deficit spending, the model will remain inconsistent. The Patinkin Supply Curve in Fig. 2 is therefore a convenient device for comparing classical with Keynesian economics.

The importance of this device is, according to Patinkin, still further enhanced, since he attributes a second aspect to its economic meaning. Patinkin states[8] that there is full employment if Y_r is so large that suppliers can supply exactly as much as they desire, *i.e.*, OT in Fig. 2. This means that point $_{FE}Y_r$ represents the full-employment level of real national income: $_{FE}Y_r - _EY_r$ is therefore a quantitative measurement for unemployment. Moreover, this unemployment can now be qualified as "involuntary," since suppliers do not act "freely": they are not all of them on their behaviour equations. In this way the difficulties which Patinkin ascribed to "traditional Keynesian economics" seem to be overcome.

So far we have only been summarising the trend of Patinkin's argument. Let us now see whether his solution is valid.

I think that Patinkin's statement that $_{FE}Y_r$ represents the full employment level of real national income implies a jump in the argument. He has obtained his "desired-supply function" A_r by adding up the Walrasian supply functions of all individual entrepreneurs: however, there seems to be no reason why entrepreneurs should "desire" self-evidently to engage all workers available at the prevailing wage-rate. In other words:

PROPOSITION I: *The difficulty involved in the model of Fig. 2 is that it purports to discuss full employment and involuntary unemployment — which are characteristics of the labour market — without explicitly including the labour market in its analysis.*

It is not very difficult to fill up this lacuna. In order to do this, we should start with the supply curve of labour (curve II in Figs. 3 or 4). If $A_r = _{FE}Y_r$ represents the full employment level of real national income, then the value of A_r is the value of Y_r in the production function

$$Y_r = Y_r (N, \overline{K}_r)$$ (2.5)

(where N = employment and $\overline{K}_r$ = stock of real capital of firms, which is a given magnitude), which value is obtained if the value of the *supply* function of labour

$$N = N_{FE}(w, p) \tag{2.6}$$

for any given set of w = wage level and p = general price level, is substituted into equation (2.5).

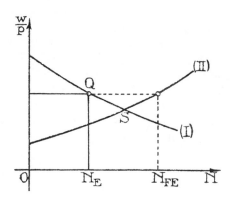

FIG. 3

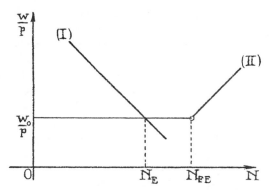

FIG. 4 (I) = demand curve for labour. (II) = supply curve for labour.

Therefore A_r now represents the time rate "people" *desire* to supply (in real terms) at a given set of w and p, the stock of real capital being given. "People" here means suppliers of finished goods plus workers; the supply curve of finished goods obtained in this way — which we may call "the Reinterpreted Patinkin Supply Curve" — is, of course, fundamentally different from the familiar one which is implicit in the conventional theory of the *firm* only.

The A_r-curve intersects the 45°-line again at point P; the ordinate through P meets the horizontal axis at a point $_{FE}Y_r$.[9] This point $_{FE}Y_r$ now indeed defines the full-employment level of real national income, as was required by Patinkin.

Quantitatively unemployment is now sharply defined by the interval $_EY_r$, $_{FE}Y_r$. Qualitatively, this unemployment is involuntary, since not all "supplying people" — especially not the workers — are on their behaviour equations (*i.e.*, their Walrasian supply equations), as can readily be seen from Fig. 3, where point Q is not on the supply curve.[10] But this applies also to the more typical case of Fig. 4, where a number of $N_E N_{FE}$ workers are not on their behaviour equations.

3. The Keynesian Supply Function: Dillard's Interpretation

PROPOSITION II: *Patinkin's complaint that the supply side of the system would have been neglected in traditional Keynesian economics is not legitimate. In the first place, Keynes himself combined an "Aggregate Supply Function"* $Z(N)$ *with his "Aggregate Demand Function"* $D(N)$; *and their point of intersection* — *which is the point at which the entrepreneurs' expectation of profits will be maximised* — *is the point of effective demand, giving the volume of employment.*[11]

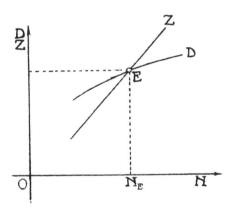

FIG. 5 Dillard's graphical presentation of the Keynesian "Aggregate" Demand and Supply Functions.

Now this passage in Keynes is not very lucid, since it fails to define very sharply *how* this pair of functions is supposed to determine effective demand. It seems therefore that any attempts to comment upon this question must necessarily contain an element of speculation as to Keynes's own intentions. Such an attempt is made by Dillard.[12]

He plots the two functions in a graph — see Fig. 5 — and assumes that each of them slants up toward the right. The point of intersection, E, is the point of effective demand.

His verbal interpretation of the two concepts is as follows. "The aggregate demand 'price' for the output of any given amount of employment is the *total* sum of money, or proceeds, which is expected from the sale of the output produced when that amount of labor is employed." The curve D represents the aggregate demand function. "A certain minimum amount of proceeds will be necessary to induce employers as a whole to offer any given aggregate amount of employment. This minimum price or proceeds which will just induce employment on a given scale is called the aggregate supply price of that amount of employment." The curve Z represents the aggregate supply function. Some pages further on Dillard declares that the aggregate supply price is the same as the total costs of entrepreneurs.[13] Hence, we may now write:

$$F = Z(N) \tag{3.1}$$

where F represents aggregate total costs.

Dillard also says that at the point of effective demand E entrepreneurs maximise their expected profits. But evidently this is not possible in the Dillard version. For in E it holds good that:

$$D = F \therefore D - F = 0$$
$$\therefore P = 0 \tag{3.2}$$

i.e., that in E entrepreneurs' net profits P are exactly zero, whilst for lower values of N the value of P is positive. Hence:

PROPOSITION III: *The Dillard version of the Keynesian Aggregate Supply and Demand Functions cannot possibly yield an exact picture, since the condition that profits are at their maximum at the point of intersection of the two curves is not fulfilled, though this is required by Keynes*[14] *himself and also by Dillard.*[15]

Dillard seems not to have noticed this inconsistency: he does not speak about it anywhere.

There is an easy way out of the difficulty involved by Dillard's interpretation: this way has been pointed out by the Belgian authors Pinxten and Declerq.[16] In order to do full justice to their position, it may be useful to remind the reader of the ambiguity of the term "aggregate" in economic literature. As a matter of fact, questions of merely verbal terminology are seldom relevant. However, even such a point can become important if it seems to be the source of a pitfall in economic reasoning. At first sight, it does not seem impossible that this may be the case here, and it seems worth while therefore to analyse the term "aggregate." This term is used in two different senses:

(1) The Robinsonian sense,[17] where "aggregate cost" is related to "marginal cost," since "marginal" cost is the first derivative of "aggregate" cost with respect to output. Mrs. Robinson opposes her concept of "aggregate" cost to "total" cost, where total cost means the sum total of fixed and variable cost. "Aggregate" and "total" cost may coincide, but they do not necessarily do so; this follows from the fact that one may write:

aggregate fixed cost + aggregate variable cost = aggregate total cost.

(2) The Keynesian sense, where "aggregate" means the same as "macro-economic": the "aggregate" demand function is the sum total of all micro-economic demand functions.

It is certain that Keynes had "macro-economic" demand and supply functions in mind when he spoke of "aggregate" functions: he used the term in the second sense. That he chose to use the word "aggregate" for this concept is, of course, merely a matter of taste — however, I shall not follow him here, since Mrs. Robinson had already used the word with another meaning. But did Keynes also use it simultaneously in the "Robinsonian" meaning?

Dillard thinks so, but we have seen that on his hypothesis the condition that profits are at their maximum at the point of intersection of the two curves is not fulfilled (see Proposition III). So I come to a new Proposition which I take from Pinxten and Declerq.

4. The Keynesian Supply Function: Pinxten and Declerq's Interpretation

PROPOSITION IV: *Dillard's interpretation of the Keynesian* D- *and* Z-*functions should be modified: the condition that profits are at their maximum at the point of intersection of the two functions will be fulfilled only if these macro-economic functions are interpreted in a marginalistic sense.*

This Proposition implies that the Robinsonian sense of the term "aggregate" does not apply here: only the first derivatives of Dillard's D- and Z-curves with respect to N are relevant. Let us call these curves the D'- and Z'-curves. I suggest that the Z'-curve may be called, verbally, "the Pinxten and Declerq Supply Function."

PROPOSITION V: *The idea of Pinxten and Declerq that nevertheless the diagram of Fig. 5 can be left unchanged is, however, not generally valid: the behaviour of the Pinxten and Declerq Supply Function should generally be depicted as in Fig.6.*

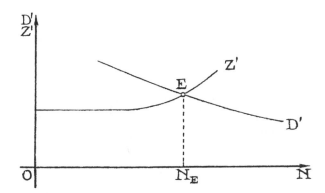

FIG. 6 A new graphical representation of the Pinxten and Declerq macro-economic Demand and Supply Functions.

Indeed, assuming for the sake of simplicity that factor cost involves only labour cost, the Pinxten and Declerq Supply Function can be written as follows:

$$Z'(N) = \frac{d(wN)}{dN}(N) \tag{4.1}$$

In the special case of depression-economics, where w is assumed to remain constant over a certain range of low values of N (see also Fig. 4), this becomes:

$$Z'(N) = w(N) \tag{4.2}$$

This fact is represented in Fig. 6, where Z' is horizontal for low values of N.

5. The Keynesian Supply Function: Fallacies in the Interpretations by Dillard and Pinxten and Declerq

It is clear that the Pinxten and Declerq Supply Curve and the Reinterpreted Patinkin Supply Curve are not identical: the one is not even a transformation of the other. This may readily be seen if we transform the one so that it can be plotted against the other in one and the same system of co-ordinate axes: the two curves do not then coincide. The curve F_r in Fig. 7 depicts a transformation of the Pinxten and Declerq Supply Curve of Fig. 6 inserted into the system of Fig. 2. Some commentary on Fig. 7 may follow here — but let us first of all agree upon a *strictly* Robinsonian use of the term "aggregate" in the subsequent text, in order to avoid confusion. (I repeat, that the attachment of just this meaning to this term is mainly a matter of taste and, up to a point, a matter of convenience.) Therefore, the word "macro-economic" will in the subsequent commentary be substituted for "aggregate" in the Keynesian sense. Figs. 2 and 6 have one common feature, *i.e.*, the macro-economic demand curve. However, this demand curve is drawn in each diagram in a different way: first, Fig. 6 runs in money terms, whilst. Fig. 2 runs in real terms; secondly, real national income is measured along the horizontal axis of Fig. 2, whilst employment is measured along that of Fig. 6; thirdly, the macro-economic demand curve of Fig. 6 is a *marginal* demand curve, whilst that of Fig. 2 is an *aggregate* demand curve. The latter point means that the easiest transformation procedure is obtained if we do not start from Fig. 6 but from Fig. 5: it is easy to see that $D_r(Y_r)$ in Fig. 2 is a transformation of $D(N)$ in Fig. 5, since Y_r is a function of N (see the production function (2.5)), and since $D = P.D_r$.

$Z(N)$ in Fig. 5 may in a similar way be transformed into a curve within the cadre of Fig. 2. The latter curve should be the picture of an equation

$$Z_r = Z_r(Y_r) \tag{5.1}$$

It follows from equation (3.1) that in the Dillard version $F_r = Z_r$, where F_r stands for macro-economic aggregate real cost; hence (5.1) may be rewritten as follows:

$$F_r = Z_r(Y_r) \tag{5.2}$$

which implies the inverse of the macro-economic production function: (5.2) is a macro-economic aggregate (factor) cost function in real terms. We need not concern ourselves here about the empirical behaviour of that function;[18] let us simply draw it as the curve F_r in Fig. 7. One thing, however, is clear: there is no reason why F_r should entirely coincide with the Reinterpreted Patinkin Supply Curve A_r in Fig. 2, which curve is copied in Fig. 7. In abandoning Fig. 6, we lose the Pinxten and Declerq point of effective demand depicted in it (point E in Fig. 6); it now becomes necessary to allow in Fig. 7 for the condition of maximal extrepreneurial profits in a different way; this is done by means of a pair of parallel tangents to the D_r-curve (in point M) and to the F_r-curve (in point N). Point $_MY_r$ in Fig. 7 now represents the value of real national income where entrepreneurial profit expectations are at their maximum: this point is analogous to point N_E in Fig. 6.

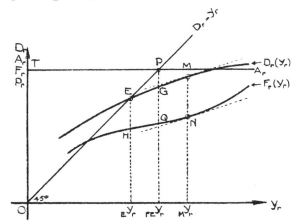

FIG. 7 A Comparison of Some Concepts of Supply in Current Keynesian Economics.

It strikes one that the points $_MY_r$ and $_EY_r$ in Fig. 7 do not necessarily coincide. In other words:

PROPOSITION VI: *The Point of Effective Demand, defined by Pinxten and Declerq* (see point E in Fig. 6 and point M in Fig. 7) *is not identical with the Point of Effective Demand or National Income as this is determined by the equality* $S = I$, *according to Keynes himself*, e.g., *on pp. 64 and 84 of the General Theory* (see point E in Fig. 1, where $S = I$, *i.e.*, point E in Figs. 2 and 7).

Here is a case of trespass against the *principium identitatis*. If this proposition be accepted, then the conclusion must necessarily follow that one of the two definitions of the Point of Effective Demand must be erroneous. Since we have already noted in § 1 that the two widely known summaries of Keynesian Economics by Lerner and Harrod concentrate fully upon point E in

Figs. 1, 2 and 7, and that they do not introduce any Supply Function,[19] it is on the surface that we should expect to find an error leading to the conclusion that point M in Fig. 7 — *i.e.*, point E in Fig. 6 — should be a definition of the Principle of Effective Demand.

Closer scrutiny reveals that the latter argument, which stems from Pinxten and Declerq and — one step farther back, as we have seen — even from Dillard, does indeed involve fallacies. Keynes rightly says on p. 77 that "the volume of employment (and consequently of output and real income) is fixed by the entrepreneur under the motive of seeking to maximise his present and prospective profits," and on p. 55 he informs us that the entrepreneurial profit is due to the macro-economic demand function "taken in conjunction with the conditions of supply"; but these correct statements do not necessarily imply that the point of intersection of macro-economic marginal demand and Pinxten and Declerq supply functions, depicted by point E in our Fig. 6, where the *sum total* of *all* entrepreneurial profits is assumed to be at its maximum, must be the point which is actually reached in this way by entrepreneurial actions (as Pinxten and Declerq do, however, state to be the case). Or:

PROPOSITION VII: *In familiar marginal analysis it is assumed that every individual firm endeavours to maximise its own (micro-economic) profits, but this assumption does not necessarily imply — in the short run, at any rate — that the sum total of all expected profits* (i.e., *macro-economic profits*) *must also be assumed to be at its maximum.*

The validity of this proposition may very briefly and comprehensively be suggested by means of two simple instances, both of them implying heroic abstractions.

First, consider a closed economy with only two firms A and B forming together a heteroduopoly (a duopoly with heterogeneous, *i.e.*, differentiated, products). Both duopolists will aim their strategies at maximising micro-profits. It is conceivable that A makes a move on the economic chess-board which makes A better and B worse off than before, since buyers go over from B to A. Let us assume that in the meantime real national income Y_r remains constant. Now it by no means follows that macro-profits — *i.e.*, the sum total of A's micro-profits and B's micro-profits — have not changed either. The result may very well be that macro-profits have risen, since the increment of A's micro-profits has been larger than the fall of B's micro-profits. Whether or not this result will be achieved depends from the situation and curvature of the micro-economic cost curves of A and B respectively. But whether or not the result mentioned above comes about, micro-profits of A and B are at their maximum *in the given situation* both *before* A made his move and *since* that time. It follows that maximum values of micro-profits at a given level of Y_r and a given distribution of demand over A and B do not at all imply that macro-profits at the same level of Y_r are also at their maximum: a shift of demand from B to A may cause macro-profits to rise.

Secondly, let us assume that in a closed economy every firm belongs to one of two industries A and B, both producing final products, while the market situation in each industry is pure competition. Let us label the sum total of the micro-profits of all firms in any one industry the semi-macro-profits of that industry. Now within any one industry i ($i = A, B$) micro-profits and semi-macro-profits of i move up and down jointly in the short run when demand for i's product rises or falls.

The distribution of macro-economic demand over A and B is in this case, where we have assumed pure competition, not influenced by entrepreneurial strategies: it is merely determined by consumers' scales of preferences, which in their turn are determined by consumers' taste patterns, prices of A and B products respectively and micro-economic money incomes. Let us assume consumers' taste patterns to be constant; changes in consumers' scales of preferences are then determined by changes in prices and money incomes only — that is, by micro-economic real incomes only. Since the distribution of national income among households is a function of the level of national income, we may regard consumers' scales of preference as determined by the level of real national income Y_r (consumers' taste patterns being given). That is, the distribution of macro-economic demand over A and B is a function of Y_r; this function must be regarded as stable, since we have assumed consumers' taste patterns to be constant.

Now, what will happen to the distribution of macro-economic demand if Y_r is allowed to rise continually, starting from a certain low value of this variable? The income elasticity of demand for A will generally not be the same as that of the demand for B. The demand for A may rise faster than that for B. With rising Y_r, semi-macro-economic profits in A and B may continue to rise, though perhaps not equally fast, and macro-economic profits will then continue to rise also.

If we assume as a special case that for very high levels of Y commodity B tends to become an inferior good, it is conceivable that the rise of the demand for B will gradually peter out and that it even begins to fall with further rising Y_r. Up from $Y_r = {}_MY_r$ the decline of B-profits may overcompensate the rise of A-profits, so that macro-economic profits begin to fall. Fig. 7 may be regarded as a picture of this special case; for $Y_r = {}_MY_r$, macro-profits are at their maximum.

The important point which should be borne in mind is that during the entire rise of Y_r *micro*-profits are *everywhere and at any moment* at their maximum — a maximum which is for any individual firm conditioned by its demand and cost behaviour at that moment. It appears therefore that maximum values of micro-profits in no way imply a maximum value of macro-profits. This is exactly what Proposition VII states.

As a matter of fact, however, in the situation depicted by Fig. 7, real national income Y_r cannot rise as far as ${}_MY_r$. Its equilibrium value is ${}_EY_r$: point E is the point of effective demand, since it is the point of *monetary equilibrium*, while point M is not relevant. But even for $Y_r = {}_EY_r$, micro-profits are at their maximum. Hence:

PROPOSITION VIII: *The Pinxten and Declerq version of the Principle of Effective Demand is fallacious: in the picture of Fig. 7, it assigns point M as the Point of Effective Demand, whilst in fact point E is the Point of Effective Demand. Point M is a useless concept.* In other words: Proposition IV is not relevant.

Thus the suggestion made by Pinxten and Declerq fails to rescue the Dillard version. Moreover, it must be conceded as an undeniable fact that Keynes himself uses his macro-economic concepts of D and Z in the *Robinsonian-aggregate* sense.[20] So far as this point is concerned, Dillard is certainly right (cf. the concluding paragraph of § 3), whereas Pinxten and Declerq are not. However, the result of accepting the latter conclusion is that the difficulty pointed out in § 3, viz., that profits in the Dillard version are exactly zero at point E in his diagram (*i.e.*, our Fig. 5), arises once more in its full sharpness. Closer scrutiny reveals that where Pinxten and Declerq have gone wrong is following Dillard in supposing that macro-economic aggregate supply price can be translated into macro-economic aggregate cost. Essentially the same error is made by A.H. Hansen, in *A Guide to Keynes*, New York, Toronto and London, 1953, p. 28. Dillard makes this statement[21] without chapter and verse; but in fact, Keynes contradicts it in the most explicit and lucid manner on p. 24, where he says quite definitely that by supply price he means "the expectation of *proceeds* which will just make it worth the while of the entrepreneurs to give that employment,"[22] whilst he defines *proceeds* as "the aggregate income (*i.e.*, factor cost *plus profit*) resulting from a given amount of employment."[23] That is to say, by supply price Keynes means cost *plus profit*. Furthermore: "The entrepreneur's profit . . . is . . . the quantity which he endeavours to maximise":[24] we must therefore take macro-economic aggregate supply price as the sum total of micro-economic aggregate factor cost *plus* the sum total of micro-economic profits, where the latter are everywhere in the economy at their maximum, which is conditioned by the behaviour of demand and cost functions as seen by individual entrepreneurs.[25] This is the genuine meaning of the Keynesian Supply Curve $Z(N)$ in Fig. 5. In short:

PROPOSITION IX: *The Dillard version of the Z(N) function is erroneous, since it does not allow for the sum total of maximised micro-profits included in the genuine Keynesian Supply Function.*

Let us now focus once again point E in Fig. 5 when this point is taken in the genuine Keynesian sense, and let us try to translate it into the language of Fig. 7. We denote again aggregate factor cost by F and aggregate profits by P; we write the sum total of all maximised micro-profits which are conditioned by the micro-economic sales and supply functions at any moment as P^{max}.

In point E in Fig. 5 it holds good that

$$D(N) = Z(N) \qquad (5.3)$$

that is, in Fig. 7:

$$D_r(Y_r) = Z_r(Y_r) \qquad (5.4)$$

Since

$$Z_r \equiv F_r + P^{max}{}_r \qquad (5.5)$$

we can rewrite (5.4) as

$$D_r(Y_r) = F_r(Y_r) + P_{max\cdot_r}(Y_r) \qquad (5.6)$$

where $P_{max_r}(Y_r)$ is the sum total of all maximised micro-profits at the demand and cost conditions regarded as given by the entrepreneur under pure competition for *any* value of Y_r. The function $Z_r(Y)_r$ indicates the volume of Y_r which entrepreneurs will produce for any value of $Z_r \equiv F_r + P_{max\cdot_r}$. The problem is now how to draw the curve $Z_r(Y_r)$ in Fig. 7.

National income consists of incomes earned by factors of production *plus* profits. Following Keynes in defining national income net of user cost, and denoting entrepreneurs' *expectations* of real national income by Y^*_r, we may write:

$$Z_r(Y_r) \equiv F_r(Y_r) + P_{max\cdot_r}(Y_r) = Y^*_r(Y_r) \qquad (5.7)$$

Now in a strictly static analysis it holds good that

$$Y^*_r = Y_r \qquad (5.8)$$

so that (5.7) can be rewritten as

$$Z_r(Y_r) = Y_r(Y_r) \qquad (5.9)$$

i.e. the 45°-line. It follows that in a strictly static analysis the 45°-line in Fig. 7 is a transformation of the curve $Z(N)$ of Fig. 5. Hence:

PROPOSITION X: *The statement made by Dillard*[26] *that the 45°-line in (our) Fig. 7 is not the same as the aggregate supply schedule* $Z(N)$ *in (our) Fig. 5, is not generally valid. In a strictly static analysis, they are indeed the same.*

The vertical distance between the 45°-line and the curve $F_r(Y_r)$ in Fig. 7 indicates entrepreneurial expected profits $P_{max\cdot_r}(Y_r)$. the latter function shows the volume of output Y_r— and thereby the volume of employment $N = N(Y_r)$ — which entrepreneurs will supply at any value of $P_{max\cdot_r}$.

The function $D_r(Y_r)$ shows consumption expenditures *plus* investment expenditures made at any value of Y_r, *i.e.*, the proceeds which entrepreneurs will *actually* make at any value of Y_r. The vertical distance between the D_r-curve and the F_r-curve shows therefore the profits P_r which entrepreneurs will *actually* make at any value of Y_r. There can be equilibrium only when for some value of Y_r, $P_r = P_{max\cdot_r}$; this is however only the case for $Y_r = {}_E Y_r$ in Fig. 7. "Thus," writes Keynes,[27] "the volume of employment is given by the point of intersection between the aggregate demand function and the aggregate supply function; for it is at this point that the entrepreneurs' expectation of profits will be maximised." It is clear that Keynes meant here by "profits," micro-economic profits. Perhaps an easier formulation might have run as follows: ". . . for it is at this point that the entrepreneurs' expectation of actual profits equals their maximised expectation of profit." We may now conclude:

PROPOSITION XI: *Keynes's analysis in pp. 24-25, as depicted in our Fig. 5, comes exactly to the same thing as the nowadays widely known graphical analysis by means of the 45°-line, as shown in our Fig. 1.*

The curve $Z(N)$ of Fig. 5, interpreted as

$$Z(N) = F(N) + P_{max\cdot}(N) \qquad (5.10)$$

can be called *The Genuine Keynesian Supply Curve*. The 45°-line of Figs. 1, 2 and 7 is essentially a transformation of this curve.

If the comment on Keynes given above is correct, Proposition II appears to rest on firm ground. It may be useful to show the validity of the latter Proposition also for the case of a generalised static Keynesian model.

6. Supply Functions in a Generalised Static Keynesian Model

Several such models have been presented by various authors.[28] I shall take here the one constructed by Don Patinkin;[29] this will provide an opportunity to see what he has to say about his own supply function in the generalised case.

Patinkin presents a generalised Keynesian model of nine equations and nine variables. He divides up the economy into three markets, viz., the market of finished goods including services (consumption goods and investment goods), the labour market and the money market; and within each market he presents two behaviour equations (one for the demand side and one for the supply side, respectively) and an equilibrium condition, as follows.

Market of finished goods:

$$D = E\,(Y, r, p)$$ $\qquad$ (6.1) $\left.\right\}$ behaviour equations
$$Y = Y\,(N_E, \overline{K})$$ $\qquad$ (6.2)
$$D = Y$$ $\qquad$ (6.3) equilibrium condition

Labour market:

$$N_E = N_E\left(\frac{w}{p}\right)$$ $\qquad$ (6.4) $\left.\right\}$ behaviour equations
$$N_{FE} = N_{FE}(w, p)$$ $\qquad$ (6.5)
$$N_E = N_{FE}$$ $\qquad$ (6.6) equilibrium condition

Money market:

$$M_D = L(Y, r, p)$$ $\qquad$ (6.7) $\left.\right\}$ behaviour equations
$$M_S = \overline{M}$$ $\qquad$ (6.8)
$$M_D = M_S$$ $\qquad$ (6.9) equilibrium condition

The nine unknown variables are: Y = national money income, r = rate of interest, p = price level, D = time rate of total money expenditures on finished goods, N_E = volume of employment determined by effective demand (*i.e.*, labour demanded by entrepreneurs or suppliers of finished goods), N_{FE} = full employment (*i.e.*, labour supplied by workers), M_D = stock of money demanded (for active and idle cash-balances), M_S = stock of money supplied (*i.e.*, money in circulation), and w = money wage level.

Equation (6.2) implies the production function. Patinkin now writes that by substituting (6.4) into (6.2) we obtain (what he calls) *the familiar aggregate supply function* (or in the terminology of the present paper: *the familiar macro-economic supply function*); and he has kindly pointed out to the present writer that this is precisely the traditional supply function which is implicit in the conventional theory of the firm. Consider a firm manufacturing one product and having one input (labour), maximising its profits subject to the restraint provided by the production function. This gives us two equations: one stating that the real wage is equal to the marginal physical productivity of labour; and a second, the production itself. We now have two alternatives: we can leave these two equations as they are — and this is what Patinkin has done in his model (see equations (6.4) and (6.2)); or we can obtain the "Familiar Supply Function" by solving out the time-rate of output as a function of real wages — and this is done, essentially, by substituting the demand function for labour (6.4) into the production function (6.2), as was indicated above.[30]

But this argument is essentially a more refined reformulation of, for instance, the passages which I have quoted in § 5 from pp. 77 and 55 of Keynes's book. I think that we are now justified in formulating the following Proposition, which is intended to fortify Proposition II:

PROPOSITION XII: *Keynes's* General Theory *implies the Familiar Supply Function: this is the second reason why Patinkin's complaint that the supply side of the system is neglected in traditional Keynesian economics is not legitimate.*

We may add to this the following, which intends simply to emphasise a point already brought forward by Patinkin himself; though the simplified analysis of Fig. 2 may help in getting across some of the basic ideas involved in Keynesian economics, a more generalised model — for instance, the one reproduced above — should be used for purposes of serious analysis. This model shows very clearly that Keynes followed Marshallian and even Walrasian–Paretian tradition in respect of his theory involving both demand and supply functions.

In summary, we have now distinguished six supply functions in Keynesian literature: the Genuine Keynesian Supply Function, the Original and the Reinterpreted Patinkin Supply Function, the Familiar Supply Function, the Dillard Supply Function and the Pinxten and Declerq Supply Function. However, only the Genuine Keynesian Supply Function, the Reinterpreted Patinkin Supply Function and the Familiar Supply Function appear to be valid concepts.

Only two problems now remain. First, what is the connection between the Patinkin Supply Curve and the "Familiar Supply Curve"?

Don Patinkin states[31] that this Familiar Supply Function differs from what I have called the Patinkin Supply Function only in this one respect, that it is now possible to drop one of the special assumptions made in the cadre of our Fig. 2:[32] that is to say, the two functions are essentially one and the same. If there were nothing more to it than that, the Patinkin Supply Curve would, according to Proposition XII, contain no fresh thought. There is, however, something more to be said, provided we understand the Patinkin Supply Curve in its "reinterpreted" version (see Proposition I and the subsequent text of § 2).

We should remember that the Reinterpreted Patinkin Supply Curve was obtained in the simple model of § 2 by substituting the value of the *supply* function of labour (2.6) into the production function (2.5). Of course, the same procedure may be applied to the generalised model of § 6: in the latter model, the Reinterpreted Patinkin Supply Function is obtained — roughly speaking — by substituting the supply function of labour (6.5) into the production function (6.2).Hence:

PROPOSITION XIII: *The Familiar Supply Function and the Reinterpreted Patinkin Supply Function are fundamentally different: the Familiar Supply Function is obtained by substituting the* demand *function for labour into the production function, whilst the Reinterpreted Patinkin Supply Function is obtained by substituting the* supply *function of labour into the production function.*

Secondly, what is the usefulness of the Reinterpreted Patinkin Supply Function? It was shown in § 2 that in the simplified model of Fig. 2 this usefulness is threefold: (1) it is an expedient for defining unemployment quantitatively; (2) it is a device for defining *involuntary* unemployment qualitatively; (3) it makes the comparison of Pigovian and Keynesian economics somewhat easier.

In the generalised model of § 6, however, its usefulness is less obvious. A potentially existent unemployment has already been defined in (6.6), if and when this equation does not hold (the case of inconsistency of the model): (1) The volume of unemployment is defined by the difference between the numerical values of N_{FE} and N; (2) unemployment is qualitatively defined as *involuntary*, since the actual volume of employment is N_E and not N_{FE}, so that workers are not on their supply function (6.5); (3) the comparison of Pigovian and Keynesian economics is made fairly easy by use of the generalised model: Pigou states that potentially existent inconsistencies of the model will always be ruled out automatically under the influence of price- and interest-adaptations: whilst the position of Keynesian economics is that this result will generally not be accomplished, since price- and interest-elasticities are too small for this.[33] We may therefore conclude that:

PROPOSITION XIV: *The Patinkin Supply Curve, even in its "Reinterpreted" version, is a superfluous concept in the cadre of a generalised Keynesian model: it does not add anything new to the complete system of Keynesian economics.* This is in full accordance with the statement of Proposition XII.

7. Concluding Remarks

Propositions II, XI and XII may be said to constitute the major results of this paper. The other Propositions are of a secondary nature. The serve on the one hand as necessary preliminary remarks and comments on the way to the three main Propositions; on the other, they embody an attempt to evaluate other writers' positions in this difficult and obstacle-ridden field.

Notes

1. I wish to acknowledge my indebtedness to Professor Don Patinkin of Jerusalem and to Mr. R.F. Harrod of Oxford, both of whom have been kind enough to supply me with many valuable suggestions relating to the contents and composition of this paper. However, these two gentlemen are in no way responsible for any defects that may appear in the argument. My thanks go also to the Rev. H.H. Hoskins of Bushey, Herts, and to Mr. N.E. Osselton of Groningen, who kindly inspected my English.

2. Keynes chose to work with "wage units." Though I agree with the opinion on this point recently expressed by J.R. Hicks, *A Contribution to the Theory of the Trade Cycle*, Oxford, 1950, Ch. II, it is not a matter on which I wish to expatiate in this paper.

3. This fact is in accordance with the contents of two widely known summaries of Keynesian economics which had Keynes's own blessing; see A.P. Lerner, "Mr. Keynes' 'General Theory of Employment, Interest and Money,'" *International Labor Review* for October 1936, reprinted in *The New Economics*, ed. S.E. Harris, New York and London, 1948, pp. 113-32, and R.F. Harrod, "Mr. Keynes and Traditional Theory," *Econometrica* for January 1937, reprinted in *The New Economics*, pp. 591-605. In neither article is a supply function introduced.

4. Don Patinkin, "Involuntary Unemployment and the Keynesian Supply Function," ECONOMIC JOURNAL, LIX (1949), pp. 360-83, with an unpublished "Mathematical Appendix," referred to in that article on p. 366 n. The article will be referred to as "Involuntary Unemployment," the appendix as "Mathematical Appendix."

5. In his "Mathematical Appendix," Patinkin points out that special assumptions must be made to obtain this result. However, since these assumptions are not relevant to my further argument, they need not bother us here. Moreover, Patinkin himself writes that the form of the curve is not very important: the one thing which is important is the fact that the curve $A_r(Y_r)$ does exist, and that its slope with respect to Y_r is smaller than that of the curve $D_r(Y_r)$. That A_r is (nearly) horizontal follows from the fact that economic theory does not show that the time rate of desired supply of entrepreneurs depends on national income; but since D_r does depend from Y_r, the slope of A_r must necessarily be smaller than that of D_r.

6. Patinkin, "Mathematical Appendix," p. 6.

7. For a convenient graphical analysis of Pigou's position see Don Patinkin, "Price Flexibility and Full Employment," *American Economic Review*, XXXVIII (1948), pp. 543-64, reprinted, with some modification, in *Readings in Monetary Theory*, ed. by F.A. Lutz and L.W. Mints, London, 1952, pp. 252-83.

8. Patinkin, "Involuntary Unemployment," section 9, p. 370.

9. The Reinterpreted Patinkin Supply Curve may or may not be horizontal. It will be horizontal in so far as w and p $\left(\text{or} \dfrac{w}{p} \right)$ remain constant with increasing Y_r. The problem whether real or money wages are relevant in Keynesian economics will not be discussed here.

10. See also L.R. Klein, *The Keynesian Revolution*, New York, 1947, pp. 74, 87 and 203.

11. J.M. Keynes, *The General Theory of Employment, Interest and Money*, London, 1936, pp. 25 *et seq*. The magnitudes $D = D(N)$ and $Z = Z(N)$ are expressed in money terms; we define here $D = p.D_r$ and $Z = p.Z_r$.

12. D. Dillard, *The Economics of John Maynard Keynes*, New York, 1948, pp. 30 *et seq*. Italics in the subsequent quotation are added.

13. Dillard, p. 37.

14. Keynes, *General Theory*, p. 25, middle of page.

15. Dillard, p. 32.

16. K. Pinxten and G. Declerq, "De effectieve vraag, kernstuk van Keynes' General Theory" (*Effective Demand, Core of Keynes's General Theory*) in the Dutch monthly *De Economist*, XCIX (1951), pp. 721-35, especially p. 728.

17. Joan Robinson, *The Economics of Imperfect Competition*, London, 1933. In the theory of the firm, she is very careful to distinguish "aggregate cost" from "total cost" (pp. 134 and 48,

respectively, of her book). One might well plead for an imitation by other authors of this very useful terminological precision, since it has proved to be very convenient for students.

18.   Nor do we allow for the special assumptions introduced by Don Patinkin in his "Mathematical Appendix," as has been pointed out before.

19.   The same point applies, *e.g.*, to Klein's *Keynesian Revolution*.

20.   See, for instance, pp. 29 and 44-5 of the *General Theory*.

21.   Dillard, p. 37: "Losses will result in either case because the proceeds received by entrepreneurs will be less than sufficient to cover the *total costs (aggregate supply price)* of the higher level of employment." Italics added.

22.   Italics added.

23.   Italics added.

24.   Keynes p. 23, bottom of page.

25.   I pass over in silence the difficulties involved in aggregation problems. It is, however, clear that Keynes's reasoning on pp. 24 *et seq.* is macro-economic, since he states that Say's Law is depicted by the entire coincidence of *D*- and *Z*-curves; this statement can only make sense if the circular flow in the economy as a whole is allowed for.

26.   Dillard, p. 35 n.

27.   Keynes, p. 25.

28.   For instance, F. Modigliani, "Liquidity Preference and the Theory of Interest and Money," *Econometrica*, XII (1944), pp. 45-88, reprinted in *Readings in Monetary Theory*, ed. by F.A. Lutz and L.W. Mints, London 1952, pp. 186-239; see especially p. 188. This model derives from the work of O. Lange and J.R. Hicks. Fundamentally the same model is used by L.R. Klein, "*The Keynesian Revolution*," p. 199.

29.   Patinkin, "Involuntary Unemployment," p. 379. This model comes to the same thing as those of Modigliani and Klein, as can easily be demonstrated.

30.   In the simple model of Fig. 7, the Familiar Supply Function is represented by the inverse of one of its two component parts, *i.e.*, the inverse of the production function in real terms; see curve F_r. When he was discussing his "aggregate supply function" on p. 25 of *The General Theory*, Keynes must, of course, have had in mind the traditional theory of the firm. We may remember that the F_r-curve in Fig. 7 is implied by the genuine Keynsian Z-curve in Fig. 5. We can say that both the Pinxten and Declerq Supply Curve and one component part of the Familiar Supply Curve are depicted by $F_r(Y_r)$ in Fig. 7. Their analytical meaning is none the less essentially different: while in the Pinxten and Declerq interpretation this curve is used in order to let the equilibrium value of Y_r be determined by the maximum of *macro*-profits, its "familiar" use involves just to let the equilibrium value of Y_r be determined by the equilibrium condition $P_r = P\text{max}_r$.

31.   Patinkin, "Involuntary Unemployment," p. 380.

32.   To wit, that the real wage level be constant. In § 2 I pointed out that Patinkin's special assumptions need not trouble us here, since they are not relevant to my argument. I showed also that a constant real wage level would cause the so-called *Reinterpreted* Patinkin Supply Curve to be horizontal (see Fig. 2).

33.   That is to say: this is the position of short-run Keynesian economics as it now stands. Keynes himself was perhaps slightly more optimistic about the interest-elasticity of the investment function; but he was not at all optimistic about price-elasticities.

90

On Keynes' Economic System. Parts I-II*

E. Lindahl

Part I

Lord Keynes' fascinating and important book "The General Theory of Employment, Interest and Money" (1936) probably stands no longer in the forefront of theoretical discussion. Instead, its central lines of thought have percolated to the text-book level, where they are usually clarified by the help of a few simple models. For pedagogical purposes a new model of this kind will be introduced here. It has been simplified as much as possible to facilitate graphic representation.[1]

The system refers to a closed economy and contains the following (macro-economic) variables:

Y : income (net)
I : investment (net)
S : saving (net)
W : wage rate (per unit)
M : volume of money
M_1 : cash balances held for trans-   all these variables are expressed
     action purposes ("trans-   in a constant value of money.
     action balances")
M_2 : cash balances held for specu-
     lation purposes ("specu-
     lation balances")
N : employment
P : average level of prices
R : average level of interest rates

For the determination of these 10 variables the following ten equations can be formed:

---

*Source: *Economic Record*, Vol. 30, May 1954, pp. 19-32 and November 1954, pp. 159-71.

$$R = R(M_2) \qquad (1)$$
$$I = I(R) \qquad (2)$$
$$S = I \qquad (3)$$
$$Y = Y(S) \qquad (4)$$
$$N = N(Y) \qquad (5)$$
$$W = W(N) \qquad (6)$$
$$M_1 = M_1(Y) \qquad (7)$$
$$M_2 = M - M_1 \qquad (8)$$
$$PM = \overline{M}^* \text{ (given parameter)} \qquad (9)$$
$$PW = \overline{W}^* \text{ (given parameter)} \qquad (10)$$

The system of equations differs from the usual variants inasmuch as the values of all variables and consequently also the volumes of money are expressed in a constant value of money; the relation between the magnitudes expressed in a current value of money and those mentioned here are denoted by an index number for the general level of prices (P). This procedure has the advantage that equations stating the relations between the level of interest rates and speculation balances (1), investment and rate of interest (2), income and saving (4), employment and income (5), can be written in a simple way without losing their validity when the value of money changes. Keynes has preferred to measure income and connected variables in wage-units, i.e. in the average wage for the unit of labour in which total employment is measured. It seems, however, doubtful whether this more complicated method of deflation gives better results.[2] Moreover, Keynes and his disciples do not measure the physical volume of money in wage units in spite of the fact that his famous liquidity function — which is the inverse of the interest function (1) mentioned above — has a more general significance when possible changes in the purchasing power of money are taken into account. On the other hand it seems reasonable that equation (7), giving the relation between transaction balances and national income, is valid, regardless of the unit in which these magnitudes are measured. However, in order to preserve the simplicity of the system, the transaction balances have been measured in a constant value of money in this equation also.

A digression of a more formal kind is that income (4) is regarded here as a function of saving, $Y(S)$, while Keynes considers consumption as a function of income and determines income as a sum of consumption and investment. But as investment is assumed to be equal to saving (all magnitudes being ex-post), this is, essentially, equivalent to making income a function of saving.[3] The latter type of relation has been chosen to facilitate the graphic treatment.

Furthermore, it may be observed that in the form of the functions, transaction balances (7) are for the sake of simplicity assumed to be proportional to national income: $M_1(Y) = kY$. The function $N(Y)$ in equation (5) is assumed to be determined by the existing technique of production; the inverse function $Y(N)$ indicates how the total volume of production increases with employment. The function $W(N)$ in equation (6) is best considered as the first derivative of the last-mentioned function, $W(N) = \dfrac{dY(N)}{dN}$; i.e. it gives the marginal productivity of labour and, consequently, the highest real wages employers are willing to pay. No function for the supply of labour has been included in the system. Instead, a given parameter $\overline{W}*$ has been introduced which gives the lowest *nominal wage* workers are willing to accept (10). The total volume of labour supplied can also be considered as a given magnitude: the parameter $N*$. By this construction it follows that the concept unemployment can be determined as the excess supply of labour existing at the current level of wages $(N* - N)$.

As the number of equations equals the number of unknowns, it should be possible to determine the latter, provided that the given functions are of a form and the given parameters have values which make a solution possible.[4]

As to the latter point it should be noticed that the volume of money ($\overline{M}*$) and money wages ($\overline{W}*$) are parameters, the values of which have not been adjusted to each other. It may seem strange to base a theoretical system on such assumptions, but it is readily shown that they are of fundamental importance for Keynes' general construction of under-employment equilibria. Since unemployment is conditioned by a certain disproportion between the fraction $\overline{M}*/\overline{W}*$ and the functions of the system, the value of the above-mentioned fraction at the functions given is too small.[5] If the volume of money is increased in relation to the money wage while the functions are unchanged, we arrive at positions of equilibrium characterized by increasing employment. At a certain relation between the two parameters, the result is full employment and a further increase leads to a position of "over-full" employment. If physical controls of different kinds are introduced (repressed inflation), the latter positions could also be described as equilibria. This reasoning can be illustrated graphically in a simple way (Fig. 1).

As already mentioned, Keynes is mainly interested in cases which result in unemployment, and it is therefore assumed in the following that the relation between $\overline{M}*$ and $\overline{W}*$ is of the type shown in figure 1.[6]

Turning to a more complete graphical illustration of our simplified variant of the Keynesian system, it is convenient to use two figures. In figure 2 the two given magnitudes, the volume of money ($\overline{M}*$) and money wages ($\overline{W}*$) — the relation between them has been assumed to correspond to the unemployment shown in figure 3 — have been introduced as two hyperbolas with a common axis for the price level. The higher the level of prices, the lower obviously are the volume of money and wages measured in real units (M and W respectively). As the decrease in real wages makes possible a greater production and, consequently, a greater total income, the higher level of prices will, at the same time as the real volume of money decreases, cause the demand for money in real units to increase, both for transaction balances (corresponding to the greater real income) and speculation balances (to make possible the lower interest level necessary for the increased investment associated with greater real income). The price level arrives at an equilibrium position when the variables M and W reach values (denoted M' and W') which are assumed for equilibrium between the variables shown in figure 3.

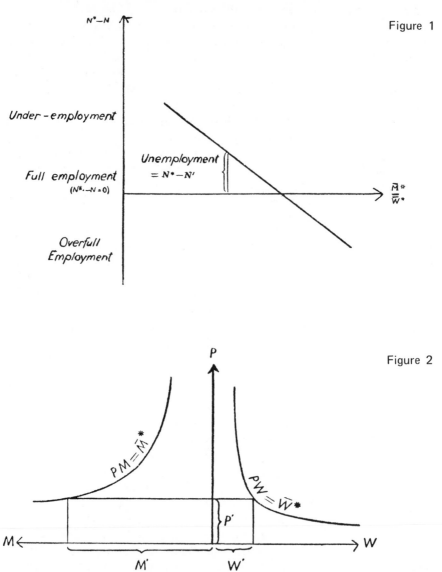

Figure 1

Figure 2

It should be observed that in figure 3 all values are measured in real units. It is convenient to start from a point where the level of interest (R) is determined by a given magnitude of the non-active holdings of money (M_2). The level of interest in its turn determines the value of investment (I) and at the same time

Figure 3

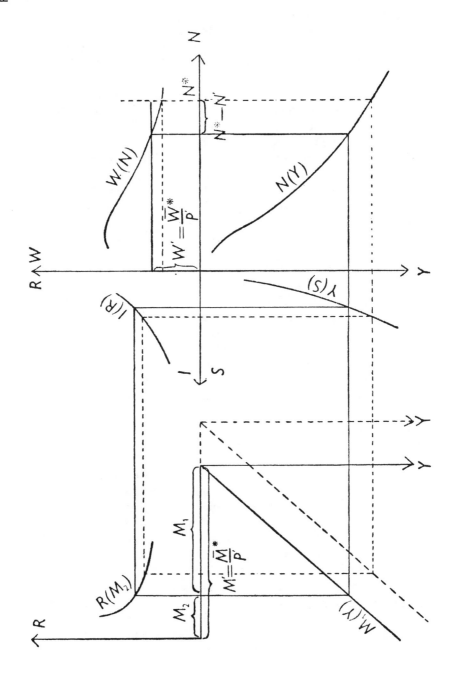

savings (S) which, according to the definitions, equals investment. Income is also determined since it is tied to saving by the relation Y. A certain value of income implies, however, on one hand a given magnitude of transaction balances (M_1) and on the other a given employment (N). Employment being determined, we also know the highest real wage which employers are willing to pay. If the money wage demanded by the workers, the parameter $\overline{W}^*$, corresponds to the highest real wage employers are willing to pay, W', an equilibrium has been established. It is assumed therefore that the price level according to the mechanism clarified by figure 2 reaches a level(P') where this condition is fulfilled, i.e. $\overline{W}^*/P' = W'$. If $\overline{W}^*$ should correspond to a higher real wage than W', this means, as is seen from the figure, that the real volume of money (M) is greater than M' which is equal to the sum of M_1 and M_2. This is not an equilibrium position. An equilibrium is attained only when the price level has risen to the level P' and real wages and real volume of money have decreased correspondingly.

If real wages are lower than W', it is necessary that the price level be lowered in order to attain equilibrium. The equilibrium constructed in this way is characterized by an amount of unemployment ($N^* - N'$) corresponding to the disproportion between the parameters $\overline{M}^*$ and $\overline{W}^*$ which was discussed with figure 1.

In constructing an equilibrium *with full employment* it is necessary to assume a different relation between the volume of money and money wages than above; the volume of money must be greater *in relation to* the money wage. In figure 3 the dotted lines show that full employment equilibrium can be reached with *unchanged functions* and at the *same level of prices*, if we assume both a greater volume of money and a lower level of wages.[7] The greater volume of money is necessary partly because speculation balances must be increased in order to make possible a lower rate of interest and, hence, a greater investment, and partly because larger transaction balances are required for the exchange of the increased national income. On the other hand, the lower level of wages is conditioned by the fact that the marginal productivity of labour decreases with increasing employment. From a traditional point of view this result does not seem very sensational. It is true that Keynes would lay heavy stress on the fact that the causation goes from increased volume of money via a lowering of the rate of interest and increased investment towards greater employment and a lower real wage, and not in the opposite direction which would perhaps be more in keeping with traditional theory. But as we are discussing an equilibrium with simultaneous interdependence of the various magnitudes, the distinction seems rather artificial.

If we drop the assumption about an unchanged level of prices and instead assume that the volume of money is unchanged, a full employment equilibrium presupposes a correspondingly greater lowering of the money wages and a somewhat smaller lowering of the price level. If we assume alternatively that money wages are kept constant, full employment requires that the price level must be raised (which implies a lowering of real wages) and that the volume of money must be increased to an extent corresponding to the increase both of transaction balances (because of the increase of national income through increased volume of production and higher prices) and of speculation balances (because of the lower rate of interest).

In this connection we might also discuss the case in which the relation between $\overline{M}*$ and $\overline{W}*$ corresponds to a position with over-employment (see figure 1), i.e. that the money wage demanded by the workers is lower than the equilibrium level at full employment. The result may either be that the employers, through their competition for labour, raise wages to an equilibrium level or that wages remain on the lower level, the competition between employers being limited through voluntary agreement or by government intervention. In the latter case the distribution of incomes is less favourable to the workers than at full employment equilibrium.

The essential features in Keynes' theory are most clearly shown if we investigate the consequences for income and employment of a change in the given functions. Assume, for example, that the investment curve $I(R)$ is higher than in figure 3 but that other functions and parameters are unchanged. The result is a new equilibrium which differs from the original in the respect that, measured in real units, investment has become greater and income has increased not only by the same amount as investment but also by an additional amount, so that the corresponding increase in saving is equal to the increase of investment; and that employment has been increased to an extent corresponding to the increase of income. A higher propensity to invest is consequently advantageous from the point of view of employment. But that is also the case with a high average propensity to consume. For if a relatively small part of the income is saved, a larger income and consequently also a higher level of employment are required in order to ensure the equality between total saving and the given investment. It also follows that the effect on income of a certain increase in investment — which can be measured by Keynes' investment multiplier — is greater if the marginal propensity to consume is relatively high, i.e. the propensity to save relatively low.[8] If we start from a position of unemployment, it is possible to say that a certain increase of the propensity to invest in relation to the propensity to save — the other parameters and functions being unchanged — leads to a new equilibrium, with income and employment at such a level that unemployment has vanished. The main point in Keynes' theory is probably exactly this that the fundamental cause of unemployment of such a kind as could be observed in England and other countries in the 1930's is that the propensity to invest had become too small in relation to the propensity to save.[9]

Before we proceed to a closer analysis of Keynes' construction we must solve two methodological problems. The first relates to the extent to which the positions treated by Keynes can be characterized as equilibria.

The concept of equilibrium is easiest to apply to stationary conditions when the development during one period is repeated without changes during the following periods. This repetition is explained by the fact that the initial stage during each period is such as to cause a certain final stage, i.e. one which leads to the same initial stage for the next period as during the first period. Despite the fact that causation runs in one direction only, it is therefore appropriate to act, when determining equilibrium conditions, as if a mutual connection existed between the initial and final stages during each period. This justifies the systems of simultaneous equations (without dated variables) which are used in the constructions of such (reiterated) processes.

It also seems reasonable to postulate an interdependence between the variables entering an economic system in the case concerning the determination of the conditions for *correctly anticipated* processes. These conditions are that the individuals have such expectations of the future that they act in ways which are necessary for their expectations to be fulfilled. It follows that the interdependence between present and future magnitudes is conditioned in this case by the fact that the latter, via correct anticipations, influence the former. If we also choose to describe such developments as equilibrium processes, this implies that we widen the concept of equilibrium to include also economic systems describing changes over time where the changes which take place from period to period do not cause any interruption in, but, on the contrary, are an expression of, the continuing adjustment of the variables to each other. The similarity to the former case lies in the fact that here also a system of simultaneous equations can be used. In this case, however, they include all dated values of variables within the time horizon considered.[10]

In the construction of these equilibrium processes it is not necessary to presume perfect foresight in the sense that all economic subjects anticipate the actual development with full certainty. It is sufficient to presume that the economic subjects which have a determining influence in their respective markets have anticipated the actual development as the *most probable* of various possibilities, in which case both their planning and their actions to a certain extent are influenced by the presence of uncertainty (the risk factor). Further, we need not presume that the anticipations should be correct for a long time ahead. But the earlier course of development must have been such as to have generated fairly correct anticipations for the relevant period. The development must, consequently, be so stable that, disregarding exogeneous factors, it does not cause any great surprise in the near future.[11]

Keynes' theory certainly does not refer to stationary equilibria but, on the contrary, shows its limitation in not being very appropriate for a treatment of those positions. As is well known, Keynes explains unemployment as a state where the propensity to save is too great in relation to the propensity to invest and always assumes that saving and investment are positive in the positions treated by him. We can, therefore, hardly believe that these positions remain entirely unchanged from period to period. The continuing accumulation of capital should bring about a successive shift of the income and investment curves which must influence the values of all variables to some degree.

If we wish to denote the positions constructed by Keynes as equilibria, we must examine the possibility of applying the concept of equilibrium in the broader meaning, which was just referred to in the discussion of the correctly anticipated processes. It then becomes evident that the Keynesian constructions can hardly be interpreted in a reasonable way unless we assume that the economic subjects base their actions on a correct (even if not quite certain) expectation of what will happen during the period. How could otherwise an inter-relation be postulated between the variables during the period? In the examination of the simplified system of equations, which has been treated in the previous part, it can be observed that the size of speculation balances influences the rate of interest which, through investment, influences income which, in its turn, influences speculation balances through transaction balances. The circle is broken most easily by assuming that the rate of interest is originally fixed at such a level that the result is the relation between the two types of balances necessary for equilibrium.[12] Of even greater significance from a methodological point of view is the mutual connection between consumption and income which is a very important part of Keynes' theory. If consumers plan to spend a certain fraction of their income during the period, but the income is determined only after the consumption purchases are finished, the only possibility of avoiding the distinction between the expected income which is the basis of the consumption plans, and the realized income, which is the result of the carrying through of the plans — a distinction which the Keynesian school are rather unwilling to use — is to make them equal, i.e. implicitly to assume that individuals correctly anticipate their income.[13]

The question whether Keynes' constructions refer to equilibrium positions has, consequently, been answered in the affirmative, provided that the concept of equilibrium can be applied to correctly anticipated processes. If we let the static theory refer to the determination of the conditions for equilibria or equilibrium processes, Keynes' theory can also be called static.

Figure 4

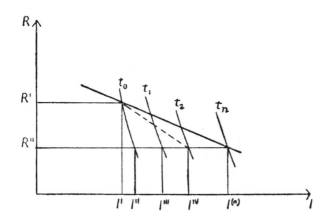

The next question which will be touched upon here is, in principle, of greater importance. It concerns the form of the functions which Keynes uses to determine the value of the variables entering his system. One difficulty which is not always properly considered is that the reaction of one variable to an assumed change of another variable is often *different in the short run and the long run*. If the time factor has not been introduced in the function, various functions can be obtained by varying the assumption about the time occurring between the original and the resulting change. Only certain kinds of these functions are applicable in static theory and, therefore, the character of the theory is dependent on the kind of function used.

The reasoning can best be clarified by an example. Assume that in an equilibrium of the Keynesian type the rate of interest is lowered from position R' to position R'' and that the effect of this on the size of investment is to be examined. It then seems likely that before plans have been adjusted to the changed position and before it is known whether the lowering of the interest rate is temporary or permanent, the increase in investment is relatively small. In figure 4 it has been assumed that investment during this first short period is increased only from I^I to I^{II}. To determine this increase of investment we can use a function which refers to the immediate reactions of the entrepreneurs to various levels of interest at the time t_o (the small steep curve). When the low rate of interest seems to be permanent, the entrepreneurs probably find it expedient to increase successively their investment per unit of time, first to I^{III}, then to I^{IV} etc. This process of expansion may be considered as terminated at the time t_n, when the investment per unit of time has reached the value I^n, a value which can then be expected to remain stable.[14] (To facilitate the following discussion it is assumed that at this point of time a new equilibrium has been reached which implies that the values of the other variables have also been adjusted to the lower level of interest.) It can be seen from the figure that the basis of these successive increases in investment is a shift of the short run investment functions (the small steep curves) up to the time t_n. *The small curve at t_1* indicates that when the interest rate is lowered from R' to R'' entrepreneurs invest the amount I^{III} if the interest rate is kept unchanged during the period, but when a new change in interest takes place they are in this position ready to adjust their investment in the way indicated immediately. The small curves at t_2 and t_n can be described in a similar way.

Apart from these short-run investment functions which, as shown, give the immediate reactions in any given position, we can form other functions which show how a change in the interest rate influences the extent of investment per unit of time, after a certain length of time has elapsed. The dotted line which connects the positions I^I and I^{IV} in the figure can thus be taken as an example of a function which shows how a change of the interest rate influences investment per unit of time after the time $t_o - t_2$ has passed. Further, it is also possible to form a function showing how investment adjusts itself to the interest level in the long run. This function has been illustrated in the figure by the line passing the positions I^l and I^n. Comparative statics refer to a comparison between various equilibrium processes and to an explanation of the divergences between them, commencing with differences between the parameters and functions taken as given in the respective systems of simultaneous equations. In comparative statics we can obviously use only long-run functions and, furthermore, only those of a certain kind; all values of variables must refer to stationary or correctly anticipated conditions, as otherwise we have no right to postulate a relation of interdependence between them. Functions of this type could be denoted as *static long-run functions*. (In figure 4 the long curve is, as has been stated earlier, an example of these functions.) In another branch of theory we can study the character of a given equilibrium, e.g. in which respects it is stable or unstable, by examining the immediate reactions to certain assumed changes. Here short-run functions should, naturally, be used, but only those which refer to the equilibrium in question. They can be called *static short-run functions*. (In the figure they are represented by the steep curves which refer to the points of time t_o and t_n.)

Starting from this important distinction between static long-run and short-run functions — which in earlier static theory was as a rule neglected by disregarding the element of time — it can be maintained that systems of simultaneous equations of the Keynesian type can be of two different kinds:

(1) Systems of static *long-run functions* which make it possible to apply the methods of comparative statics. From a system of this kind it can be seen which equilibrium corresponds to assumptions made regarding parameters and functions and how the equilibrium is shifted when these assumptions are changed. Nevertheless it is not possible to draw any definite conclusions from the system regarding the immediate effect of an assumed change of parameters or functions.

(2) Systems of static *short-run functions* which can be used only in a study of the directions of the movements initiated by an assumed change of the parameters or functions in the equilibrium situation to which the system refers. With this type of system we must start from an equilibrium (which can be determined according to the above-mentioned method) and choose the short-run functions which are valid at this position. The equilibrium situation therefore is fundamental in relation to the functions. If equilibrium is upset, for example through a change in parameters, the functions will be successively modified to a greater or lesser degree.[15] A new equilibrium in this case cannot be constructed with the aid of the original system of functions. But this system is a good starting point for the determination of the dynamic process which is induced by the disturbance of equilibrium and which in some cases may move towards a new equilibrium.

These two types of equilibrium systems show great similarities from a formal point of view: the equation systems can be built in the same way; their solution represents in both cases equilibrium positions; and if the systems are correlated, the long-run equilibrium is identical with the short-run equilibrium.

It is, therefore, important to observe that the two systems have qualities so essentially different that they serve entirely different purposes: the long-run system to determine the conditions for an equilibrium and the short-run system to determine the directions of movement from an equilibrium. It follows that the systems are complementary to each other in a useful way, and both have their given places in a rational theoretical structure. It is, however, clear that it should also contain connecting parts of a dynamic character, for it is not of very great use to know the conditions and the properties of a desirable equilibrium if we do not know the possible paths towards it.

It is remarkable that the Keynesian school has as a rule not realized, or in any case has not attached much weight to, the distinction which we have here tried to clarify. Their procedure frequently seems to combine in the same system some short-run functions (usually the interest and investment functions) and some long-run functions (especially the important consumption function or, as it has been formulated here, income as a function of saving). Commencing from this mixed system which is of little value for analysis and at any rate very difficult to handle, conclusions are sometimes drawn concerning the conditions for various equilibria (which presupposes a purely long-run system) and sometimes conclusions concerning the directions of movement from given positions (which presupposes only short-run functions). Such conclusions must naturally be more or less debatable. This criticism concerns particularly the great multitude of Keynes' more uncritical followers who interpreted and represented the master's ideas without the many qualifications that he himself had made with his strong sense of realism.

In the following we shall outline the consequences for the Keynesian constructions involved in making a clear distinction between static long-run and short-run functions.

Part II

I

When in the first part of this paper an attempt was made to give an easily comprehensible representation of Keynes' system, it was assumed that the system was of the *long-run type* which is used in comparative statics for the determination of equilibria. The question of whether the fundamental assumptions of the system concerning parameters and functions were consistent with this assumption was not touched upon in that connection. We will now discuss from various points of view this question and the possibility of certain modifications in the construction of the system.

An important assumption which is decisive for the construction of the whole system is that money wages and not *real wages* are a given parameter.[16] This assumption is undeniably justified in a short-run system which is used for a study of the immediate reactions in a certain position. Like other economic subjects the workers are to a certain extent captured by "the money illusion": a certain benefit in cash often weighs heavier than the same benefit in the form of lower prices of consumption goods and usually resistance is stronger against a decrease in real wages which is connected with a lowering of money wages than against a decrease which is caused by higher cost of living. But from this the conclusion must not be drawn that workers are, also in the long run, insensitive to the changes in real wages at given money wages, which is assumed in Keynes' system in its usual form. In any case it has been instanced that during the latest years of inflation, when higher costs of living have almost always provoked compensating demands for wages, the workers' final resort is to aim at the maintenance of a certain level of real wages. It is, however, not denied that money wages have as a rule shown themselves inflexible in the other direction and that instances are not lacking of the difficulties of adjusting money wages downwards with a falling price level. But in the construction of a static equilibrium which should be maintained for several periods during which workers will certainly have time to become conscious of the relation between money wages and real wages, it seems most reasonable in the first place to treat the case where real wages are given.

Let us therefore examine the consequences for the system if in the system of equations formerly treated, equation (10) stating that money wages are a parameter ($PW = \overline{W}*$), is replaced by a new equation $W = W*$ (11), which states that real wages are given, while the other assumptions are unchanged for the time being. Let us also assume that at the given real wage — which can be assumed to be guaranteed by an index clause in the wage agreement or even, as in Australia and New Zealand, to be regulated by law — the same amount of labour power ($N*$) is available as in the former case at the given money wage.

Returning to Fig. 3 where all values have been expressed in real units and allowing W' to represent the given real wage ($W*$),[17] we find that this line intersects the curve $W(N)$ — which indicates the highest real wages which entrepreneurs are willing to pay at various levels of employment — at a point where employment has been limited to N' and a certain unemployment ($N-N'$) exists. The question now is what this point of intersection actually means. From the point of view of "classical theory" it undoubtedly gives the equilibrium in the labour market. Could Keynes arrive at any other result from his starting points? In his system the demand for labour is not a function of wages but of real national income, which as a sum of consumption and investment, is determined by the consumption (or saving) function, the investment function, the interest function, and the division of the given volume of money into transaction and speculation balances. Only when we determine the relation between these two kinds of balances, does the money wage enter the picture, as the volume of transaction balances is dependent on the price level, for which the money wage is one of the determining factors. If the money wage had not been given, the price level could have had any height within the limits conditioned by possible redistributions between the two kinds of balances. In the same way, different positions of the rate of interest and investment would have been possible and consequently also different levels of income and employment. The connection between the wage level and employment becomes in this way less direct than in classical theory. But the whole of this construction relies upon the fact that the *money* wage is given. If the *real* wage instead is introduced as a parameter in the system, it seems difficult to avoid the consequence, that employment is immediately determined by the level of wages even though the determination takes place within the frame of a system of simultaneous equations.

If we first consider a position with higher employment than N' which corresponds to the given real wage W', it can be asserted that this is not an equilibrium. It can be assumed that entrepreneurs, who in these cases consider themselves losing by the marginal production, try to compensate this by higher prices. But since under the assumption of the constancy of the real wage money wages follow in the rise, the result is an inflationary movement which increases the demand for transaction balances and thus diminishes speculation balances with an increase in the interest level as a consequence. As a result, investment and total income decrease and employment is lowered and perhaps becomes even lower than N'. But nor do positions with lower employment than N' seem to represent a real equilibrium. Production is now at a lower level than before, and at the same time the price level and also money wages develop a tendency to fall. The result of this is a reduction of transaction balances and an increase in speculation balances which in its turn brings about a lowering of the interest rate and an increase in investment. Through this process the position is again shifted in the direction of greater income and higher employment. Even from Keynes' own starting-point one necessarily arrives at the conclusion that the position of equilibrium must coincide with the point of intersection of the curves of which one indicates the highest real wage the entrepreneurs are willing to pay (the curve $W(N)$) and the other the lowest real wage the workers are willing to accept (the line W') at different levels of employment. The short treatment Keynes himself has given does not seem to contradict this interpretation of his theory.[18]

As the real wage replaces the money wage as a parameter, Keynes' theory becomes very similar to the "classical" one, according to which the point of intersection between the curves mentioned above represents equilibrium in the labour market. According to both theories, lower real wages would make higher employment possible. And in both these systems the actual volume of money ($\overline{M}*$) has no other function than to determine, together with other factors, the absolute level of prices by the formula $P = \overline{M}*/M$ (cf. equation (9)) in Keynes' system and by similar relations in the classical system.

Lawrence R. Klein, who has given his otherwise very instructive book on Keynes the title *The Keynesian Revolution* (1947), and has been anxious to stress the distinctive features in the Keynesian system, has tried to defend the thesis that from Keynes' assumptions it is possible to arrive at another equilibrium than the traditional one, even if the supply of labour is conceived as determined by real wages.[19] Here, however, he starts from the *special* variant of the theory, according to which unemployment in a given position cannot be eliminated by a lowering of the real wage because the investment function $I(R)$ is too inelastic and/or the liquidity function $M_2(R)$ is too elastic. Consequently an increase in speculation balances would not lead to a lowering of the interest rate, and even if a lowering of the rate did evolve, the result would not be an increase in investment. We can, therefore, accept the income and employment which are results of the lowered level of investment, even if there should be in this position unemployed who are willing to work at a lower real wage than that which entrepreneurs are willing to pay. These workers cannot be employed because their employment would result in a rise in income so great that saving would exceed the level corresponding to the actual possibilities of investment.[20]

Figure 5

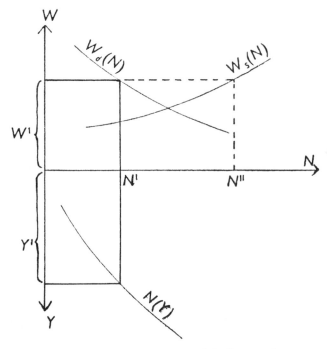

We do not deny that this extreme variant of the Keynesian system which is now and then referred to may correspond to actual cases. But it is then the question of pronounced deflationary situations and not of such equilibria which are treated in comparative statics. If the system is to be useful in determining static equilibria, it should be modified in a direction *opposite* to that suggested by Klein.

Thus the *investment function* I (R) should be given a very *elastic* form to be valid as a static long-run function. The interest level during such equilibrium processes as are treated here, and which are characterized by the fact that investors anticipate developments and make their dispositions early, could not diverge very much from the interest level which corresponds to the "marginal efficiency" of the whole stock of capital if stationary conditions are assumed.[21] This stationary equilibrium level is only slowly lowered as the stock of capital increases. The annual additions by new investment must, as a rule, be fairly small in relation to the whole stock. If two economies with roughly equal stocks of capital are compared and one has a somewhat greater annual volume of investment than the other, we can assume that the interest level in the former economy is not much lower than in the latter.

The comparison which relates to equilibrium processes is thus of an entirely different type than an examination of the effect of an unexpected change in the interest level in a certain economy. In the latter case entrepreneurs have not in advance adjusted the production apparatus for a sudden increase of capital production and the existing stock of capital has not a structure that easily permits the assimilation of fairly large annual additions of investment. In such a case, the interest level must be lowered considerably below the stationary position to have a noticeable effect on the volume of investment. We are, therefore, justified in saying that the volume of investment is in the short run rather inelastic to changes in the interest rate.[22] It is evidently this short-run investment function which Klein and many others in the Keynesian school have had in mind. It is, however, of no use in an interpretation of Keynes' system of comparative statics, if the reasoning given in previous parts of this paper is correct.

Consideration in a static way of the *liquidity function* $M_2(R)$ which is the inverse of the interest function $R(M_2)$, used in our representation of the Keynesian system, leads to even more important consequences for the formulation of the system. The reason why economic subjects keep speculation balances despite the loss of interest connected with them, is of course that they feel uncertain about the future level of interest, and therefore reckon on the possibility of a rise in the interest rate which to a greater or lesser extent lowers the capital value of bonds and other fixed interest securities. The smaller this uncertainty is, the smaller the balances become as the owners of capital invest in interest-bearing securities. During such equilibrium processes as are discussed here, the risk of a rise in the interest level seems relatively small, even if it is perhaps judged as somewhat greater at low than at high interest levels. Speculation balances are therefore relatively small and the liquidity function $M_2(R)$ becomes extremely inelastic. Under strictly static assumptions when the conditions are assumed to be permanent or correctly anticipated, speculation balances disappear completely.[23] With them we have lost the foundation for the determination of the interest level which Keynes uses in his system.[24]

It may be of interest to examine somewhat more closely how the Keynesian system of equations (as it has been presented here) will appear after the above-mentioned modifications, justified from the long-run point of view, have been made:

$$I = I(R) \qquad (2)$$
$$S = I \qquad (3)$$
$$Y = Y(S) \qquad (4)$$
$$N = N(Y) \qquad (5)$$
$$W = W(N) \qquad (6)$$
$$W = W^* \qquad (11)$$
$$M = M(Y) \qquad (7a)$$
$$PM = \overline{M}^* \qquad (9)$$

The system has been reduced by two equations but as two variables (M_1 and M_2) have disappeared, the number of equations is nevertheless still equal to the number of unknowns and the system is therefore solvable. It has, however, undergone two essential changes, disregarding the fact that the investment function $I(R)$ is here assumed to be more elastic than what is usually assumed in the Keynesian school.

Firstly, the actual volume of money ($\overline{M}^*$) has only one function — it determines (together with other factors) the height of the price level. Disregarding the absolute level of prices, we can exclude the last two equations. The remaining six are sufficient to determine the real system.

Secondly, the interest rate in this real system appears as the variable which, via investment, will satisfy the whole system. Therefore it seems suitable to replace the function $I(R)$ by the inverse function $R(I)$ which expresses more explicitly this relation, and to reformulate the whole system in accordance with it. We can in this connection either assume that real wages are given (W^*) which corresponds to the formulation of the system mentioned before (alternative I) or instead regard employment as given (N^*) and assume that workers accept the highest real wage which is in accordance with this employment (alternative II).

The real system can, however, be varied also in other ways. We can thus let interest be a parameter (R^*) determined automatically by the monetary authorities. To avoid the system being over-determined both employment and real wages must then have the character of variables which adjust themselves to the given level of interest (alternative III). The simplified variant of this alternative in which the interest rate is disregarded and investment is assumed to be determined by exogenous factors (e.g. the budget policy of the government) is often used to clarify the most essential relations in the system.[25]

Three alternative formulations of the real system are thus possible, as follows:

I	II	III
$R = R(I)$	$R = R(I)$	$I = I(R^*)$
$I = S$	$I = S$	$S = I$
$S = S(Y)$	$S = S(Y)$	$Y = Y(S)$
$Y = Y(N)$	$Y = Y(N^*)$	$N = N(Y)$
$N = N(W^*)$	$W = W(N^*)$	$W = W(N)$

All the systems are based on long-run functions and refer to a certain type of static equilibrium (correctly anticipated developments). In the construction of these equilibria a mutual connection between the various variables is postulated; in reality the conditions for equilibria are made precise by these systems. Since different variables have been chosen for parameters in the three systems, they give answers to different questions — respectively:

(i)   Which interest level makes it possible to maintain a given real wage?

(ii) Which level of interest is necessary to attain "full employment" (defined in a given way)?

(iii) What are the consequences of a given interest level for investment, income, employment and real wages? Or how can the three last-mentioned variables be determined starting from a given (annual) investment?

All the questions are of the greatest practical relevance and we can, therefore, note with satisfaction that the Keynesian system, after having obtained a consistent static form, is of considerable value as an instrument in comparative statics.[26] If some members of the Keynesian school should feel called upon to complain that the discrepancies between Keynes' system and the traditional theoretic systems have become less obvious than before,[27] they can be immediately informed that the special Keynesian features fully reappear in the more dynamic interpretation of the system to which we now proceed.

II

In the preface to the "General Theory" (p. vii) the book is characterized as a study of the forces which cause *changes* "in the scale of output and employment as a whole". According to the author's own meaning the work seems to have a more dynamic character than the preceding work "A Treatise on Money" (1930), which gave only a snapshot of a position lacking equilibrium at a given volume of production but which did not clarify the dynamic process. Nor can it be denied that the most valuable sections of the "General Theory" consist of examinations concerning the dynamic factors in our present economic system. And Keynes' immense influence on contemporary economic thinking can hardly be fully understood unless the impulses making economic theory more dynamic which emanated from his work, are considered.

But if the most important points of the book lie in the area of dynamics, how could he then explain that its constructions are mostly of a *static* character? We have already hinted at the answer to this question. The Keynesian system can be conceived as a "static short-run system" which clarifies the balance of forces in a given position. A system of this type is static with regard to its *form*: the equations refer to an equilibrium and are, therefore, of a simultaneous character. With regard to *substance* and *purpose* the system is, however, dynamic: it clarifies the actual tendencies in a certain equilibrium and can, consequently, be used for an investigation of how a movement is generated when the equilibrium is broken; furthermore, it gives material for a building of dynamic processes and for an examination of the transition from one equilibrium to another.

An interpretation of Keynes' system in this direction probably corresponds better to his actual intentions than an interpretation of it as comparative statics. And it is not denied that the system from a formal point of view stands up better to such an interpretation since several of its fundamental assumptions are, as we have just seen, more appropriate in a short-run analysis. The system thus gives room for what is generally supposed to be Keynes' most original contributions to economic theory: the introduction of the volume of employment and, also, national income as a regulator for the establishment of equilibrium between saving and investment; the determination of the interest level with the aid of the liquidity function and the connected division of the volume of money into active and non-active balances — a good move, at least from a pedagogical point of view; and generally his determination of monetary and real magnitudes in one system.

We are not here entering upon a closer examination of the form of the system from a short-run point of view, but instead shall add some reflections concerning the application of the system.

The fact that a short-run system of this type cannot be used directly for a determination of equilibria is often overlooked. For this procedure to be correct it is necessary that the short-run and long-run functions be identical, which hardly seems realistic. Strictly, the functions can be assumed to coincide only in the sense that they have the same value at the point of equilibrium (in other words, the forms of the functions are different but the solution is the same). We are, therefore, not permitted to postulate a mutual connection in respect to other values of variables in the short-run system. If a parameter or function should be changed, we can only measure the immediate reactions directly from the system, but for a determination of the process following and the new equilibrium, if it exists, an essential modification of the system in a dynamic direction must take place.

The endeavours which have been made so far to make the Keynesian system dynamic are generally based on the introduction of "lagged" variables into the functions. It has, for instance, been assumed that consumption during one period is a function not of income during the same period but of income during one or more preceding periods. Similar lags have been applied to the reactions of entrepreneurs and investors. The Keynesian simultaneous equations have, consequently, been replaced by difference equations, and the result is a dynamic system. This is undoubtedly a step in the right direction. The aim of theory is, of course, fundamentally to find models which can be tested by facts and these models must contain a determination of the relation between magnitudes during various periods.

It can, however, be questioned whether the system displayed in the "General Theory" with its static formulation and its limitation to *ex-post* magnitudes is the best base for making economic theory dynamic. In the beginning of the work Keynes introduces a distinction between "aggregate demand" and "aggregate supply", but the concepts are unfortunately not rigidly defined and are not of much use in the building of the system. If Keynes had exploited this idea in a more consistent way, he would probably have had greater understanding of such concepts as purchasing plans and sales expectations and, on the whole, of the system of concepts — including *ex-ante* and *ex-post* magnitudes as well as the differences between them — which are worked with in Swedish theory. Even the members of the Keynesian school have not been able to avoid completely the distinction between *ex-ante* and *ex-post* in their treatment of dynamic problems, but there is still a certain distrust against the more differentiated forms of the Swedish system of concepts.[28] This has unfavourable consequences for the continued work on the theory as well as for the representation of its elements in a popular form.[29]

Figure 6

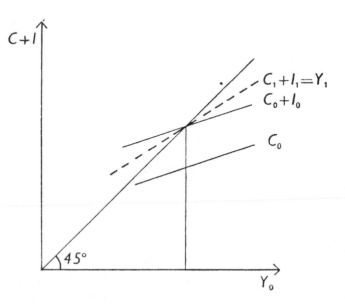

As a matter of fact Keynes had already in his "Treatise on Money" been working in this direction. The system given here was dynamic in its character

— as has just been suggested, it treated positions lacking equilibrium — and in that respect it was more general than the system in the "General Theory". No fundamental difficulties are met with in widening a system of the former type to comprise both equilibria and dynamic processes, while the making of a static system dynamic actually implies that we pass to a new system. The equations in the former system were characterized by some short-comings which during the former part of the 1930's greatly puzzled economists. Keynes solved the problems by a Gordian method: he wrote a new book with new equations, this time of a static character. The economists of the world immediately proceeded to discuss the new equations, which also had, as is well known, their weak points, and they are still discussing them. Because of important public duties during the last years of his life and of a premature death, Keynes never got the opportunity of writing a third book in which he could have remedied the short-comings of the first more general system — which does not seem very difficult from the point of view of Swedish theory — and also put into this the valuable features of the latter system. It should be an important duty for his followers to produce this work and, at the same time, put Keynes' creative contributions to economic theory in relation to the theoretical work of other schools.

It will then probably appear — at least this examination points in that direction — that Keynes' contributions as a builder of systems have been somewhat over-valued in relation to his contributions as an analyst. If the famous system of the "General Theory" is interpreted as comparative statics, it hardly appears as an essentially new creation, compared with previous systems, and if it is interpreted as a short-run balance system, it demands a dynamic complement to be of any use for economic analysis. More valuable than these systematical parts of the works are the author's thorough examinations of the factors which determine the interplay of economic forces. Keynes' greatness as an economist is, among other things, shown by the fact that he himself was not bound to his own systems and did not as a rule let the short-comings in their logical structure influence his judgment of the economic problems of the day. If we read, e.g. the little book *How to Pay for the War* (1940), in which Keynes put forward his programme for a solution of war-time financial problems, we are struck by its fresh approach; quite independent of his previous static constructions the author has here applied dynamic methods which are appropriate for this task.

In another respect also some revaluation of Keynes' theoretical contributions seems possible. What is often considered as his most important contribution to economic theory, i.e. his stressing of the fact that saving and investment are not automatically brought into equilibrium, did not, at least in Sweden, appear as a novelty in any other respect than that Keynes especially underlined the part of employment as an equalizing factor. The fundamental idea can, however, be traced to Knut Wicksell and perhaps also to other earlier economists, which is now probably recognized also in the Keynesian school. As a matter of fact, the Swedish discussion of these problems had advanced comparatively far already in the beginning of the 1930's and, what is even more important, this economic theory had, after the change of government in 1932, when Ernst Wigforss became Minister of Finance, a decisive influence on economic policy.

But even if the value of Keynes' systematical work and the novelty of his fundamental ideas are somewhat reduced, this does not much influence the appraisal of him as the leading economist of his time. Keynes had to a degree not often seen the qualities which are necessary in a good economist: constructive imagination joined with a strong sense of reality. With his rich intellectual endowment and the power of his fascinating personality, he could catch the interest of a whole generation of economists and give them new perspectives on economic problems.

Notes

This article by Professor Erik Lindahl was originally published, in Swedish, in the *Ekonomisk Tidskrift*, Vol. LV (1953): 3, pp. 186-217. With the kind permission of the author and of the editors, it has been translated for the *Economic Record* by Kurt and Margareta Eklöf and K.J. Rothwell and will be published in two parts.

1. In this discussion ideas have been used from Palander, "Keynes' allmänna teori och dess tillämpning inom ränte-, multiplikator- och pristeorien" ("Keynes' general theory and its application in the theory of interest, multiplier and price"), *Ekonomisk Tidskrift* 1942, p. 233, and Ira O. Scott, "An exposition of the Keynesian System", *Review of Economic Studies*, XIX : 1, 1950-51, p. 14. The author also wishes to take the opportunity of thanking Dr. Bent Hansen and Dr. Ragnar Bentzel for their examination of the paper and their valuable observations.

2. Cf. Alvin H. Hansen, *A Guide to Keynes*, New York, 1953, p. 44 : "Keynes' analysis could have proceeded quite as well had he adopted the price index as his deflator instead of his wage unit.... Fundamentally the matter is of no great consequence. On balance Keynes' readers would probably have preferred constant-value dollars to constant-wage-unit dollars."

3. If consumption is denoted by C, we can write
$$C = C(Y) ; I = S$$
$$Y = C + I = C(Y) + S$$
$$Y = Y(S)$$

4. It can be shown that the system of equations quoted here agrees with Keynes' line of thought, even though it shows some formal divergences from his own system, by some quotations from the well-known chapter (18) in which he gives a summary of his theory. Keynes distinguishes between "given factors", the changes in which can be disregarded in this connection, "independent variables" and "dependent variables" and defines them in the following manner:

"We take as given the existing skill and quantity of available labour, the existing quality and quantity of available equipment, the existing technique, the degree of competition, the tastes and habits of the consumer, the disutility of different intensities of labour and of the activities of supervision and organisation, as well as the social structure including the forces, other than our variables set forth below, which determine the distribution of the national income." (P. 245.)

"Thus we can sometimes regard our ultimate independent variables as consisting of (1) the three fundamental psychological factors, the psychological propensity to consume, the psychological attitude to liquidity and the psychological expectation of future yield from capital assets, (2) the wage-unit as determined by the bargains reached between employers and employed, and (3) the quantity of money as determined by the action of the central bank; so that, if we take as given the factors specified above, these variables determine the national income (or dividend) and the quantity of employment." (Pp. 246-7.)

(Professor Pigou writes about the lost quotation in his excellent little book *Keynes' General Theory, A Retrospect*, London, 1950: "This summary statement contains, as I think, Keynes' main and very important contribution to economic analysis".)

The three psychological factors correspond to the functions in our equations (4), (1) and (2).

Wages and volume of money are regarded as magnitudes determined by circumstances outside the system and can, therefore, be introduced as parameters (10 and 9) as has been done here. Our productivity functions (5 and 6) enter among Keynes' "given factors" and that is also the case with our parameter N^*, the supply of labour. Keynes conceives the curve of supply of labour as elastic up to a certain point and it is the supply at this point that has been taken as our parameter.

5. Keynes sometimes hints that the functions in the system can be conceived as formed in such a way that unemployment cannot be avoided however much the relation $\overline{M}^*/\overline{W}^*$ is increased. If the liquidity function is infinitely elastic so that an increase of the volume of money does not bring about any lowering of the interest level, or if the investment function is infinitely inelastic so that a lowering of the interest rate does not bring about increased investment, an increase of the volume of money in relation to the money wage will not have any effect on income and employment. These particular cases have been disregarded in this connection but will be touched upon later.

6. Starting from the equations laid down previously and certain assumptions about the functions in these equations, it is possible to give a more exact mathematical determination of unemployment as a function of the relation between $\overline{M}^*$ and $\overline{W}^*$. But even if the form is not of the simple linear type that has been assumed in the figure, the common-sense reasoning in the text can be upheld.

7. On this assumption the hyperbolas which correspond to $\overline{M}^*$ and $\overline{W}^*$ are shifted from the positions shown in figure 2, the hyperbola $\overline{M}^*$ upwards and the hyperbola $\overline{W}^*$ downwards.

8. The relation between the investment multiplier, $\Delta Y/\Delta I$, and the marginal propensity to consume, $\Delta C/\Delta Y$, can be written in the following way, since investment is taken to be equal to saving and saving equal to income less consumption:

$$\frac{\Delta Y}{\Delta I} = \frac{\Delta Y}{\Delta S} = \frac{\Delta Y}{\Delta Y - \Delta C} = \frac{1}{1 - \dfrac{\Delta C}{\Delta Y}}$$

If, for instance, the propensity to consume equals 0.9, the multiplier will be 10. As the propensity to consume approaches the value 1, the value of the multiplier approaches infinity.

9. It has been pointed out previously that the unemployment generated by Keynes' system (in its general formulation) is conditioned by a disproportion between the given parameters ($\overline{M}^*/\overline{W}^*$) and the given functions. It can, of course, be discussed whether the blame for the lack of adjustment and, therefore, for unemployment should be put on the parameters or on the functions. Keynes himself seems to be most inclined to answer the question in the latter direction; the fault is with the functions of investment and saving. But it is also possible to maintain that the fault is with the parameters — the volume of money and money wages. Even when the functions mentioned have a form unfavourable to full employment, unemployment can be avoided if monetary and wage policy are sufficiently adjusted to them.

10. Cf. my book *Studies in the Theory of Money and Capital*, Part 3, The Place of Capital in the Theory of Price. Cf. also Erik Lundberg "Om begreppet ekonomisk jämvikt", ("On the Concept of Economic Equilibrium"), *Ekon. Tidskr.* 1930, p. 133. For an introduction to the modern discussion, which, however, does not seem to have essentially carried forward the problem, see, among others, Samuelson *Foundations of Economic Analysis* (1947), p. 311.

11. The term "moving equilibrium" seems to be applicable in the first place to such equilibrium processes. It could, however, be extended to comprise also processes which can be characterized as "jumping equilibria", where equilibrium prevails during each period but discontinuous shifts (caused by exogeneous factors) sometimes occur at the boundary between two periods.

12. It is assumed here that the central bank, which can exercise a determining influence on the interest rate, judges the situation correctly, and that other bodies entering the capital market have fairly correct anticipations also, although the mere existence of speculation balances indicates some uncertainty inasmuch as a rise in the interest level is not considered impossible.

13. In a closer examination it is thus clear that Keynes' central equation (see note 3), $Y = C(Y) + I$ can be split into two functions (Y_o denoting the expected income):

$$Y = C(Y_o) + I$$
$$Y = Y_o$$

14. It has been hinted above that the continuing increase of capital may, ceteris paribus, be expected to lower to some degree the propensity to invest. But within the time horizons which are

considered here, this modification of I^n may be assumed to be fairly negligible in relation to the shift from I^I to I^n.

15.   Figure 4 shows how the short-run investment function which relates to the original equilibrium is successively shifted after the lowering of rate of interest at t_o.

16.   Keynes does admit (*General Theory*, p. 29) that the real wage cannot be lower than the level corresponding to "the marginal disutility of labour", but this assumption does not seem to have influenced to any great extent the formulations of his general system.

17.   This curve can also be conceived as a supply curve of labour which leads horizontally to the position of employment N* where it rises vertically. As in the case where the supply of labour was assumed to be a function of the money wage, we have preferred this simpler construction to the more usual one with the supply of labour as a continually rising function of income with a possible back turn of the curve in higher positions.

18.   Cf. *General Theory*, p. 269: "If, as in Australia, an attempt were made to fix real wages by legislation, then there would be a certain level of employment corresponding to that level of real wages; and the actual level of employment would, in a closed system, oscillate violently between that level and no employment at all, according as the rate of interest was or was not below the rate compatible with that level; whilst prices would be in unstable equilibrium when investment was at the critical level, racing to zero whenever investment was below it, and to infinity whenever it was above it. The element of stability would have to be found, if at all, in the factors controlling the quantity of money being so determined that there always existed some level of money-wages at which the quantity of money would be such as to establish a relation between the rate of interest and the marginal efficiency of capital which would maintain investment at the critical level. In this event employment would be constant (at the level appropriate to the legal real wage) with money-wages and prices fluctuating rapidly in the degree just necessary to maintain this rate of investment at the appropriate figure." From this it is evident that Keynes builds the equilibrium at constant real wages in the same way as has been done here, although he considers that this position is extremely unstable. He is, of course, right in stating that the position is more sensitive than when money-wages are kept constant, since every change in the price level receives a strengthening effect from a corresponding change in money-wages. But when the equilibrium has been established, it should not be more difficult to maintain than an equilibrium based on constant money-wages. The quoted lines convey the impression that Keynes has applied here his theory of money and interest in a too schematic way.

19.   "It hardly seems possible that Keynes could say that his major contribution to economic theory was to point out a money illusion on the part of workers as the cause of unemployment. Keynes' real contribution, to repeat, has been to show that if savings are not offset by legitimate investment outlets, failure to generate a high level of employment will follow. *Even if the Keynesian supply curve of labour is replaced by the classical supply curve in terms of real wages, there remains the problem of making savings pass into investment.*" (*Ibid.*, p. 81.)

20.   Klein elucidates his reasoning by a diagram (*ibid.*, p. 87) which is given here in a somewhat enlarged form. We assume that due to the character of the liquidity and investment functions, total real income in the economy cannot exceed Y'. In such a case employment cannot be greater than N' in spite of the fact that the real wage which entrepreneurs are ready to pay, $W_d(N)$, at this level of employment is considerably larger than the real wage which the workers demand, $W_s(N)$. Klein presumes that competition between entrepreneurs causes the real wage to rise to a maximum, W'. At this level of wages the supply of labour equals N'' and the number of unemployed is N'' − N'. In this way Klein arrives at unemployment in a formal sense — according to which every person is unemployed who at existing wages does not get the employment desired — even when the workers continually demand higher wages with increased employment. If in the previous representation of Keynes' system we had used a rising $W_s(N)$ curve instead of the one which is horizontal up to a certain point, as is illustrated by the W' line in Fig. 3, the equilibria which we constructed and found to agree with the point of intersection of the W_d and W_s curves, would not be connected with any unemployment in this sense. Cf. p. 3 and note 17.

21.   Cf. A.P. Lerner, *The Economics of Control* (New York 1945), p. 330 ff, where the question of the relation between "the marginal productivity of capital" and "the marginal efficiency of investment" is treated in an instructive way. Lerner points out that the two concepts coincide under stationary conditions, while in an expanding economy the former magnitude is higher and the latter equal to the current level of interest; it is in fact the difference between them which causes the investment. He does not, however, touch upon the question of how great the

difference will be during the equilibrium (with certain foresight) with which we are concerned here.

22. Cf. above p. 11.

23. Keynes himself has clearly realized this fact and its consequences for the theory of money as is shown in the following important passage in *General Theory*, p. 208-09: "In a static society or in a society in which for any other reason no one feels any uncertainty about the future rates of interest, the liquidity function L_2, or the propensity to hoard (as we might term it), will always be zero in equilibrium. Hence in equilibrium $M_2 = O$ and $M = M_1$; so that any change in M will cause the rate of interest to fluctuate until income reaches a level at which the change in M_1 is equal to the supposed change in M. Now $M_1 V = Y$, where V is the income-velocity of money as defined above and Y is the aggregate income. Thus, if it is practicable to measure the quantity, O, and the price, P, of current output, we have $Y = OP$; which is much the same as the Quantity Theory of Money in its traditional form."

24. As speculation balances on our assumptions form a relatively small fraction of the total volume of money, when either the level of interest is high or low, they are not very important for the determination of general equilibrium. It seems reasonable in the following to carry through the simplification of the system made possible by disregarding these balances despite the fact that we do not here assume perfect foresight.

25. The first three equations in the system denoted as alternative III can then be replaced by an equation of the following type: $Y = C(Y) + I^*$.

26. If the constructions referring to M_1 and M_2 in Fig. 3 are disregarded, the diagram can also be used to illustrate the real system sketched here which we have found is in better agreement with the demands of comparative statics.

27. The system denoted as alternative II is in fact in good agreement with Wicksell's determination of the "normal rate of interest". According to Wicksell the interest rate is normal when the volume of investment induced is equal to the (voluntary) saving arising under conditions of full employment (in the sense of equilibrium in the labour market). Wicksell also argued that the market rate of interest showed a tendency to approach this normal rate, but he did not yield to the more superficial view that competition in the capital market brings about a market rate of interest corresponding to the point of intersection of the saving and investment curves, a view justly criticized by Keynes. Wicksell's brilliant innovation in this field is the introduction of the "cumulative processes" — a counterpart to the later multiplier and accelerator theories — which are generated by the discrepancies between the market rate and the normal rate of interest and which in time force the banks to adjust their rates to the normal rates. This is certainly a mechanism altogether different from the classical one and Wicksell is, therefore, not affected by Keynes' criticism.

28. It is, however, to be regretted that one of America's leading economists, the Harvard Professor Alvin H. Hansen, has gone to the extreme (in the essay "The Robertsonian and Swedish Systems of Period Analysis", first published in the *Review of Economics and Statistics* (1950) and later reprinted in *Business Cycles and National Income* (1951) of rejecting completely the Swedish *ex-ante ex-post* analysis ("based on the divergence of planned saving and planned investment") at the same time as he applies similar distinctions ("desired/designed/saving" and "intended investment" on one hand and "actual/realised/saving and investment" on the other). It would carry us too far to reply to this criticism, which contains a confusing mixture of true and false reasoning and assertions. We shall only underline the fact that Professor Hansen has not penetrated the Swedish lines of thought — he refers only to Professor Ohlin's well-known articles in the *Economic Journal* (1937) and has misunderstood Ohlin on important points, and therefore his criticism lacks relevance.

29. In many text-books a figure similar to Fig. 6 (apart from the broken line) is used to explain the Keynesian equilibrium. The abscissa is usually taken to represent national income and the ordinate the sum of consumption and investment. This figure is, however, not satisfactory in the discussion of non-equilibrium positions. If it is possible for the $(C + I)$ line to deviate from the $45°$ line, it is necessary to interpret C and I *ex-ante* magnitudes. The *ex-ante* magnitude $C + I$ during one period cannot, however, be a function of the *ex-post* magnitude Y for the same period. But a more reasonable interpretation of the figure can be given if also the abscissa variable is interpreted as an *ex-ante* magnitude, i.e. as expected income. In the area to the left of the point of intersection, where $C_o + I_o$ exceeds Y_o, total sales of goods and services will be greater than the expectations of the sellers, which results in, on one hand, a certain disinvestment (a decrease in stocks) and, on the other hand, a certain income gain. To the right of the point of intersection the

opposite condition prevails: the expectations of the sellers are not fulfilled, and unintended increases in stock and income losses are made. The realized income (Y_1), which is represented on the figure by a broken line, will, therefore, in the former case lie above and in the latter case lie below the 45° line which represents expected income (Y_0). (The Y_1 line would coincide with the Y_0 line, if the divergences between realized and expected sales influenced only stocks and not income. In the opposite extreme, when the divergences in equations influence only income but not stocks, the Y_1 line would coincide with the ($C_0 + I_0$) line.) Already this simple application of the distinction between *ex-ante* and *ex-post* variables make clear its usefulness in the analysis of realistic cases which, as a rule, lie on one or the other side of the point of intersection.

91

Some Critical Observations on the Major Keynesian Building Blocks*

M. E. Polakoff

Introduction

It may be best to introduce this paper by making explicit the motivations and assumptions upon which it is based. Firstly, it attempts to present a rather brief survey of the more important post-Keynesian contributions which have taken place since the publication of the *General Theory*. Secondly, in so doing, it stays by and large within the Keynesian institutional framework. As a result, such fundamental problems, for example, as the relation of the State to the economy, and the practical difficulties involved in compensatory spending are not discussed. Thirdly, and for the immediate purposes of this article, the writer is interested primarily in the empirical and theoretical contributions made since 1936, and in the further development and growth of a set of analytical tools which is indispensable for purposes of fiscal and economic policy.

The Consumption Function

The emphasis upon the role played by income in determining consumption is not a novel concept originating with Keynes. Ernst Engels had initiated statistical explorations relating family income-expenditure patterns as early as the middle of the nineteenth century. Henry L. Moore, in the early twentieth century, continued this empirical work through his researches into demand functions, and E. E. Slutsky in 1915 introduced new methods in theoretical demand analysis for dealing with income changes. The Great Depression and Keynes' *General Theory*, however, shifted the focus of economic inquiry from traditional price analysis to income theory in the determination of consumer expenditures.[1]

As a result of the interest and stimulation evoked by Keynes' *General*

*Source: *Economic Journal*, Vol. 21, October 1954, pp. 141-51.

Theory and the profusion of good statistical material available, investigation developed rapidly testing the effect of income on consumption and saving. Family budget and time-series studies increased rapidly and were used to test the theoretical adequacy of the Keynesian consumption function, including its presumed stability.[2] For the Keynesian theoretical framework demanded a very precise prediction of aggregate consumption if policy was to be formulated on quantitative basis. What have been the results of such empirical studies?

Household budget studies reveal a consumption-income pattern for individual families. These studies deal with a sample of families with different incomes in a *particular* period. They, therefore, eliminate the difficulties involved in changing relationships over time. Given the distribution of income, it is then possible to derive the different consumption and saving patterns of each family. This will be a function of the size of family income at a given time and place. Although the family consumption function displays a declining average and marginal propensity to consume for families at different income levels at any *one* time, this does not mean that, for the economy as a whole, total consumers' expenditures will behave in this way as total income rises.

We now know, for example, that over the decades consumers have adjusted upward their standards of living as their incomes have risen, and the evidence suggests that, as a long-run tendency the percentage of income saved has remained fairly constant since the closing decades of the nineteenth century.[3] The secular invariance of the aggregate saving ratio cannot be explained in terms of the simple Keynesian formula which states that the saving ratio is an unique function of absolute real income, rising as income expands. One explanation is that the array of income-consumption points obtained from simultaneous observations of different families can be explained only in terms of a relationship between family consumption and relative income, measured by the position of a family in the income distribution scale.[4] This "relative income" hypothesis predicts that national consumption will be a constant proportion of national income, whatever the level of national income. The number of families at each percentile of the distribution will be the same and, consequently, the distribution of families by proportion of income devoted to consumption will be unchanged. It is true that, as the total national income rises, most families move to a higher income bracket. But this does not mean that each family, in its improved position, will save as much as a family with that size income did earlier when all incomes were lower. How much a family saves seems to depend in part on the income of other families and on the living standards created by a given level and distribution of income. As one writer points out, "Noneconomic man is greatly influenced by what others do."[5] And another states: "The *standard* of consumption or living is the level that is urgently desired and striven for, special gratification attending substantial success and substantial failure yielding bitter frustration."[6] The sociological implications of the "relative income" thesis would seem to point in the direction of assessing the importance of status distinctions upon changes in consumption and saving.

In this connection, it has been pointed out that standards may be linked to a way of life rather than to income proper.[7] Farmers appear to spend a smaller proportion of a given level of income than do city families. Also, the average and marginal propensities to consume are lower for farm than city families. The savings of farmers are used eventually in the purchase of farm machinery and equipment, as well as land. As one writer comments: "What more ostentatious or enviable possessions are there, which more capable of validating a self-picture 'urgently desired and striven for'?"[8] Concerning other socio-economic groups within the economy, it is not too clear at this juncture whether the same differences with respect to spending and saving exist for them also.[9]

The "relative income" hypothesis has been challenged recently by one writer who has come to the defense of the original Keynesian thesis that the level of consumption is a function of the level of absolute income. In order to explain the secular invariance of the aggregate saving ratio, however, he is forced to conclude that the amount of liquid assets owned by families in the economy have to be taken into consideration, as well as the absolute level of income.[10] Thus, a new variable is introduced to explain the consumption function, namely, the accumulation or decumulation of liquid and near liquid assets such as past savings in the form of demand and time deposits, government bonds, etc., or the fact that consumption not only is a function of current income but of previous income streams. This was certainly one of the more important factors determining the behaviour of the consumption function in the United States immediately after World War II and it has continued to exert a positive influence in the post-war period.

The volume of consumption and savings not only is a function of the level of income, but is dependent upon the distribution of that income. Family-budget studies have indicated that the marginal propensity to consume is different for the different income classes within the economy. Since these marginal propensities to consume are different, a redistribution of income during the course of the business cycle may give a completely unexpected turn to the marginal propensity to consume for society as a whole.[11] For purposes of forecasting and policy decision, it is absolutely imperative that changes in the distribution of income which occur during the business cycle be known in order to derive an unique consumption function for society as a whole. There is the further problem involved in assuming that the individual schedules can be aggregated in order to arrive at a group schedule. The interdependence of individual consumption expenditures makes this procedure extremely hazardous.[12]

There is also the problem of time-lags induced by changes in income during the course of the business cycle. A family whose income was $4,000 for several years and which now suffered a decline in income to $3,500 will save less out of the new income than a family whose income had been $3,000 for some time and whose income has risen now to $3,500. The former would find it quite difficult to reduce its contractual and habitual expenses very rapidly, while the latter typically would be slow to adjust to its new income level. This is consistent with the conclusion reached by two specialists in the field that the percentage of income saved depends on the relation between current income and the highest level of income reached in the past.[13] The aggregate volume of consumption and savings will be different because of these time-lags than if we could assume, as Keynes does, an instantaneous adjustment to the new income levels.

Expectations concerning the future likewise influence buying and saving. Especially with respect to durable goods, clear expectations about prices and availability can substantially influence the timing of buying. An example is the sharp rise in consumers' expenditures relative to incomes after the outbreak of the Korean crisis, when consumers rushed to anticipate the expected rise in prices and scarcity of goods.

The effect of future employment and income possibilities on expectations, as well as the importance of relative price changes, outside pressures such as saving bond drives, changes in tax rates, etc., has been pointed out as important factors in significantly shifting the schedule relationship between consumption and income from one short-run period to another.[14]

There are difficulties involved in the Keynesian thesis that real consumption is a function of real income, with its implicit assumption of rational behaviour at the consumption level.[15] This relationship presumably would not be affected by a doubling of money income and prices. But if any sort of money illusion occurred—and this seems extremely likely—then real consumption expenditures would depend not only upon changes in the level of real income but upon changes in money income and prices as well.

As a result of these and other observations made by economists in the field, it seems evident that the marginal propensity to consume is only the roughest type of guide in estimating the actual changes in consumption which are associated with short-period changes in income. Estimates of the coefficient of the income variable—the changes in consumption associated with unit changes in income—range for the United States from the low .90's to low .60's.[16] And one writer states:

> Although there was clearly an average relationship between consumption and disposable income for the post-war period (parallel to but higher than the prewar regression), this average relation frequently provided a poor guide for predicting how consumption would change from quarter to quarter as income changed. The short-period consumption function is unstable and . . . the historical relation does not tell us how the short-period relationship shifts from period to period.[17]

Concerning the propensity to consume over time, the various lines of regression drawn describe a linear consumption function which fitted closely the actual data for the prewar years. The correlation between aggregate consumption and income was remarkably high prior to the second World War. As has been pointed out, however, this is not at all surprising since consumer spending was over nine times the volume of savings during this period.[18] Thus a high correlation becomes inevitable. What is important in many cases is an estimation of savings out of disposable income since investment is the dynamic factor in the employment situation. If then comparison is made between savings and disposable income, correlating ten per cent of the whole with the whole, the technical objection to the former procedure is dispensed with. But independent calculation has shown "that the correlation between saving and income was by no means so high as between spending and income."[19] If then, as appears obvious, the saving function is unstable, or unstable within rather wide limits, the Keynesian analysis runs into trouble since investment and income also are variables. Also, public policy which must, in the nature of the case, rely on prediction becomes quantitatively impossible.

The Investment Multiplier and Fiscal Policy

The multiplier, as formulated by Keynes, supposedly "establishes a precise relationship, given the propensity to consume, between aggregate employment and income and the rate of investment."[20] Or, "it tells us that, when there is an increment of aggregate investment, income will increase by an amount which is k times the increment of investment."[21]

The multiplier rests on several assumptions. Firstly, the multiplier has no time dimension, i.e., is instantaneous in its effects. A change in investment immediately will be reflected in a multiple increase in national income. The simultaneous multiplier merely states the *ex-post* relationship between a realized change in national income and the realized change in investment in the same period. Obviously, this offers little aid for policy formulation since, in this area, decisions must proceed on an *ex-ante* basis.

Secondly, the Keynesian multiplier assumes that successive increments to income resulting from an increase in investment must either be consumed or saved, but not invested. This simplification leaves out of account many important variables which will be affected by the multiplier process. Even within the Keynesian framework certain changes will ensue. To take the interest rate as an example. If the difference between the increment in income and the increment in consumption due to an increase in investment is hoarded and liquidity preference remains constant, then the interest rate will fall and this will lead to a still further increase in investment. Or, if new investment is financed by the creation of additional money and liquidity preference remains constant, the interest rate will decline again leading to an increase in investment. Finally, if the new investment is financed by a reduction in hoards with no increase in the money supply, the liquidity preference schedule will shift lowering the interest rate and leading to a further increase in investment and income. The multiplier process is, in reality, much more complex than envisaged in the original Keynesian formulation.

Thirdly, the marginal propensity to consume is assumed to remain constant during the time in which new investment works itself out. Definitionally, this is valid but not very useful in the examination of dynamic problems.

Most neo-Keynesians, recognizing the inherent uselessness of the timeless multiplier, attempted to give the concept meaning by amplifying and expanding it into a process analysis through time. They reasonably assumed that the full multiplying effects of a change in investment are not felt immediately, and thus there may be little significance in the ratio of a current change in income to the change in investment in the same period. Logical sequences were introduced attempting to show the change in income through successive rounds or stages as a result of an increase in investment.

In addition, the importance of the acceleration principle in income determination was recognized and attempts were made to integrate it with multiplier analysis by demonstrating the induced changes in investment resulting from a previous increase in consumption.[22] Such procedure involved the recognition that investment, in part, is a function of changes in the level of income and consumption and not exogenous to the economic process. However, prediction in terms of both the multiplier and acceleration principles still would require that the marginal propensity to consume remain constant over the cycle. Should it vary for one or more of the reasons adduced in the preceding section, accurate diagnosis of the quantitative changes in income as a result of induced changes in the volume and level of investment and consumption would be impossible unless one could predict such changes in the marginal propensity to consume in advance. Unfortunately, this cannot be done as yet. Thus in rescuing the simultaneous multiplier, the neo-Keynesians left themselves open to attack via fluctuations in the MPC.

The timing problem is most important for purposes of fiscal policy. Even assuming short-run stability for the marginal propensity to consume, there is still the problem of assessing how much of an increase in investment will be spent during a certain time period, during the year, for example. Historically, the income velocity of the total money supply fell from about 3 per year in the 1920's to 2 per year in 1939 in the United States. This implies an income period of 4 months in the 1920's and 6 months in 1939. However, a substantial part of the money supply is inactive, and it has been estimated that the velocity of the active money supply was about 3.6 per year in the 1920's and about 3.25 in the late 1930's. These imply income periods of 3.3 and 3.7 months respectively.[23] Since in relating income velocity to the multiplier one is tracing the path of active money, the latter figures are the appropriate ones. Taking the 3.7 figure for purposes of rough calculation, and assuming the multiplier to be 3 with six billion dollars worth of deficit spending, the increase in income at the end of a year would be roughly thirteen billion dollars and not the eighteen billion dollars postulated by the period multiplier if one merely views the latter as a logical, non-time dimensional explanation of the increase in income resulting from an increase in investment. Since, however, even the income velocity of the active money supply is not constant in the short-run, this creates still further complications for multiplier analysis.[24]

The instability of the short-run consumption function has relegated multiplier analysis to a very insignificant role in present-day policy formulation. Instead of a neat and mechanical problem in social engineering, fiscal policy, somewhat like monetary policy, faces a significant number of variables, each operating on and partially distorting the final result. While the qualitative direction of change may be correct, quantitative prediction is more a hope of the future than a present-day reality.

The Rate of Interest

At first sight, the Keynesian theory of interest appears to run counter both to the "pure" theory of interest and also to the loanable-funds theory. This difference stems, in part, from the Keynesian denial that, on the supply side, an increase in the volume of savings tends, *ceteris paribus*, to lower the rate of interest. For Keynes, a decreased readiness to spend will not increase investment but only diminish employment through its effects on the income level. On the demand side, he denies that a rise in the marginal efficiency of capital tends, *other things being equal*, to raise the interest rate. Keynes holds that the rate of interest is the reward for parting with liquidity for a specified period. "The rate of interest is not the 'price' which brings into equilibrium the demand for resources to invest with the readiness to abstain from present consumption."[25] It is, rather, "the 'price' which equilibrates the desire to hold wealth in the form of cash with the available quantity of cash."[26]

Looking at the supply side first, is the reward for parting with liquidity completely independent of the reward for not spending on consumption, that is, for saving? Professor Robertson and other loanable-fund theorists would insist on the essential complementarity of the saving-hoarding process, interest being the reward both for *not* consuming and for *not* hoarding. As Professor Robertson states: "The fact that the rate of interest measures the marginal convenience of holding idle money need not prevent it from measuring *also* the marginal inconvenience of abstaining from consumption."[27]

On the demand side, Keynes distinguishes three motives for holding money; the transactions-motive, the precautionary-motive, and the speculative-motive. All three make up the demand for liquidity. Is this formulation and the traditional demand-for-and-supply-of loanable-funds theory really at variance?

Let us suppose there is a change in the demand for capital due to expectations on the part of entrepreneurs that the marginal efficiency of capital will change. According to the loanable-fund theorists, this will influence the interest rate. According to Keynes, however, the determinants of the marginal efficiency of capital and the interest rate are divorced from one another. But are they? Doesn't a rise or fall in the marginal efficiency of capital affect the liquidity preference schedule, causing it to shift upward or downward?

If entrepreneurs intend to increase their future expenditures due to expectations concerning increases in the marginal efficiency of capital and, if this is to be accomplished through borrowing, then in Keynes' view such action would represent an increase in liquidity preference. The demand for money has increased without either a fall in the interest rate or a rise in the volume of transactions. As borrowing proceeds, the volume of business transactions increases so that, sooner or later, the demand for money to finance the larger turnover rises. In the Keynesian lexicon, such action will lead inevitably to a rise in the interest rate since less of the existing money supply now remains to satisfy the speculative motive. Isn't the liquidity preference schedule then tied up with the marginal efficiency of capital?

In recognition of such criticism, Keynes was led to modify his original theory so that its similarity to the loanable-funds doctrine became much more obvious.[28] He now recognized the fact that the demand for money is not only a function of the transaction and speculative motives, but also of the intended new outlay or planned investment decisions of business firms. Keynes calls this latter motive the "finance" motive and points out that investment funds must be secured prior to an upsurge in business activity. He states: "During the interregnum — and during that period only — between the date when he actually makes his investment, there is an additional demand for liquidity without, as yet, any additional supply of it necessarily arising."[29] It has been cogently pointed out that "the adherents of the loanable-fund theory would merely substitute 'credits' for the word 'liquidity'" in this sentence.[30] The marginal efficiency of capital and liquidity preference curves far from being independent of one another are closely interrelated. What price terminological innovations and unusual assumptions?

As a result of such criticism, an attempt has been made to reconcile the Keynesian theory with the loanable-funds doctrine.[31] This reconciliation states that "the rate of interest is the price that equates the supply of 'credit,' or saving *plus* the net increase in the amount of money in a period, to the demand for 'credit,' or investment *plus* net 'hoarding' in the period."[32] The supply of loanable funds is then brought into equilibrium with the demand for them during the current period at the rate r'. The latter result is achieved by adding the amount of money held at the beginning of the period to the net increase in the amount of money and the net hoarding during that period.

This new formulation has been criticized, in its turn, on the grounds that it implicitly treats income as an arbitrary constant.[33] If this were true, then its theoretical base would rest upon Say's Law, with saving automatically the same as investment without any mechanism (the level of income) bringing the two schedules into equilibrium. Since the saving and investment schedules are not coincident, there can be no determinant system. On the assumption that both the saving and investment schedules are interest-inelastic, at full employment saving will be greater than investment no matter how low the rate of interest is pushed. The two schedules will intersect one another only after an adjustment is made through changes in the income level. Only after a theory of adjustment of output is introduced can the interest rate be determined for the general case. There is the further criticism of attempting to combine stock and flow concepts.[34]

Relation of the MEC and the Interest Rate

In the Keynesian system, the volume of investment is determined at the point where the interest rate is equal to the marginal efficiency of capital. The higher the interest rate, given the marginal efficiency of capital, the smaller will be the volume of investment, and vice versa.

Empirical studies made in England and the United States seem to suggest, however, that the interest rate is generally regarded by businessmen as an insignificant factor in their investment decisions.[35] Several hypotheses have been advanced as to why this is so.

One hypothesis assumes that the interest rate plays a relatively insignificant role in most investment decisions because interest is a minor element of cost for most businesses.[36] Hence, it can safely be ignored. This should not be taken to mean, however, that the interest rate is unimportant for all forms of investment. The constructional and public utility fields are especially sensitive to changes in capital costs because of the heavy initial outlay and great durability of the capital assets involved. But this does not appear to be the *general* case for most investments.

Another hypothesis states that in the real world the discount rate is more important than the interest rate.[37] In a rational and safe world, the two would be the same. In the real world, however, there are risks and uncertainties with respect to the future and the discount rate must take these into account, as well as the interest rate. Now the non-interest component — the psychological risk and uncertainty element — may far outweigh the interest component. Therefore, relatively small fluctuations in the interest rate may be of little importance so far as investment decisions are concerned.

Finally, the growing practice of internal financing enables corporate decisions to be made irrespective of fluctuations in the market rate of interest. Given retained profits and depreciation allowances, no fine marginal calculations are made by businessmen as to whether or not to proceed with investment decisions or, alternatively, to lend these funds out to others to take advantage of the current rate of interest.

According to those empirical studies which have been undertaken, the neat and determinant solution of the equilibrium volume of investment advanced by

Keynes would seem to conflict with the facts of the real world. The volume of investment would appear, by and large, to be interest-inelastic.[38]

Conclusion

The empirical and theoretical studies and contributions of the past decade-and-a-half have shed a good deal of light on Keynes' *General Theory*. Many of the Keynesian building blocks have been found either to be inadequate or lacking the necessary precision which is indispensable for purposes of *policy* and *prediction*.[39] This should not detract for one moment from the essential merits of the "Keynesian Revolution." Keynes not only rescued economic analysis from Say's Law of Markets, but his delineation of the relationships among many important economic variables and their lack of integration remains a substantial achievement in throwing light on the basic workings of our economy. What the post-Keynesian researches have done, however, is to underscore the essential complexity of our economic system and make apparent the necessary work that still remains to be done before accurate diagnosis becomes possible.

Notes

1.   Ruth Mack, "Economics of Consumption," *A Survey of Contemporary Economics*, ed. by Bernard F. Haley (Homewood, Ill.: Richard D. Irwin, 1952), II, 40. In the writer's opinion, Mrs. Mack's article is the best survey yet to appear on the economics of consumption and he is indebted to her for some of the material discussed in this section.

2.   Keynes assumed that the volume of consumption is not only a function of national income or gross national product but that this function is *relatively stable.* See, *The General Theory of Employment, Interest and Money* (New York: Harcourt, Brace and Co., 1936), p. 95.

3.   James Duesenberry, *Income, Saving and the Theory of Consumer Behavior* (Cambridge, Mass.: Harvard University Press, 1949), pp. 55-58.

Franco Modigliani, "Fluctuations in the Saving-Income Ratio: A Problem in Economic Forecasting," Conference on Research in Income and Wealth, *Studies in Income and Wealth*, Vol. XI (New York, 1949), pp. 371-441.

Dorothy S. Brady and Rose D. Friedman, "Savings and the Income Distribution," Conference on Research in Income and Wealth, *Studies in Income and Wealth*, Vol. X (New York, 1947), pp. 250-265.

4.   Duesenberry, *op. cit.*, p. 45.

5.   Mack, *op. cit.*, p. 47.

6.   J.S. Davis, "Standards and Content of Living," *American Economic Review*, March 1945, p. 3.

7.   Margaret G. Reid, "Effect of Income Concept upon Expenditure Curves of Farm Families," Conference on Research in Income and Wealth, *Studies in Income and Wealth*, Vol. XV (New York, 1952).

8.   Mack, *op. cit*, p. 55.

9.   J.N. Morgan, "The Structure of Aggregate Personal Saving," *Journal of Political Economy*, December 1951, pp. 528-34.

10.   James Tobin, "Relative Income, Absolute Income, and Saving," *Money, Trade, and Economic Growth: Essays in Honor of John Henry Williams* (New York: Macmillan Co., 1951), pp. 143 ff.

11.   Ruth Mack, "The Direction of Change in Income and the Consumption Function," *Review*

of Economic Statistics, November 1948, pp. 239-58.

12. Duesenberry, *op. cit.,* pp. 13-16, chap. 3.

13. James Duesenberry, "Income-Consumption Relations," *Income, Employment and Public Policy: Essays in Honor of Alvin H. Hansen* (New York: W.W. Norton and Co., 1948), p. 69. See also, Modigliani, *op. cit.*

14. Robert V. Rosa, "Use of Consumption Function in Short Run Forecasting," *Review of Economics and Statistics,* May 1948.

15. James Tobin, "Money Wage Rates and Employment," *The New Economics,* ed. by Seymour E. Harris (New York: Alfred A. Knopf, 1947), p. 583.

16. Mack, "Economics of Consumption," p. 65.

17. Robert Gordon, *Business Fluctuations,* (New York: Harper & Brothers, 1952), p. 83.

18. Arthur F. Burns, *The Instability of Consumer Spending,* 32nd Annual Report of the National Bureau of Economic Research (New York, 1952), pp. 8-9.

19. *Ibid.,* p. 9.

20. Keynes, *op. cit.,* p. 113.

21. *Ibid.,* p. 115.

22. Alvin H. Hansen, *Fiscal Policy and Business Cycles,* (New York: W.W. Norton and Company, 1941), pp. 274-288.

23. James W. Angell, *Investment and Business Cycles* (New York: McGraw-Hill Book Company, 1941), Chap. 9; Appendix II.

24. Gordon, *op. cit.,* p. 93n.

25. Keynes, *op. cit.,* p. 167.

26. *Ibid.*

27. D.H. Robertson, "Alternative Theories of the Rate of Interest," *Economic Journal,* September 1937, p. 431.

28. John Maynard Keynes, "The 'Ex-Ante' Theory of the Rate of Interest," *The Economic Journal,* December 1937. pp. 663-69.

29. *Ibid.,* p. 665.

30. Gottfried von Haberler, *Prosperity and Depression,* (New Revised ed.; Geneva: League of Nations, 1940), p. 213. Much of the prior discussion in this section has been influenced by Prof. Haberler's famous work.

31. Abba P. Lerner, "Alternative Formulations of the Theory of Interest," *The Economic Journal,* June 1938, pp. 211-30.

32. *Ibid.,* p. 213.

33. Lawrence R. Klein, *The Keynesian Revolution,* (New York: Macmillan and Co., 1947), pp. 120-21.

34. *Ibid.,* p. 121. For a defence of this thesis, see William Fellner and Harold M. Somers, "Alternative Monetary Approaches to Interest Theory," *Review of Economic Statistics,* February 1941, pp. 43-48.

35. H.D. Henderson, "The Significance of the Rate of Interest," *Oxford Economic Papers,* No. 1, October 1938, p. 9.

J.F. Ebersole, "The Influence of Interest Rates upon Entrepreneurial Decisions in Business," *Harvard Business Review,* Autumn 1938, pp. 35-39.

36. F.A. Lutz, "The Interest Rate and Investment in a Dynamic Economy," *American Economic Review,* December 1945, pp. 811-30.

37. Klein, *op. cit.,* p. 64.

38. For a critique of such studies, as well as a positive defense of the importance of interest rates in influencing the levels of economic activity, see W.A.L. Coulborn, "Principal Contributions to Interest Rate Theory Since Keynes' *General Theory,*" *Southern Economic Journal,* July 1953, pp. 12-22.

39. One of the major aims of this article has been to demonstrate the necessity for more precise tools of analysis than Keynes offered as a prerequisite for accurate diagnosis and prediction. It is not to be construed simply as a general criticism of Keynesian theory on the grounds of oversimplification. The writer would agree that in general oversimplification is never a very valid or very helpful criticism of theory because the essence of theory is simplification of complex experience. The criterion of a good theory is not the degree of simplification but the relevance of the abstractions in relation to the purpose for which the theory is projected. Individual concepts in a system of theory cannot be evaluated legitimately by a direct appeal to facts; they must first be evaluated in relation to each

other, and then the theory as a whole evaluated in relation to its operational meaning. Short of this, criticism becomes endless and degenerates into polemics. Having said this, however, the writer would hasten to reiterate that such an approach to questions of theory does not invalidate the need for more accurate conceptual tools if theory is to be *applied* in any meaningful or useful fashion to the actual workings of an *empirical* economy.

92

Keynes and Supply Functions*

R.G. Hawtrey

Mr. de Jong's article on *Supply Functions in Keynesian Economics* in the ECONOMIC JOURNAL for March 1954 is concerned with the interpretation of the passage in Chapter 3 of Keynes's *General Theory* dealing with Effective Demand. In that chapter are to be found an Aggregate Supply Function, Z, and an Aggregate Demand Function, D. But they are both functions of the numbers employed, N, and the condition $Z = D$ means no more than that the numbers employed are such that supply is equal to effective demand. Economists look for a pair of functions the mutual reactions of which will reflect the underlying economic determinants. But for Keynes effective demand is the single determinant. As Mr. de Jong puts it (p. 4), "real national income — and therefore employment — seems to be determined by a one-sided demand theory: thus by something *à la* von Böhm-Bawerk."

"Effective demand" is defined by Keynes not as actual demand, but as the entrepreneurs' *expectation* of proceeds of sale of their products. The Aggregate Demand Function, $D = f(N)$, is "the proceeds which entrepreneurs expect to receive from the employment of N men, and is composed of D_1, the amount which the community is expected to spend on consumption, and D_2, the amount which it is expected to devote to new investment."

The function, D, arrived at by adding together the "expectations" of many independent individuals is a very shadowy quantity. But Keynes did not leave his analysis in this rather indeterminate condition. He further elaborated the expectations which determine production in his fifth chapter, where he distinguished the short-term expectations of the manufacturer, concerned with the price he will get for his product, from the long-term expectations of the entrepreneur, concerned with the future returns from an addition to his capital equipment.

"The behaviour of each individual firm in deciding its daily output will be determined by its *short-term expectations* — expectations as to the cost of output on various possible scales, and expectations as to the sale-proceeds

*Source: *Economic Journal,* Vol. 64, December 1954, pp. 834-9.

of this output; though in the case of additions to capital equipment and even of sales to distributors, these short-term expectations will largely depend on the long-term (or medium-term) expectations of other parties." (*General Theory*, p. 47.)

If we are looking for a "supply function" we shall want to know on what grounds these expectations are based. And we learn that "the process of revision of short-term expectation is a gradual and continuous one, carried on largely in the light of realised results" (p. 50), and "producers' forecasts are more often gradually modified in the light of results than in anticipation of prospective changes" (p. 51).

A footnote (p. 51) explains that an accumulation of unsold stocks or a decline of forward orders would modify the inferences from "the mere statistics of the sale-proceeds of previous output." These indicators affect expectations before there is any actual change in prices. They are "realised results," the outcome of an actual decline of demand.

A function essentially expresses a relation to variables. Of what variables should supply be a function? When Keynes wrote (p. 30), "the propensity to consume and the rate of new investment determine between them the volume of employment," he dropped the term "expected." He was already translating "expectations" into "realised results." And throughout the book *actual* demand appears to be assumed to be the determinant of productive activity. New investment, it is true, depends on expectations, but on the expectations of the prospective users of the new capital equipment, not on those of the manufacturers and constructors.

Mr. de Jong is therefore right when he says that, according to Keynes, employment is "determined by a one-sided demand theory." Professor Patinkin proposed to modify the position by introducing a "desired-supply function," formed by aggregating the amounts which all the individual entrepreneurs would wish in the existing circumstances to supply.[1] The desired-supply function could differ from actual output, and therefore from actual demand. The difference, whenever it occurs, is a departure from equilibrium.[2]

But what is it that producers "desire"? Keynes said that they aim at maximising their profits, and Professor Patinkin, in introducing his supply curve, specified maximisation of profits as a part of its framework (p. 365). But in a later passage (p. 370) he identifies "the level of income at which suppliers are able to supply exactly what they desire" as "a full employment level of income."

Mr. de Jong proceeds to a demonstration that maximisation of profits by every individual firm does not necessarily make the sum total of all expected profits a maximum (pp. 15-17). He might have found a shorter and more general proof: maximisation of the total of profits would not occur without a concerted limitation of supply.

In the case where industry is under-employed each producer may be supposed to desire above all to get sufficient orders to employ his plant up to capacity. With a view to getting additional orders, he will cut prices, but presumably not so far that his total profit will be diminished. So long as that is so, the maximisation of each producer's profit is not inconsistent with the determination of employment by actual demand.

Full employment of capital capacity, however, is not the same thing as full employment of labour, and Mr. de Jong points out (p. 7) that "there seems no reason why entrepreneurs should 'desire' self-evidently to engage all workers available at the prevailing wage rate." He proceeds to reinterpret Professor Patinkin's supply function by introducing the supply function of labour. The numbers desiring employment depend upon the wage offered, and may be expressed as a function of the real wage $\frac{w}{p}$, where w is the wage-level and p is the general price-level. The desires in Professor Patinkin's desired-supply function are thus made to include the desires of the worker as well as of the entrepreneurs. The entrepreneurs, in suiting their action to their desires, have to take account of the condition that the supply of labour, and consequently their output, will depend on the rate of wages they offer.

Keynes did not altogether reject the classical postulate which equated the wage-level to the marginal disutility of labour. When he said that the number employed cannot exceed that which reduces the real wage to the marginal disutility of labour (*General Theory,* p. 29), he was in effect defining full employment. He expressed the employment function (Chapter 20) in terms of wage-units, with the implication that a rise in wages relative to prices would mean diminished employment. But unemployment which is "due to the refusal or inability of a unit of labour, as a result of legislation or social practices or of combination for collective bargaining or of slow response to change or of mere human obstinacy, to accept a reward corresponding to the value of the product attributable to its marginal productivity," he regarded as "voluntary" (p.6).

A rate of wages so fixed, if "voluntary," must be deemed to be in accordance with the desires of the individual wage-earner. The supply of labour is the number willing to accept employment at this rate of wages. The disutility of labour depends upon the hours of work, and has very little direct relation to the rate of wages. Hours are decided by employers, subject to collective bargaining with their workpeople. In the long run prevalent valuations of leisure in comparison with money are no doubt reflected in the agreements regarding hours, but the individual would always desire to have employment at the established rate of wages of his occupation, and would commit himself to the established hours of work without considering the disutility of the marginal hour. Short-period changes in the supply of labour are usually imposed on workpeople by employers in the shape of overtime or short-time. A supply function of labour based on the disutility principle would seem to be quite unrealistic. Mr. de Jong contrasts the supply function thus adapted to take account of the *supply* function of labour, with the "familiar" supply function, based on the *demand* function of labour. The relation of prices to costs (and therefore to the wage level) determines what output entrepreneurs will expect to be profitable, and the output they decide upon determines the numbers they will employ. When full employment is reached, competition among employers for the limited supply of labour pushes up the wage-level till its relation to the price-level is consistent with the output at full employment.

How do these versions of a supply function fit into Keynes's analysis?

The relation of the wage-level to the price-level is implicit in Keynes's use of "wage-units" in his expressions of propensity to consume, national income, saving and investment. If wages are pushed up, the number of wage-units in the expected proceeds of output is diminished, and the excess of proceeds over costs shrinks. The expectations of proceeds are arrived at through expectations of sales and of prices, and the fall in proceeds in terms of wage-units merely reflects the rise of wages relative to prices. Keynes's supply function in terms of effective demand does not differ materially from the "familiar" supply function in terms of price.

Nevertheless, Keynes dispensed with the familiar supply function.

Professor Patinkin refers in a footnote (p. 363) to "the practice of considering inventory accumulation as purchases of the firm from itself." It is this practice which makes saving and investment identically equal. It was presupposed in the assertion so positively made by Keynes in 1933 in *The Means to Prosperity* (p. 12): "For the nation as a whole, leaving on one side transactions with foreigners, its income is exactly equal to its expenditure (including in expenditure both consumption-expenditure and new capital-expenditure, but excluding intermediate exchanges from one hand to another); the two being simply different names for the same thing, my expenditure being your income." But when goods are sold *from stock,* the only income thereby generated is the seller's profit. The rest of the price represents the incomes of those who were engaged in producing the goods, incomes which had already accrued at or before the time when the goods were bought for stock. The purchase of the goods for stock is one of those "intermediate exchanges" which have to be excluded from "expenditure." Yet, if the dealer's purchases exceed his sales, the result is an addition to his capital assets, and Keynes included any such addition in "investment," and thereby deemed the goods to be purchased by the dealer on his own account.

But, if all the unsold goods in dealers' hands are thus deemed to be "sold," demand is identically equal to supply; and the formula which makes the equality of demand and supply depend on prices becomes nonsense. Keynes accordingly sought and found an alternative analysis.

Of the two components of demand, consumption and investment, investment depended on the rate of interest, and, investment once given, consumption was derived from it by the multiplier. A fall in the rate of interest would increase the demand for capital goods. There would follow an increased production of capital goods at increased prices, and the additional income thus generated would result in an increased demand for consumption goods. Increased demand means increased proceeds, partly increased production and partly higher prices required to elicit the increased production. In Keynes's analysis the increased demand is fundamental, and the rise of prices is no more than an incidental consequence. The increase in the national income is necessarily accompanied by an increase in active balances of money (Keynes's M_1), but the reduction of the rate of interest both determines the amount of investment and, in the process, provides the appropriate amount of money. Keynes attached special importance to the speculative motive, because it would interfere with the provision of the amount of money needed for full employment. If the decline in the rate of interest required to keep pace with a falling marginal efficiency of capital led people to accumulate idle cash, instead of spending either on consumption or on investment, the movement towards full employment might be barred. "Circumstances may develop," Keynes wrote (p. 172), "in which even a large increase in the quantity of money may exert a comparatively small influence on the rate of interest."

He was there assuming that there was no institutional obstacle to an indefinite increase in the supply of money. And in a later chapter he speculated on the possibility of zero interest and a euthanasia of the rentier.

A metallic standard would interpose an over-riding obstacle to a monetary expansion. The outstanding fault that Keynes saw in a metallic standard was in the desperate international competition for the limited supply of currency in order to maintain "investment." But this arose out of the limitation of the quantity of money, which, according to Keynes's theory, meant a limitation of that fall in the rate of interest which might be needed to maintain full employment.

A supply function and a demand function determine equilibrium at the point where output and demand become equal. Demand is equal to consumption, plus investment; output is equal to income, and income is equal to consumption, plus saving. If investment and saving are by definition equal, then output and demand are always equal, and their equality cannot determine an equilibrium point. The same system of definition, which excludes the classical explanation of the rate of interest as equalising saving and investment, also excludes the explanation of the price-level as equalising supply and demand.

There was no room in Keynes's analysis for functions representing either of these explanations. Yet, of course, he recognised the assumptions underlying them. He recognised that the marginal efficiency of capital and the rate of interest tended to equality. And he recognised that supply is determined by the expected excess of proceeds over costs, and so by the relation of prices to wages. But he made this determination of supply subordinate to the primary factors of his analysis: the rate of interest, investment, the multiplier, the propensity to consume.

It is possible to supplement this analysis with an account of the process by which an expanding or contracting volume of investment affects prices, and prices effect productive activity and output. The outcome would be a supply function adapted to Keynes's assumptions, but it would be subsidiary to the main analysis and not essential to it.

Notes

1. ECONOMIC JOURNAL, September 1949, p. 365.
2. *Ibid.*, p. 367.

93

Keynes and Supply Functions: A Rejoinder*

F.J. de Jong

The only point where Mr. Hawtrey seems to be attacking my argument directly has its kernel in the following sentence (see the third paragraph from the end of his Reply):

> "If investment and saving are by definition equal, then output and demand are always equal, and their equality cannot determine an equilibrium point. The same system of definition, which excludes the classical explanation of the rate of interest as equalising saving and investment, also excludes the explanation of the price level as equalising supply and demand."

This argument is directed, first, against the statement made on p. 4 of my paper that the equation

$$S_r = I_r \qquad (1.4)$$

represents a necessary and sufficient equilibrium condition.

Secondly, in the generalised model of p. 20, the equation $S = I$ is implied in

$$D = Y \qquad (6.3)$$

which is also taken as an equilibrium condition.

This can be seen from Fig. 1 on p. 4, where the 45°-line can be taken to represent *disposable income* from which derives consumption plus saving. The D_r-curve represents *earned income*, which is the same as the entrepreneurs' proceeds from their selling consumption and investment goods. Thus, within one and the same period, it holds good that:

$$\text{disposable income} = \text{consumption} + \text{saving}$$
$$\text{consumption} + \text{investment} = \text{earned income}$$

Income is determined in a unique way only *if* disposable income equals earned income, that is, *if* saving equals investment — *i.e., if* a situation of monetary equilibrium prevails (see p. 17 of my article). Paraphrasing J.G. Koopmans,[1] I define monetary equilibrium as a situation where the time rate of demand for

*Source: *Economic Journal,* Vol. 64, December 1954, pp. 840-2.

money equals the time rate of creation (supply) of money; in other words, this is a situation where the *excess* demand for money is equal to zero. The excess demand for all goods (as opposed to money) in terms of money will then also be zero so that, for one and the same period, disposable income equals earned income. This is the situation which Say had in mind when he stated his famous "law" of supply creating its own demand. However, since Say thought that this would *always* be the case, his "law" had the character of an identity[2] (demand for money *identically* equal to creation of money), whereas in the Keynesian strain of thought effective demand is determined by the equality of D and Y, which will, however, *only* be existent under *certain* values of the variables of the model. This means that the equation $D = Y$ is here taken as an equilibrium condition and therefore as a "common" equation (*i.e.*, not as an identity.)

Summarising, and taking "monetary equilibrium" in the Koopmansian way, we can state that Say thought that a situation of monetary equilibrium would always prevail by definition; Keynes, on the other hand, regarded monetary equilibrium as an equilibrium condition determining effective demand and, thereby, national income. This equilibrium condition can be written as $S = I$ (not, of course, as $S \equiv I$).[3]

Mr. Hawtrey's point is that we should write $S \equiv I$. It cannot be denied that there is indeed room for this vision in Keynes's book (see, for instance, p. 63 of the *General Theory*); this vision can even be supported by Lerner's 1936 article which met with Keynes's own approval. Is not Mr. Hawtrey's vision inconsistent with my exposition as given above?

The way out of this difficulty passes along the contradistinction of *ex ante* and *ex post* concepts. Myrdal, who is the *auctor intellectualis* of these concepts,[4] defines *ex post* savings and investments as "actually realised" savings and investments, as they can be registered in national book-keeping; *ex post,* savings must always of necessity equal investments, since in their *ex post* meaning, saving and investment involve also unintentional components.[5] Taking the concepts *ex ante*, we are concerned with the subjects' saving and investment *plans* based on their anticipations. Myrdal writes: "Had this distinction been kept in mind, much confusion about 'saving and investment' would have been avoided." This seems to me to be quite true. The argument of Mr. Hawtrey is entirely *ex post*, and only then does it hold good that $S \equiv I$.

But *ex post* concepts are not suitable for explaining how equilibrium is brought about. If Keynes's theory is to be taken as an equilibrium theory, the kernel of his argument must necessarily be taken *ex ante* lest his theory should fail to determine an equilibrium position. Although Keynes is not very lucid as to the contradistinction between *ex ante* and *ex post* concepts, a hint in the *ex ante* direction may be found on p. 64 of the *General Theory*: "The *decisions* to consume and the *decisions* to invest between them determine incomes." (Italics added.) Thus, national income is not determined by realised savings and investments, but by decisions to save and invest, *i.e.*, by *intended S* and *I* only, *i.e.*, finally, by *ex ante S* and *I*, where $S = I$ plays the part of an equilibrium condition and is therefore a "common" equation.

Notes

1. J.G. Koopmans, "Zum Problem des neutralen Geldes," in the volume *Beiträge zur Geldtheorie*, F.A. von Hayek ed., Vienna 1933, pp. 211-359, esp. p.278.

2. See the illuminating articles by Don Patinkin in *Econometrica* for 1948 (pp. 135-54), 1949 (pp. 1-27), and 1951 (pp. 134-51), and the concluding paper by K. Brunner, *ibid.,* 1951 (pp. 152-73).

3. One of the inconsistencies of the classical model was that Say's Law was taken as an identity whereas $S = I$ was *not* regarded as an identity but as an equality governed by the rate of interest.

4. G. Myrdal, *Monetary Equilibrium,* London, etc., 1939, pp. 45-7 (originally published in Swedish in the *Ekonomisk Tidsskrift* for 1931).

5. See also J. Tinbergen, *The Dynamics of Business Cycles,* Chicago, 1950, p. 162 (adapted from the Dutch original, 1942, by J.J. Polak).

94

An Evaluation of John Maynard Keynes*[1]

J.M. Gillman

A. Keynes's Three "Independent" Variables

In broad perspective, Keynes's theoretical system may be said to hold that the limits within which the oscillation of capitalist production takes place are marked off by three basic operational factors. These are: (a) the "propensity to consume," (b) the "marginal efficiency" of capital and (c) the interest rate. Keynes called these factors the independent variables — the "determinants" of his system, in which savings, investment, income and employment are the dependent variables — the "determinants." He warned, however, that his independent variables are independent only in the sense that their values cannot be inferred from one another (pp. 183-4; 245).[2]

(a) Keynes defined the propensity to consume, as the natural tendency of consumers, "as a rule and on the average," to leave an increasing margin between income and expenditures as the total income increases. As the total income rises, the portion *not* spent for consumption is increased; that is, the portion *saved* is greater. This applies especially to the wealthier segments of the population. *Their* marginal propensity to consume is characteristically "low."

Conversely, as the total income declines, consumer expenditures decline by less than the income. As the total income declines, consumption absorbs an increasing portion thereof; a decreasing portion is saved. The marginal propensity to consume then is "high." On the decline, all of the current income (and sometimes even more) tends to be consumed (pp. 28-32; 96-98).

(b) The marginal efficiency of capital Keynes defined as the *estimated expected* rate of return in the future on any *additional* capital currently to be invested. When the expected rate of profit appears likely to fall too close to the prevailing interest rate, the additional investment will not be made. This is so because interest as a payment for loans is an alternative form of income to the probable profit to be derived from productive investment.

*Source: *Science and Society*, Vol. 19 (2), Spring 1955, pp. 107-33.

The rate of profit tends to fall as new investments make the total of a community's capital assets "less scarce" — as additions increase the existing stock of capital goods. This, Keynes explains, holds especially true of advanced capitalist economies where the existing productive equipment is already large. If there is to be continued new investment, therefore, the interest rate must continually fall below the falling marginal efficiency of capital (pp. 31; 135-7; 213; 219-221).

(c) The interest rate thus appears to play a crucial role in Keynes's theoretical system. We treat of it, therefore, in detail at once, leaving his concepts of the propensity to consume and of the marginal efficiency of capital for later treatment.

B. Interest and the Interest Rate in the Keynesian System

1. *A "Psychological Phenomenon."* — We ask, first, what determines the interest rate?

Two things, said Keynes, determine the interest rate: "liquidity-preference" and the quantity of money. Liquidity-preference Keynes defined as the natural tendency of man to hold on to cash in the absence of sufficient inducement, in the form of interest, to part with it.

The quantity of money which an individual will want to hold is fixed by the amount which he has to begin with, by the degree of his current tendency toward liquidity-preference, and by the power of the counteracting pull of the current rate of interest.

So now we must find out what sort of thing this "liquidity-preference" is if we are to learn what determines the interest rate.

For this we must first learn something about, what Keynes calls, the "psychological time-preferences" inherent in the propensity to consume.

Each "individual," said Keynes, is confronted with two sets of time-preferences on which he must act. First he must make the psychological decision as to the portion of his income he will choose to spend *now*, that is, consume now, and the portion he will choose to save for spending in the future. Having decided on the portion he will save, he must make a further psychological decision: In what form to hold his savings — in the form of cash or in the form of debt?

This is where a man's liquidity-preference comes in. For reasons of certain business as well as psychological considerations, the uncertainty of future interest rates, among them, an individual will prefer to hold on to his cash. But hoards do not earn interest. He will, therefore, part with some of his money in the form of loans if the interest rate is sufficiently attractive. This is the "quantity of money" which an individual will prefer *not* to hold in the form of cash. In a word, the interest rate is the "reward for parting with liquidity for a specified period," and is determined at the point where the desire to hold a certain amount of cash is just offset by the pull of the interest rate offered for that quantity of cash (pp. 166-168).

Thus, in Keynes's words, the interest rate is "a highly psychological phenomenon" (p. 202). It is not a payment for "waiting," or "abstinence," which the neo-classical economists invented, but for *not hoarding* (p. 182); as we have just seen, for *parting* with liquidity.

Now, we ask, since interest is a part of the national income, where does the wherewithal to pay it come from? Is liquidity a productive service like labor? Does liquidity itself breed interest? Does money?

The fact is that by treating the interest rate as a psychological phenomenon Keynes abstracted interest from the realities of the business world, both as regards the forces which determine its being (and its rates) and as regards its probable effect on business decisions. This theory of interest is inadequate also historically. The time has long since passed when interest and the interest rate could be said to be determined by individual money-lenders, swaying on a balance between a hypothetical liquidity-preference and the pull of interest.

Actually, interest is a return on money capital of the same nature and origin as the return on all capital used in the capitalist production process; it is a form and a part of capitalist profit, a payment made out of the profit earned on the entire capital for the use of a particular portion thereof, even though this portion may be nothing more than a bank credit advanced on production in process. One capitalist (say, a business firm) shares his profit with another capitalist (an individual, a bank, another business firm) in return for a loan in order to make more profit, or even only to maintain the present rate of profit. He would not borrow if it did not "pay him" to do so.

Take a capitalist with a given sum of money, M, and start him in an industrial business. (Where he got this money is of no consequence for the moment; say, he inherited it). Now, a capitalist does not engage in a business venture and risk his capital for the purpose of seeing his money go through a process of reproduction only to come back intact in the original amount. He wants his money to "make" money. He wants his money, M, to come back to him enlarged to the extent of M'.

To achieve this end our capitalist must do several things. To begin with, he must part with his liquid capital, M—he must *part with liquidity*— in the form of converting it into labor-power, materials and production equipment. He then must put these production commodities through a production process which will result in their transformation into new commodities, C, which he will sell at a profit. His original M will have been "metamorphosed," as Marx described it, into M'.

In other words, in order for interest to emerge at all there must first take place a transformation of money capital into commodity capital and then back again into money capital. M must be converted to C and C to M', for profit and, therefore, for interest to emerge.

In the Keynesian schemes, both the interest and the money-supply, which, according to Keynes, is one of its determinants, are abstracted from this sphere of production, where alone they can originate, and are given an independently initiating existence. Keynes seems to ignore the fact that it is production that provides both the basis for money creation (credit) and the demand for credit-money, and that it is production which produces the income (profit) out of which alone interest can be paid, and by which alone its rate can be determined.

Keynes would have it the other way around: that money generates production and that interest is paid for that money for other reasons than those arising from production. Thus, in Keynes's view, money breeds money. Conceived in this manner, the whole question of the source of capitalist profit is circumvented; the whole question of capitalist class relations as they manifest themselves in the capitalist production process is ignored; and all the consequences that follow from these class relations can be reasoned out of existence.

If, then, we are to understand the phenomenon of interest in capitalist society, we must understand the phenomenon of profit in such a society. For that, we must know the economic and *social* origins of profit and how it is apportioned among the various forms of capital — money capital, merchant capital, industrial capital. And there is nothing "psychological" in any of these determinations, except that the businessman is a *homo sapiens,* the same as the rest of us, and except that as a businessman he must be more calculating in his business actions than he is, say, in his church or community relations.

What should be clear is that for the capitalists as a class it is of little moment in what form they get the returns on their capital, whether in the form of interest ("coupon clipping") or in the form of "profit" (from dividends), so long as the rate is satisfactory. It might make a difference to the individual capitalist. As a matter of convenience, the individual capitalist might wish to have a portion of the returns on his investment come to him in the regular-time flow of fixed interest payments, rather than in irregular and fluctuating dividends on stocks. Generally, he will "distribute his risks." He will divide his investments among various forms of securities to suit his convenience as dictated by the exigencies of the business cycle, price trends, etc. But it all comes out of the same source. It all comes out of the "earnings" of the total capital, as payment to capital ownership.

Except in times of crisis, when all money and credit relations are violently disrupted, the rate of interest, therefore, must depend primarily on the prospective profitability of the loan to the borrower, and only slightly if at all on a psychological "liquidity-preference" of the lender. It is not liquidity-preference which determines the rate of interest, but it is the rate of profit which determines the rate of interest and *so* perhaps the liquidity-preference — the reluctance to part with cash.[3]

But whatever the origin of profit, interest can be nothing more than a segment of profit, or of surplus-value, to use the Marxist terminology. Where the capitalist has his own money resources he receives his full profit. (Henry

Ford did essentially that). If he has to borrow from others, he must share it with them. When profits are low, then interest rates will tend to be low. When profits are high, interest rates will tend to be high, even though at such times liquidity-preference may be receding to the vanishing point.

It is only in times of crisis — and then it becomes one of the symptoms of crisis — that the interest rate tends to move in the opposite direction from profits, and violently so. It is then (or it used to be so), when profits fall drastically, that the interest rate may rise by leaps. It is then, that liquidity-preference may become a controlling influence. There is then a universal rush for liquidity — to "conserve" resources and to meet contractual obligations. As the pressure for liquidity becomes general, everybody trying to avoid bankruptcy, "liquidity-preference" stiffens, a "money shortage" develops and the rate of interest rises sharply as the value of disposable assets sharply falls. Obligations cannot be met and an epidemic of bankruptcies ensues. Under these conditions, "liquidity-preference" becomes so marked as to create the illusion that it has an independent existence. "On the eve of the crisis," Marx wrote,[4] "the bourgeois, with the self-sufficiency that springs from intoxicating prosperity, declares money to be a vain imagination. Commodities alone are money. But now [in a crisis] the cry is everywhere: money alone is a commodity! As the hart pants after fresh water, so pants his soul after money [as if this were] the only wealth."

In placing liquidity-preference at the bottom of the interest rate, Keynes generalized a crisis phenomenon into a universal principle. And this led him to postulate an independence for the rate of interest in relation to the rate of profit (the marginal efficiency of capital). To maintain that thesis he created the rentier whom he endowed with the psychology of liquidity-preference and placed upon him the chief responsibility for determining the interest rate. For his pains he decreed his euthanasia, together with his interest charges.

2. *Interest and Investment.* — In the Keynesian theory of the interest-investment relationship, a decline in the rate of interest increases the inducement to invest, while a rise reduces that inclination.

The historical fact is that the rate of interest does not vitally affect the rate of investment.

Mordecai Ezekiel has shown that for the United States, for the years 1921-40 which he studied, "No evidence could be found that reductions in the interest rate stimulated investment."[5]

A comprehensive empirical survey conducted for England by a group of Oxford University scholars brought forth similar results.[6] Two of the conclusions of that survey read:

> (1) There is almost universal agreement that short-term rates of interest do not directly affect investment either in stocks [inventories] or in fixed capital. . . The effect of changes in the rate is too small in comparison with the profit margins [note!] to make any difference.

(2) The majority deny that the long-term rate of interest affects investment directly. . . The majority who deny its importance give as their reasons either that they do not need to borrow for extension or that it is too small an element in comparison with depreciation, obsolescence, the uncertainty of the market for their product.[7]

The reasons given by the British businessmen for the ineffectiveness of the interest rate on investment decisions reflect with special force two long-run economic trends which Keynes ignored in this connection. One is the secular decline of interest rates over the past half century and more. The other is the growing tendency of corporations to self-financing. With the growth of giant industry and its command over financial resources, and with the growing vertical integration of industry and the spread of the holding company, more and more of corporate investment is financed from internal funds — from depreciation reserves and from undistributed profits. The more industries draw on their own resources for investment purposes, the less they need to borrow. The less they borrow, the less the interest rate affects investment decisions.[8]

The historical fact is that interest as an operating expense has been a declining fraction of capitalist enterprise. A United States Department of Commerce study of the "Financial Experience" of a representative sample of large and medium size American manufacturing firms, covering the years 1927-1951, has shown that the proportion of firms whose interest payments amounted to 10 per cent or more of profits before taxes and interest has declined from 40 per cent for 1927 to less than 6 per cent for 1951.[9] For all American corporations, that is, including public utilities, etc., as well as the manufacturing industries, interest payments are shown to have amounted to 8 per cent of earnings before taxes and interest in 1952, in contrast to 12 per cent just before World War II, and to 30 per cent in the late 1920's.[10]

3. *Sources of Investment Funds.* — Studies of the growing tendency of corporations to finance themselves from their own funds are still meager. Statistics are available for the years 1922-37 in the *Proceedings* of the Temporary National Economic Committee (the "TNEC"),[11] but none for prior years. A long-term trend cannot, therefore, be firmly established on the basis of those figures, especially since of the 16 years covered by the TNEC, 8 fell within the period of the depression when almost all investment stopped, except for replacements from depreciation reserves. Again, the distribution of the war-time investments by sources of funds, following the period covered by the TNEC, would not at all be a scientifically justifiable basis for conclusions as to trends. There was too much of an admixture of government financing in the expansion of private industry during the years 1940-45 to permit a clear-cut classification of sources of funds. The five-year amortization privilege granted on war construction especially vitiates any comparisons with previous peacetime years.[12]

If, then, we learn from the TNEC figures that in the 8 prosperous years, 1922-29, internal sources provided 78½ per cent of the total corporate financing and in the 8 depression years, 1930-37, over 94 per cent, we have, if not a reliable indication of trend, at least a measure of the degree of independence of American corporations of Keynes's rentier. That gentleman recedes further into the limbo of history when, in addition, we make allowance for corporate financing through banks and through "private placements" with insurance companies and similar fiduciary institutions.

The financing data for the postwar years are equally informative as well as instructive.

In the six years 1946-1951 the manufacturing firms to which we referred invested a total of $86 billion for capital expansion. Of this total only $14 billion, or 16 per cent, were raised by borrowing through banks or insurance companies. Over 65 per cent ($56 billion) were met from retained profits and depreciation reserves. The remaining 19 per cent were covered by assumed current liabilities, more than half of which were reserves for federal taxes, and all of which would be liquidated from future earnings.[13]

It would seem, then, that the role of interest rate as one of the principal determinants of the rate of investment, and so of the business cycle, which Keynes assigned to it, has been descending to the vanishing point, as the rate has gone down and as corporations in any event, have been drawing less and less on outside sources to finance their investment needs.

C. The Marginal Efficiency of Capital

1. *"Expectations."* — Investment is slowed, said Keynes, when expectations — the marginal efficiency of capital — decline. The marginal efficiency of capital declines as investment makes capital less scarce.

We need not linger here to show why the Keynesian concept of the marginal efficiency of capital, as expectations, does not constitute a realistic approach to an analysis of economic fluctuations. Like liquidity-preference and the interest rate, Keynes's "expectations" are a purely psychological phenomenon. They are born, he tells us, of "animal spirits" and are nurtured on the "nerves and hysteria" of stock market speculators. They lack, therefore, the tangible qualities required for analytical purposes.[14] As Schumpeter phrased it:

> Expectation acquires explanatory value only if we are made to understand *why* people expect *what* they expect. Otherwise . . . expectation conceals problems instead of solving them.[15]

After all, we need to go but a short step beyond the "science of business forecasting" to discover that the "animal spirits" which call forth the day-to-day gyrations of stock prices do not determine the next phase of the business cycle. It is not the rise or fall of stock prices which determines the rise or fall of corporate profits and corporate investment, but the other way around. It is when corporate profits and corporate investments are expected to rise or fall that stock prices tend to rise or fall, except when the "bears" make a feast of the "lambs." It is here that we should look for causes, not in the state of speculators' expectations. These, too, follow, rather than precede profits and investments. As a rule, only a small fraction of stock market transactions is channeled to new investment. For the most part they are dealings in existing stocks.

To quote Schumpeter again:

> ... those ups and downs of ... investment expenditure are themselves only a surface phenomenon and ... we must try to see what there is behind it ... Unless we do this, investment ... is a mere label for a blank space and if we fill this blank space by some such thing as expectations we are filling a blank with another blank.[16]

As "expectations," the marginal efficiency of capital has no scientific significance unless it is measured against actual profit trends, for instance, if it were a reflection of the fact that "the current yield shows signs of falling off." (*General Theory,* p.317). But then the question would arise, why is the current yield falling off? Keynes gave no clue to an answer, except that investors suddenly discover that by their investment they had made capital less scarce; that is, that profit was falling off!

2. *The Scarcity Theory of Capital.* — Keynes's answer in the form of his scarcity theory of capital is contradicted by the very essence of the capitalist process. "The only reason," Keynes said, why an asset, in the course of its use, yields a return greater than its own cost, that is, a profit, "is because it is *scarce.*" "If capital becomes less scarce, the excess yield will diminish" (p. 213). But it is precisely by making capital "less scarce" that profits are increased. The sole purpose of invention, innovations, and the whole gamut of technological improvement is to make capital "less scarce." A business firm would have no reason to add to its equipment, or improve it with new devices, except as it expected thereby to enhance or at least maintain its current rate of profit.

Keynes's scarcity theory of capital cannot answer the question of the falling rate of profit, any more than could the same theory in the hands of Adam Smith 150 years earlier. It was Smith who, following Hume, had tried to explain the falling tendency of the rate of profit as a consequence of the progress of capital accumulation and of the growing competition among the capitals.[17] But, wrote Marx, "when Adam Smith explains the fall in the rate of profit as due to the overabundance of capital, the accumulation of capital, he is speaking of a *permanent* effect, and this is wrong. On the other hand, a transitory overabundance of capital, overproduction, crisis, is something different. There are no permanent crises."[18]

The "permanent effect" which Marx had in mind in this connection is that of the law of diminishing returns which guided the thinking of most later classicists (the neo-classicists) in their search for an explanation of the falling tendency of the rate of profit. This, said Marx essentially, is a one-way theory. It works only downward, and is irreversible. As more labor is applied to the same amount of capital, this theory asserts, the output per unit of labor declines. Similarly, as more capital is put into use with the same number of laborers, the output per unit of capital declines. Either condition results in a fall of the rate of profit.

The flaw of this theory is that it assumes no progress in the capitalist production process. It assumes that the new capital is of the same quality as the old. It admits of no possible qualitative improvement in the productivity of labor by virtue of the introduction of the new capital.

Keynes's scarcity theory of capital is of this static nature.

We take as given [he wrote] the existing skill and quantity of available labor, the existing quality and quantity of available equipment, the existing technique, the degree of competition, the tastes and habits of the consumer . . . as well as the social forces . . . which determine the distribution of the national income. [*General Theory*, p. 245].

Not that he assumed these factors to be constant, but "merely that, in this place and context [he was] not considering or taking into account the effects and consequences of changes in them"! (*Ibid.*)

But not only may the new capital be an improvement over the old — it generally is; it may also revolutionize the efficiency of the old capital, thereby decreasing unit costs and increasing profits. Capital additions, or even mere replacements, are for the most part aimed at "capital-saving" as well as at labor-saving, the traditional role assigned to the introduction of a new machine. The continuous technological revolutions which capital investment produces are a basic feature of capitalism. They are, in fact, the very mechanism of the dynamism of the system. To assume that capitalism can operate on the basis of technological constancy is to project motion upon an assumption of no motion. Yet this is what Keynes essentially does in his scarcity theory of capital.

Incidentally, the technological dynamism of capitalism of which we just spoke offers a basis for at least part of an explanation of the decline of investment opportunities, which concerned Keynes so much. From purely a technological point of view it may be said that it is capital-saving investment which leads to a decrease in investment potentials, when saving potentials are rising, rather than a growing abundance of capital and a consequent falling rate of profit. If in a particular industry a decrease of investment occurs, this may be due not to an increase in the volume of its physical assets (and a presumed fall in the rate of profit because of the operation of the law of diminishing returns), but to the greater output achieved with a relatively lesser volume of capital. Investment opportunities then would diminish not because capital becomes abundant, but because the new capital makes labor more productive. This (as we show elsewhere) has indeed been the striking characteristic of 20th century capitalism: a rising labor productivity without a corresponding rise in capital assets.

Finally, it should be noted, that the law of diminishing returns — Keynes's scarcity theory of capital — cannot serve as an explanation of the business *cycle.* For so long as there is any new investment, the total volume of capital must grow and, on Keynes's terms, the rate of profit fall. That is exemplified by his view of the effects of investment in advanced capitalist countries. As the system progresses, he argued, progress becomes more difficult. As a nation's investment and income rise, more tends to be saved and, unless investment outlets can be maintained, the system of capitalist production must run down into a depression. Since, however, according to the *General Theory* investment is limited by the marginal efficiency of capital and since the marginal efficiency of capital tends to fall as with the progress of industry " capital becomes less scarce," the "progress of industry" leads to its own retrogression. True, further investment would be possible if the interest rate were depressed low enough to raise the marginal efficiency of capital. But too low an interest rate meets with the barrier of liquidity-preference of the money lenders, and the principal source of investment funds is dried up.

Thus we arrive at a theory of secular stagnation, rather than at a theory of cyclical change. And again we meet with the limitations imposed upon progress by the psychological law of the propensity to consume, the law which states that as income rises, less relatively is consumed and more is saved — more tends to be saved than is good for the system.

We must now, therefore, examine the meaning and import of the Keynesian concept of the propensity to consume. Before doing that, however, we must note that if pertinent at all, this concept applies only to the relation between individual consumer income and individual consumer saving. It cannot by any means apply to corporate income and corporate saving — increasingly the fuel that propels capitalist production.

D. The Propensity to Consume

1. *The Consumption Function.* — The place which Keynes assigned to consumption in the formation of the business cycle he based on two complementary assumptions. One, that consumption is a declining proportion of the national income. The other, that investment, through the multiplier, determines that level of income. It follows that the volume of consumption depends on the rate of investment. Investment, therefore, is largely independent

of consumption.

These assumptions do not, however, square with the realities of the business world. Consumption does not alone *depend* on income, but also helps create it. Nor, therefore, is investment the *sole* determinant of the level of income, and so of the rate of consumption. Consumption depends not only on the current income, but also on past and expected future income, thus currently creating investment opportunities which, in their turn, create new sources of consumer income. Consumption and investment are interdependent forces, moving together both up and down the business cycle, although at different rates and with different amplitudes.

We have here to be on our guard, however, not only against the proposition that all income originates in investment, but also against the proposition that all investment originates in immediate consumer demand. True, all investment can have as its ultimate justification only the satisfaction of consumer wants, even if its primary aim is the private accumulation of capital. But under capitalism the bonds between production and consumption are not so immediate as the underconsumptionists claim, nor so loose as Keynes visualized them to be. The investment in the production of automobiles, of the radio, of the electric refrigerator, and lately of television, or of the thousand other new and improved articles of consumption of today did not come in response to an existing consumer demand. On the other hand, the automobile manufacturer *et al.* will not contine to produce their products unless the market for them remains viable.

Nor does the producer of capital goods gear his investment to the immediate needs of the producers of current consumer goods. He also invests in the production of new and improved machinery and new and improved materials for the manufacture of new and improved old consumer products in anticipation of a market. So, just as we have "induced" investment (consumer demand stimulating production), we have also "induced" consumption (the production of new consumer products and services which create and stimulate consumer demand). The whole of modern "salesmanship" and the multi-billion dollar advertising industry live in this new world of the capitalist production process.

Keynes's assignment of primacy to investment over consumption was, in large part, a reaction against both the underconsumptionists who, in giving consumption the primacy, endow it with independence in the formation of the business cycle and against Say, who had postulated a virtually unbreakable unity between production and consumption. But in doing so, Keynes compounded the errors of both the underconsumptionists and Say. He over-estimated the degree of independence between investment and consumption by postulating a separation where there is organic unity.

The fact is that the relation between production and consumption cannot be treated either in the one-sided manner of the underconsumptionists or in the form of a Sayian identity. Capitalist economy is an exploitative economy. In the employment of wage-labor the capitalist constantly strives for an increasing divergence between the output of the worker and his consumption power which he gets in the form of wages. This is how the capitalist increases his profit, or surplus-value, in Marx's terminology. With an increasing capital investment per worker — with the "progress of industry," so to say — the individual worker must receive a decreasing portion of the output if the rate of profit on the invested capital is not to fall. That is, an increasing ratio of the value of the physical capital to wages requires an increase in the ratio of surplus-value to wages to prevent a fall in the rate of profit.

But capitalist economy is also a market economy. The commodities produced must be *sold* at a profit, and only such commodities are produced and only in such quantities as can so be sold. In a market economy, therefore, total production and total sales (consumption) must be held in fairly close proportionality to each other. This becomes possible in the recovery phase of the business cycle, when there are both increasing employment and a substantial reservoir of unemployed workers. Under these conditions an expansion in the aggregate of investment capital can take place without at the same time increasing the capital invested per worker. The rate of profit can be maintained without having to decrease the workers' portion of the output. Hence, in this period we can have a continuous expansion of total wage payments as employment increases, a corresponding expansion of consumer demand, and an increasing capital stock which remains in fair proportion to both wage payments and consumer demand. All this can take place without a decline in the rate of profit.

Note that both of these conditions, namely, the maintenance of the rate of profit and the maintenance of a rough proportionality between investment and consumption, are essential to the continued operation of the system. The one, because capitalist profit is the *raison d'être* of the system, the other, because, in the last analysis, investment must eventuate in consumption.

But as we approach a condition of full employment, as the industrial reserve army approaches exhaustion, and no new resources of exploitable labor are at hand, total wage payments must level off. If capitalists should then continue investment, a sharp rise in the ratio of investment capital to wages would occur and the rate of profit would fall. For to maintain the rate of profit constant under these conditions would require a sharp rise in the "rate of exploitation," in the ratio of surplus-value to wages. This would have to mean a rise in the demand for investment goods, in the face of a potentially falling demand for consumption goods. This, as we have just seen, is intolerable for any length of time in a capitalist economy. Expanded investment under capitalism justifies itself only in the possibility of the realization of an expanded surplus-value. This requires expanding markets, including, above all, an expanding market for consumer goods which under the circumstances would be leveling off.

Thus, the private accumulation of capital requires ultimately a disproportionality between production and consumption in order to maintain the rate of profit and, at the same time, a proportionality between them in order to maintain the rate of investment.

When a condition of full employment comes into sight, the conflict, the "contradiction," between these two incompatible drives comes to a head, further accumulation is negated and a crisis results. The crisis, by reconstituting the reserve army of unemployed workers, restores the conditions for a renewal of capital accumulation and for a renewal of expansion of production and consumption.

Say's Law postulated such strong bonds of unity between production and consumption as to preclude the emergence of any market problems, in the sense of limitations to the aggregate consumer demand, and hence the possibility of a general "glut." Keynes, observing the rupture between investment and consumption which occurs as a result of a crisis, projected it as a normal feature of capitalism. He did the same, we noted, with the crisis phenomenon of liquidity-preference and with the crisis phenomenon of an over-abundance of capital. He failed to see that the normal relation between investment, production and consumption is that of a dialectical unity of opposites, and so over-emphasized the degree of independence between them. He, therefore, postulated as his law of the business cycle that consumer consumption decreases and investor consumption increases (relatively) as production increases, until an intolerable relationship is created between a falling marginal efficiency of capital and a sticky interest rate. The incongruity of the assumption of a continued divergence between consumption and investment as a normal feature of a market economy seems to have escaped him entirely.

2. *Consumption and Saving.* — The double assumption, of the dependence of consumption on the income level and of the unique role of investment in the determination of that level of income, compelled Keynes to make the still further assumption that the consumption-income relationship is a stable relationship. It becomes impaired, according to Keynes, only under unusual and revolutionary circumstances.

Actually, for the vast mass of consumers this relationship is highly unstable. Numerous studies have shown that this relationship varies not only in line with Keynes's conception of the propensity to consume (as a schedule of demands), but also, as we have pointed out, in response to changing price levels, to earning prospects, and to past incomes. For the middle income families "expenditures on a number of items increase faster than income, and total expenditures press hard on the total income," according to one observer. Basing herself on American experience, this observer concluded that

> There is no clear evidence that the "psychological law" [of the propensity to consume] is a fundamental law of human nature . . . Mr. Keynes seems to have propounded a theorem which may be applicable to a particular group at particular times, not a general psychological law which may be relied

upon to describe the action of all men (or even most men) at all times.[19]

We ourselves have witnessed the experience of the postwar years when consumer expenditures not only rose with a rising income, but at times exceeded it. Less was saved from current income, past savings were used up and future savings were mortgaged in purchases on the installment plan to make up for wartime shortages or to advance living standards. In the third quarter of 1950, at the outbreak of war in Korea, the increase in consumer expenditures (to beat the renewed inflation and in anticipation of renewed wartime restrictions) exceeded the increase in consumer income. All these were abnormal times, one would say. But when on the curve of a business cycle are times "normal"? On the upgrade? On the downgrade? At the bottom? At the peak? In a period of deflation?

In all the postwar years, U.S. Department of Commerce studies have shown, consumer expenditures exceeded their average (1929-41) consumption-income relationship.[20] Especially noteworthy is the fact that this departure from "normal" occurred in the expenditures for non-durable as well as for durable goods. Here, in the case of the non-durable, there was no pressure to make up for wartime shortages as might be argued with respect to the expenditures on durables. What these studies reveal, rather, is the pressure of the upward shift of the standard of living of large segments of American consumers which resulted from the larger than normal earnings during the war years. As Americans earned more they learned to live better, to buy better food and better clothing. Rather than save more out of their higher postwar earnings, as Keynes's "law" would lead us to expect they would, American consumers spent even more than their higher earnings, by drawing on their past and future savings[21] in order to hold on to their newly acquired living habits.

Keynes's psychological law of the propensity to consume does not seem to apply in the real world.[22]

E. Policy Recommendations

> . . . for everywhere he really pleads for a definite policy, and on every page the ghost of that policy looks over the shoulder of the analyst, frames his assumptions, guides his pen. . .

Thus did Schumpeter in his first review of the *General Theory* characterize Keynes and the objectives of his book.[23]

1. *General Monetary Reform.* — In our study of Keynes thus far we have confined ourselves almost entirely to his *General Theory*. But before the *General Theory* there were his two-volume *Treatise On Money* (1930), which his biographer has characterized as his "most mature work"[24]; his *Tract On Monetary Reform* (1923), *The Economic Consequences of the Peace* and *A*

Revision of the Treaty (1919, 1922); *Indian Currency and Finance* (1913); *The End of Laissez-Faire* (1926); *The Means of Prosperity* (1933) and numerous essays and magazine and newspaper articles, and work on Royal Commissions. In all of these Keynes sought by monetary reform and through the control of the flow of saving and investment to correct what to him seemed to be the faults which were, in general, laying capitalism in Europe low and which were leading to the breakdown of British imperialism, in particular. As far back as 1924 he wrote in the London weekly *Nation* (May 24):

> I look, then, for the ultimate cure of unemployment and for the stimulus which shall initiate a cumulative prosperity to *monetary reform* — which will remove fear — and to the diversion of the National Savings from relatively barren foreign investment into *state-encouraged* constructive enterprise at home, which will inspire confidence.[25]

The abolition of the gold standard, the establishment of a gold-exchange standard, central banking operations, an international credit union, a super-national central bank (which eventually took the milder form of the International Monetary Fund and of the International Bank of Reconstruction and Development), the control of the money supply, of the interest rates,[26] of the flow of saving and investment — these were the mechanisms and methods for effecting the reforms required to cure unemployment and stimulate "cumulative prosperity," — to halt the secular decline of capitalism and to save the world from communism.[27]

When he began to work on his *Treatise On Money,* Keynes tells us, he was still uncertain regarding the relation of money to the general theory of supply and demand. When he finished it, he had "made some progress towards pushing monetary theory back to becoming a theory of output as a whole." (*General Theory,* p. vi). In the *General Theory* he shed all reservations. Here he fully committed himself to the quantity theory of money in its earliest classical sense. "So long as there is unemployment," he wrote (p. 296), "*employment* will change in the same proportion as the quantity of money and when there is full employment, *prices* will change in the same proportion as the quantity of money." (Keynes's italics).

The *General Theory* thus becomes Keynes's intellectual apparatus, his rationale, for the use of the mechanism of money as a means of mitigating unemployment which, at the time he was writing the book, was threatening the very existence of capitalism.

The reasoning is simple enough, once you grant the premises. An increase of the money-supply will lower the rate of interest. A lowered rate of interest will raise the differential between it and the marginal efficiency of capital. An increase in the money supply will also tend to raise prices and to lower real wages. That, too, will tend to widen the differential between the interest rate and the marginal efficiency of capital, as well as raise the marginal efficiency of capital itself. This widening differential will induce new investment. An increase of investment will raise the national income. This will raise employment. And so on, and so forth, in a cycle of boom and bust.

We need not here repeat the well-established objections to the quantity theory of money, in general, and to its relevance in an explanation of the formation of the business cycle, specifically. Here we concern ourselves with the question of the feasibility of Keynes's specific policy recommendations as enunciated in his *General Theory*.

2. *Specific Policy Recommendations.* — In essence these were three in number: One, that the state impose high income taxes on estates and on the personal incomes of the wealthy classes with a view of raising their propensity to consume. Two, by means of an increase of the money supply and of commodity prices, to reduce real wages as an inducement to investment. Three, as a long-range proposition, that the state undertake to control and direct the flow of saving and investment — to "organize" and "socialize" investment — "with a view to a progressive decline in the marginal efficiency of capital." (p. 325; also p. 376.) With respect to organizing and socializing investment, Keynes wrote as far back as 1926:

> I believe that some coordinated act of *intelligent* judgment is required as to the scale on which it is desirable that the community as a whole should save, the scale on which these savings should go abroad in the form of foreign investments, and whether the present organization of the investment market distributes savings along the most nationally productive channels. *I do not think that these matters could be left entirely to the chances of private judgment and private profits, as they are at present.* [28]

That coordination was to be done by the state, by the intellectual aristocracy from whose ranks, according to Keynes, the state apparatus is constituted.

None of these policy recommendations, however, did Keynes think through seriously, either as to their practical feasibility or as to their probable impact on the business cycle.

As to the first recommendation, Keynes took back with one hand what he gave with the other. In the first place, he would go no further with his high taxation than to skim a thin layer off the cream — only the "large disparities" would be removed. In the second place, he would leave the conditions which raise it undisturbed. Not only did he insist on the "social and psychological justification for significant inequalities of incomes and wealth" (p. 374), but once investment has been "socialized," the individual entrepreneur would be free to carry on as before — "the classical theory comes into its own from this point onwards" (p. 387). All capitalist class relations remain the same — the class ownership of capital and the class-determination and the class-control of the distribution of the product of industry that go with that ownership. The social and psychological needs for significant inequalities of incomes and wealth are fully met. In the "improvements in the technique of modern capitalism by the agency of collective action," Keynes wrote, "there is nothing . . . which is seriously incompatible with what seems to me to be the essential characteristic of capitalism, namely, the dependence upon the intense appeal to the *money-making* and money-loving instincts of individuals as the main motive force of the economic machine."[29]

The second recommendation is partly new only in the proposed method of its implementation. Otherwise, it is the long-standing classical idea of passing on the cost of economic crises to the underlying, working population. Only the classicists would "cut wages" as a means of restoring profitability of employment. Keynes would restore profitability of employment by raising the price of wage-goods, that is, by reducing the workers' real wages. "In general," he wrote, "an increase in employment can only occur to the accompaniment of a decline in the rate of real wages" (p. 17). It is the idea of the classicists brought in by the back door. A "Machiavellian device," Professor Ellis called it.[30]

The year before the *General Theory* was published, Professor Pigou, the official bearer of the classical tradition, had written that if a policy of wage-cuts "could be practically carried out, it would . . . be a true antidote, within limits, to slump conditions. It would not abolish, but it would effectively lessen the waste of unemployment."[31]

In America, the same year, Professor W.I. King, echoed these sentiments by declaring that if wage earners would accept a wage cut of 50 per cent, production and employment would nearly double, as costs would be cut in half and the "working man" would be able to buy twice as much goods for every dollar of wages. "He would be approximately twice as prosperous as at present."[32]

Keynes would have none of these crudities. "Whilst," he wrote (p. 9), "workers will usually resist a reduction in money-wages, it is not their practice to withdraw their labor whenever there is a rise in the price of wage-goods," Keynes's term for consumer commodities. The same idea is repeated on page 264 there.

But, regretfully comments the German ex-banker-professor L. Albert Hahn:

> If Lord Keynes has discovered the mechanism of lowering real wages through monetary manipulation, he has at the same time destroyed the working of the mechanism by drawing attention to it.[33]

3. *Keynes's "State."* — With respect to the third policy recommendation, namely, that the state organize and socialize investment, two questions arise. First is the question whether once the eggs are scrambled can they be unscrambled? Once you begin to socialize investment how long can it be before no room is left for individual private enterprise, that is, for capitalism?

The necessity for socializing investment, which follows upon the Keynesian analysis, is not alone cyclically conditioned. It is essentially a secular phenomenon, as with the progress of industry capital becomes "less scarce." It is not, therefore, a case of the state's entering into and withdrawing from the economy with the changing phases of the cycle. Socializing investment, on Keynes's premises, must become a long-run and cumulative program of government. Once, then, the need is admitted for the state to step in, it must also be admitted that it is there to stay, not as a means of saving capitalism, as Keynes assumes, but of gradually transforming it. Is capitalism ready and willing to get itself "socialized" out of existence? Keynes treated this whole question rather cavalierly. He really never followed through his own premises. But there is a prior question, which must and can be answered, yet which Keynes also ignored. It is this: Can we expect the state, which in any class society can do no more than act in the interests of its ruling class, undertake economic policies which in the end must contravene these interests? "Organizing" and "socializing" investment must mean depriving the capitalists not only of their basic means of self-perpetuation as capitalists but, if these succeed in effecting "a progressive decline in the marginal efficiency of capital," also of their sole motive for being capitalists — of their compelling drive to raise the rate of profit.

The answer, of course, is, no. No ruling class ever abolished itself, nor will the capitalist class permit its state to do it for them.

The alternative is to say with Dr. Lawrence Klein, an American Keynesian, that the capitalists can be brought "to look upon the entire system and their social responsibilities" to correct its faults.[34] But then we should be guilty with Dr. Klein of the triple illusion:

(1) that the capitalists as a class recognize any social responsibilities except such as may redound to their own benefit.

(2) that they could "correct" the basic faults of capitalism without ceasing to be capitalists.

(3) that they *would* do so if appealed to on rational grounds as Keynes and Klein would appeal.

A hundred years earlier Marx and Engels dealt with a form of economic reform, "Bourgeois Socialism" they called it, which was not unlike that entertained by Keynes and his disciples today. Bourgeois socialism, Marx and Engels pointed out, would change existing material conditions for the betterment of the working class, without altering the capitalist relations of production which determine these material conditions. But such economic reform, they said, can have substance only as a "mere figure of speech":

Free trade: For the benefit of the working class. Protective duties: For the benefit of the working class. Prison reform: For the benefit of the working class. These are the last words and the only seriously meant words of Bourgeois Socialism.

It is summed up in the phrase: The bourgeois are bourgeois — for the benefit of the working class.[35]

Keynes, according to his biographer, "believed in the supreme value of intellectual leadership, in the wisdom of the few" and that the apparatus of the state would always, in Great Britain, be in the hands of the chosen few.[36]

In his *General Theory* (p. 383) Keynes wrote:

> . . . the ideas of economists and political philosophers, both when they are right and when they are wrong, are more powerful than is commonly understood. Indeed the world is ruled by little else. Practical men, who believe themselves to be quite exempt from any intellectual influence, are usually the slaves of some defunct economist. Madmen in authority, who hear voices in the air, are distilling their frenzy from some academic scribbler of a few years back.

Little did Keynes, apparently, understand that his own thoughts and ideas did not spring from an innate wisdom, but that they were reflections of the social forces originating outside his brains; that it was such social forces which alone ultimately compel the actions of "practical" men and the ravings of "madmen in authority." Indeed, these *actions* and ravings are part of the very social forces which determine our, and determined, his thinking. Not that ideas have no effect on our actions. On the contrary, they often serve as powerful, facilitating agents in *furthering* the progress of mankind. But to exert such effects these ideas must themselves have their origins in the need to solve the ever-new problems which arise from that progress.

In the real world, it would seem capitalists are not initially impelled to act as they do by the ideas of economists and political scientists, even of such astute economists and political scientists as John Maynard Keynes.

Notes

1. Adapted from the author's manuscript on the theory of economic crises.
2. Unless otherwise indicated, page references between parentheses in this article are from his *General Theory of Employment, Interest and Money.*
3. Writing in the third quarter of the 19th century, Marx noted (*Capital*, Vol. III, p. 717): "In our times the rate of profit regulates the rate of interest; in those times [before the rise of industrial capitalism] the rate of interest regulated the rate of profit." "Those times" refers to the era of mercantilism, which was the immediate predecessor era to that of industrial capitalism. In that era loan capital was the chief means by which the merchant could command, and so derive profit from the sale of the output of the then *manu*facturer, the *handi*craftsman. Seventy-five years before that, Adam Smith had written: "It may be laid down as a maxim, that wherever a great deal can be made by the use of money, a great deal will commonly be given for the use of it; and that wherever little can be made by it, less will commonly be given for it. . . . The progress of interest, therefore, may lead us to form some notion of the progress of profit." *The Wealth of Nations.* (New York, 1906), p. 87.

4. *Capital,* Vol. I, p. 155. See the same idea in his *Critique,* p. 198, where he writes (in 1859!): "This sudden reversing from a system of credit to a system of hard cash heaps theoretical fright on top of the practical panic. . ."

5. "Statistical Investigations of Saving, Consumption, and Investment," the *American Economic Review,* March and June, 1942, pp. 22-49 and 272-307, respectively. The quoted sentence is from page 306.

6. *Oxford University Papers,* No. 1, October, 1938. Two papers:
(1) "The Significance of the Rate of Interest," by H.D. Anderson, pp. 1-13.
(2) "Summary of Replies to Questions on Effects of Interest Rates," by J.E. Meade and P.W.S. Andrews, pp. 14-31. The quoted paragraphs are from the second paper, p. 28. The survey was conducted through interviews with a selected number of British business men.

7. The predominant reasons given by American manufacturing corporations for the discrepancies between planned and actual expenditures for new plant and equipment in 1949 were: changed sales and earnings outlook, changes in the plant and equipment supply situation, and changes in plant and equipment costs. "Availability and cost" of debt and equity financing was barely mentioned, while changes in the rate of interest were not mentioned at all.
See: "Business Investment Programs and Their Realization," by Irwin Friend and Jean Bronfenbrenner, the *Survey of Current Business,* December, 1950, pp. 11-22. The statistics and the discussion of the "reasons" will be found on page 19 there.

8. For the declining interest rate through 1940 see: *Banking and Monetary Statistics,* Board of Governors of the Federal Reserve System, 1943, pp. 448 (the interest rate) and 469 (bond yields). For data since 1940 see: *The Survey of Current Business,* U.S. Department of Commerce, "1949 Statistical Supplement," and current issues.

9. *The Survey of Current Business,* November 1952, p. 7-13.

10. U.S. Department of Commerce: *Markets After the Defense Expansion,* pp. 42-43. For similar findings consult, for example, Friederich A. Lutz: "The Interest Rate and Investment in a Dynamic Economy," The *American Economic Review,* December 1945, pp. 811-830.

11. *Verbatim Record of the Proceedings,* Vol. II, March 25 to May 29, 1939, p. 430. Statistics for a selected group of 56 industrial corporations, for the years 1930-38, are given in the same volume, p. 447f.

12. This wartime five-year amortization privilege, abolished in 1946, was reenacted in the tax law passed September, 1950.

13. *Loc Cit.* p. 7, Table I. See also *S.C.B.*, March 1948, pp.10-16 and September 1954, pp. 5-7, for corroborative statistics. A news item in the New York *Times* of June 30, 1952, carried the information that by the end of that year the oil companies of America will have invested $20 billion in expansion and development since the end of World War II, of which new financing was "negligible": "Program Carried Out by Companies Plowing Back Large Part of Earnings," was given as the explanation.

14. The resort to psychology for explanations of economic behavior is not new. For an attempt to raise it into a science, see: Samuel P. Hayes, Jr., "Some Psychological Problems of Economics," in the *Psychological Bulletin* (July, 1950), pp. 289-330. Mr. Hayes cites over 30 references to psychological theories applied to economics, starting with Adam Smith's "moral sentiments" and Malthus's "Man's procreative urge," and going through Bentham's "felicific calculus," Veblen's "instinct of workmanship" down to Keynes's "propensities."

15. *Journal American Statistical Association* (December, 1936), p. 793, n. 3.

16. "A Historical Approach to the Analysis of Business Cycles," a paper read by Schumpeter at the Universities-National Bureau Conference on Business Cycle Research (November 25-29, 1949). This was one of the last two or three of Schumpeter's appearances in public. He died the following January. The quotation will be found in *Conference on Business Cycles,* National Bureau of Economic Research (New York, 1951), Gottfried Haberler, Editor, p. 153.

17. Adam Smith: *Op. cit.,* Chapter IX: "Of the Profits of Stock."

18. *Theories of Surplus Value,* p. 373, n. 1. Marx's italics.

19. Elizabeth W. Gilboy, "The Propensity to Consume," in the *Quarterly Journal of Economics* (November, 1938), p. 138 and 140. See also, Hans Staele: "Short-Period Variations in the Distribution of Income," in the *Review of Economic Statistics* (August, 1937), pp. 133-141, for similar conclusions based on statistics for Germany. Also Woytinsky, S.W.: "Relationship Between Consumers' Expenditures, Savings, and Disposable Income," *ibid.*

(February, 1946), pp. 1-11 and "Postwar Economic Perspectives," in *Social Security Bulletin*, for the same date.

20.   This information will be found in several issues of the *Survey of Current Business*, for example, those for November, 1950, April, 1951 and January, 1950. In the latter (pp. 17-20) it is shown how the demand for different goods and services responds with different degrees of sensitivity to changes in disposable income. For the years 1929-1949 the indexes of sensitivity of various goods and services ranged from less than 0.5 to over 2.0 around an average of 0.86, depending, largely, on the postponableness of the commodity or service.

21.   The rise of installment buying in the years following the war, in the face of the contemporary rise of the disposable consumer income, has been truly phenomenal.

22.   Said Colin Clark in his article, "A System of Equations Explaining the U.S. Trade Cycle, 1921-41," in *Econometrica* (April, 1948), p. 99: "The study of the consumption function has been pursued by many, often with surprising and indeed disastrous results (e.g., the widespread prediction of a depression in 1946)."

23.   In the *Journal of the American Statistical Association* (December, 1936), p. 792.

24.   Professor Harrod, in his *Life of John Maynard Keynes* writes (p. 403): "The Student of the future, if he had to choose among Keynes's works, would get the best picture of his total contribution to economics in the *Treatise.*"

25.   Quoted, *ibid.*, p. 346. Present writer's italics.

26.   "I am bold to predict," Keynes wrote in his Treatise (Vol. II, p. 384), ". . . that to the economic historians of the future the slump of 1930 may present itself as the death struggle of the [high-level] war-rates of interest and the re-emergence of the [lower-level] pre-war rates."

27.   In the fall of 1939, Professor Harrod tells us (*Life*, p. 489), "Keynes drafted a memorandum which included the idea of a Reconstruction Fund to be supported by the United States, on terms of unprecedented generosity, as soon as Hitler was overthrown, to prevent the spread of Communism to Germany." Less than ten years later the American government in the forms of the Marshall Plan and similar financial aids did exactly that on a global scale.

28.   *The End of Laissez-Faire* (London, 1926), p. 69. Present writer's italics. In his *Treatise* (Vol. II, p. 376), Keynes wrote that in a case of severe unemployment, "it is not sufficient for the Central Authority to stand ready to lend . . . The Government must itself provide a program of domestic investment."

29.   *The End of Laissez-Faire*, p. 50. Italics supplied.

30.   "The State of the 'New Economics,'" in *The American Economic Review* (March, 1949), p. 475.

31.   In his *Economics in Practice* (London, 1935), p. 51.

32.   "Employment and Wage Rates," in the New York *Times Annalist* (May 3, 1935), p. 64.

33.   *American Economic Review* (March, 1945), p. 39, in his article: "Compensating Reactions to Compensatory Spending."

34.   L.R. Klein: *The Keynesian Revolution*, p. 185.

35.   The *Communist Manifesto*.

36.   *Life*, p. 331, f.n. 192.

95

Keynes and Supply Functions. (Followed by H. Johnson's Mathematical Appendix)*

D.H. Robertson

The page references in what follows are, unless otherwise stated, to Mr. de Jong's article in this JOURNAL, March 1954.

1. The following points about Keynes' function, or as I shall call it curve, $Z = \phi(N)$ (*General Theory*, p. 25) seem to me to be clear.

(i) It is a curve of aggregate costs, in what de Jong calls the Robinsonian sense, not of marginal or average costs.

(ii) In "cost" it includes such profits as emerge when price is equated with marginal factor cost, these being, under the competitive conditions assumed in Keynes' book, the maximum profits which entrepreneurs are in a position to make. De Jong is mistaken (p. 17) in saying that Hansen has failed to perceive this; but Hansen is mistaken in describing the profits so included as "normal";[1] clearly in a position of pronounced under-employment equilibrium, if such exists, profits are likely to be below normal, in any ordinary sense of that word.[2]

(iii) It is a "familiar" supply curve in de Jong's sense (p. 23) that the factor costs included in it are costs as they present themselves to the entrepreneur, not to any other party.

2. In support of the above statement I offer the following evidence. In making some comments (no longer extant) on an earlier draft of this chapter (also, as far as I know, no longer extant) which Keynes sent me, I had misunderstood the nature of this curve, which was then somewhat confusingly labelled D', suggesting some kind or other of demand curve. In setting me right Keynes wrote as follows: "D is the sale-proceeds for which it is expected that the output from employing N men can be sold. D' is the sale-proceeds the expectation of which will cause the output from employing N men to be *produced*. It is simply the age-old Supply Function." A little farther on he alluded again to D' as "only a re-concoction of our friend the Supply

*Source: *Economic Journal*, Vol. 65, September 1955, pp. 474-8.

Function." To my complaint (anticipating apparently that of some later critics) that after this passage D' was never heard of again, he replied that it "is *frequently* heard of again. It runs through the whole book. . . . For I make the volume of output essentially depend on the conditions of demand and supply."

Certainly in his own view Keynes did not "dispense with the familiar supply function," as Hawtrey says he did.[3] And I think that on this point Keynes' own view of what he was doing can be accepted.

3. How are we to represent the intersection of D and Z on a two-dimensional diagram? Let us assume as Keynes does in *General Theory*, p. 27, that the money wage-rate does not alter (without necessarily accepting his assurance that it would make no difference if it did). We have three choices as to what to plot along the X axis — (i) real output, (ii) the money value of real output, (iii) numbers employed; and two choices of what to plot along the Y axis, (a) money sales proceeds, (b) the real value of money sales proceeds.

The method nearest to that familiar from partial analysis is (i) (a). The method suggested by Keynes' own treatment and adopted by Dillard on p. 30 of his *Economics of John Maynard Keynes* (cf. de Jong's Fig. 5, p. 9) is (iii) (a). (iii) (b) would also seem to be a plausible method.

My attempt to exhibit the behaviour of D and Z curves under these three methods led me into error, from which I have been rescued by Mr. H.G. Johnson, who, without taking any responsibility for the rest of this article, has kindly added a mathematical note at the end. Here are his results as regard Z. Under (i) (a) Z will be convex to the X axis, unless (over a range) marginal costs are rising at a sufficiently rapidly decreasing rate (the ordinary curve representing them is sufficiently concave to the X axis). Similarly under (iii) (a) Z will be convex to the X axis[4] unless (over a range) the marginal productivity of labour is falling at a sufficiently rapidly decreasing rate (the ordinary curve representing it is sufficiently convex to the origin). Under (iii) (b), on the other hand, Z will be concave to the X axis.

There remain (ii) (b), which nobody, I think, would suggest using; and (ii) (a) and (i) (b) — respectively Dillard's figure on his p. 34 and de Jong's Fig. 7 (p. 13) — in each of which Z is reduced to a mere 45° line. It is perhaps this fact that suggests to many minds that Z is bogus or otiose. But the tautological nature of Z in these popular pictures is merely the result of the fact that, unlike what occurs under (i) (a) or (iii), all the stuffing, so to speak, has been taken out of it before it is allowed to appear in the diagram.

On his own plane of reasoning then, Keynes was right. But equally Patinkin and many others have been right in intuiting that the position of "equilibrium" whose establishment is indicated by this apparatus is for a number of reasons a very precarious and inconclusive one.

4. De Jong then is justified (p. 19) in placing his point of "equilibrium" at E in his Fig. 7. But what about his verbal exposition? First, he surely leads us astray in saying that for any volume of output the intercept between the 45°

line and the curve of aggregate factor cost "indicates entrepreneurial expected profits"; what it indicates is the profits which, if they *were* expected, would suffice to elicit that volume of output.

Secondly, he issues a challenge by suddenly changing the description of his D curve to make it mean the (real value of the) sales proceeds which entrepreneurs will *actually* (his italics) receive for any volume of output. Now for this he will find no warrant on pp. 25 or 29 of the *General Theory*, or in my quotation from Keynes above, which are all deliberately framed in terms of expectation. But if he looks very carefully he will find some support on *General Theory*, p. 30, where, as I pointed out many years ago,[5] what entrepreneurs do expect is unobtrusively transformed into what they "can expect," *i.e.*, presumably what they ought to expect because that is what in fact will happen.

Let me at this point disclose, since I hope it is of more than personal interest, another excuse for having been defeated by the first draft of this crucial chapter. In addition to D and D' (now Z) there dodged through its pages another symbol Y, still further complicating the landscape. Y, it was explained to me, was actual, as contrasted with D, expected, sales proceeds or income. Y eventually dropped out; but there is an echo of his existence on *General Theory*, p. 78, where in the course of a criticism of myself, Keynes suddenly alludes to the contrast, "so vital for causal analysis," which he has "tried to make between effective demand and income," — a contrast of which the reader of the published book now hears for the first (and I think the last) time.

Is, then, de Jong's transformation of Keynes' "expected" into "actual" sales proceeds, for which this much (though no more) warrant can be found in Keynes' own pages, required in order to make the whole apparatus viable? I think that either this, or some more restricted definition of the word "expected," *is* so required. Otherwise, as I have pointed out,[6] if entrepreneurs have been reading J.B. Say and are consequently expecting that all income will be spent, the difference between Keynes' $D(N)$ and $Z(N)$ will vanish; and any disappointment which entrepreneurs suffer from expanding employment beyond the equilibrium point will have to be explained not in terms of a difference between $D(N)$ and $Z(N)$, but in terms of a difference between effective demand (*i.e.*, expected income) and income actually received.

5. I fully agree with de Jong (this JOURNAL, December 1954, pp. 840-1) that to give a fair run to this whole order of ideas we must use $S = I$ (a condition of equilibrium) and define our terms appropriately. But it is no use pretending the Keynes did this; he used $S \equiv I$ (an identity), deliberately rejected both my suggested distinction between received income and disposable income and the Swedish *ex ante* analysis, and expressed approval of his expositors who did likewise. De Jong, I think, realises this; but the chief moral of the debate (if it *is* a debate) between himself and Hawtrey seems to me to be that it would be convenient if some words other than Keynesian could be found to denote trains

of analysis which embody not only concepts which Keynes invented or made use of but also others which he expressly repudiated.

6. I agree with what I take to be Hawtrey's view (*ibid.*, p. 837) that Keynes' definition of "involuntary employment" is quite unacceptable. It was, I think, almost immediately abandoned by some of his English expositors,[7] but is defended by Hansen,[8] and not, I think, rejected by de Jong. So far as the number of adult male workers seeking work is concerned, the whole notion of a forward-rising supply curve of labour seems to be completely beside the mark.[9] As Pigou has explained,[10] in this connection the "classical" supply curve of labour must be thought of as *either* (if "thoroughgoing competition" between workers prevails) as a vertical straight line *or* (if the wage-rate is temporarily fixed by convention or collective action) as temporarily a horizontal straight line; there is no room for anything between.[11]

Mathematical Appendix

1. Let x be aggregate real output, and p be the general price level measured in wage units;[12] on Keynes' assumption of competition, the price level is determined by marginal production cost, and the latter is assumed to be rising as output increases.

Case (i) (a) plots px as a function of x. The curvature of the graph is given by $\frac{d^2(px)}{dx^2} = 2\frac{dp}{dx} + x\frac{d^2p}{dx^2}$. Since $\frac{dp}{dx}$ is positive by assumption, $\frac{d^2(px)}{dx^2}$ must be positive, indicating convexity to the X-axis, unless $\frac{d^2p}{dx^2}$ is negative (signifying a decreasing rate of increase of marginal cost) and its absolute value exceeds $\frac{2}{x}\frac{dp}{dx}$. If px is defined and possesses a derivative throughout the interval $x \geqslant 0$, and it is assumed that $px = 0$ for $x = 0$ and $\frac{dp}{dx}$ is positive for all non-negative values of x, it can be shown by the Mean Value Theorem that the graph must be convex to the X-axis over part of its range;[13] it cannot be concave throughout.

Case (ii) (b) is the reciprocal of Case (i) (a).

2. On the assumption that labour is the only variable factor, rising marginal production cost implies diminishing marginal productivity of labour.

Case (iii) (b) plots output x as a function of employment n. The curvature is given by $\frac{d^2x}{dn^2}$, which by assumption is negative, indicating concavity to the X-axis.

3. On the same assumption, the price level in wage units p will be equal to the

reciprocal of the marginal product of labour m $\left(=\dfrac{dx}{dn}\right)$. Case (iii) (a) plots

the value of output px $\left(=\dfrac{x}{m}\right)$ as a function of employment n. The curvature

is given by $\dfrac{d^2\left(\dfrac{x}{m}\right)}{dn^2} = \dfrac{1}{m^3}\left[2x\left(\dfrac{dm}{dn}\right)^2 - m^2\dfrac{dm}{dn} - mx\dfrac{d^2m}{dn^2}\right]$. Since $\dfrac{dm}{dn}$ is

negative by assumption, $\dfrac{d^2(px)}{dn^2}$ will be positive, indicating convexity to the

X-axis, unless $\dfrac{d^2m}{dn^2}$ is positive (signifying a decreasing rate of decrease of

marginal productivity of labour) and sufficiently large. As in 1 above, it can be
shown that the graph cannot be concave to the X-axis over the whole range.

4. Let c be aggregate real demand for output, assumed to depend only on
aggregate real output x. Case (i) (a) plots pc as a function of x. The curvature of

the graph is given by $\dfrac{d^2(pc)}{dx^2} = 2\dfrac{dc}{dx}\dfrac{dp}{dx} + c\dfrac{d^2p}{dx^2} + p\dfrac{d^2c}{dx^2}$, which indicates

convexity to the X-axis unless marginal cost rises at a decreasing rate or the
marginal propensity to consume decreases as output increases.

In Case (iii) (b), the curvature is given by $\dfrac{d^2c}{dn^2} = m^2\dfrac{d^2c}{dx^2} + \dfrac{dc}{dx}\dfrac{d^2x}{dn^2}$, indicating

concavity to the X-axis unless the marginal propensity to consume increases as
output increases. In Case (iii) (a), the curvature is given by

$$\dfrac{d^2\left(\dfrac{c}{m}\right)}{dn^2} = \dfrac{d^2c}{dx^2}\,m - \dfrac{1}{m^3}\left[m^2\dfrac{dm}{dn}\dfrac{dc}{dx} + mc\dfrac{d^2m}{dn^2} - 2c\left(\dfrac{dm}{dn}\right)^2\right];$$

this indicates convexity to the X-axis unless the marginal propensity to
consume decreases as output increases or the marginal productivity of labour
falls at a decreasing rate as employment increases.

Notes

1. "Current production is undertaken in *expectation* of sales proceeds adequate to cover all
costs (including normal profits)" (*A Guide to Keynes*, p. 28).
2. Hansen also slips up (*op. cit.*, p. 32) in criticising Keynes for describing aggregate demand
D as a function of employment N. For on the assumption of the validity of the multiplier analysis,
which Hansen accepts, the D_1 (consumption) component of D, and therefore D itself, is a function
of N. Hansen has, I think, mistaken Keynes' statement "$D_1 + D_2 = D = \phi(N)$" on *General
Theory*, p. 29, for a definition, — it is not, it is a condition of equilibrium, exactly equivalent to
Hansen's own "$D_1 + D_2 = D = Z$" on his p. 31.
3. This JOURNAL, December 1954, p. 837.
4. Dillard therefore puts our thoughts in a wrong direction by drawing it as a straight line, and
a 45° one at that.
5. *Essays in Monetary Theory*, p. 115.
6. *Loc. cit.*

7.   See J. Robinson, *Essays in the Theory of Employment*, pp. 10-13. Mr. Harrod, however, informs me that he still regards it as serviceable and important.

8.   Hansen admits that Keynes' exposition is confused, and would like to re-write the "second classical postulate," which Keynes says (*General Theory*, p. 5) he is attacking, as follows (*A Guide to Keynes*, p. 22): "(1) Workers will refuse the proffer of employment if the *real* wage rate is cut below the current real wage; (2) a cut in *money* wage rates is an effective means to reduce real wage rates." (2) is in order; but I cannot recognise in (1) any resemblance to any "classical" doctrine. It seems to imply that the "Classics" held that, as a result of a cut in money wages, believed by them to entail a cut in real wages, the number of unemployed men would be indefinitely *increased*. In point of fact they held that it would be *diminished*.

9.   The concept of a *backward-rising* curve may have some relevance to the connection between adult male wages and the numbers of women and juveniles seeking work.

10.   *Employment and Equilibrium*, 2nd edition, pp. 70 and 86.

11.   An intriguing puzzle arising out of Keynes' definition is the following. Suppose a man has been drawn back by "reflationary" action of some kind into employment; how long must he wait before demanding a rise in wages in order that he may be given retrospective credit for having been involuntarily, and not voluntarily, unemployed?

12. p is measured in "wage units" purely for economy of symbols; following the text § 3, the "wage unit" in terms of money is assumed constant.

13.   I am grateful to Professor Robert Strotz of Northwestern University for providing a rigorous proof of this restriction.

96

Keynes and Supply Functions: Second Rejoinder, with a Note on the Concept of Monetary Equilibrium*

F.J. de Jong

The first section of this paper is devoted to a rejoinder to the stimulating Comment of Professor Robertson. For the sake of brevity, I will avoid quoting his statements by following the articulation of his Comment. I agree with all points made by Professor Robertson which are not mentioned below in Section 1.

In a personal interview, Professor Koopmans of Amsterdam told me that, in the sketch of his concept of monetary equilibrium inserted in my first rejoinder (that to Professor Hawtrey[1]), I have misinterpreted him at a certain point. The issue of the second section of this paper will therefore be to present a brief exposition of the kernel of Koopmans' theory.

1. Rejoinder to Professor Robertson

1. In the passage from Hansen, cited by Professor Robertson, "normal profits" are explicitly subsumed under "costs." I feel that this concept of normal profits must be the same as Marshall's.[2] Normal profits in this sense are constituted of managers' salaries and interest. If this is true, I believe that one may indeed say that Hansen makes "essentially the same error" as Dillard, as I stated on p. 17.

2. The considerations of Professor Robertson and Mr. Johnson on the representation of the functions D and Z on a two-dimensional diagram are certainly very instructive. Personally, I do not think that a decreasing rate of interest of marginal costs, an increasing rate of decrease of marginal productivity of labour, and an increasing marginal propensity to consume as output increases, are — in the short run, at any rate — very probable cases. Under (iii) (a), $i.e.$, p. 30 in Dillard or p. 9, Fig. 5, in my article, the D and Z curves may therefore probably be assumed to be approximately linear over a

*Source: *Economic Journal*, Vol. 65, September 1955, pp. 479-84.

certain range, while they will become convex to the X axis as soon as employment surpasses a certain value. This result is indeed different from Dillard's picture, which I have copied in my article, especially for the matter of the D curve. But it is not quite true that Dillard draws the Z curve as a 45°-line. Incidentally, if in his diagram the straight Z curve is produced to the left, it intersects the N-axis to the right of O.

I have been puzzled by the diagram, produced by Hansen on p. 31 of his book, where the curve $Z = Z(N)$ is drawn as a 45°-line passing through the Origin. I feel that, in Hansen's exposition, where Z covers all costs (including "normal profits") and costs only, this can make sense only if a new system (iii) (c) is assumed where (c) indicates that $Z_w \equiv \dfrac{Z}{W}$ and $D_w \equiv \dfrac{D}{W}$ are plotted along the Y axis. Z_w and D_w are measured in the same units as N.[3] The 45°-line can then be regarded as the sale proceeds divided by the wage unit, the expectation of which will cause the output from employing N men to be produced. Since Z_w covers only costs, this output (according to this train of thought, at any rate) will be produced if $Z_w = N$,[4] provided that entrepreneurial *labour* is included in N and Z_w; this is required since the rewards of this labour, managerial salaries, are a constituent of normal costs and are therefore covered by Z. However, even in this interpretation, Hansen's diagram is erroneous, since his concept of Z is erroneous (see 1).

3. I fully agree with Professor Robertson that his statement:[5] "the intercept between the 45°-line and the curve of aggregate factor costs . . . indicates . . . the profits which, if they *were* expected, would suffice to elicit that volume of output," is the exact formulation. When writing the passage, criticised by Professor Robertson, I had an uneasy feeling that something in the argument went wrong, but I could not identify the obscure point. I am glad that Professor Robertson has accomplished this, and I believe also that his response to the "challenge" issued by me by suddenly changing the description of the D curve to make it mean the sales proceeds which entrepreneurs will *actually* receive for any volume of output, is the correct response. There must, however, be some bridge between Keynes' "expected" and his (and my) "actual" sales proceeds. In a stationary state these concepts coincide. In an economy which has become stationary at a certain moment a certain time must elapse before equilibrium is reached. During this time of adaptation, it may happen that entrepreneurs' expectations do not appear to come true. Under the influence of this result, entrepreneurs will change their expectations from period to period until the expectations come true, that is, until equilibrium is ultimately brought about. As soon as equilibrium prevails, "expectations" involve only what entrepreneurs "can expect" in the sense pointed out by Professor Robertson.

In some cases static analysis is a less lucid method than dynamic analysis. My conviction is that especially in matters of analysis of the circular flow of income, dynamic analysis can much more easily be understood than static analysis. Keynes wrote on p. 78: "Thus Mr. Robertson's method[6] might be

regarded as an alternative attempt to mine (being, perhaps, a first approximation to it) to make the same distinction, so vital for causal analysis, that I have
tried to make by the contrast between effective demand and income." In my
opinion, Robertson's method, as an expository device, is superior to that of
Keynes, provided that we define the "period," involved in his method, not
as the well-known Robertsonian "day" but as the income propagation period
involved in dynamic multiplier analysis.[7] If we lump all firms together to a
single giant firm[8] and all households to a single giant household, and if we
denote the receipts of the household by Y_H, the receipts of the firm by Y_F,
spontaneous or *ex ante* consumption expenditures by C, spontaneous or *ex
ante* saving by S and spontaneous or *ex ante* investment by I, it holds good
within one and the same period for a closed "anarchistic" economy that

$$Y_H = C + S \tag{1}$$
$$C + I = Y_F \tag{2}$$

while Y_H of *this* period is defined identically equal to Y_F of the *previous* period.[9]
If we label Y_H "disposable income" and Y_F "earned income," it is obvious that
these equations are just a repetition of those inserted in my first rejoinder on
p. 840. During the upswing of the business cycle, when $S < I$, it holds good that
$Y_H < Y_F$. During the downswing, the situation is characterised by $S > I$ and
$Y_H > Y_F$. I feel that Y_F may be identified with "effective demand" (or, expected
income) and Y_H with income" (or, income actually received) in the passage
quoted from Keynes, and I think that equation (2) can be regarded as the
"more restricted definition of the word 'expected' (income)" as required by
Professor Robertson.

The model will be in equilibrium only if $Y_H = Y_F$, that is, if

$$S = I \tag{3}$$

Y_F is constant in the course of time if and when the equilibrium condition (3) is
satisfied; we may therefore label this situation as *income equilibrium*.[10] When
income equilibrium prevails, entrepreneurs do expect what they "can expect"
according to Keynes' formulation (*General Theory*, p. 30).

In Keynes' book a situation of income equilibrium is always reached
immediately after a change in the *data* has occurred, since Keynes applies the
static method. Indeed, it is no great step from dynamics to statics, since in the
words of Frisch[11] "statics can be considered as a limiting case of dynamics by
stating that in the static model world all time rates of reacion are infinitely
large, whereas in the dynamic model the time rates of reaction are finite
magnitudes." Let us once more inspect Fig. 1 on p. 4 of my article in the March
1954 issue of this JOURNAL. Along the horizontal axis, disposable income is
plotted, since consumption is a function of disposable income. The intercept
between the 45°-line and the consumption function can now easily be seen to
represent savings,[12] as it should be. D denotes earned income. Point E is the
equilibrium point, which is arrived at immediately; thus, at any moment,
entrepreneurs do expect what they "can expect." In Keynes' train of thought,
the last statement is always true. However, to my mind, this is seen much more

easily if we do not start from statics but from dynamics, and switch over to statistics afterwards.

4. Professor Robertson's testimony that Keynes meant $S \equiv I$ must, of course, be accepted.[13] But if follows from this — to quote a passage from Section 3 of his Comment — that the position of equilibrium whose establishment is indicated by Keynes' apparatus is an inconclusive one. Since a word other than "Keynesian" is required to denote analyses of the type as exposed, for instance, in Subsection 3 of this rejoinder, we could perhaps best label them "neo-Keynesian."

5. I believe that Keynes himself has torpedoed the relevance of his 1936 definition of "involuntary unemployment" already in 1939.[14] I have left this problem out of consideration in my article (see p. 8 n.). As a matter of fact, I agree with the opinion of A.H. Hansen, quoted by Professor Robertson in a footnote on the last page of his Comment, and I do not think that neo-Keynesian economics should in this respect necessarily deviate from classical economics.

The question of the form of the labour supply curve is difficult. If supply of labour N_{FE} (see my article, p. 20, equation (6.5)) is defined as a flow of manhours per annum, and if, for the sake of simplicity, we define N_{FE} as a function of real wages $\dfrac{W}{p}$, the short-run form of this curve may presumably approximately be in accordance with the picture of Fig. 4 on p. 8 of my article, with this one amendment that the upward slanting part will not be linear but convex to the N-axis; it may well tend to become vertical as N grows larger. The upward-slanting part is due to the willingness of workers to work longer for higher wages (overtime). In the long run, however, the curve may be found to be sloping backward, at any rate in the vicinity of the present real wage level in the Netherlands; this is due to the fact that workers tend to shorten the weekly working time as real wages become higher.

2. A Note on the Concept of Monetary Equilibrium

On p. 25 of his *Guide to Keynes*, Hansen writes concerning Chapter 3 of Keynes' *General Theory*: "This chapter is of special significance because here, after repeated failures, an impressive attack was at long last made upon Say's law."

In fact, Say's law was already rejected three years earlier by Koopmans.[15]

The first principal line of his argument runs as follows. In a non-monetary economy goods are bartered against goods. In a monetary economy barter transactions can be divided into two complementary halves: goods are offered against money, and in exchange for money goods are demanded. The monetary economy offers an opportunity which is non-existent in a non-monetary economy, viz., to proceed no farther than a half barter transaction. If one sells a good and does not spend the money received within the same period,[16] the second stage of the barter transaction does not come off; we can label this transaction a "pure supply" (this term was, however, not used by Koopmans). If one buys a good with money which one has not "earned" during the *same* period but which one has dishoarded or received from a bank ("creation" of money), it is the first half of the barter transaction that is non-existent; Koopmans labels this transaction a "pure demand" (a term taken from H. Neisser). If in a certain period, there is net pure supply in the entire economy, the situation in that period is deflationary; if there is net pure demand, the situation is inflationary.[17] In neither case does Say's law apply. If net pure demand (or supply) is nil, monetary equilibrium — or, as Koopmans put it in 1933: a situation of "neutral money" — prevails. Monetary equilibrium is the zero-point between inflation and deflation.

If spontaneous hoarding is denoted by $\triangle L$ and spontaneous creation of money by $\triangle M$, it must hold good in any period for all individuals that *income receipts* $+ \triangle M = $ *spendings out of income* $+ \triangle L$. Income receipts can be used for C and/or S; income is spent on C and/or I. Three possible analytical definitions of monetary equilibrium are therefore: *income receipts* $=$ *income spendings*, $S = I$, and $\triangle L = \triangle M$. An essential point in this definition is that "income receipts" and "income spendings" are considered to take place within the *same* period; a lagged relationship like that in the theory of income equilibrium, where the disposable income of *this* period is identically equal to the income earned in the *previous* period, is excluded by definition.[18] This does not mean that such a lagged relationship will never exist in reality; it means only that monetary equilibrium requires a situation where the result is exactly the same *as if* this lag did not exist. Personally, I feel that this requirement is fulfilled, *inter alia*, if income equilibrium prevails; therefore, income equilibrium always implies monetary equilibrium. On the other hand, monetary equilibrium can even exist when income equilibrium does not prevail; this is the case if and when "income receipts" and "income spendings" change simultaneously at an equal rate so that their equality is not disturbed. If this vision is true, *income equilibrium is a special case of monetary equilibrium.*

If we step over to statics, Keynesian equilibrium as determined by effective demand, too, implies monetary equilibrium.

The second principal line in Koopmans' work is to demonstrate that monetary equilibrium does *not* necessarily imply constancy of any variable or set of variables in some monetary equation of exchange of the Fisherian or Robertsonian types (*e.g.*, stock of money M, flow of money MV, general price level P, money national income Y, or real national income Y_r). Pressure of space forbids me to follow up this second line.

Notes

1. This JOURNAL, December 1954, pp. 840-2.
2. A. Marshall, *Principles of Economics*, eighth edition (London, 1920), Book VI, ch. viii, esp. pp. 618-19: "Thus the whole of normal profits enter into true or long-period supply price."
3. See Keynes, *General Theory*, p. 44, top of page.
4. In this reasoning, the condition that genuine profits should be maximised is neglected; as a matter of fact, profits in the proper sense (profit as a residual income) are zero. See my criticism of Dillard and Hansen on p. 17 of my article.
5. This statement refers to Fig. 7 on p. 13 of my article, *i.e.*, case (i)(b), and the text of p. 19, middle of page. A point of historical interest is made by E. Schneider, *Einführung in die Wirtschaftstheorie*, Volume III (Tübingen, 1952), p. 100n. Schneider states that the nowadays widely applied 45°-line method was used for the first time by the Danish author, Ivar Jantzen, in an article entitled "Lidt planøkonomisk Teori" (*A Little on the Economic Theory of Planning*), which appeared in the *Nordisk Tidsskrift for Teknisk Økonomi*, I (1935); an English translation of this article is inserted in his *Basic Principles of Business Economics and National Calculation*, being a special issue of the same *Tidsskrift*, V(1939).
6. That is, the method of defining "to-day's" disposable income as being equal to "yesterday's" earned income. D.H. Robertson: "Saving and Hoarding," this JOURNAL, XLIII (1933), pp. 399-413, reprinted in *Essays in Monetary Theory*, pp. 56-82.
7. See L.A. Metzler, "Three Lags in the Circular Flow of Income," in the volume: *Income, Employment and Public Policy: Essays in Honor of Alvin H. Hansen* (New York, 1948), pp. 11-32. The lag, mentioned by Robertson (*Essays*, p. 65) represents, I think, only one of the three indicated by Metzler. I agree with those authors who state that the length of the income propagation period is equal to the reciprocal of the income velocity of *active* money, provided that payments in the financial sphere are considered to be done by means of inactive money.
8. J.R. Hicks, *The Social Framework*, 2nd edition (Oxford, 1952), p. 113.
9. For an open economy, the equations become more complicated. See the Tables in F. Machlup, *International Trade and the National Income Multiplier* (Philadelphia, 1943). His "past Y" corresponds to my Y_H, his "current Y" to my Y_F. The consecutive order of my equations (1) and (2), and — within each equation — of the terms, corresponds to the inner logic of Machlup's Tables.
10. In my first rejoinder I identified income equilibrium with monetary equilibrium as defined by Koopmans. I will show in Section 2 that this identification is illegitimate. The theory of income equilibrium is essentially a dynamised version of the Keynesian theory of effective demand.
11. R. Frisch: "Statikk og dynamikk i den økonomiske teori" (*Statics and Dynamics in Economic Theory*), *Nationalzkonomisk Tidsskrift*, LXVII (1929), pp. 321-79, esp. p. 326.
12. According to equation (1) of this rejoinder.
13. Professor Hawtrey is another witness who makes the same statement in a letter to me dated March 22, 1955. He adds to this: "Keynes would not accept my suggestion that investment should be defined to exclude undesigned increments (or decrements) in the stock of unsold goods (pp. 75-6 of *General Theory*). It is because he includes them that investment is identically equal to saving." It follows from this that Keynes' argument is entirely *ex post* and can therefore yield no conclusive equilibrium theory. To obtain such a theory, all magnitudes in the behaviour equations must be defined *ex ante*, that is, as "designed" or "spontaneous" magnitudes. If we define *ex ante* magnitudes as "either autonomous magnitudes or magnitudes in accordance with the behaviour equations concerned," induced magnitudes are also *ex ante* in so far as they are not "undesigned."
14. J.M. Keynes, "Relative Movements of Real Wages and Output," this JOURNAL, XLIX (1939), pp. 34-51. See on this: A.H. Hansen, *Monetary Theory and Fiscal Policy* (New York, 1949), pp. 119-20.
15. J.G. Koopmans, "Zum Problem des neutralen Geldes," in the volume *Beiträge zur Geldtheorie*, F.A. von Hayek ed. (Vienna, 1933), pp. 211-359.
16. The money is then either "hoarded," *i.e.*, added to the cash balance, or "annihilated," *i.e.*, handed over to the banking system.
17. Inflation is therefore not identical with rising prices. Rising prices are only a special case of inflation.
18. This is the point which I have overlooked in my first rejoinder.

97

A Graphical Exposition of the Complete Keynesian System*

W.L. Smith

The purpose of this paper is chiefly expository. A simple graphical technique is employed to exhibit the working of several variants of the Keynesian model. Many of the issues discussed have been dealt with elsewhere,[1] but it is hoped that the analysis presented here will clarify some of the issues and be useful for pedagogical purposes.

I. The Keynesian System with Flexible Wages

This system can be represented symbolically by the following five equations:

$$y = c(y, r) + i(y, r) \tag{1}$$

$$\frac{M}{p} = L(y, r) \tag{2}$$

$$y = f(N) \tag{3}$$

$$\frac{w}{p} = f'(N) \tag{4}$$

$$N = \varphi\left(\frac{w}{p}\right). \tag{5}$$

Here y = real GNP (at constant prices), r = an index of interest rates, M = money supply (in current dollars), p = index of the price level applicable to GNP, N = the volume of employment (in equivalent full-time workers), w = the money wage. The model represents a theory of short-run income determination with capital stock fixed and labor the only variable factor of production.

The working of this model is illustrated in Figure I. Figure I should be studied in clockwise fashion, beginning with Chart I (a) in the lower lefthand corner. In I (a), DD represents the demand for labor [equation (4)], and SS represents the supply of labor [equation (5)]. The level of employment and

*Source: *Southern Economic Journal*, Vol. 23 (2), October 1956, pp. 115-25.

the real wage are determined at the full employment levels, N_f and $\left(\dfrac{w}{p}\right)_f$.

Proceeding to I(b), the curve OP represents the aggregate production function [equation(3)], its shape reflecting diminishing returns.[2] With employment of N_f, y would be at the level y_f, indicated in I(b).

Figure I

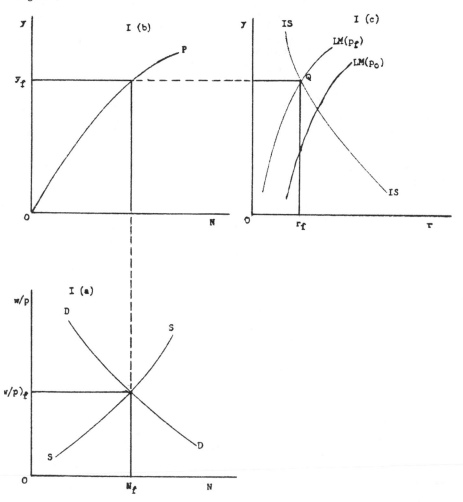

Chart I(c) is the type of diagram developed by Hicks and utilized by others to depict the condition of monetary equilibrium in the Keynesian system.[3] The *IS* curve in I(c) depicts equation(1) and indicates for each possible level of the interest rate (r) the equilibrium level of income (y) which would prevail after the multiplier had worked itself out fully.[4] We treat the stock of money as an exogenous variable determined by the monetary authority. Given M, the LM curves in I (c), of which there would be one for each possible price level (p) which might prevail, represent equation (2) in our model. For example, if the price level were held constant at p_0, the curve LM (p_0) depicts the different interest rates that would be required to preserve equilibrium in the money market at different income levels. The fact that rising income levels are associated with higher interest rates reflects the presumption that as income rises, transactions cash requirements are larger, leaving less of the fixed (in real terms) quantity of money to satisfy demands for idle balances, thus pushing up the interest rate.

If prices and wages are flexible and the situation is as depicted in Figure I, full employment will automatically be maintained, since the price level will adjust to the level p_f, establishing the LM curve in the position LM (p_f) where it will intersect the IS curve at point Q which corresponds to the full employment level of income (y_f). If, for example, the real wage is initially above $\left(\dfrac{w}{p} \right)_f$, money wages will fall due to the excess supply of labor. This will reduce costs, resulting in increased output and employment and lower prices. Falling prices shift the LM curve upward by increasing the real value of cash balances $\left(\dfrac{M}{p} \right)$, thus lowering the interest rate and expanding aggregate demand to the point where the market will absorb the output corresponding to full employment.[5]

Two important and related propositions can be set down concerning interest and money in the above model:

(1) The rate of interest is determined solely by saving and investment and is independent of the quantity of money and liquidity preference.

(2) The quantity theory of money holds for this model — that is, a change in the quantity of money will bring about an equal proportional change in the price level and will have no effect on real income or employment.

In other words the quantity of money and liquidity preference serve not to determine the interest rate, as alleged by Keynes, but the price level. As can readily be seen from Figure I, income is established at the full employment level [I (a) and I (b)], the interest rate adjusts to equate saving and investment [on the IS curve in I (c)] at this income level, and the price level adjusts so as to satisfy liquidity requirements at this interest rate [establishing the LM curve at the appropriate position in I (c)].

It is a comparatively simple matter to modify the analysis of Figure I to take account of the possible effect of changes in the real value of liquid assets on consumption (the Pigou effect).[6] The real value of the stock of liquid assets would be included in equation (1), and falling prices would then shift the IS curve to the right, thus strengthening the tendency toward full employment equilibrium. This suggests the question: Does the introduction of the Pigou effect give the quantity of money the power to change the rate of interest when prices and wages are flexible? The answer to this question cannot be deduced from the curves of Figure I, but it is not difficult to find the answer with aid of the following simple model:

$$\bar{y} = c(\bar{y}, r, a) + i(\bar{y}, r)$$
$$\frac{M}{p} = L(\bar{y}, r)$$
$$a = \frac{A}{p}.$$

Here $a =$ the real value of liquid assets which is included in the consumption function and $A =$ their money value. The last three equations of our original model are assumed to determine the real wage, employment, and real income. These equations are dropped and y is treated as a constant (having value $\bar{y}$) determined by those equations. We can now treat M and A as parameters and r, a, and p as variables, differentiate these three equations with respect to M, and solve for $\dfrac{dr}{dM}$. This gives the following expression:

$$\frac{dr}{dM} = \frac{\dfrac{c_a}{i_r} \dfrac{A}{M} (1 - \eta_{AM})}{p \left(1 + \dfrac{c_r}{i_r} + \dfrac{A}{M} \dfrac{L_r c_a}{i_r}\right)}. \tag{6}$$

In this expression, the subscripts refer to partial derivatives, e.g., $c_a = \dfrac{\delta c}{\delta a}$. Normally, the following conditions would be satisfied: $c_a > 0, i_r < 0, L_r < 0$. We cannot be sure about the sign of c_r, but it is likely to be small in any case. The coefficient η_{AM} has the following meaning:

$$\eta_{AM} = \frac{M}{A} \frac{dA}{dM} = \frac{\dfrac{dA}{A}}{\dfrac{dM}{M}}.$$

For example, if a change in M is brought about in such a way as to produce an exactly proportionate change in A, η_{AM} will be unity. Or if the change in M is not accompanied by any change in A, η_{AM} will be zero. It is apparent from the above expression that a change in the quantity of money will not affect the rate of interest if $\eta_{AM} = 1$, while an increase (decrease) in the quantity of money will lower (raise) the rate of interest of $\eta_{AM} < 1$.[7] Thus, the way in which changes in the quantity of money affect the rate of interest depends upon what asset concept is included in the consumption function (i.e., what is included in A) and how the volume of these assets is affected by monetary change. If M itself is the appropriate asset concept to include in the consumption function (i.e., if $A = M$), changes in M will not affect the interest rate, since in this case η_{AM} is equal to unity. However, the consensus of opinion seems to be that some other aggregate, such as currency, deposits, and government securities held by the non-bank public minus the public's indebtedness to the banks, is more appropriate.[8] If this concept is employed, most of the usual methods of increasing the money supply will ordinarily either leave A unchanged ($\eta_{AM}=0$) or cause it to increase less than in proportion to the increase in M ($0 < \eta_{AM} < 1$).[9] We may conclude that the Pigou effect gives monetary changes power to influence the rate of interest, even if wages and prices are fully flexible. An increase (decrease) in the quantity of money will ordinarily lower (raise) the rate of interest and also increase (decrease) investment and decrease (increase) consumption, but will not change income and employment which are determined by real forces (the last three equations of our complete model).[10,11]

II. Possibilities of Underemployment Disequilibrium

There are several possible circumstances arising from the shapes of the various schedules which might produce a situation in which, even though the relations in the above model held true, it might be impossible, at least temporarily, for equilibrium (full employment or otherwise) to be reached. The most widely discussed of these possibilities is depicted in Figure II.

II(a) and II(b) are similar to I(a) and I(b). However, the LM curves in II(c) are drawn to reflect the much-discussed possibility mentioned by Keynes[12] that the liquidity preference schedule might become infinitely elastic at some low level of interest rates [r_a in II(c)], due either to the unanimous expectations of investors that interest rates would rise when they reached this extremely low level relative to future expectations or to the cost of investments. In the case depicted, full employment (N_f) would involve a level of income of y_f. If the IS curve were at the level IS_0, the interest rate required to make investment equal to saving at income y_f would be r_f. But the infinite elasticity of the LM schedule prevents the interest rate from falling below r_a. The result would be that employment and income would be prevented from rising above the level N_a and y_a by inadequate effective demand. The real wage would hold at the level $\left(\dfrac{w}{p}\right)_a$ which is above the full employment level $\left(\dfrac{w}{p}\right)_f$. Competition for employment would reduce money wages, costs, and prices. But the falling price level, although it would increase the quantity of money in real terms, would not affect the interest rate, hence would not increase investment. As prices fell, the LM curve would take successive positions, such as $LM(p_0)$, $LM(p_1)$, $LM(p_2)$, etc., leaving the interest rate unaffected.[13]

A special case of the situation depicted in Figure II may arise if a negative interest rate is required to equate investment to full employment savings. In this case, the IS curve would cut the y-axis and lie to the left of it at an income corresponding to full employment. Then, even if there were nothing to prevent the rate of interest from approaching zero, it could not go below zero,[14] and the *LM* curve would have a floor at a zero rate, thus preventing full employment from being attained.

Figure II

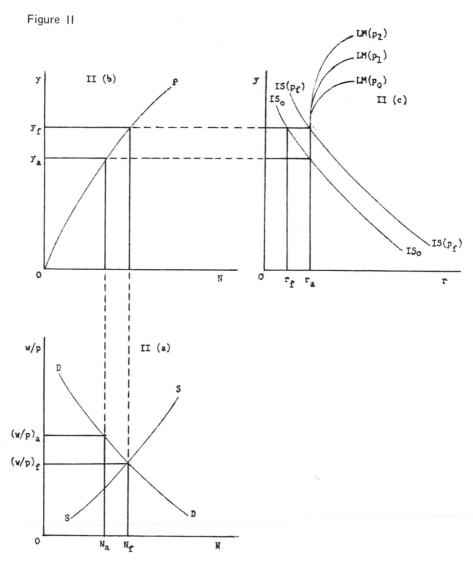

It is interesting to note that if the Pigou effect is operative, a full employment equilibrium may be attainable even in the case illustrated in Figure II. As prices fall, the real value of liquid assets increases. If this increases consumption expenditures, the *IS* curve will shift to the right until it attains the position *IS* (P_f), where a full employment equilibrium is reached.

Certain other conceivable situations which might lead to an under-employment disequilibrium are worthy of a brief mention. One possibility is that the supply of labor might exceed the demand at all levels of real wages. Such a situation seems very improbable, however, since there is reason to believe that the short-run aggregate labor is quite inelastic over a considerable range of wage rates and declines when wage rates become very low.[15]

Disequilibrium situations could also arise if (a) the demand curve for labor had a steeper slope than the supply curve at their point of intersection, or (b) the *IS* curve cut the *LM* curve in such a way that *IS* lay to the right of *LM* above their intersection and to the left of *LM* below their intersection in Figure I (c) or II (c). Actually, these are situations of unstable equilibrium rather than of disequilibrium. However, in these cases, a slight departure from equilibrium would produce a cumulative movement away from it, and the effect would be similar to a situation of disequilibrium.

III. Underemployment Equilibrium due to Wage Rigidity

Next we may consider the case in which the supply of and demand for labor are essentially the same as in Figures I and II, but for institutional or other reasons the money wage does not fall when there is an excess supply of labor.[16] This rigidity of money wages may be due to various factors, including (a) powerful trade unions which are able to prevent money wages from falling, at least temporarily, (b) statutory provisions, such as minimum wage laws, (c) failure of employers to reduce wages due to a desire to retain loyal and experienced employees and to maintain morale,[17] or (d) unwillingness of unemployed workers to accept reduced money wages even though they would be willing to work at lower real wages brought about by a rise in prices.[18]

A situation of this kind is depicted in Figure III. The fixed money wage is designated by $\bar{w}$. In order for full employment (N_f) to be attained, the price level must be at p_f (such as to make $\dfrac{\bar{w}}{p_f}$ equal to the real wage corresponding to full employment), income will be y_f, and the interest rate must reach r_f. However, in the case shown in Figure III, the quantity of money, M, is such that when p is at the level p_f, the *LM* curve $[LM(p_f)]$ intersects the *IS* curve at an income (y_0) below the full employment level and an interest rate (r_0) above the full employment level. Hence full employment cannot be sustained due to inadequate effective demand. On the other hand, if production and employment are at y_0 and N_0, with a price level such (at p_0) as to establish a real wage appropriate to this volume of employment, the *LM* curve will be at a level above $LM(p_f)$. This is because p_0 must be less than p_f in order to make $\bar{w}/p_0$ higher than $\bar{w}/p_f$. In this case production and employment will tend to rise because aggregate demand exceeds current output. Therefore, income must be between y_f and y_0, employment between N_f and N_0, the interest rate between r_f

and r_0, the price level between p_f and p_0. An equilibrium will be reached somewhere between these limits, say at N_e, y_e, p_e, and r_e.[19]

Figure II

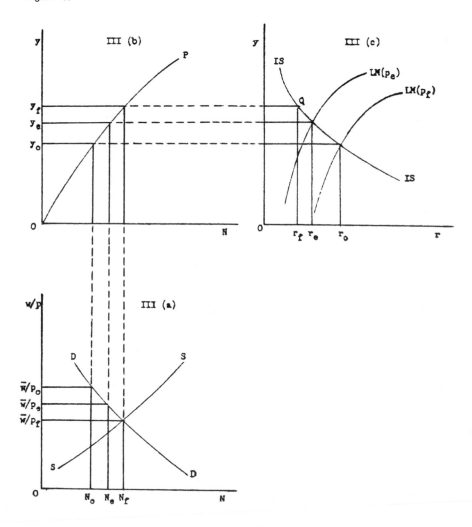

This is a case of underemployment equilibrium. It should be noted that full employment can be attained by an increase in the quantity of money (M) sufficient to shift the LM (p_f) curve to the position where it will intersect the IS curve at point Q. Two propositions can be set down here to be contrasted with the two stated in connection with Figure I.[20]

(1) Changes in the quantity of money cause changes in both the price level and the level of output and employment, and the quantity theory of money does not hold true.[21]

(2) An increase (decrease) in the quantity of money causes a decrease (increase) in the rate of interest. In this case, the interest rate is determined by the interaction of all the relations in the model. Saving, investment, liquidity preference, and the quantity of money all have a hand in its determination.

Introduction of the Pigou effect into Figure III would not prevent the occurrence of an underemployment equilibrium, although it would somewhat complicate the process of adjustment since changes in p or M would cause changes in the IS curve as well as the LM curve.

To summarize, our analysis of Figures I and III indicates that rigidity of money wages is, in general, a necessary condition for (a) the occurrence of an underemployment equilibrium, (b) the quantity of money to have an effect on the level of real income and employment. The rate of interest will not be affected by the quantity of money and liquidity preference unless (a) there is rigidity of money wages or (b) the Pigou effect is operative with $\eta_{AM} \neq 1$. Monetary theories of the rate of interest, whether of the loanable funds or liquidity preference variety, ordinarily assume rigidity (or at least stickiness) in the structure of money wages.[22]

IV. Concluding Comments

In conclusion, we would like to call the reader's attention to further uses to which our graphical technique can be put. With appropriate modifications to suit the occasion, it can be used to analyze other variations of the Keynesian model.[23] Additional factors affecting the income, employment, and price levels, such as those suggested by Hough[24] and by Lutz[25] can be quite easily introduced into the analysis through appropriate shifts in the schedules shown in our system of graphs. Fiscal policy and its relation to monetary policy can be dealt with, since fiscal policy influences the level and shape of the IS curve. Finally, it provides a useful starting point for the study of economic growth. Factors affecting the rate of growth, such as capital accumulation, population growth, technological change, etc., can be brought in by allowing for their effects on the various schedules.

Notes

The development of the technique employed in this paper is a result of discussions with many persons, particularly Professor Daniel B. Suits of the University of Michigan, to whom the writer wishes to express his thanks.

1. See particularly L.R. Klein, "Theories of Effective Demand and Employment," *Journal of Political Economy*, April 1947, LV, pp. 108-131, reprinted in R.V. Clemence (ed.), *Readings*

in Economic Analysis, Vol. I (Cambridge, Mass.: Addison-Wesley Press, 1950), pp. 260-283, and *The Keynesian Revolution* (New York: Macmillan Co., 1950), esp. Technical Appendix; F. Modigliani, "Liquidity Preference and the Theory of Interest and Money," *Econometrica*, Jan. 1944, XII, pp. 45-88, reprinted in F.A. Lutz and L.W. Mints (eds.), *Readings in Monetary Theory* (Philadelphia: Blakiston, 1951), pp. 186-239; also V. Lutz, "Real and Monetary Factors in the Determination of Employment Levels," *Quarterly Journal of Economics*, May 1952, LXVI, pp. 251-272; L. Hough, "The Price Level in Macroeconomic Models," *American Economic Review*, June 1954, LXIV, pp. 269-286.

2.   According to the mathematical formulation of our model in equations (1)-(5), the curve DD in I (a) is the derivative of curve OP in I (b), the relation reflecting the operation of the marginal productivity law under competitive conditions. This precise condition is not important, however, and we shall make no attempt to draw the curves in such a way as to fulfill it. For one thing, the presence of monopoly in the economy or failure of entrepreneurs to seek maximum profits would destroy the precision of the equations, but relations of the type depicted in Figure I would in all probability continue to hold.

3.   For a detailed discussion of this diagram, see J.R. Hicks, "Mr. Keynes and the 'Classics': A Suggested Interpretation," *Econometrica*, April 1937, V, pp. 147-159; also A.H. Hansen, *Monetary Theory and Fiscal Policy* (New York: McGraw-Hill, 1949), Chap. 5. The reader's attention is directed to the fact that we have reversed the axes of the Hicks diagram; we measure the interest rate on the horizontal axis and income on the vertical axis.

4.   It should be noted that the formal analysis in this paper falls entirely in the category of comparative statics, that is, it refers to conditions of equilibrium and changes in the equilibrium values of the variables brought about by changes in data or exogenous variables and does not pretend to describe the *paths* followed by the variables as they move from one equilibrium position to another.

5.   We abstract from the possibility of dynamic instability which may arise due to falling prices if the public has elastic expectations. See D. Patinkin, "Price Flexibility and Full Employment," *American Economic Review*, Sept. 1948, XXXVII, pp. 543-564, reprinted with slight modification in Mints and Lutz, *op. cit.*, pp. 252-283.

6.   On the Pigou effect, see A.C. Pigou, "Economic Progress in a Stable Environment," *Economica*, New Series, August, 1947, XIV, pp. 180-188, reprinted in Lutz and Mints, *op. cit.*, pp. 241-251; Patinkin, *op. cit.*; G. Ackley, "The Wealth-Saving Relationship," *Journal of Political Economy*, April 1951, LIX, pp. 154-161; M. Cohen, "Liquid Assets and the Consumption Function," *Review of Economics and Statistics*, May 1954, XXXVI, pp. 202-211; and bibliography in the latter two articles.

7.   We assume that $c_r \leq 0$, or if $c_r > 0$, $1 + \dfrac{A}{M} \dfrac{L_r c_a}{i_r} > \left| \dfrac{c_r}{i_r} \right|$, so that the denominator of (6) is positive.

8.   The question of what asset concept is appropriate is discussed in Patinkin, *op. cit.*, Cohen, *op. cit.*, and J. Tobin, "Asset Holdings and Spending Decisions," *American Economic Review Papers and Proceedings*, May 1952, XLII, pp. 109-123.

9.   Open market purchases of government securities by the central bank from the non-bank public will leave A unchanged, since the initial purchase transaction will result in a decline in the public's security holdings and an equal increase in M, while any induced expansion of loans and investments by the banks will result in an increase in M offset by an equal increase in the public's indebtedness to the banks. On the other hand if the Treasury prints currency and gives it to the public, A will be increased by the same absolute amount as M but the increase in A will be proportionately smaller than the increase in M (provided the public's holdings of government securities exceed its indebtedness to the banks so that $A > M$).

10.   The fact that the existence of a wealth effect on savings may confer upon the quantity of money the power to affect the rate of interest even with flexible wages is demonstrated in L.A. Metzler, "Wealth, Saving, and the Rate of Interest," *Journal of Political Economy*, April 1951, LIX, pp. 93-116. Metzler's conclusions, which differ from those given here, can be attributed to assumptions that he makes, particularly the assumption that the only assets are money and common stock.

11.   If the supply of labor is affected by the real value of wealth held by workers, changes in the quantity of money may affect output and employment by shifting the SS curve in Figure I (a).

Also, even though monetary change does not affect the *current* level of income and employment, if, due to the operation of the Pigou effect, it changes the interest rate and thereby investment, it may affect the *future* level of employment, since the change in capital stock will ordinarily shift the demand for labor [DD curve in Figure I(a)] at a future date. Both these points are mentioned in V. Lutz, *op. cit.*

12. J.M. Keynes, *General Theory of Employment, Interest, and Money* (New York: Harcourt, Brace and Co., 1936), pp. 201-204.

13. Equations (1)-(5) above apply to the situations covered in both Figure I and Figure II. In the latter case, however, the equations are mathematically inconsistent and do not possess a solution. Mathematics does not tell us what will happen in this case (although the additional conditions necessary to describe the results could be expressed mathematically). The statements made above concerning the results (i.e., that income will be y_a, prices and wages will fall together, etc.) are propositions in economics.

14. Since the money rate of interest cannot be negative, as long as it costs nothing to hold money. In fact, a zero rate of interest would be impossible, since in this case property values would be infinite; however, the rate might *approach* zero. The *real* rate of interest *ex post*, may be negative due to inflation, but this is not relevant to our problem. On this, see I. Fisher, *The Theory of Interest* (New York: Macmillan Co., 1930), Chaps. II, XIX, and pp. 282-286.

15. On the probable shape of the short-run aggregative supply of labor, see G.F. Bloom and H.R. Northrup, *Economics of Labour Relations* (Homewood, Ill.; Richard D. Irwin, 1954), pp. 250-253.

16. We will assume that this rigidity does not prevail in an upward direction — i.e., money wages will rise when there is an excess demand for labor.

17. See A. Rees, "Wage Determination and Involuntary Unemployment," *Journal of Political Economy*, April 1951, LLX, pp. 143-153.

18. Keynes, *op. cit.*, Chap. 2; J. Tobin, "Money Wage Rates and Employment," in S.E. Harris (ed.), *The New Economics* (New York: Knopf, 1947), pp. 572-587.

19. In the case depicted in Figure III, an additional equation $w = \bar{w}$ is added to equations (1)-(5) above. This gives six equations and only five unknown ($y, N, p, w,$ and r). Such a system of equations is *overdetermined* and does not in general, possess a solution. If the quantity of money is treated as a variable which is adjusted so as to maintain full employment, we have six equations and six unknowns and there will be a solution (unless the equations are inconsistent).

20. See p. 4, *supra*.

21. In the limiting case in which the DD curve has a horizontal stage which includes the current level of employment, the entire effect of an increase in M is on y, with no change in p. A considerable part of Keynes' *General Theory* (prior to the discussion of wages and prices in Book V) has reference primarily to this situation.

22. The relative merits of loanable funds and liquidity preference types of monetary interest theories we do not consider, except to say that when appropriately formulated, the two are equivalent.

23. For example, the models with which Modigliani begins his analysis (*op. cit.*, pp. 46-48 in original, pp. 187-190 in *Readings in Monetary Theory*). Analysis of these models requires some alteration in the graphical technique, since he assumes that consumption, investment, and the demand for money, all in current dollars, depend upon money income and the rate of interest, thus introducing "money illusions" into his scheme at several points.

24. *Op. cit.*

25. *Op. cit.*

98

What is Surviving? An Appraisal of Keynesian Economics on its Twentieth Anniversary*

W. Fellner

In the twenty years that have elapsed since the publication of John Maynard Keynes's *General Theory of Employment, Interest and Money* this work has come to mean different things to different economists. Not even in the first approximation is the "Keynesian influence" a well-defined concept. I think it is impossible to understand the problem with which this anniversary session is concerned unless we are willing to distinguish between at least three meanings of the Keynesian influence.

To avoid frequent repetition of lengthy phrases, I will speak here of (1) cyclical Keynesianism, (2) stagnationist Keynesianism, and (3) fundamental-theoretical Keynesianism. Anticipating the conclusions, I will add that in my opinion "cyclical Keynesianism" has survived these twenty years and will continue to be influential doctrine in the predictable future. "Stagnationist Keynesianism" and "fundamental-theoretical Keynesianism" have received hard blows, and they might not survive, or at least not in much strength. I shall also argue that specific analytical tools of the Keynesian system will retain their usefulness in contexts where it is advisable to disregard the equilibrating faculty of changes in the general price level.

Let us first turn to what, for the sake of brevity, I have called "cyclical Keynesianism."

Given the general price level, saving obviously does not have to be equal to planned investment at the capacity level of output. There may take place an unplanned (unexpected) accumulation of inventories,[1] coupled with the hoarding of previously active money or with failure of new-money creation to keep pace with the increase in output; or there may take place an unplanned reduction of inventories, coupled with dishoarding or with new-money creation that exceeds the increase in output. The first of these cases is that in which planned investment falls short of savings and the second that in which

*Source: *American Economic Review*, Vol. 47, May 1957, pp. 67-76.

planned investment exceeds savings. In the second case, where planned investment exceeds savings at a stable price level, it is at least in principle always possible to restore the balance by restrictive credit policies. But in the first case, where saving exceeds planned investment at a stable price level, it is not always possible to restore the balance by the conventional easy money policies of central banks.

Conventional central bank techniques can supply more reserves to the banks, and they can reduce interest rates on government securities to very low levels, although they presumably cannot reduce these rates quite to zero. This leaves the rates on business loans subject to a positive (and perhaps not even so very low) floor level. If, to begin with, full capacity saving exceeds planned investment at the given price level and if we limit ourselves to conventional easy money policies, it is unpredictable how much of the new money will go into additional investment and how much into idle deposits. In a period of major depression tendencies, most of it is quite likely to go into idle deposits. As long as we assume constancy of the general price level, compensatory fiscal as well as monetary policies may be needed to avoid large-scale cyclical unemployment and excess capacity.

But why assume constancy or near constancy of the general price level? The logic of the matter leads us to the question whether in the absence of wage and price rigidity the saving-investment balance would or would not become restored at the capacity level of output by changes in the level of money wages and prices. The logic of the matter should lead us to this question of price-level adjustments at any event, even if conventional easy money policies were generally reliable means of restoring balance, because even the conventional central bank techniques are interferences, and the logic of the matter inevitably brings up the question whether a market economy is self-adjusting through changes in money wages and prices.

It is a characteristic property of what I here call cyclical Keynesianism that it by-passes the question of the consequences of money-wage and price adjustments with an answer that is evasive and yet not meaningless. The answer is that when we are faced with the problems of business cycle policy we frequently wish to proceed as if a self-adjustment mechanism via significant changes in the general wage and price level did not exist. We wish to do this because even if in a free market economy such an adjustment mechanism should exist, it is likely to be a very sluggish mechanism, operating with lags and detours and impeded by institutional obstacles the existence of which, even in a reasonably free market economy, we should not overlook. Therefore, when a discrepancy develops between full employment savings and planned capital formation, cyclical Keynesianism favors policies that work toward restoration of the balance without reliance on significant changes in the general level of money wages and prices. These policies include countercyclical regulation of the relationship between fiscal revenues and fiscal expenditures as well as central bank techniques.

This brief account has moved on thoroughly familiar ground; it raises the question whether cyclical Keynesianism should be called Keynesianism at all. At least in some countries compensatory central bank action has a history that is more than a century old, and the objectives of compensatory central bank policy have been those of cyclical Keynesianism. Toward the end of the nineteenth century and in the beginning of the present, Wicksell's work convinced many economists that in business cycle analysis it is fruitful to attribute an important role to saving-investment discrepancies. From the twenties on, Robertson in England and a prominent group of economists in Sweden have been using brands of their own of the saving-investment analysis. Their conclusions fall under the heading of cyclical Keynesianism, to some extent even with respect to countercyclical fiscal policy. In connection with these contributions it is anachronistic to speak of Keynesianism. The *General Theory* was published in 1936; even the *Treatise on Money* was published after the decade of the twenties (1930). The truth of the matter is that the Keynesian contribution came after a long sequence of important antecedents and that any intelligent presentation of so-called "Keynesian" views requires integrating the Keynesian formal apparatus with analytical elements to be found in the writings of the preceding period. Yet Keynes's contribution to the problem now considered was very significant, and in doctrinal history it is by no means uncommon to associate approaches primarily with the names of writers who toward the end of a historical sequence gave a doctrine a particularly effective formulation. This is why cyclical Keynesianism may after all not be a misleading term, although it is a term which does not do justice to the contributions of the pioneers.

I think it is exceedingly likely that the world would have been spared many tragic events if around 1930 cyclical Keynesianism had been generally accepted doctrine. The German case provides perhaps the most convincing argument in support of this thesis, particularly in view of the fact that world politics has become so lastingly and decisively influenced by what happened in Germany during the thirties. Extended mass unemployment was unquestionably the most powerful among the factors responsible for Hitler's rise to power in January, 1933, and therefore for World War II and for its aftermath. It is impossible to match the German illustration with equally strong ones from other countries, but given the general characteristics of contemporary Western social systems, failure to engage in compensatory fiscal as well as monetary policy during periods of severe depression would have exceedingly grave consequences everywhere. Nor can a single country succeed in its compensatory policies all by itself; that is to say, without some degree of international co-operation in these matters.

One's enthusiasm for cyclical Keynesianism may well become tempered by a tendency on the part of governments to adopt compensatory policies in an asymmetrical fashion, with the result that at the end chronic inflationary pressure is produced. This is an acute danger particularly in an environment where money wage increases, such as exceed the rate of increase in productivity whenever full employment exists, may force a choice between inflation and some amount of unemployment. In such an environment the pressures of the social system might very well tip the efforts of compensatory policy in the inflationary direction.

In their advising capacity economic experts should not overlook this danger. Still, it seems to me very much preferable to try to cope with this danger by urging a less-than-perfectionist attitude to the problem of full employment than to refrain from using strong policies when we become faced with strong cyclical swings. Indeed, it seems inconceivable that any responsible government should revert to the prewar policies in this regard.

On the other hand, the inclination to resort immediately to fiscal policy, even when the economy is faced with weak or moderate swings, is also connected with the influence of cyclical Keynesianism. This attitude, which plays down the promise of compensatory central bank policies to a wholly unwarranted extent, was based on an unreasonable version of cyclical Keynesianism. Fortunately, this attitude has recently been weakening. It is true that central bank policies cannot cope with significant tendencies toward instability all by themselves, but they can do much to counteract weak or moderate tendencies toward instability, and they have the great advantage of prompt adjustability. This is being increasingly recognized.

Let me now turn to what I have called "stagnationist Keynesianism."

The basic premises of stagnationist Keynesianism include those of cyclical Keynesianism and also a further premise. It is postulated that when at the capacity level of output planned investment begins to fall short of saving by a significant margin, conventional easy money policies are insufficient to restore balance, and that the wage-price flexibility mechanism either cannot or should not be relied upon to restore it. This is implied in cyclical Keynesianism, too. In addition, stagnationist Keynesianism implies that in advanced industrial economies such under-investment or oversaving tends to become the typical state of affairs. Thus, we are supposed to get a tendency toward chronic unemployment; that is, toward a level of underutilization where saving ceases to be greater than planned investment.

Stagnationist Keynesianism had a very great impact on the thinking of economists in the decade following the publication of the *General Theory*. The number of converts was especially great in the United States. Even now it is not uncommon to try to explain away the characteristics of all decades other than the thirties by the hypothesis that these other decades have had some exceptional property.

By now the stagnationist predictions have acquired a very substantial degree of implausibility. From the outset the proponents of the doctrine were faced with the difficulty that by the logic of their argument the evils of stagnation should have emerged gradually during a span that started a long time ago, about the turn of the century or even earlier. The logic of the argument, as I see it, is centered on the assumption that a gradually mounting pressure of diminishing returns reduces the rate of return to investors on the amount of new investment which would be required to match full employment savings. Innovations, it is then argued, should be expected to become increasingly insufficient to offset this growing pressure of diminishing returns.

Yet the process of capitalist expansion into vacant or primitive areas started to slow very much earlier than in the thirties. The same is true of the proportionate rate of growth of the population. Surely, in the United States and also in the world of Western capitalism taken as a whole, the rate of increase in "utilized land" and in the labor supply (the increase in land-plus-labor, so to speak) was much smaller relative to the rate of increase in the capital stock about 1900 than several decades earlier. By the turn of the century, innovations were surely performing against a "mounting pressure of diminishing returns." They have been performing against a mounting pressure for a long time. In the long run they have been offsetting this mounting tendency quite successfully. We have been adjusting to a rising scarcity of land-plus-labor relative to capital.

Perhaps the best way of expressing this is to say that Keynes and the stagnationists were right in maintaining, or at least implying in their argument, that changes in the relative resource positions of advanced economies call for certain adjustments. To be more specific here than the stagnationist literature has been, one or more of the following adjustments is needed if profit rates are not to fall to very low levels: (1) more plentiful innovating activity (that is, innovating activity that raises output per unit of resource-inputs more than was the case in earlier phases); or (2) relatively more land-and-laborsaving and relatively less capitalsaving innovating activity (that is, innovating activity that has a more favorable effect on the relative share of capital than did the earlier innovations); (3) a lower propensity to save (lower investment-output ratio), corresponding to the lower rate of acquisition of new resources which are complementary with capital.

Keynes and the stagnationists seem to have been wrong in implying that we shall not get some combination of these adjustments. Advanced economies seem to have been getting both the first and the third of these adjustments; that is, more plentiful innovating activity and a lowering of the investment-output ratio. There is a presumption, it seems to me, that in this connection the emphasis should be placed more on accelerated innovating activity than on the lowering of the investment-output ratio. In the United States, for example, each unit of new capital formation seems to bring more increase in output now than was the case in earlier periods; an increased rate of technological-organizational progress (more plentiful innovating activity) appears to be the most plausible explanation of this. There exists no good reason to assume that historically we would be running into diminishing returns on any major scale, or with much consistency, even if the saving-output or investment-output ratio were the same now as it was two or three generations ago. The saving-output or investment-output ratio has become lower, but it would be far-fetched to argue that with somewhat higher saving Western economies would be running into diminishing returns to the extent of generating chronic deflationary pressure.

In the Western world, investment opportunities have so far stayed plentiful indeed, except in periods of cyclical depression (some of which, however, were of considerable duration). Technological-organizational advance may very well prove to be a self-accelerating process. At any rate, the thesis of secular stagnation must by now explain away five decades or more as atypical decades when it represents a single decade as reflecting allegedly typical conditions in advanced industrial systems. Innovations have been sufficiently plentiful and their land and laborsaving character has stayed sufficiently pronounced to prevent any appreciable secular lowering of rates of return to investors.

Even if economic stagnation should in the future become the typical state of affairs in Western societies, the question of whether the reasons are Keynesian or Schumpeterian would, of course, stay controversial, since net rates of return to investors are influenced by redistributive political measures as well as by the relative factor supplies in our economies. But the main point here is that stagnationist predictions cannot at present properly be derived by projecting into the future the observable long-run relations of the past.

Notwithstanding favorable secular trends, the influence of stagnationist Keynesianism may wane only gradually. In fact, its influence has been on the decline for some time, but this has been a slow decline. The dangers of a stagnationist bias in professional opinion are not negligible. Experts with a stagnationist bias are apt to suggest strong antideflationary measures when we move into a cyclical phase which later turns out to be one of minor recession; in other words, a policy of cyclical Keynesianism may become distinctly lopsided (inflationary on balance) if the policy is administered by experts who are under the influence of stagnationist Keynesianism. Furthermore, in times of severe cyclical depression such experts may show a tendency to favor not merely those antideflationary public policies which at the same time provide incentives for a subsequent full recovery of private investment, but also some public investment policies which discount, so to speak, the inability of private investment ever to recover to its former significance.

On the whole, my own view is therefore that while stagnationist Keynesianism has raised questions of very great analytical and practical interest (and in this sense has been very fruitful), much harm could develop from a stagnationist attitude to problems of economic policy. I feel that it is exceedingly important to divorce a reasonable version of cyclical Keynesianism from stagnationist Keynesianism or, as we might prefer to put it, to hasten the gradual process by which the two are becoming divorced from one another.

The third and last meaning of Keynesianism to be considered in the present paper is that which we have called "fundamental-theoretical Keynesianism." I here mean the theoretical position that denies the Pigou effect or Patinkin's "real balance effect." The positions which in this paper were called those of cyclical Keynesianism and of stagnationist Keynesianism can afford to by-pass the fundamental question of whether, in the event of threatening demand insufficiency at a given price level, a fall in money wage rates and in prices would not always raise effective demand to the size consistent with full utilization. If we disregard problems of transition (expectational spirals and the like), perfect flexibility of money wage rates and of prices could have this beneficial consequence by raising the real value of the already existing money hoards and by thus encouraging the use of money for the purchase of goods. This was pointed out already by Haberler in the early stages of the controversy about the *General Theory*. Cyclical and stagnationist Keynesianism were defined as implying either that the reasoning which establishes the real balance effect of price reductions is invalid or that the reasoning, while theoretically valid, lacks practical significance. This is somewhat evasive. What I call here fundamental-theoretical Keyesianism differs from the other two types of Keynesianism in that it is not evasive concerning the real balance effect of money wage and price reductions. Fundamental-theoretical Keynesianism denies the existence of this effect.

It might perhaps be objected that Keynes did not argue for the position which we here define as that of fundamental-theoretical Keynesianism. Into the analytical framework which he introduced Keynes did not incorporate the real balance effect (this statement will scarcely be contradicted), but the reasons why he failed to do so are not quite obvious. From the outset he may have omitted from his formal system those analytical elements which (had he included them) he would have had to disregard at the end because of his conviction that lags, frictions, and institutional rigidities render the real balance effect practically insignificant. On the whole I believe, however, that Keynes's failure to develop a clear-cut verbal argument with respect to the real balance effect, which at the same time is absent from his formal system, should lead us to contrast his views with the views of those who do attribute theoretical importance to the real balance effect. This is why I speak of fundamental-theoretical Keynesianism when I mean denial of the theoretical validity of the real balance effect.

It seems to me that the anti-Keynesian reasoning which establishes the real balance effect is valid reasoning, but that a theoretical system which relies on the equilibrating faculty of the real balance effect should recognize that the rate of growth may depend importantly on how much or how little use the economy is allowed to make of general price changes in equilibrating itself.

Let us for a moment completely disregard lags in the adjustment process and also rigidities of a sociological-political character. Even on these assumptions, there remains the difficulty that it is impossible to describe a series of appreciable, consecutive price reductions without thereby postulating a very high real rate of interest. This means little growth or, if we carry the assumption far enough, perhaps no growth. If price reductions instead of monetary expansion were used as a means of satisfying the desire for additional real balances, the real rate of interest might have to rise regardless of how far the money rate of interest is lowered. After all, the money rate is subject to a floor, perhaps somewhere near the zero level. Growth rates would be reduced, and if the size of the required price reductions were great enough even for relatively small rates of growth, stationary or near-stationary equilibrium would be the only analytical result consistent with these assumptions.

To put it briefly, with the aid of the real balance effect of price changes it is possible to describe a process which will eliminate any demand for additional real balances and hence any possible deficiency of effective demand; but if the demand for real balances were equated with the supply of real balances by this mechanism instead of by the proper degree of monetary expansion, the growth process might be harmed or even destroyed. This is the tentative conclusion which the present state of the controversy suggests to me concerning the real balance effect. While this conclusion is non-Keynesian, it is obviously influenced by analytical developments which were greatly stimulated by Keynes's work. If we reject fundamental-theoretical Keynesianism, we may view the Keynesian analytical apparatus as a simplifying device which disregards the equilibrating faculty of changes in the general price level. For the reasons here indicated, it seems to me that this is frequently a very useful simplification in the theory of long-run growth as well as in the analysis of countercyclical policies.

In this anniversary session I should perhaps have spent less time trying to analyze problems in detail and more time making general observations. Yet the main general observation which I would like to offer did require reference to detail. Some important specific ideas of the *General Theory* have become incorporated into widely accepted economic theory, although it is not at all obvious just how Keynesian or Robertsonian or neo-Wicksellian or neo-classical the integrated product is. The ideas that have thus found their way into the main stream of doctrinal development are those of cyclical Keynesian-ism rather than of stagnationist or of fundamental-theoretical Keynesianism. Also, there has recently developed a good deal of awareness of differences between reasonable versions of cyclical Keynesianism, which allow for the efficacy of central bank policy in periods of moderate disturbance, and extreme or unreasonable versions of cyclical Keynesianism which place all the emphasis on fiscal policy. But the elements of Keynesian theory that have found their way into the main stream of doctrinal history do not tell the full story. Even where the present generation and the next are unlikely to go along with Keynes's answers, they will find that Keynes posed problems in a fruitful fashion. They will want to move with Keynes over some sections of his analytical route, although they presumably will not wish to stay on Keynes's route right to the stage of definite conclusions. This is what I was trying to say in a somewhat detailed discussion of specific propositions.

To be sure, while Keynes called his book of twenty years ago a *General*

Theory of Employment, Interest and Money, the number of significant problems in that area which he left outside the scope of the book is quite large. The list of neglected or omitted problems includes the relationship between incentives and the equalitarian currents of our epoch, monopoly and competition, the possible coexistence of inflationary tendencies and of full use of equipment with the underemployment of labor, and the effect of technological progress on relative factor prices. Still, the range of problems on which he has compelled us to agree or to disagree with him is wide. For this posterity will be grateful to him. Much has met his eye and it would be ungracious to complain that not even more has. After all, economists have continued to derive inspiration from more works than one and from more brilliant thinkers than one. None can deny Keynes a prominent place among these men and the *General Theory* a prominent place among these works.

Note

1.   As long as we assume constancy of the general price level, we may perhaps postulate that planned and realized savings are always equal. But even if these two magnitudes should be unequal, this need not create the same disturbance as the inequality of planned and realized investment. Therefore, I shall engage in no discussion of unexpected savings here.

99

The Influence of Keynesian Economics on Contemporary Thought*

D. Dillard

In appraising the influence of Keynesian economics one is immediately confronted with the question whether Keynesian economics refers exclusively to tools of analysis like the propensity to consume, the marginal efficiency of capital, and liquidity preference, or whether it also embodies a substantive contribution; that is, quantitative and qualitative judgments about institutional and historical developments. Among the great majority of academicians and professionals, Keynesian economics probably means tools of analysis, and the influence here should be judged in terms of the acceptance or rejection of Keynesian concepts. To the world outside academic halls, economics is thought of in more substantive terms, and consequently Keynesian economics should be judged in this connection in terms of its influence on policy and ideology.

Academic economists are also interested in policy questions, but they are inclined to evaluate Keynesian economics as a conceptual system which per se has nothing to do with policy and ideology. This enables many who do not agree with Keynes's views on economic policy to utilize in good conscience the Keynesian tools of analysis and even to consider themselves Keynesians. In this sense there is much validity in the statement, "We are all good Keynesians now," although for the peace of mind of a minority who may feel ill at ease in this category, the statement should be amended to read, "We are nearly all Keynesians now." In this connection one should bear in mind that Keynes was careful not to say classical economics is wrong. His main criticism was its irrelevance to explanations of unemployment. Keynesian economics supplements rather than supplants the theory of resource allocation. Under conditions of full employment the classical theory comes into its own.

*Source: *American Economic Review*, Vol. 47, May 1957, pp. 77-87.

I. Present Status of the Technical Concepts

One simple but significant measure of the influence of Keynesianism on contemporary economics is obtained by comparing the textbook of today with that of twenty years ago. The changes have been profound. National income analysis, born in 1936, now sits at the head of the table even before attaining its twenty-first birthday. The theory of the firm — twenty years older and considerably heavier — has been dethroned, and in some cases the marginal cost–marginal revenue analysis is looked upon as a stepchild and has been relegated to the annex. The numerous progeny, which might be called problem children, receive less attention than before because the new young master demands so much attention. Money plays a more important part in family affairs because King Macro has a special affinity for liquidity preference. Family relations are good, but some members lack a clear idea of how they are related to each other.

My belief is that all the major parts of Keynes's economics remain pretty much as he devised them, with, of course, the inevitable refinements and additions. Any significant body of theory must possess organic unity; that is, consist of concepts, theorems, and propositions — all of which are related to each other and to the system as a whole. In the nature of the case the removal of any major part would greatly weaken the whole theory. It is easier to abandon an entire system than to abandon major parts of a system. If a body of theory survives, because it is useful or for any other reason, additions are more likely than excisions.

The Keynesian consumption function has stood up pretty well in the light of many theoretical critiques and statistical investigations. Keynes claimed only that the relation of consumption to income is a "fairly stable function." He recognized the influence of other variables and warned that they must not be forgotten. No one, to my knowledge, has denied his main point; namely, that income is the principal variable upon which consumption depends.

The most important addition to Keynesian theory, in my judgment, has been the long-term consumption function, as a supplement to Keynes's short-term consumption function. Duesenberry's type of long-term consumption function is important, not only as a piece of technical apparatus, but also because the idea embodied in it moderates the basic message of the *General Theory*. The size of the gap which must be filled by investment increases much less rapidly than is implied by Keynes, because of the upward movement of the short-term function. The range of instability and the threat of stagnation are thereby reduced, although by no means eliminated.

One conceptual problem arising in connection with the stability of the consumption function is the use of "consumption" to mean expenditure of money rather than the actual process of using goods and services. If a consumer's durable purchased in period one lasts for several periods, the current expenditure in period one exceeds the actual consumption, when the latter term is defined as utilization of the good; and in the subsequent periods the actual consumption exceeds the expenditure. A bunching of purchases of durables such as occurred at the outbreak of the Korean conflict in 1950 and of automobiles during the first three quarters of 1955 may yield data which show consumption increasing faster than income, because consumers are investing in durables at a rapid rate. Instability of the consumption function may be more apparent than real, depending on which definition of consumption is chosen. If actual consumption is preferred to money expenditure as a measure of consumption, then data on consumer inventories are needed to determine how nearly the two measures of consumption correspond.

Keynes claimed more novelty for his liquidity-preference theory than subsequent commentators have been willing to concede. While the loanable-funds theory of interest seems to hold a lead in popularity among economists, the liquidity-preference theory is still very much in evidence. The consensus appears to be that there is no significant difference between these two theories of interest. Perhaps the most important refinement of the Keynesian theory of interest has been made by Professors Hicks and Hansen. The point at issue, however, is really a minor one. In his formal model Keynes did not take account of the influence of changes in the level of income on the quantity of money available for speculative balances. Professor Hansen is technically correct that the interest rate is indeterminate until income is known. Other logical refinements in the Hicks-Hansen model show the relation of productivity and thrift in the determination of the Keynesian interest rate. Logical completeness has its virtue but simplicity has its charm. Keynes preferred charm to virtue.

The marginal efficiency concept has undergone less alteration than either of the other two basic schedules in the original Keynesian construction. In its purely formal properties it was less original with Keynes than the consumption function or the liquidity-preference function. Keynes's contribution here relates to the uncertainty of expectations on long-term investments rather than to the formal concept of the marginal efficiency of capital. Further study of Keynes leads me to the conviction that uncertain expectations constituted for him the most important single premise in his monetary theory of production.[1] For those Keynesians who emphasize the irrationality of the investment process, the marginal efficiency of capital is the most vital concept in the entire system.

Hardly any concept or proposition in Keynes's *General Theory* has gone unchallenged, but most, although not all, of these criticisms lack operational meaning. A typical performance is for a critic to deliver a vigorous refutation of Keynes, only to acknowledge that the criticism has no practical significance. For example, almost no one any longer recommends money-wage cuts as a remedy for unemployment, but writers are still showing that if wages and prices are completely flexible and if the expectational effect is not unfavorable, wage cuts would eliminate unemployment. Other examples of this type of criticism pertain to the Pigou effect, equilibrium at less than full employment, Say's law of markets, the flattening out of the liquidity-preference schedule, and propositions invoking the completely un-Keynesian assumption of unchanging expectations.

Models constructed by theorists with no feel for practical policy are frequently so unrealistic in their assumptions — and therefore in their conclusions — that they can have no conceivable utility except to test the capacity of our students in logical gymnastics. Keynes may not always have been more logical than his adversaries but what he said was usually more relevant to the problems of actual experience.

II. Keynesian Influence in its Broader Aspects

In discussing the influence of Keynesian economics on policy, institutions, and ideology, I take as my text Alfred Marshall's statement that poverty constitutes the most important problem and the chief justification for the study of economics. My thesis is that the essential difference between pre-Keynesian and Keynesian economics resides in attitudes toward a solution of the problem of poverty. The shift from what may be called the economics of scarcity to the economics of potential plenty reflects nothing less than recognition on the level of economic analysis of the age of mass production, a movement that had its roots in the nineteenth century but the concrete manifestations of which became abundantly clear only in the twentieth century. Economic historians sometimes speak of this as the second industrial revolution. Since Keynesian economics reflects the most far-reaching economic development of the twentieth century, it can hardly be viewed as a passing fancy of the Great Depression of the thirties, even though it was that great catastrophe which precipitated a Keynesian vision of twenty years into a system of analytical techniques which we know as the general theory of employment.

During the Great Depression, economists continued to teach that the economic principle is concerned with the allocation of scarce resources and that economic problems are therefore problems of scarcity. No one would deny to economists the right to define their subject in any manner they wish, but little common sense was needed to understand that scarcity was not the economic problem. How false, therefore, were the teachings of the economists in a pragmatic, historical, and operational sense. How shockingly realistic it must have seemed to hungry men, living in the shadows of smokeless chimneys and praying for the offer of a job, to be told that workers employ the means of production and thereby determine the volume of employment. How frustrating to be told in the midst of incalculable social waste and involuntary unemployment that the solution of our economic needs lay in frugality and hard work. The orthodox economists were violating their first maxim that science should deal with what is rather than what should be.

The old ideology of scarcity, frugality, and abstinence was discredited by the sheer force of circumstances. Keynes moved in to fill the vacuum with what Professor Schumpeter was wont to call a "vision," defined as a "preanalytic cognitive act." Adumbrations of Keynes's vision ran through his earlier writings but it was first clearly perceived in the *Means to Prosperity* (1933) and received theoretical implementation in the *General Theory* (1936). Keynes verbalized his vision in the opening sentence of the *Means to Prosperity* as follows: "If our poverty were due to famine or earthquake or war — if we lacked material things and the resources to produce them, we could not expect to find the Means to Prosperity except in hard work, abstinence, and invention. In fact, our predicament is notoriously of another kind."

Following Professor Rogin, we shall speak of Keynes's insight as the optimistic hypothesis of abundance. It takes on momentous significance, not because Keynes was the first to express the idea that poverty is unnecessary, but because he was the first to elevate it to a leading principle of economics which found wide acceptance in an age in which it was consistent with the underlying technological conditions of mass production and the underlying political institutions of mass democracy.

Prior to the Great Depression, economics was pervaded by the pessimistic hypothesis of scarcity. It finds clear expression in the Malthusian principle of population and in the law of diminishing returns. Marshall struggled to give some operational meaning other than unavoidable poverty to the economic principle of scarcity, and Professor Pigou elevated "welfare economics" to the forefront of economic discussion. They continued, however, to attribute poverty to the limitations of human and material nature. Keynes, on the contrary, embraced the heresy which attributes poverty to social and economic institutions.

The revolution in thought led by Keynes could have happened only against a backdrop of severe crisis. Keynes was ideally suited to lead a two-front war on classical theory and practice because he had one foot in the world of affairs and the other in King's College. His position seemed realistic in the light of the prevailing predicament of the economy and it satisfied the requirements of the science among the younger generation of economists and even won many converts from the older generation. The crisis gave his ideas greater influence than the *General Theory* would merit as a sheer intellectual *tour de force*.

The Keynesian vision of abundance pervades all the concepts and *obiter dicta* of the *General Theory* but is most forcefully represented by the principle of effective demand. This is Keynes's answer to Marshall's most important problem of poverty. Immediately following his preliminary summary of the principle of effective demand in Chapter 3, Keynes says: "This analysis supplies us with an explanation of the paradox of poverty in the midst of plenty." The principle of effective demand is well known. In a potentially wealthy society, everyone cannot be put to work producing consumers' goods because there would not be enough demand to buy back all the consumers' goods produced. Some means must be found to disperse additional income, most of which will be spent on consumers' goods, without bringing onto the market any current consumers' goods to be sold. "Investment" is the activity which injects the additional income. Normally it takes the form of producing capital goods, but the same function of disbursing income may result from payments for leaf raking, building battleships, fighting wars, or by refunding income taxes paid in previous years. My purpose here is to show how the principle of effective demand followed from the optimistic hypothesis of abundance and how it countered the pessimistic hypothesis of scarcity, frugality, abstinence, and hard work.

The optimistic hypothesis of abundance is manifest in many other facets of the Keynesian analysis: in the notion that the marginal efficiency of capital may fall to zero in a couple of generations of full production; in the view that interest rewards no genuine sacrifice any more than the rent of land; in the attitude toward a large public debt; in the passive role assigned to saving; in the criticism of "sound finance"; and in the view that equality of income is fully compatible with progress in the accumulation of wealth. Lest there be any misunderstanding, it should be pointed out that the hypothesis of abundance applies only to advanced capitalist countries. Keynesian economics is not very germane to underdeveloped countries, where abundance is not a short-term possibility and the classical medicine for poverty applies.

Loan expenditure was Keynes's means to prosperity during the depression. This involved, of course, deliberately unbalanced budgets and ran counter to accepted principles of public finance. In 1930, the British Treasury cut the salaries of school teachers and retrenched on other expenditures in order to try to bring the budget into balance. President Hoover was so outraged by Keynes's ideas that he referred to deficit spending and related recommendations as "Operation Cuttlefish" and branded Keynes, along with Marx and Mussolini, as one of the three greatest enemies of modern civilization. Franklin D. Roosevelt, who later supported deficit spending, in the campaign of 1932 leveled a blistering attack against President Hoover for failing to balance the budget and called for drastic reductions in federal expenditures. Professional economists had little wisdom to offer in pointing a way of escape from the crisis. Keynes, however, knew what should be done, and his prescription of loan expenditure has now become a standard remedy for depressions. The acceptance of deficit financing as a respectable type of public policy is one of the remarkable changes in public thinking for which Keynesian economics has been primarily responsible.

Another way to express the operational meaning of Keynesian economics is in terms of a repudiation of the theoretical foundations of laissez faire, on the one hand, and the theoretical sanction for a mixed economy, on the other hand. In much the same way that Marx the socialist presents a theory of capitalism as the basis for an argument for socialism, so Keynes the interventionist presents a theory of laissez faire as the basis for an argument for a mixed economy. If the economic system is not self-adjusting, then positive steps are needed to insure full employment. By refraining in the *General Theory* from blueprinting the type of intervention that would be required to overcome the paradox of poverty in the midst of potential plenty, Keynes leaves open a flexible view of the future, with, however, the direction clearly indicated. The concluding chapter of the *General Theory* states the social philosophy of a mixed economy. The degree of the mix is flexible, but the area of government activity will be much larger than under the limping laissez faire existing in the United States and the United Kingdom at the onset of the Great Depression. Private property is neither defended nor attacked on economic grounds. Keynes always maintained that the issue of private versus public ownership of the means of production is unimportant. So long as private ownership in the means of production does not militate against the realization of abundance, it should be encouraged because of its many noneconomic advantages. But the shift in emphasis from thrift to expenditure weakens the hallowed place which private property held in classical economics.

Even the verbal acceptance of a new social philosophy is important because it opens an avenue through which new ideas may reach statesmen receptive to innovations in policy. In the postwar world, nearly all nations have adopted full or high-level employment programs. Both major political parties in the United States and nearly all political parties in other countries are committed on paper to use the power of government to prevent another general breakdown of the economic system. The Employment Act of 1946 in the United States is an important manifestation of the new Keynesian-type social philosophy. One of the culminating steps in this direction occurred in 1952 when General Eisenhower pledged all-out use of federal authority to prevent large-scale unemployment.

Although statesmen from F.D.R. to President Eisenhower have endorsed Keynesian-type policies against depression, there is little evidence that what has happened to the level of economic activity has been much influenced by these ideas. The United States entered the second World War with an unliquidated depression of vast proportions with no solution, except war, in sight. Since then the nation has experienced a decade and a half of war and postwar boom. Eleven years of postwar prosperity bring us now to the same relative position where the nation stood in 1929. The feeling is strong, as it was before 1929, that there will be no more major depressions. A new New Era philosophy is developing among economists, businessmen, and the public. Confidence that events will cease to resemble the past at this particular juncture in history rests, in no small part, upon the belief in the adequacy of Keynesian-type policies: built-in stabilizers, monetary policy, and fiscal policy. This appears a strange and dangerous illusion into which we have fallen — the illusion of economic stability. Although actual events have been little influenced during the past twenty years by Keynesian economics, we now implicitly put our faith in the conscious application of this type of policy to save us from the fate which has characterized capitalist development with increasing intensity during the past century and a half. We have the arrogance to assume that from now on we shall do what has never been done before. We seem to think that because we now know the causes of depressions and stagnation, we shall therefore prevent them from recurring. Such faith in human intelligence is admirable but hardly justified from experience. The burden of proof is upon those who believe that a New Era has really come to pass this time. History does not repeat itself, but neither does it suddenly reverse itself. It is not another 1929 to 1932 that we have most to fear, but another 1936 to 1939.

It is as important not to overestimate the influence of Keynesian economics as it is not to underestimate it. The power of ideas to control events is, at best, limited and works with moderate influence only over very long periods of time. Keynes himself erred in overstating the influence of ideas. In the closing paragraph of the *General Theory* he wrote: "The ideas of economists and political philosophers, both when they are right and when they are wrong, are more powerful than is commonly understood. Indeed the world is ruled by little else." My reading of history does not bear out this faith in the power of ideas to influence events. Professor Pigou seemed closer to the truth in the closing paragraph of his presidential address to the Royal Economic Society: "The hope that an advance in economic knowledge will appreciably affect actual happenings is, I fear, a slender one. It is not likely that there will be a market for our produce." Here is one example, at least, in which Professor Pigou admits that supply does not create its own demand!

The most that an economist can be expected to do is to clarify great issues and point to the direction of their solution. The *sine qua non* of greatness, therefore, is insight into contemporary historical problems. As Professor Schumpeter says, a new vision, such as Keynes's vision of abundance, is necessarily associated in its genesis with an ideology; that is, with value judgments, a point of view, a set of interests, and selection and emphasis as among the facts which are more important and those which are less important in the total complex of a social predicament. For the vision to become a part of science, according to Professor Schumpeter's methodology, it must be purged of its ideological content because economic theory (science) is neutral with respect to value judgments and practical policy. Consequently, Schumpeter accused Keynes of the Ricardian vice of "offering in the garb of general scientific truth, advice which carries meaning only with reference to the practical exigencies of the unique historical situation of a given time and country." In his review of the *General Theory* Schumpeter said of Keynes: "... everywhere he really pleads for a definite policy, and on every page the ghost of that policy looks over the shoulder of the analyst, frames his assumptions, guides his pen . . . It is vital to renounce communion with any attempt to revive the Ricardian practice . . . Economics will never have nor merit any authority until that unholy alliance is dissolved. This book throws us back again." I submit that this judgment which sees the *General Theory* as a great misfortune for economic theory was wrong, and that on the contrary it did more than any other event in this century to vitalize economic science. The Ricardian vice is really a virtue, or if not a virtue, let us defend the vice. The great stature of Ricardo as well as of Keynes as economists stems from the fact that they did take positive stands on the great issues of their times. My reading of the history of economic theory raises this to a general truth about the development of our discipline. In striving for neutrality economists typically achieve sterility. Fortunately Keynes was not one of the neutralists and was thereby better qualified to promote the science. To be scientific one must be objective in the sense of being guided by the facts of experience, but one does not have to be neutral in the sense of refusing to state propositions which have operational significance for practice. In order for economists to be influential in the Ricardian and Keynesian sense, their programs, which represent the operational meaning of their theories, must be consistent with the underlying historical and institutional conditions of the age and be capable of political implementation. Ricardo's program for repeal of the Corn Laws was consistent with the best allocation of resources as between agriculture and industry and with the growing political power of the industrial capitalists as represented, for example, by the Great Reform Act of 1832. Keynes's program for full employment is an answer to capitalist instability and is consistent with the growth of mass democracy, with its willingness to act through the state if private enterprise does not make available sufficient employment opportunities. While it is unfortunate that a theory about a variant environment cannot be both historically relevant and universally valid, this is one of the facts of life mere mortals should learn to accept.

In the very long run, the influence of great ideas upon the future course of events cannot be predicted, but the subject merits speculation. Perhaps the most important contribution of Keynesian economics will turn out to be a higher stage of rationalization of economic life — in the Max Weber sense of rationalization — through the impetus it has given to national income analysis and accounting. As Werner Sombart and others have pointed out, modern capitalism would have been impossible without rational business calculation in the form of double-entry bookkeeping. The great age of business enterprise is characterized by the extreme rationality of business accounting, on the one hand, and the complete lack of conscious calculation for the economy as a whole, on the other hand. Slowly we seem to be entering an era in which the scope of conscious calculation extends beyond the individual firm to the economic system as a whole. This is a logical inference from the demise of laissez faire. A system of conscious calculation on an economy-wide basis means that economic decisions are made in terms of their effect on the size of the national income rather than upon the profits and losses of private business. When accounting is made in terms of national income, many of the most difficult economic problems are automatically solved. For example, since unemployed workers contribute nothing to national income, it is desirable, in terms of national income accounting, that they be employed so long as they produce anything more than nothing. Hence the conscious direction of economic affairs in these accounting terms would immediately result in the disappearance of unemployment. The great social irrationality of unemployment, which so perplexed Keynes's generation, would turn out to be no problem at all. The visible hand of the national income accountant would replace the invisible hand of Adam Smith.

Note

1.   The term, "Monetary Theory of Production," was the title Keynes gave to his lectures at Cambridge during the early thirties. For discussion of this concept in relation to the central theme of the *General Theory*, see my "The Theory of a Monetary Economy," in *Post-Keynesian Economics* (Rutgers University Press, 1954), edited by Kenneth K. Kurihara, p. 3-30.

100

Keynesian Economics After Twenty Years: Discussion*

D.M. Wright, W.A. Salant and T. Scitovsky

David McCord Wright: I accept Professor Dillard's standard that the value of a theory is to be judged by its ability to yield policy conclusions relevant to the contemporary scene. But I also find it shockingly unrealistic that stagnation (of the capital glut variety) should still be treated as the great danger in this time of world-wide shortages in most countries and of inflationary pressure in practically all of them.

Professor Dillard says that it has now been shown that there is no significant difference between the loanable fund and liquidity-preference theories. This statement at once says too much and too little. I agree that various definitional schemes can be drawn up formally assimilating them. But, when we leave tautology, there are a number of different cases, in some of which the two theories do yield the same results but in others of which they do not.

A diagram (below) will, I hope, help to make the matter clearer.

We assume a given full employment gross national product level. The abcissa measures amounts of saving and of investment. The ordinates percentages of interest and expected profit. Planned saving is assumed (for simplicity's sake) to be interest inelastic in the short run. Accordingly it is indicated by a straight vertical line.

Three marginal efficiency of capital schedules are drawn: MEC_1, MEC_2, MEC_3. Each is a schedule of the expected marginal return at various levels of planned investment, at the given initial GNP level, and under various general conditions of expectation and technical change, over a time period, say, of six months to one year.

MEC_1 is drawn intersecting the saving line at 4 per cent. It is evident, by elementary economic logic, that 4 per cent is the only equilibrium interest rate.

*Source: *American Economic Review*, Vol. 47, May 1957, pp. 88-95.

If the rate be higher, planned saving will exceed planned investment and income will begin to fall. If the rate be lower, planned investment will exceed planned saving, and, barring rationing of credit (since full employment is initially assumed), inflation will begin.

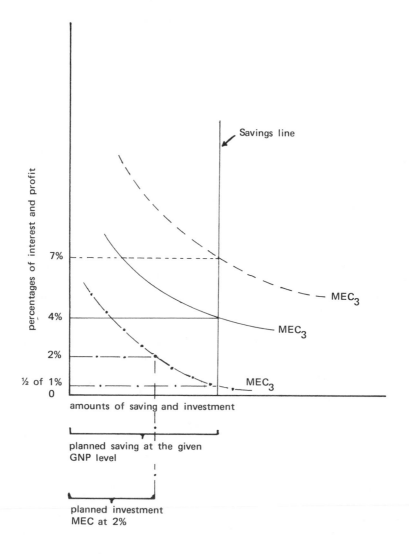

In MEC_2 the schedule cuts the saving line at 7 per cent. It is again evident that barring inflation or credit rationing, the rate of interest must rise, and that 7 per cent is the only equilibrium figure. Some Keynesians of the type I have called "stream-lined" seem to think that Keynes's statement that the rate of interest is "solely" determined by the interaction of liquidity preference and the quantity of money excludes any effect of an upward shift in the MEC schedule upon the interest rate. This is a mistake, as I have shown in my "Future of Keynesian Economics" article in the *Review* (June, 1945). A rise in the MEC schedule will cause a rise in the L_1 or transactions demand for liquidity. Businessmen attracted by the higher general set of profit expectation will seek new transactions balances or finance wherewith to exploit them. If language makes one any happier, one can say they wish to provide for expected or proposed higher income activity levels.

It is true that the rise in the money rate may be temporarily prevented by a drop in the L_2 demand for liquidity due to a decline in the speculative motive. This operates, however, as an increase in velocity. It will (barring positive offsetting action by the monetary authorities) cause inflation. But once the inflationary impetus of the released funds is exhausted, the rate will rise to the proper equilibrium figure. It will be seen that the end result is thus the same for liquidity preference or loanable funds. Keynes's schema does, however, make especially evident the possibility of an interim inflationary movement. I doubt, however, that this part of his analysis would have surprised either Ricardo, Smith, Mill, or Hume.

The really important Keynesian case is shown in our MEC_3 schedule. There the pure loanable funds theorist would have it that the rate of interest would fall to ½ of 1 per cent, or even lower, and thus planned investment would continue to equal planned saving. But Keynes, by his L_2 speculative motive analysis, which I need not repeat, shows that it may stick at, say 2 per cent. In that case, planned investment falls far below planned savings, and a general decline in gross national product levels will begin.

Some students have asked me what would make the MEC schedule shift? Surely it is obvious that a general rise or fall in the general state of expectation can be brought about by new discovery, new governments, new changes in social policy, the opening up of new areas.

The diagram and explanation I have given merely make clearer the analysis I published in 1945 which was approved by Keynes himself in writing as well as by Sir Dennis Robertson. Remember, also, that Keynes told Professor John H. Williams that he was trying to educate the English to the need for a higher rate of interest after the war, and that I have letters from him saying that he expects the problem after the war will be inflation, not unemployment. Failure to recognize the relativity of Keynes's teaching is not merely bad economics but bad Keynesianism!

Keynes's theory does not prove that an increase in (planned) saving or a rise in the interest rate would reduce actual saving. This would only be true "assuming no favorable change in the investment schedule." Yet Klein's text contains the mistake concerning saving, Dillard's concerning the interest rate. And there are others equally dogmatic. Furthermore, it is not necessarily true (though here I speak primarily for myself) that one has to rely on an upward shift in the MEC schedule. For if the saving line shifts to the right and the

MEC curve remains unchanged, then reduced consumption outlay could conceivably release balances adequate to satisfy any increase in the L_2 demand for liquidity due to the speculative motive. Why would the *MEC* curve not necessarily fall? Because investment and consumption are not necessarily linked by any fixed mechanical relationship. The investment might mostly be autonomous.

One of the principal troubles is, I believe, that Keynes's disciples have depended too much upon oral tradition concerning what he said and not paid enough attention to what he wrote. I could illustrate with several anecdotes from my own experience the difference between a teacher extemporizing in his rooms or seminar and his writings. We economists must realize that we only make progress and are scientific to the extent that we remain conscious of the multiple variety of the social process. The persistence today of stream-lined Keynesianism — I mean such doctrines as that the rate of interest is a purely monetary phenomenon in reality and not by definition, or that an increased attempt to save, or a higher rate of interest, must mean a fall in realized saving, or that capital glut is inevitable as the economy expands — is only possible because of a massive collapse of respect for fact, scholarly accuracy, and scientific conscience in a large part of the economics profession.

William A. Salant: Professor Fellner has expressed the view that what he calls cyclical Keynesism has won wide acceptance, but he adds that this variety of Keynesianism is the work not only of Keynes himself but also of such predecessors as Wicksell and Robertson. I should like to define what I conceive to be the character of Keynes's contribution. This will require a brief discussion of the relation between the so-called "classical" system, the work of the forerunners referred to by Fellner, and the Keynesian system.

It was in the spirit of classical and neoclassical analysis that a smoothly working economic system would tend toward equilibrium at full employment. (In this context "smoothly working" can be taken to mean dynamically stable and free of rigidities.) This implied that a reduction in any component of effective demand would set in motion a set of responses that would restore aggregate demand (in real, though not necessarily in money, terms) to a full employment level. The system might be compared to an automatic pilot which maintains a stable course by compensating for external disturbances. The automatic mechanism by which full employment was maintained or restored was not very clearly spelled out by classical and neoclassical writers; indeed, we have learned a good deal about how the classical system was supposed to work in the discussion stimulated by the *General Theory*. It is clear, however, that the interest rate was the key stabilizing force, assisted by variations in the level of costs and prices, operating either through their effects on the interest rate or directly on the real value of monetary assets.

Students of the saving-investment process, beginning with Wicksell, focused attention on forces that could alter the level of aggregate demand.

These forces could be classified into those affecting saving, investment, hoarding, and the quantity of money. These writers devoted a good deal of attention to the problem of action by the monetary authority designed to counteract the disturbing forces. They accepted a stable price level (or, in some cases, stable per capita money incomes) as a desirable objective of policy, either as a means to stabilization of output or as an end in itself. In this connection, they did not always distinguish between the impact of disturbing forces on prices and on output, but their emphasis was generally on the price level. Perhaps it is fair to say that they assumed that falling prices would have a depressing effect on output and rising prices a stimulating effect, while output would be in equilibrium at full employment when prices (or money incomes) were stabilized. It should be added that a good part of the explanation for the emphasis on prices undoubtedly lies in the fact that fluctuations in prices were both more violent and more clearly revealed by the available statistics than fluctuations in output and employment.

These writers dealt with disturbances in the equilibrium of the classical system. Some of them advocated intervention by the monetary authority in order to offset these disturbances rather than reliance on the automatic self-correcting forces inherent in the system. They did not, however, provide an alternative theory of the determination of the level of output. The Keynesian system did provide such a theory.

In order to bring out sharply the features of the Keynesian analysis which I regard as distinctive, I shall add to Fellner's three types of Keynesianism a fourth, which might be called "contingent" or "conditional" Keynesianism. This subspecies takes as its point of departure the assumption that the classical stabilizers are inoperative, that the automatic pilot is switched off. Under what conditions they will in fact become inoperative, how the classical system has to be modified in order to attain this result, is a problem of the type that Fellner calls fundamental-theoretical; contingent Keynesianism simply "evades" it, to borrow another word from Fellner, and I shall not attempt to deal with it.

Using as its point of departure the assumption that neither interest rate nor price and cost variations stabilize aggregate demand, contingent Keynesianism tells us that, given the level of investment and the consumption function, real income will be in equilibrium at that point at which saving and investment are equated. The classical stabilizers having been rendered inoperative, real income must perform the entire job of equating saving and investment. This is, of course, a stripped-down economy-model of Keynesianism. It is clearly related to Fellner's cyclical Keynesianism. Whether it is part of a continuous line of development or a mutation comparable to that which took place on the historic day when a soccer player first picked up the ball and ran with it, thus inventing rugby, I shall not attempt to judge.

A notable feature of the Keynesian system is that it lends itself to development in many directions, and such development has flourished in the two decades since the publication of the *General Theory*. The system can be enlarged by the insertion of elements omitted from its early versions, such as foreign trade and government, and by the disaggregation of aggregate variables. The simple hypotheses, such as the original consumption function, can be replaced by more complex and, it is hoped, more realistic ones such as the Brady-Duesenberry-Modigliani relative income hypothesis. The essentially static Keynesian system can be made dynamic by the insertion of lags, the introduction of rates of change as variables, or by allowance for changes in the capital stock resulting from investment, as in the Samuelson multiplier-accelerator model, the Metzler inventory model, and the Harrod-Domar growth models.

As regards the stagnationist form of Keynesianism, Fellner concludes that it has not made a significant theoretical contribution. But it would appear that stagnationism, as distinct from other forms of Keynesianism, is not primarily a matter of theory at all, but rather a set of quantitative judgments as to the future position of the investment and consumption functions. It is true enough that stagnationist forebodings have not been borne out (an unrepentant stagnationist might want to add the word "yet") in that the forties and fifties have been periods of inflation rather than stagnation. Quite apart from the influence of the war and the cold war, however, it should be recalled that the stagnationist case rested heavily on the projection of a declining rate of population growth — a projection that has proved far off the mark. To this extent, the actual course of events has discredited one of the noneconomic assumptions of stagnationism rather than its economic forecasts, which, whatever their merits, remain largely untested.

Tibor Scitovsky: Being the last speaker at a session that ends a long and tiring day, I am in no state to embark on a scholarly analysis; and you, probably, are no longer in a state to listen to such. Besides, I have not much quarrel with the theses presented in the two papers. So I shall just elaborate on a remark of Professor Dillard's and make the very simple point that Keynes has very much simplified economic theory, rendered it more realistic, and has thereby given the further development of economics a tremendous push.

Professor Fellner is right, of course, in saying that most of the ingredients of Keynes's theory, and most of the policy conclusions as well, were known to many people before Keynes. As Professor Whitehead has put it: "Everything of importance has already been said before, by someone who did not discover it." Keynes co-ordinated already known bits of economic theorizing, supplied some missing links, and created a coherent theory of employment out of it. To call this, as Professor Fellner calls it, giving a particularly effective formulation to known doctrines, is in my opinion an understatement.

One of Keynes's main contributions — and the one crucial for employment theory — was the notion of underemployment equilibrium. Maybe this has led to no insights that were new to Wicksell or Sir Dennis Robertson; but it has accomplished something much more important. It has rendered speculation about the level of prosperity and what determines the level of prosperity very much simpler than it has ever been; and it has established a common language and common ground between the economist and the public.

Let us bear in mind that before the *General Theory* unemployment was regarded as the result of friction, temporary disequilibrium, or the monopoly power of labor unions. This meant that the business cycle had to be explained within a theoretical framework that made no allowance for the possibility of variations in employment and income. It also meant that business cycle policy had to be formulated without the benefit of a conceptually satisfactory measure of prosperity, such as the level of income or output or employment. This may sound absurd to us today; but it was Keynes's *General Theory* that made us realize its absurdity.

Many business cycle theorists did admit, of course, the possibility of unemployment. Pigou even used the percentage employed as an index of prosperity; but this was a concession to common sense rather than an integral part of the theory. The price level, the degree of roundaboutness, the proportion of investment in total output — these were the theoretically important variables in terms of which the business cycle was measured and explained. Hence, to be a competent business cycle theorist by the standards of the time, one had to master the nebulous concepts and teutonic complexity of capital theory. No wonder if most people shied away and only the very best, such as Wicksell or Sir Dennis, managed to evolve business cycle theories and policies that have stood the test of time. The great majority of economists settled down to a kind of schizophrenia. They believed in and taught a logically elegant price theory; and at the same time they adhered to a monetary and business cycle theory that was sometimes good, sometimes bad, but almost always incompatible with their price theory.

Keynes's concept of underemployment equilibrium has changed all this. It has harmonized, or at least rendered compatible, price theory and employment theory; and it has made employment theory simple. Let us bear in mind that this is the part of economics that is the most relevant to human welfare and human suffering, and it is thanks to Keynes that this humanly most important part of economics has become simple enough to be taught in introductory courses to elementary students. I think it is very important to be able to show the relevance of economic theory to human and social problems at an early stage. After all, young people become economists, not — or at least I hope not — with a view to raising their potential earning power, but out of an idealistic concern with human and social problems. In the days, however, when I was a student, a young man would spend years in studying indifference maps, budget lines, elasticities of substitution, marginal this and marginal that; and only when these studies have ground away all his compassion for human and social problems, only then would he be considered ready for the higher mysteries of capital theory and business cycle study.

In the meantime, of course, we have learnt that employment and business cycle theory are not nearly as simple as Keynes and the early Keynesians believed. But we still have an employment theory; and we can still start out from a simple, universally intelligible, and almost universally accepted first approximation; and proceed from there to explore the higher complexities of the consumption function or investment function or of dynamic growth models. Thanks to Keynes, economic theory today is of a piece; and the economist need no longer live with an inner conflict between his theory and his common sense.

With the same stroke with which Keynes resolved the conflict within the economist's breast, he has also eliminated the conflict between the economist and the public. The notion of underemployment equilibrium, the use of national income, or gross national product, or employment as the basic variable, have given the economist a language and a conceptual framework that the public understands and appreciates. This is not to say, of course, that today the public fully understands the economist. After all, the *New Yorker*, a short while ago, thought it funny that the Harvard Club of New Jersey should have introduced Professor Seymour Harris at a banquet as "an economist well qualified to tell you why there will be no depression and what to do when it comes." Obviously, we economists see nothing funny or incompatible in this at all.

Nevertheless, I do think that there is today closer contact and greater interaction between economists on the one hand and practical politicians and the public on the other. I realize that the economist's greater influence on practical affairs is, in the opinion of some, a mixed blessing; but you will surely all agree that the economist's greater awareness of his public responsibilities — his recognition of economics as a social science and not merely a logical exercise — is a good thing. And I cannot help feeling that Keynes had a large part of the responsibility for this aspect of the economist's attitude today.

101

Malthus and Keynes:
A Reconsideration*

B.A. Corry

I

In the past few years the view has solidified that Malthus was one of the most important precursors of the Keynesian way of thinking. This view was given its main impetus by Keynes himself, first in the memoir on Malthus[1] and later in the *General Theory*.[2] It bears testimony to the revolutionay nature of Keynes' contribution that prior to his work very little attention was paid to this element in Malthus' thought. This is true not only of general histories of economic thought,[3] but also of the specialised works devoted solely to Malthus. Bonar,[4] for example, devoted only a few pages to Malthus' treatment of the possibility of overproduction, whilst Palgrave gave only a paragraph to this topic.[5]

There are, of course, one or two exceptions to this early appraisal of Malthus' work; John Lalor is perhaps the most interesting of these, and as early as 1851 he was prepared to rate Malthus' theorising in this field higher than his contribution to population economics.[6] But in general a glance at the standard histories before the "Keynesian Revolution" will confirm that this aspect of Malthus was largely ignored.

It is often said that the question of overproduction was, after all, only a minor part of Malthus' total contribution and hence did not warrant much consideration, but there is very little evidence for this view. It is one of the predominant themes in the Ricardo-Malthus correspondence and occupies nearly a third of Malthus' Principles.

Keynes changed all this. Malthus' fear of over-saving now receives an honourable mention in the "new" histories, and some writers claim to have found many of the "building blocks" of the *General Theory* in Malthus. In particular, the writings of Hansen, Lambert and O'Leary may be mentioned.[7]

In my view this attempt to set up Malthus as a forerunner of Keynes is of doubtful validity. My criticism is not merely that the functional relationships making up the theoretical framework of the *General Theory* are not to be found in Malthus. It is more fundamental than this. I also object to the view, stated so strongly by Keynes, that "the almost total obliteration of Malthus' line of

*Source: *Economic Journal,* Vol. 69, December 1959, pp. 717-24.

approach and the complete domination of Ricardo's for a period of a hundred years has been a disaster to the progress of economics."[8]

In what follows I shall investigate rather more closely than has so far been the case the exact nature of Malthus' dispute with the orthodox school, and seek to show, first, that Malthus was not in fact an analytic forerunner of Keynes, and second, that victory for Malthus in his dispute with Ricardo over the effects of capital accumulation would probably not have hastened the development of Keynesian economics.[9]

II

Various parts of the Keynesian system have in their time been highlighted as the "essence" of the contribution. For example, the consumption function has been described by some writers as the key to Keynes' break with the Classics,[10] but clearly this is not so. With a mechanism to ensure the equality of planned saving and investment, the fact that a percentage of national income is not consumed does not necessarily present any problems of aggregate demand. On the other hand, there does seem to be general agreement about the fact that one of the important differences between Keynes and the Classics concerns the assumptions made about the savings-investment mechanism. Professor Paul Samuelson has put this point of view clearly in the following terms:

> "I myself believe the broad significance of the *General Theory* to be in fact that it provides a relatively realistic, complete system for analyzing the level of effective demand and its fluctuations. More narrowly, I conceive the heart of its contribution to be that subset of its equations which relate to the propensity to consume and to saving in relation to offsets-to-saving. In addition to linking saving explicitly to income, there is an equally important denial of the implicit 'classical' axiom that motivated investment is *indefinitely expansible or contractable,* so that whatever people *try* to save will always be fully invested. It is not important whether we deny this by reason of expectations, interest rate rigidity, investment inelasticity with respect to over-all price changes and the interest rate, capital or investment satiation, secular factors of a technological and political nature, or what have you. But it is vital for business-cycle analysis that we do assume definite amounts of investment which are highly variable over time in response to a myriad of exogenous and endogenous factors, *and which are not automatically equilibriated to full employment saving levels by any internal efficacious economic process.*"[11]

Now an essential feature of Classical macro-economics was the equality of saving and investment; the Classics were prepared to admit the possibility of a breakdown in the economic system if uncompensated hoarding were to be attempted, but generally speaking, its occurrence on any significant scale was thought to involve an assumption of irrational behaviour.[12] At the root of Classical (and Neo-Classical) economics was the "saving is spending" theorem, and this clearly has to be sharply contrasted with the Keynesian approach. As Keynes himself pointed out:

"Contemporary thought is still deeply steeped in the notion that if people do not spend their money in one way they will spend it in another. Post-war economists seldom, indeed, succeed in maintaining this standpoint *consistently*; for their thought today is too much permeated with the contrary tendency and with facts of experience too obviously inconsistent with their former view. But they have not drawn sufficiently far-reaching consequences; and have not revised their fundamental theory."[13]

It is against this background that we must look at Malthus' contribution.

III

The first point to make clear is that throughout his analysis Malthus assumed that an act of saving was always translated into an act of investment, that is to say, he assumed the equality of *ex ante* saving and *ex ante* investment. Thus in this respect Malthus was at one with the orthodox Classical school; as Professor Robbins has remarked, "unfortunately Malthus has insisted that savings were always invested; he spurned the suggestion that they were often hoarded."[14]

Take the following quotation from Malthus:

"A third very serious error of [Say, James Mill and Ricardo] and practically the most important of the three, consists in supposing that accumulation ensures demand; or that the consumption of the labourers employed by those whose object is to save, will create such an effectual demand for commodities as to encourage a continued increase of produce.

"Mr. Ricardo observes, that 'If £10,000 were given to a man having £100,000 per annum, he would not lock it up in a chest, but would either increase his expenses by £10,000, employ it himself productively, or lend it to some other person for that purpose; in either case demand would be increased, although it would be for different objects. If he increased his expenses, his effectual demand might probably be for buildings, furniture, or some such enjoyment. If he employed his £10,000 productively, his effectual demand would be for food, clothing, and raw materials, which might set new labourers to work. But still it would be *demand*.'

"Upon this principle it is supposed that if the richer portion of society were to forego their accustomed conveniences and luxuries with a view to accumulation, the only effect would be a direction of nearly the whole capital of the country to the production of necessaries, which would lead to a great increase of cultivation and population. But this is precisely the case in which Mr. Ricardo distinctly allows that there might be a universal glut; for there would undoubtedly be more necessaries produced than would be sufficient for the existing demand."[15]

It is clear from this pasage that Malthus assumed that savings "became" investment, and to reiterate within such a model it is not possible to deduce that lack of effective demand is caused by oversaving.[16] What problem, then, was it that really troubled Malthus? His starting-point was the (obvious) fact that unemployment was a normal feature of capitalist economies. "The actual wealth of all states with which we are acquainted is very far short of their powers of production."[17] Somehow or other this situation was due to "overproduction" caused by a deficiency of effective demand.

At this point it is important to distinguish two possible interpretations of the concept of overproduction. First, "general" overproduction caused by an excess of planned saving over planned investment — which was ruled out by assumption both in Malthus and orthodox Classical reasoning. Secondly, the idea that the translation of "revenue into capital" led to a falling rate of profit and if continued would kill the motive for further accumulation. It is in this second sense that Malthus' fears must be interpreted; assuming profits to be determined by a simple relationship between investment and consumption, then a switch from consumption to investment would (inevitably) produce a lower monetary return than had been expected: if profits had only been "normal" to begin with, the transfer would result in a stagnation in economic activity. The way out of such a situation, Malthus argued, was to stimulate "unproductive" consumption. To summarise this view in Malthus' own words: "it appears to be quite . . . certain that an inordinate passion for accumulation must inevitably lead to a supply of commodities beyond what the structure and habits of . . . society will permit to be profitably consumed."[18]

Using this second definition of overproduction, it is easy to show that Malthus and Ricardo were in basic agreement concerning its logical possibility, a point which comes out clearly in their correspondence. The typical case Malthus considered was the switch to a higher rate of capital accumulation financed by means of a decrease in luxury spending; continued for a sufficient length there would be a point where nobody wanted the extra output, the rate of profit would be below the minimum necessary for net capital accumulation.

In a sense Ricardo was in complete agreement with all of this, provided that this hypothetical case of Malthus' really did occur. "I affirm with you," he wrote to Malthus, "that 'if the farmer has no adequate market for his produce, he will soon cease to distribute more necessaries to his labourers,' with a view to the production of more necessaries."[19]

And when Malthus wrote to say:

"I also fancy that I am fortified with new arguments to prove demonstratively that a neat revenue is *absolutely impossible* under the determination to employ the whole produce in the production of necessaries, and consequently that if there is not an adequate taste for luxuries and conveniences, or unproductive labour, there must necessarily be a general glut."[20]

Ricardo replied: ". . . with a very slight alteration I should entirely concur in your proposition."[21]

Moreover, Ricardo agreed that if Malthus' diagnosis were correct, interventionist measures to maintain total output were required.[22]

So far I have argued that in so far as the dispute between Malthus and Ricardo was about the possibility of a rate of profit insufficient to promote capital accumulation, the two writers were in basic agreement, but a great deal of the heat generated in the controversy was due to the fact that they did not realise this. Malthus fought for a confession that conditions could be thought up which would produce a general glut; Ricardo, equally fervently, regarded such conditions as unrealistic. As usual, a great deal of the misunderstanding was due to imprecise language and terminology, and in addition one cannot help feeling that neither side had a particular desire to end the controversy — it was, after all, one way of keeping the friendship going.

Each accused the other of wilful refusal to understand; Ricardo complained to James Mill:

"I think he [Malthus] has not understood himself, for what are all his attacks on Say and me, surely not because we have said in all cases there would be motives sufficient to push production to its utmost extent . . ."[23]

Whilst Malthus's apparent frustration appears in a letter to Ricardo:

"I am either unfortunate in my explanations, or your mind is so entirely prepossessed with your own views on the subject of our discussion, that you will not give to any statement, which departs from them the degree of attention which is necessary to put you in possession of what is meant."[24]

What has been said so far may be summarised in the following manner: Malthus' main concern was with the effects of a declining rate of profit caused by "excessive" capital accumulation. Unfortunately within the framework of orthodox Classical theory a falling rate of profit was not necessarily a disequilibriating force. The rate of interest (a real phenomenon determined mainly by the rate of profit) equated saving and investment, hence a change in it merely altered the allocation of total spending between consumption and investment. As Keynes himself pointed out, Malthus had no alternative theory of interest to offer, so that ultimately his idea of excessive capital accumulation rested on the assumption that investment was independent of its rate of return.

IV

In this section some of the policy implications of Malthus' analysis will be examined, to elaborate the point that he had much less in common with Keynes than is usually supposed.

First of all, what did Malthus have to say about the effect of wage cuts on the volume of employment? It will be recalled that within the framework of the *General Theory* direct effects are zero — although there is some possibility of secondary effects via the rate of interest. Malthus, on the other hand, thought that full employment would eventually be achieved through wage reductions. In writing of the post-1815 situation he mentions the consequences of a "sudden abundance of corn," it reduced prices,

> "the consequence of which was that, in the midst of plenty, thousands were thrown out of employment — a most painful but almost unavoidable peliminary to a fall in the money wages of labour, *which it is obvious* could alone enable the general income of the country to employ the same number of labourers as before, and, after a period of severe check to the increase of wealth, to recommence a progressive movement."[25]

This is straightforward Classical reasoning with the idea of a "wages fund" lurking in the background.

Let us now take a look at the "Malthusian policy for full employment," for it is here that the apparent Keynesian nature emerges most strikingly; probably it is the use of the term "effectual demand" that has misled people. Malthus argued (in clear contrast to Keynes) that, starting from a low level of economic activity, the only way to increase effective demand was to raise consumption or "unproductive expenditures." As he put it: "the greatest stimulus to the continued production of commodities, taken altogether, is an increase in the exchangeable value of the whole mass, before a greater value of capital has been employed upon them."[26]

Or in more explicit terms: "a country with great powers of production should possess a body of consumers who are not themselves engaged in production."[27]

All this followed from Malthus' concern with the effects of a falling rate of profit, and the possibility of an equilibrium situation[28] where further investment was unprofitable.

> "It is undoubtedly possible by parsimony [Malthus wrote] to devote at once a much larger share than usual of the produce of any country to the maintenance of productive labour; and suppose this to be done, it is quite true that the labourers so employed are consumers as well as those engaged

in personal services, and that as far as the labourers are concerned, there would be no diminution of consumption or demand. But . . . the consumption and demand occasioned by the workmen employed in productive labour can never *alone* furnish a motive to the accumulation and employment of capital."

The only expenditure that investment created was the wages of the labour directly involved, hence —

"it is impossible that the increased quantity of commodities, obtained by the increased number of productive labourers, should find purchasers, without such a fall of price as would probably sink their value below that of the outlay, or, at least, so reduce profits as very greatly to diminish both the power and the will to save."[29]

There seem to be some peculiar assumptions involved here: there are no multiplier effects and investment is replaced in total every period.

There is, finally, the question of the social control of the saving-investment process. Perhaps the most important implication of Keynes' work was the notion that in an unregulated capitalist economy, full employment was fortuitous; hence given maximum production as an end, government control of aggregate saving and investment was necessary. But Malthus did not think along these lines; for him *laissez-faire* was the guiding rule. At the end of the *Principles* he sums up the position thus:

"Saving, as I have before said, is, in numerous instances, a most sacred private duty. How far a just sense of this duty, together with the desire of bettering our condition so strongly implanted in the human breast, may sometimes, and in some states of society, occasion a greater tendency to parsimony that is consistent with the most effective encouragement to the growth of public wealth, it is difficult to say; but whether this tendency, if let alone, be ever too great or not, no one could think of interfering with it, even in its caprices. There is no reason, however, for giving an additional sanction to it, by calling it a public duty. The market for national capital will be supplied, like other markets, without the aid of patriotism. And in leaving the whole question of saving to the uninfluenced operation of individual interest and individual feelings, we shall best conform to that great principle of political economy laid down by Adam Smith, which teaches us a general maxim, liable to very few exceptions, that the wealth of nations is best secured by allowing every person, as long as he adheres to the rules of justice, to pursue his own interest in his own way."[30]

V

The conclusion must surely be that victory for Malthus would not necessarily have led to the happy results that Keynes supposed. There appears to be little in the Malthusian analysis which bears affinity to the model of the *General Theory*. Needless to say, this does not imply that victory for the Ricardian approach was a "good thing." The fundamental weakness of Classical economics was its failure to work out a coherent analysis of the determination of income and employment in the short run. And whilst it is true that Ricardo, at least, emphasised that his analysis was meant as a contribution towards the theory of long-period equilibrium, one cannot escape the conclusion that by and large the orthodox Classical group were prepared to let this long-run analysis serve without modification as a description of the economic system at all points of time.

Malthus was undoubtedly a better observer of the economic scene than his opponents — he was aware that full employment was not the norm — but it cannot be said that his analysis provides an explanation of this phenomenon. Probably critics have been misled by Malthus' policy proposals, for to a certain extent they are not dissimilar to what a "Keynesian" would recommend. But a vague feeling that something is wrong does not justify the overthrow of a particular analytic framework. When a particular theory has been falsified it must be replaced with another theory, but Malthus did not do this, he did not break through the inner logic of Classical macro-economics.[31]

Notes

I should like to acknowledge the advice of Professor Lionel Robbins, Mr. Piero Sraffa, Mr. Kurt Klappholz and Mr. G.C. Archibald in the preparation of this paper.

1.   "Robert Malthus: the First of the Cambridge Economists," *Essays in Biography* (1933).

2.   *The General Theory of Employment, Interest and Money,* Chapter 26.

3.   *E.g.,* L.H. Haney, *History of Economic Thought* (1917), p. 204, "As to overproduction, Malthus differed with the majority of his contemporaries in believing it possible as a general condition, his moral being that there are limits to parsimony or saving. He was clearly in error."

4.   James Bonar, *Malthus and his Work* (1924).

5.   *Palgrave's Dictionary of Political Economy* (Ed. by H. Higgs, 1925), Vol. 11, article on Malthus.

6.   John Lalor, *Money and Morals* (Preface). Mention should also be made of J.M. Robertson's *The Fallacy of Saving* (1892).

7.   A.H. Hansen, *Business Cycles and National Income*; Paul Lambert, "Keynes and Malthus," *Weltwirtschaftliches Archiv*, 1955; Preface to J. Stassart, *Malthus et la Population*; J.J. O'Leary, "Malthus and Keynes," *Journal of Political Economy*, 1952; "Malthus's General Theory of Employment and the Post-Napoleonic Depressions," *Journal of Economic History*, 1943. Professor Lambert seems to have taken up the most extreme position on this point. He argues that "le parenté entre les deux auteurs est plus intime encore que Keynes en l'a cru." The reasons he gives for this view appear to ignore the question of the *ex ante* equality — or otherwise — of savings and investment. Cf. the Preface to Stassart, *op. cit.,* p. 14. Professor Robbins allowed me to see some correspondence he had had on this subject with Professor Lambert which was helpful in clarifying this issue.

8. J.M. Keynes, *Essays in Biography,* pp. 140-1.

9. There are, of course, certain contemporary economists who have never accepted this new verdict on Malthus; R.F. Harrod, for example, has written, "I cannot believe that Malthus, splendid as he was as a population theorist, contributed much of value to economics, in which he was always muddled." *The Life of John Maynard Keynes,* p. 460.

10. "It has been my conviction for years that the great contribution of Keynes' *General Theory* was the clear and specific formulation of the consumption function." A.H. Hansen in *The New Economics* (ed. S.E. Harris), p. 135.

11. Paul A. Samuelson, "The General Theory (3)" in the *New Economics* (ed. S.E. Harris), pp. 150-1.

12. This statement requires qualification: there are instances in the classical literature of discussions of the effects of sudden changes in the demand for money. Perhaps the *locus classicus* here is J.S. Mill's, "Of the Influence of Consumption upon Production."

13. J.M. Keynes, *The General Theory of Employment, Interest and Money,* p. 20.

14. L.C. Robbins, *Robert Torrens and the Evolution of Classical Economics*, p. 248. See also Schumpeter, *History of Economic Analysis,* p. 641 n.

15. *Principles of Political Economy,* 2nd ed., pp. 322-3.

16. For our purposes it is immaterial whether we assume that savers are entrepreneurs, or that there is a flexible rate of interest. Classical macro-economics contains both assumptions.

17. Malthus, *op. cit.,* p. 329.

18. Malthus, *op. cit.,* p. 325.

19. *Works of David Ricardo* (ed. P. Sraffa), Vol. VIII, p. 278. Letter dated October 9, 1820.

20. *Ibid.,* Vol. VIII, p. 285. Letter dated October 26, 1820.

21. *Ibid.,* Vol. VIII, p. 300. Letter dated November 24, 1820.

22. For more on Malthus' attitude towards public works see the present author's "The Theory of the Economic Effects of Public Expenditure in English Classical Economics," *Economica*, 1958.

23. *Economica,* 1958, Vol. IX, p. 13. Letter dated July 9, 1821.

24. *Ibid.,* Vol. IX, p. 90. Letter dated October 9, 1821.

25. Malthus, *op. cit.,* p. 393, my italics.

26. Malthus, *op. cit.,* p. 361.

27. *Ibid.,* p. 398.

28. A situation where only normal profits were being earned.

29. *Ibid.,* pp. 314-15.

30. Malthus, *op. cit.,* p. 434.

31. It may be added here that in the present writer's opinion this breakthrough was Keynes' greatest achievement.

102

Keynes and the Classics:
A Dynamical Perspective*

R. Clower

Although it is possible to draw various purely technical distinctions between modern and pre-Keynesian economics, it is mainly with respect to matters of intellectual orientation that the two are strikingly different. Many and diverse reasons have been advanced to explain why this should be so, most of them plausible, all of them fairly elaborate. The purpose of this note is to add an element of unity and simplicity to these explanations by suggesting a straightforward dynamical interpretation of the foundations of Keynesian and classical thought.

I

The entire discussion is developed in terms of the market for labor in a pure consumption economy of the sort described by Keynes in his preliminary skirmish with classical theory in Chapter 2 of the *General Theory*.[1] Omitting background details for the sake of brevity, let us begin with the relevant labor supply and demand functions, represented in the accompanying diagram by the curves S_L and D_L, respectively. Any point in the diagram corresponds to a pair of values of employment, N, and the real wage rate, w/p. From the standpoint of *some* dynamical system, moreover, every point in the diagram may be presumed to represent a potentially attainable "state" of the labor market or, alternatively, a potentially observable *employment situation*. On casual empirical grounds, however, it is plausible to restrict attention to situations described by a more narrowly circumscribed set of points, obtained as follows.

First, notice that any point on the demand curve for labor defines an employment situation which, if attained, is optimal for firms; i.e., any such state satisfies the (maximum profit) condition of equality between the marginal physical product of labor and the real wage rate.[2] Similarly, any point on the

*Source: *Quarterly Journal of Economics*, Vol. 74, May 1960, pp. 318-23.

supply curve represents an employment situation which, if attained, is optimal for households; i.e., any such point satisfies the (utility maximization) condition of equality between the marginal utility of the real wage and the marginal disutility of labor.[3] On the other hand, points in the diagram to the *right* either of the demand curve or of the supply curve (the shaded area in the diagram) represent employment situations that are nonoptimal for firms, nonoptimal for households, or nonoptimal for both. Assuming that a "short demand" always dominates a "long supply" and that a "short supply" always dominates a "long demand," situations defined by such points cannot occur in a system of voluntary trading and may be ignored accordingly.[4]

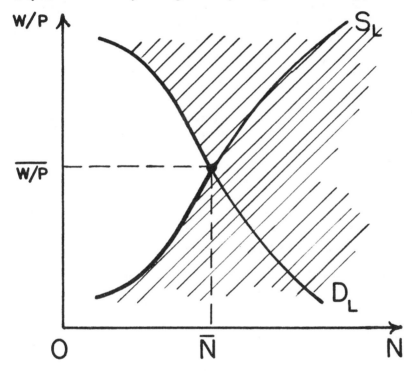

Points to the *left* both of the demand and of the supply curves (the unshaded area of the diagram) represent employment situations that are acceptable (though not optimal) for both firms and households; i.e., situations in which the real wage is less than the marginal product of labor and in which, simultaneously, the marginal utility of the real wage is greater than the marginal disutility of work. Situations of this kind are plausibly considered to be dynamically attainable, hence potentially observable; but they cannot be maintained more than momentarily because households and firms share a *mutual* desire to increase employment and output under these circumstances. In short, such states represent situations of "frictional" underemployment (and underproduction) which, on grounds of transiency, may be ignored.[5]

We are left with states represented by points: (i) on the supply curve and to the left of the demand curve; (ii) on the demand curve and to the left of the supply curve; (iii) on the supply curve *and* on the demand curve.

Taking these in reverse order, any situation defined by the intersection of the demand and supply curves (the point (N, w/p) in the diagram, for example) corresponds to a classical (and Keynesian) state of full employment. On the basis of elementary empirical considerations, it is clearly plausible to suppose that states of this sort, if attained, tend to be maintained indefinitely in the absence of exogenous "shocks." (By Walras' Law applied to a "labor and goods" economy, supply-demand equality in the labor market necessarily implies supply-demand equality in the goods market.)

On the other hand, any point which lies on the demand curve but above the supply curve (case (ii), above) refers to a state of *involuntary unemployment* in the sense of Keynes; i.e., at a lower level of the real wage rate, the demand for and supply of labor both exceed the level of employment associated with the given point.[6] Under the latter circumstances, the marginal utility of the real wage exceeds the marginal disutility of labor, whereas the marginal product of labor is equal to the real wage; hence *households alone* have an incentive to expand employment. By analogy with situations of a similar sort experienced in practice, it is natural to regard these as "depression" states of the model.

The interesting thing about "depression" states is that it is not directly plausible to say that they cannot persist indefinitely. No doubt it can be asserted, with good reason, that any particular "depression" state will tend to be transitory; the relevant question, however, is whether the transition is towards a state of "full employment" or whether one "depression" state tends to be followed by another "depression" state, and so on, *indefinitely*. This is clearly a dynamical stability question, and casual empirical considerations might be used to support either point of view. To say anything useful about such "conflict of interest" situations, therefore, everyday knowledge has to be supplemented by a fairly detailed specification of the dynamical assumptions underlying the market adjustment process.[7] Provided one is willing to admit the existence of multiperiod planning horizons, for example, it is easy to formulate a dynamical model of a pure consumption economy in which the presence of excess supply in the labor market is associated with a tendency for the real wage, and so excess supply, either to fall or to rise over time. In slightly more general models, moreover, one does not need to resort to expectational phenomena to get similar results.

So much for "depression" states. Proceeding finally to situations defined by points on the supply curve but below the demand curve (case (i), above), we have to do with what might be called states of *involuntary underproduction*. All such states describe situations of "full employment" in the Keynesian sense (i.e., no "involuntary unemployment");[8] since the real wage rate is less than the marginal product of labor in these cases, however, labor is in short supply from the standpoint of business firms. One might be inclined to argue that situations of this kind will soon be eliminated through a competitive "bidding up" of money wages by employers; but matters are not so simple. For we have to deal once more with a conflict of interest situation in which the reactions of employees to the actions of employers cannot be specified on the basis of casual empirical considerations. One possibility (and it is nothing more than this) is that competitive bidding for labor will entail continually rising money prices along with continually rising money wages. On this ground, and to emphasize the analogy with "depression" states of involuntary unemployment, it is natural to regard situations of involuntary underproduction as "inflation" states of our model.

II

The preceding discussion of alternative possible employment situations is basically neutral in its assignment of "probabilities of occurrence" to states of full employment, states of involuntary unemployment, and states of involuntary underproduction. In effect, it is based on the assumption that probable employment states are distributed more or less symmetrically about a mean position of full employment equilibrium.

By contrast, classical doctrine rests on the assumption that the entire probability distribution is concentrated at a single point. This might be weakened slightly; e.g., it is consistent with the general tenor of classical thought to admit that other than full employment positions are possible, but to assert that the equilibrium state of full employment is stable and so heavily damped that the probability of observing a nonequilibrium employment situation is almost negligible. Nevertheless, it is hard to deny the essential correctness of the Keynesian view that ". . . the postulates of the classical theory are applicable to a special case only and not to the general case, the situation it assumes being a limiting point of the possible positions of equilibrium."[9]

The Keynesian assignment of "probabilities of occurrence" is motivated by the conviction that "depression" states are the rule rather than the exception, and the Keynesian distribution of probable employment states is correspondingly skewed to give major weight to situations of involuntary unemployment. In the light of recent history, this view has lost some of the plausibility that it had during the years of the Great Depression; but that is largely beside the point. The important thing is that the Keynesian perspective, unlike that of the classics, leads naturally to an analysis of the ". . . dynamical development [of output and employment] as distinct from the instantaneous picture . . ."[10] For the most part, therefore, Keynes dealt with *disequilibrium* states; with states which, if recognized at all by classical writers, were never systematically analyzed. He was encouraged accordingly to create new analytical tools (the "consumption function," the "marginal efficiency of capital schedule," the "liquidity preference function"), better suited — at least in his opinion — to deal with disequilibrium phenomena. To make the probability of occurrence of disequilibrium states seem vastly greater than that of full employment equilibrium states, moreover, Keynes emphasized volatile factors like expectations and concentrated attention on speculative aspects of asset-holding phenomena. To be sure, the analytical methods adopted were those of traditional comparative statics rather than those of modern dynamics; but the situations studied had an obvious dynamical "flavor," and that is what has counted in the long run.

On this interpretation, *the essential formal difference between Keynes and the classics is more one of subject matter than of underlying postulates.* Classical theory is mainly concerned with equilibrium states, but does not specifically deny the existence of other possibilities; Keynesian theory is mainly concerned with disequilibrium states, but allows for the (very slight) possibility of "full employment." To say only this, however, would be to overlook the ultimate source of the Keynesian Revolution. Although Keynes himself never made a complete transition from statical to dynamical modes of thought, his work prompted many of his near contemporaries to do precisely this,[11] and so wrought a fundamental change in intellectual perspective in the space of a few years. Nor was this aspect of his work lost to Keynes: "The ideas which [I have] expressed so laboriously are extremely simple and should be obvious. The difficulty lies, not in the new ideas, but in escaping from the old ones, which ramify, for those brought up as most of us have been, into every corner of our minds."[12]

Nothing could be simpler in principle than a shift from statical to dynamical habits of thought; neither, however, could anything be more difficult in practice. The fruits of the Keynesian Revolution have been, and are being, gathered primarily by a new generation of economists, a generation that has finally accustomed itself to thinking in terms of points and planes instead of curves and crosses.

Notes

1. J.M. Keynes, *General Theory of Employment, Interest, and Money* (New York, 1936).
2. *Ibid.,* p. 5, Postulate I.
3. *Ibid.,* p. 5, Postulate II.
4. *Ibid.,* p. 12.
5. *Ibid.,* p. 6.
6. *Ibid.,* p. 15.
7. *Ibid.,* pp. 15-19. The issue seems obvious now, but it was not so clear in 1936.
8. *Ibid.,* pp. 15-16.
9. *Ibid.,* p. 3.
10. *Ibid.,* Preface, p. vii.
11. It is only necessary to mention such names as Harrod, Domar, Hicks, Modigliani, Samuelson, Goodwin, Duesenberry and Patinkin in order to appreciate the significance of this comment.
12. *Op. cit.,* Preface, p. viii.

103

The Critics of Keynesian Economics*[1]

D.J.J. Botha

Die Majorität einigt sich und über die Widerstrebenden wird langsam aber sicher zur Tagesordnung übergegangen. E.v. Böhm-Bawerk, *Positive Theorie des Kapitales*.

It is now a quarter of a century since J.M. Keynes' *The General Theory of Employment, Interest and Money* was first published. Measured in terms of its influence on academic thought, both *pro* and *contra*, as also on public policy, this book has been compared with the *Wealth of Nations* and *Das Kapital*. Like Adam Smith and Karl Marx, Keynes reacted strongly to economic policy and economic conditions obtaining at the time: by discrediting the "invisible hand" approach of *laissez-faire* theorists inspired by Smith he proposed a virtual revolution in economic outlook — a revolution which, unlike Marx's, was primarily aimed at bolstering the basic economic structure of Western democratic society,[2] which at that time had already succumbed to the onslaught of totalitarianism in a number of countries on the Continent.

Since the publication of the *General Theory* Keynesian economics may be said to have gone through two phases, viz., the more narrow[3] *pro* and *anti*-Keynesian, followed by the so-called "post-Keynesian". The book under review may be said to be concerned mainly with the narrow anti-Keynesian approach. Although it is well-nigh impossible to draw definite lines of demarcation, it might be said that in the post-Keynesian phase those who previously had or might have been pro-Keynesian (e.g. the younger generation) began to extend Keynes' analysis in various directions, so as not only to improve on the purely theoretical aspects of the book[4], but also to allow for changes in the nature of the issues of the day. Keynes himself also did not neglect the latter, as is proved by his *How to Pay for the War*, containing as it does prescriptions for policy under circumstances opposite to those which constituted the background against which the *General Theory* had been written.

*Source: *South African Journal of Economics*, Vol. 31, June 1963, pp. 81-102.

The first phase has now passed into the realm of doctrinal history — the polemics between the narrow Keynesians and anti-Keynesians has died down, the front-line has shifted, and any new attempts to refute *conventional* Keynesianism at this late stage, as in the book under review, can justifiably be construed as a Charge of the Light Brigade — excellently performed (in places), without adding to our store of knowledge or settling old issues in a definitive way.

Mr. Hazlitt's book contains twenty-two essays of widely different standards on various aspects of Keynes' work reprinted from journals and books, most of which appeared before the 'fifties. These could be divided into three groups. First, there are two extracts from Say's *Traité d'Économie Politique* (1803) and Mill's *Some Unsettled Questions* (1844), which, according to the Editor, refute Keynes' ideas "in advance". The second group consists of an interesting collection of papers and reviews (of the *General Theory*) by Viner, Knight, Mantoux, Modigliani, Williams, Hutt, etc. The final group consists of a number of papers by lesser-known authors as also the Editor's *Introduction*, whose journalistic style of writing and apparent lack of objectivity are the main detracting elements in this work, and whose contributions could have been omitted without impairing the value of the book as a work of reference.

There is, therefore, nothing "new" in this book. The first two groups of articles, however, constitute an interesting source of reference not only from the point of view of *Dogmengeschichte* but also in regard to the early reactions to the *General Theory*, which provide a good cross-section of the views of some of the more narrow anti-Keynesians. To claim anything more than this, as the Editor does with great zest, is to put a wrong stamp on the book as a whole: it is *not* the "final refutation of Keynesianism". It merely contains reprints of a number of articles in which Keynes was attacked along well-known lines, and which formed the subject of debate some years ago. In the past, the few dissenters failed in their attempts to convert their fellow-economists. Apparently they would also fail to do so now. In practice developments have been rather such as those mentioned by Böhm-Bawerk when writing about conflicting views on the theory of capital (see motto above): leaving the dissenters behind, the majority joined forces and proceeded with constructive work — in this case positive, not negative criticism.

To appraise each of these essays in turn would not be a rewarding task. Nor would a discussion of *obiter dicta* which in the past had formed the subject of controversy. In the following we shall briefly discuss the works of Say and Mill reprinted here, followed by a review of two essays which contain perhaps the most succinct arguments in regard to some general aspects of the anti-Keynesian view, viz., those by Viner and Hutt.

Most anti-Keynesians (and perhaps others) are of the opinion that Keynes had been greatly influenced by Continental thinking. Wicksell and some German writers have often been mentioned in this connection[5]. Whether or not this is true is difficult to judge. Although Keynes once made the rather odd statement that he could understand German only when the subject dealt with something with which he was already familiar, and that new ideas were veiled from him by language difficulties, this was probably not intended to be taken seriously.[6] For his numerous quotations from German works on mathematics in the *Treatise on Probability*, on psychoanalysis in the *Treatise on Money*, etc., as also the fact that (as we are told) on occasion he briefly addressed a meeting on the Continent in German, bear testimony to the contrary. Perhaps Keynes himself came nearest the truth when he wrote: "There are many small indications, not lending themselves to quotation, by which one writer can feel whether another writer has at the back of his head the same root-ideas or different ones. On this test I feel that what I am trying to say is the same at root as what Wicksell was trying to say."[7] Be that as it may, we are primarily concerned here not with priorities but rather with the more important question of the use to which scattered (and fruitful) ideas have been put.

I. Say and Mill on Say's Law. The Say–Malthus Controversy

The first essay reprinted in the book is a translation of an extract from Say's *Traité d'Économie Politique*.[8] The editor is of the opinion that "few economists who have ventured to refute (Say's) law in recent years, in fact, reveal any acquaintance with it in its original form."[9] There appears, however, to be nothing new in this extract, all the major points having been discussed exhaustively in the literature. For example, the main objection to Say's law is left unanswered, viz., unlike Walras' law, which refers to both commodities and money, Say's law relates to commodities only and can, therefore, hold only in a barter economy.

This is better illustrated as follows. Let there be n goods in the economy, of which $(n\text{-}1)$ are commodities and the nth money. Let p_i be the price of an arbitrary good and D_i and S_i its demand and supply ($i = 1, 2, \ldots, n$). Walras' law now states:

$$\sum_1^n p_i D_i \equiv \sum_1^n p_i S_i \tag{1}$$

or, the money value of goods bought is identically equal to the money value of goods sold. Say's law is, however, more restrictive. Write p_j for the price of an arbitrary commodity (excluding money), and D_j and S_j for its demand and supply, respectively ($j = 1, 2, \ldots, n\text{-}1$). Then, according to Say, in a money economy:

$$\sum_1^{n-1} p_j D_j \equiv \sum_1^{n-1} p_j S_j \tag{2}$$

or, the money value of commodities bought is identically equal to the money value of commodities sold (excluding money). Here nothing is said in regard to the nth good (money), but it is implied that the identity (2) hold only when the demand for and supply of money are identically equal, i.e.

$$D_n \equiv S_n \qquad\qquad (3)$$

where $p_n = 1$.

But this is unrealistic. Once money is introduced, a *reine Nachfrage*,[10] a demand expressed in terms of money, not commodities, becomes possible, i.e. the identity (2) is violated. This can happen when money is withdrawn from circulation (hoarding) or is created. The "classical" theory contends that a supply of money presupposes a sale of goods in the past, so that (2) ultimately holds. But this cannot be accepted. Although a supply of money usually (but not always) presupposes a sale of goods in the past, this does not materially affect the argument, for there is no telling what period of time has elapsed between the earlier supply of goods and the present demand, during which anything can happen. Apparently Say was conscious of the importance of the length of this period of time, but he did not analyse its consequences (nor did Mill): "Money performs but a momentary function in this double exchange; and *when the transaction is finally closed*, it will always be found, that one kind of commodity has been exchanged for another."[11]

The problem is that we do not know *when* "the transaction is finally closed." For, as Marshall so succinctly said in the *Principles*, though men have the power to purchase, they may not choose to use it. Or, as Marx had written: "No one can sell unless someone else purchases. But no one is forthwith bound to purchase, because he has just sold."[12] We may, if we so wish, pursue this matter even further back in history. Already in 1820 Malthus in his *Principles of Political Economy* rejected Say's law as being "utterly unfounded"[13], although his refutation in the *Principles* was not as convincing as that of e.g. Marx. We shall return to Malthus below.

J.S. Mill, in an essay written in 1830 (published 1844), defends Say's law in terms almost identical to those used by Say himself.[14] Mill starts by criticising the "immense importance attached to consumption" (p. 24). This is wrong, for "what a country wants to make it richer is never consumption, but production."[15] Government, therefore, need not concern itself with consumption, for everything that can be produced will be consumed "until the wants of all who possess the means of producing are completely satisfied, and their production will not increase any farther" (p. 26). From this follows Mill's two directives for Governments: *first*, producers should be left free to employ the means of production in the best ways possible and, *second*, those who at present lack the means of producing "to the extent of their desire to consume", shall be afforded every opportunity to their "acquiring the means, that, becoming producers, they may be enabled to consume."

In this passive way, according to Mill, Government would indirectly encourage production. It ought not to do so directly. For "the utility of a large government expenditure, for the purpose of encouraging industry, is no longer maintained."[16] Government expenditure on such a scale would call for more taxes, which, he maintains, defeat their own purpose: "It is no longer supposed that you benefit the producer by taking his money, provided you give it to him again in exchange for his goods."[17]

The foregoing represents the first of two aspects of Mill's paper to which attention will be drawn here. It is a good example of the classical view that all Government interference in economic affairs is repugnant to private enterprise. The second aspect relates to the "doctrine of the impossibility of an excess of all commodities" (p. 41). This doctrine states that there can never be a deficiency in aggregate demand — those offering commodities for sale desire to purchase others in exchange for it, and are, therefore, "buyers by the mere fact of (their) being sellers."[18] Mill then rightly states that this would hold only in a barter economy. In a money economy, however, buying and selling *ultimately* is "nothing but barter" (p. 41). Thus Mill with great clarity anticipates Marx, Marshall and Neisser in this respect: "Although he who sells, really sells only to buy, he needs not buy at the same moment when he sells; and he does not therefore necessarily add to the *immediate* demand for one commodity when he adds to the supply of another."[19] Consequently, there may be periods characterised by a general excess of supply or of demand (depressions and booms) which are "of no uncommon occurrence" (p. 42).

But, we are told, this state can only be a temporary one and must be followed by a reaction of corresponding violence.[20] Mill then proceeds to analyse the meaning of an excess supply (demand). An excess supply refers to commodities only, i.e. the supply of commodities compared to that of money: "there cannot be an excess of all other commodities, and an excess of money at the same time."[21] But this is not borne out by his analysis, in which he shows that, owing to expectations in regard to e.g. future prices, individuals may prefer to hoard money (money is "collected in masses, and hoarded"), commodities become abundant and might fall in price. The result, which Mill does not mention, is that *both* commodities and money may then be in excess supply.

It is at this point that we are told that an excess supply of all commodities (a general, not a partial over-production) is *only short-lived*. It is, says Mill, of the "utmost importance" to observe this. However, two sentences further on he states that 'there *cannot* be excessive production of commodities in general."[22] In the rest of Mill's paper this apparent contradiction is not solved or explained, and he ends by summarizing his views as follows: (*a*) there cannot be a permanent excess of production, but (*b*) "there may be a temporary excess of any one article considered separately, so may there of commodities generally, *not in consequence of over-production, but of a want of commercial confidence.*"[23]

The latter half of (*b*) is interesting. Here a distinction is drawn implicitly between the supply and demand aspects to exchange which, again, anticipates the views of Marx, Marshall, Neisser, etc., in regard to the rupture between supply and demand in a money, as contrasted with a barter, economy.

Whether the distinction drawn in the above sentence is a fundamental one in that context is, however, open to doubt. For over-production is a relative concept, and we are here primarily concerned not with causation but with the possibility of the *existence*, or otherwise, of over-production.

Mill's analysis in this paper has been referred to as the "fullest and best considered statement of Say's law to be found in the works of the classical economists."[24] Mill has, of course, shown with admirable clarity that over-production *per se* is *possible* and "of no uncommon occurrence." But his emphasis on the temporary nature of it in practice — introduced rather as a *deus ex machina* — is not well-founded. However, let us assume this phenomenon to be a temporary one. The crucial question then is *for how long can it continue?* Over-production lasting six months might cause a few bankruptcies — if two, or three, years it might ruin the country.

In short, Mill's analysis is inconclusive. Say's law cannot be accepted. The mere possibility of over-production justifies the existence of a body of thought that aims at lifting the economy out of the doldrums caused by the existence of temporary over-production, that is when its "temporary" nature is such as to cause anxiety.

The two extracts from Say and Mill published by Hazlitt refer to only one side[25] of the question in regard to Say's law. The other one is much more interesting. It is this: *already in the nineteenth century Say's law gave rise to a controversy in which Say came off a poor second best.* We refer, of course, to the correspondence between Say and Malthus.[26] No reference is made to this in *Hazlitt*. In a book on anti-Keynesian economics this omission is a serious one indeed. Malthus, in many respects the intellectual forerunner of Keynes,[27] persuasively argued *inter alia*, that a widespread increase in saving would reduce income (*vide* Mill above on this point); and that a glut could be occasioned by an inordinate increase in output, which could lead to prices falling below costs, production being checked for the time being. To this Say retorted by *defining* (in his second letter to Malthus) a "product" as something having a market value in excess of its cost of production (if not, it is the "sterile result of ineffective effort"). This clearly was mere prevarication. For Malthus afterwards pointed out that "within the very last year" prices had dropped below costs in the cotton, woollen and silk industries, which rendered the arguments of Say and James Mill "to be utterly without foundation."[28]

Thus already in the nineteenth century Say's position had become quite indefensible. And yet Malthus' view did not prevail — partly because, as Keynes said, he had to appeal to facts of common observation, and failed to "furnish an alternative construction,"[29] and partly, perhaps more importantly, as Lambert has pointed out recently, because the implications of Malthus' views, viz., the salutary effects on economic activity of spending rather than saving, *were morally repugnant in the nineteenth century.*[30] To his orthodox readers his views appeared to revolt against the established order of things. The result in fact was, as Lambert has said, that Say admitted defeat (from

Malthus) *while raising the flag of victory.*[31]

II. Contemporary Anti-Keynesianism

The claim that Say and Mill, in the extracts reproduced in this book, have refuted Keynes "in advance" is, therefore, open to very serious doubt. In turning now to the contemporary scene, we are confronted by a vast literature of which the articles selected by Mr. Hazlitt represent a good cross-section, including both the meritorious and others. Among the former category special reference is made below to those by J. Viner and W.H. Hutt, containing as they do references not only to "pure" theory but also to policy implications. We would be better able, however, to view these in perspective if we prefaced our discussion by a brief outline of the rationale of classical theory as represented in the work of Professor Pigou.

1. Classical Theory: The Rôle of the Pigou-effect

Fundamentally, classical theory claims that a free-market economy automatically tends towards full employment. Basic to this theory is the assumption of flexible wages and prices. There are two versions to be distinguished: classical theory "proper" and classical theory in its modern garb, as amended by Pigou, Scitovszky and Haberler to meet the onslaught of the Keynesian views.[32]

In regard to the former, it is well-known that classical theorists (Smith, James Mill, J.S. Mill, etc.) lauded parsimony as the *sine qua non* of economic progress. This constitutes the basis of Adam Smith's thesis of non-intervention in economic affairs by Government: saving is equated with spending and, since each is performed by a different set of people, this points to a self-regulating mechanism within the economy.[33] An increase in investment was held to lead to a declining rate of profit which, in turn, regulated the saving-investment process, viz., if profits fell to too low a level the supply of savings would dwindle, the rate of interest would rise and the increase in investment would be arrested. The rate of interest was flexible, there was no interference from the side of the monetary authorities, and any changes in the propensities to save and invest would be reflected in a change in the rate of interest.[34] With wages flexible, the effect on employment of a cut in wages was assumed to depend on the labour-supply function. The supply of labour was an increasing function of the wage rate, and employment was assumed to be full, or tended to be so.[35] Thus employment, given the stock of capital, was a function of the wage rate. Involuntary unemployment was not ruled out, but its existence was regarded the result of a wage rate that was too high — yet given wage flexibility this could not last for long:[36] the excess supply of labour would force the wage rate down until full employment was re-established.

In regard to the "modern" version of classical theory, this has perhaps been best analysed by Professor Pigou in his *Employment and Equilibrium* (1941) and two well-known papers.[37] Briefly, his argument is as follows:

Assume an economy with zero net investment, a fixed working population and a constant stock of money. Market equilibrium is established throughout, and the Government does not interfere by either fixing prices or controlling investment in order to regulate employment. *Thorough-going* equilibrium will be established when there is equality between the marginal rate of return from capital and the representative man's rate of time preference. Next, assume that in a particular year net investment becomes positive. The economy will then move away from equilibrium temporarily but will ultimately return to it with a larger stock of capital, zero net investment and positive rate of interest.[38]

This is shown to be possible in either of two ways. First, assume *saving is a function of the yield from investment only*. Thus at a zero rate of interest saving will be nil. The initial rise in investment now signifies an excess of the rate of return i over the rate of time preference R, thus providing a stimulus for a further increase in investment. With the working population fixed, however, the rate of return may be assumed to become continually smaller — but it cannot drop to zero, since *before* it reaches zero it will have become equal to R (the representative man's rate of time preference being positive) and establish a "thorough-going" equilibrium.

But assume, secondly, that saving is a function of the yield *and* the amenity-value of unspent income (e.g. wealth desired for reasons of prestige, security, etc.). Now saving at a zero rate of interest becomes possible. For while previously a stationary equilibrium is attained at $R = i$, this is now the case when $R = (i + a)$ where a is the amenity-value of savings. Thus depending on the size of a, the rate of interest may fall to zero *before* the latter equality is satisfied. Apparently we are here presented with a dilemma: since i cannot be negative, it may be impossible for the equality $R = (i + a)$ to be satisfied and for the economy to reach a new stationary equilibrium with a larger stock of capital and higher real incomes.

The answer to this question is a two-fold one: the Keynesian and the Pigouvian. According to Keynes with $R < (i + a)$ and $i = 0$, people would still want to save. But there would be no inducement to invest, and the quantity of money in circulation, income velocity and nominal income would diminish. With *wages rigid* this would lead to unemployment of resources. Further, the R would not be unaffected: as incomes decrease, the rate of time preference of the representative man would increase to R' and, if incomes drop sufficiently, the above inequality changes to $R' = (i + a)$, with $i = 0$ and $R' > R$, that is, the new rate of time preference is equal to the amenity-value of savings. A new equilibrium is established with lower real incomes and a lower level of employment — assuming that the initial wage *rate* is maintained.

Pigou, however, is more optimistic. He rightly criticises Keynes' assumption of rigid wages despite the growing unemployment, and instead assumes a continual *fall in wage rates*, nominal income and prices. In this way the level of employment and real income would be maintained. However — and this is the Pigou-effect — a lower price level spells a higher real value of cash balances, and the higher the latter becomes, the lower would tend to be the amenity-value a of such balances, until eventually the equality $R = (i + a)$ is established with $i = 0$. Then a new equilibrium is reached at the zero rate of interest and a lower money income and prices, while real income and employment have been maintained.

This, in outline, is the rationale of the Pigou-effect.[39] It apparently constitutes a strong argument in favour of a downward flexibility of wage rates, which has been propagated by other modern clasical writers, e.g. those discussed below. The important difference, however, is that while these writers advocated *wage cuts as a matter of practical policy*, Pigou regards his model as an "academic exercise" only, for it is "extremely improbable that (the assumptions in the model) will ever be satisfied in practice."[40]

2. *Wage Reductions and the Sales Lag* (J. Viner)

Professor Viner, in his review article (1937) of the *General Theory* emphatically denounces Keynes' interpretation of the "classical" view on the effects of a cut in money-wages, and instead presents a concise and admirably clear summary of the received doctrine on this point.[41]

Classical theory, according to Viner, "looks to wage-reductions during a depression to restore profit-margins, thus to restore the investment-morale of entrepreneurs and to give them again a credit status which will enable them to finance any investment they may wish to make."[42] This, says Viner, assumes the existence of a lag between the lowering of wage rates and the consequent reduction in sales at previous prices. During this lag marginal costs are lower than prices (the implicit assumption here apparently being that of perfect competition), which would render increases in output profitable, assuming the demand would be forthcoming. Then inventory and replacement investment is assumed to increase wages sufficiently to provide the means with which the increased output can be bought — "and the gain in employment . . . is expected to release for expenditure the emergency reserves of the wage-earning class."[43] Assuming then that a large part of entrepreneurial expenditures can be postponed without affecting output (although possibly increasing costs of production), "the supporters of this doctrine maintain that recovery of a profit margin can lead for a time to an increase in entrepreneurs' expenditures many times the increase in their net income, or, alternatively, the reduction in their net loss. They do not contend that this is certain to occur, but . . . they say that it is a reasonable probability."[44]

Thus far Professor Viner. In brief, it is argued that a cut in wages might lead to a drop in sales, but only after a lag. This lag is all-important, for during this interval buying could be sustained by consumers' drawing on cash reserves, so that profits might rise, entrepreneurs become more confident, and output might expand. Increased output could lead to increased wages which, in turn, could be used in buying the extra output.

As stated here, this theory rests on very unsure foundations. It apparently does not take sufficiently into consideration the stark economic realities of a depression, which an uncomfortably large number of workmen have experienced to a far greater degree than some economists appear to be willing to allow for in their theories. The same holds for the paper discussed below.

There is no telling whether a reduction in wages will in fact lead to a decline in sales only after a lag. More must be known about the nature and extent of such reductions, their expected incidence and the state of the economy generally. A wage reduction in the very early stages of a depression might have a lagged effect on sales, when consumers might be willing to fall back on cash reserves in the hope of a speedy recovery, as mentioned by Viner. But it is uncertain whether this would in fact happen, for much depends on expectations. When the early stages of what eventually appears to be a severe depression are mistakenly regarded as merely a temporary and short-lived recession, consumers might react in the way outlined by Viner.[45] When, on the other hand, the signs of the times are correctly interpreted, a wage reduction would probably affect sales without any appreciable lag, which would tend to aggravate the situation and accelerate the onset of the depression proper.

In the depths of the depression the effects on which Viner's theory rests are most unlikely to materialise. For one thing, wages will then already be low so that any further reduction is bound to force consumers into buying the barest essentials only. For another, the cash reserves assumed to be brought into play following the wage reduction may confidently be expected to be non-existent (except for the higher income classes), so that any sustained buying and, consequently, recovery of profit-margins could be ruled out.

The foregoing are general observations in regard to a theory couched in equally general terms. Viner's theory rests heavily on an assumption about consumer behaviour which apparently is a function of rational calculation only (which has not been analysed), and not on the vicissitudes of individual behaviour.

3. Selective Wage Reductions, Induced Employment and the Law of Compensating Price Movements (W.H. Hutt)

Viner's defence of the classical doctrine of wage flexibility as a means of ensuring full employment has been strongly supported by Professor W.H. Hutt some seventeen years later in a paper published in this Journal.[46] Unlike Viner, Hutt had written at a time when classical and Keynesian economists could be considered as having discussed exhaustively the relationship between wage rates and employment. His contribution, therefore, contains a number of subtleties that are absent from that of Viner's. Let us briefly summarize his arguments.[47]

Firstly (*pp.* 391-2)*:* Keynesians think in terms of aggregates, assuming that wage-rate reductions imply a drop in total earnings. And a change in wage-rates is regarded as a blanket change. On the contrary, what is wanted is not a uniform but a *selective* reduction in wage-rates. Even if equi-proportional wage cuts were enacted during a period of high unemployment, "aggregate and average earnings might still tend to increase, owing to the redistribution of workers over the different wage groups."

Secondly (p. 393): The relations between wage-rates and total wages received should be considered in relation to the price-system as a whole. The Keynesians appear to neglect the synchronising function of prices, i.e. the price of a commodity determines its rate of consumption or the rate at which it moves to the next stage of production. The co-ordination of the different rates of flow is effected through price changes: *cet. par.* a price rise causes a reduction in the rate of flow, and *vice versa* for a fall in price.

Thirdly (pp. 390-92): Keynes' followers not only regard costs as limiting output, but also as calling forth output through demand. This cannot be accepted. Defenders of price flexibility advocate only such cost adjustments as would increase real income — and, in regard to wages, *only such wage rate reductions as would increase, not decrease, aggregate wages received, and hence the total demand for wage-goods.*

Finally (p. 392): If there is unemployment among, say, carpenters, a cut in their wages would, according to Keynesian theory, reduce their incomes and expenditures, even assuming their employment is restored. This could cause the demand for labour of other workers to fall. Advocates of price flexibility, on the other hand, do not assume that the fall in carpenters' wages and in the price of their product would directly increase the employment of carpenters, but that this would rather be *induced "as a result of wage-rate and price reductions on the part of persons who ultimately buy the carpenter's services"* (italics in original). It is assumed that in *other* industries the reduction results in the release of "withheld capacity" and that the increased flow of goods "becomes demand through being priced to permit its full sale. *This is the argument which the Keynesians should answer"* (italics added).

It is impossible to discuss these arguments in detail here. The first three paragraphs will be considered together. If an equi-proportionate wage-cut is to lead to higher aggregate earnings this would apparently be due to a sales lag which might give rise to greater output (*à la* Viner) — i.e. *not* due to a redistribution of workers between industries as Hutt mentions, which is less likely to happen when labour is in excess supply.[48] However, a sales lag, as we have seen, is unlikely to occur under these circumstances and, even if it did, may not have the desired effect on expectations. Further, if a reduction is engineered selectively, apparently this would be mainly in respect of the highly-paid occupations. To expect a higher total wage bill and a general recovery to follow from this would be expecting the impossible: the greater the contribution to national output of industries introducing the cut the more the expected rise in output would be — but the greater also the reduction in total purchasing power.

In this theory, as in Viner's, expectations apparently play no rôle. This is best shown in the second résumé above. We are told that Keynesians neglect the synchronising function of prices, i.e. the rate of consumption of a commodity is determined by its price, and the different rates of flow are co-ordinated through price changes. This is true in static price theory, which rests heavily on the *ceteris paribus* clause. The latter condition is briefly mentioned in the above. However, it usually does not hold in practice. It is indeed true that *cet. par.* a drop in price (e.g. wages) would call forth an increase in demand (e.g. for labour) but it is also true that this need not follow when the demand for output is not expected to rise following the reduction in wages. Then employment might not increase at all.

We now turn to what we believe constitutes the core of the "classical" theory in regard to the desirability of a downward flexibility of wage rates. It is contained in the final paragraph of the above résumé. This passage is of extraordinary interest. In Professor J.G. Koopmans' classic paper *Zum Problem des Neutralen Geldes*, published three years before the *General Theory*, a long section (52 pp.) is devoted to *Das angebliche "Gesetz der kompensatorischen Preisänderungen" und dessen Widerlegung* (the so-called Law of Compensating Price Changes and its Refutation).[49] This "law" Professor Koopmans apparently rather mysteriously attributes to the then current thinking without mentioning any well-known authors, which tends to leave the student of to-day not well-versed in pre-Keynesian literature rather baffled. Confronted by such an explicit defence of the "classical" theory as in the fourth résumé above, however, Koopmans' analysis falls into perspective. In fact, the whole of his analysis of this "law" is relevant here and can be applied to destroy Hutt's argument to its foundations. Reference can only be made here to the more salient points of this part of Koopmans' work.

The "classical" view (*vide* above) appears to be that a lowering of wages and prices in an industry suffering from unemployment would enable consumers buying the products of that industry to spend more on *other* goods, resulting in an increase in demand and, therefore, output of those *other* industries.[50] This formulation corresponds with that of Koopmans who states the "Law of Compensating Price Movements" for both a rise and a fall in prices.[51] According to Koopmans, the Law states that a fall in the prices of one or more goods might lead to a reduction in consumer outlay on them, thus setting free purchasing power which could be expended on *other* goods, the prices of which may then rise — or, in its modern[52] version, demand, and therefore employment may rise in those industries.

This, in brief, is the rationale of the "classical" theory of a downward flexibility of wages as a possible remedy for unemployment. The arguments against this view are very fundamental. It is true that in a barter economy in which there is no *numéraire* a fall, say, in the price of one good will cause a corresponding rise in the prices of other goods in terms of the first. For example, let in one situation x units of a commodity exchange against y of another and z of a third, etc.; if at a later point in time $2x$ units exchange against y and z, the first commodity will have become cheaper *vis-à-vis* the other two. Here we have a change in relative prices and a lowering of the price of one good affecting its exchange ratio with respect to all other goods, the ratios as amongst those other goods remaining the same: commodity x has become half as expensive as before to those offering y and z, whereas y and z have doubled in price to those offering x.

The same reasoning, says Koopmans, is apparently followed in those theories in which it is held that in a *monetary* economy there are instances when changes in individual money prices cannot cause a change in the general price level, since these initial individual changes would be offset by opposite changes in the money prices of *other* goods — this offsetting change being the result of buyers spending less on goods the prices of which have fallen and more on other goods. This, in essence, is also Hutt's argument.[53]

Nothing of the kind is, however, likely to happen in a monetary economy. There is no telling how buyers would react to a fall in the price of a particular commodity. On the demand side, it is possible that consumer outlay on that commodity may either rise or fall, depending on the price-elasticity of demand for that commodity. If demand for a particular commodity is generally elastic, outlay would probably rise — but not necessarily so, for if a further drop in price is *expected*, outlay might even diminish. If, further, demand is inelastic, outlay may be expected to fall. Assuming consumer income has, on the whole, remained unchanged (a not very realistic assumption during a depression), more may be spent on other goods *or savings may increase*. The latter is likely to happen when consumers desire to increase their cash reserves (which may be low in the circumstances, in contrast to Viner's view above) against unforeseen contingencies, or because of an expected further fall in prices in the near future. In this case classical theory will not hold. The former reaction (increased outlay on other goods) is of the kind assumed in classical theory. But the expected result will still be absent if, on the supply side, idle capacity exists in those industries to which consumer buying is switched, i.e. when output can be increased without employing more labour. Of course, there may be a rise in profits and wages in those industries and in the amounts paid to suppliers of raw materials. This might set in motion a multiplier process, the extent of which depends on the size of the switch in buying, if at all, and the nature and extent of the spending lags involved.

All this is assumed to follow from the initial reduction in wages and prices in the first industry. The problem is to know on what scale such a reduction should take place in order to spark off a process that would restore activity generally, bearing in mind the *caveats* mentioned above. Obviously, it is impossible to answer this question in a definitive way. It has apparently also worried the author under review here, who conveniently relegates it to a footnote.[54] Price and wage reductions, he writes, would cause severe distributive injustices if engineered on a small scale and confined to individual trades. This poses a serious problem to anyone trying to comprehend the "classical" line of thought on this important question. First, we are told that selective, not uniform, wage reductions are required to restore activity; and that such reductions could lead to a rise in the aggregate wage bill. But then we are warned that these selective reductions, if administered on a small scale, might result in a *lowering* of the total wage bill accompanied by "severe distributive injustices". We are not given any indication as to the nature of the selective wage reductions that would *not* cause distributive injustices — and, more important, no criteria are given for the basis on which individual industries are to be singled out for a selective cut in wages.

Professor Hutt is, of course, not unaware of some of the objections raised above. But he disposes of them in an unsatisfactory manner. He ends this section of his paper with the perplexing statement that since a policy favouring a change in the value of money would have the effect of throwing the price system out of co-ordination, therefore "if the value of the money unit is expected to rise, then until the necessary adjustments have all taken place, 'willingness to buy' must necessarily fall off."[55] This possibility merits serious consideration. However, the author hastens to add in a footnote that this is "no conclusive argument" against policies aiming at raising the value of money (*i.e.* lowering wages). But no reasons are advanced in support of this view. Having sown the seeds of doubt the author leaves the reader to fend for himself.

4. Anti-Keynesianism, Statics and Dynamics

The extensive criticism and qualification of the "orthodox" Keynesian theory in the years following the publication of the *General Theory* have been interpreted by the anti-Keynesians as proof of the fallacies of "Keynesianism". The latter part of Professor Hutt's article is devoted to these later developments.[56] Again, let us first summarise his views:

1. Keynesian theory is static; if it is made dynamic, Keynes' arguments for underemployment equilibrium with price flexibility fall away. In fact, some neo-Keynesians (e.g. Patinkin) explicitly argue that Keynes' underemployment equilibrium must be rejected. Flexibility, says Patinkin[57] will cause a drop in wages following an excess supply of labour, i.e. the system will not continue unchanged through time as under equilibrium conditions. Thus, by definition, price flexibility and under-employment are incompatible. *Ergo*, says Hutt, by definition, price flexibility is "inconsistent with wasteful idleness",[58] *even under dynamic conditions*. Then price flexibility requires a continuous adjustment of prices so as to establish harmony between current and expected prices. "Under such adjustments, even unemployment *dis*-equilibrium is ruled out."[59] The stark truth, therefore, is that wasteful idleness can be eliminated either through a continuous (*a*) adjustment of prices or (*b*) dilution of the value of money. But the latter is a "tragically evil method" of rectifying price disharmonies because of the harmful effects of inflation. The

former, however, is a "policy which has never been experimentally tested":[60] in no country has it been deliberately attempted to "increase income by reducing all prices which appear to be above the natural scarcity level so that all prices and wage-rates below the natural scarcity level may rise."[61] Actual policy has favoured the Keynesian view that "disharmonies in the wage-structure must not be tackled but offset", which is politically a more attractive method.

2. "The abandonment of the theory of under-employment equilibrium under price flexibility means that the Say law stands once again inviolate as the basic economic reality in the light of which all economic thinking is illuminated."[62] This has had extremely serious consequences for Keynesian economics. "The apparent revolution wrought by Keynes after 1936 has been reversed by a bloodless counter-revolution conducted unwittingly by higher critics who tried very hard to be faithful".[63]

Professor Hutt's attack on the Keynesian theory of under-employment equilibrium is perhaps the most forceful in this volume.[64] We believe, however, his conclusions on the incompatibility of price flexibility and wasteful idleness to be premature. His case rests heavily on a static application of the marginal calculus to the exclusion of the all-important factor *expectations*, as is shown above. The onus is on him to show that selective price reductions would indeed have the salutary effects on activity mentioned in classical theory; the reader is apparently expected to accept it in good faith. But, as we have argued above, the evidence against it is overwhelming. A second important (and related) factor neglected in the argument is *time*. The kind of adjustment envisaged here has a *time dimension*: the time period during which it is accomplished would lead to consequences which classical theory does not consider. This was mentioned above.

The rôle of time has been analysed much more incisively by Patinkin than it would appear from Hutt's brief quotation in his paper. We have here, *im Grunde*, Mill's views on Say's law all over again. Mill, as we have seen, regards a general over-production as a short-lived phenomenon — *how* short we do not know — so that, on the whole, Say's law should be vindicated. Hutt, on the other hand, quoting Patinkin, holds that with flexible prices excess supply of labour would force wage rates down and restore activity on an equilibrium level. Under-employment equilibrium is ruled out by definition, and Say's law comes into its own as "the basic economic reality in the light of which all economic thinking is illuminated."

Professor Hutt surprisingly does not criticise Patinkin's analysis of the rôle of time in this adjustment process.[65] Patinkin shows that "even granted full flexibility of prices, it is still highly possible that a deflationary policy will not work, due to the dynamic factors involved".[66] These, according to Patinkin, are twofold: first, an anti-depression policy, in order to be effective, must achieve its objectives *rapidly*; second, price reductions cannot be instantaneous, i.e. we have, *nolens volens*, to consider the transition process prior to the attainment of the new equilibrium position. It is this process which pre- (and anti-)Keynesian theorists failed to recognise[67]. It is also during this transition phase, as we have shown, that expectations might take a turn for the worse, with consequences that are difficult to foresee.[68]

Finally, it has been said that the Keynesian theory is not dynamic. This is true on Mr. Harrod's interpretation of dynamics: there is no growth of capital in the *General Theory*, which makes the model of less interest from the point of view of development over time.[69] But we might also interpret *dynamic* in the Frisch-Hicks sense, *static* as a method of analysis and *stationary* the absence of development over time. Thus a static model could be dynamic, i.e. when one or more variables contain a time subscript. In the *post*-Keynesian model this is true of consumption if a lagged income-consumption relationship is posited; it is true of the Keynesian theory of investment and of money, expectations playing a rôle in regard to both the marginal efficiency of capital and liquidity preference.

5. Anti-Keynesianism: Some General Considerations

The value of money was a major dependent variable in the "classical" theory. The disastrous events of the early 'thirties, however, shifted the emphasis away from money to the employment of resources, as in Keynes' theory, which advocated unorthodox policies of spending, both from income and borrowing, to lift the economy to a higher level of activity. As a result, he has been criticised (in this respect) on two major fronts, viz. his *inflationary* bias and his leanings toward *Socialism*.

In regard to the former, Professor Von Mises writes: "It is the pseudo-philosophy of those who can think of nothing else than to dissipate the capital accumulated by previous generations".[70] Viner is equally critical: "In a world organised in accordance with Keynes' specifications there would be a constant race between the printing press and the business agents of the trade unions", unemployment being eliminated only if the printing press could maintain the lead.[71] And in regard to the latter (Socialism) one of the contributors to Mr. Hazlitt's volume writes: "(The *General Theory* contains) the most subtle and mischievous assault on orthodox capitalism and free enterprise that has appeared in the English language."[72]

Keynes did indeed make some rather bold and, as it turned out, provocative suggestions in regard to the socialization of investment. But the doleful prognostications quoted above (to which most anti-Keynesians would subscribe) cannot be said to have been substantiated. A careful reading of what Keynes said on this subject should dispel the idea that his theory aimed at undermining the free-enterprise system, as the following shows: "I conceive therefore, that a somewhat comprehensive socialization of investment will prove the only means of securing an approximation to full employment". He added, however, that public authority will have to co-operate with private enterprise, and that he did *not* envisage "a system of State Socialism which would embrace most of the economic life of the community".[73] The State need not *own* the instruments of production; the primary object is for the State to be able to "determine the aggregate amount of resources devoted to augmenting the instruments and the basic rate of reward to those who own them".[74] Keynes was acutely aware of the virtues of private enterprise (efficiency, decentralisation and the "play of self-interest", p. 380), and held that the totalitarian systems "seem to solve the problem of unemployment at the expense of efficiency and of freedom".[75]

Planning is, of course, anathema to all anti-Keynesians. But since price flexibility alone is likely to be insufficient to restore *confidence* in times of crisis, more direct action becomes imperative. Admittedly, if carried to excess, this could smother private initiative. What is required is a policy based on mutual trust and a determination on the side of Government to foster private enterprise while at the same time curbing the activities of the ambitious civil servant, and institute only such controls or to take a hand in production which is calculated ultimately to benefit the private sector. This is the basis of the *économie orientée*, which raises problems that are often related as much to politics as they are to economics. The necessity for well-directed intervention had been stressed by Keynes at least a decade before publication of the *General Theory*: "The important thing for Government is not to do things which individuals are doing already, and to do them a little better or a little worse; but to do those things which at present are not done at all".[76]

A more mundane, but equally serious, charge against Keynesian theory concerns *inflation* (see above) which, it is claimed, is a necessary concomitant of Government deficit expenditure, a measure which Governments, under the influence of Keynes' teaching, have tended to regard as a panacea for preventing a slowing-down of economic activity. This is, of course, a complex subject, and we shall have to confine ourselves to a few generalities only. *First*, as Einzig has said: "Broadly speaking, the history of mankind is the history of rising prices,"[77] a trend which, even considering prolonged intervals of constant or falling prices, could be traced back for approximately four thousand years.[78] *Second*, to this anti-Keynesians would add that Keynes' theory has *exacerbated this tendency*, as is proved by the history of prices over the last century and a half.[79] One may indeed assume this to be one of the consequences — a very serious one no doubt — of the application of Keynes' teaching. *Another is the effect on unemployment*. Anti-Keynesians seldom discuss these two effects simultaneously. If one did, however, one would be faced by an alternative involving economic policy at the highest level: should the value of money be stabilised regardless of the consequences, or should unemployment be eliminated, whatever the effects may be on the purchasing power of money?[80] The answer to this question in practice involves a value judgement in regard to which the economist is unlikely to have the final say.

On the whole, anti-Keynesians favour policies that would not harm the interest of the wealth-owning classes. The *ideal*, naturally, should be for policy to be harmful to the interests of neither group, i.e. for a "monetary equilibrium" to be maintained at a high-employment level. It is interesting to quote Keynes' view on this matter, twelve years before the publication of the *General Theory*: "Thus Inflation is unjust and Deflation is inexpedient. Of the two perhaps Deflation is, if we rule out exaggerated inflations such as that of Germany, the worse; *because it is worse in an impoverished world, to provoke unemployment than to disappoint the rentier*. But it is not necessary that we should weigh one evil against the other. It is easier to agree that both evils are to be shunned.[81]

A *third* general observation is the following. There is an important difference between the Keynesian prescriptions of the middle 'thirties, framed against the background of one of the most severe and widespread depressions in history, on the one hand, and, on the other, the manner in which these prescriptions have subsequently been applied under widely different conditions. Lamentable though this may be, it cannot be ascribed to ill-conceived and maladroit Government action only. For Government policy is to an important extent a function of the social philosophy obtaining at the time: e.g. in the 'thirties ten per cent. unemployed was regarded as a tolerable percentage, whereas today few democratically-elected Governments would survive a persistent unemployment of such magnitude. This points to the influence of not only the work of Keynes (and Beveridge) but also of militant trade unionism in the industrially-advanced countries, and a greater consciousness in the public mind of matters affecting the welfare of labour. As a result, wages have become rigid downwards but flexible upwards, thereby aggravating the conflict inherent in the fundamental aims of economic policy.

It is fitting to conclude with a brief reference to the views of the great classical economist David Hume (1752), on the *beneficial effects of inflation*.[82] After clearly discussing a rise in accounting prices and a rise in money prices — without apparently being aware of the difference[83] — he continues: ". . . in every kingdom, into which money begins to flow in greater abundance than formerly, everything takes a new face: labour and industry gain life; the merchant becomes more enterprising, the manufacturer more diligent and skilful, and even the farmer follows his plough with greater alacrity and attention."[84]

Hume then goes on to explain *why* a rise in the supply of money should have this effect, and in so doing *discloses a greater awareness than some of the "modern classicals" of the importance of the passage of time in economic processes (cf. supra)*. The greater abundance of gold and silver, he says, causes a rise in commodity prices, *but not immediately*. In fact, "some time is required before the money circulates through the whole state, and makes its effect be felt on all ranks of people. At first, no alteration is perceived; by degrees the price rises, first of one commodity, then of another; till the whole at last reaches a just proportion with the new quantity of specie which is in the kingdom."[85] In conformity with what later became known as the classical idea of the "veil of money" he then concludes that "it is only in this interval or intermediate situation, between the acquisition of money and rise of prices, that the encreasing quantity of gold and silver is favourable to industry."[86]

In the last analysis, therefore, money cannot be a "veil" only, despite Hume's implicit claim to the contrary. For the "domestic happiness of a state", we read, it is immaterial whether "money be in a greater or less quantity". *However*, it is "good policy" to keep money "still encreasing", for in this way the "spirit of industry in the nation" is kept alive. Hume is acutely aware of the difference between equilibrium situations and transition periods, and because of the beneficial effects during the latter following an increase in the quantity of money, and the deleterious effects following a decrease, he strongly favours an inflationary policy as the only method (of the two) of increasing "real power and riches."[87]

This does not, of course, constitute a plea in favour of perpetual inflation. It is the marginal effects of an inflationary in contrast to a deflationary policy which in a period of low economic activity appear to speed up the recovery.

In the book under review it is alleged that the Keynesians themselves by their constructive criticism — mostly expressed *sotto voce* — have qualified Keynesian theory beyond recognition. This is more or less true. We may describe this development in either of two ways. Like the anti-Keynesians we may regard it as conclusive evidence of the fallacy of the Keynesian doctrines. From the point of view of *Dogmengeschichte* Keynesianism should then be regarded as a mere aberration. This is the negative view. On the positive side we may interpret it as another example of how a pioneering[88] work has stimulated thought to such an extent as to render obsolete large parts of the original contribution. In *this* respect Keynes was not a pioneer; to a greater or lesser degree a similar development took place in the case of the early authors of the Subjective Value Theory, of Böhm-Bawerk on the theories of Capital and Interest, Wicksell on Monetary Equilibrium, etc. But we cannot for that reason value these works less highly.

Thus the work done in the post-Keynesian era justifies the conclusion — a not very startling one — that the *General Theory* has been superseded in some important respects by the contributions of economists who drew their inspiration mainly from Keynes' work.[89] But not in all respects. The lasting contributions of the *General Theory* are rather of a general nature: the emphasis on the relationship between demand (expenditure) and income (which had been dormant in the 19th century economics — i.e. Malthus' effective demand); and the emphasis on macro-relationships, which led away from Marshallian partial analysis to an analysis of general equilibrium conditions, which Keynes (unlike Walras) presented in such a manner that they could be subjected to empirical testing.

But then, Hazlitt *cum suis* would argue, the post-Keynesian developments indeed prove the fallacy of the Keynesian doctrines on most specific issues. Again, this is a negative view which cannot be accepted. The anti-Keynesian approach appears to be a *cri-de-coeur* for a return to "classical" theory as it existed prior to the publication of Keyne' *General Theory*. And for anybody desiring to acquaint himself with the views of this school, this is the volume to consult.

Notes

1.   Review of *The Critics of Keynesian Economics*, by H. Hazlitt (Ed.) New York, 1960. In what follows this will be referred to as *Hazlitt*. I wish to express my gratitude to Dr. Jan Graaff for his valuable and constructive criticism of this paper. He cannot, of course be associated with views expressed here or with any errors that may remain. I also wish to record my indebtedness to Professor W.H. Hutt, University of Cape Town, whose energetic and tenacious defence of the anti-Keynesian views, both in conversation and in print, has greatly assisted me in reaching clarity on a number of points discussed below.

2.   Anti-Keynesians would not agree with this view. This is discussed below. The above should not be interpreted as implying that all pre-Keynesian economists had belonged to the *laissez-faire* school.

3.   *Narrow* is used here not as an emotive expression. It refers to a particular approach, seen within the context of doctrinal history.

4.   Keynes was averse from economic analysis in which the mind was — to use a telling expression of his — "trying to catch its own tail". And yet few of his predecessors and contemporaries have been better equipped for higher analysis, as his work in mathematics well shows.

5.   Cf. L. Albert Hahn, Continental European Pre-Keynesian, *Hazlitt*, pp. 287-303. Hahn claims that "all that is wrong and exaggerated in Keynes I said much earlier and more clearly," (*ibid.*, p. 287), and quotes numerous passages from the *General Theory* and his well-known *Volkswirtschaftliches Theorie des Bankkredits* (1920) in support of his view.

6.   J.M. Keynes, *A Treatise on Money*, London, 1930, Vol. I, p. 199, *n.* 2.

7.   *Ibid.*, p. 198, *n.* 3. It would be interesting to speculate on the extent to which Keynes had been influenced by Wicksell, whose work he knew well (*vide* the references in the *Treatise*) and towards which he was, on the whole, not unsympathetic. The affinity between Lundberg's *Studies in the Theory of Economic Expansion* (1937) and the *General Theory*, is a pointer in this direction.

Wicksell and Keynes knew each other personally. As early as 1916 Keynes wrote in a letter: "... I have delivered my evening lecture at the Admiralty; and I have testified before the wicked leering faces of the Hampstead Tribunal to the genuineness of James's conscientious objections. Oh, and I have brought out the March E.J. and entertained a Swedish Professor" — who, we are told, was Wicksell. Cf. R.F. Harrod, *The Life of John Maynard Keynes*, London, 1951, p. 211. In view of this it is surprising to read Schumpeter's statement in discussing the origins of Keynes' consumption function (he mentions the names of Malthus and Wicksell): "Wicksell he then hardly knew." Cf. J.A. Schumpeter, *A History of Economic Analysis*, New York, 1954, p. 1176, *n.* 12.

8.·   *Ibid.*, pp. 12-22.

9.   *Ibid.*, p. 11.

10.   Cf. H. Neisser, *Der Tauschwert des Geldes*, Jena, 1928, p. 13.

11.   *Ibid.*, p. 15. Italics added.

12.   K. Marx, *Capital*, Modern Library, New York, p. 127. On the same page we read: "Nothing can be more childish than the dogma, that because every sale is a purchase, and every purchase a sale, therefore the circulation of commodities necessarily implies an equilibrium of sales and purchases. If this means that the number of actual sales is equal to the number of purchases, it is mere tautology. But its real purport is to prove that every seller brings his buyer to market with him. Nothing of the kind."

13.   T.R. Malthus, *Principles of Political Economy*, Blackwell, 1951 (reprint), p. 315.

14.   Hazlitt, *ibid.*, pp. 24-45, esp. pp. 39-45.

15.   *Ibid.*, p. 26. And J.B. Say, *ibid.*, p. 21.: "Thus it is the aim of good government to

stimulate production, of bad government to encourage consumption."

16. *Ibid.*, p. 25.

17. *Ibid.*, Or again, it is fallacious to assume "that the man who steals money out of a shop, provided he expends it all again at the same shop, is a benefactor to the tradesman whom he robs."

18. *Ibid.*, p. 41. Mill then continues: "The sellers and the buyers for all commodities taken together, must, by the metaphysical necessity of the case, be an exact equipoise to each other; and if there be more sellers than buyers of one thing, there must be more buyers than sellers for another." Apparently it is this view that Marx has referred to as a tautology. Cf. *n.* 12 above.

19. *Ibid.*, p. 42. Italics in original.

20. "An overstocked state of the market is always *temporary* and is generally followed by a more than common briskness of demand" (p. 42). "It is . . . of the utmost importance to observe that excess of all commodities . . . means only a *temporary* fall in their value relatively to money" (p. 43). Italics added.

21. *Ibid.*, p. 43.

22. *Ibid.*, p. 44. Italics added. Apparently this should read: "There cannot be a *permanent* excess in the production of commodities in general."

23. *Ibid.*, p. 45. Italics added.

24. Cf. Hazlitt's introduction to Mill's essay, p. 23.

25. I.e. an uncritical statement of the "law" only.

26. Cf. J.B. Say *Letters to T.R. Malthus on Political Economy and Stagnation of Commerce* (1821), London, 1936 (reprint). This publication contains five letters by Say addressed to Malthus. The full Say-Malthus correspondence appeared under the title *Mélanges et correspondence d'Économie Politique*, Paris, 1833.

27. It is sufficient to mention here only the concept *effective demand* — "an idea which struck him . . . as he rode on horse-back from Hastings to Town . . .". Cf. J.M. Keynes, Robert Malthus, the First of the Cambridge Economists, in *Essays in Biography*, London, 1951 (reprint), p. 103.

28. T.R. Malthus, *Definitions in Political Economy*, London, 1827, pp. 65, 67. James Mill had argued that a drop in price below cost somewhere in the economy would be accompanied by a *rise* in price by an equivalent amount above cost elsewhere. To this Malthus replied: "I doubt, indeed, much, whether satisfactory evidence could be brought to show that a single million's worth of goods has risen above the cost of production, while seventy millions' worth have fallen below it." *Ibid.*, p. 66. (Malthus estimated the drop in prices below costs in the cotton, woollen and silk industries to be of the order of seventy million pounds.)

29. J.M. Keynes, *The General Theory*, p. 32.

30. P. Lambert, The Law of Markets prior to J.B. Say and the Say-Malthus Debate, *International Economic Papers No. 6*, London, 1956, p. 22. Cf. also Keynes, writing on the pre-1914 world: "The duty of 'saving' became nine-tenths of virtue and the growth of the cake (national income) the object of true religion." *The Economic Consequences of the Peace*, London, 1920, p. 17.

31. *Ibid.*, p. 19. And yet Malthus would have been the first to deplore the extremes to which his views have led (*via* Keynes) in some countries — i.e. the affluent societies: spending for the sake of spending, on the part of consumers, and, on that of entrepreneurs, the planned obsolescence to exploit the exaggerated importance which the consumer attaches to new designs. "Lord Lauderdale appears to have gone as much too far in deprecating accumulation, as some other writers in recommending it. This tendency to extremes is one of the great sources of error in political economy, where so much depends upon proportions." T.R. Malthus, *Principles of Political Economy*, p. 314, note.

32. T. Scitovszky, Capital Accumulation, Employment and Price Rigidity, *Review of Economic Studies*, 1940-41, pp. 69-88; G. Haberler, *Prosperity and Depression*, pp. 491-503. For references to Pigou's work, see *n.* 37 below.

33. "What is annually saved is as regularly consumed as what is annually spent . . ." *And*: capital is increased by parsimony and diminished by "prodigality and misconduct." A. Smith, *The Wealth of Nations*, Cannan ed., Vol. I, p. 320.

34. Classical theorists, e.g. Smith, Ricardo, J.S. Mill, argued that the quantity of money had no effect on the rate of interest.

35. Cf. also A.C. Pigou: ". . . full employment does, indeed, not always exist, but always *tends* to be established." *Employment and Equilibrium*, London, 1941, p. 78.

36. The question arises: *for how long?* (See below). Of course, some classical economists

held divergent views. *E.g.* Robert Torrens (in his *Letter to the Right Honourable the Earl of Liverpool*) and J. Cruickshank argued that flexible wages in a period of falling prices might well aggravate the situation. According to the latter, a cut in wages might lead to insurrection on the part of labour, and "this in all probability would terminate in the ruin of the British Empire." And paradoxically Malthus, despite his effective-demand approach, believed that a reduction in wages would lead to full employment. Cf. B.A. Corry, *Money, Saving and Investment in English Economics, 1800-1850*, London, 1962, p. 27.

37.   The Classical Stationary State, *Economic Journal*, 1943, and Economic Progress in a Stable Environment, *Economica*, 1947, reprinted in *Readings in Monetary Theory*, London, 1952.

38.   Pigou (*Economica*, 1947) merely assumes a positive net investment takes place in year 1, and that it eventually returns to zero. The path of investment over time is not analysed.

39.   This question cannot be analysed further here. A full *Dogmengeschichte* will probably have to start at least as far back as Walras' *Études d'économie politique appliquée*, and end with the reaction to Patinkin's *Money, Interest and Prices*.

40.   Pigou, *op. cit., Readings in Monetary Theory*, p. 251.

41.   J. Viner, Mr. Keynes on the Causes of Unemployment, *Quarterly Journal of Economics*, Vol. 51, 1936-37, pp. 147-67, reprinted in *Hazlitt*, pp. 46-65.

42.   *Hazlitt*, pp. 60-61.

43.   *Ibid.*, p. 61.

44.   *Ibid.*, p. 61.

45.   Or they might not, depending on the living standards made possible by the wage prior to the decrease. A cut in subsistence wages could lead to a narrowing of the range of goods bought and might turn some commodities, e.g. foodstuffs like bread, into a Giffen good. (This recently happened in Russia following the rise in prices — drop in real income — of certain foodstuffs, e.g. meat). Further, if, as is stated in the text, the lagged effect is present but the downturn nevertheless continues, this would imply that Viner's theory does not hold.

46.   W.H. Hutt, The Significance of Price Flexibility, *S.A. Journal of Economics*, 1954, pp. 40-51, reprinted in *Hazlitt*, pp. 386-403. This paper constitutes the most recent and explicit defence of the anti-Keynesian view (on wages and employment) in the book reviewed here.

47.   Cf. *Hazlitt*, pp. 389-396, *S.A.J.E.*, pp. 42-46.

48.   When during a period of "high unemployment" for every man on a job, say, two are waiting to take his place, a redistribution of labour may be expected to take the form of the unemployed moving into paid occupations rather than the lower-paid moving to better-paid occupations. Total wages may indeed rise following the rise in output, but the question still remains whether industry would expand output merely because of the drop in wages. If this happens, as Hutt reasons, it would imply that either expectations are neglected, or assumed to favour expansion. The former is unpardonable, the latter unrealistic.

49.   J.G. Koopmans, Zum Problem des Neutralen Geldes, published in *Beiträge zur Geldtheorie*, ed. F.A. Hayek, Vienna, 1933. (Other contributors to this Volume include Fanno, Holtrop and Myrdal). We are not alone in thinking that Koopmans' essay (148 pp.) ranks with the very best of contributions in the whole field of monetay theory, and is comparable with the best that Keynes ever wrote. (He shows, *inter alia*, that none of the variables in the Fisher equation can be accepted as a criterion for monetary stability). In a conversation recently Professor Hayek gave it as his opinion that Koopmans' essay is perhaps the best in this volume. Reference to aspects of Koopmans' theory is made in e.g. F.J. de Jong, Keynes and Supply Functions, A Second Rejoinder, *Economic Journal*, September 1955, pp. 479-84, esp. pp. 483-4, and the present reviewer's *A Study in the Theory of Monetary Equilibrium*, Leiden, 1959, Ch. VI. Neither of these, however, does any justice to the originality and rigour of Koopmans' work.

50.   This is how we interpret the final paragraph of the above summary. The original passage is, however, not free from ambiguity (*Hazlitt*, p. 392. *S.A.J.E.*, pp. 43-4). For reference is made to a reduction in carpenters' wages, and the fact that this would *induce* an increase in their employment "as the result of wage-rate and price reductions on the part of persons who ultimately buy the carpenters' services". What is presumably meant here is that the latter persons *benefit by* the price reduction in the first industry and *not* that *their* wages are also reduced as is implied here. They may not — but could — buy more from the first industry, and could thus switch purchasing power to other industries which, in turn, are assumed to "release withheld capacity". This is discussed below. If, however, this passage is interpreted as meaning that a wage cut in one industry

would lead to wage and price reductions in *other* industries, this implies that activity would be restored if lower prices and wages obtained all round. Why this should be so is not clear. For in order to reach the lower level of wages and prices, the economy will have to undergo a slow and painful process of downward adjustment of wages (price reductions being lagged behind wage reductions) which cuts buying power and is not calculated to restore the confidence of the entrepreneurial classes.

painful process of downward adjustment of wages (price reductions being lagged behind) which cuts buying power and is not calculated to restore the confidence of the entrepreneurial classes.

51. *Zum Problem* etc. p. 291.

52. Koopmans does not discuss the effect of this law on employment.

53. *Vide* above, especially *n.* 41.

54. *Hazlitt*, p. 392, *n.* 17 and *S.A.J.E.*, p. 43, *n.* 17.

55. *Hazlitt*, p. 396, and *n.* 26; *S.A.J.E.*, p. 46.

56. *Hazlitt*, pp. 396-403; *S.A.J.E.*, pp. 46-51.

57. D. Patinkin, Price Flexibility and Full Employment, *American Economic Review*, 1948, pp. 543-64, reprinted (with additions) in *Readings in Monetary Theory*, pp. 252-83.

58. *Hazlitt*, p. 400, *S.A.J.E.*, p. 49.

59. *Ibid.*

60. *Hazlitt*, p. 403, *S.A.J.E.*, p. 51.

61. *Ibid.*

62. *Hazlitt*, p. 402, *S.A.J.E.*, p. 50.

63. *Ibid.*

64. Cf. also A.F. Burns, Keynes' Theory of Underemployment Equilibrium (1954), *Hazlitt*, pp. 404-410.

65. Patinkin, *Readings*, pp. 271-77.

66. *Ibid.*, p. 272.

67. We need not, for the purposes of this review, consider the question whether *all* pre-Keynesian theorists were guilty of this charge.

68. Pigou, as we have seen, takes a more realistic view: to him a process set in motion by price and wage reductions is a mere "academic exercise", not a matter of practical policy. Hutt, on the other hand, while admitting that this is a policy that has "never been experimentally tested" (*Hazlitt*, p. 403) clearly implies that it should be given a chance to prove itself, given an absence of rigidities in the system. But this presumably would refer to an economy in which economic processes take place in mechanical fashion, expectations being ruled out altogether.

69. J.M. Keynes, *The General Theory*, p. 245. Here Keynes states that the labour supply, capital equipment, technique, degree of competition, etc., are assumed constant. However, as Pigou pointed out in his review of the *General Theory* (*Economica*, 1936), throughout the main part of the book, Keynes assumes new investment is undertaken every year.

70. L. Von Mises, Lord Keynes and Say's Law, *Hazlitt*, p. 320.

71. J. Viner, *Hazlitt, op. cit.*, p. 49.

72. Joseph Stagg Lawrence, Lord Keynes and the Financial Community, *Hazlitt*, p. 345. It is interesting — and amusing — that some of the authors included in this book condemn Keynesianism in terms identical to those used by contemporary Soviet critics of Keynes who, incidentally, do *not* consider Keynesian theory to lead ultimately to the Utopia of a planned economy. Cf. *e.g.* L'Alter, The Multiplier and Acceleration Principle in Bourgeois Political Economy, *Mirovaia Ekonomika i Mezhdunarodnye Otnosheniia*, No. 1, 1960.

73. J.M. Keynes, *The General Theory*, p. 378.

74. Keynes, *ibid.*

75. Keynes, *ibid.*, p. 381.

76. J.M. Keynes, *The End of Laissez-Faire*, London, 1926, pp. 46-7. This counsel appears to be more (but not necessarily *only*) apposite in the case of a less-developed economy, endeavouring to raise its rate of capital accumulation than in that of a mature economy suffering from unemployment of resources.

77. P. Einzig, *Inflation*, London, 1952, p. 26.

78. The implication in anti-Keynesian writings that Keynes was indifferent to the deleterious effects of inflation is ill-founded. Already in *The Economic Consequences of the Peace*, London, 1920 (pp. 220-1) Keynes wrote: "There is no subtler, no surer means of overturning the existing basis of society than to debauch the currency. The process engages all the hidden forces of economic law on the side of destruction, and does it in a manner which not one man in a million is able to diagnose." Also, Keynes' analysis in the *Tract on Monetary Reform* (1924) of the pros

and cons of inflation and deflation must be regarded as one of the best in the literature. Cf. *n.* 81 below, and the relevant passage in the text. In the *General Theory*, of course, Keynes remains relatively silent on these issues — a fact to which the anti-Keynesian would point with alacrity. But then, the *General Theory* referred to conditions in which inflation was the very last eventuality worthy of serious consideration.

79.   For example, U.S. statistics show a sharp rise in prices during the American Revolution at the end of the 18th century, the War of 1812, the Civil War, during the 'sixties and the first World War. In each case this rise was promptly followed by an equally sharp drop in prices to approximately the pre-war level. This experience was not repeated in respect of the second World War and the Korean War. For the last quarter century prices have shown no marked drop at all.

80.   I.e. more bluntly: should the real value of assets (wealth) be preserved, or should as many members of the community as possible be gainfully employed?

81.   J.M. Keynes, *A Tract on Monetary Reform*, London, 1924, p. 40 (italics added). The passage following alludes to a view brought forward much more forcibly in the *General Theory*, viz., the harmful effects on the economy of the two group "savers" and "investors" acting independently, and the desirability of freeing "ourselves from the deep distrust which exists against allowing the regulation of the standard of value to be the subject of *deliberate decisions*" (Italics in original).

82.   J.S. Mill emphatically rejected Hume's arguments in regard to the desirability of inflation, while Adam Smith did so rather perfunctorily. "One of the great puzzles in the analysis of (Smith's) work is to sort out his attitude towards Hume's appraisal of the effects of inflation." B.A. Corry, *Money, Saving and Investment in English Economics, 1800-1850*, London, 1962, p. 52, *n.* 1.

83.   A greater quantity of money, said Hume, "can have no effect, either good or bad, taking a nation within itself." It is the same as though "on a merchant's books . . . instead of the Arabian method of notation, which requires few characters, he should make use of the Roman, which requires a great many" — increase in accounting prices. *And then*: "But notwithstanding this conclusion . . . it is certain, that, since the discovery of the mines in America, industry has encreased in all the nations of Europe . . . and this may justly be ascribed, amongst other reasons, to the encrease of gold and silver" — increase in money prices. Cf. *David Hume, Writings on Economics*, E. Rotwein (ed), London, 1955, p. 37.

84.   *Ibid.*, p. 37.

85.   *Ibid.*, p. 38.

86.   *Ibid.*, p. 38.

87.   The relevant passage is worth quoting: "A nation, whose money decreases, is actually, at that time, weaker and more miserable than another nation, which possesses no more money, but is on the encreasing hand. This will be easily accounted for, if we consider, that the alterations in the quantity of money, either on one side or the other, are not immediately attended with proportionable alterations in the price of commodities. There is always an interval before matters be adjusted to their new situation; and this interval is as pernicious to industry, when gold and silver are diminishing, as it is advantageous when these metals are encreasing. The workman has not the same employment from the manufacturer and merchant; though he pays the same price for everything in the market. The farmer cannot dispose of his corn and cattle; though he must pay the same rent to his landlord. The poverty, and beggary, and sloth, which must ensue, are easily foreseen." *Ibid.*, p. 40.

88.   Most anti-Keynesians, of course, would not attribute any originality to Keynes' work, *e.g.* Hazlitt, p. 3: "What is original in the book is not true; and what is true is not original." This hostile view is surely too narrow. As we have said above, we are less interested in priorities than in the question of the use made of ideas scattered through the earlier literature.

89.   This is a development which Keynes would no doubt have welcomed. *E.g.* Modigliani's classic *Liquidity Preference and the Theory of Interest and Money* reprinted in *Hazlitt*, pp. 132-84, should be classified among these (post-Keynesians) rather than with the anti-Keynesians. For an incisive and impartial analysis of Keynesian and post-Keynesian theory, see H.G. Johnson, *The General Theory* after Twenty-five years, *American Economic Review, Papers and Proceedings*, May, 1961, reprinted (with bibliographical references) in H.G. Johnson, *Money, Trade and Economic Growth*, London, 1962, pp. 126-47. A more biased (anti-Keynesian) discussion is that of J.R. Schlesinger, "After Twenty Years: The General Theory", *Quarterly Journal of Economics*, 1956, pp. 581-602.

104

Keynes's Finance Motive*

P. Davidson

In *The General Theory*, Keynes distinguishes between three motives for holding cash '(i) the transactions-motive, i.e. the need of cash for the current transaction of personal and business exchanges; (ii) the precautionary-motive, i.e. the desire for security as to the future cash equivalent of a certain proportion of total resources; and (iii) the speculative-motive, i.e. the object of securing profit from knowing better than the market what the future will bring forth' [11, p. 170]. Keynes recognized that 'money held for each of these three purposes forms, nevertheless, a single pool, which the holder is under no necessity to segregate into three water-tight compartments' [11, p. 195]; however, he did suggest that these three categories formed an exhaustive set and that all other reasons for holding money (e.g. the income motive or the business motive) are merely sub-categories of these three major divisions [11, pp. 194-200]. According to Keynes, the quantity of money demanded for transactions and precautionary purposes 'is not very sensitive to changes in the rate of interest' [11, p. 171]; rather it 'is mainly a resultant of the general activity of the economic system and of the level of money-income' [11, p. 196]; the quantity of money demanded for speculative purposes, on the other hand, responds to 'changes in the rate of interest as given by changes in the prices of bonds and debts of various maturities' [11, p. 197]. Although Keynes did not actually use the terms in *The General Theory*, the money held to satisfy the first two motives is usually called active balances, while money held for speculative purposes is customarily referred to as idle balances.

In reply to Ohlin's lengthy criticism [14] of his position, in a 1937 review and restatement of his ideas, Keynes introduced a new and somewhat novel purpose for demanding money, namely, *the finance motive* [9]. Keynes argues that if the level of investment was unchanged, then the money held to 'finance' new investments was a constant amount and could therefore be lumped under a subcategory of the transactions motive, where capital goods transactions are involved. In other words, entrepreneurs typically hold some cash balances to assure themselves that they will be able to carry out investment plans. These

*Source: *Oxford Economic Papers*, Vol. 17, March 1965, pp. 47-65.

balances can be looked upon as transactions balances, since given the marginal efficiency of capital schedule, the rate of interest, and the consumption function, there will be a unique level of investment demand for any given level of output, i.e. for any given output level, there will be a certain volume of planned investment transactions for which transactions balances will be maintained.

'But', Keynes argued, 'if decisions to invest are (e.g.) increasing, the extra finance involved will constitute an additional demand for money' [**9**, p. 247]. Thus, according to Keynes, the finance motive was an important additional component of the aggregate money-demand function when the decision to change the level of investment occurred. For example, if the marginal efficiency of capital schedule were to shift outwards because of improved profits expectations, then for any given level of output and rate of interest, entrepreneurs would desire to engage in more investment transactions than before; consequently when the marginal efficiency of capital function shifts, it gives rise to an additional demand for cash balances [cf. **18**, pp. 20-22].

To clarify the essence of the finance motive, and to indicate why it is not properly taken into account in the discussion of the transactions motive, Keynes wrote:

> It follows that, if the liquidity-preferences of the public (as distinct from the entrepreneurial investors) and of the banks are unchanged, an excess in the finance required by current ex-ante output (it is not necessary to write 'investment', since the same is true of *any* output which has to be planned ahead) over the finance released by current ex-post output will lead to a rise in the rate of interest; and a decrease will lead to a fall. I should not have previously overlooked this point, since it is the coping-stone of the liquidity theory of the rate of interest. I allowed, it is true, for the effect of an increase in *actual* activity on the demand for money. But I did not allow for the effect of an increase in *planned* activity, which is superimposed on the former. . . . Just as an increase in actual activity must (as I have always explained) raise the rate of interest unless either the banks or the rest of the public become more willing to release cash, so (as I now add) an increase in planned activity must have a similar, superimposed influence [**10**, p. 667].

Considering that Keynes felt that the finance motive was the coping-stone of his liquidity preference theory, it is surprising to see that the concept has practically disappeared from the literature.[1]

There was, however, a very clear practical illustration of this point offered by Keynes about a year later when his attention was devoted to the imminent rearmament programme and the prospect of war. In a letter printed in the 18 April 1939 edition of the London *Times*, Keynes elucidated his reasoning still further. The immediate question was how to finance the pending additional government expenditures for rearmament. Keynes argued that 'If an attempt is made to borrow them [the savings which will result from the increased production of non-consumption (war) goods] before they exist, as the Treasury have done once or twice lately, a stringency in the money market must result, since, pending the expenditure, the liquid resources acquired by the Treasury must be at the expense of the normal liquid resources of the banks and of the public.' In other words, an increase in planned governmental expenditures will normally result in an increase in the aggregate demand for money function, even before the expenditures are undertaken.

Is the finance motive really as significant as Keynes believed? And if it is, why has it been given short shrift and almost vanished by neglect in the post-Keynesian literature? The rest of this paper will be devoted to answering these questions. We will show that the almost ubiquitous adoption of a strained and somewhat distorted variant of the Keynesian system resulted in the omission of the finance motive *and* the incorrect specification of the transactions demand for money function. As a consequence of these imperfections in the model, a needless theoretical controversy about the independence of the real and monetary subsectors developed[2] which has led subsequent work into many blind avenues, for, as will be argued below, the finance motive provides the link to demonstrate that the aggregate demand for money function is *not* independent of events in the real sector. Thus an unnecessary polarization has occurred to beguile some, and bedevil others, more interested in comprehending Keynes's own thought.

The Finance Motive

Most writers have simply ignored the finance motive[3] by popularizing, in the name of Keynes, a macroeconomic system which made it easy to completely abrogate the finance motive. This system, which is pedagogically centred about the familiar 45-degree diagram[4] (Fig. 1), and which (by definition) prevents the analysis of nonequilibrium positions (i.e. positions off the 45-degree line), has achieved such popularity that it is, if not unfair, impossible, at this date, to associate it with any one economist. Consequently, in what follows, the writings of Hansen have been chosen merely as a familiar example and should not be interpreted as suggesting that Professor Hansen is either the sole or even the primary source of the error.

According to Hansen, the demand for transactions balances function, L_t, shows 'the *desired* volume of active or "transactions" cash balances at various levels of income Y' [6, p. 61]. Thus Hansen writes the demand for transactions balances as

$$L_t = kY \tag{1}$$

where k is a constant. He thereupon plots the function as the straight line L_t emanating from the origin (Fig. 2). The implication of Hansen's diagram is that the demand for transactions balances is a function of the 45-degree line (i.e. the output identity line). In other words, Hansen has made the quantity of money demanded for transactions purposes a function of the actual level of output at each level of output.

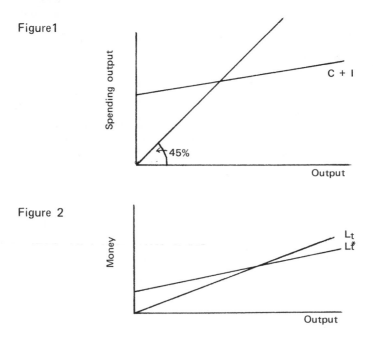

Figure 1

Figure 2

Once we go back to Keynes, however, it is clear that in his writings on the finance motive, the quantity of money demanded for transactions balances is not directly related to output, rather it is associated with planned or expected spending propensities, i.e. it is a function of the aggregate demand for goods (the $C+I$ line in Fig. 1), which, in turn, is a function of the level of output. The quantity of money demanded, therefore, is only indirectly related to the level of output via the aggregate demand function. In other words, Keynes's transactions-demand concept is functionally related to, in the simplest case, the summation of the consumption function and the investment demand function. If we assume that the quantity of money demanded for transactions balances is equal to some fraction of the aggregate demand for goods at each level of output, then the transactions-demand-for-money function would be drawn as L_t^* rather than L_t in Fig. 2 (since it is related to the $C+I$ line rather than the 45-degree line in Fig. 1).[5]

Much more is involved here than merely a geometric misrepresentation of the demand for transactions balances, for it now becomes obvious that the relationship between the quantity of money demanded for transactions and the level of output is a 'function of a function', rather than a simple direct relationship. Thus, to trace out the change in the quantity of transactions money demanded for a given change in output it is necessary to obtain the change in the quantity demanded of transactions balances for a given change in aggregate demand *and* the change in aggregate demand for a given change in output.[6] In other words, the change in the quantity of money demanded for transactions purposes depends not only on changes in output, but also on the relationship of the change in the level of aggregate demand with a change in output (e.g. given the level of investment, on the marginal propensity to consume). Furthermore, given the customary payments period in the economy, it follows that if consumers and/or investors decide to spend more at any given level of income (an upward shift in the aggregate demand function), then there will be an increase in the demand for money for the purchase of goods *at each level of output* (an upward shift on the L_t^* function).

Let us summarize symbolically the argument as developed so far. The demand for transactions balances should be written as

$$L_t^* = \alpha C + \beta I \qquad (2)$$

where α and β are constants ($0 \leqslant \alpha \leqslant 1; 0 \leqslant \beta \leqslant 1$) whose magnitudes depend primarily on the frequency of payments and the overlapping of payments and receipts in the system, and C and I are the real consumption and investment functions respectively. Assuming linear functions merely for algebraic simplicity, the consumption function may be written as

$$C = a_1 + b_1 Y \qquad (3)$$

where a_1 is a constant ($\geqslant 0$) and b_1 is the marginal propensity to consume. The investment-demand function, on a linear conception, is:

$$I = a_2 - b_2 i \qquad (4)$$

where a_2 and b_2 are constants, and i is the rate of interest. Combining equations (3) and (4) into (2) we obtain

$$L_t^* = \alpha a_1 + \beta a_2 + \alpha b_1 Y - \beta b_2 i. \qquad (5)$$

If we assume a constant rate of interest (which is implicit in the usual 45-degree diagram), then the fourth term on the right-hand side of equation (5) is a constant; thus, equation (5) appears to be similar to Hansen's equation (1) except that the function does not emanate from the origin.

There is, however, a significant analytical difference between equations (1) and (5). In Hansen's system, the parameter k of equation (1) depends only on the customary length of the payments period in the economy, and consequently, the equation is entirely independent of the behavioural parameters of the real sector [equations (3) and (4)]. Thus, as long as the conventional payments period is unchanged, the magnitude of k is fixed, and therefore Hansen's transactions demand for money function is stable — even if the parameters of the aggregate demand-function change. On the other hand, equation (5) shows that some of the parameters (the a's and the b's) are common to both the transactions demand for money function *and* the real consumption- and investment-demand functions. Thus, according to equation (5), even if the payments period is unchanged (i.e. α and β are constant), any change in either the investment demand or the consumption functions will result in a shift of the entire transactions demand for money schedule; or as Keynes noted, any 'increase in planned activity' will result in an increased demand for money *at each level of output*. Accordingly, any change in the parameters of the aggregate-demand function (contrary to Hansen's system) will result in a shift in the L_t^* function. The demand for money function is *not* independent of changes in the real sector.

It is the shift in the L_t^* function induced by a change in spending propensities that Keynes was describing when he discussed the finance motive.[7] Whenever there is a shift in the aggregate-demand function, there will be a concomitant shift in the demand for money schedule. Consequently, when there is an increase in planned investment, for example, the equilibrium quantity of money demanded will ultimately increase for two reasons: (1) a shift in the L_t^* function (i.e. the finance motive), and (2) a movement along the new L_t^* function as output increases and induces further spending via the multiplier. It is the shift in the L_t^* function which puts additional pressure on the rate of interest.[8]

Thus, every upward shift of the aggregate-demand function (the $C + I$ line in Fig. 1) implies the prevalence of a 'finance motive' as spending units switch over from one money-demand function to a higher one. Once this change has occurred, spending units will maintain larger transactions balances than before *at each level of output*. At that point the dynamic finance motive merges with the static concept of the transactions motive. The finance motive thus evolves as one of the dynamic elements in the static Keynesian model [18, pp. 80-87]; its major contribution is in macro-economic path analysis rather than in comparative statics.

Implications of the Analysis

It is useful to distil three important implications of the analysis before further elaborating on it. These are:

1. Since the demand for money function is not as stable as Hansen's formulation implies (i.e. it varies every time the aggregate-demand function shifts), and since it does not emanate from the origin, *even if the rate of interest is a constant*, there is no reason to expect a constant relationship between the demand for money for transactions purposes and the level of output. In other words, and in the language of monetary theorists, we should *not* expect the income velocity of money to be constant. The recognition of the 'finance motive' concept prepares us for some clearer understanding of monetary phenomena.

For example, Friedman, recognizing that the income velocity of money is a demand-oriented phenomenon, has attempted to estimate the income elasticity of demand for money. He has found that observed short-run variations in income velocity imply an income elasticity less than unity, whereas secular evidence indicates an elasticity which exceeds unity [**3**, pp. 328-30]. In a novel (and perhaps somewhat forced) explanation, Friedman tries to reconcile these conflicting short-run and secular estimates of elasticity by imputing differences between 'permanent' income and prices and measured income and prices [**3**, pp. 334-8]. Our finance motive analysis, however, suggests a much simpler explanation which is entirely consistent with Friedman's short-run and secular estimates. If the short-run demand for transactions-balances function has a positive intercept and is either a straight line or concave to the abscissa, then:

$$\frac{dL_t^*}{dY} < \frac{L_t^*}{Y}.$$

It therefore follows that the income elasticity of demand for transactions balances will be less than unity along the entire function.[9] In other words, given the normal aggregate consumption and investment functions and the rate of interest, we would expect Friedman to find out that as the economy moved toward equilibrium, short-run movements in output will be accompanied by less than proportional changes in the quantity of money demanded by spending units.

Observed secular changes in the quantity of money demanded, on the other hand, are most likely the result of viewing particular demand points on different L_t^* functions as the latter shifts through time in response to changes in the parameters of the system. The 'income elasticity' calculated from observations which cut across short-run L_t^* functions will obviously be larger in magnitude than the elasticity measured along any one L_t^* function and might easily result in estimates which exceed unity. This secular 'elasticity' measurement, however, has little or no relationship to the usual concept of income elasticity which assumes a given preference scheme (i.e. given behavioural parameters).

2. A shift in *any* component of the aggregate demand for money function will induce a concomitant shift in the transaction demand for money function. Thus, when Keynes linked the finance motive with changes in the decision to invest, he was, as he readily admitted, discussing 'only a special case' of the finance motive[10] [**9**, p. 247].

Generally speaking, the finance motive will be involved whenever the aggregate demand function is changed. For example, if we add a government spending function (assuming, for the moment, no change in the $C + I$ line in Fig. 1) then we would have to shift up to the L_t^* function (in Fig. 2) to include government's demand for transactions balances. Furthermore, to the extent that the quantity of money demanded per dollar of consumption is different from the quantity demanded per dollar of planned investment (i.e. $\alpha \neq \beta$) or planned government spending (or planned foreigners' purchases for that matter), then the total demand for transactions balances will depend upon the composition of aggregate demand (at each level of output), while the latter, in turn, will depend at least in part on the distribution of income [cf. **11**, p. 201]. To illustrate, if income is redistributed from spending units which have high liquidity needs to units which have lower liquidity needs to carry out a given volume of planned expenditures, then even with the same level of aggregate demand for goods, the quantity of money demanded will be reduced. For example, to the extent that consumers have less leeway in matching their receipts to their obligations (because of less flexible consumer credit institutions), consumers may require higher balances per dollar of planned expenditures than business firms.[11] Thus, the composition of aggregate demand as well as the level of output may be an important determinant of the demand for cash balances.

At the level of public policy, as well as correct theory, it thus appears that once the L_t^* function is related to the components of the aggregate demand function rather than to the 45-degree line, some important insights appear. For example, if the economy is initially at some output level, say Y_1, and if the government decides to increase its purchases of new goods and services by x dollars (on the assumption that the supply of money is unchanged), the magnitude of the impact on the rate of interest at the original Y_1 level (as well as at any other Y level) will depend on whether the government 'finances' the increased expenditure by borrowing or by taxation[12] (this was noted earlier in the revealing quotation from Keynes regarding war finance). This suggests that even before an expansionary activity occurs, a planned increase in government spending will affect the money market through the demand for new balances to finance and fund the projected outlay. Assuming investment demand to be relatively inelastic to changes in the rate of interest, the magnitude of the impact on the money market will be greater if the government borrows rather than increases taxes to finance the expenditure, since borrowing will result in the addition of the government component to the aggregate demand function; while financing via income-taxes, for example, will reduce the consumption component while elevating the government component. Thus, in the latter case, we should not expect the aggregate demand curve to be elevated as much as in the former case: the shift in the L_t^* function will be less with taxation than with borrowing. (Hansen's L_t function, on the other hand, portends a complete absence of impact on the money market until after the increase in economic activity actually occurs.)[13]

3. If the demand for transactions balances is related to the aggregate demand function, then a straight-line L_t function which emanates from the origin belongs to the world of Say's Law — a world where the aggregate demand function coincides with the 45-degree line,[14] i.e. a world where the aggregate demand function is linear and homogeneous with respect to output. In such a world, however, 'money is but a veil' and there exists a dichotomy between the

real and monetary sectors so that there can be no monetary obstacle to full employment for the real and monetary factors are completely independent[15] [cf. **8**, pp. 282-3]. Once, however, it is recognized that the demand for transactions balances is a function of aggregate demand, which, in turn, *is not homogeneous with respect to output*, then the demand for money function is not homogeneous with respect to output. It therefore follows that the system cannot be dichotomized into independent monetary and real subsets since the scale of activity is an important determinant of the level of aggregate demand and, therefore, of the quantity of money demanded. (Certainly, Keynes believed that the analytical separation of the real and monetary sectors was wrong [**11**, p. 293].)

The Finance Motive and the Interdependence of the Real and Monetary Sectors

The inappropriateness of attempting to dichotomize the system into independent real and monetary subsets can be clarified by utilizing the more general Hicksian *IS-LM* framework where both the rate of interest and the level of output are simultaneously determined, rather than relying on the 45-degree diagram which assumes a constant rate of interest. The *IS-LM* system has the advantage of showing both the real sector and the monetary sector on the same diagram; consequently, interdependence can be visually observed if when one function shifts, the other is concomitantly displaced.

Figure 3

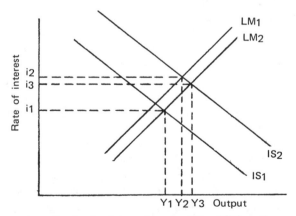

In Hicks's system, the basic determinants of the *IS*-function are the marginal efficiency of capital schedule and the aggregate consumption function, while the *LM*-function is based on the money demand and supply functions [**7**]. The *IS*-function may be derived by combining equations (3) and (4) with the output identity $Y \equiv C + I$:

$$Y = a_1 + b_1 Y + a_2 - b_2 i, \tag{6}$$

or
$$Y = \left(\frac{1}{1 - b_1}\right)(a_1 + a_2 - b_2 i). \tag{7}$$

Equation (7) is the *IS* function; it traces out all the values of output and the rate of interest which are compatible with the investment demand and consumption functions. In Fig. 3 it is plotted as the downward sloping IS_1 line, since as the rate of interest declines, according to equation (7), the level of output will rise.

The demand for money equation can be derived by adding the speculative and precautionary demand functions to the demand for transactions-balances function. Since we are only interested in the implications of the finance motive, i.e. of shifts in the transactions-demand function, we do not have to specify the form of the precautionary and speculative demand functions, we may merely assume them as given and constant (or varying directly with the transactions demand function). Thus the demand for money function can be derived from equation (5) as:

$$L = \alpha a_1 + \beta a_2 + \alpha b_1 Y - \beta b_2 i + \sigma, \tag{8}$$

where L is the total demand for money, and σ stands for the unspecified precautionary and speculative demand functions.

Given an exogenously determined supply of money, $\bar{m}$, and letting the demand for money equal the supply of money, we obtain the *LM* function as:

$$i = \frac{a_2}{b_2} + \left(\frac{\alpha}{\beta b_2}\right)(a_1 + b_1 Y) - \frac{1}{\beta b_2}\,\bar{m} + \frac{1}{\beta b_2}\,\sigma. \tag{9}$$

Thus, given α and β, and the a's and the b's, once outside of the liquidity trap, the *LM* function is plotted as upward sloping (see LM_1 in Fig. 3) since, as Y increases, the rate of interest rises. The values of i and Y which satisfy both (7) and (9) simultaneously are revealed as the equilibrium rate of interest and the equilibrium level of output of the system (i_1 and Y_1 in Fig. 3).

The interdependence of the money market [equation (9)] on the real sector [equation (7)] is now easily demonstrated. For example, suppose an outward shift of the investment demand function [equation (3)] is posited. In other words, assume a_2 increases. It follows from equation (7) that at each rate of interest, the Y ordinate of the *IS* function will increase by an amount equal to the change in a_2 multiplied by $1/1(1 - b_1)$; this means simply that the *IS* function moves outward to IS_2 in Fig. 3. Observe that whereas in Hansen's system, the *LM function would remain unchanged when the IS curve shifts* [**6,** pp. 77-80], it can be seen from equation (9) that when a_2 increases, the i ordinate of the *LM* function will increase by an amount equal to the change in a_2 multiplied by $(1/b_2)$ at each output level. Thus, the whole *LM* function shifts upward to LM_2 in Fig. 3, so that the new equilibrium level of output and rate of interest (Y_2 and i_2, respectively) are higher than before.[16] In a similar manner, equivalent simultaneous shifts in the *IS* and *LM* functions can be demonstrated whenever any of the parameters of the consumption or investment demand functions change.

The inevitable conclusion is that the system cannot be dichotomized into independent real and monetary subsets; consequently, it is not correct to separate monetary economics from real economics as has often been done.[17] It is important to note that the interdependence of the real and monetary sectors does not require the fine theoretical point (which may have little practical significance) of a real balance effect (cf. [15, pp. 105-15], [13, pp. 83-84, 88], [8, pp. 282-5]). That so much controversy about the possible independence of the real and monetary sectors has appeared in the post-Keynesian literature is surprising in view of Keynes's warning that the 'division of Economics between the Theory of Value and Distribution on the one hand and the Theory of Money on the other hand is, I think, a false division' [11, p. 293]. Had the interconnexion between the finance motive, the transactions motive, and the aggregate-demand function been understood originally, much of this barren controversy could have been avoided.[18]

Once the finance motive concept is understood, it is easy to demonstrate the correctness of Keynes's *obiter dictum* that an overdraft system is an 'ideal system for mitigating the effects on the banking system of an increased demand for ex-ante finance' [10, p. 669]. For example, if there is an outward shift of the *IS* function from IS_1 to IS_2 as profit expectations rise, and if the resulting increase in demand for cash to finance the additional investment plans can be furnished by overdrafts, then the supply schedule of money will increase *pari passu* with the increase in the demand for money function. Consequently, the *LM* function will not shift; rather it will remain firm as LM_1 so that the equilibrium level of output will expand to Y_3 while the equilibrium rate of interest increases only to i_3 (Fig. 3). Consequently, as Keynes noted, 'to the extent that the overdraft system is employed and unused overdrafts ignored by the banking system, there is no superimposed pressure resulting from planned activity over and above the pressure resulting from actual activity. In this event the transition from a lower to a higher scale of activity may be accomplished with less pressure on the demand for liquidity and the rate of interest' [10, p. 669].

The Role of Productivity and Thrift: a Digression

With the aid of Fig. 3, it is now easy to demonstrate that much of the controversy between Robertson and Keynes on the role of productivity and thrift in determining the rate of interest is mainly a semantic confusion between movements along the demand schedule for money and shifts in the schedule.[19] An increase in the productivity (i.e. expected profitability) of capital would induce an outward shift in the *IS* curve (from IS_1 to IS_2 in Fig. 3) and, as we have already argued, a concomitant shift in the demand for money schedule so that given the supply of money, the *LM* curve is elevated from LM_1 to LM_2.

Since LM_2 lies above LM_1, Robertson was correct when he argued that an increase in productivity will raise the rate of interest (*at each level of output*) as the demand for money function shifts [cf. **17**, pp. 10-12]. On the other hand, Keynes was correct when he stressed that, given the supply of money, the increase in the equilibrium quantity of money demanded (due to the finance motive shifting the L_f^* function 'superimposed' upon a movement along the L_r^* schedule as output increased) caused the equilibrium rate of interest to rise from i_1 to i_2 [e.g. **9**, p. 247]. Since Keynes was discussing a movement from one equilibrium rate of interest to another, he stressed changes in spending propensities and output as the producer of changes in the equilibrium quantity of money demanded and in the rate of interest; whereas Robertson was essentially viewing the impact of changes in 'productivity' on the entire demand for money schedule.

The discussion of the role of thrift was enshrouded in the same confusion. An increase in thrift (i.e. a downward shift of the consumption function) would result in an inward movement of the IS function (say from IS_2 to IS_1) and a reduction in the demand for money schedule, so that the LM curve would be depressed (say from LM_2 to LM_1). Here again, we can see that Robertson, in arguing that an increase in thrift lowers the rate of interest (at each level of output), is emphasizing the shift in the entire demand for money schedule, while Keynes stressed the fall in the equilibrium rate of interest from i_2 to i_1, which resulted from a decline in the equilibrium quantity of money demanded as spending propensities and output fell [**11**, pp. 98, 183-5, 372].

Some Concluding Remarks

From the argument above it seems to follow that the disappearance of the finance motive from the post-Keynesian literature has led to some omissions and some confusions, making for wrong theoretical constructions and an inadequate understanding of certain policy implications of money supplies in a growing economy where 'finance' must be provided or deflationary pressures emerge via the rate of interest.

It is provocative to speculate briefly on this aspect for the theory of growth. For example, Gurley and Shaw argue that the growth of non-monetary intermediaries will reduce the growth in the demand for money by spending units, and consequently 'reduces the required growth of the money stock' necessary for a policy of expansion [**4**, p. 228]. Furthermore, Gurley and Shaw claim that 'a favorable climate for the growth of non-monetary intermediaries is one in which there is an expansion of national output based primarily on private expenditures . . . that are financed to a great degree by external means' [**4**, p. 228], since such circumstances will induce the expansion of financial intermediaries and ultimately lower the demand for money.

Gurley and Shaw's thesis can be made more specific by using our Fig. 3. If when the marginal efficiency of capital increases so that the *IS* schedule shifts from IS_1 to IS_2, in the absence of either an overdraft system, or financial intermediaries, or specific action by the Monetary Authority, the supply of money would be unchanged, and the new equilibrium levels will be i_2 and Y_2. If financial intermediaries are in the system and *if* they are induced to expand their activities *pari passu* as output expands, then the ultimate equilibrium level of output will be higher than Y_2 and the rate of interest will be lower than i_2 (say, Y_3 and i_3 in Fig. 3). This movement from the original equilibrium values of Y_1 and i_1, to Y_3 and i_3 can be looked upon as occurring in two stages. In the first instance, the outward shift of the *IS* function has increased the demand for money function as planned spending increases. The resulting increase in economic activity, if Gurley and Shaw are correct, simulates the growth of non-monetary intermediaries who are able to reduce the liquidity needs of spending units for any level of planned expenditures by rearranging the overlap of payments and receipts via the sale of financial assets of high liquidity. Thus, in the second stage, the demand for money function is reduced as the intermediaries grow. The final result on the demand for money function depends upon the magnitude of these two countervailing forces. As a first approximation, we may assume that they just neutralize each other, so that despite the constancy of the money supply the relevant *LM* function may be LM_1 instead of LM_2. Thus, Gurley and Shaw's system of nonmonetary intermediaries suggests a somewhat different, and perhaps more difficult, path than Keynes's overdraft system for avoiding shortage of liquidity as plans for expansion are made.[20]

On the theoretical plane, the omission of the finance motive has led to an undue concern with dichotomized models and has resulted in ignoring one strand of thought (e.g. [1], [20], [22]) which suggests that any such effort is, in effect, returning us to Say's Law and barter models, almost a perversion of what should have been learned from Keynes. Small wonder then that many 'Keynesian' models proclaim unemployment an attribute almost solely to rigidities in the wage structure. On the other hand, recognition of the finance motive reveals almost another 'liquidity trap'; this one will restrain expansion in the economy as consumption and investment plans are prepared in advance of actual expenditures unless the Monetary Authority is alert to this phenomenon and have taken appropriate measures to alleviate the strain. As Keynes cogently argues, the development of the analytical concept of the finance motive highlights the fact that

the banks hold the key position in the transition from a lower to a higher scale of activity. If they refuse to relax [i.e. to provide additional finance], the growing congestion of the short-term loan market or the new issue market, as the case may be, will inhibit the improvement, no matter how thrifty the public purpose (sic) to be out of their future income. On the other hand, there will always be *exactly* enough ex-post saving to take up the ex-post investment and so release the finance which the latter had been previously employing. *The investment market can become congested through shortage of cash. It can never become congested through shortage of saving. This is the most fundamental of my conclusions within this field* [**10**, pp. 668-9, italics added].

It is at this level that the finance motive deserves more attention and investigation than it has received. For theory to neglect any relationship which can be important, cannot help but close either avenue of investigation. Our analysis has already indicated that the finance motive can be used to shed new insights into the income velocity of money, the income elasticity of demand for money, macroeconomic path analysis and economic expansion, and the relationship of the real and monetary sectors. Other problems in monetary theory may prove tractable once the 'finance motive' is better understood.

Appendix[21]

In the traditional (e.g. Hansen's) formulation, the demand for transactions (L_t) [and precautionary (L_p)] balances are usually taken as a linear function of the level of output,

$$L_t + L_p = kY \tag{10}$$

while the speculative demand function (L_s) is assumed to be inversely related to the rate of interest (outside the liquidity trap). If, for algebraic simplicity, we assume a linear relationship, then the speculative demand for money balances can be written as:

$$L_s = \lambda_1 - \lambda_2 i, \quad \text{for } i > i_0 \tag{11}$$

where i_0 is the liquidity trap value of i. Combining equations (10) and (11) with an exogenously determined money supply, $\bar{m}$, the traditional LM function can be written as

$$i = \frac{\lambda_1 - \bar{m}}{\lambda_2} + \left(\frac{k}{\lambda_2}\right) Y. \tag{12}$$

Equation (12) is traditionally interpreted as indicating the rate of interest in the money market which will bring the total demand for money into equilibrium with the total supply of money for any given level of output.

The equilibrium level of output for the economy is obtained by solving equations (6) and (12) simultaneously as

$$Y^* = \frac{\lambda_2(a_1 + a_2) + (\bar{m} - \lambda_1) b_2}{\lambda_2(1 - b_1) + kb_2} \tag{13}$$

while the equlibrium rate of interest is

$$i^* = \frac{k(a_1 + a_2) + (\lambda_1 - \bar{m})(1 - b_1)}{\lambda_2(1 - b_1) + kb_2}. \tag{14}$$

With the finance motive system stressed in this paper, on the other hand, the transactions (and precautionary) demand for money is related to the aggregate demand function, i.e.

$$L_t + L_p = \alpha C + \beta I. \tag{15}$$

Substituting the consumption and investment demand functions [equations (3) and (4)] into equation (15) yields

$$L_t + L_p = \alpha(a_1 + b_1 Y) + \beta(a_2 - b_2 i). \tag{16}$$

Combining equation (16) with equation (11) and equating the sum to the exogenously determined supply of money, the *LM* function can be written as

$$i = \frac{\alpha a_1 + \beta a_2 + \lambda_1 - \overline{m}}{\beta b_2 + \lambda_2} + \frac{\alpha b_1}{\beta b_2 + \lambda_2} Y. \tag{17}$$

Solving equations (6) and (17) simultaneously, the equilibrium level of output in this system is given by

$$Y^* = \frac{\lambda_2(a_1 + a_2) + (m - \lambda_1)b_2 - (\alpha - \beta)a_1 b_2}{\lambda_2(1 - b_1) + \beta b_2 + (\alpha - \beta)b_1 b_2} \tag{18}$$

while the equilibrium rate of interest for the entire system is

$$i^* = \frac{\alpha a_1 + \beta a_2 + (\lambda_1 - \overline{m})(1 - b_1) + (\alpha - \beta)a_2 b_1}{\lambda_2(1 - b_1) + \beta b_2 + (\alpha - \beta)b_1 b_2}. \tag{19}$$

A comparison of equations (13) and (18) shows that, if, *and only if* $\alpha = \beta = k$, then the equilibrium level of output in both the traditional and finance motive systems will be identical. This result can be interpreted with the help of Fig. 4.

Figure 4

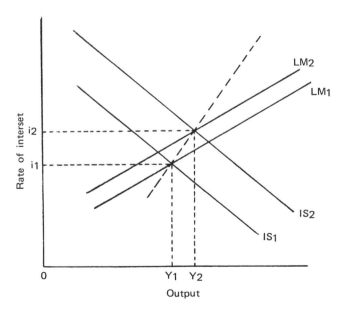

If, as we have argued in this paper, the demand for transactions balances is a function of the aggregate demand for goods, then when IS_1 shifts to IS_2 (in Fig. 4), the LM_1 function shifts to LM_2, and the equilibrium values for Y and i rise from Y_1 to Y_2, and i_1 to i_2, respectively. The locus of equilibrium points which will be derived for given shifts in the IS and LM functions is given by the dashed line in Fig. 4, and would be algebraically represented by equation (12). This implies, however, that the traditional interpretation of equation (12) is incorrect. This equation does not show the rate of interest in the money market which brings the demand for money into equilibrium with the supply of money *for any level of output*; rather, if $\alpha = \beta = k$, equation (12) indicates the various combinations of rates of interest and output levels which will bring about simultaneous equilibrium in both the commodity and money markets, given specified changes in the real behavioural parameters of the aggregate demand function.

On the other hand, in the more realistic case where $\alpha \neq \beta \neq k$, the equilibrium level of employment of the traditional system as derived via equation (13) will be different from the result obtained via (18), once the finance motive is recognized. Consequently, when $\alpha \neq \beta$, the traditional approach tends to suggest that for a given shift in IS, the resulting equilibrium level of output (say Y_3 in Fig. 3) will differ from the resulting equilibrium level of output (say Y_2 in Fig. 3) which would occur, if the transactions demand is related to the aggregate demand function rather than to the level of output.[22]

Consequently, only in the case where $\alpha = \beta = k$, can the traditional algebraic formulation of the LM function be salvaged by re-interpreting it as a sort of long-run growth path which results from shifting short-run IS and LM functions. (This analogy to the micro-concepts of short-run and long-run curves is admittedly somewhat forced, but it may help clarify my position to some readers.)

In the more general (and more realistic case) where $\alpha \neq \beta$, the traditional formulation does *not* correctly describe the equilibrium expansion path of the system, and should, therefore, be discarded.

Notes

The author is grateful to C.F. Carter, Miles Fleming, Sir Roy F. Harrod, Helen Raffel, Eugene Smolensky, Sidney Weintraub, and Charles R. Whittlesey for helpful comments at various stages.
  1.   Only a few 'Keynesians' even discuss it (e.g. [**18**, pp. 20-22, 80-87], [**20**, p. 135]).

  2.   For an example of a popular post-Keynesian model showing this independence of subsectors, see [**12**]. For a discussion of some aspects of the dichotomization of the real and monetary sectors, see [**15**, pp. 105-15, 454-9].

  3.   Tsiang is an important exception in that he discusses the finance motive before discarding it as unimportant. Tsiang argues (as did Keynes) that all transactions must be financed. Tsiang, however, then jumps to the incorrect conclusion that the ' "finance" and transactions demand for money ... are really the same thing' [**19**, p. 547]. Thus, Tsiang implies that Keynes's coping-stone is really a redundancy.

4. Had an alternative geometrical apparatus using aggregate supply and demand functions (as developed by Weintraub [20, Ch. 2]) been adopted, the omission of the finance motive and the incorrect specification of the transactions demand for money function would probably not have occurred. With Weintraub's scheme, it would have been obvious, I believe, to relate the demand for money schedule with the demand for goods function.

5. Keynes, of course, recognized that the demand for transactions balances was not only related to the aggregate demand function, but also via 'the business motive' to the parameters of the aggregate supply function (i.e. to the price of inputs, production functions, degree of industry integration, and the degree of monopoly) [11, pp. 195-6]. To make the following analysis comparable to the usual post-Keynesian treatments of liquidity preference, however, we shall make the explicit assumption (which is implicit in the works of others) that, either (1) there is no change in the aggregate supply function, or (2) any change in the quantity of money demanded for 'the business motive' occurs only *pari passu* with changes in the aggregate demand function. Accordingly, we can focus our attention entirely on aggregate demand.

6. Symbolically this can be stated as

$$\frac{dL_t^*}{dY} = \frac{dL_t^*}{dD} \frac{dD}{dY}$$

where D is aggregate demand.

7. In the case of war finance, discussed by Keynes in 1939, what was involved was an increase in the government component of aggregate demand which was to be financed by borrowing before the actual spending occurred.

8. As we will show below, it was this aspect that led D.H. Robertson to utter the triumphal note that Keynes has at last restored productivity 'to something like its rightful place in governing the rate of interest from the side of demand' [16, p. 317].

9. Letting E_m represent the income elasticity of demand for money, the elasticity can be defined as

$$E_m \equiv \left(\frac{dL_t^*}{dY}\right)\left(\frac{Y}{L_t}\right).$$

It follows therefore that the income elasticity of demand for money is greater than (equal to, less than) unity, when (dL_t^*/dY) is greater than (equal to, less than) L_t^*/Y.

Keynes believed that the income velocity was not constant, and furthermore, he suggested that the elasticity of demand for money would normally be less than unity at less than full employment [11, pp. 304-6, also see 11, pp. 201, 299].

10. Keynes's justification for linking the finance motive to changes in planned investment was his belief that planned investment is 'subject to special fluctuations of its own' [9, p. 247]. In his discussion of war finance, however, Keynes was generalizing the finance motive to other components of aggregate demand.

11. In a recent article [2], Miles Fleming carefully analyses the implications of business firms changing their timing of payments via the use of trade credit.

12. In either case, of course, the equilibrium rate of interest and the equilibrium level of output will rise.

13. Hahn, in a similar case, noted that the traditional liquidity preference theory 'predicts that the rate of interest will remain constant' when, for example, the (original) Y_1 level is a disequilibrium level; that is, when '*ex ante* $S <$ *ex ante* I' or, more generally stated, if aggregate demand exceeds aggregate supply at the disequilibrium level of Y_1 [5, p. 62]. On the other hand, Hahn claims that the loanable-funds approach correctly indicates that there will be a rise in the rate of interest *at the* Y_1 *level* when aggregate demand rises above aggregate supply. Consequently, Hahn attempts to correct the traditional liquidity preference approach to this disequilibrium situation by introducing the demand for finance via a 'subtransactions' mechanism among investors, holders of cash, and producers of capital goods, as people attempt 'to substitute bonds for capital goods' [5, p. 63].

Nevertheless, Hahn is not entirely happy with his amended version of liquidity preference and he concludes that his 'period analysis is highly artificial. . . . This probably means that L.F. [loanable funds] as here formulated is more useful than L.P. [liquidity preference], since *we will never be able to find a time when the rate of interest is independent of the demand for "finance"* ' [5, p. 64, italics added].

Under the interpretation of the finance motive given in this paper, there is no reason to resort to Hahn's 'highly artificial' period analysis. We are always dealing with a situation involving an aggregate demand level for each level of output — even in the example cited by Hahn. Thus when aggregate demand is increased above aggregate supply *at a given level of output*, if the finance motive is then correctly introduced, the liquidity preference approach will demonstrate that the rate of interest must increase, even at the original (disequilibrium) level of output — for there is a need for more money to enforce the increased demand for goods.

Finally, it should be noted that the analysis presented in this paper firmly supports Hahn's assertion that the rate of interest is never independent of the demand for 'finance'.

14.   The case where the aggregate demand function is a straight line emanating from the origin at an angle other than 45 degrees is a trivial case, since the only solution to the system occurs at a zero level of output.

15.   In a world of Say's Law (e.g. a Robinson Crusoe economy), value theory can, of course, be treated independently of monetary theory.

16.   Since normally $b_2 > 1$, while $1 - b_1 < 1$, a change in a_2 will have a larger impact on the IS function (7) than on the LM equation (9), that is the IS curve will shift more than the LM curve so that the new intersect will always be to the north-east of the original intersection.

In Hansen's traditional system, since the LM curve is not displaced, the new equilibrium level of output and rate of interest is Y_3 and i_3 respectively.

For completeness, it should be pointed out that the traditional (e.g. Hansen's) algebraic formulation of the LM function can, given a restrictive and highly unrealistic assumption, be resuscitated by reinterpreting it as representing the loci of equilibrium points (a sort of long-run equilibrium path) traced out as *both* the short-run IS and LM functions shift in response to changes in the parameters of the spending propensities. In the following Appendix, it is demonstrated that if, *and only if* $\alpha = \beta$ (that is, if the additional quantity of transactions money demanded for an additional dollar of planned consumption is *always* equal to the additional quantity of transactions money demanded for an additional dollar of planned investment spending, or planned government, or planned foreigners' purchases), then a money sector function based on equation (8) being written in the traditional algebraic form of $L = kY + \sigma$ (where $k = \alpha = \beta$) describes an equilibrium path which cuts across shifting LM curves, when the latter are displaced as a result of shifts in the IS function.

(I am extremely grateful to Sir Roy F. Harrod for bringing this possibility initially to my attention, and to Helen Raffel for providing me with a basic mathematical proof for clarifying this point.)

17.   It can be shown that value theory provides the logical underpinnings for macroeconomic and monetary theory [1, Ch. 9-13] [20, Ch. 2, 8].

18.   Weintraub has criticized the common Keynesian models which he calls 'Classical Keynesianism', for reverting, in the name of Keynes, to barter concepts where, for example, price level phenomena have no real effects [22].

19.   Since we have demonstrated that the economy cannot be divided into independent real and monetary subsets, it should not be surprising to find that the 'real' variables of productivity and thrift have an impact on the monetary sector.

20.   Although an analysis of international liquidity problems with planned expansion of world trade is beyond the scope of this paper, it would appear that Keynes's 'Bancor' plan envisaged a different path for solving international liquidity problems (via liquidity supply creating aspects, including overdrafts) than the development of international non-monetary intermediaries such as the IMF and IBRD.

In a paper entitled 'Plan to Increase International Monetary Liquidity' (to be published by the Joint Economic Committee), Sir Roy Harrod proposes a system of automatic annual increases in 'drawing rights' by members of the IMF. Under his plan, current drawing rights plus additional annual increments would automatically become an inseparable part of the member's deposit, and could be used at the member's own discretion at any time. Harrod further proposes that 'deposits at the IMF should constitute what may be called international legal tender'. Harrod presents forceful arguments to show why such a plan will overcome the already serious problem of international liquidity shortage, and would also provide necessary additional liquidity for future expansion of international trade.

Conceptually, Harrod's proposal has some properties similar to an overdraft system, except that Harrod would not have any interest charges for the use of these additional drawing rights (overdrafts), nor would he require individual members to pay the fund back for the drawing rights used. His plan would allow the supply of international liquidity to increase *pari passu* with increased demand for liquidity resulting from the necessity of financing planned expansion of world trade, and would convert the IMF from a nonmonetary intermediary to an institution performing a liquidity creating supply function.

21. This appendix is based on a mathematical proof provided for me by Helen Raffel. Any errors occurring in the interpretation of this proof are mine alone.

22. A similar comparison of equations (14) and (19) indicates that when $\alpha = \beta = k$ the equilibrium rate of interest is the same in the two systems, but when $\alpha \neq \beta \neq k$, the equilibrium rate of interest differs in the two systems.

References

1. DAVIDSON, P., and SMOLENSKY, E., *Aggregate Supply and Demand Analysis*, New York, 1964.
2. FLEMING, M., 'The timing of payments and the demand for money', *Economica*, May 1964, 31, pp. 132-57.
3. FRIEDMAN, M., 'The demand for money: some theoretical and empirical results', *Journal of Political Economy*, Aug. 1959, 67, pp. 327-51.
4. GURLEY, J.G., and SHAW, E.S., *Money in a Theory of Finance*, Washington, 1960.
5. HAHN, F.H., 'The rate of interest and general equilibrium analysis', *Economic Journal*, Mar. 1955, 65, pp. 52-66.
6. HANSEN, A., *Monetary Theory and Fiscal Policy*, New York, 1949.
7. HICKS, J.R., 'Mr. Keynes and the "classics": A suggested interpretation', *Econometrica*, Apr. 1937, 5, pp. 147-59.
8. _____ 'A rehabilitation of "classical" economics?', *Economic Journal*, June 1957, 67, pp. 278-89.
9. KEYNES, J.M., 'Alternative theories of the rate of interest', *Economic Journal*, June 1937, 47, pp. 241-52.
10. _____ 'The ex-ante theory of the rate of interest', *Economic Journal*, Dec. 1937, 47, pp. 663-9.
11. _____ *The General Theory of Employment, Interest, and Money*, New York, 1936.
12. MODIGLIANI, F., 'Liquidity preference and the theory of interest and money', *Econometrica*, Jan, 1944, 12, pp. 45-88; reprinted in *Readings in Monetary Theory*, New York, 1951, pp. 186-239.
13. _____ 'The monetary mechanism and its interaction with real phenomena', *Review of Economics and Statistics*, Feb. 1963, suppl., 45, pp. 79-107.
14. OHLIN, B., 'Some notes on the Stockhom theory of savings and investments II', *Economic Journal*, June 1937, 47, pp. 221-40.
15. PATINKIN, D., *Money, Interest, and Prices*, Evanston, 1956.
16. ROBERTSON, D.H., 'Mr. Keynes and "Finance"', *Economic Journal*, June 1938, 48, pp. 314-18.
17. _____ *Essays on Monetary Theory*, London, 1948.
18. ROBINSON, J., *The Rate of Interest and Other Essays*, London, 1952.
19. TSIANG, S.C., 'Liquidity preference and loanable funds theories, multiplier and velocity analyses: a synthesis', *American Economic Review*, Sept. 1956, 46, pp. 540-64.
20. WEINTRAUB, S., *An Approach to the Theory of Income Distribution*, Philadelphia, 1958.
21. _____ 'The Keynesian theory of inflation: the two faces of Janus?', *International Economic Review*, May 1960, 1, pp. 143-55.
22. _____ *Classical Keynesianism, Monetary Theory, and the Price Level*, Philadelphia, 1961.

105

Keynesian Revisions*

W.H. Hutt

The purpose of this essay is to discuss the significance of a very welcome symposium of contributions from nine leading economists, edited by Robert Leckachman and entitled *Keynes' General Theory — Reports of Three Decades*.[1] Each contributor has two articles, one of which is a reprint of a contribution published nearly two or three decades ago, and one a specially written recent article. Of the former (most of which were of considerable importance in the clarification of Keynesian doctrine), four were published in 1936, one in 1937 and four in 1946. The contributors are Haberler, Harrod, Lerner, Reddaway, Austin Robinson, Samuelson, Paul Sweezy and Viner.

The most striking thing about the new essays presented is the evidence they afford the discerning reader of the gradual — albeit reluctant — abandonment of critical logical elements in Keynes' argument. The *retreat* can be perceived, in varying degrees of clarity, in eight out of the nine new contributions, as well as in the Editor's Introduction. The exception is by Harrod.

Two essays are by friendly and respectful non-Keynesian critics, Haberler and Viner. Both make it obvious that, in their opinion, the crucial originality of the *General Theory* — the unemployment equilibrium thesis — cannot be sustained (pp. 291 and 255 respectively). The other contributors would probably all still describe themselves as Keynesians. Their position is not so unequivocal as that of the two non-Keynesians. We propose here to deal particularly with those passages in the symposium which most clearly disclose (for the perspicacious student) the wish to find an escape from the untenable doctrines which, developed mainly on the unemployment equilibrium notion as foundation, have become the new orthodoxy.

Austin Robinson is cautious and modest. He explicitly disclaims the suggestion that Keynes' contribution lay in asking new questions or in forcing economists to re-examine existing answers. What he did do, says Robinson, was to force economists to "ask what are the factors that determine the level of employment as a whole, not only in a full-employment long period but also in a short period" (p. 90). Yet Robinson here attributes to Keynes credit for

*Source: *South African Journal of Economics*, Vol. 33, June 1965, pp. 101-13.

stimulating a form of questioning which, we should have said, was almost monopolising the minds of pre-Keynesian economists between 1920 and the publication of the *General Theory*. Indeed, concern with the very issue to which Robinson refers (aroused by 'classical' teachings at the London School of Economics) not only inspired the present reviewer's choice of post-graduate studies but prompted his decision to seek leisure for the study of the subject by entering academic life in 1928. Believing that the root causes of chronic unemployment could be found in the method of pricing labour, he was led to an examination of the theory of collective bargaining, a venture which culminated, in 1930, in the publication of a book with that title. That his youthful judgement was correct seems to be borne out by the fact that former or present Keynesians are now being forced[2] to admit that the over-pricing of labour *does* lie at the root of the unemployment phenomenon, both in its short-run and its long-run manifestations.

Obviously, then, Robinson gives Keynes the wrong sort of credit. Surely, Keynes' contribution (whether judged to have been valuable or the reverse) consisted in the disturbance of what had seemed to be settled convictions; and the disturbance was caused, not through his drawing attention to overlooked issues, but in the putting forward of a quite different diagnosis of the causes (both short-run and long-run) of unemployment. Keynes insisted that the factors responsible for a condition of worsening idleness of productive resources were not those his 'classical' predecessors and contemporaries believed they had identified.

Before Keynes, it had been generally held that unemployment and recession persisted because productive services came to be priced higher than the community could afford to pay out of uninflated income or too high in relation to price expectations. The pricing of capacity into idleness in any one field caused, it was thought, a contraction of real income which, confronting in turn rigidity of prices, set going a general cumulative decline in all or most fields.[3] (See, for instance, Lavington, *The Trade Cycle*, 1928.) Resistances to co-ordinative price or wage-rate adjustments prevented immediate or early recovery.

The essential novelty in Keynes' contribution — the crux of his challenge to the 'classics' — can be found in his contention that this is an inherently defective diagnosis. Market-selected downward adjustments of wage-rates and prices are incapable, he argued, of restoring full employment once there has been a departure from that condition. Such adjustments aggravate, they do not mitigate the recession. Unemployment can, indeed, exist in equilibrium, the Say Law is therefore invalidated, and the Austrian theory of fluctuations is refuted. (According to the Austrian theory, under currency convertibility the correction of a period of inadvertent or reckless inflation, requiring as it does recourse to rectifying deflation, is necessarily accompanied by cyclical recession, with unemployment when wage-rate and price rigidities are permitted, until the economy is reco-ordinated by automatic reactions or deliberate steps taken which break down the rigidities.)

The thesis of the *General Theory* involves not only a denial that full employment requires the co-ordination of the economy through price adjustments (to changes in preference[4] and changes in resource availability) but the assertion that the maintenance of activity is achievable by the maintenance of expenditure on 'consumption' *plus* 'investment'.[5]

Yet the Keynesians' own policy of validating wage-rates (which have been raised beyond the reach of uninflated income, or fixed inconsistently with expectations) by the 'maintenance of effective demand', itself relies upon price adjustments. In so far as it achieves its purpose, it is *via* the crude adjustments in *relative* prices (cost-price ratios) which can be effected through the use of monetary or fiscal policy to reduce the real value of the money unit.

In respect of practical judgement and policy recommendations, the non-Keynesians believed that in a chronic depression such as, say, that which was plaguing Britain in the 1930's, just a little wage-rate reasonableness could have transformed depression into prosperity, have saved the pound sterling and have permitted Britain to keep faith with those who had trusted her pledge to pursue a 'sound money' policy (i.e., to honour her monetary obligations). This was at a time when one of the two most influential British apologists for the trade-union movement, Sidney Webb (subjected as he then was to the strains of Government responsibility), could remark (privately, not publically) to the other most influential apologist, Beatrice Webb, that the leaders of the trade-union movement were 'pigs'.[6]

It was, however, common cause that, given wage-rate inflexibility, the Keynesian remedy (i.e., the maintenance of a market rate of interest below the 'natural' level) could restore and maintain full employment without denying labour unions the right continuously to price the product of labour out of range of uninflated income. But, Keynes' critics warned, this could only be achieved at the expense of creeping inflation, together with a proliferation of central controls (presaged to some extent in the *General Theory* itself),[7] the magnification of State power and a growing sacrifice of personal freedom. The actual course of subsequent history has, of course, wholly justified their warnings.[8]

But what of the core of Keynesian *theory*? To what extent has intellectual speculation strengthened, weakened or perhaps demolished the edifice which Keynes and his disciples had erected by 1946? The careful reader of Leckachman's symposium is likely to be struck by the uneasiness of most of the would-be Keynesians. In some cases, "what Keynes really meant" clearly becomes "what Keynes ought to have meant".

Accepting Modigliani and Haberler as having first explicitly challenged the Keynesians on the unemployment equilibrium issue,[9] we can regard Patinkin as having led the retreat in 1948. In his case, however, it was a partial retreat. He put forward the notion of 'unemployment *dis*equilibrium' and sought to explain the disequilibrium as due to the failure to adjust prices to expectations. The present reviewer's reply to that suggestion (published in this *Journal* in 1954) was to the effect that the price flexibility envisaged in 'classical' theory (as essential for the co-ordination of the economy) implies adjustments to changes in expectations as well as to changes in currently expressed demands. If such flexibility can be created (it was argued) prices may be fixed so that the full potential flow of productive services can become output (irrespective of the proportion of that output which is to be decumulated through consumption — immediately, in the near future, or in the distant future).

But in the symposium under review, we find Lerner obliquely disclaiming the unemployment equilibrium thesis, without reliance upon Patinkin's argument about expectations. With a surprising casualness, he dismisses the most crucial issue in the whole Keynesian controversy by the bland assertion that 'equilibrium' or 'disequilibrium' is "purely a matter of terminology" (p. 231).[10] We certainly cannot accept this. It is *not* just a question of terminology. If Keynes had merely elaborated the truth that price rigidities in face of changing circumstances create disequilibrium, his followers could not have told a credulous world that a shattering new insight of an economist of genius had wrought a revolution in thought.

Similarly Samuelson, describing the unemployment equilibrium thesis as "revolution not evolution, . . . the most shocking view in the *General Theory*", which brought "Smith's Invisible Hand under direct attack", says that "what is most shocking in a book is not necessarily most important and lasting. Had Keynes begun his first few chapters with the simple statement that he found it realistic to assume that modern capitalistic societies had money wage rates that were sticky and resistant to downward price movements, most of his insights would have remained just as valid" (p. 332). The impression left by this passage is wholly unacceptable. The retreat that Samuelson is now admitting by implication is much more judiciously recorded by Haberler who contends that "it is now almost generally recognised that the Keynesian theoretical system proper . . . depends on the assumption of wage rigidity. If that assumption is not made, the Keynesian system simply breaks down" (p. 291). "As soon as we assume wage rigidity and wage push, . . . the main difference between Keynes and the classics disappears, and with it vanishes what many Keynesians regard as Keynes' greatest achievement — the demonstration of the possibility of underemployment equilibrium"[11] (p. 293).

During a period of sabbatical leave in 1949, the reviewer tried unsuccessfully to get some of the Keynesians at the London School of Economics to admit that, in the light of Modigliani's criticism,[12] the propositions of the *General Theory* would have to depend solely upon the assumption of wage-rate (or price) rigidity. He could get no frank agreement on this point; but he was asked by Hayek to write a paper on the topic which he read to the Mont Pelerin Society in June of that year.[12] During a subsequent leave, in 1956, after having circulated copies of his 1954 article on *The Significance of Price Flexibility*, which appeared in this *Journal*, he still failed to elicit any unequivocal admission that the unemployment equilibrium thesis had to be abandoned.

There is, however, a wider retreat from Keynesiansism than that caused directly by the collapse of its chief logical support. This is well reflected in Leckachman's Introduction. He says (about the contributions he has edited): "What is notable" is that, with the exception of Samuelson's article, "they have comparatively little to do with Keynesian diagnoses"; and he refers to the revival, in the 1960's, of the "venerable gold standard justification of internal deflation", although, "few are willing to argue for the concomitant wage and price reductions" (p. 4). He refers also, just as though he was writing in 1930-31, to "frictional impediments which represent labour market imperfections", and to "the behaviour of exactly those large economic units whose activities are so imperfectly comprehended within the Keynesian economic framework". He agrees that, "by abstracting from the degree of competition, Keynes in fact denied the importance of variations in market organisation to the workings of his apparatus" (p. 4).

It has, I suggest, been the actual course of contemporary experience rather than academic criticism which has begun to destroy Keynesian faith in the doctrines of the *General Theory*. Yet I do not observe that any of the contributors to Leckachman's symposium has perceived (or at any rate referred to) the chief reason for the counter-revolution which is now taking place. The gradual inflation on which the Keynesians have, in the past, placed so much reliance has become purposeless because it has come to be expected. When the continuous depreciation of the money unit is anticipated, its crude co-ordinative virtues are lost. Entrepreneurs wishing to borrow must raise their interest offer; and wage-rates tend to rise *pari passu* with or even ahead of prices, largely because prospective yields are raised through the confidence of managements that inflationary expansion will justify higher prices. It has been for this reason, I suggest, that in spite of creeping inflation *and* a menacing build-up of latent inflation,[14] unemployment in the United States has averaged more than six per cent. and never fallen below five and a half per cent. since 1958 (until the early months of 1965). Unemployment of this intensity for so prolonged a period was, indeed, never experienced in the pre-Keynesian era. Small wonder that Lerner complains that in the "public discussion the balanced budget seems to have regained the reverence it enjoyed in 1931" (p. 223) and that "the ancient fallacies [the 'classical' fallacies] have been able to creep back on the stage, pretending that they are the new 'common-sense' " (p. 223).

Lerner blames this trend not on a growing recognition of the purposelessness of Keynesian policy (through its anticipation) but on the Keynesians who have laid themselves open to "Counter attack by their failure to look deeply enough at the nature of the weakness in the 'automatic tendencies' to full employment" (p. 228). He does not accuse them of failing to understand unemployment equilibrium but of misconceptions about the nature of price rigidities. He charges them with having wrongly believed that these rigidities "could be put right by monetary and fiscal 'aids', which, by quickly increasing (or decreasing) investment and consumption just when the automatic forces were trying to do this, would be acting only as amplifiers or servo-mechanisms to increase their power". But, he argues, "wages and prices are 'sticky downwards' . . . because they are not determined by the automatic forces of demand and supply but are decreed by individuals or committees who have the power to countermand the automatic market forces . . . (which are) *inhibited* by these men or committees who are wage and price *administrators*" (p. 228).

In the light of this passage, one feels almost that Lerner must be subtly ironic when he complains that the public is turning away from "Keynesian enlightenment to classical and pre-classical superstitions"; for he has himself re-stated as gospel exactly the 'classical' beliefs that Keynes tried to upset! His approving re-assertion of the 'classical' position combined with expressions of hostility to it is, indeed, so confusing that the reviewer's impression of ironic intention became even greater on re-reading the essay. Or is it perhaps Lerner's 'tactic of persuasion' to represent his approval of 'classical' thought as an attack upon it? Does he (intuitively or shrewdly) feel that, unless he poses as an unrepentant Keynesian he will be denied a hearing?

Or does he simply wish to challenge the usual *policy inferences* from 'classical' theory? If so, we meet the difficulty that 'classical' *theory* does not automatically justify the rejection of his policy recommendations. He asks for the central determination of wage-rates and prices, the aim of the controls being to "make the administered prices move in something like the way prices would move in a perfectly competitive economy" (p. 230). He wishes, presumably, to bring wage-rates and prices down to the level at which they can restore the full flow of income. (The *implied* rejection of the unemployment equilibrium thesis is obvious.)

Now those who (like Lerner) have come to believe that the only practicable way to combat the perpetual tendency of labour unions to reduce the flow of uninflated wages and income is for *the State* to reduce wage-rates, are merely suggesting particular institutional arrangements for securing co-ordinative adjustments, the need for which has been exposed by 'pure theory'.[15] 'Classical' economists will, we think, reject one facet only of Lerner's proposals *on purely theoretical grounds*. We refer to his insistence that the central price administrators "would pay as little attention to profits or losses as is paid by the forces of demand in a perfectly competitive market" (p. 230). Unless he means by this something quite different from what most readers will understand, the older economists would certainly have rejected it. Surely, in a 'perfectly competitive market', i.e., in the ideal co-ordination which Lerner is envisaging, the costs of all inputs (whether for replacement or net accumulation) will be incurred in the expectation of output values which exceed the costs by more than the rate of interest on input values. That is simply another way of saying that all truly co-ordinative investment decisions are motivated by the prospect of profits (or the avoidance of losses) on all increments of input. But if Lerner merely means by the passage quoted that the controls he proposes would aim at being as ruthless as market-expressed competition in reducing such capital values as have been inflated by contrived scarcity, he will encounter no 'classical' opposition on this score. The dissolution of contrived scarcity in respect of any activity, having reduced the prospective income stream from that activity (and hence its present discounted value), will in no way weaken the co-ordinative force of the profit incentive.

The objection of most economists who accept the 'classical' analysis to Lerner's proposals will otherwise be based, I believe, not on dissatisfaction with the *theoretical* arguments he now presents but on a difference in practical judgement, namely, that centrally administered prices are *less* likely to reflect natural scarcities, as distinct from contrived scarcities, than those determined when entrepreneurial decision-making is subjected — as far as is practicable — to the social discipline of the *free* market. Such critics will feel that Lerner *tacitly assumes* that a discipline similar to — or even more effective than — the loss-avoidance, profit-seeking sanctions will restrain the politicians, or the officials subject to them, when they make pricing decisions. *Typical* 'classical' economists will, therefore, think along quite different lines. They will attempt to envisage the institutional changes needed to create *market* freedom. Some believe for instance (and they have *prima facie* a very strong case) that the application of the United States anti-trust laws to the whole economy, instead of to the politically weak sector alone, would be quite sufficient not only to eliminate tendencies to unemployment in the absence of inflation but to create greater social justice.[16] But for nearly three decades economists have been inhibited from dispassionate study of the relative merits of the two approaches, or of the complementarity of collective and market initiatives, precisely because the 'Keynesian revolution' following 1936 erected the 'unemployment equilibrium' barrier.

Paul Sweezy's position is not essentially different from Lerner's on this issue; but he claims to remain both a Keynesian and a Marxist; he still gives Keynes credit for "freeing economics from the tyranny of Say's Law, and exploding the myth of capitalism as a self-adjusting system . . .;" yet he retracts as 'misleading' his (Sweezy's) 1946 assertion that Keynes' analysis "shows that depression and unemployment . . . are the norms to which the economy tends" (p. 305). Keynes actually believed, Sweezy now claims, that the self-adjustment process does not work owing to defects in "the structure of the system". Given the structure, he says, Keynes "gave reasons (essentially downward rigidity of wages and interest rates) why it could not generate full employment in the absence of a strong inducement to invest" (p. 306).[17] But this is not unemployment equilibrium! On the contrary, the passage tacitly admits the self-adjustment process, with the simple qualification that the 'structure' may be such that its frustration is permitted.

How, then, can Sweezy still cling to the unemployment equilibrium idea and the inference from it that the Say Law must be rejected? He tries now to rely wholly and entirely upon price and wage-rate rigidity, and especially upon the influence of 'administered' prices. Accepting Berle and Means' emphasis on the domination of the economy by huge corporations, he argues that "by no stretch of the imagination" can they "be assumed to behave like the entrepreneurs of classical and neoclassical theory" (p. 308). Yet that was not *Keynes'* argument at all. If it had been, and if the pre-Keynesian 'classical' writers had accepted that the realities were, indeed, as Berle and Means represent them, they would have agreed with Keynes' diagnosis even though they might have rejected his prescription. For even if modern corporations do possess and abuse an arbitrary power, effectively uncontrollable by anti-trust, such as Berle and Means contend, that does not amount to a 'contradiction' of the Say Law 'by every day experience', as Sweezy asserts in 1963 (p. 309). On the contrary, it illustrates that Law. The withdrawal of the supply of any type of valuable output is the withdrawal of a source of demands for non-competing output.

Curiously enough, in a recent attack on the United States Steel industry, G.C. Means, who builds on his joint work with Berle, promises a future study of how the exercise of the large corporations' power to 'administer' prices, "*prevents the operation* of Say's Law and accounts for wide swings in business activity".[18] And if certain 'classical' economists (Sweezy calls them 'bourgeois economists'), such as Petersen, reject the view that the large corporations are to blame for pricing part of the potential output beyond reach of uninflated income, again that is due to their practical judgement about the effects.[19] It is significant that Sweezy does not mention the power of the labour unions exerted *through* the great American corporations. Yet, to take the case of the United States Steel Corporation, in 1964 its employees received $1,795 million and its stockholders $135.5 million with $103.3 million being ploughed back.[20] If it is borne in mind also that its purchases were $1,404.8 million, what *measure* of responsibility for price rigidity can be attributed to concern for interest of stockholders? Only if, through the privileged position of organised labour, the managements of the great corporations have been somehow coerced into acting as agents for the unions can Sweezy's thesis be defended. It should be easy to determine whether, in depression, the residual claims of stockholders decline less rapidly than the contractual receipts of employees. But to the extent to which Keynes himself based his argument upon rigidities in exchange values, it was the adverse effect of wage-rate rigidities upon the marginal efficiency of capital — prospective profits — which he blamed for unemployment.

Reddaway's position is less clear. But he also *seems* to suggest that when Keynes "accused the classical economists of assuming that the economic system contained within itself some force which would produce continuous full employment" (pp. 115-6), he was assuming that governments were impassive in respect of the factors which (presumably by keeping wage-rates and prices too high) are creating unemployment. At any rate, that is the interpretation I place on Reddaway's rather puzzling phrase: "Full employment is neither guaranteed by the automatic working of the system, nor yet an implausible assumption to take as first approximation, since the government may well make this a high-priority objective" (p. 116). But Reddaway himself discusses the 'managed economy' with no reference at all to the fundamental question of co-ordination through relative prices.

Champernowne takes a quite different line. He admits that "the argument on which Keynes himself most relied" (pp. 190-1) — "the main object" of the *General Theory* — "may be regarded as that of refuting the thesis that the cause of heavy unemployment is the insistence by wage earners on high real wages" (p. 175).[21] He says that "even if money wages" (meaning money wage-rates) "were flexible, this would not cure unemployment but would *cause violent instability*" (p. 176, our italics). This formulation shifts the argument from a charge that the reduction of those wage-rates which (in depression) are pricing output out of range of income would aggravate instead of relieve *unemployment*, to the charge that the ability and willingness of producers to adjust money values so as to permit the full utilisation of demanded productive services must somehow *create instability*. Flexibility would not, argues Champernowne, allow "an orderly return to full employment" but "would result in the economy being driven either to a state of reckless inflation with money wages, prices, effective demand, and (initially) employment all shooting up, or else to a state of panic with money wages, prices, employment, and effective demand plunging into a bottomless sink. [Keynes] regarded the relative stability actually found in the economic system as being due to the stickiness of money wages" (p. 191). Presumably, this is an admission that downward adjustments *can* restore full employment in a depressed economy but in a *disorderly* way, the full employment condition being highly unstable.

It is true that there are passages in the *General Theory* which would justify the last sentence quoted; but they contradict other passages in which, as a second line of defence, Keynes fell back upon the same stickiness to explain unemployment and depression. And it is this same stickiness which an increasing number of Keynesians are now blaming for the alleged instabilities of the so-called 'free market' economy. The rift in the Keynesian camp could hardly be greater.

Pre-Keynesian 'classical' economists are sometimes accused of having believed that a prolonged period of severe unemployment or under-employment can alone provide the incentives required for the co-ordinative adjustment of wage-rates. They certainly *did* believe that recession creates entrepreneurial opportunities for the profitable utilisation of potentially valuable, under-utilised or idle capacity. But they recognised also that these incentives could be frustrated by legal enactment or the private coercive power of collusion (or possibly an element of 'natural monopoly' which is inherent when large-scale operations are economic). They did *not* hold that policy should be passive in respect of such obstacles to co-ordination.

Now, rather paradoxically, we find *soi-disant* Keynesians arguing that, in the contemporary institutional set-up, unemployment *has* a sort of disciplinary purpose. Lerner contends, for instance, that as communities become richer, "the greater becomes the intensity of unemployment needed to prevent prices from rising. Only when unemployment exceeds this degree of intensity is the market strong enough to overcome the power of the wage and price administrators and induce price revisions . . ." Even under expansionist monetary and fiscal policy "the operating automatic tendency . . . is for employment to move not towards *full employment* . . . but toward the *price stability level of employment* . . . [at less than full employment] . . . where the market forces tending to reduce prices are just able to balance the administrors' efforts to raise them" (p. 229).

But the failure of orthodox Keynesian monetary and fiscal measures to prevent chronic unemployment is not due to growth in the wealth of communities. It is due to the concensus of expectations about the speed and duration of inflationary policy, combined with the right of those who can shield themselves against market discipline to exploit the price mechanism for private advantage. Admittedly, persistent unemployment of labour (with idleness in other resources) acts as a deterrent to rising labour union claims and monopolistic pricing generally, and it probably strengthens the ability and willingness of managements to protect their customers (the consumers to whom they are, of course, ultimately responsible) against exploitation by organised labour. However, what is most important about the argument we have been discussing is its tacit admission of Keynesian error in logic and inefficacy in policy.

Samuelson makes very much the same point as Lerner, but he does not frankly admit (as does Lerner) the break-down in practice of monetary and fiscal measures to maintain employment, and he is deliberately non-committal in respect of suggested reforms. "I leave all this as an open question," he says. And referring to proposals for meeting the dilemmas caused by anticipation of inflation, he comments, in what reads like a sort of jocular cynicism: "Conservatives say, 'Treat labour rough. Legislate and prosecute. Bargain hard . . . ' Radicals say, 'Use direct price and wage controls . . . ' Optimists in between say, 'Be clever. Think up new devices which preserve freedom, prosperity, and price flexibility' . . . " (p. 340).

This is hardly a responsible manner in which to deal with the great problem at issue. Is it not obvious that we are now compelled to think out afresh the permissible role and scope of collective bargaining? We need to re-examine, I suggest, without preconceptions or inhibitions imposed by political loyalties, whether the private use of coercive power is the only effective method, or a tolerable method, of protecting employees from managerial tyranny or monopsonistic exploitation (by corporate managements acting individually or in collusion).

The line that Samuelson is taking as an adviser to the Treasury and the President of the United States is by no means as neutral as the phrase "I leave all this as an open question" would suggest. He is now advocating "some degree of price increase", as the cost to be incurred for a reduction of unemployment.[22] He does not specify the speed or duration of the inflation he advocates. But if his advice is followed, it must inevitably entail more stringent exchange controls, other restrictions on the market economy and an accelerated trend in the totalitarian direction.

In spite of the ignominious failure of the policies which Keynes seemed to have made respectable, his disciples are, not surprisingly, reluctant to recommend their abandonment. They are now tending to defend Keynesianism by attacking the old 'classical' precepts of 'balanced budgets' and 'sound money', as though those precepts defined the whole scope of alternative policy; and they do so by scornful references and unintended misrepresentations. Thus, Reddaway (saying that he is going to discuss "the effects of increased thrift", but going on to discuss "the effects of a decreased readiness to spend . . ." (p. 113), under the assumption of a closed system) imagines the consequences of a policy involving "a balanced budget and a stable quantity of money", the economy being left "to look after itself". He remarks that "it may seem fanciful to younger readers to imagine that a government might react in this way" (whether towards increased thrift or an increased demand for money is not clear) and says that "the British Labour Government adopted just such a policy in its 1931 budget, which it presented with a great display of self-righteousness" (p. 113 and pp. 114-5n). But Reddaway ought to have told his younger readers that what was 'fanciful' about that policy was not Britain's adherence to the policy of keeping faith (for no other monetary policy could, in then existing circumstances, have saved sterling) but the policy of subsidizing idleness and passively permitting, in Beatrice Webb's words, recorded in her diary at that very time, "the sabotage of British industry by trade union pigheadedness".

Pre-Keynesian 'classical' economics no more condemned governmental borrowing as such than it condemned business borrowing. But deficit spending *is* all too frequently the concomitant of inflationary policy; and in the days when it was thought conducive to the efficient co-ordination of the economy for the economic measuring rod — the money unit — to have a defined permanent value, a period of inflation implied ultimate resort either to rectifying deflation or the bankruptcy of the credit system (devaluation). The essence of 'sound money' was simply the honouring of the maxim, "we must keep faith with those whom we have persuaded to accept our word that we shall convert at the agreed parity".[23]

Unfortunately, nearly all discussions of Keynesian fiscal policy appear to be grounded in error through the assumption that taxation is deflationary and the remission of taxation inflationary. The fallacy here is an exact parallel of the equally false notion that saving is deflationary and consumption inflationary. But an increase in taxation *may* lead to a reduced wish to consume (a reduced wish, by private persons and the State, to decumulate the stock of assets which is in process of concurrent replacement or growth), and hence, *ceteris paribus*, to a fall in the 'natural' level of interest, so that any existing unchanged market rate of interest will become deflationary. This is the cause of the confusion.

We have emphasized here the evidence afforded in the symposium of a general retreat from the most revolutionary thesis in the *General Theory*. But a host of subsidiary fallacies can be identified at different places in the book reviewed.[24] Nearly all of them have served, by obscuring fundamental issues, to perpetuate the crucial unemployment equilibrium error: confusion between the determinants of the rate of interest and the determinants of its deviation from the 'natural' level; confusion of expenditure with consumption; confusion of expenditure with demand; confusion of expenditure with income generation; confusion of the act of saving with the entrepreneurial act of determining the form in which assets shall be replaced or accumulated; confusion of saving-preference with liquidity-preference (in the broad sense of demand for the services of money); confusion between inflation and expansion (growth); seriously defective concepts of savings and investment as independent magnitudes; fallacious notions that the 'administrative' (as distinct from the market) fixing of wage-rates and prices can cause inflation or deflation, or that the imposition or lifting of taxation can itself exert a deflationary or inflationary influence, or that saving is deflationary and consumption inflationary, or that money rationally retained has a yield of *nil*, or that the source of demands can be found in consumption rather than in production, or that income consists of money receipts instead of being the money valuation of output;[25] fallacious models such as the multiplier and the accelerator; and the failure to perceive the simple truth that the real value of the money unit (and hence the money valuation of income) is a matter either of contract or of discretion (i.e., of monetary policy responding to demand for the services of money).

Every one of these fallacies or defective concepts, which the reviewer has attempted elsewhere to expose,[26] is to be discerned in the Keynesian contributions to the symposium we have been discussing; and each has, we believe, played some part in rendering plausible and perpetuating the unemployment equilibrium thesis. It has done so through clouding understanding of the nature of changing economic preferences and the operation of the mechanism of response in an exchange economy. But although they have hindered, they have not prevented a growing perception that the notion of price adjustments being self-frustrating must be abandoned and the Say Law once again accepted as the most fundament of all economic principles. In his 1946 contribution Sweezy admitted that "the Keynesian attacks, though they appear to be directed against a variety of specific theories, all fall to the ground if the validity of Say's Law is assumed" (p. 300). Here, we believe Sweezy to have been right. But the subsidiary fallacies we have just listed are likely, for an unpredictable period, to continue to hinder both logical analysis and efforts at constructive policy thinking. Through the force of intellectual fashion and awe of authority, models and constructions which derive meaning only from the unemployment equilibrium thesis will probably continue to dominate the teaching of economics in most universities at least for the next decade.

We conclude, in Haberler's words, that although "it is now almost generally recognised that . . . what many Keynesians regard as Keynes' great achievement . . . vanishes" (pp. 291 and 293), the retreat is still in progress. The Keynesians have lost a critical battle in the warfare of ideas, but the mopping up process is unlikely to be short.

Notes

1. Macmillan, 1964, 30s. net.
2. We discuss the 'force' which is compelling their admission on p. 9.
3. This is, of course, a heroic over-simplification. We have to explain why services priced out of one utilisation do not seek or find alternative employment in less productive utilisations. This is discussed fully in the writer's *Theory of Idle Resources,* particularly on pp. 139-140.
4. The word 'preference' must be taken to cover *inter alia* time-preference, liquidity-preference, risk-preference and leisure-preference.
5. Logically, this means, although the Keynesians do not seem to understand the meaning, expenditure on replacement *plus* net accumulation of assets.
6. See the reviewer's article in this *Journal,* June, 1964, p. 84, n.
7. The *General Theory* was, of course, contradictory on this point. In January, 1939, a liberal-minded Keynesian convert in London, to refute the writer's forecasts, indignantly referred him to the enigmatical last chapter with its approving references to 'classical doctrine'.
8. By 1944, Beveridge (or his advisers whose ideas he presented) was prepared to admit and defend the totalitarian implications.
9. McCord Wright's challenge of 1945 was more general and, I feel, an attempt rather to rehabilitate than attack Keynesianism. Nevertheless it was an important factor in the gradual emergence of a scepticism which Keynesian leaders could not ignore.
10. Lerner's actual words are: " . . . less-than-full-employment-equilibrium (or disequilibrium for this is purely a matter of terminology) . . . " (p. 231).
11. Haberler shows, incidentally, that "growth theory has . . . slowly and laboriously worked its way back to the classical position" (p. 293).
12. Modigliani, "Liquidity Preference and the Theory of Interest and Money," *Econometrica,* Jan. 1944.
13.. When the reviewer wrote that paper, he had not read through to Haberler's sceptical article in *The New Economics* (Ed. Harris) which had been published in the U.K. in 1948.
14. In the form of an enormous accumulation of time deposits, semi-liquid funds in building societies and other finance institutions, consumer indebtedness, hire purchase debt and mortgage indebtedness.
15. Thus, the reviewer himself has, for more than thirty years, always defined competition as "the substitution of the least-cost method of achieving any economic objective, *irrespective of the institutional arrangements which may be necessary to achieve that method*". Curiously enough, a discussion with Lerner in 1933, already referred to in this *Journal* (March, 1954), inspired this definition.
16. Especially if suspicions of political discrimination on the prosecution side could be removed.
17. Sweezy admits that Keynes did not explain "why the inducement to invest should be

chronically weak" (p. 306), such reasons as he did suggest being poor theory and superficial history (p. 307).

18.   G.C. Means, *Pricing Power and the Public Interest: A Study Based on Steel*, p. xx (our italics).

19.   W. H. Petersen, *Steel Price Administration: Myth and Reality,* in Shoeck & Wiggins (Eds.), *Central Planning and Mercantilism.*

20.   U.S. Steel Corporation, *1964 Annual Report*, p. 29.

21.   Champernowne's formulation reflects conceptual confusion or loose writing which happens seriously to misrepresent the 'classical' thesis that Keynes attacked. The older economists believed that the forcing up of wage-rates *reduced* real *wages*, in the sense of the flow of wages, and hence reduced the average earnings of labour. When they thought of wage-rates (the prices of different kinds of labour) having been fixed too high they envisaged 'wages' as having been forced too low.

22.   Quoted by G.C. Wiegand in the *Commercial and Financial Chronicle*, March 4th, 1965.

23.   President Johnson is reported recently to have referred to that system as one "which brought us all to disaster in the early 1930's". That is what his advisers told him. Actually it is the biggest libel of a beneficent institution in economic history.

24.   They are mostly, but not entirely, Keynesian fallacies.

25.   'Real income' also having meaning only as a *money* valuation — in terms of an abstractly conceived unit of constant 'real value'.

26.   *Keynesianism — Retrospect and Prospect.*

106

Keynes After Thirty Years (with Special Reference to the United States)*

A.H. Hansen

I The Challenge to Neo-classicism

In the early nineteenth century the great economic dualists were Ricardo and Malthus. In our century it was Keynes versus Pigou. In his *Retrospective View of Keynes's General Theory*, Professor Pigou paid high tribute to Keynes[1]. "Nobody before him, so far as I know," said Pigou, "had brought all the relevant factors, real and monetary at once, together in a single formal scheme, through which their interplay could be coherently investigated." Professor Pigou singled out the following paragraph from Chapter 18 of the *General Theory* as the kernel of Keynes's contribution to economic thinking[2]: "Thus we can sometimes regard our ultimate independent variables as consisting of (1) the three fundamental psychological factors, namely, the psychological propensity to consume, the psychological attitude to liquidity and the psychological expectation of future yield from capital assets, (2) the wage-unit as determined by the bargains reached between employers and employed, and (3) the quantity of money as determined by the action of the central bank; so that, if we take as given the factors specified above, these variables determine the national income (or dividend) and the quantity of employment."

Here we have the investment multiplier, the marginal efficiency of investment schedule, the consumption function, the liquidity preference schedule, the quantity of money, and the wage unit (the back-bone of the price level). "This summary statement," said Pigou, "contains . . . Keynes's main and very important contribution to economic analysis"[3]. And he added that were he not afraid his audience might feel insulted, he would read it over again.

With the battery of weapons so brilliantly outlined in Chapter 18, and

*Source: *Weltwirtschaftliches Archiv*, Vol. 97, Hft 2, 1966, pp. 213-31.

more fully expounded in the volume as a whole, Keynes undertook the herculean task of attempting to demolish not indeed the micro-economics of neo-classicism — this Keynes accepted in full — but rather the neo-classical sophisticated mystique of automatic adjustment of wages and interest rates — the mechanism, it was believed, by which the self-sustaining economy tended to produce full employment.

The great virtue of Keynes's work, as also of the giant classicals — Adam Smith, Ricardo, Malthus, and Mill — was the grand magnificent sweep which it gave us of the overall determining forces at work in the economy. Neo-classicism had descended from the lofty mountain tops of the great classicals to the lower ground in search for petty details in an effort to cement minor cracks in a vast superstructure. Though not altogether without merit, this had directed the attention of economists away from the great issues. Pigou himself characterized the neo-classicism of 1936 as follows[4]: "After Marshall's main work was finished, economic thought on fundamental issues moved little, at all events in this country. We were pedestrians, perhaps a little complacent. Keynes's *Treatise on Money* and later his *General Theory* broke resoundingly that dogmatic slumber. Whether in agreement or disagreement with him discussion and controversy sprang up and spread over the whole world. Economics and economists came alive. The period of tranquillity was ended. A period of active, and, so far as might be, creative thought was born. For this the credit is almost wholly due to Keynes."

The shift in emphasis from analysis of price effects to analysis of income effects stimulated statistical research throughout the world. Econometric studies of the consumption function, the investment multiplier, liquidity preference opened up rich fields for empirical work. The empty boxes were progressively filled, not just hit and miss in the hope that a mere accumulation of facts might turn up something, but within the meaningful pattern of the Keynesian theoretical structure. New analytical insights pointed the way to the areas where empirical research might be rewarding.

The neo-classicism of the early nineteenth century had become a powerful resistant to social and economic reform. Economic analysis could usually be counted upon to show why novel proposals (whether guarantees of bank deposits or social security or other "common-sense" programs) were unworkable and rested on a misunderstanding of an intricate self-regulating mechanism. Confronted with the overwhelming problems of the great depression, neo-classical economics stood helpless. Since the turn of the century it had become largely an escape from reality.

To this, however, one important qualification must be made. Following the publication of Mitchell's *Business Cycles*[5] in 1913, great interest, both theoretical and statistical, had been aroused in the problem of economic fluctuations. But the contributions of Mitchell and his followers were primarily statistical. The most significant theoretical advances in this area had already appeared in the work of continental writers —

Tugan-Baranowski, Spiethoff, Wicksell, Schumpeter, Aftalion[6].

With respect to business cycle *policy*, the leading innovators were Wicksell, Irving Fisher, and Keynes — the Keynes of the Monetary Reform[7] and the Treatise[8]. These men constituted the "avant garde" of economic thinking — neo-classical rebels, so-to-speak, who ventured to challenge the thesis that the economy had best be left to the automatic functioning of a laissez-faire system. Instead they proposed deliberate control of the monetary mechanism through the Central Bank as a means of ironing out the cycle. Yet this break-away from the rigid neo-classical orthodoxy did not strike deeply at the basic thesis of a self-sustaining economy. Central bank control of the money supply and the rate of interest spelled no serious government intrusion into the aggregate spending stream. The role of government, properly speaking, was not affected.

A number of bold explorers into the dangerous territory of macro-economics could possibly be counted in a loose sense as fore-runners of Keynes. All had, however, been laughed out of court. To enter the fray anew took courage. Keynes foresaw quite clearly that his opponents would make an effort to class him with the cranks that had already fallen by the wayside. He therefore deliberately brought this aspect of the matter out into the open by writing a discerning and illuminating chapter on Mandeville, Malthus, Hobson and Gesell. All these had tried their hand at macro-economics, but all had miserably failed to meet the onslaught of orthodox theory. A good neo-classicist could always show that these rebels just did not understand the intricacies of sophisticated economics. Nobody but a fool or a superman with supreme confidence in his own skill, and in the armor he had donned for the fray, would dare to attack the firmly established orthodoxy. Even so notable a theorist as Aftalion, though respected for his masterly work on business cycles, had been brushed aside by British and American reviewers for his attack on Say's law.

Keynes, supremely confident of his own competence as a good classicist and in his academic credentials, was not a man to fear a good fight. He expected it and was prepared. Time and again one is impressed with the skill with which he anticipated the shafts of his critics. Time and again the answer could already be found in the *General Theory*.

That it took the courage of a superb master of his subject is, however, by no means self-evident to the present generation of young economists who wonder what the noise was all about. Keynes's antagonists were sure that he was quite wrong, but the present generation finds it difficult to believe that he said anything new.

II Early Stages in the Great Debate

On New Year's day, 1935, in a letter to George Bernard Shaw, Keynes wrote[9]: "I believe myself to be writing a book on economic theory which will largely revolutionize — not, I suppose, at once but in the course of the next ten years — the way the world thinks about economic problems."

The progress of the Keynesian revolution over the past three decades can perhaps best be traced by taking account of the changing character of the opposition he aroused. Keynesian doctrines in the first stage had to face complete and total opposition. Then step by step, the critics retreated more or less from ground formerly held. Finally in the third stage they became in effect the "Loyal Opposition." That this last stage has by now been reached in the United States must have been apparent to anyone who attended the recent Washington Celebration of the twentieth anniversary of the Employment Act of 1946. Once this last stage is reached the oft-heard phrase "We are all Keynesians now" begins to have at least some measure of real content and meaning.

Already by 1950 the "loyal opposition" stage had been reached in academic circles[10]. But it took another decade before that stage was reached in the United States in the area of practical politics.

The United Nations Monetary and Financial Conference of forty-four nations at Bretton Woods in July, 1944, marks one milestone in the Keynesian revolution. No one attending that conference could fail to note the breath of fresh air in an intellectual climate permeated with Keynesian thinking. Keynes was the commanding figure, the guiding architect. His great prestige had won over the British Treasury without which there would have been no Bretton Woods.

A new role of government — this was the resounding note that dominated the Conference. Deliberate governmental policy was to supplant the automatic functioning of the economy.

Shortly before the Bretton Woods Conference the British government had issued (May, 1944) a pioneering White Paper on Employment Policy[11]. Keynes was indeed the Treasury economist, but the White Paper, it must not be forgotten, was a government document, and as such it disclosed cautious restraint. A bolder statement, untrammeled by Treasury traditions, was issued in June, 1944, under the name of Sir William Beveridge[12], though the volume was in fact a cooperative effort in which a number of brilliant Cambridge University Keynesians had participated. And finally, in October, 1944, six young economists of the Oxford Institute of Statistics issued the Economics of Full Employment — a thoroughgoing Keynesian document[13].

Immediately after the publication of the *General Theory*, numerous critical articles began to appear in the scientific journals, notably in England and America. Keynes, as editor of the world renowned *Economic Journal*, kept a sharp eye on the debates and wasted little time in answering his critics.

Also in the United States the pot was boiling. A hot debate was initiated by the Hearings in May, 1939, before the Temporary National Economic Committee of the Congress of the United States[14] — the so-called TNEC. The

Committee invited me to lead off in the Hearings on Saving and Investment[15], and I used this occasion to expound the Keynesian analysis of the great depression from which we were still suffering. This analysis was supplemented by statistical materials presented by Laughlin Currie, then Assistant Director of the Division of Research and Statistics of the Board of Governors of the Federal Reserve System.

Keynes's *General Theory* had already in the preceding two years occupied the center of the stage in the Fiscal Policy Seminar (conducted by John H. Williams[16] and myself) at Harvard University. Government economists not infrequently participated in this seminar, and it became the center from which Keynesian thinking spread to other universities[17]. But it was the Hearings before the TNEC that opened the debate in Washington and before the general public. There emerged vigorous discussion in the public press, in the weekly and monthly magazines (e.g. *Fortune* Magazine, New York) and in the scientific economic journals. The new Keynesian doctrines met sharp opposition.

The British White Paper, alluded to above, represented a major change in official thinking. The Report affirmed the belief that the maintenance of an adequate level of expenditures in goods and services may no longer be realized automatically. At the onslaught of the 1930 depression the British government had, it should be remembered, instituted an economy program. Curtailment, less spending, more saving — these were the pre-Keynesian remedies for depression and unemployment. The White Paper in sharp contrast stated that "the first step in a policy of maintaining general employment must be to prevent total expenditure . . . from falling away"[18].

Clearly all this involved a sharp break with two main principles that had guided governments in the past; first, that government expenditures should be kept down to the barest minimum; and second, that government income and expenditure should be balanced[19]. The governments' role was to be that of complete neutrality, leaving the field for the automatic functioning of the economy. These principles, if violated, would, it was believed, destroy confidence. The "confidence argument" remains to this day as an obstacle to progressive reform[20].

Canada issued two notable documents in April and August 1945 — just within Keynes's ten-year forecast[21]. The government declared it was not only prepared to accept large deficits but will "deliberately plan for them in periods of threatened unemployment." The "modern governmental budget must be a balance-wheel of the economy."

III The U.S. Employment Act of 1946

In the United States as elsewhere world shaking events were stirring men's minds. The devastating depression, the expenditures incurred in the Second

World War, the sky-rocketing public debt paradoxically parallelled by a vast increase in private and business savings — all this shook orthodox preconceptions. Before the war conventional financial wisdom opined that the Federal government could not float more than a 2-billion-dollar bond issue. The war raised the ante. Within five years over 200 billion dollars of U.S. securities had been absorbed. Mental horizons were being widened.

It was in this new milieu of public opinion coupled with the dreadful memory of the great depression and the fear that this could happen again that the Employment Act of 1946 was passed.

President Roosevelt had already outlined an economic bill of rights in his State of the Union message of January, 1944 — the right to have "a useful and remunerative job"[22]. Governor Dewey, Republican candidate for President, said in his Seattle speech in September, 1944[23]: "If at any time there are not sufficient jobs in private employment to go around, the government can and must create job opportunities because there must be jobs for all in this country of ours." Campaign speeches are, however, no guarantee of governmental responsibility. This required an Act of Congress. The Murray Full Employment Bill of 1945 went all the way. But the Employment Act of 1946 as passed softened the language so as to blunt the assumption of full governmental responsibility for full employment.

The Employment Act did indeed represent a modest step toward counter-cyclical fiscal policy. Still the Congress remained highly conservative, and the influential press was strongly anti-Keynesian. Congress was caught up in a dilemma. War-time expenditures had indeed brought undreamed of prosperity. But in war-time "all bets are off," and one could not believe that such things can go on forever. Peace-time reform measures, even social security, were regarded with suspicion. The New Deal seemed to many to violate the "natural order." How to reconcile the two goals of "fiscal integrity" and full employment remained unresolved.

The 1946 Employment Act is studiously vague. It can mean all things to all men. Its real importance is the machinery it set up — The President's Annual Economic Report, the Council of Economic Advisers, and the Joint Economic Committee of the Congress[24]. This institutional setup compelled discussion and debate.

Ever since the Second World War the American economy has done moderately well compared with earlier times. This may, however, have had little to do with the Employment Act or Keynesian economics. The post-war scarcities, the huge defense budget, the government contracts, the new technologies, the rapid population growth, the mass market for consumer durables of all kinds — these spontaneous forces, not government intervention, held the stage.

The post-war re-stocking boom came to a halt in 1948. There followed a period of uncertainty and indecision. Indeed in the sharp recession of 1949 (unemployment rising to 7.6 per cent in February, 1950) instead of a vigorous anti-recession policy, the President and his Council of Economic Advisers continued to be obsessed with the fear of inflation though actually prices had reached a peak in August, 1948, and continued to decline until the Korean war turned the tide. The famous tax cut of 1948 (engineered by Senator Taft, who was certainly no Keynesian) was vigorously opposed both by the President and his economic advisers. In July, 1949, the Council stated with apparent pride that it had not urged anti-cyclical federal spending. Instead the Council (not unlike a later Council under Eisenhower) stressed "its confidence in the internal recuperative forces"[25]. At the depth of the recession the Report argued that the public debt should be reduced.

Congressional opinion remained overwhelmingly skeptical about enthroning fiscal policy as a major instrument of economic control. Outside of Congress, bankers, businessmen, and journalists continued their vigorous opposition to Keynesian economics.

The Korean war shifted the problem from depression to inflation. Orthodoxy and Keynesianism under these conditions tend to join hands though there remained sharp differences as to means. It is a pity that during the Korean episode the President's Economic Reports reverted to orthodox slogans about balanced budgets instead of giving the country a sophisticated discussion of the role of fiscal policy as the balance-wheel of the economy.

IV   The Eisenhower Administration and Fiscal Policy

Enter the Eisenhower Administration in January, 1953. Barely installed, a recession set in. Remembering the Hoover depression many feared the Republican return to power. Eisenhower hastened to re-assure the country. The government, he said, would use all its vast powers to prevent a depression.

The change of administration, after twenty years of Democratic rule, at first threatened the demise of the Employment Act of 1946. Powerful Republican opposition had developed to the entire set-up including the Council of Economic Advisers. President Eisenhower, however, stood firm. Fortunately, Arthur Burns, highly respected and able spokesman for the moderate conservatists, accepted the responsible position of chairman of the Council in this highly critical period.

In two earlier articles (the 1946 Annual Report of the National Bureau of Economic Research; and the Review of Economics and Statistics, November, 1947) Burns[26] had noted that the world had, following the publication of the *General Theory*, "moved swiftly in a Keynesian direction"[27]. He cited the epoch making announcement of the British White Paper and noted that also in the United States these ideas were being actively debated. He expressed doubt about the wisdom of these governmental pronouncements, fearful that in the existing state of economic knowledge, the governments might have assumed too great a responsibility. Later, as chairman of the CEA, he remained skeptical and preferred cautious and restrained governmental actions, confident that a vigorous economy would move forward largely on its own steam. Built-in automaticity, he favored. And he did not reject deliberate governmental intervention in the event of a threatened cumulative down-spin. Indeed the Council under his leadership acknowledged[28] that "unless the Government is prepared and willing to use its vast powers to help maintain employment and purchasing power, even a minor readjustment may be converted into a spiralling contraction." The once fashionable theory that a sharp liquidation was good for the economy could not be trusted.

The Council, moreover, accepted fiscal policy as a major policy weapon. The key to governmental planning for economic growth is, it said, the Federal budget. The Council recognized[29] that "automatic stabilizers cannot be counted on to do more than restrain either an upward or a downward tendency of the economy." In view of this limitation "the Government will not hesitate to make greater use of monetary, debt management, and credit policy, . . . or to reduce taxes, or to expand on a large scale the construction of useful public works, or to take any other steps that may be necessary."

The next Economic Report (January, 1955) was equally firm in the declaration[30] that the "Government will shoulder its full responsibility." Both these Reports were written in the closing months of 1953 and 1954 — in short against the background of the 1954 recession. The country was worried. These two Reports constitute the high water mark of Republican acceptance of fiscal policy as a necessary and effective anti-depression weapon.

The Joint Economic Committee enthusiastically welcomed both Reports. The Committee unanimously accepted the view that the Federal government may be called upon to act promptly and vigorously, accepting a deficit as the most appropriate fiscal policy.

Something had clearly happened. The Joint Economic Committee, composed of both Republicans and Democrats, was in a new mood. There was unanimous support for a strong positive fiscal program. The Committee was especially reassured to find an increasing acceptance in the President's Reports of "the theory that the balanced budget, 'hard money,' and reconstruction of the Federal debt structure are not to be regarded as ends in themselves"[31].

But now the tune changed. The President's January, 1956, Report reflected a swing toward orthodoxy. The economy had moved during the year 1955 into high prosperity. Confidence in the self-sustaining economy was revived. Once again the general tone tended to minimize the responsibility of government. Indeed it was argued that the Administration had kept the economy strong and growing by restricting government expenditures. No longer could we find re-assuring statements about compensatory fiscal policy. Both in the State of the Union message and in the Budget message, the balanced budget principle, not the compensatory principle, was set forth as the appropriate criterion for expenditures and tax policy.

The Joint Economic Committee was not slow to notice the new trend in the President's thinking. Especially significant is the fact that the Committee firmly re-stated its position that the basic guide to Federal fiscal policy should be the state of the national economy. The President, however, now plumped for the balanced budget. The Democratic members of the Committee bemoaned the fact that while the President's earlier Reports had represented progress in economic thinking, the January, 1956, Report was burdened throughout with strong political overtones. Fiscal orthodoxy was back in the saddle.

The Democratic members of the Committee re-iterated in a firm statement their belief[32] that "fiscal integrity, if it is not to be a hollow phrase, calls for using the Federal Government's fiscal powers deliberately in such a way as to minimize economic fluctuations from the path of steady growth." Referring specifically to the vigorously orthodox position taken by Secretary Humphrey, they noted that "the Secretary of the Treasury apparently does not now accept this generally held principle of fiscal policy."

Then came the severe recession of 1958. The economy shifted into a lower gear. Semi-stagnation and high unemployment rates were defended as necessary to combat inflation and the menacing deficit in the balance-of-payments. A tax cut had indeed been seriously considered in the spring of 1958. But as it turned out, the trough of the recession was reached in April, and the Administration took pride in the fact that a tax cut had apparently not been needed. It was in fact desperately needed to close the gap resulting from the geologic displacement, so to speak, that left the economy throughout 1958—63 some 40 to 50 billions of dollars below its potential capacity.

V An Intermediate Step Toward Keynesianism

In the meantime an educational process had been going on for some years led by liberal-minded businessmen (mostly moderate Republicans) who had organized in the late forties the Committee for Economic Development, known as the CED. The fiscal policy principles associated with this group amounted to a conservative version of Keynesianism. The Committee had already issued in November, 1947, a basic document on "Taxes and the Budget"[33]. It called for a tax structure which would balance the cash budget at "full employment." Expenditures would move on a trend line (not cyclically) and the tax rate structure also on a trend rate adjusted from time to time so as to balance accounts at full employment. Cyclically, reliance was placed on the built-in stabilizers. And finally a new dimension was added — the principle of marginal budget balancing.

All these formulations made obvious concessions to fiscal orthodoxy — a compromise which served as a useful bridge toward Keynesian thinking. Moderate in character, and couched in part in conventional terms, such a program could and did play an important educational role among men of affairs both in Congress and in business.

A manifesto on marginal budget balancing and built-in stabilizers — the so-called Princeton Manifesto[34] — had, moreover, been issued by leading economists in September, 1949. The substance of this manifesto was competently presented to the Joint Economic Committee, and its recommendations were embodied in the Douglas sub-committee report early in 1950[35]. This clearly helps to explain the advanced fiscal policy pronouncements in the Joint Economic Committee in 1954—55.

The CED program could easily be misinterpreted. Budgetary surpluses, generated by economic growth, were (so it seemed to say) to be eliminated by tax reduction. In fact, however, it is precisely in periods of surging spontaneous expansion that a budgetary surplus may be needed to restrain inflation. The true meaning of the CED program was that taxes should be set low enough so that the tax take would not dissipate the steam needed to produce full employment. If, however, the steam in the boiler exceeded or fell below this amount, taxes should in Keynesian theory be increased or reduced respectively. The CED was not altogether unaware of these matters, but public understanding often lagged behind.

Especially appealing was the emphasis on automaticity. Once installed, the built-in stabilizers and the agreed upon tax structure became a part of the "natural order." No bureaucrat would operate the mechanism. The economy would remain in effect self-sustaining.

This line of reasoning overlooks the fact that the system of built-in stabilizers rests upon a massive government budget — a budget big enough so that the automatically created deficits and surpluses can exert powerful countercyclical movements.

Two world wars in one generation together with a technological revolution with its concomitant upsurge of urbanization and population growth — all this had forced upon governments everywhere in the western world massive governmental expenditures. Fiscal policy could no longer remain an academic exercise. Keynesian thinking had arrived, one could say, just in time.

Keynes once complained that governments seemingly cannot be persuaded to spend except for war. Wars do indeed leave behind them the aftermath of enlarged budgets — the so-called "displacement effect." The War of 1812 raised U.S. federal expenditures from 0.6 per cent of aggregate national income before the war to 1.5 per cent after peace was restored; the Civil War to 3.0 per cent; World War I to 4.5 per cent; the great depression to 11.0 per cent; and World War II to 17.0 per cent[36]. U.S. defense expenditures increased from 11.6 billion dollars in 1948 to 50 billion dollars in 1965. In addition, urbanization and industrialization created pressures for increased outlays on social welfare. Federal government transfer payments (social security, grants to state and local governments) increased from 15.7 billion dollars in 1948 to 55.1 billion dollars in 1965. Defense and social welfare expenditures together have lifted the cash budget to a level at which the automatic swings of tax receipts and expenditures (notably the corporate taxes on the one side and the unemployment benefits on the other) exert a strong stabilizing influence upon the economy[37].

Equipped with a large budget and progressive federal tax system, automatic fiscal policy could now play a large role. This established fact made converts to a half-way Keynesian position. Automatic fiscal policy was welcomed but increases in the budget were deplored. President Eisenhower struggled to hold expenditures down. But the pressure was on. Cash expenditures grew from 70 billion dollars in 1954 to 95 billion dollars in 1960.

The moderate conservatists believed with Pigou that the basic economic problem is simply one of "lapses from full employment." The Keynesian view was that a continuous, sustained fiscal program is needed to insure stable growth at continuing full employment.

The 1961 argument between President Kennedy's Council of Economic Advisers and Arthur Burns about the so-called "gap" between actual and potential GNP illustrates the point. Burns' chief quarrel with the Council was, as he expressed it[38], that they seemed to lack "faith in the capacity of private enterprise to generate full employment." Hence, as he put it, "the Council has — quite logically — been urging active Federal intervention." This Burns believed unnecessary except to prevent a serious cumulative depression.

VI "The New Economics"

This brings us to the last stage in the progress of Keynesian thinking in the United States. The inauguration of President Kennedy introduced a new day in public acceptance of modern fiscal policy. A new group of convinced and highly competent Keynesians filled virtually all the important economic posts in Washington, including among others, the Council of Economic Advisers, the Bureau of the Budget, and the Treasury Department. Among the distinguished economists (to name only a few) who played a highly important role in the Kennedy-Johnson Administration were the following: Walter Heller, David Bell, J.K. Galbraith, Paul A. Samuelson, Seymour Harris, Kermit Gordon, Charles Schultze, Gardner Ackley, James Tobin, John P. Lewis, Otto Eckstein, Arthur Okun, James Duesenberry, and Robert Solow. A fruitful close contact was, moreover, maintained with leading economists outside of the government, notably Joseph Pechman and Walter Salant of the Brookings Institution and Gerhard Colm of the National

Planning Association. Seymour Harris, as Senior Economic Consultant at the Treasury Department, assembled monthly a group of some twenty (mostly university economists) for the discussion of fiscal and monetary problems confronting the Treasury.

Keynesian ideas were now for the first time in full bloom — twenty-five years after the appearance of the *General Theory*[39]. The Reports of the Council of Economic Advisers, the State of the Union Message and the Budget Message became for the first time genuine Keynesian documents. Lively ideas flooded almost every page. The "full-employment surplus," the "gap," the "fiscal drag," brilliantly illuminated by ingenious diagrams and charts, struck fire. The "new economics" was picked up by the leading newspapers and magazines. A process of public education began. Government documents became textbooks on fiscal policy. President Kennedy himself became, one might say, a professor of economics, as witness his famous Yale Commencement Address in June, 1962[40].

Yet as it turned out, the program that was put into effect could properly be called, as Professor Galbraith has pointed out, "conservative Keynesianism" with emphasis on tax reduction rather than on expenditures. Keynesian fiscal policy should aim to achieve three goals: (1) full employment, (2) stable growth with reasonably stable prices, and (3) optimum social priorities. The first two goals can be achieved reasonably well, as far as fiscal policy goes, by manipulating the tax structure. The third goal requires, especially in the United States, enormous increases in federal expenditures to correct the gross imbalance between the private and the public sector.

The spectacular expansionist policies of the Kennedy-Johnson Administration took the form of four tax reductions: (1) the investment tax credit of 1962, (2) the accelerated depreciation guide lines, (3) the famous tax cut of 1964, and (4) the 1965 cut in excises. It was of course notably the tax cut of 1964 that broke new ground by forestalling the historically anticipated recession and boosting the prolonged expansion to a 5.5 per cent growth rate.

A substantial tax cut in the midst of a good recovery and with the Administrative budget still in deficit represents a landmark in public thinking on economic problems. How did it happen?

Businessmen had for years longingly hoped for both a balanced budget and tax reduction. But they had been taught by the Eisenhower Administration that tax reduction must wait until the budget is balanced. Eisenhower had been compelled to accept a peace-time budget deficit of over 12 billion dollars in 1958 and had, moreover, produced a recession in 1960 by deliberately balancing the budget. The "full-employment surplus" and the "fiscal drag" theory appeared to offer an explanation of this conundrum. Under the "new dispensation" businessmen were persuaded to settle for a tax cut without waiting for the balanced budget[41].

In the Kennedy and Johnson Administration federal cash expenditures increased no faster relative to GNP than under Eisenhower. Under Eisenhower federal cash payments increased from 69.7 billion dollars in 1954 to 95.6 billion dollars in 1959, or an average of 5.2 billion dollars per year. Under Kennedy-Johnson, federal cash payments increased from 94.7 billion dollars in 1960 to 127.9 billion dollars in 1965, an average of 6.6 billion dollars per year. But the average GNP for the Eisenhower period was 426 billion dollars and for the Kennedy-Johnson period, 580 billion dollars. In terms of the current GNP the average increase per annum in cash payments was 1.2 per cent of income under Eisenhower and slightly below that under Kennedy-Johnson.

Note, however, that the figures just cited above omitted the fateful year, 1960. Hard pressed by ardent fiscal conservatists, notably Secretary Humphrey, the Eisenhower Administration made the fatal mistake of cutting the Administrative budget by 4 billion dollars in the fiscal year 1960. The Administration budget was indeed at long last balanced at 1.2 billion dollars, but at the cost of the 1960 recession.

VII The Current Status of Keynesianism in the United States

With this experience behind us, where do we now stand with respect to the Keynesian Revolution? Employing the language used by Keynes himself in his famous letter to Shaw, we could perhaps say that Keynes had indeed "largely" revolutionized the way America thinks about economic problems. But we still have a long way to go. Even with respect to tax policy I suspect that many people look upon the recent tax cut as an episode — a "shot in the arm" — a program that cannot prudently be repeated very often.

Some conservatists, however, have seized upon the "fiscal drag" concept as a powerful weapon, stolen from the Keynesian arsenal, with which to achieve a progressive year by year reduction in federal taxes — a device to capture all the fruits of technological progress for the private sector. Social priorities are thrown to the winds. Government expenditures are to be held, as far as possible, to present or even lower levels.

The great fiscal policy debate in years to come will center not so much on full employment but rather on the burning issue of social priorities. The "Loyal Opposition" has moved an important step forward. The first stage, as noted above, involved acceptance of active fiscal policy, if the economy (a) dipped below the "tolerable bottom" where serious cumulative depression threatens or (b) is pushing up through the "inflation ceiling." In between these two levels the self-sustaining economy was to be given free range to operate on its own, assisted by the built-in stabilizers. The new stage in the progress toward Keynesianism involves the acceptance of active fiscal policy within the area *between* the "tolerable bottom" and the "inflation ceiling" with the proviso, however, that such active fiscal policy take the form of tax reduction — such reduction to be cancelled, however, if the economy is heating. The conservatists have learned, perhaps too well, the "new economics" lesson about the "fiscal drag."

There thus remains much unfinished business. Shall irresponsible advertising continue to control people's minds, propelling the economy on to an ever-increasing output of gadgets, or shall we in earnest tackle the problems of the Great Society — air pollution, water pollution, ugly scrap heaps on the roadside, destruction of nature's beauty, slums; and on the positive side, the poverty program, housing, education, medical schools, hospitals, nursing homes, urban renewal, urban transportation, government support of the creative and performing arts. The political battles of the future will of necessity be fought over the size of the government budget.

In addition to the Council of Economic Advisers, we now need a new Act of Congress creating a Council of Social Values[42] to help redress the present unequal emphasis on material things. This act should require the President each year, aided by his Council, to make a report to the Congress and to the people on our cultural goals. This report should set forth the goals for the coming year and should indicate the programs and policies necessary to achieve those goals.

President Eisenhower in his last public address before leaving office warned the nation about another pressing problem — the danger to our economy inherent in our vast military-business complex. To ward off corruption and inefficiency will be no easy task as Secretary McNamara has discovered. The new role of government, not as supplier but as buyer on an undreamed of scale, raises problems about the functioning of the price system unknown to neo-classical economics. Moreover, disarmament — if and when it comes as ardently hoped for — will greatly complicate the management of a peace-time economy.

Fortunately, we shall not allow this problem to take us totally by surprise. The government has already issued (July, 1965) an excellent Report of the Committee on the Economic Impact of Defense and Disarmament under the chairmanship of Gardner Ackley[43]. The Report stays clear of vague complacencies. It is based on good Keynesian economics. The magnitudes are enormous, and the needed adjustments will reach colossal proportions.

VIII What About Europe?

A final word about the miracle of post-war European prosperity. Is this also a part of the Keynesian Revolution? With the sole exception of Sweden (a country that was developing during the Great Depression an active fiscal policy on its own) all European countries were at that time following orthodox reliance upon the self-generating forces of recovery, fearful that active government intervention might destroy the revival of "confidence" upon which they built their hopes.

The impact of Keynesian thinking may well have been greatest in the

Anglo-Saxon world. Still in this age of instantaneous communication, new ideas penetrate rapidly throughout the globe. To what extent Keynesian thinking has influenced continental governmental policy I leave to others to say. The post-war European growth miracle is a complex phenomenon. The Marshall aid program with its multiplier effect was itself an injection of governmental active intervention unknown to the pre-war world. Since 1940 the United States has poured over 100 billion dollars into the economies of the free world. The gigantic post-war budgets (inexorably imposed upon all western governments by an increasing industrialization, revolutionary technological developments, and a rapidly growing urbanization) far from being a burden, have powerfully sustained and fed an ever increasing aggregate demand. Technology and capital formation have raised productivity to a level at which the incomes of the masses can afford expensive consumer durables, the purchase of which has in turn opened up large new investment outlets. All this together has produced the post-war European miracle. Keynesian thinking may have played a role not so much possibly, as an activating force but rather in terms of melting away the icy walls of dogmatic resistance to the process of change.

Notes

1. A.C. Pigou, *Keynes's 'General Theory'*, *A Retrospective View*, London, 1950, p. 65.
2. *Ibid.*, p. 20. — John Maynard Keynes, *The General Theory of Employment, Interest and Money*, London, 1936, pp. 246sq.
3. Pigou, *op. cit.*, p. 20.
4. *Idem*, "The Economist", in: *John Maynard Keynes, 1883 — 1946, Fellow and Bursar*, A Memoir Prep. by the Direction of the Council of King's College, Cambridge, 1949, pp. 21sq.
5. Wesley C. Mitchell, *Business Cycles*, Berkeley, Calif., 1913.
6. See my *Business Cycles and National Income*, New York, 1951, Chapters 16—18.
7. John Maynard Keynes, *Monetary Reform*, New York, 1924.
8. *Idem, A Treatise on Money*, London, 1930, 2 Vols.
9. R.F. Harrod, *The Life of John Maynard Keynes*, London, 1951, p. 462.
10. It should be noted that Pigou never moved beyond the "loyal opposition" stage. In his *Lapses From Full Employment*, London, 1945, he openly admitted (as also in the Memoir paper) that Keynes had won the argument on wage flexibility. In the Preface, p. V, he stated that he no longer favored "attacking the problem of unemployment by manipulating wages rather than by manipulating demand." This represented a big step toward Keynesianism. But he still denied the under-employment equilibrium. He believed that mere *stabilization* of aggregate demand would permit automatic wage adjustment so as to provide full employment.
11. *Employment Policy*, Presented by the Minister of Reconstruction to Parliament by Command of His Majesty, May 1944, Cmd. 6527, London.
12. William H. Beveridge, *Full Employment in a Free Society*, London, 1944.
13. *The Economics of Full Employment*, Six Studies in Applied Economics Prep. at The Oxford University Institute of Statistics, Oxford, 1944.
14. This Committee was authorized and directed to make a full and complete study and investigation with respect to the concentration of economic power in, and financial control over, production and distribution of goods and services. The Committee consisted of six members of Congress and leading officials of the Department of Justice, the Securities Exchange Commission, the Federal Trade Commission, the Department of Labor, the Treasury Department, and the Commerce Department.

15. See: *Investigation of Concentration of Economic Power,* Hearings Before the Temporary National Economic Committee, Congress of the United States, 77th Congress, 1st Session, Pursuant to Public Resolution No. 113 (75th Congress), Authorizing and Directing a Select Committee to Make a Full and Complete Study and Investigation With Respect to the Concentration of Economic Power in, and Financial Control over, Production and Distribution of Goods and Services, P. 9: *Savings and Investment,* Washington 1940, pp. 3495 to 3520; 3538—3559; 3837—3859.

16. Professor Williams, distinguished monetary economist, was consistently an able, liberal-minded critic of Keynesian thinking.

17. See my *Fiscal Policy and Business Cycles,* New York, 1941, which grew in considerable measure out of these seminar discussions. It became the standard reference book on modern fiscal policy and there evolved around it for several years a lively critical literature.

18. *Employment Policy, op. cit.*, p. 16.

19. A budgetary deficit in depression, said the government White Paper (see *Employment Policy, op. cit.,* pp. 24sqq.), must be tolerated in order to help maintain the national income, but it is nonetheless an unwelcome guest. Keynes himself never explored thoroughly the public debt problem. It remained for his disciples to undertake this task — a highly important one. Had the old dogmas about debt burden continued to prevail, Keynesian fiscal policy would have been severely crippled.

20. Government expenditures were regarded as (a) *ineffective* because funds raised from taxation or by borrowing from the public simply reduced private spending, or (b) *dangerous* because funds borrowed from the banking system were believed to be inflationary and destructive of confidence.

21. *Employment and Income With Special Reference to The Initial Period of Reconstruction,* Pres. to Parliament by The Minister of Reconstruction, April 1945, Ottawa, 1945, and Dominion-Provincial Conference on Reconstruction, August, 1945.

22. Franklin D. Roosevelt, *Selected Speeches, Messages, Press Conferences, and Letters,* Ed. With an Introd. by Basil Rauch, "Annual Message to Congress, January 11, 1944", New York and Toronto, 1957, p. 347.

23. See my *Economic Policy and Full Employment,* New York and London, 1947.

24. See *Employment Act of 1946, As Amended, With Related Laws and Rules of the Joint Economic Committee, Congress of the United States,* 89th Congress, 2d Session, February 1966, Washington, 1966, Sec. 3, 4 and 5.

25. *The Midyear Economic Report of the President to the Congress, July 11, 1949,* Together With a Report: *The Economic Situation at Midyear 1949,* by the Council of Economic Advisers, Washington, 1949.

26. Arthur F. Burns, *Economic Research and the Keynesian Thinking of Our Times,* Twenty-Sixth Annual Report of the National Bureau of Economic Research, New York, 1946 — *Idem,* "Keynesian Economics Once Again", *The Review of Economic Statistics,* Vol. XXIX, Cambridge, Mass., 1947, pp. 252sqq.

27. *Idem, Economic Research and the Keynesian Thinking of Our Times, op. cit.,* p. 11.

28. *Economic Report of the President,* Transmitted to the Congress, January 28, 1954, Washington, 1954, pp. 7; also Chapters 4 and 12.

29. *Ibid.,* pp. 112sq.

30. *Economic Report of the President,* Transmitted to the Congress, January 20, 1955, Washington, 1955, p. VI.

31. *Report of the Joint Committee on the Economic Report on the January 1955 Economic Report of the President With Supplemental Views and the Economic Outlook for 1955,* Prep. by the Committee Staff, March 14, 1955, Senate, 84th Congress, 1st Session, Report No. 60, Washington, 1955, p. 12.

32. *Report of the Joint Committee on the Economic Report on the January 1956 Economic Report of the President With Supplemental and Minority Views and the Economic Outlook for 1956,* Prep. by the Committee Staff, March 1, 1956, Senate, 84th Congress, 2d Session, Report No. 606, Washington, 1956, p. 32.

33. *Taxes and the Budget: A Program for Prosperity in a Free Economy,* A Statement on National Policy by The Research and Policy Committee of the Committee for Economic Development, New York, November, 1947.

34. *Federal Expenditure and Revenue Policies,* Hearing Before the Joint Committee on

the Economic Report, Congress of the United States, 81st Congress, 1st Session Pursuant to Sec. 5(A) of Public Law 304, 79th Congress, September 23, 1949, Washington, D.C., 1949.

35.   *Monetary, Credit, and Fiscal Policies,* Report of the Subcommittee on Monetary, Credit, and Fiscal Policies of the Joint Committee on the Economic Report, Congress of the United States, Pursuant to S. Con. Res. 26, Presented by Mr. O'Mahoney, January 23, 1950, Senate, 81st Congress, 2d Session, Document No. 129, Washington, 1950.

36.   Of course military expenditures *during* the war constituted a far higher per cent of GNP.

37.   The Roosevelt New Deal measures had already laid the groundwork for an effective fiscal policy. New Deal institutional arrangements had opened up responsible and manageable outlèts for government spending, including Social Security, Unemployment Insurance, Federal housing programs, the Federal highway system, Rural Electrification, Tennessee Valley Authority, Federal Works Agency, together with the numerous Federal loan and credit institutions.

38.   See his recent book, *The Management of Prosperity,* New York, 1966. He favors a systematic year by year tax reduction program which includes a limited delegation of power to the President to suspend the reductions if conditions justify such action.

39.   The growing interest in Keynesian thinking is attested to by the recent appearance in the United States of a paper-back edition of the *General Theory.* Also, the number of foreign language translations of my *Guide to Keynes* (*A Guide to Keynes*, Economics Handbook Series, New York, London and Toronto, 1953) continues to grow especially in recent years. Keynes retains his place in the center of the stage in well-nigh every economic journal or new book on economic policy.

40.   "Commencement Address at Yale University, June 11, 1962", in: *John F. Kennedy,* Containing the Public Messages, Speeches, and Statements of the President, January 1 to December 31, 1962, Public Papers of the Presidents of the United States, Washington, 1963, pp. 470sqq.

41.   That the "new economics" has not dispelled the old slogans is abundantly clear from the preamble contained in Section 1 of the Revenue Act of 1964: "It is the sense of Congress that the tax reduction provided by this Act through stimulation of the economy, will, after a brief transitional period, raise (rather than lower) revenues and that such revenue increases should first be used to eliminate the deficits in the administrative budgets and then to reduce the public debt. To further the objective of obtaining balanced budgets in the near future, Congress by this action, recognizes the importance of taking all reasonable means to restrain Government spending . . ." *Revenue Act of 1964 With Explanation,* Based on the New Law as Approved by the President, February 26, 1964 (P.L. 88—272), Chicago, Illinois, 1964, p. 136 (Sec. 1).

42.   See my *Economic Issues of the 1960's,* Economics Handbook Series, New York, Toronto and London, 1960, pp. 91sq.

43.   *Report of the Committee on the Economic Impact of Defense and Disarmament,* Superintendent of Documents, Washington, D.C., July, 1965, pp. IX, 92.

107

Keynes and the Keynesians:
A Suggested Interpretation*

A. Leijonhufvud

I

One must be careful in applying the epithet "Keynesian" nowadays. I propose to use it in the broadest possible sense and let "Keynesian economics" be synonymous with the "majority school" macroeconomics which has evolved out of the debates triggered by Keynes's *General Theory* (*GT*). Keynesian economics, in this popular sense, is far from being a homogenous doctrine. The common denominator, which lends some justification to the identification of a majority school, is the class of models generally used. The prototype of these models dates back to the famous paper by Hicks [6] the title of which I have taken the liberty of paraphrasing. This standard model appears to me a singularly inadequate vehicle for the interpretation of Keynes's ideas. The juxtaposition of Keynes and the Keynesians in my title is based on this contention.

Within the majority school, at least two major factions live in recently peaceful but nonetheless uneasy coexistence. With more brevity than accuracy, they may be labeled the "Revolutionary Orthodoxy" and the "Neoclassical Resurgence." Both employ the standard model but with different specifications of the various elasticities and adjustment velocities. In its more extreme orthodox form, the model is supplied with wage rigidity, liquidity trap, and a constant capital-output ratio, and manifests a more or less universal "elasticity pessimism," particularly with regard to the interest-elasticities of "real" variables. The orthodoxy tends to slight monetary in favor of fiscal stabilization policies. The neoclassical faction may be sufficiently characterized by negating these statements. As described, the orthodoxy is hardly a very reputable position at the present time. Its influence in the currently most fashionable fields has been steadily diminishing, but it seems to have found a refuge in business cycle theory—and, of course, in the teaching of undergraduate macroeconomics.

*Source: *American Economic Review*, Vol. 57(2), May 1967, pp. 401-10.

The terms of the truce between the two factions comprise two propositions: (1) the model which Keynes called his "general theory" is but a special case of the classical theory, obtained by imposing certain restrictive assumptions on the latter; and (2) the Keynesian special case is nonetheless important because, as it happens, it is more relevant to the real world than the general (equilibrium) theory. Together the two propositions make a compromise acceptable to both parties, permitting a decent burial of the major issues which almost everyone has grown tired of debating—namely, the roles of relative values and of money—and, between them, the role of the interest rate—in the "Keynesian system." Keynes thought he had made a major contribution towards a synthesis of the theory of money and "our fundamental theory of value" (*GT*, pp. vi-vii). But the truce between the orthodox and the neoclassicists is based on the common understanding that his system was *sui generis*—a theory in which neither relative values nor monetary phenomena are "important."

This compromise defines, as briefly as seems possible, the result of what Clower aptly calls the "Keynesian Counterrevolution" [4].

II

That a model with wage rigidity as its main distinguishing feature should become widely accepted as crystallizing the experience of the unprecedented wage deflation of the Great Depression is one of the more curious aspects of the development of Keynesianism, comparable in this regard to the orthodox view that "money is unimportant"—a conclusion presumably prompted by the worst banking debacle in U.S. history. The emphasis on the "rigidity" of wages, which one finds in the New Economics, reveals the judgment that wages did not fall enough in the early 1930's. Keynes, in contrast, judged that they declined too much by far. It has been noted before that, to Keynes, wage rigidity was a policy recommendation and not a behavioural assumption (e.g.,[11]).

Keynes's theory was dynamic. His model was static. The method of trying to analyze dynamic processes with a comparative static apparatus Keynes borrowed from Marshall. The crucial difference lies in Keynes's inversion of the ranking of price- and quantity-adjustment velocities underlying Marshall's distinction between the "market day" and the "short run." The initial response to a decline in demand is a quantity adjustment. Clower's investigation of a system, which responds to deflationary disturbances in the first instance by quantity adjustments, shows that the characteristic Keynesian income-constrained, or "multiplier," process can be explicated in terms of a general equilibrium framework [4]. Such a model departs from the traditional Walrasian full employment model only in one, eminently reasonable, respect: trading at "false prices"—i.e., prices which do not allow the realization of all desired transactions—may take place. Transactors who fail to realize their desired sales, e.g., in the labor market, will curtail their effective demands in other markets. This implies the amplification of the initial disturbance typical of Keynes's multiplier analysis.

The strong assumption of "rigid" wages is not necessary to the explanation of such system behavior. It is sufficient only to give up the equally strong assumption of instantaneous price adjustments. Systems with finite price velocities will show Keynesian multiplier responses to initial changes in the rate of money expenditures. It is not necessary, moreover, to rely on "monopolies," labor unions, minimum wage laws, or other institutional constraints on the utility maximizing behavior of individual transactors in order to explain finite price velocities. Keynes, in contrast to many New Economists, was adamantly opposed to theories which "blamed" depressions on such obstacles to price adjustments. The implied proposition that, if "competition" could only be restored, "automatic forces" would take care of the employment problem was one of his pet hates. Atomistic markets do not mean instantaneous price adjustments. A system of atomistic markets would also show Keynesian adjustment behavior.

In Walrasian general equilibrium theory, all transactors are regarded as price takers. As noted by Arrow, "there is no one left over whose job it is to make a decision on price" [2, p. 43]. The job, in fact, is entrusted to a *deus ex machina*: Walras' auctioneer is assumed to inform all traders of the prices at which all markets are going to clear. This always trustworthy information is supplied at zero cost. Traders never have to wrestle with situations in which demands and supplies do not mesh; all can plan on facing perfectly elastic demand and supply schedules without fear of ever having their trading plans disappointed. All goods are perfectly "liquid," their full market values being at any time instantaneously realizable. Money can be added to such models only by artifice.

Alchian has shown that the emergence of unemployed resources is a predictable consequence of a decline in demand when traders do not have perfect information on what the new market clearing price would be [1, Chap. 31]. The price obtainable for the services of a resource which has become "unemployed" will depend upon the costs expended in searching for the highest bidder. In this sense, the resources is "illiquid." The seller's reservation price will be conditioned by past experiences as well as by observation of the prices at which comparable services are currently traded (*GT*, p. 264). Reservation price will be adjusted gradually as search continues. Meanwhile the resource remains unemployed. To this analysis one need only add that the loss of receipts from its services will constrain the owner's effective demand for other products—a feedback effect which provides the rationale of the multiplier-analysis of a system of atomistic ("competitive") markets.

To make the transition from Walras' world to Keynes' world, it is thus sufficient to dispense with the assumed tatonnement mechanism. The removal of the auctioneer simply means that the generation of the information needed to coordinate economic activities in a large system where decision making is decentralized will take time and will involve economic costs. No other "classical" assumptions need be relinquished. Apart from the absence of the auctioneer, the system remains as before: (1) individual traders still "maximize utility" (or profit)—one need not assume that they are constrained from bargaining on their own, nor that they are "money illusioned" or otherwise irrational; (2) price incentives are still effective—there is no inconsistency between Keynes's general "elasticity optimism" and his theory of unemployment. When price elasticities are assumed to be generally significant, one admits the potentiality of controlling the activities of individual traders by means of prices so as to coordinate them in an efficient manner. It is not necessary to deny the existence of a vector of nonnegative prices and interest rates consistent with the full utilization of resources. To be a Keynesian, one need only realize the difficulties of finding the market clearing vector.

III

It is a widely held view that the main weaknesses of Keynesian theory derive from Keynes's neglect of the influence of capital and real asset values on behavior (e.g., [8, pp. 9, 11, 17]; [12, p. 636]). It is above all on this crucial point that the standard model has proved to be a most seriously misleading framework for the interpretation of Keynes's theory. This is readily perceived if we compare the "aggregative structures" of the standard model and the *General Theory* model. In either case, we are usually dealing with but three price relations, so that the relevant level of aggregation is that of four-good models:

Standard Model	General Theory
Commodities	Consumer goods
Bonds	Nonmoney assets
Money	Money
Labor services	Labor services

The aggregate production function makes the standard model a "one-commodity model." The price of capital goods in terms of consumer goods is fixed. The money wage is "rigid," and the current value of physical assets is tied down within the presumably narrow range of short-run fluctuations in the "real" wage rate. Relative prices are, indeed, allowed little play in this construction. "Money" includes only means of payment, while all claims to cash come under the heading of "bonds."

The four-good structure of the *General Theory* is a condensed version of the model of the *Treatise on Money* (*TM*) with its richer menu of short-term assets. All titles to prospective income streams are lumped together in "nonmoney assets." Bond streams and equity streams are treated as perfect substitutes, a simplification which Keynes achieved through some quite mechanical manipulations of risk and liquidity premia (*GT*, Chap. 17). The fundamental property which distinguishes nonmoney assets both from consumables and from money is that the former are "long" while the latter two are "short"—attributes which, in Keynes's usage, were consistently equated with "fixed" (or "illiquid") and "liquid," respectively (cf. *TM*, V:I, p. 248). The typical nonmoney assets are bonds with long term to maturity and titles to physical assets with a very long "duration of use or consumption." Basically, Keynes's method of aggregation differentiates between goods with a relatively high and a relatively low interest elasticity of present value. Thus the two distinctions are questions of degree. As a matter of course, the definition of money includes all types of deposits, since their interest elasticity of present value is zero, but "such instruments as treasury bills" can also be included when convenient (*GT*, p. 167 n.).

Keynes's alleged neglect of capital is attributed to his preoccupation with the short run in which the stock of physical capital is fixed. The critique presumes that Keynes worked with the standard model in which the value of such assets in terms of consumables is a constant. But in Keynes's two-commodity model, this price is, in principle, a short-run variable and, as a consequence, so is the potential command over current consumables which the existing stock of assets represents. The current price of nonmoney assets is determined by expectations with regard to the "stream of annuities" in prospect and by the rate at which these anticipated future receipts are discounted. The relevant rate is always the long rate of interest. In the analysis of short-run "equilibrium," the state of expectation (alias the marginal efficiency of capital) is assumed to be given, and the price of assets then varies with "the" interest rate.

In Keynes's short run, "a decline in the interest rate" and "a rise in the market prices of capital goods, equities, and bonds" are interchangeable descriptions of the same event. Since the representative nonmoney asset is very long-lived, its interest elasticity of present value is quite high. The price elasticity of the output of augmentable income sources is very high. The aggregative structure of this model leaves no room for elasticity pessimism with regard to the relationship between investment and the (long) rate of interest. It does not even seem to have occurred to Keynes that investment might be exceedingly interest inelastic, as later Keynesians would have it. Instead, he was concerned to convince the reader that it is reasonable to assume that "a moderate change in the prospective yield of capital-assets or in the rate of interest will not involve an indefinitely great change in the rate of investment" (*GT*, p. 252).

The relationship between saving and the interest rate is of less quantitative significance, but Keynes's ideas on the subject are of considerable interest and give some clues to his theory of liquidity preference. The criticisms of his supposed neglect of wealth as a variable influencing behavior have been directed in particular against the *ad hoc* "psychological law" on which he based the consumption-income relation. This line of criticism ignores the "windfall effect" which "should be classified amongst the major factors capable of causing short-period changes in the propensity to consume" (*GT*, pp. 92-94). This second psychological law of consumption states simply that the propensity to consume out of current income will be higher the higher the value of household net worth in terms of consumer goods. A decline in the propensity to consume may, therefore, be caused either by a decline in the marginal efficiency of capital (*GT*, p. 319) or by a rise in the long rate (*GT*, p. 94; *TM*, V:I, pp. 196-97). In the short run the marginal efficiency is taken as given and, so, it is the interest rate which concerns us.

The usual interpretation focuses on the passages in which Keynes argued that "changes in the rate of time-discount" will not significantly influence saving. In my opinion, these well-known passages express the assumption that household preferences exhibit a high degree of intertemporal complementarity, so that the intertemporal substitution effects of interest movements may be ignored. Consequently, the windfall effect of such changes must be interpreted as a wealth effect.

Hicks has shown that the wealth effect of a decline in interest will be positive if the average period of the income-stream anticipated by the representative household exceeds the average period of its planned "standard stream" [7, especially pp. 184-88]. Households who anticipate the receipt of streams which are, roughly speaking, "longer" than their planned consumption streams are made wealthier by a decline in the interest rate. The present value of net worth increases in greater proportion than the present cost of the old consumption plan, and the consumption plan can thus be raised throughout.

This brings our discussion of the *General Theory* into pretty unfamiliar territory. But Keynes's "vision" was of a world in which the indicated conditions generally hold. In this world, currently active households must, directly or indirectly, hold their net worth in the form of titles to streams which run beyond their consumption horizon. The duration of the relevant consumption plan is sadly constrained by the fact that "in the long run, we are all dead." But the great bulk of the "fixed capital of the modern world" is of a very long-term nature (e.g., *TM*, V:II, pp. 98, 364), and is thus destined to survive the generation which now owns it. This is the basis for the wealth effect of changes in asset values.

Keynes's *Gestalt*-conception of the world resembles Cassel's. Cassel used the wealth effect to argue the "necessity of interest" [3], an argument which Keynes paraphrased (*GT*, p. 94). The same conception underlies Keynes's liquidity preference theory of the term structure of interest. Mortal beings cannot hold land, buildings, corporate equities, British consols, or other permanent income sources "to maturity." Induced by the productivity of roundabout processes to invest his savings in such income sources, the representative, risk-averting transactor must suffer "capital uncertainty." Forward markets, therefore, will generally show a "constitutional weakness" on the demand side [7, p. 146]. The relevance of the duration structure of the system's physical capital has been missed by the modern critics of the Keynes-Hicks theory of the term structure of interest rates [10, pp. 14-16] [9, pp. 347-48].

The recent discussion has dealt with the term structure problem as if financial markets existed in a vacuum. But the "real forces of productivity and thrift" should be brought in. The above references to the productivity of roundabout processes (*GT*, Chap. 16) and the wealth effect indicates that they are not totally ignored in Keynes's general theory of liquidity preference. The question why short streams should command a premium over long streams is, after all, not so different from the old question why present goods should command a premium over future goods. Keynes is on classical ground when he argues that the essential problem with which a theory of asset prices must deal derives from the postponement of the option to consume, and that other factors influencing asset prices are subsidiary: "we do not devise a productivity theory of smelly or risky processes as such" (*GT*, p. 215).

IV

Having sketched Keynes's treatment on intertemporal prices and intertemporal choices, we can now consider how "changing views about the future are capable of influencing the quantity of employment" (*GT*, p. vii). This was Keynes's central theme.

"It is by reason of the existence of durable equipment that the economic future is linked to the present" (*GT*, p. 146). The price of augmentable nonmoney assets in terms of the wage unit determines the rate of investment. The same price in terms of consumables determines the propensity to consume. This price is the focal point of Keynes's analysis of changes in employment.

If the "right" level of asset prices can be maintained, investment will be maintained and employment at the going money wage stabilized. If a decline in the marginal efficiency of capital occurs, maintenance of the prices of long-lived physical assets and equities requires a corresponding drop in the long rate and thus a rise in bond prices. To Keynes, "the role intelligible explanation" (*GT*, p. 201) of why this will normally not occur is that bear speculators will shift into savings deposits. If financial intermediaries do not "operate in the opposite direction" (*TM*, V:I, pp. 142-43), bond prices will not rise to the full extent required and demand prices for capital goods and equities will fall. This lag of market rate behind the natural or "neutral" rate (*GT*, p. 243) will be associated with the emergence of excess demand for money—which always spells contraction. "The importance of money essentially flows from its being a link between the present and the future" (*GT*, p. 293).

Contraction ensues because nonmoney asset prices are "wrong." As before, "false prices" reveal an information failure. There are two parts to this information failure: (1) Mechanisms are lacking which would ensure that the entrepreneurial expectations guiding current investment mesh with savers' plans for future consumption: "If saving consisted not merely in abstaining from present consumption but in placing simultaneously a specific order for future consumption, the effect might indeed be quite different" (*GT*, p. 210). (2) There is an alternative "circuit" by which the appropriate information could be transmitted, since savers must demand stores of value in the present. But the financial markets cannot be relied upon to perform the information function without fail. Keynes spent an entire chapter in a mournful diatribe on the Casino-activities of the organized exchanges and on the failure of investors, who are not obliged to hold assets to maturity, to even attempt "forecasting the prospective yield of assets over their whole life" (*GT*, Chap. 12).

Whereas Keynes had an exceedingly broad conception of "liquidity preference," in the Keynesian literature the term has acquired the narrow meaning of "demand for money," and this demand is usually discussed in terms of the choice between means of payment and one of the close substitutes which Keynes included in his own definition of money. Modern monetary theorists have come to take an increasingly dim view of his speculative demand, primarily on the grounds that the underlying assumption of inelastic expectations represents a "special case" which is unseemly in a model aspiring to the status of a "general theory" [5, pp. 145-51] [13] [8, p. 10] [9, p. 344]. But it is only in the hypothetical world of Walrasian tatonnements that all the information required to coordinate the economic activities of a myriad traders is produced *de novo* on each market day. In any other construction, traders must rely heavily on "memory" rather than fresh information. In the orthodox model, with its interest inelasticity of both saving and investment, there is admittedly no "real" reason why traders' past experience should be of a narrow normal range of long rates. In Keynes's model, there are reasons. In imperfect information models, inelastic expectations are not confined to the bond market. The explanation of the emergence of unemployed resources in atomistic markets also relies on inelastic expectations. To stress "speculative behavior" of this sort does not mean that one reverts to the old notion of a Walrasian system adjusting slowly because of "frictions." The multiplier feedbacks mean that the system tends to respond to parametric disturbances in a "deviation-amplifying" manner—behavior which cannot be analyzed with the pre-Keynesian apparatus.

A truly vast literature has grown out of the Pigou-effect idea, despite almost universal agreement on its "practical" irrelevance. The original reason for this strange development was dissatisfaction with Keynes's assertion that the only hope from deflation lies "in the effect of the abundance of money in terms of the wage-unit on the rate of interest" (*GT*, p. 253). This was perceived as a denial of the logic of classical theory. Viewing Keynes's position through the glasses of the standard one-commodity model, it was concluded that it could only be explained on the assumption that he had overlooked the direct effect of an increase in real net worth on the demand for commodities (e.g., [11, pp. 269-70] [12, Note K:1]). The one-commodity interpretation entirely misses Keynes's point: that the trouble arises from inappropriately low prices of augmentable nonmoney assets relative to both wages and consumer goods prices. Relative values are wrong. Absolute prices will "rush violently between zero and infinity" (*GT*, pp. 239, 269-70), if price-level movements do not lead to a "correction" of relative prices through either a fall in long rates or an induced rise in the marginal efficiency of capital (*GT*, p. 263). It is hard to see a denial of "our fundamental theory of value" in this argument.

V

We can now come back to the "terms of the truce" between the neoclassicists and the Keynesian orthodox. I have argued that, in Keynes's theory: (1) transactors do maximize utility and profit in the manner assumed in classical analysis, also in making decisions on saving and investment; (2) price incentives are effective and this includes intertemporal price incentives—changes in interest rates or expected future spot prices (*GT*, *loc. cit.*) will significantly affect present behavior; (3) the existence of a hypothetical vector of nonnegative prices and interest rates which, if once established, would bring full resource utilization is not denied.

The only thing which Keynes "removed" from the foundations of classical theory was the *deus ex machina*—the auctioneer which is assumed to furnish, without charge, all the information needed to obtain the perfect coordination of the activities of all traders in the present and through the future.

Which, then, is the more "general theory" and which the "special case"? Must one not grant Keynes his claim to having tackled the more general problems?

Walras' model, it has often been noted, was patterned on Newtonian mechanics. On the latter, Norbert Wiener once commented: "Here there emerges a very interesting distinction between the physics of our grandfathers and that of the present day. In nineteenth century physics, it seemed to cost nothing to get information" [14, p. 29]. In context, the statement refers to Maxwell's Demon—not, of course, to Walras' auctioneer. But, *mutatis mutandis*, it would have served admirably as a motto for Keynes's work. It has not been the main theme of Keynesian economics.[1]

Note

1.   The paper is an attempt to summarize some of the conclusions of a lengthy manuscript, "On Keynesian Economics and the Economics of Keynes: A Study in Monetary Theory," to be submitted as a doctoral dissertation to Northwestern University.

References

GT: John Maynard Keynes, The General Theory of Employment, *Interest and Money* (London, 1936).
TM: _____, *A Treatise on Money*, Vols. I and II (London, 1930).
1.   Armen A. Alchian and William R. Allen, *University Economics* (Belmont, Calif., 1964).
2.   Kenneth J. Arrow, "Towards a Theory of Price Adjustment," in M. Abramowitz, *et. al.*, *The Allocation of Economic Resources* (Stanford, 1959).
3.   Gustav Cassel, *The Nature and Necessity of Interest* (1903).
4.   Robert W. Clower, "The Keynesian Counterrevolution: A Theoretical Appraisal," in F.H. Hahn and F.P. Brechling, eds., *The Theory of Interest Rates* (London, 1965).
5.   William Fellner, *Monetary Policies and Full Employment* (Berkeley, 1946).
6.   John R. Hicks, "Mr. Keynes and the 'Classics': A Suggested Interpretation," *Econometrica*, 1937.
7.   _____, *Value and Capital*, 2nd ed. (Oxford, 1946).
8.   Harry G. Johnson, "The General Theory After Twenty-Five Years," *A.E.R.*, May, 1961.
9.   _____, "Monetary Theory and Policy," *A.E.R.*, June, 1962.
10.   David Meiselman, *The Term Structure of Interest Rates* (Englewood Cliffs, N.J., 1962).
11.   Don Patinkin, "Price Flexibility and Full Employment," *A.E.R.*, 1948, as reprinted in F.A. Lutz and L.M. Mints, eds., *Readings in Monetary Theory* (Homewood, Ill., 1951).
12.   _____, *Money, Interest, and Prices*, 2nd ed. (New York, 1965).
13.   James Tobin, "Liquidity Preference as Behavior Towards Risk," *Rev. of Econ. Studies*, 1958.
14.   Norbert Wiener, *The Human Use of Human Beings*, 2nd ed. (New York, 1964).

108

Keynes and the Monetarists*

S. Weintraub

Now, as I have often pointed out to my students, some of whom have been
brought up in sporting circles, high-brow opinion is like a hunted hare; if you
stand in the same place . . . it can be relied upon to come round to you
in circle. D.H. Robertson, *Economic Commentaries* (London 1956), 81.

Undoubtedly the late Sir Dennis Robertson, and Keynes himself, would have
approved the modern monetarist inscription that "money matters." Both
might be astonished to learn that any economist thought otherwise. Near
death, Keynes was engrossed in plans for guiding the world banks toward
establishing a viable international monetary order; the man who gave currency
to the concept of monetary management can hardly be accused of ignoring
monetary influences.[1]

In the light of modern controversy it is of some importance to examine how
and where money enters into Keynes' system. Intended below is some contrast
of Keynes' ideas on output levels and inflation, and their monetary implications, with the views of Milton Friedman, the most prominent monetarist. This
should permit a judgement on the possible rapprochement of ideas or the
identification of any impassable chasm. It will prove convenient to commence
with Friedman's Monetarist doctrines for their directness should afford ready
contrast with the "two-theories" that can be demarcated in Keynes.

The Friedman Monetarist View

In his exposition of monetary phenomena Professor Friedman usually
connects the changes in the money aggregate to changes in money *income*,
thereby transforming the old into the new quantity theory of money.[2] In the
hands of Jean Bodin, John Locke, Richard Cantillon, and the two Davids,
Hume and Ricardo, changes in the money stock compelled changes in the price
level (P) with due recognition of transitional effects on output (Q) and

*Source: *Canadian Journal of Economics*, Vol. 4 (1), February 1971, pp. 37-49.

employment (N).

While the predictive superiority of models is not under review here, Professor Friedman has deployed income models of the following nature which convey his thinking on the pervasive influence of money supplies:[3]

$$\Delta Y = V' \, \Delta M \qquad (1)$$

$$\text{d} \log Y \, (T)/\text{d} \log M(T) = f(y_p, \, \delta, \hat{w}) \qquad (2)$$

where $Y =$ money income; $M =$ money supply; $V' =$ marginal income velocity of money; $y_p =$ permanent income; $\delta =$ other variables; $\hat{w} =$ elasticity of price level to money income.

From the above, and in the analytic statement which is erected firmly on a modernised version of the Cambridge demand function for money (embodying several of Keynes' liquidity-preference ingredients), Friedman espouses his rules for monetary policy to achieve steadier growth in the economy *sans* inflation.[4] While conceding that the past record discloses some feedback tendencies tracking the other way, Professor Friedman extracts as the main lesson that of the governing power of money; he traces the causal train running from $\Delta M \rightarrow \Delta P$ and, in conditions of unemployment either under cyclical recession or labour force growth, from $\Delta M \rightarrow \Delta Q$, with a variable time lag historically, as low as 4 months and as high as 29 months.[5]

Reflecting on his inductive studies Professor Friedman concludes, nonetheless, that the money income split between $Q \, \Delta \, P$ and $P \, \Delta \, Q$ subsequent upon Δm is obscure:[6] "The general subject of the division of changes in money income between prices and quantity badly needs more investigation." Also: "none of our leading economic theories has much to say about it."

Despite the inability of his statistical techniques to isolate the prices ΔP impact, Profesor Friedman insists on the "close link between money changes" and macro phenomena so that "if you want to control prices and incomes," money supplies provide the lever.[7]

A Monetarist Version of Inflation

In the title essay of his recent collection of writings Friedman invites us to visualize a helicopter dropping dollar bills over an economy in settled equilibrium, to double the existing cash holdings.[8] Through his M_d equation of money-demand, with each individual seeking to maintain his representative real holdings, the doubled expenditure will double prices and nominal income: with Q unchanged P must yield.

This is a revival of David Hume's parable of imagining each Englishman awakening to find an extra £5 note "slipt into his pocket." Hume also recounts that P will ascend to reflect the greater money supply.[9] Professor Friedman includes repeated helicopter "raids": P will rise at the same pace as M, with proper reservations for anticipations and uncertainty.

Over time, barring only the other determinants of M_d — the expectation of inflation especially — and the Q — changes, P responds to M; inflation is inherently a monetary phenomenon. The system "gets out of order" when M

"behaves erratically, when either its rate of increase is sharply stepped up — which will mean price inflation — or sharply contracted — which will mean economic depression . . ."[10]

Money Wages

In the monetarist doctrine full employment ensues from the automatic market forces establishing appropriate prices and factor incomes reflecting the ultimate real relations regardless of the size of M.[11] Missing in the usual monetarist version of inflation is any stress on average money wages (w).[12] But this lack is not inadvertent for there are other passages in which the wage-price spiral is either rejected or denounced as of no significance.[13] The reasoning seems to be based on the contemplation of a system in general equilibrium, in which one M is fixed, through an implicit stipulation of the velocity of money (V), MV governs Y.

With Y settled, given the demand and cost phenomena, product prices are resolved. Adjusted simultaneously are factor prices. To "explain" factor prices the system is opened, and the "partial" equilibrium theory generally utilized invokes the principle of "derived-demand," to wit, that product prices determine factor prices.[14]

Disorderly Labour Markets?

In the monetarist vision then, once M is introduced and supplemented by the real forces, full equilibrium will be established and the endogenous P-Y-Q-w-N-r variables will be ordered.

Suppose that in this tranquil Walrasian image there is an increase in w, sponsored by a new sentiment that permits this to happen. Union leaders propose and business leaders defer. Clearly, with M (and V) rigid then P *must* rise, and Q and N *must* drop: unemployment will occur as the demand for nominal money balances increases because of the price rise, and interest rates rise, depressing investment. This is scarcely a novel conclusion; non-Keynesians long ago concluded that Keynes' unemployment theory was erected on wage rigidity.[15]

We shall return to the implications of this analysis shortly for it is just at this point that the monetarist position is faced with the ultimate hard implication of espousing unemployment on the presumption that the wage level will right itself mechanistically without any direct intervention in the form of incomes or wage policy. Conceptually, the wage level may be resistant to this self-correcting dependence so that the outcome partakes features of the worst of both worlds, of unacceptable rates of inflation with persistent wage hikes and excessive unemployment, as in the United States in 1957-9 and 1969-70.

Further, the dilemma cannot be escaped by arguing that over time improvements in labour productivity will simply neutralize the wage gains. For the facts are likely to be such that the progress of the calendar will also report new wage increases so that the same issues remain though with altered impacts, depending on the size of the wage-productivity ingredients in the new mix of relations.

The P- and Q-Theories of Keynes

With minor qualification the monetarist position rests on the causal relation of $\Delta M \rightarrow \Delta Y$ with an intervening time lag. Noting:

$$dY = PdQ + QdP, \text{ or} \tag{3a}$$
$$dY/Y = dQ/Q + dP/P. \tag{3b}$$

Professor Friedman admits to some obscurity surrounding the magnitude of the respective $P \Delta Q$ and $Q \Delta P$ portions of the ΔY variation ensuing upon an exogenous ΔM change.

Despite some failures in subsequent interpretations of his work, Keynes was concerned with this very issue.[16] Two core themes are distinguishable in *The General Theory*. One, of course, delineates the employment-output determinants: this is the N (or Q) -theory. The other is Keynes' price level theory, a P-theory. Of these two facets of Keynesianism the Q-theory has achieved far greater prominence in exposition and application than the P-theory. Our account will reverse this practice. Although the elaboration of each theory will be brief, some attempt will be made to explore the monetary implications of each theory for evidence of agreement with and dissent from the monetarist point of view.

The Q-*Theory*

In the Great Depression it was inevitable that Keynes' N-precepts were spotlighted. The message was codified and transferred to the textbooks by means of the 45° diagram of Hansen and Samuelson, with further generalization in Hicks' *IS-LM* interpretation: this Q-distillation bears the "Keynesian" label.[17]

These models are so commonplace that there is no need to dwell on them. They run in terms of real output and thus assume, implicitly, a constant price level — at least until "full employment." Inflation is thus effectively precluded. So far as their monetary implications go, barring the absolute liquidity preferences that would mark only the special circumstances of the 1930s which discouraged Keynes' faith in monetary policy, we would have:

$$(\partial Q/\partial I)\,(\partial I/\partial r)\,(dr/dM) > 0, \text{ with} \tag{4a}$$
$$\partial Q/\partial I > 0 \text{ and } \partial I/\partial r < 0 > dr/dM \tag{4b}$$

where $I = $ real investment, $r = $ the level of interest rates.

More money would thus yield more output in amount related to the investment function and the multiplier. For Keynes, the "law of returns" would also be a factor for there could be some price level perturbations, say, under diminishing returns. For the money increment to match up with the output increment, and any associated price eruption to evoke the output, we would

have:
$$V\Delta M + M\Delta V + \Delta V\Delta M = P\Delta Q + Q\Delta P + \Delta P\Delta Q. \qquad (5a)$$
If $\Delta V = 0$, and availing ourselves of the truism $V = PQ/M$, then:
$$(Q\Delta M/M\Delta Q) = 1 + (Q\Delta P/P\Delta Q) + \Delta P/P. \qquad (5b)$$
Writing E_{mq} for the elasticity on the left side, *though viewing money as the independent variable for policy*, and recognizing the right side parentheses as the reciprocal of the (aggregate) supply elasticity (E_s), we have:
$$E_{mq} = 1 + (1 + \Delta Q/Q)/E_s. \qquad (5c)$$

In equation 5c, by working in constant dollars so long as there is unemployment, Keynesians really view $E_s = \infty$, so that a one per cent money variation has an output *potential* of one per cent, with the precise outcome hinging on the investment and liquidity functions (and thus, implicitly, on the ΔV variation). Monetarists would generally share this view, but with an appropriate ΔV qualifier being more central and explicit. Keynes, on the other hand, would also give attention to the "laws of return," and some latent price perturbations accompanying the output flow after a money injection — even with money wages (the "wage-unit") constant. To Keynes, E_s would be neither zero nor infinite; its magnitude would depend on the productivity of the available labour and the state of idle equipment. "Diminishing-returns inflation," while not normally a serious phenomenon in an employment upswing, could not be summarily precluded.

Nonetheless, in the over-all monetary implications of equation 5a there is nothing *in principle* to separate Keynes from either Keynesians or monetarists: more money is generally indispensable for higher output-employment levels. The money increment in equation 5a, whose exact amount is imperfectly predictable because of changes in the average velocity of money (which Keynes thought would vary because of volatility in the speculative motive) is causal, as in the monetarist view. The money injection required to budge Q in amount ΔQ can be described as the *stimulative* aspect of monetary policy. In older terminology it has its analogue in the *Currency Principle* which viewed money as transmitting a causal influence in governing macroeconomic phenomena.

There can be little serious dispute then, so far as the Q-theory goes, in identifying Keynes with the monetarists under conditions of unemployment and interest rate-investment sensitivity to larger money supplies, with wages rigid *and constant returns* under pure competition so that price movements were precluded. In this Keynesian model that has largely dominated the literature the P-aspects were effectively suppressed; the mitigating factor was that nobody suspected that cumulative inflation would mar the post-war scene. Through Keynesian insights, unemployment has been *nearly* eradicated. Inflation is our new devil. Hence Keynes must now be appraised in the perspective of inflation theory.

Keynesian Caricatures: the "Symmetrical" Theory

Keynes' inflation ideas have been badly caricatured, even by dedicated Keynesians.[18] For whereas Keynes deliberately chose wage-units as his "deflator," Keynesians blithely made the translation in *real* terms — "constant dollars" — despite his admonitions.[19] For Q-theory this probably made no difference; for the P-theory it does. Working in real terms Keynesians evolved a neat — albeit erroneous — symmetry, with unemployment on one side of the full employment equilibrium and inflation on the other.[20] Overlooked entirely was the obvious fact that most of the post-war world suffered concomitant unemployment *and* inflation. There was also the analytical anomaly of expounding inflation in a model of constant prices.

Phillips Curve as Anti-Keynes

Lately, with the Phillips curve grafted on to the Keynesian apparatus a plausible theory of inflation has emerged. The Q-determinants (with labour force) transmit simultaneously the unemployment forces: unemployment rates thereupon govern the wage *increments* which impel P-perturbations.

Phillips curves, with their trade-off fixation, imbed some complacency into modern Keynesianism. Technically, proponents are apt to overlook Phillips' empirical curve-fittings in an analytic leap toward smooth functions which suppress an immanent range of indeterminateness. Philosophically, Phillips curve addiction perpetrates a cruel hoax on Keynes in its invitation to abide *some* unemployment and *some* inflation; it has led some Keynesians to abdicate the promised land of full employment for the comfort of vague but possible price damping.[21] It has led others to brush off inflation as unimportant. Keynes' entire intellectual commitment was to use reason to eradicate economic ailments rather than to "trade-off" one ill for another malady.[22]

Keynes on Wages and Prices: The P-*Theory*

Once Keynes assumes a given wage unit — interpreted here as an average money wage level and structure — only his Q- or N-theory really surfaces. *Given w*, P is determinate: while P may rise as N advances because of some diminishing returns, or some rise in monopoly power accompanying shifts in the consumption function or the investment level, the P-perturbations are probably small. For the Q-theory, therefore, "constant-dollar" Keynesianism is amply representative of Keynes.

Once w alters, the conventional Keynesianism fails: nothing really happens either under the 45° approach or the *IS-LM* coverage. Of course, this dichotomization of Keynes into two isolated and independent core theories need not arise; a unified approach would serve both ends for there are some indubitable interactions between w, P, r, Q, and N. Keynes himself, in his negelected chapters on w and P interdependence (*The General Theory*, chaps. 19-21), sketched in his own masterly way the key consequences of a general cut in wages. Noting that wage cuts were frequently recommended as the remedy for unemployment, Keynes concluded that lowering w would compel a (nearly) proportionate fall in P.[23] Employment might increase, *if the nominal money supply was unchanged*, because the curtailed demand for money at the lower P would depress r: a general fall in w was thus revealed to be a roundabout method of expanding *real* cash balances and reducing r; the ends of monetary policy would thereby be accomplished through trade union acquiescence. In the prevailing moods of the Great Depression the N-effects would be minimal. This is one of the more percipient analyses of *The General Theory*.

Prices and Unit Wage Costs

The price level in Keynes depends substantially on the relation of w to the average productivity of labour (A).[24] A relative rise in w would raise unit labour costs and spur a higher P. Monopoly power is also admitted while *expectations of the future enter through user costs*; the monetarist stress on "inflationary expectations" could cite Keynes' priority. With minor latitude Keynes' P-theory can be transcribed as $P = kw/A$, where k = the mark-up of prices over unit labour costs or the reciprocal of the wage share. With k "nearly" constant, unit labour costs dominate the P-outcome.

Monetary Aspects

The monetary implications of Keynes' P-theory follow readily. Lowering w and thus P, with Q unchanged, r may fall if M is fixed. The r-reduction may stimulate I, and thus Q and N. A higher w would spark the opposite sequence. To offset any unemployment incidence the M-total would have to expand. Keynes *always* advocated action to increase M and reduce r so long as unemployment prevailed, the state of liquidity preferences permitting. There can be little question on this, or on his view that with an increase of employment, and M constant, that interest rates would edge upwards. To reverse the argument and make it at least partially relevant to contemporary inflation, with higher wage and price levels we would have (when output growth has been retarded)

$$\Delta (MV) = Q\Delta P \text{ or } (P\Delta M/M\Delta P) = 1, \text{ if } \Delta V = \Delta Q = 0. \quad (6)$$

For Keynes, once a wage movement had occurred through trade union success at the bargaining table, the money supply would have to be enlarged to avert unemployment following a higher demand for money and higher interest rates if M is unchanged. The causal impetus, however, resides in the ΔP advance (following Δw). Monetary action which is geared to maintain the Q-level might be described as performing a *sustaining* function, or merely "meeting the needs of trade" in the language of the older Banking School.[25]

It is with respect to the execution of the "sustaining" function that Keynes' analysis deviates from the monetarist position. The money increment is not a causal factor; it is an effect of "business conditions" which Friedman acknowledges as occurring empirically — but not assigned by him the form of an inflation anti-climax, as the foregoing interpretation of Keynes would have it. Further, for Keynes the demand for more money implicit in equation 6 tends to *compel* sustaining operations on the part of the monetary authorities. Thus increments in the money supply are not envisaged as descending from a helicopter but as reflecting: (1) the higher wage and price levels, which (2) induce an increased demand for nominal money quantities, which (3) is then relieved by the monetary authorities acknowledging the unpalatable political, social, and economic facts of unemployment in the midst of an inflation about which they are practically impotent. On the inflation front, rather than indicting their actions in expanding the money supply as causing the unwanted price phenomena, the monetary authorities are instead engaged in scotching the other ailment, that of unemployment; in the generation of inflation they are neither culpable agents nor willing accomplices.

Liquidity-Preference Proper

Even these brief remarks stamp Keynes as a monetarist, cognizant that "money matters." Keynes' monetarism would also lean to the provision of more money to sate the "speculative-demand" for cash balances whenever "liquidity-preference-proper" threatened to lift the r-structure and impede full employment. Whenever individuals (or institutions) wanted green cheese-money, the green cheese factory — the central bank — had to produce such objects of fancy (*The General Theory*, p. 235). Only more money could check a Q-N deterioration: an unresponsive M would indeed matter. In a monetarist version these aspects of a greater demand for money would be subsumed, presumably, in a change in money velocity (ΔV) at higher interest rates. Keynes' monetary analysis sought out the source or cause of such variations: velocity changes were the necessary accompaniment of the behavioural relations described.

The Friedman Monetarist Rules

The spirit and feasibility of a theory can often be tested in its strategy for policy. Professor Friedman has listed three alternative proposals; all of them are a throwback to discussions in the 1930s. He writes:[26] ". . . I have always emphasized that a *steady* and known rate of increase in the quantity of money is more important than the precise numerical value of the rate of increase."

Let us consider his monetary prescriptions. In all cases we shall enunciate the rule and then comment on the M, P, and w path. The t-subscript will denote the year, with t-n referring to the date at which the policy commences.[27]

Rule 1. A Constant M

The first proposal involves holding M constant. Friedman declares this policy would accomplish "a decline in prices of about 4 to 5 per cent a year, if the real demand for money continues to rise with real income as it has on the average of the past century" (p. 46).

Rule 1: $M_t = M_{t-1} = M_{t-2} = M_{t-3} = \ldots = M_{t-n}$;

P-series: $P_t = 0.95\, P_{t-1} = 0.95^2\, P_{t-2} = \ldots 0.95^n\, P_{t-n}$;

w-series: $w_t = (1-e)\, w_{t-1} = (1-e)^2\, w_{t-2} = \ldots (1-e)^n\, w_{t-n}$.

On rule 1 the money wage level would fall at a rate (approximately) equal to the growth of the labour force (e), with e in the 1 per cent — 2 per cent range. Reflecting on the path of w is enough to dispel confidence in the immediate implementation of rule 1. Even if full employment could proceed under P-deflation, the requisite of a falling w would presage severe union strife, for it is a progamme to secure labour's assent to falling money wages.

Rule 2. Constant w

Retaining rule 1 as a "long-run" objective, but "too drastic" for the near future, Friedman announces "a more limited policy objective might be to stabilize the price of factor services" (p. 46). On his estimates of unitary income elasticity of demand for real cash balances "this would require for the United States a rise in the quantity of money of about 1 per cent per year, to match the growth in population and labour force." For a somewhat higher elasticity, a 2 per cent money increment would be in order.

Rule 2: $w_t = w_{t-1} = w_{t-2} = \ldots w_{t-n}$;

M-series: $M_t = 1.02M_{t-1} = (1.02)^2 M_{t-2} = \ldots = (1.02)^n M_{t-n}$;

P-series: $P_t = 0.97 P_{t-1} = (0.97)^2 P_{t-2} = \ldots = (0.97)^n P_{t-n}$.

Friedman appears reticent about specifying money wages and instead, talks of the prices of "factor services." Surely wages *must* be paramount.[28] The P-series assumes that technological factors raise output by about 3 per cent per annum. Unquestionably this rule imposes a powerful discipline on labour, to forego, on average, increases in money wages.

Rule 3. A Constant M-Growth

Because of the recent tendencies of P to rise by some 3 per cent to 5 per cent per annum, Professor Friedman renounces rule 2 as involving "serious transitional costs." Despite his attachment to rule 2, as a concession to tradition and "a near-consensus in the profession, that a stable level of prices of final products was a desirable policy objective," he recommends a 4 to 5 per cent annual increase in the monetary total (of currency outside the banks plus all commercial bank demand *and* time deposits) as the most appropriate rule for current implementation (pp. 47-8).

Rule 3: $M_t = 1.05 M_{t-1} = (1.05)^2 M_{t-2} = \ldots = (1.05)^n M_{t-n}$;

P-series: $P_t = P_{t-1} = P_{t-2} = \ldots P_{t-n}$;

w-series: $(w/A)_t = (w/A)_{t-1} = \ldots = (w/A)_{t-n}$; $(w_t / w_{t-1}) = (A_t / A_{t-1})$.

The w-series follows on the presumption that if P is to be stable, unit labour costs over time will also have to be (nearly) stable.

This last relationship is important: Friedman proposes to achieve, through monetary policy, a time pattern in which w is synchronized with A.[29] Whereas in Keynes this wage path would require trade union concession or legislative compliance, Friedman promises to order the result indirectly, through adherence to his monetary rule. Labour would be expected to make the adjustment "voluntarily," undoubtedly through the pain of unemployment. "Disorderly" wage demands would exact a penalty: prices would rise and unemployment would ensue.

Agreement and Dispute

On the relation of money to output and employment it appears that there is little to distinguish Friedman from Keynes; Keynesianism and monetarism effectively coincide. It is on the price level or inflation that the camps divide, into monetarist and wage sects. For Keynes the wage-productivity mesh was decisive. For Friedman it is the dual of money supply and output. In protesting some interpretations of his position, Friedman writes:[30] "The price level is then a joint outcome of the monetary forces determining nominal income and the real forces determining real income." Also: "I regard the description of our position as 'money is all that matters for changes in *nominal* income and for *short-run* changes in real income' as an exaggeration but one that gives the right flavor of our conclusions."

Thus the dispute must ultimately revolve about the respective theories of the price level and the policies advanced to combat inflation. The trend of wages under Friedman's projected rule 3 becomes particularly crucial; although under all of his rules there is an embodied wage policy, under rule 3 it has tended to be submerged. Presumably, unemployment is to be meted out if labour does not yield to the monetary clamp. Recent wage trends suggest that the theory may be incorporating an unduly sanguine estimate of future labour market behaviour.

This optimistic wage trend assessment of Monetarism has not received the attention it deserves. For to stabilize P and w/A under rule 3 the instrument elected is that of a constant M-growth. Yet Friedman himself is the authority for the view that while ΔM bears a good relationship to ΔY, the split between $Q\Delta P$ and $P\Delta Q$ is vague. It is thus doubtful that the M-policy will hold P and w/A firm with (nearly) full employment unless the monetary rule succeeds in foisting a new docility on labour, or an imposed discipline through new laws, signifying either a voluntary or a legislated incomes policy.

For its policy success, unless it is to lead to unacceptable levels of both unemployment and inflation, Friedman's rule must therefore also secure labour's compliance; again we see the convergence in the theories: *both entail an appropriate wage trend.* Friedman assumes it can be achieved indirectly and harmoniously; others equally dedicated to *P*-stability contend that new institutions are needed to induce labour, through cajolery or coercion, to adopt a more reasonable wage stance.

Skepticism thus persists on the viability of Rule 3 unless its policies, when confronted by excessive annual wage demands and the persistence of unemployment, are enunciated. To keep paying the price of unemployment and unrealized output, with its damage to human lives, is undoubtedly harsh: a rule should not compound human misery. Can the rule curb union adamancy for 10, 12, or even 30 per cent annual increases in money wages?

In short: what is the monetarist programme for coping with unruly wage demands? For action in the face of persistent unemployment? If these events occur, what is the contingency plan? It would help to have the monetarist view on these matters; it is evasive to contend that it cannot happen. It may happen, just as it has happened under the less mechanistic monetary policies of the past.

Final Note: Keynes as the Monetarist

The monetarists are the modern descendants of the Currency School: set the monetary course and the economy can be charted while further thought with respect to Q, N, P, and w is superfluous. Inherently, the monetarists believe, along with Mill, that money *doesn't* matter — except under the wrong rule. Delicate monetary parries in combatting unexpected major convulsions or minor disruptions in the evolving economy are rejected.

Keynes regarded money as a lubricating prerequisite to sustain the transactions purposes and to sate the liquidity demands which might take unpredictable turns. In his view, monetary policy could have decisive influence on the outcome when unusual events erupted. Conceivably, Keynes may be better suited for the honorific monetarist title than those who insist that by implementing a single rule, money, thereafter, does not matter.

Notes

An earlier version of this paper was presented at the meetings of the Canadian Economics Association, Winnipeg, June 1970.

1. The 1969 adoption of SDRS by the IMF is a belated vindication of Keynes' plan to enlarge interntional monetary reserves. For a bibliography of Keynes' writings on money, see S.E. Harris, ed., *The New Economics* (New York, 1947).

2. In some passages the old quantity theory survives among the monetarists. Karl Brunner writes: "An assemblage of all the inflationary experiences, new and old, demonstrates that the monetarist thesis explains the whole range of experience with respect to both occurrences and orders of magnitude." See Karl Brunner, "The Drift Into Persistent Inflation," *The Wharton Quarterly*, IV, no. 1 (fall 1969), 26. Friedman: "Inflation is always and everywhere a monetary phenomenon . . ." See M. Friedman, "What Price Guideposts," in George Schultz and Robert

Aliber, eds., *Guidelines, Informal Controls, and the Market Place* (Chicago, 1966), 18. Darryl R. Francis, President of the *FRB* of St. Louis: "The growth of money is thus the key to inflation . . . ," in "Controlling Inflation," Federal Reserve Bank of St. Louis, *Monthly Review*, 51, no. 9 (Sept. 1969), 11.

3. Milton Friedman, *The Optimum Quantity of Money and Other Essays* (Chicago, 1969), 226; Milton Friedman and David Meiselman, "The Relative Stability of Monetary Velocity and the Investment Multiplier in the United States," in Commission on Money and Credit, *Stabilization Policies* (Englewood Cliffs, 1963), 171.

4. On the Keynesian ingredients, see Don Patinkin, "The Chicago Tradition, the Quantity Theory, and Friedman," *Journal of Money, Credit and Banking*, 1, no. 1 (Feb. 1969).

5. Friedman, *The Optimum Quantity of Money*, 215; also M. Friedman, *A Program For Monetary Stability* (New York, 1959), 87-8.

6. Friedman, *The Optimum Quantity of Money*, 279; also, with David Meiselman, "The Relative Stability of Monetary Velocity and the Investment Multiplier In The United States," 172. Anna Schwartz remarks: "indeed, this issue of the forces determining the division of a change in income between prices and output is perhaps the major gap in our present knowledge of monetary relations and effects." See A. Schwartz, "Why Money Matters," *Lloyds Bank Review*, 94 (Oct. 1969), 11.

7. Friedman, *The Optimum Quantity of Money*, 170, 179.

8. *Ibid.*, chap. 1.

9. David Hume, "Of Interest," *Political Discourses* (1752).

10. Friedman, *The Optimum Quantity of Money*, 278.

11. John Stuart Mill, who is quoted with favour by Friedman, wrote long ago: "There cannot, in short, be intrinsically a more insignificant thing, in the economy of society, than money; except in the character of a contrivance for sparing time and labour." And "it only exerts a distinct and independent influence of its own when it gets out of order." *Principles of Political Economy* (1848). Ashley edition, (London, 1915), 488.

12. The word "wages" does not appear in the index of *The Optimum Quantity of Money* though a few inconclusive passages are devoted to the subject. Anna Schwartz likewise fails to refer to wages in the article cited in n. 6.

13. In an earlier article Friedman has written: "The crucial fallacy is the so-called 'wage-price spiral'." See M. Friedman, "The Case for Flexible Exchange Rates," *Essays in Positive Economics* (Chicago, 1953), 181.

14. Apparently, Keynes' castigation of this theory has never been pondered. J.M. Keynes, *The General Theory of Employment, Interest and Money* (London, 1936), 257-60. Cf. my criticism based on J.M. Keynes, *An Approach to the Theory of Distribution* (Philadelphia, 1958), 14-18.

15. Gottfred Haberler, *Prosperity and Depression* (London, 1958); Don Patinkin, *Money, Interest and Prices* (New York, 1956).

16. Axel Leijonhufvud, *On Keynesian Economics and The Economics of Keynes* (New York, 1968), 132n.

17. On the importance attached to the 45° diagram, likening it to Marshallian demand and supply curves in micro-theory, see P.A. Samuelson, "The Simple Mathematics of Income Determination," in *Income, Employment and Public Policy: Essays In Honor of Alvin H. Hansen* (New York, 1948), 135.

18. Cf. my earlier critique in *Classical Keynesianism, Monetary Theory, and the Price Level* (Philadelphia, 1961), chap. 11.

19. On this issue of the choice of units (which I regard as vital for the *P*-theory), Alvin Hansen wrote: "Fundamentally the matter is of no great consequence." See *A Guide to Keynes* (New York, 1953), 44.

20. For an early statement of the "symmetrical" theory, see Robert L. Bishop, "Alternative Expansionist Fiscal Policies: a Diagrammatic Analysis," in *Essays In Honor of Alvin H. Hansen.* Cf. the remarks on "an overly simple model which my generation of economists learned and taught," by James Tobin, "Unemployment and Inflation: The Cruel Dilemma," in Almarin Phillips and O.E. Williamson, eds., *Prices: Issues In Theory, Practice and Public Policy* (Philadelphia, 1967), 101. Keynes had cautioned earlier that deflation in employment and inflation in prices were not symmetrical concepts, *The General Theory*, 291-303.

21. I have suggested, in all seriousness, that those who advocate unemployment through

public policy as an inflation remedy should be the first to joint the ranks of the unemployed to ensure the success of the policy. Cf. R.F. Harrod: "I would suggest that any policy measures deliberately designed to increase the level of unemployment are morally wrong." *Towards A New Economic Policy* (Manchester, 1967), 16.

22. Keynes wrote: "... by acting on the pessimistic hypothesis we can keep ourselves forever in the pit of want." J.M. Keynes, *Essays in Persuasion* (London, 1931), vii-viii.

23. Keynes, *The General Theory*, 12, 295, 302.

24. For Keynesian corroboration of this interpretation of the especial importance of money wages for inflation, cf. R.F. Harrod, *Reforming The World's Money* (London, 1965), 26-27; R.F. Kahn, Radcliffe Commission, *Memorandum of Evidence* 3 (1958), 140; Nicholas Kaldor, "Economic Growth and Inflation," *Economica*, XXVI (Nov. 1959), 292; A.P. Lerner, "Employment Theory and Employment Policy," *American Economic Review*, Proceedings, LVII (May 1967); Joan Robinson, review, *Economic Journal* (Sept. 1938), 510.

25. See Lloyd W. Mints, *A History of Banking Theory* Chicago, 1945).

26. Friedman, *The Optimum Quantity of Money*, 48. Page references in this section are to this work. Cf. some parallel remarks in my "Incomes Policy in the Monetarist Programme," *The Bankers' Magazine*, CCX (Aug. 1970), 75.

27. While Professor Friedman's lags are thus not correctly reproduced, the results will apply along the ultimate path traversed.

28. Cf. Keynes: "The maintenance of a stable general level of money wages is ... the most advisable policy for a closed system; whilst the same conclusion would hold good for an open system, provided that equilibrium with the rest of the world can be secured by means of fluctuating exchanges." *The General Theory*, 270.

29. On the option "of allowing wages to rise slowly whilst keeping prices stable," Keynes wrote that "on the whole my preference is for the latter alternative . . ." *Ibid.*, 271.

30. Milton Friedman, "A Theoretical Framework For Monetary Analysis," *Journal of Political Economy*, 78, no. 2 (March-April 1970), 217.

109

Soviet Views on Keynes:
A Review Article Surveying the Literature*

J.M. Letiche

In writing this paper I benefited greatly from information provided by visiting scholars (at Berkeley) from the Soviet Union, Hungary, Czechoslovakia, Poland, and Yugoslavia. To them, and to the following friends and colleagues, I am deeply indebted not only for stimulating discussions and research cooperation but also for observations based on personal experience — particularly on issues of fundamental disagreement: Carlo M. Cipolla, Gerard Debreu, Howard S. Ellis, Oldrich Kýn, Abba P. Lerner, Mark Perlman, Richard Roehl, and Benjamin Ward.

The purpose of this article is to present an extended review of *An analysis of Soviet views on John Maynard Keynes* by Carl B. Turner (Durham, N.C.: Duke University Press, 1969, pp. vii, 183; $6.50) in the spirit expressed by the late Jacob Viner — teacher and fatherly friend — in a letter dated June 25, 1969: "What is usually referred to as 'scientific objectivity' . . . I prefer to label as 'scholarly objectivity' (because science as it is, once it goes beyond laboratory processes or reporting on actual observations, does not impress me as being strikingly more objective than *some* theological writing, old and recent, I know, or even than *some* poetry I know)."

Carl B. Turner has written an important, objective, and disturbing book on the Soviet economic literature from 1917 to 1964 on Keynes' work.[1] His Chapters I and II provide background by citing the judgments of Lenin and other Soviet authorities on Keynes' writings before the *General theory*. Chapters III and IV examine the relevant Soviet literature during the period 1936-48, including the expurgated "official" Russian translation of the *General theory* that appeared only in 1948. Chapters V and VI review the pertinent books and articles published between 1949 and 1956, the years just before and after Stalin's death in 1953. Chapter VII presents the Soviet reappraisals of Keynes in the comparatively relaxed period 1956-63, and Chapter VIII formulates Turner's conclusions.

*Source: *Journal of Economic Literature*, Vol. 9 (2), June 1971, pp. 442-58.

I

Lenin made numerous and extensive references to Keynes. By Marxian standards, he held him in high regard for his penetrating analysis of contemporary economic problems. Understandably, Lenin was sympathetic to Keynes' conclusions in *The economic consequences of the Peace*, and particularly to his advocacy of cancelling all war debts and normalizing commercial relations with the Soviet Union. These recommendations were the more "edifying," noted Lenin, because they "were given by an avowed bourgeois, a ruthless opponent of bolshevism, which he, as an English philistine, pictures in an ugly, savage, and brutal manner" [48, p. 10]. The epithets notwithstanding, up to the publication of the *General theory*, Lenin's relatively favorable evaluation of Keynes was representative of the Soviet position. Turner cites an entry on Keynes, written before 1936, in the first edition of the *Great Soviet encyclopedia;* formulated in a scholarly manner, it contains not a disparaging word about the man or his work. The entry lists Keynes' "main" books that appeared between 1913 and 1931; it reveals that three of them were expeditiously translated into Russian [48, pp. 12-13]. Surprisingly, no mention was made of *A treatise on probability* [25, 1921].

The pattern changed radically after the publication of the *General theory*. In examining the reasons for this change — many of which can be deduced from Turner's survey — the reader is furnished with new material for an appraisal of the determinants of Soviet acceptance or rejection of Keynesian views.

The first thorough and creditable review of the *General theory* with allowance made for Marxian interpolations appeared in 1946, written by I. G. Blyumin. Turner generously exaggerates when he states that it brought Soviet economists substantially up to date on Keynesian economics. It did, however, make an important contribution toward that end and raised several interesting issues. Contending that Keynes had disregarded the previous history of inflation and underestimated its dangers. Blyumin questioned whether increased employment could long be achieved by reducing real wages through "inflationary" measures. This presentation, at least by implication, distorted Keynes' argument and recommendations. At one juncture, Keynes originally did formulate his theory in a way which suggested that the increase in employment brought about by an increase in spending would be accompanied by a fall in the real wage. But soon after the publication of the *General theory* it was recognized that the change in the real wage — whether it goes up or down — is hardly relevant and does not affect the important proposition that the increase in spending increases employment. In fact, Keynes favored a stabilized wage policy with, if necessary, a small rise in prices to eliminate involuntary unemployment in the short run but rising wages with stable prices in the long run [21, Keynes, 1936, pp. 15-17, 269-71]. Blyumin also devoted considerable space to a critique of Keynes' treatment of interest as a purely monetary phenomenon. His criticism charged Keynes with excluding the labor theory of value from an organic part of the argument in his discussion of the marginal efficiency of capital, and with disregarding the interdependence between the source of profit, the role of self-financing, and the rate of interest in analyzing the determinants of investment. His strongest rebuke was directed against Keynes' omission of a thorough treatment of monopoly and its relation to the "basis of the capitalist class" in generating economic crises. Blyumin considered the "euthanasia of the *rentier*" an obsolete concept which, in any event, applied only to the small *rentier*, not to financial giants. As Turner observes, Blyumin believed Keynes had identified himself with the self-interest of the bourgeoisie who regarded his doctrine as an antidote "to radical plans of socialist democracy" and, he adds sarcastically, to the "wicked Bolshevik planners" [48, pp. 36-40, 41]. The Keynesian program to save capitalism, Blyumin maintained, had a Utopian character. He, therefore, predicted that the effectiveness of Keynes' proposals in regulating capitalism would be negligible. As was characteristic of the time, he closed his review with an "authoritative" statement — a quotation from Stalin! [48, p. 41].

Although reference had been made in the Soviet literature to the *General theory* before the appearance of this review, the commentaries were surprisingly unsystematic, diffuse, and imperceptive. Following Blyumin's review, the number of articles increased and the critical tone became more severe. This was particularly so after the publication in 1948, of N. N. Lyubimov's "official" translation. It included a 45-page introductory article by Blyumin whose name also appeared on the title page. Several of Keynes' passages were omitted, *e.g.,* "The authoritarian state systems of today seem to solve the problem of unemployment at the expense of efficiency and of freedom" [21, p. 381 and 48, p. 70], and editorial comments were added. Turner's study shows, I believe, that with the appearance of Lyubimov's translation in 1948 a turning point occurred in the Soviet treatment of Keynes.

II

As the Cold War grew colder the tone of Soviet economic writing increasingly became that of a "party science." By 1950 one Soviet economist described Keynes as "an open ideologist of imperialist wars"; another claimed "he was even more reactionary than, say, Marshall and Malthus" [48, pp. 77, 84]. More generally, Kochetkov wrote: "Keynesianism was the ideological basis for fascism and cosmopolitanism, and Keynesians were the worst enemies of the working class" [48, p. 84]. By 1952, Blyumin presented Keynes as a "cynical intriguer, the worst enemy of the working class and the toiling masses, and the trusted servant of contemporary imperialism" [48, p. 114]. In 1953, the *Great Soviet encyclopedia* had a new entry on Keynes:

All the activity of Keynes, the zealous enemy of the working class and apologist of the fascist imperialist bourgeoisie, was directed to strengthening the power of the monopolies under the cover of demagogic "anti-crises" phrases . . . . [48, p. 115]

On his international influence, Turner shows the representative Soviet view to be:

> The reactionary militaristic theory of Keynes, which is preached by contemporary Keynesians, the American economists Boulding and Ayres, the English reactionary Beveridge, and others, is now used by the most aggressive circles of American and English monopoly capital, who are acquiring fabulous profits, for the future redistribution of the national income in their favor with the help of the bourgeois state.
>
> The false, reactionary theory of the redistribution of national income that is based on Keynesian ideas is openly accepted by the right-wing socialists and especially the laborites in the service of Anglo-American imperialism. [48, p. 120]

Much of the discussion, whatever comic relief it provides, had manifestly degenerated into vituperation. Keynes' character, and that of other Western economists, was maligned. The emerging form of economic organization, institutions and planning in Western countries was misunderstood and distorted. The interpretation of American, British, French, Indian, Yugoslav, etc., foreign policies as conspiratorial assumed Stalinist proportions. Those who dared disagree with the authoritative position, such as the academician Varga, were down-graded.

In effect, long before the end of World War II, the work done under the auspices of Soviet institutes of economics — as well as the universities — tended to interpret Western economic theory in terms of an "imperialist coalition" and its alleged endeavor to redivide the world. But these efforts failed to fructify in improved explanation of Western economic reality or in theoretical economic advance. In the adaptation and application of Western economic concepts to concrete national problems, however, outstanding Soviet engineers and economists made important contributions both to economic performance and to economic theory.[2] These contributions often were brought about by indirection: in the theory of capital, rent, prices and profits. Since about 1958, under the intellectual stimulus of L. V. Kantorovich and leadership of the late V. S. Nemchinov, Soviet economists have to an increasing extent been catching up and — in some instances — making independent contributions to mathematical programming, input-output analysis, matrix models for economic regions, choice of techniques, optimal growth, investment, decomposition, foreign trade, decision, and forecasting theory.[3]

Turner points out that between 1936 and 1948 Soviet economists paid more attention to Keynes' writings on such practical, applied subjects as "The Policy of Government Storage of Foodstuffs and Raw Materials" [23, pp.

449-60] or *How to pay for the War* [22, 1940], and to the *General theory*. He suggests that the lack of a translation was partly responsible for the neglect of Keynes' major work. But on this matter it is impossible to distinguish between cause and effect, for on previous occasions Soviet authorities had arranged for the rapid translation of Keynes' books.

III

Although Turner raised the important question as to why Soviet economists long neglected the *General theory*, he provides only cursory suggestions and practically no analysis on the problem. Following, therefore, are my views on this issue.

1. By the latter 1930s, the Soviet Union — at whatever cost — could avoid mass unemployment. The main issues to which the *General theory* was directed therefore had little direct relevance to the Soviet economy. It was even claimed by a few that the Keynesian multiplier, predicated on the working of a market mechanism, was not directly applicable to a Soviet-type economy. This is true in the sense that if the Soviet Union were successful in achieving a certain growing level of income, real or monetary, any multiplier would have to be zero because any deviation from plan would be offset. The same, however, is theoretically just as true for a market enterprise economy which achieves a planned level of income.

2. Soviet economic planning has been oriented toward long-run growth trends with emphasis on heavy industry, geographical diversification, existing structural differences between developed and semi-developed regions, and "optimal allocation" among plants and industries. The *General theory* introduced no new tools to help solve these problems. For the improvement of an output-plan worked out centrally, Soviet economists later found input-output techniques and linear programming more useful guides.

3. Before the Second World War, Soviet economists analyzing capitalist countries had become so accustomed to formulating their views in traditional Marxian terms that many appeared unprepared — as were many Western economists — for the arduous intellectual task of mastering the *General theory*.

4. Until the mid-1940s, most Soviet economists did not know the Keynesian literature. Those who had read the *General theory*, I have been repeatedly told by Marxian economists, often as not were genuinely unconvinced by it. They were perplexed that a distinguished economist such as Keynes would, on scientific grounds, omit discussion of technical change, capital formation, and economic growth from a volume designed to explain the root causes of capitalist instability. Consequently, some Russian economists regarded the book as "apologetic," "unsophisticated," or "vulgar economics," undeserving of scientific attention.

5. During the postwar (WW II) Stalinist era, practically all Soviet economists seemed to believe in the inevitability of Western economic collapse and in the irreconcilability of the "two" economic systems. They were therefore inhibited from considering seriously a theory that endeavored to show the possibility of capitalist countries developing into reasonably full-employment, mixed economies.

6. The *General theory* gave rise to fear of a formidable, intellectual-political challenge. Its conclusions contravened the Stalinist predictions that capitalist countries are inherently unable to promote national economic planning. By formulating the contrary view, Keynes had in effect disputed the inevitability of Socialism in the form of Communist-ruled centrally planned economies.

Given the different structures of the Soviet Union and Western countries, it should not be surprising that at certain times important theories originating in the West would be rejected in the Soviet Union without overt discussion. This is likely to occur in sensitive periods if the conclusions are unacceptable on political grounds. Such conclusions, if later discussed in the professional literature, are often deemed to have been derived from false premises and/or to have led to "ideologically" untenable results. This, to a considerable extent, happened with regard to the *General theory* from 1936 to 1946, and continued in a more virulent, open manner from 1946 to 1956.

It should also be expected that some Western theories would remain unknown in the Socialist countries, while certain Marxian concepts would be kept alive by dogma rather than benefiting from critical reappraisal or justified demise.[4] Thus, as late as 1959, I. N. Dvorkin held that Keynesian inflationary policies only impoverished the workers and that the law of absolute impoverishment was still in force [48, p. 130]. For most Soviet writers the labor theory of value remained inviolable, although some give the impression of using it for other than the actual purposes; and marginal analysis remained ideologically in disrepute. This, at the very time of a resurgence in the use of mathematical economics in the Soviet Union!

Three groups could readily be distinguished: 1) the "official" and sympathetic ideologues who, by continually proclaiming the traditional position, preserved vitality for much that could have been forgotten without loss; 2) the deservedly distinguished mathematical and literary theoretical economists who pioneered in the introduction of more modern technical techniques; and 3) the competently secure government economists who were predisposed toward a pragmatic functional approach. But neither these nor the more mathematical and theoretical economists directly challenged the outworn orthodoxy. Indeed, when a Polish economist raised a related issue, he was cautioned by a Russian economist that the demand to "enrich" Marxism by means of Keynesian theory was "The miserable role of revisionism . . . it opens the doors widely for bourgeois ideology to penetrate the ranks of the proletariat" [48, p. 132].

IV

With the advent of peaceful coexistence, the Soviet literature on Keynes flourished in volume, objectivity, diversity, and form. Its tone mellowed from vituperation to refutation. Publication of various gradations in Keynesian thought by Western economists appeared. Theories of "mixed capitalism" were published. Western writings on post-Keynesian dynamics, on oligopoly, economic growth, monetary and fiscal theory, as well as policy, were accorded justifiable attention. As a result, Soviet misunderstanding of Western economies — with attendant erroneous economic predictions — was substantially reduced.

However, a fundamental transformation in the Soviet approach to economic analysis, understandably, did not occur. The less restricted Soviet interpretation of the Western economic literature, and the more objective emergent Soviet writings on the Russian economy, were doubtless complementary products of the freer intellectual environment. But these two phenomena, although interrelated, stem from different sources and have their own streams of existence: the treatment of foreign economic literature appears to have been determined primarily by political, nationalistic forces; the history of Soviet economic analysis has been strongly influenced by Marxian ideological principles. This has impaired even the best Soviet appraisals of Keynesian and more modern Western economic thought. Witness the quality of professional criticism:

> The methodological faults of the Keynesian theory of full employment [are] . . . the subjective-psychological method, the many exchange equations, and the unemployment resulting from insufficient demand [48, p. 152].

And:

> Many of Keynes' ideals to this very day [1963] are the basis of bourgeois interpretations of capitalist reproduction, the theoretical base of various anti-crisis programs, and are used in the theories of "democratic socialism." Therefore the thorough criticism of Keynes' theory in Blyumin's work has not lost its relevance for the present times [48, p. 152].

There is warranted agreement among Russian economists that their more recent criticism of "bourgeois economics" represents a considerable improvement over that of the Stalin period. But the main point is invariably missed. The weakness of much of the Soviet economic literature appears to stem from the historical attrition of theoretical, as compared with applied, economic work. This emphasis is reflected in the basic Russian view that Keynesian economics was successful because it was the most suitable ideological weapon of contemporary capitalism, rather than because it was a formidable intellectual achievement with a superior analytical apparatus for the explanation and eradication of mass unemployment. Accordingly, Keynesian influences are still regarded in the Soviet Union as a form of revisionism to be deplored. Russian economists have been forewarned against a merging of Marxism with Keynesianism. This would be regarded as a step toward peaceful coexistence on the ideological front, a step which the official position has so far categorically disallowed.[5]

Marxian economists have become increasingly aware of the difficulty in communicating with economists of the Western tradition. In applying Marxian theory to problems posed by Keynes in his *Treatise on money* and in the *General theory*, Erdös writes:

> He [Keynes] analysed them by the methods of what he calls classical economics [sic!], while we, by our means, hope to obtain more appropriate answers. Others will have to judge the final result of this attempt, which is not as yet complete. But no one will be surprised to find that the results of this approach in so far as they are already available, though far from identical with those derived by Keynes nevertheless strike the Western-trained economist as quite familiar. This will not prevent one or the other economist, for instance in Hungary, finding them novel. Hence I must ask the indulgence of both groups of possible readers: one will have to excuse the undue prolixity of my explanations, while the others must forgive the unjustifiable brevity.[6]

Erdös judges correctly, I believe, that the results he has so far obtained are familiar to the Western-trained economist. This notwithstanding, he is to be commended for placing emphasis on scholarly objectivity in interpreting Marxian and non-Marxian writings. All economists, he states, should become acquainted with the *General theory* and its effects on the development of diverse schools of economic thought.[7] Furthermore, he deems it important that the international labor movement study the actual conditions and possibilities of the capitalist countries, including their economic principles. He regards Keynes' *General theory* as an effective beginning for this task. But the reasons he gives for these aims are strictly of the applied Marxian variety:

> ... it is necessary to go beyond a criticism of Keynes' methodology to a practical critique of Keynesian policies. Theories regarding the possibility of various forms of state intervention, and their limitations, have to be elaborated on a scientific basis, so that laborers in capitalist countries can resolutely demand correct economic policies rather than remain passive and nihilistic. Hungarian economists have already contributed to this useful theoretical work. The publication of the *General theory* in Hungarian will doubtless assist its continuance.[8]

V

Oskar Lange also had occasion to be concerned about the tone and method of professional discussion, particularly in regard to the development of Marxian and Western economics. Known to our profession (and certainly to me, his student) as a brilliant teacher, a leading American professor of economics, as well as a Marxian theorist, he was in an admirable position to carry back to Eastern Europe a sophisticated understanding of Keynesian thought as it existed in this country in the decade of publication of the *General theory*. But for many years thereafter his scientific work seems to have ceased. In a remarkable but little known essay written in 1943 [29, pp. 378-384] (before he returned from the United States to Poland), he noted that Keynesian principles could — and should — be applied to neo-Marxist theories of imperialism. Mass unemployment gives to all classes in society a stake in imperialist expansion. For the working class, this stake is much more one of employment opportunities than higher real wages, as had been assumed in Lenin's theory of the corruption of the working class by imperialism. Hence, Keynesian economics leads to a theory of imperialism different from the one held by Hilferding and Lenin, which was formulated in terms of exportation of surplus capital. In essence, it acquires the character of a "people's imperialism" which *e.g.*, under fascism, binds together all social classes and eliminates the class struggle by granting to the members of each class a stake in imperialist expansion. Lange thought the situation explained the idological success of German fascism with the working class. It also explained, he asserted, why fascism cannot be overthrown by internal class conflict but only by external military defeat.

As regards the Marxian theoretical apparatus specifically, Lange stressed the need for comparing Marxian economics with "modern marginal analysis," and critically evaluating it in these terms. He objected to the view that modern economic theory was devoid of social significance. *Per contra,* to act on the assumption that the Marxian approach alone can yield economic theory endowed with this attribute (social significance), cannot but result in a loss of important achievements of modern economics and failure to benefit from the latter's criticism of Marxian theory.

This had already occurred. In the Marxian theory of prices, Lange pointed out, the organic composition of capital and the rate of turnover of capital are taken as given. These assumptions are contradicted by experience: both depend on prices and the rate of interest. The Marxian theory is inadequate to take this into account and, to do so, resort must be had to the concept of marginal productivity. Moreover, the Marxian theory presupposes constant physical returns (to scale?) in each industry. When industries are subject to increasing or decreasing returns, demand must be introduced explicitly in the determination of prices. Again, this leads to marginal analysis. Further, the labor theory of value is not applicable to the labor market, because the equilibrating mechanism resulting from mobility of capital and labor between different industries does not operate in this market (*sic*). Nor does a solution by means of the "reserve army" save the labor theory of value. There remains also the difficulty of reducing skilled labor to common labor. Lange doubted whether such a reduction could be made without running into the vicious circle of making the reduction through reference to relative wage rates, *i.e.*, to prices.

By renouncing the methods of marginal analysis, Lange concluded, Marxian theory deprives itself of a powerful tool for analyzing the dynamics of wage-rate determination, monopoly and oligopoly. Marxian theory could be greatly strengthened, he advised, by the incorporation of modern monetary theory and the tools of mathematical dynamic economics. Most Western academic economists, he thought, use modern analytical techniques in a way which deprives them of social signficance. However, addressing himself to Marxist economists, he wrote:

> But, before we decide to reject them and to revert to an obsolete theory like the labor theory of value (which is open to all the unanswered objections enumerated above), we would have to prove that they can not be used fruitfully in a way which is socially significant. We would have to prove, too, that the labor theory of value can be improved to meet all the objections raised against it [29, 1943, p. 382].

Lange considered the Marxist attachment to the labor theory of value a cardinal stumbling block to the fusion of Marxian and Western economic theory. He noted that Marxians interpret market processes in terms of objective social relations appearing in the course of production; *i.e.*, in the economic process as a social bond emerging among men as producers. But they believe marginal analysis interprets market processes in terms of subjective relations appearing in the course of market exchange *i.e.*, in the economic process as man satisfying his personal economic advantage. Marxists therefore concentrate their analysis on relations of the former type: "man-thing-man." They reject as useless the work on relations of the latter type: "man-thing." In doing so, however, Lange points out that these Marxists miss the very intent of Marxian theory. Its purpose, he maintains, is to treat economics not merely as the study of social relations between men, but as the study of a specific type of social relations; *viz.*, those which result from the relation of men to things as objects of satisfaction of their wants. It is the interplay of relations between men and things and social relations between men which is at the core of the theory of historical materialism.

To meet the needs of Marxian theory, the analysis of the relations between men and things considered as want-satisfying objects is therefore indispensable. "There is no reason," Lange observes, "why Marxists should be satisfied with the utterly crude treatment of this subject given by Marx, rather than accept the achievements of modern marginal economics in this field" [29,

1943, p. 383].[9] Lange was willing to accept the suggestion of other Marxists that the labor theory of value might be used as a sociological theory of imputation in conjunction with marginalist price theory. Because marginal theory, he states, deals with relations of "man to things," imputation of part of the value product to non-human agents of production — capital and land — would entail consistent economic analysis. Economic sociology, however, is concerned with relations between men. In consequence, he alleges that imputation to non-human agents in this sphere of analysis would be meaningless. Here the labor theory of value would, presumably, not be open to the usual objections. But even for this purpose he recognized that the concept would be strained. There still remains the problem of reducing different kinds of labor to a common unit, and the notion of "surplus labor" is arbitrary because of the indeterminateness of the concept of "necessary labour." In any event, Lange acknowledged that a sociological interpretation can be given to economic processes in a much more straightforward and precise manner than by means of such "a stretched use of the labor theory of value" [29, 1943, p. 383].[10]

The fundamental problem of modern marginal analysis — pure economics — Lange insisted, is the use of scarce resources. The fundamental problem of Marxian analysis — economic sociology — is the class structure of society. The two problems are strictly interrelated: for the theory of the class structure of society can be expressed in terms of the way in which society is organized to make use of scarce resources. This approach, Lange believed, would permit treating the problems posed by Marxian theory by means of much more satisfactory techniques than Marxists had heretofore employed.[11] Research along these lines, Lange stated, would absorb the major contributions of Marxian theory without being hampered by its limitations. Even more important, it would clear the path for further developments. By clinging to the traditional apparatus of Marxian theory — and Lange rightly singled out the labor theory of value for particular attention — he feared that Marxists would submit in matters of economic science to a spirit of traditionalism and conservatism to which they would certainly refuse to submit in matters of social policy.

Conclusions

1. The appraisal of the Soviet economic literature on Keynes from 1917 to 1964 published in Turner's book demonstrates that politico-nationalist forces primarily determined the extent of Soviet acceptance and/or rejection of Keynesian — and more recent Western — economic writings. Given this restraint, the advance of Soviet economic theory was further hindered by the bounds of Marxian "ideological" principles. In many instances, the retention of obsolete concepts seriously impaired the quality of economic analysis. Key

aspects of Keynesian economics continued to be misinterepreted. With the advent of peaceful coexistence, Soviet economists were able to introduce and to absorb much modern economic theory within the limits set by allegiance to Marxian principles. Keynesian theory was more objectively presented and criticized with resulting improvement in Soviet perception of Western economies and reduction in erroneous economic forecasts.

2. The ideological factor in traditional Marxian economic theory — with the labor theory of value and its relation to national and international "capitalist class exploitation" as its core — readily lent itself to the political misuse of the Soviet economic profession. This was shown to be particularly true in the harsh interpretations of Keynes, the man and his work, during the Stalinist era. Although virtually all economic theorizing suffers from an ideological element (and institutions the world over have ways of generating ideas congenial to themselves), traditional Marxian economic theory has been burdened by a deliberately ideological vocabulary. With rapidly changing ends and increasing availability of alternative means, this has become a serious handicap to Soviet economists endeavoring to forge new economic principles for the efficient guidance of the Soviet economy. In partial consquence, a small but noted group of Soviet economists has turned to the greater use of mathematics in economics, thereby widening the gulf between what Soviet economists term "theoretical" as compared with "mathematical" economics. The experience has proved that a technical economic vocabulary, as free as possible from ideological valuations, is essential not only for defining modern economic concepts, but also for representing, explaining, and testing basic premises and fundamental national and international economic relationships.

3. The Soviet advance in modern economic analysis appears first to have substantially spread in the theoretical non-mathematical literature. Some Russian mathematical economic writings had their "proximate" antecedents in the 1920s and 1930s, to say nothing of the celebrated earlier work, but it was only after 1958 that the various branches of mathematical economics made their gigantic strides. The growth of econometrics, however, appears to have been hindered by a lack of recognition on the part of the "planning organs" — and by many Soviet economists — of the practical usefulness of these techniques. Although Soviet economists in none of these fields have made a frontal attack against the antiquated concepts of traditional Marxian economic theory, "mathematical economics" has served as a stimulus for strengthening "economic theory" and as a rarified force for revising obsolete concepts.

4. The remarkable essay by Oskar Lange on the *rapprochement* of Marxian and modern economics, with its conclusions attested to by the works of Joan Robinson, pointed out that none of the important propositions which have been expressed in terms of the labor theory of value can not be better expressed without it. Since the mid-1950s, as an ever larger body of modern economic principles has been introduced and developed in the Soviet Union, there has been a growing recognition that they have nothing inherently "capitalistic" or

"socialistic" about them. For the effective allocation of resources — abstracting from the different principles of distribution — increasing attention has also been devoted to the process of imputation in regard to land and capital, as well as to labor. A small number of Soviet mathematical economists have recognized the weaknesses and misuse of the Marxian value concept for the determination of optimum factor and product prices, for the efficient planning of investment, and for the guidance of optimum national output. Most Soviet economists have given passive support to these views by discreet silence. However, no disagreement has arisen on the inviolability of the "Marxian system" as a method of dialectical materialism, with the related view among Soviet economists that the labor theory of value remains immutable as an argument in "capitalist exploitation" and the "laws of motion of capitalist society." Distinguished Soviet economists have been unaware of, or find it incumbent "to discover" and "to prove" within the Marxian framework, otherwise well known modern propositions, endeavoring to show that their formulation, rather than that of other Marxists, is a correct or consistent interpretation of Marx. This is yet a more determined form of "ideology" — a refusal to recognize that the Marxian "economic system" or "model," like others — may in general be no more inviolable than that of many economic concepts.

As regards economic sociology, Lange's position notwithstanding, the Marxian *value* concepts are as inapplicable for the explanation of "capitalist exploitation" or its "law of motion" as they are for the explanation of other capitalist phenomenon. The human agent throughout recorded history has been inextricably linked with the discovery and use of capital. As an historical process, capital inherently contains previously existing capital as well as "embodied" labor. A distinction must carefully be drawn between tools of analysis used to explain and guide an economic system under given conditions and concepts used as norms for socio-economic purposes. As I interpret several distinguished Soviet economists, they consider Marxian *value* concepts as "a social welfare criterion" for optimum distribution and as surrogate criteria for the allocation of "socially necessary resources" among competing public and private uses, including provision for future needs. In a socialist economy, such "norms," with all their technical limitations, might serve as a useful benchmark for long-run analysis, demonstrating that existing product and factor prices do not necessarily conform with optimum social valuations. While inapplicable even for this purpose to Western economies, it might well stimulate East-West research into allocation criteria applicable to both socialist and non-socialist countries.

5. Although Marxian economists have emphasized the need for theory to explain the process of development of an economic system over time, their attention has been riveted to a fundamental Marxian law: the evolution of an economic system is a self-generating dialectical process in which contradictions occurring within the system produce its continual motion and develop-

ment. Our analysis has shown that before 1956, Soviet economic literature suffered primarily from obsolete basic premises and from contradictions between the "partial" and the "aggregative" elements ("parts" and "wholes") in the Marxian economic system. This form of obsolescence was even more important than the extremely slow development of new Marxian concepts, hypothesis and theories to explain the changing structural relations and growth of the Soviet economy. The primary thesis of this review, confirmed by the examination of the Soviet economic literature during two postwar periods — before and after 1956 — is that the method and tone of "discussion" are of primary importance for scholarly objectivity and theoretical economic advance. After 1956 the freer intellectual environment in the Soviet Union, even within comparatively narrow limits, produced a much stronger positive force than the restraining influence of "ideological truths" of traditional Marxian concepts and systems of concepts.

Further evolution along these lines is indispensable for accelerating the development of Soviet economic theory and thereby narrowing the gap between Soviet "economic theory" and "mathematical economics." This would contribute not only to professional confidence and coherence within the Soviet Union but to the *rapprochement* between East and West in analytical economic thought. The views of Marxian and non-Marxian economists have been converging on the conclusion that the results of such modern analysis would tend to demonstrate advantages to the Soviet Union of gradually moving toward a centrally planned but decentralized market economy with increased delegation of decision-making powers to directors responsible for integrating the production-distribution networks.[12] These problems, and the conclusions reached in this paper, are closely related to Turner's contribution. They required, however, distinct identification and appraisal.

Notes

1. My references to Turner's book will be made mainly in the text in the form "[48, 1969, p. –]." References to the *General theory* will be to the first American printing [21, 1936].

2. For discussion of the pre-1945 contributions, see especially Norman Kaplan [17, 1952] and Gregory Grossman [9, 1953]. Whether it be termed "a dialectic of scientific cognition" (Lange) or "an economic logic that has nothing specifically 'capitalist' about it" (Pareto and Barone), Isaac Guelfat has endeavored to show that Soviet economists have independently "discovered" many Western economic principles. See *e.g.*, his discussion on "Land Rent" and the survey "From Kantorovich to the Lieberman-Trapeznikov School" [10, 1969, pp. 76—94, 131—49]. As objective achievements in the history of economic analysis, predictably, the "discoveries" cited therein do not appear impressive.

3. For a comprehensive treatment of these advances, see Alfred Zauberman (with contributions by A. Bergstrom, T. Kronsjö, and E.J. Mishan) [53, 1967], esp. on "Reconciling Leontief with Marx," pp. 34—38, the "Link-Up with Russian Thought of the Early 1900s," pp. 47—55, and Part II: On Planning Techniques in Pricing, Profit Guidance, Efficiency of Investment, and Foreign Trade. For particular topics, *cf.* also Maurice Dobb [5, 1969], Part II; C.H. Feinstein, ed. [8, 1967], esp. the essays by economists from the centrally planned economies: P. Erdös, L.H. Hejl, M. Kalecki, A.A. Konüs, O. Kýn, O. Lange, B. Sekerka, O. Sik,

and Sh. Ya. Turetsky; John P. Hardt, Marvin Hoffenberg, Norman Kaplan, and Herbert S. Levine, eds. [11, 1967]; and Benjamin Ward [51, 1967, Ch. VII].

4. Péter Erdös, a Hungarian economist, has observed that "economic ideas which have long ago become commonplace in one camp, in the other remain totally unknown; or else, and no less frequently, are known but wholly rejected." See his "The Application of Marx's Model of Expanded Reproduction to Trade Cycle Theory" [7, 1967, p. 59].

5. For references on this issue, including the program of the Twenty-Second Congress of the CPSU, see Turner [48, pp. 154—56]. The lack of primary source materials on Marxist views regarding the relation between Keynesian and Marxian economics and on variant reasons for the success of the *General theory* makes it worthwhile to present *in extenso* a translation of Péter Erdös' "Foreword to the Hungarian translation of *The general theory of employment, interest and money*" as an appendix to this article.

6. See [7, 1967, p. 60]. To avoid misunderstanding, it is important to distinguish between various uses of the term "classical economics." It was invented by Marx, who used it synonymously with "the classical school of political economy which dates from William Petty [1623—89] in England and Boisguillebert [1648—1714] in France, and closes with Ricardo [1772—1823] in the former country and Sismondi [1773—1842] in the latter." Karl Marx, [34, 1859, p. 56]: in *Capital*, Marx speaks of " . . . Adam Smith and David Ricardo, the best representatives of this school" [35, Vol. I, p. 36]. Keynes, however, included in "The Classical School the *followers* of Ricardo . . . who adopted and perfected the theory of the Ricardian economics, including (for example) J.S. Mill, Marshall, Edgeworth, and Prof. Pigou" [21, 1936, p. 3, n. 1; italics in original]. Even with respect to this definition, Keynes referred to his approach as "our point of *departure* from the classical system," [21, 1936, p. 17, italics supplied].

7. See "Foreword" in Appendix (p. 474). The Soviet economic literature on Keynes throughout the 1960s has continued to demonstrate a critical but increasingly objective tone; no fundamental change in interpretation has occurred, however, since the publication of Turner's book. But some recognition has been given to structural changes in capitalism. See L. Al'ter [1, No. 4, 1964, p. 75], where the author admits that Leontief's input-output approach has a scientific direction ("nauchnoe napravlenie"), but is imbued with notions of vulgar bourgeois political economy; Al'ter [2, 1966] interprets attempts to dynamize Keynesian and post-Keynesian thought in accord with ongoing structural changes in capitalism. No mention is made of previous Khrushchevian claims of "overtaking and surpassing" the United States. *Cf.*, however the ideological tone in M.N. Ryndina [43, 1964] and, particularly, in Y. Varga's [50, 1963, pp. 304—29] "The Reason for the Popularity of Keynesian Theories." Also, the writings of I. Osadchaia [39, 1965 and 40, 1967] on post-Keynesian economics represent a mellowing of criticism, as well as a differentiation among neo-Keynesians and their critics. For the more objective tone in the Polish, Czechoslovakian, and Hungarian literature, respectively, see M. Kalecki [15, 1963]; L. Urban, ed., with contributions by R. Budinová, M. Rumler, A. Tlustý, J. Janis, O. Kýn, J. Chlumský [49, 1967]; and Janos Kornai [27, 1971].

8. See Appendix, p. 474. The reaction in Western countries to the form of Soviet planning must also be borne in mind. "Planning," writes Karl W. Rothschild, "had to be refused as the thin end of the bad wedge of socialism. The market had to be extolled as the one and only means of running a 'free society.'" [42, 1967, p. 170]. In 1944 this position found its formulation in F. von Hayek's *Road to serfdom* [14]. As a fervent liberal in the wider sense, Keynes wrote to Hayek: "In my opinion it is a grand book. We all have the greatest reason to be grateful to you for saying so well what needs so much to be said. You will not expect me to accept quite all the economic dicta in it. But morally and philosophically I find myself in agreement with virtually the whole of it; and not only in agreement with it, but in a deeply moved agreement" (cited by R.F. Harrod [13, 1970, pp. 105—06]). Joseph A. Schumpeter took even a more extreme position, questioning "whether analytical work of the kind that is [was] being turned out [in the Soviet Union] is really preferable to total suspension of such work." [44, 1954, p. 1158, n. 9]. The record, as noted, appears to have disproved this view; moreover, the growing worldwide tendency to separate the fundamental capitalism-socialism debate from the planning-market debate clearly would have been approved by both Keynes and Schumpeter.

In his letter to Hayek, however, Keynes further wrote: "I should therefore conclude your theme rather differently . . . what we want is not no planning . . . we almost certainly want more . . . Moderate planning will be safe if those carrying it out are rightly oriented in their own minds and hearts to the moral issue . . . Your greatest danger ahead is the probably practical failure of the application of your philosophy in the U.S. in a fairly extreme form"—June 28, 1944 [12, 1951, pp. 436—37].

9. Lange's later writings took a stronger Marxian tone but, if I interpret him correctly, his position on these issues remained consistent [28, 1963, pp. 231—264]. In a historical discussion on the way in which Western economists have used "subjective economics," however, Lange claims that they extended the principle of maximization employed in capitalist enterprise to all economic activity in all historico-social conditions. He concedes that they formulated certain "praxiological principles of behavior," the science of rational activity, of which "the economic principle" is one: "rational human behavior directed to the maximum realization of a given end" [28, 1963, p. 187]. But these principles, he writes, are not economic laws; *i.e.,* laws operating in objective reality. "They are methodological rules of behavior forming the subject matter of praxiology — a discipline auxiliary to political economy like logic, mathematics, statistics, econometrics, and so on. As political economy, the subjectivist theory must be reckoned a failure" [28, 1963, p. 264]. In an otherwise provocative mathematical book, Lange, on the other hand, presents a doctrinaire position on the theory of dialectical materialism [30, 1965, pp. 1—3, 72—75]. In reviewing another of Lange's books, *Theory of reproduction and accumulation,* Domenico Mario Nuti observes that Lange's work has been highly influential and successful as an attempt to translate modern economic theory into the Marxian categories commonly used in Eastern Europe, but "the book suffers from the sterility of the Marxian system of definition and classification of economic categories which should not be identified with the substance of the Marxian approach to political economy" [38, 1970, p. 341]. See also Joan Robinson, [41, 1947, p. 20]. Yet, in 1967, A.A. Konüs, a competent economist with Gosplan, still insisted upon the adherence to "the fundamental formulae of the labour theory of value" [26, 1967, p. 83]. A comparatively small number of Soviet economists, however, have used mathematical economics as an instrument for theoretical advance and as a stimulus for revision of dogma and obsolete concepts, acknowledging the use of marginal analysis for the process of imputation with respect to all relevant inputs and noting the misuse by some authors, even within the Marxian framework, of the labor theory of value as an average concept for optimum factor and product pricing. See A.L. Lur'e [32, 1966, p.27]: " . . . optimal valuations and the prices that correspond to them will be *proportional* to the socially necessary labor expenditures if by these are meant the marginal increments in labor on the scale of the entire socialist economy corresponding to a unit increase of one or another resource." Also see the article (1969) by Lur'e, [33, esp. pp. 199—212]. His presentation is definitely *not* representative of the Soviet economic literature in general. The earlier formulation by V.V. Novozhilov is noteworthy [37, 1939].

10. To a considerable extent, this has been done in the modern applications of economic sociology to the study of roles, organizations, and institutions that specialize in economic activities. See the article by Neil J. Smelser, [45, 1968, pp. 500—06].

11. *E.g.,* he refers to Abba Lerner's use of Joan Robinson's theory of rent as a basis for a theory of social stratification. See A.P. Lerner, [31, 1939, pp. 557-67]. In a similar vein, an important common concept underlies at least three recent applications of economic theory to problems hitherto not generally considered to fall within its range; *viz.,* the social utility or disutility of any structurally integrated group whose behavior can be analyzed in terms of collective upon individual interest, *e.g.,* a trade-off by discriminators between a willingness to sacrifice material gain and a psychological gain derived from discrimination [3, Becker, 1957; 6, Downs, 1957 and 4, Breton, 1964]. The above-mentioned concept can readily be integrated into the Paretian Welfare Theory [47, Tarascio, 1969, esp. Table 1, p. 5].

12. For converging views among Marxian and non-Marxian economists referred to *supra*, see V.S. Nemchinov [36, 1936], L.V. Kantorovich [16, 1964], Alfred Zauberman [53, 1967], Clark Kerr [18, 1969], Chs. IX and X on "New 'Inherent Contradictions' " and "The Future of Pluralism," pp. 115-130, and János Kornai [27, 1971], esp. Parts III and IV. The materials contained in [46, 1970] also should prove useful; to date they have been unavailable to me.

References

1. AL'TER, L. "Teoriia i praktika kapitalisticheskogo regulirovaniia" ("Theory and Practice of Capitalist Controls"), *Mirovaia ekonomika i mezhdunarodnye otnosheniia*, No. 3,

1964, pp. 63-72, and No. 4, 1964, pp. 71-79.

2. _____, 'Metodologicheskie problemy teorii ekonomicheskogo rosta: ("Methodological Problems of Economic Growth Theory"), *Mirovaia ekonomika i mezhdunarodnye otnosheniia*, No. 10, 1966, pp. 17-28, and No. 12, 1966, pp. 78-88.

3. BECKER, G. S. *The economics of discrimination*. Chicago: University of Chicago Press, 1957.

4. BRETON, A. "The Economics of Nationalism," *J. Polit. Econ.*, August 1964, 72, pp. 376-86.

5. DOBB, M. *Welfare economics and the economics of socialism*. Part II. Cambridge: Cambridge University Press, 1969.

6. DOWNS, A. "An Economic Theory of Political Action in a Democracy," *J. Polit. Econ.*, April 1957, 66, pp. 135-50.

7. ERDÖS, P. "The Application of Marx's Model of Expanded Reproduction to Trade Cycle Theory" in *Socialism, capitalism, and economic growth* ed. by C. H. FEINSTEIN. Cambridge: Cambridge University Press, 1967.

8. FEINSTEIN, C. H., ed. *Socialism, capitalism and economic growth*. Cambridge: Cambridge University Press, 1967.

9. GROSSMAN, G. "Scarce Capital and Soviet Doctrine," *Quart. J. Econ.*, August 1953, 67, pp. 311-43.

10. GUELFAT, I. *Economic thought in the Soviet Union*. C.I.R.I.E.C. Liege and Martinus Nijhoff, The Hague, 1969.

11. HARDT, J. P.; HOFFENBERG, M.; KAPLAN, N. AND LEVINE, H. S., eds. *Mathematics and computers in Soviet economic planning*. New Haven and London: Yale University Press, 1967.

12. HARROD, R. F. *The life of John Maynard Keynes*. New York: Harcourt, Brace and Company, 1951.

13. _____, Review of *Roads to freedom. Essays in honour of Friedrich A. von Hayek*, in *Econ. J.*, March 1970, pp. 105-106.

14. VON HAYEK, F. A. *Road to Serfdom*. Chicago: University of Chicago Press, 1944.

15. KALECKI, M. *Zarys teorii wzrostu gospodarki socjalistycznej (An outline of a theory of growth for the socialist economy)* Warszawa: PWN, 1963.

16. KANTOROVICH, L. V. *Planirovanie i ekonomiko-matematicheskie metody*. Moscow: "Nauka," 1964, tr. from Russian (in part), as "A Dynamic Model of Optimum Planning," *Mathematical Studies in Economics and Statistics in the USSR and Eastern Europe*, Winter 1964-65, 1(2), pp. 41-67.

17. KAPLAN, N. "Investment Alternatives in Soviet Economic Theory," *J. Polit. Econ.*, April 1952, 60, pp. 133-144.

18. KERR, C. *Marshall, Marx and modern times*. Cambridge: Cambridge University Press, 1969.

19. KEYNES, J. M. *A foglalkoztatás, a kamat és a pénz általános elmélete*, tr. by PÉTER ERDÖS. Budapest: Közgazdasági Kiadó, 1959.

20. _____, *The economic consequences of the Peace*. New York: Harcourt, Brace and Company, 1919.

21. _____, *The general theory of employment, interest and money*. New York: Harcourt, Brace and Company, 1936.

22. _____, *How to pay for the War: A radical plan for the Chancellor of the Exchequer*. New York: Harcourt, Brace and Company, 1940.

23. _____, "The Policy of Government Storage of Foodstuffs and Raw Materials," *Econ. J.*, Sept. 1938, 48, pp. 449-60.

24. _____, *A treatise on money*. 2. vols. London: Macmillan and Co., Ltd., 1930.

25. _____, *A treatise on probability*. London: Macmillan and Co., Ltd., [1921] 1952.

26. KONÜS, A. A. "On the Tendency for the Rate of Profit to Fall" in *Socialism, capitalism and economic growth* ed. by C. H. FEINSTEIN. Cambridge: Cambridge University Press, 1967.

27. KORNAI, J. *Anti equilibrium: On economic systems theory and the tasks of research*. Amsterdam. North-Holland Publishing Company, 1971.

28. LANGE, O. *Political economy*, Vol. I. Tr. by A. H. WALKER. New York: Pergamon Press, 1963.

29. _____, Review of *The theory of capitalist development* by PAUL M. SWEEZY in *J. of Philosophy*, July 1943, *40*(14), pp. 378-84.

30. _____, *Wholes and parts, a general theory of system behavior*. London: Pergamon Press (original published in Poland, 1962, tr. by EUGENIUSZ LEPA), 1965.

31. LERNER, A. P. "From Vulgar Political Economy to Vulgar Marxism," *J. Polit. Econ.*, August 1939, *47*, pp. 557-67.

32. LUR'E, A. L. 'Abstraktnaia model' optimal'nogo khoziaistvennogo protsessa; ob'ektivno obuslovlennye otsenki," *Ekonomika i Matematicheski Metody*, 1966, *2*(1), pp. 12-30; trans. from the Russian as "An Abstract Model of an Optimal Economic Process and Objectively Determined Valuations (Shadow Prices)," *Mathematical Studies in Economics and Statistics in the USSR and Eastern Europe*, Winter 1966-67, *3*(2), pp. 3-35.

33. _____, "O raschetakh normy effektivnosti i ob odnoproduktovoi neprerivnoi modeli narodnogo knoziaistva," *Ekonomika i Matematicheskie Metody*, 1969, *5*(3), pp. 366-77; trans. from the Russian as "Concerning Calculations of the Norm of Effectiveness and a One-Product Continuous Model of the National Economy," *Matekon*, Winter, 1969-70, *7*(2), pp. 196-216.

34. MARX, K. *A contribution to the critique of political economy*. Chicago: Charles H. Kerr and Company (KARL KAUTSKY, ed. of original edition, 1859), tr. from the 2nd German edition by N. I. STONE (Chicago: Charles H. Kerr and Company, 1904).

35. _____, *Capital*. Vol. I. Chicago: Britannica Great Books, 1952; Vols. II and III. Chicago: C. H. Kerr and Company, 1909.

36. NEMCHINOV, V. S. "Osnovnye kontury modeli planovogo tsenoobrazovaniia," *Voprosy ekonomiki*, 1963, No. 12, pp. 105-21; tr. from Russian as "The Basic Contours of the Model of Planned Price-Formation," *Mathematical Studies in Economics and Statistics in the USSR and Eastern Europe*, Winter 1964-65, *1*(2), pp. 3-40.

37. NOVOZHILOV, V. V. "On Choosing Between Investment Projects," trans. from Russian by B. WARD, *International economic papers* (London: Macmillan Co., 1956), pp. 66-87. Originally published in *Transactions of the Leningrad Industrial Institute*, 1939, and in *Transactions of the Leningrad Polytechnic Institute*, 1946.

38. NUTI, D. M. Review of *Theory of reproduction and accumulation* by OSKAR LANGE in *Econ. J.*, June 1970, p. 341.

39. OSADCHALA, I. "Evoliutsiia keinsianstva" ("Evolution of Keynesianism"), *Mirovaia ekonomika i mezhdunarodnye otnosheniia*, 1965, No. 2, pp. 61-72.

40. _____, " 'Neoklassicheskaia' teoriia rosta v sovremennoi burzhuaznoi politicheskoi ekonomii" (" 'Neo-classical Growth' Theory in Modern Bourgeois Political Economy"), *Mirovaia ekonomika i mezhdunarodnye otnosheniia*, 1967, No. 3. pp. 17-28.

41. ROBINSON, J. *An essay in Marxian economics*. London: Macmillan Co., Ltd., 1947.

42. ROTHSCHILD, K. W. "Socialism, Planning, Economic Growth" in *Socialism, capitalism and economic growth* ed. by C. H. FEINSTEIN. Cambridge: Cambridge University Press, 1967.

43. RYNDINA, M. N. *Kritika osnovnykh napravlenii sovremennoi burzhuaznoi politicheskoi ekonomii* (*Critique of the main directions of current bourgeois political economy*). Moscow: "Mysl," 1964.

44. SCHUMPETER, J. A. *History of economic analysis*. Edited by E. B. SCHUMPETER. New York: Oxford University Press, 1954.

45. SMELSER, N. J. "Economy and Society," *International Encyclopedia of the Social Sciences*. Vol. IV. The Macmillan Company and The Free Press, 1968, pp. 500-06.

46. *Strukturnye izmeneniaa i novye napravleniia v razvitii politicheskoi ekonomii pri kapitalizme*. Materialy mezhdunarodnoi konferentsii ekonomistov-marksistov. (*Structural changes and new directions in the development of political economy under capitalism*. Materials of International Conference of Marxist Economists), Bratislava, 1970.

47. TARASCIO, V. J. "Paretian Welfare Theory: Some Neglected Aspects," *J. Polit. Econ.*, Jan.-Feb. 1969. *77*, pp. 1-20.

48. TURNER, CARL B. *An analysis of Soviet views on John Maynard Keynes*. Durham, N.C.: Duke University Press, 1969.

49. URBAN, L. ed. *Eseje o teoriích ekonomického růstu* (*Essays on theories of economic growth*) with contributions by R. BUDÍNOVÁ, M. RUMLER, A TLUSTÝ, J. JANIS, O. KÝN, and J. CHLUMSKÝ. Praha: Academia, 1967.

50.   VARGA, Y. *Politico-economic problems of capitalism.* Moscow: Progress Publishers, 1968. Tr. from the Russian (1963) by DON. DANEMANIS.
51.   WARD, N. *The socialist economy.* New York: Random House, 1967.
52.   VON WIESER, F. *Social economics.* Tr. A. FORD HINRICHS. London: George Allen & Unwin, Ltd., 1927.
53.   ZAUBERMAN, A. *Aspects of planometrics.* New Haven: Yale University Press, 1967.
54.   _____, "The Rapprochement Between East and West in Mathematical-Economic Thought," *Manchester School Econ. Soc. Stud.*, March 1969, pp. 1-21.

Appendix by Péter Erdös[1]

It is to be expected that our economists will greet with considerable satisfaction the publication of the Hungarian-language edition of J. M. Keynes' most important work. In fact, all economists ought to be acquainted with the *General theory* and its effect on the development of diverse schools of economic thought.

It will be clear to the great majority of Hungarian economists why this book was among the first by nonsocialist authors to be selected for publication. As they know, it upset and divided bourgeois economists into two groups; it led to a variety of economic policies which, at least in outline, became the ideological basis of the developing state monopoly capitalism. Today we may encounter Keynesians of diverse gradations as well as anti-Kenyesians among bourgeois economists, but they all draw on the categories appearing in Keynes' book.

Great success is by no means always a sign of great genius. Even Keynes' most ardent admirers do not regard him as an exceptional genius in the history of economic thought. This translation will provide the opportunity for Hungarian readers to form their own judgment. Those properly trained in Marxist writings, and not via second-rate Marxian commentaries, cannot be mistaken in this regard. There is no doubt, however, that Keynes was one of the most prominent bourgeois economic theorists of the past half-century. The Hungarian reader has no reason to complain: he is being presented with one of the best works of its kind.

How to explain Keynes' world-wide success? Firstly, the timing was important. The *General theory* appeared during the devastating depression of the 1930s, when Keynes could well say that "at the present moment people are unusually expectant of a more fundamental diagnosis; more particularly ready to receive it . . . . "[2]

Secondly, the economic theories of reproduction and crises then in vogue among bourgeois economists were incredibly *simpliste.* Immediately arising out of this ignorance was the fact that the policies they advocated tended to aggravate the crisis rather than mitigate it.

Thirdly, there was concern among capitalists that recurrence of a crisis of such depth would inevitably threaten the survival of the capitalist system itself. They hoped that Keynes could be of some help to avoid such a recurrence.

Fourthly — and a particularly important factor — was the huge sharpening of the general crisis of capitalism — leading to the beginning of the transformation of monopoly capitalism into state monopoly capitalism. This made it possible to apply relatively coordinated anti-crisis policies, enabling diagnosis to be followed by more or less effective therapy.

Fifthly, Kenyes' success was of course partly due to his pointing out that of all the complex interrelations of reproduction, the rate of investment is correlated with business fluctuations. The volume of investment is one of the most important levers which a capitalist government can use to mitigate a crisis — if and only if it knows how to handle it correctly and is in a position to do so. Keynes concluded that such regulation was the task of government.

At that time a challenge of this magnitude to the dogma of Say — so primitive and apologetic but, within the realm of bourgeois economics, seemingly unshakable — required considerable scientific courage for a bourgeois economist.

In modern bourgeois literature we are sometimes confronted with opinions that deny that Say's dogma was widely accepted when Keynes successfully attacked it. To show how incorrect these opinions are, note the following passage by von Wieser, one of the triad of the Austrian school, a passage reprinted in 1924:

> Those who speak of the appreciation of money [*i.e.,* a fall in the price level, ed.] misjudge the power of this historical value for which every business man makes allowance in calculating his costs and prices. The appreciation of money would thwart the anticipations of every business man, would depress all sales prices and would decrease or wipe out all expected profits. Should it go still further, it would become impossible to recover costs incurred and would bring in its train a universal crises which would be more ruinous than any crises engendered by overproduction in particular industries. . . . An old doctrine asserts correctly that a condition of "general overproduction" cannot arise. Partial overproduction is possible inasmuch as a particular type of production may be excessive, passing the general limit and reaching a point at which sales cannot be affected for the surplus product. "General overproduction" is inconceivable. A condition which would seem to warrant the use of this term would not be overproduction at all but would be a general production of surplus. The increased volume of product would bring with them increased sales, "wares being paid for by wares," natural values exchanging for other natural values. Where natural values increase in adjusted proportions there will be no difficulty in arranging for payments without provoking crises.[3]

This passage, I repeat, was written by a leader of the Austrian school of economics in 1924, five years before the outbreak of the greatest crisis of general overproduction known in history. It was written 100 years after the outbreak of the first crisis of general overproduction, and exactly 65 years after the publication by Marx of " Zur Kritik der politischen Ökonomie," containing a very clear refutation of Say's dogma.[4]

Marxists in 1936 did not have to read Keynes' book for a proof either of the actual existence of crises of general overproduction or of the inherent tendencies to unemployment in capitalism, even independent of cyclical business fluctuations. Nor was the task so set for Keynes. He had to explain these facts while shunning Marx's theories, completely ignoring his theoretical achievements, and analyzing the world under perfectly competitive assumptions, using the marginal productivity theory of distribution developed by John Bates Clark: the point being that workers are paid the value of their marginal product. Therefore, by definition, there can be no exploitation. Keynes' task was to demonstrate that capitalism, in spite of its inherent defects, was the only worthwhile social order within which the economic system should be analyzed.

In this foreword to the *General theory*, there is no place for any criticism of Keynes' scientific methodology. The interested reader will find a detailed critique in the book by Csapó László, *The state of monopolistic capitalism*. The expert will at least derive some intellectual satisfaction from observing the difficult obstacles overcome by Keynes. He did, of course, believe in his methods and results. In effect, he carried out the wishes of the bourgeoisie; but he did so wholeheartedly and in accord with his conscience. He naively believed in the analytical tools offered by what he calls "the classical school of economics" and this renders his problem-solving even more amusing, *e.g.,* his attempt to prove the existence of a specific role for money, a problem solved long before by Marxists. But Keynes, responding to his class instincts, was unable to accept these methods of solution.

These are not points on which the reader should dwell. It was not long ago that, sarcastically, we used to dismiss Keynes as a physician of capitalism, desiring to create a perpetually viable system. If a physician's task was to render unhealable patients healthy and immortal, then Keynes would have deserved little but scorn. Perhaps, by his counsel, he really did hope to assist in enabling capitalism to last forever. But there is a branch of medicine, geriatrics, which aims to make old age as enduring and endurable as possible. In this sense, a physician can perhaps prolong capitalism. Whether the life of capitalism should be extended, and whether it could be extended, are two different considerations.

Capitalism is undoubtedly in its old age. State monopoly capitalism is a symptom of its old age, but it is also a form of accommodation of the aged organism to the requirements of the physiology of old age. Our days now are characterized by the struggle between an increasingly senile capitalism and the progressively strong and young socialism. We shall do everything we can to see that this struggle is resolved, not amidst the horror of atomic war, but within a framework of peaceful competition.

The prospects of such a peaceful competition are very good, but even though the promise of a favorable outcome appears most excellent, we cannot be certain until the victory. It will not be an easy victory. Aged capitalism exhibits an astonishing degree of tenacity. It is clear that the measures of state monopoly capitalism are not *a priori* ineffectual; indeed, we are all sometimes surprised by the degree of their effectiveness. It is true today as it has been in the past: there is no situation from which capitalism could not find a means of escape; it does not collapse automatically, it has to be overthrown.

Therefore, in connection with Keynesian economics, the international labor movement faces two kinds of tasks. First, it has to study the actual conditions and possibilities of our adversaries, including the economic principles which they accept. Keynes' work forms the basis of much of this thought, and therefore constitutes an effective beginning for this task. Second, we have to understand that the working class in capitalist countries, and under state monopoly capitalism, must not primarily be opposed to all acts of interference by the state in the economy. On the contrary, it must formulate it own positive claims. And, since the measures of state monopoly capitalism are chosen and explained in Keynesian terms, and since the major part of the working class in capitalist countries sympathizes with Keynesian policies, it is necessary to go beyond a criticism of Keynes' methodology to a practical critique of Keynesian policies. Theories regarding the possibility of various forms of state intervention, and their limitations, have to be elaborated on a scientific basis, so that laborers in capitalist countries can resolutely demand correct economic policies rather than remain passive and nihilistic. Hungarian economists have already contributed to this useful theoretical work. The publication of the *General theory* in Hungarian will doubtless assist its continuance.

Notes

1. John Maynard Keynes, A *foglalkoztatas, a kamat es a penz altalanos elmelete* tr. from the English by Peter Erdös. (Budapest: Kozgazdasagi Kiado, 1959, pp. 430, with illustrations.) Professor Erdös' translation into English of his Foreword to this volume has been edited by J.M. Letiche, with Erdös' translations of quotations from third sources replaced by the original published English versions.

2. Keynes' sentence ends as follows: "eager to try it out, if it should be even plausible." (*General theory*, p. 33.) Ed.

3. Friedrich von Wieser, *Social economics*, trans. by A. Ford Hinrichs (London: George Allen & Unwin, Ltd., 1927), p. 285; first published as "Theorie der Gesellschaftlichen Wirtschaft," Vol. I. Part II of *Grundriss der Sozialökonomik*, 1914; the 2nd edition to which Erdös refers appeared in 1924.

4. There are, understandably, many differences between Professor Erdös and myself on questions of theory and fact as to the reasons for the success of the *General theory,* but I must record an inability to find a theoretically satisfactory refutation of Say's Law in Marx, which Keynes did provide. If the refutation is interpreted to mean the existence of general over-production and unemployment in capitalism, Marx certainly did claim that; but Marx did not anticipate Keynes in claiming that deficiency of effective demand could be due to downward inflexibility of wages (or prices). For specific statements contrary to Say's Law in the former sense, see *e.g., Karl Marx, A contribution to the critique of political economy,* [34, pp. 123—25]; *Capital*, Vol. I, *op. cit.*, pp. 51—52, 216—219, and more generally, Ch. 25; Vol. II

(Chicago: C.H. Kerr and Company, 1909), pp. 460—476; and Vol. III (Chicago: C.H. Kerr and Company, 1909), pp. 309—313, and 567—569; for specific statements indicating that Marx did not anticipate the Keynesian argument against Say's Law, see *A contribution to the critique of political economy, op. cit.,* pp. 182—183; *Capital,* Vol. I, pp. 72—73, 306—397; and Vol. II, pp. 392—396. Cf. also Joan Robinson [41, Chs. VI and X, and sources cited therein].

110

Was Keynes a 'Keynesian'?
A Review Article*

H.I. Grossman

Axel Leijonhufvud has recently provided us with an insightful and refreshing reappraisal of the so-called Keynesian revolution in his *On Keynesian Economics and the Economics of Keynes* [8, 1968]. In light of the significance and importance of this book, it is disappointing that, although the reviewers have been very complimentary, the published discussion seems to have offered little in the way of critical evaluation of Leijonhufvud's arguments. This paper attempts to remedy this situation.

Leijonhufvud argues convincingly that popular Keynesianism, as well as its offspring, the so-called neoclassical synthesis, does not have an adequate choice-theoretic, *i.e.,* microeconomic, basis. This view seems to be finding wide and warranted acceptance. In addition, Leijonhufvud argues that, although this defect pervades popular Keynesianism, it does not characterize Keynes' own writings. Leijonhufvud suggests that Keynes himself would have been unsympathetic with the development of popular "Keynesian" macroeconomic theory. This paper argues, to the contrary, that this latter contention is not consistent with a complete and careful reading of the *General theory*. My analysis will suggest that Keynes' thinking was both substantially in accord with that of his popularizers and similarly deficient.

Leijonhufvud's argument emphasizes the interpretation of the Keynesian consumption function developed by R. W. Clower in his "The Keynesian Counter-Revolution: A Theoretical Appraisal" [3, 1965]. I certainly accept Leijonhufvud's contention that Clower's conception, which is discussed more fully below, provides the choice-theoretic basis for macroeconomic theory, which popular Keynesianism lacks.[1] However, Leijonhufvud also suggests that Clower's conception may be attributed to Keynes himself.[2] This latter is the hypothesis at issue. Leijonhufvud can point to no specific content in Keynes' writing which explicitly supports this attribution. His argument (pp. 91-102) seems to amount to the following: Keynes' discussion is dreadfully confusing, but Clower's interpretation offers the only conceivable way to make sense of it.[3] Therefore, Keynes must have had Clower's idea in mind.

*Source: *Journal of Economic Literature*, Vol. 10 (1), March 1972, pp. 26-30.

My analysis will focus upon Keynes' treatment of the demand for labor services, a part of Keynes' model which Leijonhufvud largely neglects. This particular aspect of the *General theory* is both central and completely unambiguous and, as we shall see, is clearly inconsistent with Leijonhufvud's hypothesis regarding the basic conceptions which Keynes himself harbored. This inconsistency suggests an alternative hypothesis — namely, that Keynes had nothing like Clower's conception in mind and that Keynes' own formulation of the consumption function was simply *ad hoc*.[4]

1. Leijonhufvud's Argument

Leijonhufvud cites a number of instances in which standard popularizations of the *General theory* are inconsistent with either the letter or the spirit of what Keynes actually wrote. However, according to Leijonhufvud, the most significant blunder of the popularizers was their failure to appreciate the essential nature of Keynes' revolutionary paradigm.[5] In this view, Keynes rejected the classical theory of markets, in both its Walrasian and Marshallian forms, essentially because it focused upon market-clearing conditions.[6] Following on this rejection, Keynes' central theoretical objective in the *General theory* was to develop an alternative analytical paradigm which would focus upon the inter-relation of markets which chronically failed to clear.

According to Leijonhufvud, Clower's interpretation of the Keynesian consumption function exemplifies Keynes' revolutionary analytical conception. The failure of a market to clear implies that actual quantities transacted diverge either from the quantities supplied or from the quantities demanded. From the stand-point of the individual, these divergences appear as constraints, to which their behavior in other markets must conform. In Clower's interpretation, the dependence of consumption demand upon income arises as a manifestation of excess supply in the labor market. Clower stresses that such a dependence is inconsistent with the classical paradigm, in which income itself is a choice variable. Thus, the consumption function exemplifies the articulation of Keynes' new paradigm, in which analysis focuses on the implications for one market of the failure of other markets to clear. However, in most other respects, Keynes' efforts to define and articulate this new paradigm clearly faltered, but—Leijonhufvud suggests—only because Keynes lacked sufficient technical apparatus and patience with technical detail.

Unfortunately, the "Keynesians," those writers who popularized the *General theory*, failed to perceive what Keynes, according to Leijonhufvud, was essentially trying to do. In their hands, Keynes' model appeared to fit into the classical paradigm, albeit as a novel case in which certain of the behavioral functions had exotic properties.[7] Leijonhufvud argues that this popular interpretation, which has led to a denigration of Keynes' theoretical inventiveness, does Keynes a great injustice. The "Keynesians" should have recognized, as Clower eventually did, that Keynes' consumption function was essentially inconsistent with the classical paradigm. Once the consumption function is understood and appreciated, the true nature of Keynes' intentions and the true significance of his contribution becomes clear.

Leijonhufvud's hypothesis is that Keynes himself viewed and understood his system in the way in which Clower and Leijonhufvud have interpreted it, and that the popularization of Keynes' model as a special case of the classical paradigm was inconsistent with Keynes' own insight and motivation. It seems to me that this hypothesis is untenable. Of course, the consumption function, as interpreted by Clower, turns out to be an important, even revolutionary, conception. However, another completely unambiguous aspect of the *General theory* suggests very strongly that Keynes himself did not appreciate the essential conceptual departure which the consumption function exemplifies. If, instead, Keynes' specification of the consumption function was simply *ad hoc*, and no passage in the *General theory* explicitly avers otherwise, then there is really no basis for thinking that Keynes would have disavowed attempts to fit his analysis into the general market-clearing framework of the classical paradigm.

2. Keynes' Treatment of Labor Demand

The aspect of the *General theory* to which I draw attention is Keynes' treatment of the demand for labor services. Keynes assumed, in explicit accord with received pre-Keynesian doctrine, that, the demand for labor is inversely and uniquely related to the level of real wages.[8] Given this assumption, cyclical variations in the amount of unemployment, reflecting changes in the quantity of labor demanded, must imply countercyclical variation in real wage rates. However, despite repeated attempts, such a pattern of real wages has not been observed.[9] Interestingly, Keynes himself acknowledged the evidence and was clearly disturbed by it. In the *Economic Journal* of March 1939 he offered a rather contrived explanation in terms of monopoly and procyclical variation in demand elasticities.[10]

In addition to being inconsistent with the facts, Keynes' classical labor demand function led him and his popularizers to surprisingly classical policy implications. In particular, Keynes accepted the view that the unemployment of the depression was not solely a monetary phenomena—that it did not result solely from money values being too high in relation to the nominal money stock and level of autonomous expenditures—but that it involved also a real maladjustment in the form of too high a real wage rate. Consequently, Keynes also accepted the view that, given the nominal wage rate, inflation of the price level was necessarily concomitant to a reduction in unemployment.

Expansionary monetary or fiscal policy would only work by creating an excess demand for current output, thereby causing the price level to rise and the real wage rate to fall.

3. Labor Demand Under Non-Market-Clearing Conditions

The irony of this situation is that the analytical paradigm which Clower has used to rationalize the Keynesian consumption function also provides a basis for rejecting the classical analysis of labor demand. In particular, a consistent application of this paradigm implies that the quantity of employment is not uniquely associated with the real wage. Such an analysis apparently was first suggested by Patinkin in 1949 and developed further in Chapter 13 of his *Money, interest and prices*. Patinkin assumed that depressions are characterised by excess supply in the market for current output.[11] Consequently, sales are constrained by the level of aggregate demand, and producers tend to employ only sufficient labor to produce what they are able to sell. They are forced by inadequate demand to operate in a region in which the marginal product of labor exceeds the real wage rate.

In this situation, the level of employment is unaffected by changes in real wages, but it does respond directly to changes in the level of aggregate demand, even with the real wage rate unchanged. Patinkin's analysis thus reconciles theory with fact and explains why unemployment need not involve the classical bogey-man of structural maladjustment. Patinkin's analysis also provides a clear distinction between, on the one hand, the classical unemployment problem associated with excessive real wages and, on the other hand, unemployment which results solely from a deficiency of aggregate demand and which is consistent with real wages which are at or below the level consistent with general equilibrium. Indeed, Patinkin's theory is truly neoclassical, and, in that respect, is, as he suggests, more Keynesian than Keynes' own discussion.

According to Clower's interpretation, consumption demand depends upon aggregate demand, represented by national income, because of the existence of excess supply in the labor market. According to Patinkin's analysis, effective labor demand and employment depend upon aggregate demand, represented by national product, because of the existence of excess supply in the market for current output. Essentially, what Patinkin did was to apply to the labor demand function the same logic by which Clower interpreted the Keynesian consumption function.[12]

The obvious question is why did Keynes himself fail to do this.[13] Keynes would certainly have welcomed a theory like Patinkin's, in that it would have been more consistent with the facts and would have provided a stronger case for the value and necessity of expansionary monetary and fiscal policy. Moreover, Patinkin's theory, together with the consumption function, enables a complete break with the "habitual modes of thought of Classical Economics."

The most plausible answer surely is that Keynes did not have in mind anything resembling Clower's interpretation of the consumption function. The consumption function was a key link in Keynes' theory, but its specification was apparently *ad hoc* and Keynes' surely did not appreciate the essential sense in which it was inconsistent with the classical theory of markets. Keynes' treatment of the labor demand function suggests that the development of popular Keynesianism was not inconsistent with his own thinking, and that he had no vision of the sort attributed to him by Leijonhufvud.[14]

However, Keynes' suggestion that the basic precepts of the classical theory of markets might be questioned certainly encouraged economists to reflect critically upon "habitual modes of thought." By so doing, Keynes helped to set the stage for development of the new paradigm, which Leijonhufvud discusses, focusing upon the interrelation of markets which fail to clear. But neither Keynes' writings nor the heated controversy and popularization which followed upon the publication of the *General theory* seems to have involved such a shift in analytical framework. We must attribute the first conscious attempts to articulate this new paradigm to post-Keynesianism and to such writers as Patinkin and Clower.

Notes

1.   For further development of this approach, see R.J. Barro and H.I. Grossman [1, 1971] and Grossman [4, 1971].

2.   "One must conclude, I believe, that Keynes' theory, although obscurely expressed and doubtlessly not all that clear even in his own mind, was still in substance that to which Clower has recently given a precise statement"—Leijonhufvud, p. 102. Clower suggests the same hypothesis, but rather more tentatively. "It is another question whether Keynes can reasonably be considered to have had [the Clower] theory of household behavior at the back of his mind when he wrote the *General theory*. For my part, I do not think that there can be any serious doubt that he did, although I can find no direct evidence in any of his writings to show that he ever thought explicitly in these terms" [3, Clower, 1965, p. 120].

3.   Clower makes this point explicitly, "Keynes either had [the Clower theory] at the back of his mind, or most of the *General theory* is theoretical nonsense" [3, Clower, 1965, p. 120].

4.   In a recent paper, Leland Yeager advances this same hypothesis without specifically referring to Keynes' treatment of the labor demand. "Upon re-reading the *General theory*, I was struck by how much of what Keynes says does resemble the supposedly vulgar Keynesianism of the income-expenditure theory" [12, Yeager, 1971].

5.   It should be clear that I am not taking issue with Leijonhufvud's other contentions. For more on these, see Leijonhufvud [9, 1969].

6.   Walras incorporated the privilege of recontracting into his tatonnement mechanism for finding the general market-clearing price vector. Marshall had prices respond instantaneously to any momentary discrepancy between quantities supplied and demanded. Either assumption assures that actual transactions take place only under market-clearing conditions.

7.   In particular, consumption demand depended primarily upon income, the demand for money balances depended significantly upon the rate of interest, and the labor supply function had a peculiar kink and horizontal segment with respect to the nominal wage rate.

8. In the *General theory* (p. 17) Keynes wrote, " . . . with a given organization, equipment and technique, real wages and the volume of output (and hence of employment) are uniquely correlated, so that, in general, an increase in employment can only occur to the accompaniment of a decline in the rate of real wages. Thus, I am not disputing this vital fact which the classical economists have (rightly) asserted. . . . The real wage earned by a unit of labour has a unique inverse correlation with the volume of employment." Keynes' treatment of the demand for money as depending upon income accords with his treatment of consumption, whereas his classical treatment of investment demand parallels his treatment of labor demand.

9. For a review of the evidence see E. Kuh [7, 1966] and R.G. Bodkin [2, 1969].

10. Other writers have attempted to explain this discrepancy in terms of a fixed proportions production function in the short run.

11. In contrast, Keynes' treatment of the labor demand function implies that the market for current output is clearing. The *General theory* seems perfectly consistent on this point. Keynes implies throughout that prices, as contrasted with wages, adjust instantaneously to bring the quantity demanded into line with the quantity supplied, the latter being fixed in the short run. Thus Leijonhufvud would seem to have no basis for his contention that Keynes generally reversed the Marshallian rankings of relative price and quantity adjustment speeds.

12. For a detailed comparison of those theories and a development of their interrelationship, see the article by R.J. Barro and H.I. Grossman [1, 1971].

13. The logical complementarity between the Clower and Patinkin ideas is so natural that Leijonhufvud, having digested Clower's interpretation, proceeds to incorporate the essence of Patinkin's theory into his discussion, and implicitly attributes it to Keynes, despite the absence of any textual basis for this attribution. For example, "In Keynesian disequilibrium, firms, like households, are to some extent constrained by their inability to sell what they want at the prices of the moment" [8, Leijonhufvud, 1968, p. 57]. Also, " . . . producers will not be willing to absorb the excess supply of labour at a wage corresponding to the real wage that would 'solve' the Walrasian problem" [8, p. 90]. In contrast, the *General theory* repeatedly assumes that firms refer only to the real wage rate in determining their demand for labor, and Keynes never even suggests the notion of a sales constraint. Leijonhufvud makes no reference to Patinkin in this context and apparently does not appreciate either that these assertions contradict Keynes' assumption that employment and real wages are uniquely related, or the implications of this theory for the cyclical pattern of real wages.

14. Interpreted within Leijonhufvud's analytical framework, the *General theory* deals with the case in which the market for current output is clearing while the market for labor services is in excess supply. The interpretation implies that Keynes' analysis is limited to a very narrowly defined range of wage-price vectors. Had Keynes' thinking tended along these lines, he certainly would not have proclaimed the generality of his discussion.

References

1. BARRO, R.J., and GROSSMAN, H.I. "A General Disequilibrium Model of Income and Employment," *Amer. Econ. Rev.*, March 1971, *61*(1), pp. 82-93.
2. BODKIN, R.G. "Real Wages and Cyclical Variations in Employment," *Can. J. Econ.*, August 1969, *2*(3), pp. 353-74.
3. CLOWER, R.W. "The Keynesian Counter-Revolution: A Theoretical Appraisal" in F.H. HAHN and F.P.R. BRECHLING, eds., *The theory of interest rates.* London, 1965.
4. GROSSMAN, H.I. "Money, Interest and Prices in Market Disequilibrium," *J. Polit. Econ.*, Sept.-Oct. 1971, *79*(5), pp. 943-61.
5. KEYNES, J.M. *The general theory of employment, interest and money.* New York, 1936.
6. _____, "Relative Movements of Real Wages and Output," *Econ. J.*, March 1939, *49*, pp. 34-51.
7. KUH, E. "Unemployment, Production Functions and Effective Demand," *J. Polit. Econ.*, June 1966, *74*(3), pp. 238-49.
8. LEIJONHUFVUD, A. *On Keynesian economics and the economics of Keynes.* New York: Oxford University Press, 1968.
9. _____, *Keynes and the classics.* London: Institute of Economic Affairs, 1969.

10. PATINKIN, D. "Involuntary Unemployment and the Keynesian Supply Function," *Econ. J.*, 1949, *59*, pp. 360-83.
11. _____, *Money, interest and prices.* Second Edition. New York, 1965.
12. YEAGER, L. "The Keynesian Diversion," unpublished manuscript, 1971.